THE OFFENSIVE INTERNET

The Offensive Internet

Speech, Privacy, and Reputation

Edited by
Saul Levmore and Martha C. Nussbaum

HARVARD UNIVERSITY PRESS
Cambridge, Massachusetts, and London, England   2010

Library of Congress Cataloging-in-Publication Data

The offensive Internet : speech, privacy, and reputation / edited by Saul Levmore
and Martha C. Nussbaum.
     p. cm.
  Includes bibliographical references and index.
  ISBN 978-0-674-05089-1 (alk. paper)
   1. Internet—Law and legislation—United States.   2. Libel and slander—United States.
3. Privacy, Right of—United States.   4. Reputation (Law)—United States.   5. Privacy,
Right of—United States.   I. Levmore, Saul X.   II. Nussbaum, Martha Craven, 1947–
   KF390.5.C6O344 2010
   343.7309'944—dc22

                                                              2010022409

Contents

III Speech

IV Privacy

THE OFFENSIVE INTERNET

Introduction

SAUL LEVMORE AND MARTHA C. NUSSBAUM

In many ways the Internet has succeeded in remaking us as inhabitants of a small village. No one is a stranger either in the village or on the Internet; in both settings the savvy citizen knows how to process information. The Internet may be offensive to some, as the title of this book warns, but it benefits far more than it offends the well-informed. If we know something of American history, and now wish to know whether Betsy Ross really made that first flag, the Internet allows us to work our way through noisy websites to the few that seem ably written and reliable. Similarly, we can, as never before, find a hotel on some vacation island that serves our preferences, even as many competitor hotels exaggerate their own qualities, and even as amateur reviewers carry on about the manner in which they were wronged at the reception desk. But no medium, and certainly not one with such low entry barriers, can protect the ignorant except perhaps with extraordinary regulation and consumer protection. If we wish to learn how to pronounce names in Korean, we can visit what seems like a terrific website, but must hope that the site does not mislead, for most of us cannot there distinguish fidelity from fraud. In the case of pronunciation, as opposed to hotel quality, it is unlikely that someone profits by misleading those who search for information, so we tend to trust the website. In all these things, the Internet is a valuable medium for a far-flung world. In the days when one's reach could extend no farther than one's own village, gossip and experience protected, or at least covered, the terrain. Social norms and some legal rules worked to create an atmosphere, or market of sorts, in which one could operate reasonably well. In a more cosmopolitan world, the Internet helps re-create the world of the village, where one learned to trust here and to avoid there. If one needed shoes to be repaired, there was good information about the village shoemakers; if one needs a camera today, there is excellent information on the Internet. In both places, self-promotion and misleading information can be overcome. The key tool in the village was personal experience, or what we might now call repeat play, while on the Internet it is the fact of numerous, communicative players.

In the absence of personal experience, it is especially difficult to become well-informed about people. In the village and on the Internet one can ask about a shoemaker or a camera, and in both cases a great deal of information will be forthcoming from people who have experienced those services or that item. But information about the shoemaker's character is somewhat more difficult to obtain because reputations are often deservedly—or undeservedly—made or broken by one or two important events. If one defrauds another or heroically rescues someone from a fire, life in the village will be far worse or much better, as this episode comes to be known. If honor is claimed where it is undeserved, or honesty is misreported as fraud by a competitor, our hero must hope that the truth will win out because of repeat or multiple play. If one does evil, one must try to recover by doing good, and eventually reputations can be redeemed. But the tendency of some humans to harass others, and even to inflict emotional harm, casts some doubt on the reliability of reputations. If one tries to escape the past by moving to another village, it is likely that the newcomer will be mistrusted. In the village, every longtime resident knows whom to ask about a third party, but in the cosmopolitan world it is rare to find but one degree of separation between an employer and an applicant, or a landlord and prospective tenant. "Googling" a target is therefore the best one can do, though that is more like asking a randomly chosen person for a reference. In contrast, a village elder or other known source likely has personal knowledge of the target and also some reputation of his or her own.

Googling, like other Internet searching strategies, is fraught with peril. In the first place, it is cheap to slur someone on the Internet, for it can be done with a few keystrokes, with complete anonymity, and—as we will see repeatedly in this book—with no fear that the Internet forum provider on whose website the slur is found will somehow be held responsible for incorrect, mean-spirited, or defamatory statements. And yet someone who searches a name and finds a slur might rationally decline to hire or trust that named person because there is no reason to take a risk when there are so many other, untainted applicants or contacts. In the village, one might make further inquiries, and one might discover that the source of the slur is the problem. On the Internet it is very difficult to do so. Inasmuch as positive information on the Internet is often a product of self-presentation, such positive information is unlikely to offset even a single negative revelation or fabrication in the mind of the inquirer. Moreover, as Cass Sunstein explores in the essay "Believing False Rumors," certain kinds of false rumors spread especially well on the Internet because of social cascades and group polarization.

The speed with which reputations can be made and altered is just one way in which the Internet has changed everything. It is surely the case that most of the changes are for the better but, sadly, the Internet is a curse when one is the subject of negative information, whether self-presented, and then indelible, or communicated by others. And yet the Internet has changed nothing, which is to say it has returned us to the world of the village. In both settings, we wonder what can be done about irrepressible information that is not to our liking. We are drawn to horror stories of bullying, harassment, and sordid pasts, real or not. It is this question that dominates the present volume. The Internet can be offensive to many of its users and an absolute nightmare for those who cannot escape harassment on it.

One reaction to false information is to regulate the providers of information. In the village, an unfavorable credit report disciplined borrowers, but an unfair credit report presented a serious flaw in the social and economic fabric. It could be overcome by experience, as others vouched for the unfairly maligned debtor. Eventually, perhaps because information traveled far beyond the village, fair credit reporting became a part of law, and law sought to protect individuals from false disclosures and even from mere errors in their records. This is the analogy that Frank Pasquale suggests to us in his essay "Reputation Regulation: Disclosure and the Challenge of Clandestinely Commensurating Computing." Pasquale encourages us to develop a "Fair Reputation Reporting Act." He takes aim at employers, and others who use information: asking them to explain the nature and source of information they use is like asking banks to disclose their lending decisions. In the world of credit it has been important to provide consumers with access to the intermediaries who collect information and sell it to lenders. It is possible that the analogy demands that we think of forcing Internet forum providers to disclose their sources and to give those who have unfavorable reputations the chance to correct misinformation. If so, we would have a very different cyberspace, because anonymity is at present a common feature in that domain.

Providers of false information on the Internet can also be regulated with rules drawn from tort law, much as defamation and other law came to the village. Anupam Chander, in "Youthful Indiscretion in an Internet Age," would regulate the Internet, like the village, with a narrowly drawn tort meant to deter the public disclosure of information plainly meant to be private. Danielle Citron's "Civil Rights in Our Information Age" shares Chander's sense that hurtful (and "low-value") speech on the Internet disproportionately affects women, and she advances the idea of cyberspace civil rights law. Martha Nussbaum's essay "Objectification and Internet Misogyny" also focuses on suits brought by injured victims. Her inquiry into the source of the attacks on victims leads to a call for the success of suits by women who are assaulted, but it suggests that the problems reflected in these Internet episodes will not truly be solved without large-scale social change. All three of these authors presumably favor the presence of similar legal tools in the village, where assaults may be met with social sanctions but where they can, in modern times, be treated with legal remedies as well.

Regulation can take the form of advance instructions, or structural change, rather than the availability of punitive or compensatory remedies following a harm. One possibility is to rely on private institutions more than law itself. Just as employers can create safe work environments, whether encouraged to do so by law or not, other institutions can play a role in controlling harassment and other ills. Karen Bradshaw and Souvik Saha, in "Academic Administrators and the Challenge of Social Networking Websites," concentrate on what schools might do to influence behavior on social-networking sites. Educational and other institutions are often able to exert extraordinary and extralegal influence over their constituents, though it must be said that the "offensive Internet" reaches well beyond where schools, churches, and employers may choose to go.

More of our authors look not to educators but to Internet forum providers as the means of combating the offensive Internet. They may well be the best problem solvers, or least cost avoiders, because their reach is coextensive with the Internet. Brian Leiter, in "Cleaning Cyber-Cesspools: Google and Free Speech," makes progress with the observation that search engines, like that managed by Google, influence the construction of cyberspace cesspools by the means with which they array sites in response to a search request. Daniel Solove's essay "Speech, Privacy, and Reputation on the Internet" is more anxious about invasions of privacy than the facts of harassment, but he too is inclined to lessen the problem not with a tort but with instructions to forum providers. He recommends, as do other authors in this volume, a notice-and-takedown policy, of the kind found in copyright law. A provider would be informed that something offensive was in the air, and the provider could or should then remove the offensive communication—though there would be sanctions against those who abused the notice-and-takedown policy. Saul Levmore takes a similar tack in "The Internet's Anonymity Problem," but is more inclined to think the problem can be solved by eliminating much of the anonymity that reigns on the Internet. With the exception of Solove, we might say that these authors seek to reform the Internet so that it is yet more like the village. Old solutions are sometimes appropriate for new problems.

Old solutions will probably not do if the Internet's problem is truly new and different. Ruben Rodrigues's "Privacy on Social Networks: Norms, Markets, and Natural Monopoly" argues that social-networking sites have such substantial natural monopolies—because users want to be where everyone else is also located—that the normal remedy of exit, from where one finds one's privacy invaded for instance, is too costly. If this is so, it is important to emphasize that much of the offense on the Internet takes place on blogs or on other sites that do not have this natural monopoly feature. The larger question is, of course, whether understanding the novelty of the Internet is the key to combating its offenses.

Speech

Thus far, we have thought about the offensive Internet from the perspective of defending one's reputation, or discouraging harassing attacks on it. The promise of our title, however, is that the importance and value of speech should also be taken into account. The balance between valuable speech and offensive speech is hardly a novel one, peculiar to the Internet. Our authors refer to speech that harasses, bullies, threatens, defames, invades privacy, and inflicts reputational damage as well as emotional distress. But non-Internet speech also does these things. When we consider how to prevent such damages, or to remedy them once they have occurred, we immediately have to consider the possibility that our proposals will place unjustifiable limits on free speech. But what is freedom of speech? Why is it valuable? And what types of harm might be sufficient to justify its regulation? These are general human questions but if our purpose is to think about directions for legal regulation, we ought to think in the context of the First Amendment, which constrains limitations on speech.

According to a popular misconception, freedom of speech is an absolute, and the First Amendment protects all speech from any type of government regulation. We often hear any proposal to limit or regulate speech described, without further argument, as censorship or as "a violation of the First Amendment." But the absolutist view of the First Amendment is implausible, and it has never prevailed. Regulation of speech is uncontroversially constitutional with respect to threats, bribery, defamatory statements, fighting words, fraud, copyright, plagiarism, and more. What courts have said is that the First Amendment, properly understood, does not protect these forms of speech. Moreover, few people would defend the position that the "marketplace of ideas" should be trusted to sort out the problems posed by fraud, bribery, and their cousins.

One question, then, is whether offensive speech on the Internet deserves First Amendment protection. The answer is far from obvious, and cannot be arrived at by treating the First Amendment as self-explanatory. It calls for patient work with both legal doctrine and more general theories of speech. A good starting place is Geoffrey Stone's essay "Privacy, the First Amendment, and the Internet," which presents a broader normative account of First Amendment protections than do our other essays. But before getting to details, it is useful to step back and ask whether disparate approaches—as collected in this volume—can connect on the question of Internet offense. Why might abstract philosophical analysis as well as law-and-economics approaches illuminate difficult legal issues about speech?

The First Amendment is concise and abstract: "Congress shall make no law abridging the freedom of speech." But what is "abridging," and what sort of "freedom" is protected for what sorts of "speech"? The difficulty and indeterminacy of these questions can be appreciated from the evident fact that our understanding of what the First Amendment protects has changed over the years. For much of our history, for example, it was generally agreed that the First Amendment did not protect the political speech of dissidents during wartime. Today that sort of speech would seem to most interpreters (and to the public) to lie right at the heart of the First Amendment's protections. When judges or legal thinkers grapple with the difficult issues posed by the constitutional text, it is natural for them to look for help in other theoretical understandings of free speech that offer more in the way of analysis and rationale.

If the interpreter is an "originalist," who believes that the Constitution should best be interpreted in keeping with the public meaning of its text at the time of the Founding, he or she might look at philosophical theories to determine what the public culture of that time thought about speech. Temporally, such an inquiry might not be strictly limited to the time of the Founding, because the First Amendment was not incorporated—that is, applied to those other (nonfederal) acts—until after the Civil War. For the meaning of the Bill of Rights at the time of incorporation, we might therefore look at mid-nineteenth–century ideas. Later philosophical theories might also be considered, insofar as they render explicit ideas that were already part of the public culture at an earlier time. Thomas Scanlon's theory of free speech—based, as it is, on Kantian ideas of autonomy and respect that were highly influential by the late eighteenth century—and Alexander Meiklejohn's theory, which conceives of protected speech as that which contributes to democratic deliberation—and which almost certainly has strong historical antecedents—would probably both pass this test.

The non-originalist is even more interested in philosophical theories. An interpreter of a disputed text might simply try to arrive at a deeper understanding of goals and purposes that animate the text. But philosophical theory is unlikely to be conclusive. These theories are ahistorical and transnational, while drafters and judges inhabit a particular legal tradition and must consider relevant precedents and conventions. They cannot simply ask what is best, but rather ask what is best justified in light of the available text, precedents, and history. Theories are sometimes most useful where these materials leave room for fine distinctions.

One difficult area of our First Amendment doctrine concerns the category of "low-value speech." As Geoffrey Stone points out, our tradition has recognized that some speech is of "high value" and deserves very strong protection. That sort of speech can be regulated only in very narrow circumstances, where it is "likely to produce a clear and present danger of a serious substantive evil." Terminiello v. Chicago, 337 U.S. 1, 3 (1949). But the Supreme Court regards other forms of speech as of "low value," less deserving of protection. If the low-value speech inflicts harm, regulation is often permitted. Unfortunately, the line between these categories has not been well drawn. Theories of the First Amendment here come into play. John Deigh, Brian Leiter, and Danielle Citron agree on the theories of free speech that are particularly useful for constitutional interpreters to ponder, along with the materials already noted. Each of these theories focuses on a different core value: truth, autonomy, and democratic deliberation. A short introduction to these theories is useful for readers embarking on this volume.

For John Stuart Mill, the main point of free speech protections is to help society arrive at the truth. When speech is restricted, people may fail to discover the errors embedded in their current ways of thinking. Even if their opinions are true, they may be incomplete, and suppressed material may help citizens reach a more comprehensive understanding. And even if the suppressed opinions are false, they may help people by sharpening their understanding of the true views and preventing lazy or complacent endorsement. On Mill's view of speech, speech that is not part of an argument aimed at truth—purely emotive speech, bullying speech, and speech that does not make truth-claims at all—deserves no particular protection.

The second prominent theory of speech focuses on autonomy; we owe people access to a wide range of opinions because we respect them as free beings who are entitled to make their own choices. Restriction of speech stifles awareness of options and in this way threatens autonomy. Within this view, speech that itself diminishes autonomy by insulting, denigrating, or intimidating others is ripe for regulation rather than protection.

Finally, there is again Alexander Meiklejohn's influential account of the First Amendment, which holds that the key purpose underlying a system of free speech is the preservation of the sort of open debate that is a necessary part of democracy. Meiklejohn's view, which has had great influence on legal doctrine, is that political speech, whether in public settings or simply on matters of political interest, is at the core of the First Amendment. Other forms of speech—including commercial speech and perhaps artistic expression—are less important for the First Amendment, and can be more readily regulated.

These three theories are binary in that they identify a category of high-value speech worthy of serious protection, and thus also identify, if only by elimination, all other speech as low value. In reality, things are not so convenient, and theories of free speech sometimes recognize additional categories. For example, artistic speech will often be regarded as more important than threatening speech or bribery, but not nearly as important as recognizable political speech. Most of the authors in this volume are content to proceed with the understanding that offensive speech on the Internet is, for the most part, not of the high-value sort. Deigh and Leiter demonstrate that none of the major philosophical theories gives us reason to think that repeated slurs, or cyber bullying, are high-value speech. And, as a matter of law, harmful non-newsworthy speech about private figures (for most of the cyber bullying is of classmates and neighbors rather than celebrities) has not been held to deserve First Amendment protection. There is, to be sure, room to argue about what is newsworthy, or relevant to political discourse, and Geoffrey Stone, for one, fears that we risk endangering free speech if we understand low-value speech to include most of the communications discussed in this volume, simply because it invades privacy or inflicts emotional distress. Under that last view, the low-value category should be restricted to threats, bribery, and only a very few other, narrowly constructed subcategories. Citron and Solove disagree. Citron points out that the Court has upheld enhanced penalties for crimes expressing hatred, denying that the expressive aspect of that activity is protected by the First Amendment, so long as the law is framed broadly and does not involve discrimination on the basis of the ideas expressed. Both point out that bullying, harassment, and hate speech deter or suppress valuable speech, so the net result of intelligent government regulation may well be *more* valuable speech. This is certainly the majority position of our authors. All of our authors think that speech on the Internet may be regulated at least as much as speech in other venues and media, and many take particular aim at one section of the Communications Decency Act, which has been interpreted to immunize the operators of websites and blogs against liability for comments posted by others. A withdrawal of that immunity could, without constitutional difficulty, restore the symmetry between website operators and publishers of newspapers, who can of course be sued for damages if they publish defamatory material.

Privacy

If a focus on reputation and then on the First Amendment reminds us that the Internet presents old problems in new clothing, then a spotlight on privacy clarifies the novelty of the Internet. A bit of information once thought confidential may now blanket the globe with the help of the Internet; a false and defamatory accusation about a person may become a constituent part of that person's Internet identity, where it affects relationships and employment opportunities for all time. A romantic breakup can lead to retaliation on the Internet, where details of a sexual relationship can injure one of the party's reputations and mental equanimity. How should law respond to these new, or at least more intense, threats to privacy, and are these responses consistent with free speech requirements?

Privacy can refer to a number of distinct ideas, or interests. There is the value of *seclusion,* which is the right to be beyond the gaze of others. There is *intimacy,* in which one chooses with whom to share certain information and experiences. There is also the interest in *secrecy,* which is to information as seclusion is to the physical person. And then there is *autonomy,* which is the set of private choices each person makes. These ideas are not unconnected. Thus, sexual relationships—a constant topic of offensive communications on the Internet—are often kept from prying eyes in ways that reflect all four of these interests. In the realm of sex, autonomy is probably the most controversial, but we can at least surmise that those who insist on a right of autonomy in this sphere often do so because they think that sexual choices are particularly intimate and self-defining.

The four privacy interests, or meanings, can also diverge. A married couple might value intimacy and seclusion, but not resist the inference that they are engaging in sexual activity with one another. The lack of secrecy does not mean they welcome others into their bedrooms or intimate conversations. And then a secret and secluded relationship may have no intimacy, as might be the case between a client and a commercial sex worker. There is even more divergence when we add to seclusion the special zone that we call home, though this is not a well-articulated idea in law. Even in the home the government is likely to have every right to police such things as domestic violence and child abuse. In any event, if the privacy interest, and perhaps the special treatment of the home, is understood to involve an element of autonomy, then there may be room for its expansion to other zones, including the Internet.

All four of these notions of privacy make appearances in these essays, though it is not always clear which privacy interest an author holds most dear. The confusion is found in constitutional law itself, and may simply derive from the fact that we use the word "privacy" to mean so many things. When we say that medical information and financial records are private, we refer to autonomy or a version of secrecy, because the information is obviously known to some strangers, is maintained in a non-secluded place, and is not normally an important ingredient of intimacy. Solove argues that we have overindulged the secrecy aspect of privacy, and have therefore been deficient in protecting information that people have communicated to a small circle of intimates. He observes a generational shift, such that a new generation that has not known seclusion is more concerned with the ability to control the access others have to information about them. A more nuanced understanding of privacy could generate doctrines that would protect information even if it has been previously divulged. Pasquale also looks to new constructions in order to restore to individuals the control that the Internet has weakened. Stone draws a very different conclusion about the Internet era. For him, the era of informational privacy is over, and we will just have to learn to live with it. "Once information is out of the bottle, once we share it with others, once others know it, we can no longer hope to put it back. If that era ever existed, it is now the past."

It is clear that new thinking is required if privacy is to flourish in the Information Age, and especially so where the intimacy and secrecy interests are concerned. The problem is not simply one of dissemination and selective control, but also one of choosing among competing interests. In "Collective Privacy," Lior Strahilevitz focuses attention on the fact that privacy disputes often emerge not when something entirely secret is made public, but rather when information shared carefully is then revealed more broadly by the first recipient. If the revelation concerns multiple individuals, then there will often be privacy collective action problems, because the individuals may have disparate views of the value of confidentiality or revelation. Strahilevitz suggests that law identify the party best able to resolve the privacy issue, and require that person's consent.

Privacy, speech, and reputation can be thought of as separate topics, but they come together rather often where the offensive Internet is concerned. Most of these essays explore connections among all three of these values, or subjects. If the Internet is truly different from the village, it is not just because one is global and the other local. In the village, privacy and reputation were important matters, and threats to these interests were often dealt with in kind or, perhaps, through exit. In the Internet era, the means we have of controlling threats to privacy and reputation all involve constraints on speech, so that there are three balls in the air rather than two. With so many ideas in play, and human relationships at stake, it is no wonder that these essays are both informative and provocative.

PART I

The Internet and Its Problems

CHAPTER 1

Speech, Privacy, and Reputation on the Internet

DANIEL J. SOLOVE

He has a name, but most people just know him as "the Star Wars Kid." In fact, he is known around the world by tens of millions of people. Unfortunately, his notoriety stems from one of the most embarrassing moments in his life.

In 2002, as a 15-year-old, the Star Wars Kid videotaped himself waving around a golf-ball retriever while pretending it was a light saber. Without the help of the professional choreographers working on the *Star Wars* movies, he stumbled around awkwardly in the video. The video was found by some of the boy's tormentors, who uploaded it to an Internet video site. It went viral with a multitude of fans. All across the blogosphere, people started mocking the boy, making fun of him for being pudgy, awkward, and nerdy.

Several remixed videos of the Star Wars Kid started popping up, adorned with special effects. People edited the video to make the golf-ball retriever glow like a light saber. They added *Star Wars* music to the video. Others mashed it up with other movies. Dozens of embellished versions were created. The Star Wars Kid appeared in a video game and on the television shows *Family Guy* and *South Park*. It is one thing to be teased by classmates in school, but imagine being ridiculed by masses the world over. The teenager dropped out of school and had to seek counseling. What happened to the Star Wars Kid can happen to anyone, and it can happen in an instant. Today, collecting personal information has become second nature. More and more people have cell phone cameras, digital audio recorders, web cameras, and other recording technologies that readily capture details about their lives. For the first time in history nearly anybody can disseminate information around the world. People do not need to be famous enough to be interviewed by the mainstream media. With the Internet, anybody can reach a global audience.

For centuries—perhaps since the dawn of human society—people have spread rumors, gossiped about each other, and engaged in shaming for social transgressions. These social practices are now moving over to the Internet, where they are taking on new dimensions. Gossip used to travel in local circles. It rarely spread widely and would be forgotten over time. On the Internet, however, gossip is no longer ephemeral. As with gossip, the Internet is having similar effects on the practice of shaming. Once localized and fleeting, shaming online creates a permanent record of people's past transgressions—a digital scarlet letter.

Although a common argument is that more information will be useful in judging each other, there are many reasons why less information can be preferable. Personal information taken out of context often does not foster a more accurate impression of other people. In fact, it can result in hasty and hypocritical judgments, as well as severe misunderstandings. There is a grave danger that people will enslave themselves and each other by making their past mistakes permanently and readily available for the rest of their lives. The long-standing value of giving people a second chance, of allowing people to reinvent themselves, might soon become a relic of a bygone era. This has profound effects on people's freedom to experiment, to grow, and to change.

We must protect privacy to ensure that the freedom of the Internet does not make us less free. But to do so, we must rethink our notions of privacy and recalibrate the way privacy is balanced against freedom of speech.

The Rise of Generation Google

Before the Internet, gossip would spread by word of mouth and remain within the boundaries of a social circle. Private details would be confined to a diary and kept locked in a desk drawer. Social networking spawned by the Internet allows communities worldwide to revert to the close-knit culture of preindustrial society, in which nearly every member of a tribe or a farming hamlet knew everything about the neighbors. Except that now the "villagers" span the globe.

In the village of yesteryear, people had to live under the ever-present judgmental eye of their fellow villagers. The small village mythos of bygone days—a sunny happy place, where everybody got along—is an idealized image. A brief dip into history and literature (such as Nathaniel Hawthorne's *The Scarlet Letter*) shows a world rife with oppressive norms, with nosy neighbors and communities ready to condemn, often unfairly. One example of the problematic nature of community nosiness was the common double standard imposed on women who committed extramarital sex—women were watched much more carefully and condemned much more readily than men. While social control can be good, not all is, and sometimes it can be downright unfair, stifling, misguided, and cruel.

One of the benefits of the modern world was that people could escape from the oppressiveness of the small village fishbowl. But no longer. We now live in a "global village," to use Marshall McLuhan's term. The return of the village fishbowl comes with a pernicious twist. In the small village, people knew each other well, and disreputable information would be judged within the context of a person's entire life. Now, people are judged out of context based on information fragments found online. The amount of these fragments is vastly increasing and the kind of information involved is becoming more personal and potentially discreditable.

College students have begun to share salacious details about their schoolmates. Until it was shut down in 2009, a website called JuicyCampus served as an electronic bulletin board where students nationwide posted anonymously and without verification a sordid array of tidbits about sex, drugs, and drunkenness. Another site, Don't Date Him Girl, invites women to post complaints about the men they have dated, along with real names and actual photographs. On a site called AutoAdmit, users spread gossip, lies, and invective about others, including two female students at Yale Law School. As Danielle Citron observes: "Thirty-nine posters targeted named students on the site's message board. The posters, writing under pseudonyms, generated hundreds of threatening, sexually-explicit, and allegedly defamatory comments about the victims."[1]

The number of young people using social-networking websites such as Facebook and MySpace is staggering. At most college campuses, more than 90 percent of students maintain their own sites. I call the people growing up today "Generation Google." For them, many fragments of personal information will reside on the Internet forever, accessible to this and future generations through a simple Google search.

The new openness on the Internet is both good and bad. People can now spread their ideas everywhere without reliance on publishers, broadcasters, or other traditional gatekeepers. This enhances free speech and individual expression and communication. But these changes also create profound threats to privacy and reputations. The *New York Times* is not likely to care about the latest gossip at Dubuque Senior High School or Oregon State University. Bloggers and others communicating online may care a great deal. For them, stories and rumors about friends, enemies, family members, bosses, coworkers, and others are all prime fodder for Internet postings.

Broad-based exposure of personal information diminishes the ability to protect reputation by shaping the image that is presented to others. Reputation plays an important role in society, and preserving private details of one's life is essential to it. We look to people's reputations to decide whether to make friends, go on a date, hire a new employee, or undertake a prospective business deal.

Some would argue that the decline of privacy might allow people to be less inhibited and more honest. But when everybody's transgressions are exposed, people may not judge one another less harshly. Having your personal information may fail to improve my judgment of you. It may, in fact, increase the likelihood that I will hastily condemn you. Moreover, the loss of privacy might inhibit freedom. Elevated visibility that comes with living in a transparent online world means you may never overcome past mistakes.

People want to have the option of "starting over," of reinventing themselves throughout their lives. As American philosopher John Dewey once said, a person is not "something complete, perfect, [or] finished," but is "something moving, changing, discrete, and above all initiating instead of final."[2] In the past, episodes of youthful experimentation and foolishness were eventually forgotten, giving us an opportunity to start anew, to change, and to grow. But with so much information online, it is harder to make these moments forgettable. People must now live with the digital baggage of their pasts.

This openness means that the opportunities for members of Generation Google might be limited because of something they did years ago as wild teenagers. Their intimate secrets may be revealed by other people they know. Or they might become the unwitting victim of a false rumor. Many people will face significant consequences from having their personal information online.

Employers and others increasingly look at applicants' social-networking website profile pages when making their hiring decisions. College admissions officers also use social-networking sites like Facebook and MySpace to make decisions on applicants. According to a survey of 500 colleges, 10 percent of admissions personnel stated that they examine social-networking websites when making decisions about applicants, and 38 percent found that the online information had a negative impact.[3] In some cases, the information they gleaned led them to turn down applicants.[4]

Most colleges lack policies with regard to when and how college admissions officers can use social-networking website profiles in making admissions decisions.[5] Moreover, many companies and college and graduate school admissions officers lack a policy or guidelines about the appropriate and inappropriate use of the information they find online about a candidate. Policies are sorely needed, as there are many issues that need to be thought about: Should information found online about an applicant be used? When? How heavily should it be relied upon? What kinds of things should negatively impact an applicant? Information about sex life? Drug use? Drinking? Bad behavior? What steps should be taken to make sure that the information is accurate? Should a distinction be made between information that people post about themselves and information that others have posted about them, perhaps invading their privacy without their consent? What steps should be taken to make sure that the information used in fact relates to the applicant and not to somebody else with the same name? Should people be notified that information online was used against them and given an opportunity to be heard to explain it?

In most contexts involving hiring or other important decisions affecting people's lives, not enough thought has been devoted to the issue of when and how that online data should be used in the decision-making process. Nor are parents and educators devoting enough attention to the issue. Therefore, it is not just Generation Google that is being careless about online gossip and rumors. Those who are using the data to make decisions about people also need to ponder the consequences of their own behavior.

Rethinking Privacy

There are a surprising number of torts, statutes, and other legal protections of privacy. The problem is that they are currently so weak they cannot serve as an adequate response to the burgeoning problems caused by the spread of online gossip. One of the primary problems with the law is that it is bogged down by antiquated conceptions of privacy.

Can we prevent a future in which so much information about people's private lives circulates beyond their control? Some technologists and legal scholars flatly say no. Privacy, they maintain, is just not compatible with a world in which information flows so freely. As Scott McNealy of Sun

Microsystems once famously declared: "You already have zero privacy. Get over it."[6] Countless books and articles have heralded the "end," "death" and "destruction" of privacy.[7]

Those proclamations are wrongheaded at best. It is still possible to protect privacy, but doing so requires that we rethink outdated understandings of the concept. A long-standing and antiquated conception of privacy is that it involves secrecy and is lost once information is disclosed. I call this the "secrecy paradigm." If any information is exposed to others, many courts, policy makers, and commentators conclude that it is not private since it is no longer hidden or concealed.

The secrecy paradigm leads to two very significant limits on privacy protection that cripple privacy law. First, the secrecy paradigm holds that when a person appears in a public place, she no longer has a reasonable expectation of privacy. The problem with this view is that so much of our lives occur in public places, and modern technology enables information to be captured so readily in cell phone cameras, video, and audio recording devices, and other surveillance technologies. We frequently have conversations in restaurants where we expect to be partially overheard by people near us, but we do not expect our entire conversations to be recorded and disclosed to the world. Likewise, we expect others in the drugstore to see what we are purchasing, but we expect that they do not know who we are or care about what we are buying. For all purposes, we are anonymous. If this anonymity disappears, we lose a lot of freedom that we currently enjoy in our daily lives.

Second, the secrecy paradigm views information exposed to others as no longer secret, and hence, no longer private. However, in today's Information Age, it is nearly impossible to expect much information to be completely secret. So many companies and other individuals hold pieces of information about our lives. But that should not mean that information is not private. Although we share secrets with others, the law should recognize that we have expectations of trust and confidentiality. In particular Professor Neil Richards and I propose expanding the breach of confidentiality tort, which provides a remedy when a duty of confidentiality is breached.[8] In the United States, the tort applies to professional relationships, such as doctor-patient and attorney-client. But in England, it applies to a broader array of relationships, such as those among family and friends. Expanding the American version of the tort could provide considerable protection against the spread of gossip online.

If the law abandoned the secrecy paradigm and recognized greater protections of privacy in public as well as confidentiality, this would go a long way in helping to protect against spurious rumors and gossip spreading online.

As the generation growing up today understands, privacy is not all-or-nothing as the secrecy paradigm holds. Members of this generation know that personal information is routinely shared with countless others, and that they leave a trail of data wherever they go. The more subtle understanding of privacy embraced by Generation Google recognizes that a person should retain some control over personal information that becomes publicly available. This generation wants a say in how private details of their lives are disseminated.

The issue of control over personal information came to the fore in 2006, when Facebook launched a feature called News Feeds, which sent a notice to people's friends registered with the service when their profile was changed or updated. To the surprise of those who run Facebook, many of its users reacted with outrage. Nearly 700,000 of them complained. At first blush, the outcry over News Feeds seems baffling. Many of the users who protested had profiles completely accessible to the public. So why did they think it was a privacy violation to alert their friends to changes in their profiles?

Instead of viewing privacy as secrets hidden away in a dark closet, they considered the issue a matter of accessibility. They figured most people would not scrutinize their profiles carefully enough to notice minor changes and updates. They could make changes inconspicuously. But Facebook's News Feeds made information more noticeable. The privacy objection was not about secrecy, but about accessibility.

In 2007 Facebook encountered another privacy outcry when it launched an advertising system with two parts, called Social Ads and Beacon. With Social Ads, whenever users wrote something positive about a product or a movie, Facebook would use their names, images, and words in advertisements sent to friends in the hope that an endorsement would induce other users to purchase a product more than a generic advertisement. With Beacon, Facebook made data-sharing deals with a variety of other commercial websites. If a Facebook user bought a movie ticket on Fandango or an item on another site, that information would pop up in the user's public profile.

Facebook rolled out these programs without adequately informing its users. People unwittingly found themselves shilling products on their friends' websites. And some people were shocked to see their private purchases on other websites suddenly displayed to the public as part of their profiles that appeared on the Facebook site.

The outcry and an ensuing online petition called for Facebook to reform its practices—a document that quickly attracted tens of thousands of signatures and ultimately led to several changes. As witnessed in these instances, privacy does not always involve sharing of secrets. Facebook users did not want their identities used to endorse products with Social Ads. It is one thing to write about how much one enjoys a movie or album; it is another to be used on a billboard to pitch products to others.

Protecting privacy extends beyond the mere keeping of secrets. It also involves providing greater rights to control how information is disseminated and used. There are some who contend that it is too late to protect privacy because so much information is already out there. David Brin argues that the *"djinn* cannot be crammed back into its bottle" and that "[l]ight *is* going to shine into every corner of our lives."[9] But even if information is already exposed in some contexts, this does not mean that protecting privacy with respect to that information is futile.

In some areas, U.S. law has a well-developed system of controlling information. Copyright recognizes strong rights for public information, protecting a wide range of works, from movies to software. Procuring copyright protection does not require locking a work of intellect behind closed doors. You can read a copyrighted magazine, make a duplicate for your own use, and lend it to others. But you cannot do whatever you want: for instance, photocopying it from cover to cover or selling bootleg copies in the street. Copyright law tries to achieve a balance between freedom and control, even though it still must wrestle with the ongoing controversies in a digital age.

The appropriation tort, one of the U.S. privacy torts, bears some similarities to copyright law. The tort prevents the use of someone else's name or likeness for financial benefit. Unfortunately, the law has developed in a way that is often ineffective against the type of privacy threats now cropping up. Copyright primarily functions as a form of property right, protecting works of self-expression, such as a song or painting.

To cope with increased threats to privacy, the scope of the appropriation tort should be expanded. The broadening might embody the original early twentieth-century interpretation of this principle of common law, which conceived of privacy as more than a means to protect property: "The right to withdraw from the public gaze at such times as a person may see fit . . . is embraced within the right of personal liberty," declared the Georgia Supreme

Court in 1905.[10] Today, however, the tort does not apply when a person's name or image appears in news, art, literature, or on social-networking sites. At the same time the appropriation tort protects against using someone's name or picture without consent to advertise products, it allows these representations to be used in a news story. This limitation is significant, since it means the tort would rarely apply to Internet-related postings.

Any expansion of the appropriation tort must be balanced against the competing need to allow legitimate news gathering and dissemination of public information. The tort should probably apply only when photographs and other personal information are used in ways that are not of public concern—a criterion that will inevitably be subject to ongoing judicial deliberation.

Appropriation is not the only common-law privacy tort that needs an overhaul to become more relevant in an era of networked digital communications. We already have many legal tools to protect privacy, but they are currently crippled by conceptions of privacy that prevent them from working effectively. A broader development of the law should take into account problematic uses of personal information illustrated by the Star Wars Kid or Facebook's Beacon service.

Ideally, most of these disputes should be resolved without recourse to the courts, but the broad reach of electronic networking will probably necessitate changes in common law. The threats to privacy are formidable, and people are starting to realize how strongly they regard privacy as a basic right. Toward this goal, society must develop a new and more nuanced conception of public and private life—one that acknowledges that more personal information is going to be available yet protects some choice over how that information is shared and distributed.

Reforming the CDA §230

In addition to failing to adequately protect privacy, the law is hampered because it overprotects free speech. In particular, the Communications Decency Act (CDA) §230 promotes a culture of irresponsibility when it comes to speech online. The CDA §230 states: "No provider or user of an interactive computer service shall be treated as the publisher or speaker of any information provided by another information content provider."[11] Most courts have interpreted §230 to immunize the operators of websites or blogs against liability for comments posted by others.[12]

This rule is generally sound, for the author of a blog should not be responsible for a comment posted by another. However, most courts have gone further—they have held that the immunity applies even when a blogger, ISP, or website operator fails to remove a comment despite having knowledge that it is defamatory or invasive of privacy.[13] This extension of §230 does nothing to prevent irresponsibility when it comes to privacy-invasive speech that harms others.

For example, in 2007, a website called JuicyCampus encouraged college students to post rumors and gossip about each other.[14] As a *Newsweek* article reported: "The posts have devolved from innocuous tales of secret crushes to racist tirades and lurid finger-pointing about drug use and sex, often with the alleged culprit identified by first and last name."[15] Some titles of posts included the "Best BlowJ" and "GUYS WITH STDS!" and the "Dumbest Duke Student."

JuicyCampus flaunted its §230 immunity. Since JuicyCampus did not supply the gossip and rumor itself, it could claim immunity for the comments others posted. According to JuicyCampus's FAQs:

> Is JuicyCampus liable for the content posted on the site?
>
> No. JuicyCampus is not the author of the posts on the site. Rather, JuicyCampus is the provider of an interactive computer service. Pursuant to Title 47 U.S.C. Section 230, JuicyCampus is immune from liability arising from content posted by users.[16]

The website deliberately tried to cloak gossip and rumormongers with anonymity. The FAQs stated:

> Is the site really anonymous?
>
> Yes. We don't ask for your name, email address, or other personally identifiable information in order for you to make a post. In fact, we prefer not to know who you are.[17]

Those who were the subject of gossip or rumor on JuicyCampus were helpless to do much about it. According to the website's FAQs:

> How do I remove a post that someone else made?
>
> You can't. Only we can remove posts made by others, and generally we don't. We do remove spam, but otherwise it's pretty rare.[18]

JuicyCampus shut down in 2009, a victim of the bad economy.[19] Although JuicyCampus is gone, the problems it raises persist, for there are countless other websites that encourage and spread rumor and gossip in irresponsible ways. Websites like JuicyCampus are a prime illustration of why §230 goes too far, promoting the dissemination of harmful gossip and rumor. This is why I recommend that §230 be modified to have a notice-and-takedown system rather than complete unmitigated immunity. Whenever bloggers or website operators know that a comment posted by another is tortious, the law should create an incentive for them to remove it. If a person promptly removes a tortious comment after being notified, then that person would be immune. If the person fails to remove the comment, only then would the person be subjected to potential liability.[20]

In a thoughtful response to this proposal, Amber Taylor argues that notice and takedown will open up a Pandora's box of problems. She points to the Digital Millennium Copyright Act (DMCA), which contains a notice-and-takedown procedure for information that violates copyright law.[21] A person will not be held liable for a copyright violation for improperly posting copyrighted material if, after receiving notice from the copyright holder, she "responds expeditiously to remove, or disable access to, the material that is claimed to be infringing or to be the subject of infringing activity."[22] Taylor contends that "[Solove] does not recognize that his own proposal would result in over-enforcement of privacy norms, since the threat of litigation is often enough for webmasters to take down protected speech."[23] Likewise, in a similar critique of my proposal, Professor Rebecca Tushnet argues:

> Given how easily notice and takedown can be abused, and how rarely posters challenge notices (which must seem very high-stakes indeed to nonlawyers), I am unenthusiastic about this idea unless the procedure was made very transparent and the penalties for ISPs were pretty limited.[24]

These criticisms are formidable, especially in light of how the DMCA notice-and-takedown system for copyright violations has been abused. The DMCA regime is fraught with problems, as zealous copyright owners are making overbroad takedown requests for material that is fair use. YouTube, for example, quickly removes any videos upon receiving a takedown request, even when there is a good argument for fair use. And for the blogger, it is difficult not to be shaking in one's boots when receiving a nasty takedown letter from a corporate lawyer threatening the apocalypse if one does not comply. Facing such a leviathan, with the muscular copyright law in its corner and armed with the threat of huge statutory damages, the wisest course of action is to back down and take down.

Would notice and takedown for defamatory or privacy-invasive speech run into similar problems? I do not believe it would for several reasons. First, abusing the notice-and-takedown system should be penalized.[25] Those who wrongly issue takedown threats for material that is not defamatory or invasive of privacy should be punished for making unjustified claims. Second, the entities enforcing copyright law are often very wealthy, powerful, and aggressive. Significant amounts of money are at stake. The DMCA takedown notices are part of a corporate campaign to stop music piracy and to push beyond for even greater control over content, often threatening fair use. In contrast, most privacy or defamation plaintiffs are ordinary individuals, without the ability to hire armies of lawyers or to pursue cases relentlessly to the four corners of the globe. Most individuals who request information be taken down to protect their personal reputations lack the litigating power of the music or movie industry, and the stakes are much lower.

The damages for defamation and invasion of privacy actions should be limited. This will prevent predatory lawsuits that aim to extort money. More importantly, mediation should be required before any lawsuit can proceed to trial. Most cases should not proceed to trial. The law should primarily function to incentivize parties to resolve their disputes. The measures I propose will push law into this function and prevent opportunistic litigation as well as help keep costs under control.

A related objection is that a notice-and-takedown regime will result in excessive takedown. Website operators will err on the side of takedown even when they believe that a comment is not tortious because they want to avoid the hassle of litigation and the risk that they might be incorrect. Although this is a valid objection, it should not deter us from lessening §230 immunity in the manner I propose. The risk of excessive takedown objection can be made against any potential liability for speech. Taken to its logical extreme, the excessive takedown objection suggests that if we truly want free speech uninhibited by any chilling effect from potential litigation, there should be absolute immunity for speech—immunity should be expanded to apply to all speech, whether online or offline, whether one is the speaker or not. Few would argue, however, in favor of such a broad immunity. Excessive takedown is always a concern, but the law already accounts for and deals with that risk. Lessening §230 immunity is unlikely to increase the existing risk of excessive takedown in a dramatic fashion.

Part of the analysis of how minor modifications to §230 immunity will impact speech depends upon empirical questions that remain unanswered: How often will people attempt to request to have information taken down? How frequently will such a notice-and-takedown system be abused? I do not think there will be rampant abuse. Nor do I predict a barrage of takedown requests. Indeed, even under our current system, where §230 immunizes bloggers for comments of others, there is no reason why a person should not at least ask for something to be taken down—at worst, the blogger says no. I am not aware of much evidence that takedown requests are currently out of control, and I doubt changing the system from voluntary takedown to a more mandatory takedown will result in a sudden tsunami of problems. But this is a guess. The only way to find out for certain is to experiment. The costs of leaving the law as it is are real and significant—people's lives are being ruined, their future opportunities are being limited, their freedom to grow, develop, and achieve their dreams is being hampered. Given these costs, something should be done to address the problem, even if there is some risk to free speech. The risk is likely to be small, but it is impossible to know for certain. If altering §230 immunity suddenly leads to widespread abuses and excessive chilling of non-tortious speech, then the law can always be restored.

The balance between privacy and free speech is currently out of kilter. My proposals might tip the balance too much in the privacy direction, but given the status quo of a balance tipped too far on the side of speech, I believe it is worth tinkering with the scale and taking the risk. In the unlikely event that the balance shifts too far toward privacy, adjustments can be made. The objections to my proposals certainly suggest caution, as there is indeed a risk of rampant abuses, but that is a risk, not a certainty, and we should not let it paralyze us from trying to fix an existing problematic imbalance.

The most effective solutions encourage norm change, and that occurs not just through the law but through increasing people's awareness of the consequences of their online speech. Currently, I see both in the law and in the discourse an exaltation of speech over privacy, a strong sentiment that people should be able to say whatever they want with impunity. Shaping these norms into a better balance between free speech and privacy is key if we are going to make any headway in addressing these problems.

Whom Should We Protect?

Some people, like the Star Wars Kid, are the unwitting victims of those who release their personal information online. Others willingly expose their own personal information online and may later want to remove or conceal it. Should these two instances be treated differently? Regarding the non-consensual victim of personal information disclosure, I believe that the law should provide strong protection. As for the person who self-exposes, that person is engaging in risky behavior and cedes some rights to privacy. But what if that person is a juvenile who lacks judgment? Suppose later on, as an adult, she regrets what she posted about herself online and wants it removed and others who disseminated it to take it off their websites. This is a tricky problem. I believe that there should be some limited right to retract information, especially for minors, though developing the contours of such a right would require a much lengthier exposition than is possible here.

Another issue when it comes to self-exposure is the degree of exposure. Suppose a person discloses information on a Facebook page that is set up so that only the person's friends can view it. Suppose the person has fifty friends. Is the information still private? I believe there is a good argument that it is.[26] Even though the data is disseminated to quite a few people, it is clear that the person has explicitly limited the visibility of the information to a select group of people. There should be an implicit understanding of confidentiality in this instance. A stranger who finds a way to pry into the person's Facebook page is committing an intrusion, for she is accessing information she is not authorized to see. If one of the person's friends were to disseminate the information beyond the group of friends, such a disclosure could be understood to be a breach of confidentiality. Abandoning antiquated notions of privacy would be an important first step in working out an appropriate law and policy to deal with situations like these.

One common response to the growing loss of privacy due to online speech is that in the future, Generation Google will develop a much lesser expectation of privacy. Technology has led to a generational divide. On one side are high school and college students whose lives virtually revolve around social-networking sites and blogs. On the other side are their parents, for whom recollection of the past often remains locked in fading memories or, at best, in books, photographs, and videos. For the current generation, the past is preserved on the Internet, potentially forever. And this change raises the question of how much privacy people can expect—or even desire—in an age of ubiquitous networking. For example, Taylor contends in a critique of my calls for greater privacy protection:

> The experience of living online will only become more universalized, giving people more of a basis for judging people and information they encounter there. Privacy will recede from the heights it achieved during our brief period of wealth and atomization. Present notions of reputation will no longer apply; as multiple personas become more difficult to maintain. All this will result in a more accurate and humanized representation: we are who we are, warts and all, and the exposure of actions and beliefs that we now keep under wraps will result in changes in social norms. We need not fear the future, and despite Solove's concerns, the temporary dislocation of the present is no great danger either.[27]

Exposing all our warts, however, will not improve our judgments of others or create a world where the norms people champion yet secretly transgress disappear. People are often hypocritical. Many social norms are idealized standards of behavior. When all our warts are exposed, we might still condemn. It is not clear that exposing people's foibles will change norms—it might just hurt those who get exposed. Perhaps if we had 100 percent information on 100 percent of the people, things might change, but that is unlikely to occur. Whose curtains will get ripped down and whose won't will likely be haphazard. And so a utopia where we all judge each other openly, fairly, and without hypocrisy might never exist. Instead there will be a world where more people are hurt and condemned when their private lives are suddenly exposed.

Moreover, I dispute claims that Generation Google will grow to eschew privacy and love living completely exposed. When members of Generation Google are adults with teenage children, will they celebrate their child's loss of privacy, happily helping them upload their naked pictures to the Internet? Will these parents help edit their children's typos and grammar on their tell-all sex diaries? Or will they be even more cognizant than parents today about the dangers of overexposure? I believe the latter. I believe they will learn the consequences of losing privacy, and they will better educate their own children based on their experiences. Ultimately, only time will tell. Looking back on history, the advent of new technologies frequently raised cries of the inevitable death of privacy. Nevertheless, privacy has persisted as a major social desire and goal. People have long worried that future generations would not care about privacy, but privacy still has not died, and people still care about it.

The Internet is creating new and vexing threats to privacy as people have an unprecedented ability to gather and spread information about each other around the world. To address these problems, we need to rethink privacy for the Information Age. If we fail to do so, we will face severe limitations on freedom and self-development now and in the future.

CHAPTER 2

Civil Rights in Our Information Age

DANIELLE KEATS CITRON

The Internet is a double-edged sword. While it can facilitate the empowerment of people who often face discrimination, it can also be exploited to disenfranchise those very same individuals. Anonymous mobs employ collaborative technologies to terrorize and silence women, people of color, and other minorities. The harassment typically includes threats of sexual violence, postings of individuals' home addresses alongside the suggestion that they should be raped, and technological attacks that shut down blogs and websites. Cyber mobs brand targeted individuals as inferior beings and as sexual objects.

Not surprisingly, the abuse has a profound impact upon targeted individuals. It may intimidate them, chasing them offline. It may convince them to disguise their online identities. When individuals go offline or assume pseudonyms to avoid bigoted cyber attacks, they miss innumerable economic and social opportunities. They suffer feelings of shame and isolation. Cyber mobs effectively deny people the right to participate in online life as equals.

Consider these examples.[1] Kathy Sierra, a programmer and game developer, maintained a popular blog on software development called "Creating Passionate Users." In 2007, anonymous individuals attacked Ms. Sierra on her blog and two other websites. Posters threatened rape and strangulation. They revealed her home address and Social Security number. They posted doctored photographs of Ms. Sierra. One picture featured her with a noose beside her neck; the other depicted her screaming while being suffocated by lingerie. After the attack, Ms. Sierra canceled speaking engagements and feared leaving her yard. She suspended her blog, even though it enhanced her reputation in the technical community. In April 2009, she explained that her "blog [once] was in the Technorati Top 100. I have not blogged there—or anywhere—since."[2]

Posters on a white supremacist website targeted Bonnie Jouhari, a civil rights advocate and mother of a biracial girl. They posted her child's picture and Ms. Jouhari's home address. The site showed an animated picture of Ms. Jouhari's workplace exploding in flames next to the threat that "race traitors" are "hung from the neck from the nearest tree or lamp post." Posters included bomb-making instructions beneath the picture. After Ms. Jouhari and her daughter began receiving harassing phone calls at home and at work, she left her job and moved. Ms. Jouhari has explained that neither she nor her daughter maintains a driver's license, voter registration card, or bank account because they fear creating a public record of their whereabouts.[3]

Many view these attacks as isolated instances of cyber bullying. They characterize them as random pranks or the by-products of soured relationships. But anonymous mobs accomplish something far more systematic than that. Rather than attacking a random mix of individuals, cyber mobs disproportionately target women. The nonprofit organization Working to Halt Online Abuse explains that, from 2000 to 2007, 72.5 percent of the individuals reporting cyber harassment identified themselves as women and 22 percent identified themselves as men. Half of those individuals had no relationship with their attackers.[4] Similarly, the National Center for Victims of Crimes' Stalking Resource Center reports that approximately 60 percent of online harassment cases involve male attackers and female targets. Cyber mobs often target lesbian and/or nonwhite women with particular virulence. They also focus on men of color, religious minorities, and gay men.

These cyber assaults also inflict a wider array of injuries than isolated pranks or fights between adversaries. When online mobs attack individuals because of their race, gender, or other protected characteristic, they damage individuals, their groups, and society in unique ways. Traditional criminal and tort law can reach some of their injuries, such as the tarnished reputations, emotional distress caused by threats, and privacy invasions. But they fall short of a complete response because they fail to address the gender- and race-based nature of the damage.

Civil rights laws are designed to respond to such harm. Antidiscrimination laws guarantee the right to be free of unequal treatment on the basis of race, gender, or other protected characteristics. Cyber mobs violate those guarantees when they shut down income-generating blogs because the bloggers are women or African American. They transgress civil rights laws when they terrorize individuals with rape threats because of their race, gender, or other protected characteristic. Civil rights remedies would combat a cyber mob's interference with individuals' right to work and participate in discourse online as equals.

This essay explores the destructive nature of today's online mobs. It examines how the Internet's features magnify dangerous online mob behavior. It rejects the notion that targeted individuals can, and should, combat cyber mobs on their own. Instead, it offers a comprehensive legal response to combat today's cyber mobs. It emphasizes the important role that traditional criminal and tort remedies would play in addressing the online abuse and acknowledges their limitations. It argues that civil rights laws can compensate for these shortcomings by reaching the damage that a cyber mob's discrimination inflicts upon individuals, groups, and society. I shall then respond to concerns that protecting civil rights online would compromise our commitment to free speech. I explain why a legal response comports with First Amendment doctrine and how a robust protection of cyber civil rights would promote more valuable speech than it would inhibit.

Anonymous Mobs of the Twenty-first Century

Cyber mobs attack women and minorities in several ways. They terrorize individuals with threats of sexual violence and doctored photographs, often encouraging others to physically assault individuals and providing their home addresses. Online mobs invade individuals' privacy, hacking into their personal computers and email accounts to obtain confidential information and then posting it online. Attackers post reputation-harming statements online, accusing individuals of having mental illnesses and sexually transmitted diseases. They send the damaging statements to employers and manipulate search engines to ensure that the statements appear prominently in searches of targeted individuals' names. Attackers use technology to drive targeted individuals offline. Groups coordinate denial-of-service attacks that close sites and blogs. Cyber mobs routinely use all of these tools in their attacks.

In response, targeted individuals abandon income-generating blogs and websites or maintain them under gender-disguising pseudonyms. They withdraw from online discussion groups. They employ passwords to eliminate their websites' connectivity to a wider, and potentially threatening, audience. They close comments on blog posts, foreclosing productive conversations along with abusive ones.

Cyber mobs can be very brutal. In 2007, the social-networking site Auto-Admit hosted group attacks on named female law students. Thirty-nine posters targeted the women on the site's message board. The posters, writing under pseudonyms, generated hundreds of threatening, sexually explicit, and damaging statements about the female law students.[5] Posters threatened them with violence. One poster asserted that a named female student should "get raped." That remark led to many additional threats. A poster promised: "I'll force myself on [the identified student]" and "sodomize" her "repeatedly." Another said that the student "deserves to be raped so that her little fantasy world can be shattered by real life."

Discussion threads suggested that the posters had physical access to the women. A poster described a woman's attire at the school gym. Others mentioned meeting the women, describing what they looked like and where they spent their summer. Some provided updates on sightings of particular women. A poster provided the email address of a female law student under a thread entitled "Mad at [named individual]? Email her."

Posters asserted damaging statements about the women. One claimed that a woman spent time in a drug rehabilitation center. Others remarked that the woman appeared in *Playboy*. Posters claimed that another female student had a sexually transmitted disease. Others provided her purported "subpar" LSAT score. Posters spread the alleged lies offline to ruin the women's reputations. One poster urged the group to tell top law firms about the female student's LSAT score "before she gets an offer." Posters emailed damaging statements to her former employer; they admonished the employer that clients would "not want to be represented by someone who is not of the highest character value."

The posters also engaged in the practice known as "Google bombing" to ensure that anyone searching the female students' names would see the damaging statements. Google bombing raises the ranking of a web page discussing someone if posters link to it in as many other web pages as possible. This helps ensure a web page's prominence because search engines rank a web page highly in a search of a person's name if an overwhelming number of sites link to that page. Posters provided instructions on how to engage in "Google bombing" and made plain their goal: "We're not going to let that bitch have her own blog be the first result from googling her name!"

Posters admitted their desire to intimidate and harm the female students. After one of the women did not get a summer job, a poster asked if the other "bitch got what she deserved too?" Another said, "I'm doing cartwheels knowing this stupid Jew bitch is getting her self esteem raped." A poster explained that the women were targeted "just for being women."

Similarly, a group called Anonymous has devoted itself to terrorizing and silencing hundreds of women on the web. For instance, in 2007, Anonymous used message boards and wikis to plan an attack on a nineteen-year-old woman who maintained a video blog on Japanese language and video games. Group members hacked into her email, obtaining her personal information, and published her home address, passwords, and private medical history on various sites. The group posted a doctored photograph of the woman atop naked bodies. Underneath the photograph appeared the warning: "We will rape her at full force in her vagina, mouth, and ass." Another picture depicted the woman with men brutally raping her. Group members saturated her video blog with sexually violent material and took down her videos. When her live journal or video blog would reappear, Anonymous urged its members to "rape" and "nuke [her site] from orbit."

Anonymous maintains a list of women's issues sites and blogs that it claims to have forced offline. The list includes names of shuttered sites with a line crossed through them and the accompanying message: "[d]own due to excessive bandwidth—great success." When a site reappears online, Anonymous tells its members: "It's back! Show no mercy." The group takes credit for closing more than 100 feminist websites and blogs.[6] Targeted female bloggers and website operators confirm these claims. A victim explained, "[b]eing silenced for over two weeks felt infuriating, stifling, imprisoned by gang rapists just waiting for me to try to get up from underneath their weight so they could stomp on me again."[7]

In August 2008, an online mob attacked a woman who blogged about the film *The Dark Knight*. A poster threatened: "Get a life you two dollar whore blogger, The Dark Knight doesn't suck, you suck! Don't ever post another blog unless you want to get ganged up." Another poster urged: "if you were my wife I would beat you." Others disparaged her intellect: "This is why women are TOO STUPID to think critically and intelligently about film; AND business for that matter" and "Why don't you make yourself useful and go have a baby." The woman explained that of the nearly 200 comments, only three failed to mention her gender in a threatening and disparaging manner. To stop the harassment, she closed the comments and deleted fifty of the most violent ones.[8]

Online mobs target African American and Hispanic women as well. As blogger "La Chola" explains, women-of-color bloggers consistently receive horrific emails and comments threatening violent sexual assault, death, and attacks against family members.[9] After the author of "Ask This Black Woman" posted commentary about a video game, anonymous posters attacked her on her blog and other sites. She received death threats. Posters told her to "[g]et back into the cotton fields, you filthy [n***r]" and threatened to overrun her blog.[10]

Cyber mobs inflict serious injuries. Targeted people who curtail their online activities or go offline incur serious costs. They lose advertising income generated from blogs and websites. They miss opportunities to advance their professional reputations through blogging. They cannot network effectively online if they assume pseudonyms to deflect the abuse. As technology blogger Robert Scoble explains, women who lack a robust online presence are "never going to be included in the [technology] industry." Moreover, damaging online statements can destroy reputations because employers use Google results in assessing candidates. They may decline to interview or hire someone because the statements suggest that the person attracts unwanted controversy.

Online harassment also produces serious emotional and physical suffering. Targeted individuals feel a sustained loss of personal security. They fear that online threats of sexual violence will be realized. Their anxiety is particularly acute as the posters' anonymity vanquishes any cues that might alleviate their concerns. Their emotional distress often produces physical symptoms, such as anorexia nervosa, depression, headaches, and suicide. Posts providing individuals' home addresses alongside the suggestion that they should be raped or killed have led to offline stalking.

The Internet's Role in Aggravating Cyber Mob Behavior

Social science research on group behavior suggests that the Internet will intensify the destructiveness of gender and race-based harassment. It identifies several factors exacerbating the dangerousness of groups. Groups with homogenous views tend to become more extreme when they deliberate.[11] Their members gain confidence in their preconceived ideas as discussions tend to feature many arguments supporting them and few tilting the other way. Hearing agreement from others bolsters group members' confidence, entrenching and radicalizing their views.

Group members often lack a sense of personal responsibility for their acts.[12] According to one school of thought, this occurs because people in groups fail to see themselves as distinct individuals. Another school of thought explains that people behave aggressively because they believe that when immersed in a group they cannot be observed and caught.

Groups are more destructive when they dehumanize their victims.[13] When group members view victims as devoid of humanity and personal identity, they feel free to attack without regret. They are also more aggressive when authority figures support their efforts.[14] Social scientists emphasize a perceived leader's role in accelerating dangerous group behavior. Southern newspapers in the early 1900s explicitly legitimated violence by reporting that lynch mobs included prominent members of the white community. Federal authorities implicitly encouraged the Ku Klux Klan by failing to enforce civil rights laws.[15]

The Internet magnifies the dangerousness of group behavior in each of these respects. Web 2.0 platforms create a feeling of closeness among like-minded individuals. Because online group members tend to affirm each other's negative views, they become more extreme and destructive. Individuals do and say things online they would never consider doing or saying offline because they feel anonymous and do not fear getting caught. Cyber mobs also see victims as digital images that can be eviscerated without regret.

Moreover, site operators who refuse to dismantle destructive posts reinforce, and effectively encourage, negative behavior. Their refusal can stem from a libertarian "You Own Your Own Words" philosophy or irresponsibility bred from the belief that they enjoy broad statutory immunity from liability for the postings of others. In turn, negative posts that remain online constitute calls to action that generate others in a snowball effect. In cyberspace, the accelerants of dangerous group behavior are pervasive, deepening the problem of today's abusive cyber mobs.

Some suggest that the market can solve this serious social problem. They assert that targeted individuals can defeat destructive cyber mobs by recruiting advocacy groups to defend them. They envision women's groups coordinating efforts to rebuild a targeted individual's reputation online by engaging in "Google bombing" to optimize positive posts produced in a search of a victim's name. They point to groups like Reputation Defender that have helped cyber harassment victims establish an online presence to offset destructive postings.

Such a response, however, would be inadequate. It would not remove the threats and lies that terrorize and silence individuals. In defamatory attacks, it is inconceivable that all of the damage will be erased. Because so many people will see the material, some will inevitably miss the individual's response while others will not believe, or only partially believe, it. This is especially true when dealing with attacks on someone's character because the targeted individual does not have an affirmative case she is trying to convey—she is only seeking to dispel the harm from the mob's attack. Moreover, people seeing a disproportionate number of her rebuttals will not counterbalance those who have seen none.

The efforts of advocacy groups may be unable to drown out the assaults of cyber mobs. Consider the case of Nicole Catsouras, who died in a horrific car crash. Gruesome photographs of the carnage appeared on the Internet, spreading to over 1,500 sites. Posters urged cohorts to harass her family and facilitated this harassment by providing the family's home address. The woman's family asked sites to remove the pictures but to no avail. Tracking down anonymous posters proved impossible for the family, and the pictures remained online.

Countermeasures also run the risk of sustaining the life of the attacks rather than slowing them down. Because the very purpose of many online attacks is to force individuals off the web, mobs are likely to respond with venom against those who not only stay online but try to fight back. A targeted individual would likely conclude that more people will see the defamatory or threatening material if she responds than if she does not.

This view ignores the social harm resulting from an online mob's attacks. If working and expressing opinions online subjects someone to the risk of assault, even if the damage is only temporary, the result will change the kind of people who engage in cyber discourse. Members of a targeted group will experience stigma and go offline. These attacks undermine our commitment to full and equal participation in public life in a manner that victims cannot, and should not, address on their own.

A Comprehensive Legal Approach to Cyber Mobs

Because private mechanisms cannot provide a meaningful solution to today's cyber mobs, a legal response is in order. A comprehensive response would include traditional criminal prosecutions, tort remedies, and civil rights actions. Supplementing traditional criminal and tort law remedies with civil rights ones is crucial to reach all of the harm that cyber mobs inflict.

Traditional criminal and tort law remedies can address some of the harm that targeted individuals' experience. Criminal law would punish a cyber mob's members for sending code that shuts down someone's blog. It criminalizes online harassment. For instance, the Violence Against Women Act (VAWA) punishes anyone using a telecommunications device without disclosing his identity and with the intent to "abuse, threaten or harass any person who receives the communication."[16] Some states criminalize posting messages with the intent to urge or incite others to harass a victim.[17] California authorities obtained a guilty plea from a defendant who terrorized a woman by impersonating her in chat rooms and bulletin boards, where the defendant posted the victim's home address alongside the suggestion that she fantasized about being raped.

Tort law would provide redress for a cyber mob's faulty actions. Individuals can sue cyber mobs for defamation if online lies injure their reputation. They can seek money damages for emotional distress that cyber mobs intentionally or recklessly cause. They can also bring privacy claims against cyber mobs that publicly disclose private facts that would be "highly offensive to the reasonable person."[18]

These traditional remedies have an important, yet limited role in combating cyber mobs. They express society's disapproval of online threats, computer crimes, and tortious conduct. They punish cyber mobs for socially unacceptable conduct, such as harassment and computer crimes. They secure compensation for damaged reputations and emotional distress. They serve as a deterrent when cyber mobs see that the cost of their conduct exceeds its benefits.

Now, let's explore the limitations of traditional remedies. Traditional criminal and tort law cannot reach the harm experienced by individuals, their groups, and society due to cyber mobs' interference with their right to equal treatment. Traditional remedies simply are not designed to redress the suffering caused by discrimination, both to individuals and to the public at large. Defamation law, for example, remedies a plaintiff's reputational harm caused by online falsehoods. It does not, however, redress the harm inflicted upon the person's group or society. Nor does defamation law address the stigma and economic injuries that individuals experience when they are targeted because of their race, gender, or other personal characteristic.

Civil rights laws compensate for these shortcomings. They respond to harms inflicted when cyber mobs deprive individuals of their right to equal treatment. They address the unique harms suffered by targeted individuals. Civil rights laws respond to a cyber mob's interference with a person's work because of her race, gender, or other protected characteristic. They would tackle the professional sabotage perpetrated by the anonymous posters whose threats of violence and doctored photographs drove Ms. Sierra and Ms. Jouhari offline. They would respond to the anonymous posters' technological attacks that shut down women's issues websites because the site operators were female. Whereas traditional criminal and tort law fail to address the economic harm caused by discrimination, civil rights laws do.

Civil rights laws also address the corrosive stigmatization of targeted individuals. They recognize victims' feelings of humiliation and inferiority.[19] They redress the alienation that individuals experience when they assume gender-disguising names or downplay stereotypically female attributes, such as compassion, to deflect a cyber mob's abuse. Civil rights laws prevent, punish, and redress this psychic damage.

Civil rights laws respond to the harm experienced by a targeted individual's group. Nontargeted group members often experience cyber attacks as if they happened to them personally. When anonymous posters threatened to rape Ms. Sierra, other female bloggers felt targeted and at risk. When a cyber mob threatened to kill the author of the "Ask This Black Woman" blog and told her to "[g]et back into the cotton fields, you filthy [n***r]," the website operator wasn't the only one who felt threatened. African American readers felt intimidated and threatened. Nontargeted group members may go offline or assume pseudonyms to avoid being targeted. This has psychic and economic costs that civil rights laws recognize and remedy.

Civil rights laws address the harm that cyber mobs inflict upon society. The public experiences a serious loss when targeted individuals and nontargeted group members stop contributing to our online marketplace and discourse due to cyber mobs' abuse. It suffers because online mob attacks entrench gender and racial hierarchy in cyberspace. Sexually demeaning comments and rape threats suggest men's power over women. They reinforce gendered stereotypes, casting men as dominant in the bedroom and at work and women as subservient sexual objects who are not fit to work online. Threats laden with racial epithets operate in a similar fashion, suggesting that African Americans are inferior to white individuals. These messages stake out the Internet as a space for white men. Civil rights laws respond to this systemic harm.

Federal and state antidiscrimination laws offer various means to combat cyber mobs. They would criminalize some of a cyber mob's abusive behavior. The Civil Rights Act of 1968 punishes "force or threat[s] of force" designed to intimidate or interfere with a person's private employment due to that person's race, religion, or national origin.[20] Courts have sustained convictions of defendants who made death threats over employees' email and voice mail.[21] A court upheld the prosecution of a defendant who left messages on an Arab American's voice mail that threatened "the only good Arab is a dead Arab." Similarly, a jury convicted a defendant under this statute for sending an email under the name "Asian Hater" to sixty Asian students that read: "I personally will make it my life career [sic] to find and kill everyone of you personally."[22]

Current law should be amended to criminalize online threats made because of a victim's gender or sexual orientation. VAWA is a profitable place to begin this effort. Although the Supreme Court struck down VAWA's regulation of gender-motivated violence on the grounds that such criminal conduct did not substantially affect interstate commerce to justify congressional action under the Commerce Clause, Congress could amend VAWA pursuant to its power to regulate an instrumentality of interstate commerce—the Internet—to punish anonymous cyber mobs that threaten individuals because of their gender or sexual orientation. The Department of Justice would presumably support such a development as it currently encourages federal prosecutors to seek hate crime penalty enhancements for defendants who subject victims to cyber harassment because of their race, color, religion, national origin, or sexual orientation.[23]

Civil rights laws also sanction private lawsuits against cyber mobs for their discriminatory actions. Section 1981 of Title 42 of the U.S. Code guarantees members of racial minorities "the same right in every State . . . to make and enforce contracts . . . as is enjoyed by white citizens."[24] Section 1981 permits lawsuits against private individuals without the need for state action because Congress enacted the statute under its power to enforce the Thirteenth Amendment. Courts have allowed plaintiffs to bring Section 1981 claims against masked mobs that used tactics of intimidation to prevent members of racial minorities from "making a living" in their chosen field.[25]

Women can sue a cyber mob's members under Title VII of the Civil Rights Act of 1964 for preventing them from making a living because of their sex.[26] Title VII actions can be asserted against private actors because Congress enacted Title VII pursuant to a valid exercise of its power to regulate interstate commerce. Just after Congress passed Title VII, courts upheld discrimination claims where masked defendants engaged in intimidation tactics to prevent plaintiffs from pursuing their chosen careers.[27] Although recent Title VII decisions focus on employer-employee relationships, courts should look to those early cases in deciding whether women can bring sex discrimination claims against anonymous cyber mobs that interfere with their online work because of their gender. Doing so would honor Title VII's goal of eliminating discrimination in women's employment opportunities.

Congress recognized the dangers that anonymous mobs pose to individuals' right to equal treatment during Reconstruction. It enacted the Ku Klux Klan Act of 1871 to reach the destructive conduct of Klan members who conspired to deprive individuals of their basic rights under the cloak of anonymity. Section 2 of the 1871 Act, now codified at Section 1985(3) of Title 42, allows damage suits against two or more people who conspire or go in disguise on the highway to deprive any person of the equal protection of the laws.[28] Section 241 of Title 42 similarly establishes criminal penalties for "two or more persons [who] go in disguise on the highway" to hinder a person's "free exercise or enjoyment of any right or privilege" secured by the Constitution or federal law.[29]

Today's anonymous cyber mobs go on the information superhighway to deprive individuals of their essential rights to engage in discourse and participate in society as equals just as masked Klan members went on public highways to interfere with victims' basic rights. Nonetheless, efforts to apply these statutes to online mobs face formidable obstacles. In 1875, the Supreme Court narrowed their reach by requiring state action.[30] Although relaxing this ruling somewhat in 1971,[31] the Court more recently held that Sections 1985(3) and 241 only cover private conspiracies "aimed at interfering with rights that are 'protected against private, as well as official, encroachment.' "[32] For the Court, freedom of speech is not such a right.

The Court noted that Congress "no doubt" can proscribe private efforts to deny rights secured only against official interference, such as free speech, under its power to regulate interstate commerce, but held that Section 1985(3) was not such a provision. Congress should follow this suggestion and enact a law that would proscribe an anonymous cyber mob's conspiracy to deprive individuals of their right to exercise free speech under its power to regulate interstate commerce. Congress should permit targeted individuals to bring damage suits against cyber mobs, much as Section 1985(3) supplements Section 241.

Some may insist that regulating a cyber mob's attacks would interfere with our commitment to free speech. This is simply not the case. A cyber civil rights agenda comports with First Amendment doctrine and free speech values.

First Amendment jurisprudence would not immunize a cyber mob's conduct from regulation. The Supreme Court has held that the First Amendment permits restrictions on speech that offers "such slight social value as a step to truth that any benefit that may be derived from [it] is clearly outweighed by the social interest in order and morality."[33] This is equally true for threats, defamation, intentional infliction of emotional distress, and civil rights violations.

The First Amendment does not prohibit states from using criminal and civil law to forbid threats. Threats fall outside of the First Amendment's protection and for good reason. Consider an uncontroversial example. Suppose a person tells another that he will kill her the next time she leaves her house. While he makes this threat by speaking, that fact does not provide him with a defense to either criminal prosecution or civil suit. A threat of violence is both a crime and a tort, even though it is accomplished via words. All speaking is not protected, despite the seemingly blanket promise of the First Amendment that "Congress shall make no law abridging the freedom of speech." Bribery, blackmail, and threats are commonplace examples of speech that is not only forbidden but criminalized. Threats of violence made via new technologies are not immunized from penalty on free speech grounds.

These issues become more complicated with crimes that are interwoven with arguably expressive activity. Is the burning of a cross on the lawn of an African American family best characterized as a threat? Or is the expression of a view about race, though noxious, protected by the First Amendment? In Virginia v. Black, the Court answered these questions when it held that a state may ban cross burning if the defendant carried it out with the intent to intimidate. As the Court explained, the First Amendment does not protect "true threats" that communicate a serious intention to commit violence against particular individuals. The Court noted that the speaker need not actually intend to commit a violent act because the prohibition of "true threats" protects individuals from the fear of violence and the disruption that such fear engenders. It distinguished cross burnings done with the intent to intimidate, which it deemed a proscribable "true threat," from cross burning for other purposes, which it held constituted a protected expression of viewpoint.

The Court's reasoning is important here. A cyber mob's postings can constitute "true threats" if they convey a serious intention to inflict bodily harm upon the targeted individual, even if they combine the threatening language with protected offensive views. The anonymous posters arguably conveyed a serious intention to inflict bodily harm upon Kathy Sierra with their rape threats, doctored photographs, and revelation of her home address. The same is true for the individuals who posted a picture of Ms. Jouhari's workplace exploding in flames next to a warning that "race traitors" will be lynched. These threats, and others like them, are afforded no protection under First Amendment law.

The First Amendment does not protect falsehoods that damage reputations.[34] A cyber mob cannot avoid defamation liability on the grounds that their comments are too outrageous to be believed.[35] To the contrary, reputation-harming falsehoods enjoy no First Amendment protection if they assert or imply facts. For instance, the claim that a female law student had an infectious disease or mental illness is a fact that could be proved true or false for defamation purposes. Although public figures such as Kathy Sierra must prove defendants acted with "actual malice" if defamatory statements concern matters on which the public has a justified and important interest, they need not do so here because the public has no important and justified interest in rape threats, Social Security numbers, and doctored photographs.

The First Amendment does not bar antidiscrimination actions even though civil rights violations often communicate bigoted views. As the Supreme Court has held, the First Amendment poses no obstacle to civil rights claims because they proscribe defendants' unequal treatment of individuals and the unique harm that such discrimination inflicts, not the offensive messages that defendants send.

Wisconsin v. Mitchell demonstrates this point. There, the Court considered a First Amendment challenge to a Wisconsin statute enhancing the penalty of certain crimes if the perpetrator selected the victim because of race, religion, color, disability, sexual orientation, national origin, or ancestry.[36] The

Court unanimously rejected the defendant's claim that the statute punished him for his racist views. It explained that the statute did not transgress the First Amendment because it penalized the defendant's discriminatory motive for his conduct, not his bigoted ideas.

The Court analogized the Wisconsin statute to federal and state antidiscrimination laws, which, it explained, were immune from First Amendment challenge. It specifically pointed to Title VII and Section 1981 as civil rights laws that do not infringe upon defendants' First Amendment rights because they proscribe discriminatory motive (e.g., Title VII's prohibition of employment discrimination "because of" a protected characteristic), not the expression of bigoted ideas. The Court deemed both statutes "permissible content-neutral regulation[s] of conduct." It emphasized that the state was justified in singling out bias-inspired conduct due to the great individual and societal harm that it inflicts.

The *Mitchell* Court specifically distinguished R.A.V. v. City of St. Paul,[37] a case involving a city ordinance that criminalized conduct an individual "knows or has reasonable grounds to know arouses anger, alarm, or resentment in others on the basis of race, color, creed, religion, or gender." *R.A.V.* found the ordinance unconstitutional because it discriminated on the basis of the expressions' content—certain bigoted expressions were proscribed by the ordinance, yet those that gave offense in other ways were not. The *Mitchell* Court explained that "whereas the ordinance struck down in *R.A.V.* was explicitly directed at expression (*i.e.*, 'speech' or 'messages'), the [Wisconsin] statute in this case is aimed at conduct unprotected by the First Amendment." It concluded that Wisconsin's desire to address bias-inspired conduct "provides an adequate explanation for its penalty-enhancement provision over and above mere disagreement with offenders' beliefs or biases." In short, the *Mitchell* Court made clear that the First Amendment erects no barrier to the enforcement of antidiscrimination laws that regulate bias-inspired conduct and the special harm it inflicts, whereas it prohibits laws that discriminate on the basis of the ideas expressed like the one addressed in *R.A.V.*

Applying civil rights statutes to the attacks of cyber mobs falls clearly on the *Mitchell* side of this line. The statutes' proscriptions turn on an online mob's choice of victim and the distinct harm to victims, their communities, and society that a defendant's abusive conduct produces, rather than on the opinions that either the victims or the attackers express. Intimidating Ms. Sierra with rape threats and sexually demeaning comments so that she shuts down her income-generating blog is equally offensive, and equally proscribed, no matter the anonymous perpetrators' specific views. This is true when a cyber mob prevents a woman of color from securing gainful employment with sexual threats, damaging statements, and lies. Many online attacks have included racist, sexist, or other bigoted language; others have not. When law punishes online attackers due to the special severity of the social harm produced by targeting individuals because of their gender or race, and not due to the particular opinions that the attackers or victims express, it does not transgress the First Amendment.

Not only does a cyber civil rights agenda comport with First Amendment doctrine, it is consistent with prominent free speech theories that emphasize the importance of autonomy, political deliberation, cultural innovation, and the promotion of truth. Let's address the notion that protecting free speech promotes individual autonomy. On this view, free speech facilitates self-mastery, allowing people to author their own narratives and engage in political discourse. Autonomy and dignity require equitable and effective participation in political self-government, and thus the regulation of certain speech, such as racist and sexist speech, is a necessary prerequisite to secure equal citizenship.

Restraining a mob's most destructive assaults is essential to defending the expressive autonomy of its victims. Preventing mobs from driving vulnerable people offline would advance the reasons why we protect free speech in the first place, even though it would inevitably chill some speech of online mobs. Free from mob attacks, individuals, such as Ms. Sierra, might continue to blog, join online discussions, and express themselves on public issues. Protecting them from discrimination, defamation, threats, and technological attacks would allow them to be candid about their ideas.

Although online mobs express themselves through their assaults, their actions directly implicate their targets' self-determination and ability to participate in political and social discourse. Self-expression should receive little protection if its sole purpose is to extinguish the self-expression of another. As Owen Fiss argues, sometimes we must lower the voices of some to permit the self-expression of others.[38] Similarly, Cass Sunstein contends that threats, libel, and sexual and racial harassment constitute low-value speech of little First Amendment consequence.[39] Rarely is that more true than when one group of voices consciously exploits the Internet to silence others and to hide themselves to escape social responsibility for their actions.

Now, let's discuss the argument that expression deserves protection when it involves deliberation about public issues. A cyber mob's threats, lies, and discrimination, however, do not involve discussion of issues related to public life. Quite the contrary, they deprive vulnerable individuals of their right to engage in online discussions of public issues.

On a different note, democratic culture theorists like Jack Balkin argue that free speech promotes "democracy in the widest possible sense, not merely at the level of governance, or at the level of deliberation, but at the level of culture, where we interact, create, build communities, and build ourselves."[40] Freedom of expression permits innovation in a networked age where people join together to create works of art, gossip, and parody online. It can dissolve unjust social barriers of rank and privilege. Similarly, Diane Zimmerman highlights the role of gossip as generating intimacy and a sense of community among disparate groups.[41] She explains that gossip provides people a way to learn about social groups to which they do not belong and fosters relationships by giving strangers the means to bridge awkward silences when thrown together in social situations.

To be sure, online mobs engage in gossip. But their attacks have little to do with building bonds among disparate communities. Instead, rape threats, lies, damaging photographs, and denial-of-service attacks preclude connections among differently minded group members and sever a victim's connections with her own community. An online mob's attacks inflict serious social harm rather than generating ideas in popular culture or enforcing positive social norms. Defeating such discrimination outweighs any contribution that online mobs make to our cultural interaction and exchange.

Some may insist upon protecting an online mob's attacks in order to promote truth. On this view, any silencing of speech prevents us from better understanding the world in which we live. Justice Holmes drew from this theory when he articulated the notion of the marketplace of ideas: "that the best test of truth is the power of the thought to get itself accepted in the competition of the market."[42] The marketplace-of-ideas metaphor places no special premium on political discussion, but rather captures the idea that "truth must be experimentally determined from the properties of the experience itself."[43]

An extreme version of truth-seeking theory might insist the market should sort out online mobs' deceptions and assaults. Though to do so, the theory would have to consider a Social Security number a truthful fact that contributes to an understanding of that person. A more plausible vision of truth-seeking theory, however, is not served with the disclosure of a person's personal identifying information. Rather than revealing a fact to be tested in the marketplace, a Social Security number is simply a key to a person's credit and bank accounts. In this context, it is a weapon, not a truth or half-truth to be tested in the marketplace. Rape and death threats similarly tell us nothing about the victims—no truths are contested there. This is equally true of denial-of-service attacks. Even where online mobs make factual assertions, the anonymity of online communications prevents the marketplace of ideas from performing its curative function. And as Daniel Solove notes, "truth isn't the only value at stake."[44]

Although members of an online mob may transgress a variety of laws, victims are often unable to press their claims against posters who cannot be identified. This can occur when posters use anonymizing technologies that break the link between their IP addresses and real identities and when websites hosting attacks fail to track IP addresses. To be sure, it is sometimes possible to figure out the identity of posters. All too often, however, abusive posters cannot be identified.

Efforts to rein in online mobs may falter if the posters cannot be held responsible for their civil rights violations, crimes, and torts. Generally, the operators of destructive websites either have information that could help identify abusive posters or have made a conscious decision not to obtain or retain that information. Some website operators function as crowd leaders, influencing the mobs' destructiveness. Deterring websites devoted to abusive attacks on individuals plays a crucial role in inhibiting a destructive mob's coordination and efficacy. Thus, holding accountable the operators of websites that facilitate anonymous attacks may hold the key to protecting the civil rights of individuals set upon by online mobs.

Nonetheless, current law provides a barrier to website operator liability. Courts have broadly interpreted section 230 of the Communications Decency Act to immunize website operators from liability for content created by others.[45] Despite the fact that Section 230 promises "[p]rotection for private blocking and screening of offensive material," courts nonetheless read it to shield operators of sites purveying such material. These efforts to read a sweeping immunity into Section 230 have prevented courts from exploring what standard of care ought to apply to ISPs and website operators.

Broad immunity for operators of abusive websites eliminates incentives for better behavior by those in the best position to minimize harm. As Daniel

Solove explains, such immunity can "foster irresponsibility."[46] With blanket immunity, site operators have no reason to take down false or injurious material or to collect and retain identities of posters. As a result, objectionable posts remain online and searchable by employers, often migrating across the web to become effectively irretrievable, while plaintiffs continue to be unable to find and recover damages from wrongdoers. As judges, legislators, activists, and scholars begin to devote attention to online threats to civil rights, they should reconsider this sweeping immunity of website operators.

Cyber mobs inflict serious injuries that law must address. Combating their cyber assaults requires a comprehensive approach, one that includes traditional criminal prosecutions, tort remedies, and civil rights actions. Together, traditional remedies and antidiscrimination laws have great potential to deter, punish, and remedy the abuse of online mobs.

The Internet has two faces. One propels us forward with exciting opportunities for women and minorities to work, network, and spread their ideas online. The other brings us back to a time when anonymous mobs prevented vulnerable people from participating in society as equals. We can harness law's coercive power to reverse the backward-looking trend without sacrificing our commitment to free speech.

CHAPTER 3

The Internet's Anonymity Problem

SAUL LEVMORE

As social problems go, juvenile and destructive communications on the Internet are a modest matter. These communications are often offensive and noisy, and at times they are defamatory. They are likely to attract viewers in search of amusement, but repel those looking for information. In venues where juvenile and false communications come in great volume, they may discourage or camouflage serious contributions. There are media, and especially Internet websites, where such communications predominate, and others where they mingle with more valuable contributions that might well be lost if strong steps were taken to eliminate those deemed odious. When offensive communications are dispatched by identified senders they do not seem to present a new problem, even when the medium is the Internet with its remarkable reach. The sender's reputational interest, the law of defamation and harassment, and the influence of our tradition of free speech create an environment that is not much different from that found in other media. The same is often true where the sender is unidentified, but where a publisher or other intermediary is responsible. It is anonymous and pseudonymous communications, particularly in the blogosphere where such speech is routine, that are more problematic. One can be the victim of soapbox invectives, crude thoughts recorded on a bathroom wall, malignant lines printed in a letter to the editor of a newspaper, hurtful statements or footage broadcast on television, or the same nasty words written in a comment on a blog site. The likelihood of injury seems greatest in the last of these settings, and it is there that the injured party is least protected by law.

But does the Internet require special legal attention? Novelty often raises the questions of whether new law is required and whether law ought to be neutral in a competitive environment. Infant industries often make claims for special treatment, and the evolution of law is in part the story of law-makers' coming to terms with claims of novelty. Lawyers may overestimate the effect of legal rules on reality, but lawmakers are inclined to exaggerate the need for new rules when they observe new realities. Few politicians campaign on the claim that change is unnecessary, much as few law schools boast that they teach old law for new environments. And yet new terrain is often governed well by old rules. Security interests in airplanes are essentially the same as security interests in ox carts. When we turn to the development of the Internet, we can be sure that a judicial opinion, academic contribution, or legislative initiative will make the rhetorical move of emphasizing the Internet's ubiquity, speed, and multi-jurisdictional reach. But novelty is itself ubiquitous, and we ought to value stability in law, be wary of interest groups, and careful not to impose law in a way that distorts competition among industries. By sketching the level of regulation we find in competing media, as well as the cases for and against regulation, I show that the Internet is not only the most hospitable medium for offensive communications, but also that it does not deserve the lightest touch among the media.

One method of evaluating claims of novelty is to turn to a favorite tool of law and economics, and to ask what a hypothetical bargain among users, or all citizens, would look like with respect to the regulation of these communications on the Internet. I grapple with the question of whether the interest in, or legal rule protecting, free speech trumps this democratic, or market, bargain. I intend to leave the reader with the conclusion that novelty and free speech claims have probably protected the Internet from legal regulation in a manner that has generated excessive costs to the targets of offensive speech and perhaps to Internet entrepreneurs as well. Non-anonymity, or identifiability, is one route to reducing these costs; privileging a notice-and-takedown policy is another.

The Internet and Its Competitors

The Internet is hardly the medium with the highest density of anonymous or offensive communications. A high school's bathroom stalls may be the winner in that category. But Facebook, or a similar Internet site visited and easily discovered by the same high school's students, may well be the canvas of choice for the contemporary offensive graffitist. It is useful then to compare these, and then other media, in order to think about the legal environment in which juvenile—as well as mature but false—communications take place.

Environments, or media, can be compared from the perspective of the law or from that of the communicator. For one who wishes to communicate nasty remarks about a classmate, employer, or competitor, considerations of social standing, legal consequences, audience size, interactvity, and effort are all likely to play roles. A juvenile posting will have real bite—whether on an Internet site, on handbills left around a building, or on the bathroom wall—if something more than a simple slur is produced. Details can generate a defamation claim, unless author and publisher can remain unknown, and they also make possible the communication of socially useful, if painful, information. "Amy X is a slut"[1] is quintessentially juvenile, especially as a signal of interest, and no fun for Amy X or her true friends to read. Still, it is not clear that anyone suffers grave harm, not just because of the familiar aphorism about sticks and stones but also because of the irony that the more commonplace such taunts are, the less seriously anyone will take them. One response to the slut slur is for one's friends to shout out a thousand claims of that status attached to all sorts of people in order to diminish further the value of the first communication. The alternative and not unknown reaction is for an informed or well-intentioned passerby to attempt to expunge the offensive message so that it is not further communicated. Such short messages are typical of bathroom wall postings, and do not even attempt to convey much information. In contrast, "Y stole $150 from me" or "Z loved a dog behind Bartlett Hall," are slight rewordings of observed markings, and I hesitate to be so crude as to refer to them in print except that they are unusual. The details make these claims slightly more memorable and even credible, though not for the usual reason that details facilitate falsification. The claim that Y is a thief, if true, is a good example of an anonymous insult that might provide socially useful information—either because it deters other thieves, who fear shaming, or because it warns others to be wary of Y. The same cannot easily be said for the other comment. I hesitate to label these as unusual examples of *effective* juvenile communications because we do not know the authors' aims or knowledge. Each author ran the small risk of attracting vandalism or defamation charges, or perhaps even revenge by an informed target. Revenge may well be the most serious risk; it is ironic that the target will have more success in identifying the culprit if the original claim is detailed and true, or at least based on some real events. I return to accuracy and social utility below, but for now let us assume that the communications are exaggerations or outright falsehoods and, at best, a juvenile reaction to something about Y or Z that the writer finds distasteful.

When the offensive graffitist uses the bathroom wall he runs up against the medium's constraints; the Internet now provides a superior medium for one who wishes to spread juvenile or malicious speech. One can scratch or spray paint a wall for a variety of reasons, but the audience for that speech is limited, and the greater the offense with respect to both content and audience, the more quickly the communication will be erased. Moreover, the juvenilist who works on the bathroom wall with paint or knife must work quickly to avoid detection and prosecution. Thus, a longer and often more credible message is hard to cast. In obvious contrast, the juvenilist on the Internet is empowered by the ability to communicate in leisurely fashion and to do so from afar. The old-fashioned graffitist risks disciplinary action in a school or workplace, and police attention elsewhere, because in a real environment the graffitist has committed a crime—namely vandalism— even as he is open to a claim of defamation. On the Internet there is no vandalism and, with respect to defamation, the risk of detection and social sanction is close to zero so long as the author chooses a site where anonymity is secure.

The bathroom wall is a noteworthy precursor of the Internet, not only because such graffiti has surely decreased since the Internet came to life, but also because vandalism and defamation claims threatened those graffitists who could not be certain that they would remain unidentified. The same is true for graffitists in more public places, where their work can have great political and artistic significance. Anonymity is important in order to avoid prosecution, and in some cases to escape unpleasant social sanctions. In any event, the Internet has emerged as the site of choice for many users. Whether the goal is to injure with offensive speech or to spread socially useful information about another, the Internet is more appealing than the table or the wall; anonymity is more assured, it has the potential to reach a larger audience, it keeps messages alive, and it is searchable by interested parties who can then reproduce what they like for further publication. Cutting in the other direction is the fact that the Internet does not always offer a site densely visited by a target audience. This remaining advantage of conventional graffiti is, however, certain to disappear, as the Internet's capacity to host new sites, specializing in audiences with a variety of common interests, is limitless.

The Internet, the bathroom wall, and most other media have in common the ability of an intermediary[2] to comply with a request that an offensive comment be deleted. The intermediary may adopt one of several practices. It may choose to avoid litigation or injury by practicing a notice-and-takedown policy, so that complaints bring about a kind of (automatic but slightly delayed) censorship. The intermediary may also monitor the site and preemptively remove communications it fears give offense. Alternatively, the intermediary may seek to distance itself from the activities that take place on its site, holding itself out as something of a utility provider rather than responsible manager. Even if the intermediary is otherwise proactive, it may be disinclined to erase when to do so leaves it vulnerable to claims of censorship. Facebook, for example, declines to play the role of arbiter of that which shall be deemed offensive. Similarly, a site like Ripoffreport.com encourages consumers to "get justice!" and share information by posting their complaints about merchants; this intermediary's business model makes no allowance for monitoring or removing false information. Noncommercial sites may also be passively managed, albeit for different reasons. In the case of a university-run blog, for example, interventions run the risk of bad publicity because the industry is one in which free speech is especially exalted.

The juvenilist prefers an inactive intermediary, much as the graffitist prefers a landlord without paint or cleanser. But even if the intermediary is on guard, the author is worse off than the traditional graffitist only in the sense that cleansing can be quick and cheap. The owner of a marked-up wall might delete graffiti in order to discourage yet more graffiti, to avoid offending customers, or to avoid legal claims by those who are slurred. The intermediary might fear liability because there is, in principle, legal liability for the failure of a tavern keeper, for example, to remove defamatory graffiti when it can be viewed by others and in this way further "published."[3]

The Internet is the natural and well-evolved successor to the bathroom wall. Some offending authors must value the tactile experience, spontaneity, or even risk of the restroom, but most modern juvenilists and commercial warriors can be counted on to prefer the rhythm of the keyboard, the reduced probability of detection, and the enhanced, searching, and often easily targeted audience. This preference for the Internet is not entirely the product of legal rules, but it is apparent that laws, or the absence of effective laws, pertaining to vandalism, defamation, and owner liability contribute to the emergence of the Internet as the medium of choice for a variety of communications we might rather do without.

It would be possible to argue that the bathroom wall deserves less legal oversight than the Internet, inasmuch as the wall is more easily cleansed and its small audience implies less harm. But the law favors the Internet, and so the questions then are whether it similarly favors some other media, and whether the case for regulation is weaker or stronger elsewhere. There is no need for a full catalogue here, but a few items of comparison are revealing. Moreover, an exhaustive comparison is unlikely to convince all readers that the Internet is particularly favored, because there are factors that militate for and against regulation in each medium, as well as in others not included here.

Consider, next, radio and television, where the case for regulation—whether in the form of content controls or equal access rules—derives from the scarcity of airwaves and, for some advocates, the presence of children in the audience. The case for lighter regulation (than on the Internet) might come from the greater need for advertiser or subscriber support in these broadcast media, inasmuch as both groups would exercise influence over content. In any event, radio and television stations could broadcast more anonymous messages, but they do not, and the threat of legal intervention plays some role in this state of affairs.[4]

Newspapers have also come to eschew anonymity. They occasionally withhold the names of letter writers, especially where there is a plausible case for whistle-blower protection and, of course, reporters carefully protect the identities of some sources. But, again, these are cases where the danger of anonymity is reduced by the presence of an active intermediary, subject to suit. The reporter's and editor's reputation allows for the anonymity of a source; in contrast, even the intermediary may be anonymous on Internet gossip sites. When the intermediary is passive, as the owner of the bathroom wall might be, there is no vouching for the anonymous source. In print and other media, the legal system might well decide to favor political speech by rarely asking for the identity of a confidential source, but it is clear that the anonymous juvenilist, or for that matter the complaining consumer, does not find a comfortable home in print media, and especially not in any with wide circulation. Note that bookstores, newsstand owners, and logging companies go unregulated when it comes to offensive communications they make possible, but the law's selection of a (different) least cost-avoider intermediary is nothing new.[5]

In each of these comparisons, the low cost of entry on the Internet is striking. In the case of newspapers and magazines, the cost of paper, publication, and distribution surely cause the intermediary to screen content. An Internet site might choose to incorporate all comments on a subject, perhaps because the cost of screening exceeds the implicit cost of losing audience members who do not want to wade through low-quality or offensive contributions. Except perhaps for the case of a very local newspaper, one that did not screen submissions for publication would not only lose readers' attention but also would need to absorb the cost of printing and distributing the unwanted communications. On the Internet, many readers might wish for less, but in the case of newspapers we worry that there are too few voices rather than too many, or at least we did so before the arrival of online "newspapers." Scarcity of this sort means that the intermediary can be counted on to eliminate juvenile speech, and this in turn means that there is less need for legal regulation. An argument for legal intervention is easiest to advance with the claim that in such an environment the government should be neutral, lest the scarcity empower the very government at which valuable, critical speech might be directed.

It is useful to include the soapbox in this sketch. There is something charming about free speech as practiced on that stage, especially when it is observed as a tourist and directed at governments and persons one hardly knows. In terms of comparison to the Internet and other media, there are social sanctions for offensive speech on the soapbox because the speaker is identifiable. In addition, the speaker normally addresses a small audience, and potential listeners cannot search for subjects of interest. Along all these dimensions, we would expect more regulation on the Internet than on the soapbox—and yet it is the soapbox orator who is removed if deemed to cause a disturbance or to be defamatory.[6]

It is plain that the Internet is an outlier, nearly free of regulation. Offending speakers find it easy to communicate anonymously and thus to avoid any direct defamation or other legal claims. A substantial number of hospitable Internet providers promise to protect Internet protocol, or IP, addresses and other threats to anonymity. Under the terms of the Communications Decency Act of 1996 "no provider or user of an interactive computer service shall be treated as the publisher or speaker of any information provided by another information content provider."[7] To the extent that the original reason for this immunity was to allow the new medium to flourish and experiment, it seems that a reasonable test period has now passed. The absence of effective legal regulation on the Internet has made it the preferred medium for juvenile communications, and perhaps for unfiltered communications more generally.

Targets of slurs are not the only ones injured by an unfettered medium like the Internet. Any medium with neither access cost nor legal intervention will generate a high noise-to-signal ratio and most communications will be of low value. Thus, a free wall for graffitists, without periodic cleansing, will be of low value to readers and juvenile authors alike, because the volume of junk will reduce the audience.

It is, therefore, unsurprising that sites like Amazon.com and Cnet.com work to delete juvenile and even superfluous contributions. The policy requires effort, some automated and some expensive, but it is necessary in order to keep a valuable, popular site alive, especially when the site is intended to provide a very particular kind of service.[8] If the Internet's first anonymity problem is represented by the costs imposed on Amy X, then its second anonymity problem is that Internet entrepreneurs with interactive sites are essentially obliged to spend resources in order to control the content of these sites, lest a high noise-to-signal ratio destroy the value of the medium to its users. The problem is ironic because one of the Internet's claims to singularity is the low barrier to entry for provider and user alike, and it is this very feature that makes juvenile communication so easy. The problem is that juvenile communications destroy the low-cost resource. Even if the entrepreneur-intermediary requires identifiability, and even if that greatly reduces the noise, the intermediary must police its own rules. In some settings law can help, as it does with trespass on property, for example. In other cases we may see sites emerge that predicate access on the provision of credit card numbers—not to guarantee purchases but rather to identify the participants.

I suspect that in the long run law will settle on some sort of intermediate identification regime in which IP addresses are made available to those who claim injury, and wish to sue or make demands of offenders, if these claimants can overcome some modest hurdle. Note, however, the perverse feature that these claimants risk further injury by drawing attention to themselves for bringing suit. Consider, once again, Ripoffreports, where a potential consumer can search for negative reports about businesses. Juvenile or otherwise false reports both harm the target and reduce the value of the site, but the Communications Decency Act probably protects the provider. It is interesting that on this site those who complain usually provide their given names and

hometowns; some angry consumers provide complete personal information. It is possible that they do so in order to signal reliability, but also plausible that they do so in the hope of extracting appeasement from offending
businesses. My intuition is that these consumers do not need anything like
whistle-blower protection, so that anonymity, and the withholding of *their*
IP addresses, is not an important feature of the information exchange.

When an intermediary does require speakers to identify themselves, or
where it screens offensive comments, another provider can try to satisfy
the demand for offense or anonymity by appealing to the same audience
with a parallel site. JuicyCampus.com, a now-defunct website, was one such
innovator. The site promoted "online anonymous free speech on college
campuses," and it used anonymous servers to assure users that they would
not be identified. The content was occasionally informative but very often
malicious and salacious. JuicyCampus provided a venue that even better-
targeted sites, namely university websites, declined to provide. Universities
have their own websites, of course, and they limit access and control uses.
A class discussion group may be anonymous or not, depending on which
the teacher thinks will be more productive.[9] In the event of an offensive
comment, the webmaster will delete the remark; if the author is identifiable, there will probably be a sanction. JuicyCampus operated outside any
university's control but was organized and searchable by school name, as is
its successor. In theory, these websites could support intellectual threads,
unvarnished discussion of events at named universities, and frank advice
for prospective students. In fact, they quickly evolve into mere collection
points for juvenile gossip and worse. I like to think that JuicyCampus
failed because it could not attract sufficient advertising revenue; advertisers hesitate to attach their names to filth, and too much noise reduces
readership. JuicyCampus "improved" on the bathroom stall by accommo-
dating longer messages and by enabling searches of its contents, but the
bathroom stall serves another, mundane purpose, and its construction and
maintenance are thus subsidized for reasons unrelated to its role in the
communication of information. Other sites, and especially those arranged
around subjects of common interest, like law school admissions or law firm
gossip, are positively learned compared to JuicyCampus, and they may survive with modest advertising revenues, or simply as hobbies. Still, where
there is no active censor, comments often sink to the lowest common
denominator. A site might provide information about law firm salaries or
college political groups but then also seek nominations for the "hottest as-

sociate" or the "most hypocritical libertarians." Few people are deeply offended by inclusion on such lists, but personal recognition is often one step removed from additional, ruder comments. Participants appear to self-select on these sites; in some settings a juvenile majority emerges, and the silent majority ignores the site or samples the minority's handiwork from a distance. In many more settings, the civil majority silences the crude minority, which then congregates on a very few sites.

I have emphasized that one cost of Internet anonymity is that a successful site must monitor and censor in order to inhibit what might become overwhelming noise. A complete bar on anonymity is costly both because of enforcement costs and because anonymous provocateurs may attract a valuable audience. Law could help with both by extending defamation law and by enforcing contracts. Requiring and enforcing identifiability would not, of course, reduce a provider's costs to zero. Even if a newspaper receives only signed letters, it would bore readers if it published all that it received. A plausible long-run equilibrium involves some mix of identifiability and central control. One compromise strategy for newspapers as well as the Internet is to permit some known participants to communicate at will, while others are funneled through a gatekeeper. In a newspaper this reflects the difference between a reporter's sources and letter writers. On the Internet, such a site would have more posts and fewer comments than we have become accustomed to observing. One elaborate version of this mix is found on Wikipedia. This ever-changing online encyclopedia thrives through a combination of informed posts, or entries, followed by numerous modifications, or comments, made by many readers, some of whom make a hobby, or even a life, of Wikipedia. The product reflects both the wisdom of crowds as well as the hard work of more skilled labor than a conventional encyclopedia can possibly employ—even in a virtual edition where it too could provide subscribers with ongoing updates and improvements. Wikipedia does attract vandals and ideologues, but their marks can be expunged by subsequent improvers, some of whom seem to take responsibility for selected topics. The good soldiers are remarkably vigilant. Apparently, juvenile or noisy posts are commonly excised on weekends, suggesting that much of the "central control" is accomplished by volunteers, numbering perhaps 75,000, who are otherwise occupied on workdays. But there is more than a dedicated workforce behind the site's success. Even when it was more hospitable to vandals or juveniles, Wikipedia flourished; it has improved by eliminating anonymity in ingenious fashion.

Any contribution or revision made to a Wikipedia entry is recorded on a separate, linked history page. This page details the substance of the revision, the date and time it is made, and some information about the contributor. Contributors to Wikipedia essentially agree to be identified on the history page by their IP addresses, and this identification discourages misbehavior. Any reader can, with some effort, locate the author of an offensive comment; there is no need to bring suit against an Internet forum provider who is disinclined to reveal the identity of its subscribers. Alternatively, a regular contributor can register with Wikipedia, and then be known by his or her chosen moniker, while only the central monitor, a Wikipedia insider, knows the user's true identity, or IP address. Wikipedia can take action if such a contributor's edits or contributions are unwanted; in some cases, Wikipedia will reveal a registrant's IP address. With these and other rules of participation (including rules against multiple personalities that might be used to develop false consensus)[10] Wikipedia has flourished, even though it must be a tempting target for juvenilists. And yet, this success is uninspiring because it is built on an expensive strategy with volunteers, dispute resolution mechanisms, and some central control.[11]

Anonymity can, of course, be privately and socially useful, and anonymous communications are sometimes encouraged by the intended audience. Thus, a manufacturer might encourage feedback by seeking anonymous reviews of its products, and politicians appreciate anonymous polls. A university's website is unlikely to accommodate negative information about a professor because that might discourage applicants or supportive alumni, but the same university is apt to encourage anonymous student evaluations of its faculty's teaching, and then permit or encourage fellow students to read these evaluations. Moreover, the university is probably the most efficient collector of these evaluations. It can solicit information from those who are registered for a course; it can set aside class time or even deny grades until evaluations are completed; and it can best exclude the noise that might be generated by "evaluations" submitted by those who did not really take the course in question.[12]

The great promise of anonymity is that important information or viewpoints might be chilled if authors know they will be identified. Only an uncensored site, open to anonymity, would report that "Amy X is a slut who gave me an STD." It might appear that we are confronted with a tradeoff that is familiar in the free speech literature. Even if most communication of a certain kind is useless or offensive, the free speech advocate opposes regulation because it might chill or eliminate some valuable communications. In this case, regulation runs the risk of eliminating the remarks about sexually transmitted diseases—some of which might be true and therefore valuable.

This description is, however, insufficiently sensitive to the availability of alternatives. Altruists or angry victims who seek to communicate their knowledge can contact public health officials, or in some cases a university administrator, who would speak with the alleged agent of infection. At a minimum, an official would communicate the possibility of tort liability. The gossip approach may deter others from contact with the reported source of infection, while the local health official is inclined to focus on the disease and thus on the person providing the information as well as on persons said to have transmitted the infection. It is possible, but unlikely, that the first strategy is superior to the second from a social point of view, but that is something the local authority may have decided against. Lawmakers appear to have calculated that the goal of disease prevention is better served by a tool other than broad-gauge disclosure, or gossip.

Similarly, the consumer who posts on Ripoffreports has other options. In both cases, the Internet provides a low-cost method of spreading information and in both cases it can be seen, optimistically, as a check on lawmakers. It is difficult to see why anonymity should be more valuable for commerce than for disease. But even in the former instance, a responsible intermediary, with the capacity to disclose the IP address associated with what turns out to be a *false* report, would seem to improve the exchange of information.

There is no reason to think that anonymity ought to play the same role in different media, because each has unique characteristics. If one wants to argue for present law, which is to say for Internet forum provider immunity, then one points to the cost of monitoring by the provider, the difficulty of collecting revenues in order to offset this cost, and the ability of an unhappy audience to steer clear of a site.[13] But if one wants to argue for regulation, then one emphasizes the low cost to the juvenilist or speaker of falsehoods, the gravity of the injuries, the harms propagated under the current regime, the ease of giving up (at the very least) IP addresses in order to make direct lawsuits or social sanctions possible, and the ease of following a notice-and-takedown policy—a strategy that I return to below.[14] This last option is neither costless to the intermediary nor an unambiguous social benefit, but it is a useful reminder that while it is catchy to say that the Internet has an anonymity problem, the real problem is one of offensive or noisy information, and the challenge is to devise low-cost methods of improving the exchange of information.

Bargaining for Non-Anonymity or More

I have suggested that we ought to be less distracted by novelty and more concerned with using familiar legal rules to solve identifiable social problems. Defamation and other law might be applied to an Internet provider much as it is to a newspaper publisher or the owner of a graffiti-laden wall. The case for owner immunity, and certainly for Internet exceptionalism, is a weak one. Moreover, the striking thing about the Internet is the low cost of entry, and this characteristic can be used to argue for and against legal regulation. For this reason I have hinted, if only by the title of this essay, that near immunity for Internet forum providers might be maintained in return for law, or perhaps social practice, "requiring" Internet providers to do their best to reveal or make available the identity of speakers. Non-anonymity would surely reduce the problem of juvenile communications as well as that of vengeful rather than informative consumer (and other) reactions. If so, identifiability will raise the value of the medium to most users. There are alternatives to identifiability that might better level the playing field among media, and there are remedies that might suit providers or posters who have little capacity to monitor communications. But the immediate task is to make the case for some regulation of these Internet sites. My strategy is to resort to the well-known guidepost of a hypothetical bargain among participants, or all citizens. Such a mechanism, or metaphor, might be especially apt if we think of the Internet provider as a fairly passive entrepreneur.

Begin with juvenilism, and consider the community of all who are affected by the anonymity problem. The group includes juvenilists as well as those who are plausible targets of the various communications. Participants in a communal bargain or vote need not be certain of their future roles or preferences when they bargain for prices or rules. We might imagine 1,000 people, with most deriving some pleasure from gossip about acquaintances, and a subset enjoying gossip about persons they do not know. A minority of 200, say, gain some pleasure from inflicting emotional harm on others; and a very few persons so enjoy attention or pity that they gain utility when they are the object of derision. It might be fun for some to read, and for a few to write, that "Amy X is a slut," and even if they think this improbable, the communication may help them imagine it so. In this market, Amy X may be harmed. Some targets do not mind such communications, or they may believe that ignoring slurs is the surest way to decrease their cost. But if the target feels injured, she might pay for the taunters to cease, especially if repeated publication increases the sting. She might feel emotional pain or be anxious that the taunts will reduce her future social and economic prospects. If Amy X's loss exceeds the aggregate gains of her taunters, even if added to the small gains of the passive onlookers (minus the losses from other interested parties), then it is easy to see that there could be a bargain to forego taunts. But even if not, so long as the target's loss is significantly greater than any single taunter's or onlooker's gain, then the bargain will be the same, as many of the onlookers and taunters reason that they might themselves be targets in a subsequent round. At the time of the imagined bargain, before the identity of the target is known, there must be many more persons who prefer not to slur and be slurred than who like the opportunity to behave in juvenile fashion toward others.

The simple argument for legal intervention is that there is probably a market failure. Amy X cannot locate her anonymous or pseudonymous taunters in order to pay them to cease their activity; she certainly cannot locate them in advance, before any harm is done. Moreover, if the bargain could be arranged, there is the hazard that extortionists will taunt, or threaten to taunt, in order to extract payments. The obvious analogy is to physical assault. Every legal system makes it actionable for A to kick B. We do not say that, without legal intervention, an unhappy B could simply pay A to stop kicking. Again, the problem with relying on market transactions is that it would be easy to threaten B with a kick in order to extract payment. Legal systems choose the baseline of a kick-free existence because there are surely more people who dislike (and more money would be paid to prevent) being kicked than who would gain from kicking. If the liability or property rule were reversed, there would be threats—even by persons who gained no utility from kicking—and even something of a moral hazard as opportunistic players taunted and kicked simply to establish their reputations as persons requiring payment.

The market failure is not easily solved. A forum provider cannot simply offer a choice between a free-for-all and a taunt-free, sanitary environment because it must have a means of dealing with those who choose to offend the taunt-free rule. In a world without legal sanctions nothing stops people from taunting those who choose the sanitary site. We might interpret the behavior of some celebrities as an implicit endorsement of such a two-tier scheme for specialized publications and websites. Put differently, for some people the hypothetical bargain may plausibly produce a different outcome from the civility suggested here. A Hollywood celebrity might tolerate or welcome attention to such a degree as to prefer to pay for more attention rather than less, even if the attention is sometimes hostile on its face. PerezHilton.com is one such site, and tabloids, like the *National Enquirer,* are thus its competitors. The law of "public figures" implicitly recognizes this fact when it allows more criticism and comment regarding public, rather than private, persons.

Even private citizens are not safe on websites like AbovetheLaw.com, though they might be more protected in a legal regime that followed the hypothetical bargain model. When that website, a favorite of law firm associates and law students, asks "Who is the hottest associate at firm Z?" the responses might be appealing to many of those who are mentioned without their consent, both because they might have agreed (hypothetically, at least, and in advance) to participate in the game and because exposure to harshness is sometimes the price of flattery. Anonymity and the absence of a consent process may indeed generate utility for the subjects. If the cost of legal intervention, perhaps in the form of a ban on complete anonymity, is the decline of "hottest associate" contests, I doubt this will be a stain on the legal system or the social fabric. In other contexts, broad consent may reduce any such losses. Thus, a college may normally require identifiability on Internet sites it controls, but it may encourage anonymity where course evaluations are at issue—perhaps by asking all instructors to agree to the anonymous responses and posts.

I do not claim that a hypothetical bargain of the sort described here would necessarily produce an agreement to ban anonymity. Anonymity might elicit valuable communications, and certainly more passionate expressions of support for various positions. Moreover, as we have seen, identifiability and reliability can require an army of volunteers or other resources. It is plausible that some bargains or votes would result in an agreement to bar interactive communication, to require the registration of those who wish to communicate in a forum, or to deploy what amounts to a notice-and-takedown policy. Each of these comes with costs. A notice-and-takedown policy is probably the most expensive of these to execute, though less costly than ongoing censorship.[15] It does not help targets who will not quickly know they have been maligned. Nor can they be easily protected through an opt-out policy. Juvenile communications often identify their targets by given names, or description and location. A sensitive subject, Y, will thus find it difficult to arrange in advance for the absence of comments about Y.

Notice and takedown is more attractive in some settings than in others. If the Internet's anonymity problem includes commercial slurs on a site like Ripoffreports, then it is important to see that the notice-and-takedown alternative is problematic. Information on the site is of little value if a business can merely ask the intermediary to remove any complaint against it. It is of little value to users if the site asks them to balance complaints and compliments, if only because the compliments might be planted by the targeted business. And if the intermediary must evaluate the complaint in order to decide whether to maintain or remove it, then the high cost of intermediation is obvious and the apparent technological leap of the Internet largely lost.

Finally, the hypothetical bargain approach runs the danger of underestimating the taste for taunting, much as speed limits may underestimate the preference of some citizens for speed and danger. If so, it may be useful to contemplate a site in which these speedsters and taunters can congregate with like-minded peers. There are fraternities that can be thought of as implicitly coordinating around such a norm, and there is no reason to deny the possibility or health of a virtual community of this kind. But Amy X and other targets need not be taunted by this group, any more than they need to be kicked by someone, and it is hard to see how a bargain would lead to an equilibrium in which she would be willing to be slurred without personally knowing about it. Amy X's future social and economic prospects are diminished even by slurs of which she is unaware.

When Law Trumps Bargains

In many cases it is a small leap from hypothetical bargains to laws. Laws are produced by popular and legislative votes, or by the voters' agents, and will often reflect the same preferences, and intense preferences, that produce bargains. Still, there are plainly situations where constitutional rules trump the market or the majority will. Many constitutional protections, like those that discourage warrantless wiretapping or torture of citizens, probably do track majority sentiments, but others do not. In the case of communications and expression, the majority has much less patience for something like flag burning or a "F___ the Draft" logo than does the law.[16] It is unlikely that there would be a bargain for the current, constitutional result. It is noteworthy, however, that where law is tolerant of such unpopular speech, the speaker is remarkably identifiable. My claim here is that the bathroom wall and its successors will provide more useful communications if some policy, including one requiring the identification of authors or vetting by intermediaries, reduces noise—and juvenile offense—in the process. It is difficult to see why this majoritarian-supported policy need offend constitutional law if it, or a comparable convention, does not do so in other media.

One barrier to bringing the Internet into line with other media is that citizens who like high-quality speech, and who think they might get more of it with *more,* or at least some, regulation are dispersed and unlikely to form political pressure groups. Law often comes about, and indeed overreacts, because politicians or litigants respond to the appearance of a social problem. Cyber bullying may be a social problem that energizes politicians, perhaps in the direction of anti-anonymity, but there will also be interest groups that press for Internet exceptionalism, even as they do not argue for the deregulation of competing media. It is therefore not obvious that the problem of the virtual bathroom wall will be solved by law.

One easy step for law would be the repeal of Section 230 of the Communications Decency Act, so that an Internet provider would be like a newspaper publisher. It is easy to imagine a compromise in which the provider retains immunity by promising to enforce non-anonymity or, in some settings, a notice-and-takedown rule or a notice-and-response (by the target or other interested parties) convention.

It is interesting and unfortunate that well-developed Internet networking sites do not yet provide sophisticated speech and information exchanges. Facebook and other social-networking sites make it easy for J to find K's friends, but not for J and L to get together because they share an interest in humanitarian relief in Darfur. Even Ripoffreports is surprisingly unhelpful, though there are sites, like Angie's List, that share positive and negative recommendations of vendors. But on all these sites there is a great deal of noise; there is no incentive to file reports, or accurate reports; and many searches yield no information. One cannot use Facebook to find others who used a given auto repair shop. It is not yet about these communities of interest, perhaps because, with the current architecture, it would be overwhelming to deal with the hundreds or even thousands of interests we each have.

There is, of course, the prospect of change through private action rather than through legal regulation. Over time, I anticipate that more Internet entrepreneurs will limit participation or require identification. There will remain a few sites that remind us of JuicyCampus, occupying a niche like that in which we find porn shops in city centers, at the periphery of most social interaction. The effort law takes to limit their poison to consenting adults will rise and fall. "Respectable" sites will require identification (non-anonymity) and this will severely limit sites where people comment on a professor or classmate's anatomy or alleged promiscuity. There will be some loss of opportunities to flatter, criticize, and convey information. But inasmuch as this information would have been lost in the midst of much noise, most of us will not and should not mourn the loss.

CHAPTER 4

Objectification and Internet Misogyny

M ARTHA C. NUSSBAUM

> Beati in regno coelesti videbunt poenas damnatorum, ut beatitudo illis magis complaceat.
> Blissful, in the kingdom of heaven, they will see the sufferings of the damned, so that their bliss should be more delightful to them.
>
> Thomas Aquinas, Summa Theologiae,
> quoted in Nietzsche, *Genealogy of Morals*[1]

Internet Objectification

Much of the damage done by the spread of gossip and slander on the Internet is damage to women. A significant proportion of the harmful material involves what feminists have called "objectification": treating women as objects for men's use and abuse. Getting clear about the concept of objectification is important as a prelude to seeing what is morally and legally problematic about some common forms of expression on Internet gossip sites.

Objectification has long been a cherished feminist concept, but it has not always been analyzed with the requisite clarity and complexity. I have argued that it is properly seen as a cluster concept, with no single set of necessary and sufficient conditions.[2] If, however, we want to understand what is wrong with objectification in the context of gender relations, we will do well to focus on the idea of (mere) instrumental use: the objectifier treats the objectified as a mere tool of his ends, not as an end in herself.

To objectify, further, always involves conferring on the object a spoiled, or stigmatized, identity, a compromised status. To objectify publicly is a variety of shame punishment. Pursuing that connection helps us to understand the specific type of objectification that occurs on Internet gossip sites.[3]

But what is really going on, when a woman is objectified, hence stigmatized, in an objectionable way? I argue that we can understand the malice underlying much male objectification of women on the Internet by pondering (a version of) Friedrich Nietzsche's analysis of *ressentiment* and the "slave revolt" in morality. People who feel themselves to be weak or inadequate vis à vis some other group of people seek to validate themselves by creating an entire world in which these people are no longer glorious, autonomous, or happy, a world in which they themselves enjoy complete power over those who formerly held power over them.

Beginning with the objectification of female celebrities and moving to the objectification of fellow law students, the essay studies the operation of ressentiment on the Internet, looking at how relatively powerless people gain enormous power over the lives of particular women by using the specific properties of the Internet: its ability to create a whole world in which an objectified version of the person replaces the real person; its ability to disseminate this spoiled identity widely and rapidly; and its ability to cause large-scale disruptions in the real world, as the abuse colors daily life and the spread of the hostile material through search engines such as Google affects job opportunities.

Finally, asking what sort of weakness or injury drives this massive outpouring of ressentiment, I turn to a psychological study of teenage boys in America that explains widespread aggression in terms of a pernicious overgrowth of shame about weakness and need, together with a diseased norm of masculinity that exalts total control and penalizes need and compassion.

Objectification: A Cluster Concept

The concept of objectification has been often used in feminist theory without clarification. In order to get clear about the harms involved in objectification we need to do more analysis.[4]

To objectify a person is to treat her as a thing, an object, although, being a person, she is not really a (mere) thing. So far so good. But there are many different ways in which a woman's human personhood may be denied, and objectification should therefore be viewed as a cluster concept, involving seven distinct ideas, seven ways to treat a person as a thing:

1. *Instrumentality:* the objectifier treats the object as a tool of his or her purposes.
2. *Denial of Autonomy:* the objectifier treats the object as lacking in autonomy and self-determination.

3. *Inertness:* the objectifier treats the object as lacking in agency, and perhaps also in activity.
4. *Fungibility:* the objectifier treats the object as interchangeable (a) with other objects of the same type, and/or (b) with objects of other types.
5. *Violability:* the objectifier treats the object as lacking in boundary integrity, as something that it is permissible to break up, smash, break into.
6. *Ownership:* the objectifier treats the object as something that is owned by another, can be bought or sold, etc.
7. *Denial of Subjectivity:* the objectifier treats the object as something whose experience and feelings (if any) need not be taken into account.

These different ways of objectifying a human being can be seen both in the context of sexual relations and in other contexts (slavery, labor relations, etc.). The seven are distinct notions, giving rise to different types of objectification, interrelated in a variety of complicated ways. We should think of the concept as involving a family of interweaving criteria, rather than as having a single set of necessary and sufficient conditions.

In the context of gender and sexuality, however, the key feature that makes objectification morally objectionable is instrumentality, the use of a woman as a mere means to the objectifier's ends. The treatment of a woman not as an end in herself but as a mere tool of the ends of others is the central target of feminist criticisms of objectification, and the idea of use as a mere means typically explains the presence of some of the other features, insofar as they are present in an objectionable form. Objectification is thus a notion at home in the world of Kantian ethics, whose key contrast—between treating humanity as an end and treating it as a mere means—it captures well.

Both Kant and Catharine MacKinnon are mistaken in suggesting that objectification, in the context of sexual relations, can be assessed on the basis of an isolated piece or episode of behavior.[5] A full moral assessment requires an understanding of context and relationship. In the context of an overall relationship of intimacy and reciprocity, it may be fine, or even great, to treat the person, at times, as a nonautonomous animal body. Kant suggests that focusing on a person as an animal body entails, in and of itself, a morally objectionable denial of humanity, which a relationship of trust and care can render relatively harm-free, but never morally appropriate. (Thus he thinks that what goes on in sex is always morally bad, although marriage can make it less harmful.) I argue that this view is wrong. The overall context of an instance of objectification may justify the conclusion that the behavior, though certainly involving objectification, is not morally objectionable, and it may even be wonderful, involving an embrace of the body that often eludes us in daily life.

In standard pornographic examples of objectification, however, the larger context (insofar as there is one) does not remove the moral worry in the way that a respectful and loving relationship would. Even if a pornographic film or novel has a thin story line, the woman is presented throughout as a mere thing who exists only as a tool of male desires, and who may be manipulated with impunity. Often this manipulation involves the deliberate infliction of pain.

In her new book *Sexual Solipsism*,[6] feminist philosopher Rae Langton proposes several additions to this analysis. In addition to my seven varieties of objectification, she proposes adding:

8. *Reduction to Body:* one treats it as identified with its body, or body parts.[7]
9. *Reduction to Appearance:* one treats it primarily in terms of how it looks, or how it appears to the senses.
10. *Silencing:* one treats it as silent, lacking the capacity to speak.[8]

These are valuable additions. Langton's Reduction to Body is a central feature of many of my examples. (Indeed, it is that very identification with body that I hold to be a potentially valuable part of sexual objectification in the context of respect and trust.) I failed to single it out as a separate category because I took it to be implicit in several of the others, such as Denial of Autonomy and Denial of Subjectivity, but Langton seems correct when she says that it deserves separate recognition. Reduction to Appearance is also an important one to focus on, suggested by several of the others on my list but surely not entailed by any of them. Both Reduction to Body and Reduction to Appearance turn out to be key aspects of Internet objectification, so it is important to recognize them explicitly. So often, high-achieving women are treated, on Internet gossip sites, as if they are no more than a photo, or a set of body parts. Finally, Silencing is surely linked closely to the categories of autonomy-denial and inertness, but again, it is a distinct idea, and an important one to add when we consider Internet harassment, since one of its most persistent effects is to prevent women from expressing feminist views or maintaining feminist websites.

Another suggestion of Langton's is also valuable, both in general and in the Internet context. She suggests that autonomy-denial has two species that need to be carefully distinguished.⁹ One case is the failure to *ascribe* autonomy in the first place, as with a child or a domestic animal. A very different case is what she calls *autonomy-violation:* the objectifier forcibly removes, or curtails, the woman's autonomy. Autonomy-violation is pervasive in pornographic sexual objectification. Langton's distinction is implicit in some of my examples, but I do not give it the theoretical weight that it deserves. I would, however, qualify Langton's analysis in the following way: sometimes the sexual objectification of women involves simple *autonomy-denial*—as when a woman is infantilized, treated as a lower species, or is simply not accorded full adulthood. That sort of autonomy-denial figures in pornography, prominently including Internet pornography.

Nonetheless, as Langton says, the more common pornographic scenario involves autonomy-violation: the scenario represents the woman as an agent, attempting to control her own destiny, and the man removes that freedom; sexual pleasure is found in the ability to exert control over the woman's options, removing her ability to refuse consent, to depart from the situation, and so forth. This distinction is particularly important when we think about Internet defamation, for often what is resented is a woman's freedom, agency, and good name, and pleasure is taken in destroying these things—first in fantasy, and then, given the Internet's power to affect job opportunities, in reality. The objectifier puts the objectified person in a position of helplessness. Not knowing where the abuse is coming from or how to stop it, but affected by it pervasively in her daily activities, she loses agency and employment opportunities.

In the spirit of Langton's analysis, I think we should add a similar distinction in the area of subjectivity. Sometimes one may deny subjectivity by treating a person as a thing that has no inner world, a mere automaton. That happens at times in pornographic scenarios, and it happens ubiquitously in human treatment of nonhuman animals. There is also, however, *subjectivity-violation,* in which pleasure is taken in invading and colonizing the person's inner world. Threatening and demeaning behavior often has the effect of taking over someone's thoughts, making the person unable to focus on work and friendship in the usual way. A great deal of the harm caused by pornographic Internet attacks on women involves subjectivity-violation.

Objectification and Shaming

To objectify is to treat as a mere thing, a tool of the purposes of the objectifier, an entity whose subjective feelings need not be taken into account, or whose feelings, like her autonomy, may be willfully violated. Given that the objectified is a human being, objectification confers a spoiled, or stigmatized, identity, and is thus a species of shaming.[10]

All societies inflict shame on relatively powerless groups, asking them to blush for what they are. Penalties based on the idea of shame are one common manifestation of this tendency: people are asked to wear a sign, or a symbol, identifying them as bearers of a stigmatized identity, or placed in an undignified position (i.e., in the stocks or pillory) for public viewing. Shame justice is justice by the mob: the dominant group are asked to take delight in the discomfort of the excluded and stigmatized.

Women, so often an underclass in many societies, are stigmatized in many ways, but gender-based objectification is one very prominent form of social shaming. Objectification says, "You claim to be a full human being, but you are much less than that. You are a mere thing, because I can use you that way. Your autonomy can be snatched away, your feelings ignored or violated." Despite its ubiquity, objectification is a very extreme form of shaming. Shaming always involves giving someone a stigmatized, spoiled identity. But the gap between human and thing is vast, so objectification involves an extreme form of spoiling: a statement that the person no longer counts in the universe of the human.

As both Langton and Andrea Dworkin have observed, women are often objectified, thereby spoiled, by being identified with their body parts ("Tits," "Cunt"). Brian Leiter has documented that AutoAdmit has nearly 300 threads with "cunt" in the subject line. The very fact of having those female parts is taken as sufficient to confer a spoiled identity, which can then become the object of pornographic ridicule. Typical examples of this sort occur all over Internet gossip sites, but perhaps it will suffice to focus on the site AutoAdmit. Here are several examples from the complaint filed by two female students at Yale Law School, which details the harassment they endured on that site:

> [Doe II] of YLS has huge fake titties.
> YLS 1L [DOE II] has huge fake titties and is universally hated.
> [DOE I] is a dumbass bitch and [DOE II] is a slut.

> Just don't FUCK her, she has herpes.
>
> I wish to rape [DOE I} and {DOE II] in the ass.

Such examples, utterly typical of what AutoAdmit purveys, show a real person being turned into a set of body parts, and diseased body parts at that.

Often, as we see in the last example—extremely common on the Auto-Admit site—the objectification takes the form of rape-fantasy, where pleasure is derived from violent autonomy-violation. "Jill" is written about as follows:

> I want to brutally rape that Jill slut.
>
> I'm 98% sure that she should be raped (if only in Internet Land).
>
> She's a normal-sized girl that I'd bang violently.
>
> Maybe you'd have to kill her afterwards [this in a thread titled, "Be honest, everyone here would FUCK THE SHIT out of Jill Feministe"].

A perceptive writer, Jill reflected about her abuse, later, on a feminist site. She notes that objectification moves in two directions: If the woman is agreed to be ugly, she is pilloried as an ugly set of body parts. If she is pretty, then she becomes a bimbo or a whore. "When you're held up to a subjective physical standard, to people who have no personal investment in you as a person, *you cannot win.*"[11] (Notice that the reason you can't win is that you're already reduced to appearance: you've lost subjectivity, autonomy, and the moral status of being an end.)

In daily life, there are some barriers to a woman's conversion from "whole and usual" into a mere set of stigmatized organs. The woman is there in three dimensions, and she does things that may disrupt the objectifying fantasy. She might do something kind; or make a good argument; or show a capacity for empathetic understanding; or get mad and protest. At least sometimes, such signs of humanity have an impact on male objectifiers. The Internet is different. The whole world of gossip sites is a construct, and the woman is present only insofar as the male objectifier puts her there. She is even less real than the models in *Playboy,* airbrushed though they are: they at least have faces that rather resemble the faces of real women. The Internet world is a self-enclosed, self-nourishing world that is remarkably resistant to the reality outside. Indeed, it prides itself on being *its own reality,* by contrast to the merely fictitious world of friendship and human interaction. Of DOE I, a poster calling himself Spanky wrote, "Clearly she deserves to be raped so that her little fantasy world can be shattered by real life."

At the same time, the shaming inflicted by Internet objectification spills back into the real world, damaging women's employment prospects and their self-esteem. Autonomy-violation in the fantasy becomes autonomy-violation (and silencing) in reality. The AutoAdmit lawsuit carefully details the way in which threads on the site get onto Google, and impact a woman's job search. The impact on identity in daily life is at least as severe. "Jill" continues:

> I'm a fairly self-confident person. I don't usually feel like I'm being evaluated on my looks. . . . But for the last two months of school, I was absolutely neurotic, glaring at anyone I didn't know who made eye contact with me, and doing my best to not let myself check that stupid board to see what they were saying.

Notice here the importance of the idea of subjectivity-violation. Jill's subjectivity was not simply ignored. That would be bad enough. But the aim, and the "achievement," of the objectifiers was to take over her mind, make it impossible for her to think happy thoughts, to do her work in the normal way, to pursue friendships and sexual relationships with confidence. In that way, Internet abuse is very similar to stalking, or is, perhaps, a form of stalking.

Objectifying Famous Women

Why? What is going on when (some) men treat women they don't even know as bearers of a spoiled identity, as mere tools of their fantasy, violating their autonomy and hijacking their subjectivity?

Some objectification of women might be called merely traditional. Throughout human history, women have been treated as objects of possession and exchange, the way men treat a cow or a sports car. Men seem to be reared, in so many times and places, to think of women as sets of body parts, beautiful or ugly, and to speak of them as if they were not autonomous or feeling beings. So it's the man who manages to perceive a woman as a whole human being who requires explaining, in many cultures at least.

To say, "It's traditional," and "It's part of culture" is not to dispense with the need for an account. But perhaps we should begin with the more obviously malign cases, asking where their malice comes from, and later ask how deeply rooted in culture and tradition it is. So: what is the cruelty of AutoAdmit all about?

Objectification of women, both on the Internet and in other media, often focuses on women who are public figures: actresses, politicians, sports figures, and so on. Endless gossip surrounds their divorces, their sexual escapades, their drug use—and in the typical cases the treatment of these story lines involves all the classic features of objectification. The woman's story is used as a tool of fantasy, and her feelings are not taken into account. Both men and women objectify the famous, treating them as fantasy objects, and both men and women are objectified, but there is a recognizably distinct strand of the phenomenon that partakes of the general characteristics of male objectification of women, involving a pornographic delight in the misadventures of female celebrities.

When men objectify the models in *Playboy*, there is little obvious cruelty involved, and how could there be? These women don't have a story, they are just models, and any suffering or hurt they experience in life is concealed from view. Even a frown will not be shown, so skillfully airbrushed is the usual photograph. When, by contrast, a man objectifies Britney Spears, or Marilyn Monroe, the narrative of suffering and reversal is central to the pleasure that he experiences. The reader of objectifying star fiction cannot actually influence the life of the star. Somehow, though, the idea of the powerful being brought low is integral to the sexiness of these reports and the type of sexual fantasy that they evoke. Significantly, one sad event in a famous person's life that is never the occasion for objectifying eroticization is *loss of celebrity*. To many celebrities, this might be the worst loss of all, but if the world at large has become bored with someone, the porno world is too.

Now I turn to Nietzsche. Here I do not pretend to be doing Nietzsche scholarship. I want only to extract a set of ideas from *The Genealogy of Morals* and to use them to explain what underlies the objectification and shaming of famous women.

Ressentiment is a reactive emotion inspired by the feeling of weakness. A group feels itself weak and inadequate, in a world that values certain attributes that its members don't have. Another group of people in the society does have those attributes, and the goal of ressentiment is to bring those people down and get power over them. Unable to win on the terms of the strong (unable, say, to beat Homeric heroes in a contest of strength), the weak find another way to get power. They create a system of values that ranks them high and the powerful low. In the case of Nietzsche's Christians, they create moral values of altruism and self-denial that they are capable of exemplifying, and then use these values to denigrate the behavior of the heroes. So it's the hatred of the powerful that explains the creation of the new set of values.

On one common account, ressentiment is strategic: the weak want to get power for themselves and to punish the powerful. According to R. J. Wallace's perceptive reconstruction, however (and let's not worry whether it is really the right account of Nietzsche), there is something deeper going on: the weak need to affirm themselves, relieving the psychic distress that comes with subordination, by creating a virtual world, an expressive world, in which they hold sway.[12] (Wallace notes that the ascetic priests described by Nietzsche probably do take a purely strategic approach to the new values: without really believing them, they use them to get power over those who previously held power over them.)

The revenge of the powerless is merely imaginary, in the following sense: they do not really have physical or social power, they are still economically and socially oppressed. But in fantasy, they dominate the world. As Nietzsche graphically shows, the Christian world picture creates a universe in which the weak indeed inherit the earth, in the sense that Christian eschatology informs them that they will be rewarded in heaven, and will even be able to witness the penalties of the damned. Nietzsche makes much of this feature of the Christian world, suggesting that the fantasy of vindication in the afterlife is a source of psychic affirmation and pleasure in this one.

Now let us return to the objectification of famous women. And let us consider objectification not simply of the fan-mag sort, but the more aggressive and sordid pornographic objectifying that often takes place on the Internet when well-known people are discussed. (As I've noted, the fan-mag sort involves men as well as women, but the more pornographic variety is primarily directed at women by men.) Here we see something like a "slave revolt": the powerful are depicted as suffering, powerless, prone to disasters of all sorts (and yet somehow sexy and glamorous. Meanwhile, the unknown person who fantasizes about them can feel affirmed and empowered. In fantasy, he creates a world in which celebrities are no longer autonomous, or happy, or free, a world in which he enjoys power over those who once held power over him. It's not just their troubles he imagines, he imagines himself having sexual power over them.

This is a slave revolt of sorts: and yet it does not create new values. There's a veneer of that, in that fame is taken to be a source of disaster, obscurity of safety—but the gaze of the pornographer remains fixed on fame, not obscurity, and the things that celebrity brings with it—glamor, money, nice clothes, fancy cars—these things are not really repudiated. And the pornographic blogger still does not have them. So his fantasy of having power over those who in the real world have power over him is unstable, always subject to unmasking. It hasn't really remade the world.

Moreover, the pornographer doesn't really impinge on the celebrity's world, or not for long. He can blog to his heart's content, but it's very likely that Julia Roberts will never know of his fantasies and they will have no impact on her life. So that's another way the fantasy is vulnerable: it just doesn't work, it doesn't really do anything to the self-confidence of the powerful, the way that Nietzsche's slave revolt eventually, over time, did have an impact on the self-confidence of the former master types. Objectification is directed at power, but it succeeds only to the extent that the powerful are vulnerable.

The objectifier might do better with a minor celebrity, because someone who is only a little bit famous may take the trouble to read what is said about her, and to get upset by it. Some minor celebrities are addicted to Googling themselves, and fasten on any abuse and get obsessed with it. And if the minor celebrity is part of the same narrower world as the pornographer—a law firm, a university—the objectifier may be able to feel satisfaction at having the power to disrupt the well-being of people who in daily life have fame and autonomy and achievements that he does not have.

Here, then, we are moving closer to the slave revolt. Achievement, glamor, literary productivity, and other forms of worldly power are reconfigured as sources of vulnerability to abuse, and the obscure position of the objectifier is reconfigured as a position of immense power.

Note that this power of the obscure to disrupt the lives of the powerful has been immensely magnified, more or less created, by the Internet. Before the emergence of our Internet-suffused environment, if you didn't like some big shot in the university, or in some other profession touching on your life, you had the power to insult and objectify that person in personal fantasy, and perhaps to circulate that porno vision to a few friends, but you could not spread it very far, or get that person's attention. You would have to hesitate before publicizing your abuse, or mailing it to the person, because you would put yourself in a vulnerable position by so doing. Now, by contrast, your view of the target circulates all over the world, and such publicity often has a major impact on the life of the target. Meanwhile, you are protected by anonymity.

The Internet has this power because of its ability to circulate information rapidly, at little to no cost, to every corner of the globe, and also because of its own quite autonomous existence, a virtual world set over against the world of reality, and frequently impervious to protests from that other world. Search engines magnify that power. A pernicious statement on a website might have little or no effect; but if it becomes highly ranked on a Google search of the target's name, it assumes in the reader's mind an importance disproportionate to its relevance. Nietzsche's Christians achieved that kind of insulation from critique only by arduous efforts of conversion and political/military conquest. After spreading their vision of the afterlife around the world by conversion and bloodthirsty battle, they could enjoy their fantasy of viewing the punishments of the damned to their hearts' content. But that took centuries of work. By contrast, the Internet objectifier doesn't have to convert anyone or go to war against anyone: he has only to know how to get his vision of a person onto Google, and presto, it flies around the globe. Who needs the Crusades? With a little savvy he can create a world in which his target exists only as a thing, a spoiled identity, and he, the spoiler, has complete power.

Objectification of Fellow Students

Now we arrive at the case of AutoAdmit, and other cases like it. The women objectified on AutoAdmit are not famous at all. At most, they are locally known as attractive women, or good students, or whatever. The anonymous commentators objectify them, treating them as mere sets of body parts, mere appearances. This treatment shames them, giving them a spoiled identity. They are also constructed as violable, threatened with rape and other violence.[13]

But there's a difference between celebrity objects and these other targets: what the objectifier does can really change the woman's life in major ways. When the objectified is Julia Roberts, the porno world is smaller and weaker than the real world. When it is Professor X (some big shot in the world of scholarship, but relatively unknown outside it), the porno world is large enough, perhaps, to get the attention of Professor X, but still is not very large. When the target is DOE I, the porno world can define her in the eyes of the entire world, because there's no counterweight, no other way she exists in the eyes of the world at large. So, the analogue to Nietzsche's picture of Christian eschatology is far closer. Through the power of Internet connectivity, the objectifier can create an entire world in which DOE I exists as a mere thing, a cunt, a set of tits. And then he can watch with malicious delight as this construct damns DOE I in the eyes of employers, clients, and prospective friends and lovers. (As with all objectification, the assault presupposes that DOE I is not really just a set of tits, that she has feelings and autonomy to be violated.) Thus the objectifier violates both DOE I's autonomy and her subjectivity far more effectively than he ever would be able to violate the humanity of a celebrity. In effect he hijacks her agency more or less completely, by colonizing her mind, her social relationships, her access to employment.

Many real-world consequences follow. In law schools, women who are the targets of Internet objectification may stop participating in class. (One Harvard law student whom I won't name told me that she entirely stopped attending her discussion section as the result of anonymous Internet harassment, on the section blog, clearly from a member of the section.) In many other related ways, their relationships with faculty and peers may be affected. When they begin to look for work, employers may learn of the material circulated about them. Even if prospective employers are clear that they are victims and that the rumors are false, knowing the pornographic depictions may taint their view of these women, just as knowledge of a rape victim's identity often colors people's associations with her. DOE I and DOE II, good students at Yale, got no job offers.

Is this objectification motivated by ressentiment, and, if so, of what? In the case of the celebrity, it is easy enough to identify the targets of ressentiment: fame, money, glamor, sexiness, achievement. But what is it that makes DOE I and DOE II the objects of misogynistic hatred, and can it be analogized at all to the case of the celebrity? Well, what seems to set these men off is competitive achievement: much turns on fabricating lies about the students' LSAT scores, for example. These women are high achievers in a world of tremendous male anxiety, and they are attractive and independent as well. This may be enough to make anxious, highly competitive men want to blot them out, spoil their identities so that they will no longer be out there as part of the competition. Insecure about their own futures in law, they delight in the spectacle of pain inflicted on those uppity women who dare to compete with them for grades, jobs, and clerkships.

In effect, these men are restoring the patriarchal world before the advent of sex equality, the world in which women were just tools of male purposes. In the real world, women today are threats to male autonomy, job security,

and pride (as newly freed slaves were to lower-class whites in the Reconstruction South). In the fantasy world of the Internet, there is no such
threat, because men have total power over women's futures, their self-
esteem, their relations with others. So in a deep sense there is something
like "revaluation of values" going on here, far more, in fact, than in the
celebrity case, only it is retrogressive: the objectifier restores the world of
yesteryear, in which women had no right to be more than tits and cunt. And
then he makes this revaluation real and effective in the real world, through
the pervasive power of the Internet over multiple dimensions of human
opportunity.

According to Wallace's Nietzsche, the gratification of the rebelling slaves
is achieved in fantasy, albeit a fantasy so powerful that it can completely
dominate a society's picture of human relations, as Christian eschatology
did, thus indirectly influencing social relations in the real world. The Christian's pleasure is one of anticipation, as he foresees the time when the weak
will gloat over the damnation of the strong.

In the case of AutoAdmit, the gratification is still subjective, as all gratification is, but it does not require much anticipation, since the deleterious
effects on the prospects of DOE I and DOE II begin as soon as slanders are
published. The Internet, moreover, blurs the distinction between fantasy
and reality, in that the objectifier's fantasy is out there, a piece of every
reader's reality, and it also shapes reality.

What is distinctive about the Internet is that it is its own world, and a
world in which values can be remade, in something like the way in which
Christian eschatology creates a world of value inversion. The person who
was free, happy, and autonomous can be turned into a thing there and
damned, silenced, violated for all the world and all time. Meanwhile, the
objectifier, anonymous and hidden, becomes like the blissful in Christian
heaven, safely shielded from accident or pain, as secure as in the womb,
watching the penalties of the damned. As in the passage from Aquinas that
Nietzsche quotes, his awareness of the torments of the damned make his
own security from shaming more delightful to him.

What Lies Beneath

What lies behind the ressentiment of the Internet objectifier? At this point
all diagnoses are speculative, but mine has some solid empirical work to
back it up. In *Hiding from Humanity*, I argue that all human beings suffer, to

some extent, from an emotion that I call *primitive shame,* a shame at the very fact of helplessness. From blissful completeness in the womb, human beings are born into a world that they do not control. The precocious cognitive maturity of the human infant, combined with its extreme physical helplessness—a combination unknown in any other species—leads to long periods during which a child can fasten on wanted objects but can do nothing to ensure their arrival. Growing awareness of this situation leads not only to fear (lest the objects not arrive) and anger (at those who withhold them), but also to a feeling of helplessness that contrasts painfully with the expectation of being attended to constantly, which all children form to some extent—what psychologists call "infantile omnipotence." The thought is, "I am the center of the world—and yet, here I am, cold, hungry, and wet." A painful emotion arises. Primitive shame, like all shame, is a pain at not having some desired trait or perfection. What makes it primitive shame is that the state inspiring pain is imperfect humanity itself, the ills and incompletenesses that are a part of our worldly condition, since we do not live in the womb.

As life goes on, primitive shame may be transformed in various ways. Children learn that they are part of a world of interdependent beings, and that they can help one another out. They also learn to fend for themselves, and to be less helpless. All of this diminishes shame. Nonetheless, to the extent that completeness and fullness are still craved, shame will remain on the scene, since no human being is ever in total control. When people become aware of mortality, something nobody fails to want to control and surmount, shame at lack of control increases.

So, all human beings feel shame at a very deep level in their personalities—some more, some less. And one very handy way of discharging primitive shame is to turn some other group of people into the shamed ones. The shaming of others creates safety for the shamer.[14]

A social fact that augments shame is the tendency of some societies to define the ideal adult as self-sufficient, independent, lacking in deep needs with respect to others. In many societies, such pictures are held out to young people—but far more often to males than to females. The idea of the "real man" as someone who is never weak, never dependent, always in control, is a very common feature of developmental patterns in countless societies, but certainly in ours, which so strongly valorizes the lone cowboy who can provide for himself without the help of any others. Women, by contrast, are more often taught that maturity includes interdependency with others.[15] Thus lack of control will be more alarming to someone who has bought into the male myth than someone reared on a different norm.

But of course the idea of total control is a myth, unmasked every day by life itself. So an undercurrent of shame runs through the psyche of any person who lives by that myth: I'm supposed to be the "real man," controlling everything, but I feel that I don't control my own world, in countless ways. Psychologists Dan Kindlon and Michael Thompson have spent years studying disturbed adolescent boys in the United States. They conclude that a "dominant image of masculinity that requires strength and stoicism" leads to the formation of a "culture of cruelty," in which the shame boys feel at not being totally in control is turned outward toward the humiliation of others.[16] "With every lesson in dominance, fear, and betrayal, a boy is tutored away from trust, empathy, and relationship."[17] This peer culture is reinforced by the use of shame as a motivator in sports, as players must strive to avoid humiliation.

Meanwhile, patterns of talk about emotions in the culture enhance the growth of shame and aggression, since adults, very much including mothers, typically assume that boys are not interested in talking about emotions, whereas girls are far more interested.[18] So boys don't learn a language to name and reflect on their own insecurities, and this makes it all the more likely that they will turn them outward in the form of aggression. Repeatedly, Kindlon and Thompson found that boys could not talk about their feelings, or imagine how their actions affected those of others.[19] Thus skills that might have helped boys come to terms with their own weakness, diminishing shame, remain uncultivated, and primitive shame, augmented by the culture, lurks, unaddressed.

This undercurrent of shame then leads to a vicious ratcheting process: whenever inner reality signals to the boy his own failure to exemplify the desired (but impossible) norm, the need to humiliate someone else becomes more acute. But this project of domination is itself fraught with anxiety; ultimately it increases shame rather than diminishing it.

At just the time when the "culture of cruelty" is reaching its height, boys are going through puberty and experiencing constant sexual arousal. The peer culture now tells them that kindness and empathy are "soft" feelings and that only domination is good. They now learn from other boys that sex is all about control, and that tenderness and softness are bad.[20] Boys are very anxious about sexual performance, and yet they cannot show fear or pain to other boys. What they can show is hostility and anger. Real intimacy, the psychologists note, requires "sensitivity, respect, and tenderness." And yet, just as they are becoming interested in girls, boys are subjected to a culture that stigmatizes these qualities as feminine, and teaches them that "power, dominance, and denial of sensitivity" are the good qualities.[21]

Meanwhile, boys masturbate frequently, and they find that experience satisfying in part because it is an experience that they can control. But the culture of cruelty shapes a boy's fantasies, building up "a library of sexual memories" in which he is in complete control over women who, in real life, may terrify him.[22] Given the way in which his culture values control, he soon learns to prefer the fantasy world, in which women are objects he can manipulate. He then seeks to replicate that fantasy world in reality by treating women as mere objects and attempting to dominate them. The ubiquitous presence of pornographic images reinforcing that way of treating women strengthens the habit of viewing women in this way.

In short, what Kindlon and Thompson find as a result of their detailed empirical study is very much what my analysis of "primitive shame" has suggested. All human beings feel anxiety and shame about lack of control, in various areas of life. Sexuality is one area where these anxieties are extremely prominent. But culture greatly influences how those anxieties develop and whether shame will be to some extent renounced in favor of compassion, or converted into aggressive objectifying behavior.

This is where the males of AutoAdmit are coming from. They fit perfectly into the Kindlon/Thompson analysis, and we can see how the Internet facilitates a young man's aggressive response to women, viewed as powerful, secure, and out of reach. In fantasy, he can dominate and punish them, remaining utterly secure himself. Shaming comes from shame, untutored and even augmented by a culture of maleness that teaches that any status short of total control is weak and shameful.

Law?

Does this analysis have any implications for law? First of all, it suggests the urgent importance of figuring out how to make it possible for plaintiffs like DOE I and DOE II to win. At present it is very difficult for them to do so, and this situation needs everyone's attention. Beyond this, my analysis suggests that the behavior of the anonymous AutoAdmit writers is best understood as a gender-based hate crime. That way of understanding what is happening may or may not lead to any concrete steps for law and policy:

much depends on one's view of the whole category of hate crime, and the justifiability of treating it as a separate category.

As Saul Levmore's essay argues, the anonymity of the AutoAdmit writers is a major source of their freedom to create for themselves a shame-free zone in which they can inflict shame on others: so my analysis suggests the importance of requiring identification as a condition of posting. Such requirements are already in force on many university sites, and it would be good if this became the norm of good practice everywhere. There will still be irresponsible outliers, but their outlier status would be plain, and both readers and employers would beware of the information they received there.

Removing anonymity goes to the heart of the "slave revolt": for the ability of the bloggers to create a new world in which they exercise power and the women are humiliated depends on their ability to insulate their Internet selves from responsibility in the real world, while ensuring real-world consequences for the woman. The world of AutoAdmit can accomplish the goals of ressentiment precisely because it is sealed at one end and not at the other, so to speak: the real watcher, securely masked, enjoys the real-world torment of the target woman that flows from her torment in cyberspace.

More generally, my analysis suggests that we should be much less deferential to this sort of anonymous speech in close-knit communities (such as law schools) than in the broader public sphere. Julia Roberts is unlikely to suffer serious harms from Internet abuse. The harms suffered by DOE I and DOE II are real and major. We need to prevent this unhealthy phenomenon from corrupting the climate of instruction and conversation in our university communities, though perhaps we need not be as vigilant about the public sphere more generally. Regulation must consider the size of the community, the status of the objectified victim, and the likelihood of serious damage, both to individuals and to the community.

The more general conclusion suggested by my analysis, however, is cultural rather than legal. The culture of shame/domination that leads to the world of AutoAdmit is not immutable. Changing it, however, requires not just reining in some pathological bad apples: it requires changing pervasive cultural patterns of thinking and talking about masculinity. Part of this change may be produced through more responsible images of masculinity in the media and the public culture.

Most of the work, however, can be implemented only on the individual level. As Kindlon and Thompson conclude:

It is the responsibility of people who raise boys to train them specifically to be good, empathic partners to girls and women. It can be done, by fathers who model respect for women in the family and in the wider world, by mothers who help sons understand a girl's point of view, and by anyone in a boy's life who helps him see his connectedness to others as a positive thing. What will not work is to ignore this need for guidance, leaving boys to their own devices, winking at their dominating and reckless behavior, and forcing girls and women to pay the price for this cultural and personal negligence.[23]

That's easy to say, hard to do—particularly in the midst of a culture that values aggression and domination and devalues empathy and connection. Can it be done one family at a time? It is difficult for parents to counteract the tremendous influence of the peer culture. A boy who is connected and loving at home soon enters the culture Kindlon and Thompson describe, and is very likely to learn, there, to feel shame about the "soft" and "feminine" values he has been exhibiting at home. Families sometimes prevail: not all male law students become AutoAdmit objectifiers. Universities and law schools can also play their part in shaping culture. Nonetheless, it is not enough to call the behavior exhibited on this and other sites pathological, or the work of isolated nuts. It is rooted in American culture itself, and in one form or another in most cultures of masculinity in the world.

Above all, however, what we really need is what Nietzsche, I am sure, would have hated most of all: a true "slave revolt," a "revaluation of values" that would put the "morality of pity" (i.e., a morality centrally based upon compassion for weakness and suffering) in place of the will to power as a key social aspiration. Or, even more radically, a revolution that would show that the need to dominate is a form of weakness, the ability to allow another person to be whole and real a sign of strength. *Pace* Nietzsche, this "slave revolt" would not be inspired by ressentiment. It would be an attempt to undo the work of ressentiment, and it would be inspired by compassion, respect for the dignity of each human individual, and a sense of human interdependence. (Mohandas Gandhi was one leader who successfully conducted such a "slave revolt" for a time, convincing his followers that respect and compassion are stronger and more manly than aggression. But then, of course, he was shot by someone who described himself as motivated by feelings of humiliated masculinity on behalf of all Indian males—who were being lured, as Nathuram Godse saw it, into an unmanly and shamefully nonaggressive style of life.)

The culture of gender-based objectification is tenacious, and the Internet has made it more difficult to combat. Many individual men are wonderful, but the culture of masculinity around the world, and perhaps especially in America, remains deeply diseased. Andrea Dworkin wrote in 1974: "[W]omen are objects, commodities, some deemed more expensive than others—but it is only by asserting one's humanness every time, in all situations, that one becomes someone as opposed to something. That, after all, is the core of our struggle."[24] As we consider Internet norms, we must, then, ask: How can we facilitate those assertions of humanness? And how can we ensure that the voices who make those assertions will not be silenced by pornographic hate?

PART II

Reputation

CHAPTER 5

Believing False Rumors

CASS R. SUNSTEIN

With the rise of the Internet, false rumors are ubiquitous. Many of them involve famous people. For example, numerous Americans have believed that Barack Obama is a Muslim, that he was not born in the United States, and that he "pals around with terrorists." False rumors are pervasive about the allegedly terrible acts, beliefs, and motivations of public officials and about the allegedly scandalous private lives not only of those officials, but of many other people with a high public profile.

In the era of the Internet, it is easy to spread false rumors about almost anyone. A student, a professor, a banker, an employer, an insurance broker, a real estate agent—each of these is vulnerable to an allegation that can have a painful, damaging, or even devastating effect. If the allegation appears on the Internet, those who Google the relevant name will immediately learn about it. The allegation will help to define the person. The false rumor can involve organizations—the Central Intelligence Agency, General Motors, Bank of America, the Boy Scouts, the Catholic Church—as well as individuals. And because material on the Internet tends to have considerable longevity, and may even be permanent (for all practical purposes), a false rumor can have an enduring effect.

My goal here is to specify some of the mechanisms that lead to the acceptance of false rumors, even destructive and bizarre ones. When people believe false rumors, they are often perfectly rational in the sense that they are led, quite sensibly in light of their existing knowledge, to accept falsehoods. This problem is especially acute on the Internet. Rumors often arise and gain traction because they fit with, and support, the prior convictions of those who accept them.

As we shall see, false rumors end up spreading through two processes: social cascades and group polarization. People often rely on what other people believe, or seem to believe, and the informational signals given by others can ensure widespread belief in false rumors. The discussion has a straightforward implication for politics and law: the processes that underlie the "marketplace of ideas" sometimes work poorly because they ensure that many people will converge on falsehoods rather than truth. It is not at all clear what, if anything, the law should or can do about the matter, but it is reasonable to conclude that a "chilling effect" on the transmission of destructive falsehoods about human beings and their institutions can be highly desirable. Without such an effect the marketplace of ideas will predictably lead many people to accept damaging falsehoods about both individuals and institutions, sometimes to the detriment of democracy itself.

Rumors as Informational Cascades

To see how informational cascades work, imagine a deliberating group that is deciding whether some person or group has engaged in unfair or even outrageous conduct, warranting disapproval or some kind of punishment or reprisal.[1] Assume that the group members are announcing their views in sequence. From his own knowledge and experience, each member has at least a little private information about what that person or group has done. But each member also attends, reasonably enough, to the judgments of others. Andrews is the first to speak; perhaps he is a propagator of the rumor. Starting or spreading a rumor, he suggests that bad conduct has indeed occurred. Barnes now knows Andrews's judgment; it is clear that she too should certainly conclude that there was such conduct if she agrees independently with Andrews. But if her independent judgment is otherwise, she would—if she trusts Andrews no more and no less than she trusts herself—be indifferent about what to think or do, and she might simply flip a coin.

Now turn to a third person, Carlton. Suppose that both Andrews and Barnes have said that outrageous conduct has occurred, but that Carlton's own information, though not conclusive, suggests that they are wrong. In that event, Carlton might well ignore what he knows and follow Andrews and Barnes. It is likely, after all, that both Andrews and Barnes had reasons for their conclusion, and unless Carlton thinks that his own information is better than theirs, he should follow their lead. If he does, Carlton is in a cascade.

Now suppose that Carlton is speaking in response to what Andrews and Barnes did, not on the basis of his own information, and also that subsequent deliberators know what Andrews, Barnes, and Carlton said. On reasonable assumptions, they will do exactly what Carlton did: accept the view that bad or outrageous conduct has occurred regardless of their private information (which, we are supposing, is relevant but inconclusive). This will happen even if Andrews initially blundered. That initial blunder, in short, can start a process by which a number of people participate in creating serious mistakes. This sort of process happens on the Internet every day.

If this is what is happening, there are two major social problems. First, people will believe a falsehood, possibly a damaging one. They might well disapprove of a third party, or favor punishment or some kind of sanction against that person, even if the rumor is baseless. Second, those who are in the cascade do not disclose any information or doubts that they privately hold. In the example just given, the judgment of group members will not reflect the overall knowledge, or the aggregate knowledge, of those within the group—even if the information held by individual members, if actually revealed and aggregated, would produce a better and quite different conclusion. The reason for the problem is that individuals are following the lead of those who came before.

With respect to rumors, of course, people start with diverse levels of information. Most or many will lack any relevant information at all; they might simply follow the informational signals of their predecessors, including the propagators. Other people will have some relevant information, but not enough to overcome the signal given by the shared beliefs of many others, at least of those others are trusted. Still other people will have some relevant information, but are nonetheless motivated to accept or to reject the false rumor. When rumors spread, it is often through a process in which they are accepted by people with low thresholds for acceptance, and eventually through others as well, simply because most people think that so many people cannot be wrong. A tipping point can be reached in which large numbers of people accept a false rumor even though it is quite baseless.

Informational cascades often do occur in the real world. For a seemingly distant example, offering illumination on the mechanisms of rumor transmission, consider a study of music downloads. Matthew Salganik and his coauthors[2] created an artificial music market, with 14,341 participants who were visitors to a website popular with young people. The participants were given a list of previously unknown songs from unknown bands. They were asked to listen to a brief selection of any songs that interested them, to decide which songs (if any) to download, and to assign a rating to the songs they chose. About half of the participants were asked to make their decisions independently, based on the names of the bands and the songs and their own judgment about the quality of the music. The other half could see how many times each song had been downloaded by other participants. These participants were also randomly assigned to one or another of eight possible "worlds," with each evolving on its own; those in any particular world could see only the downloads in their own world. Two key questions were whether people would be affected by the choices of others—and whether different music would become popular in the different "worlds."

Informational cascades developed. In all eight worlds, individuals were far more likely to download songs that had been previously downloaded in significant numbers, and far less likely to download songs that had not been so popular. Most strikingly, the success of songs was quite unpredictable, and the songs that did well or poorly in the control group, where people did not see other people's judgments, could perform very differently in the "social influence worlds." In those worlds, most songs could become very popular or very unpopular, with much depending on the choices of the first downloaders. The identical song could be a hit or a failure, simply because other people, at the start, were seen to choose to download it or not. As Salganik and his coauthors put it: "In general, the 'best' songs never do very badly, and the 'worst' songs never do extremely well," but (and this is the remarkable point) "almost any other result is possible."[3]

We can easily see an analogue to the domain of rumor transmission. Alleged facts do spread from one "world" to another—and in different worlds, people will believe different "facts." Rumor propagators will have terrific success in some worlds but none at all in others. Quality, in terms of correspondence to the truth, might not matter a great deal. We can see in this light why some social groups will hold, quite tenaciously, to false rumors, while other groups will treat them as implausible or even ridiculous. The differential success of rumors provides a real-world analogue to the science fictional concept of "parallel worlds." Consider in this regard the existence of widely divergent group judgments about the origins and causes of AIDS—with some groups believing, falsely, that the first cases were observed in Africa as a result of sexual relations between human beings and monkeys, and with other groups believing, also falsely, that the virus was produced in government laboratories.[4] Consider also the existence of widely divergent views, including rumors, about the causes of the 9/11 attacks—views that attribute the attacks to many sources, including Israel and the United States.

The multiple views about AIDS and the attacks of 9/11 are products of social interactions and in particular of cascade effects. False rumors often spread as a result. When groups come to believe some alleged fact about the egregious misconduct of (say) the United States, or the foolishness or terrible misdeeds of a public or private figure, an informational cascade is often at work. Indeed, cascadelike processes are sufficient to explain divergences across groups—but as we shall see, divergent prior beliefs are important as well.

Rumors as Reputational Cascades

In a reputational cascade, people think that they know what is right, or what is likely to be right, but they nonetheless go along with the group or the crowd in order to maintain the good opinion of others. Suppose that Albert suggests that a certain political figure is corrupt and that Barbara concurs with Albert, not because she actually thinks that Albert is right, but because she does not wish to seem, to Albert, to be ignorant or indifferent to official corruption. (Albert may or may not be a propagator.) If Albert and Barbara say that the official is corrupt, Cynthia might not contradict them publicly and might even appear to share their judgment—not because she believes that judgment to be correct, but because she does not want to face their hostility or lose their good opinion.

It should be easy to see how this process might generate a cascade. Once Albert, Barbara, and Cynthia offer a united front on the issue, their friend David might be reluctant to contradict them even if he thinks that they are wrong. The apparently shared view of Albert, Barbara, and Cynthia carry information; that view might be right. But even if David is skeptical or has reason to believe that they are wrong, he might not want to take them on publicly. The problem, of course, is that the group will not hear what David knows. Reputational cascades often help to account for the spread of a false or disgusting rumor. Especially when people live in some kind of enclave, they may silence themselves in the face of an emerging judgment or opinion even if they believe it to be wrong. Often, people will be suspicious of a rumor, or believe that it is not true, but they will not contradict the judgment of the relevant group, largely in order to avoid social sanctions.

In the actual world of group decisions, people are of course uncertain whether publicly expressed statements are a product of independent knowledge, participation in an informational cascade, or reputational pressure.

Much of the time, listeners and observers often overstate the extent to which the actions of others are based on independent information rather than social pressures. False rumors spread and are sometimes quite robust as a result. And here too, of course, diverse thresholds matter a great deal. Jones may not silence himself, or agree with the relevant group, unless the reputational pressure is intense; Smith might more easily be led to go along with the crowd. But if most of the world consists of people like Smith, then Jones might eventually yield.

Rumors and Group Polarization

As we shall now see, deliberation among like-minded people often entrenches false rumors.[5] The explanations here overlap with those that account for social cascades, and here too we can understand why some groups will believe rumors that seem ludicrously implausible in others.

The Basic Finding

What happens when group members deliberate with one another? A standard answer is *group polarization:* Like-minded people typically end up in a more extreme position in line with their pre-deliberation tendencies.[6] In keeping with the subject at hand, let us focus on beliefs about facts, rather than values. If, for example, people tend to believe that the nation's leader is a criminal, or that some corporate executive is a scoundrel, their belief to this effect will be strengthened after they speak together. In the context of rumor transmission, the implication is simple: if group members begin with an antecedent commitment to a rumor, internal deliberations will strengthen that belief. The antecedent commitment might involve a specific claim, including a bit of gossip. Or it might involve a more general belief with which the rumor easily fits. The key point is that internal deliberations should entrench the rumor.

With respect to group polarization, the initial experiments involved risk-taking behavior. What happens when risk-inclined people talk with other people who are risk inclined? The answer is that they become still more risk inclined.[7] Consider, for example, the questions whether to take a new job, to invest in a foreign country, to escape from a prisoner-of-war camp, or to run for political office.[8] For many decisions, members of deliberating groups became significantly more disposed to take risks after a brief period of collective discussion. On the basis of such evidence, it became standard to believe that deliberation produced a systematic "risky shift." For a significant period, the major consequence of group discussion, it was thought, was to produce that risky shift—a thought that would bear on many parts of social life, because groups are often asked to decided whether to take a gamble or instead to take precautions.

But later studies drew this conclusion into serious question. On many of the same questions on which Americans displayed a risky shift, Taiwanese subjects showed a "cautious shift."[9] On most of the topics just listed, deliberation led citizens of Taiwan to become significantly less risk inclined than they were before they started to talk. Nor was the cautious shift limited to the Taiwanese. Among Americans, deliberation sometimes produced a cautious shift as well, as risk-averse people became more reluctant to take certain risks after they talked with one another.[10]

At first glance, it seemed hard to reconcile these competing findings, but the reconciliation turned out to be simple: *the pre-deliberation median is the best predictor of the direction of the shift.*[11] When group members are disposed toward risk taking, a risky shift is observed. Where members are disposed toward caution, a cautious shift is observed. It follows that the striking difference between American and Taiwanese subjects is not a product of any cultural difference in how people behave in groups. It results from a difference in the pre-deliberation medians of the Americans and the Taiwanese on the key questions.[12] Thus the risky shift and the cautious shift are both subsumed under the general rubric of group polarization.

In the behavioral laboratory, group polarization has been shown in a remarkably wide range of contexts, many bearing directly on transmission of rumors.[13] How good-looking are people in slides? Group deliberation produces more extreme judgments about that question: if individuals think that someone is good-looking, the group is likely to think that that person is devastatingly attractive.[14] (Movie stars undoubtedly benefit from this process.) Group polarization also occurs for obscure factual questions, such as how far Sodom (on the Dead Sea) is below sea level.[15] Even burglars show a shift in the cautious direction when they discuss prospective criminal endeavors.[16]

In the domains of rumor transmission, several studies are especially relevant (though they do not involve factual claims). After deliberation, groups of people turn out to be far more inclined to protest apparently unfair behavior than was their median member before discussion began.[17] Consider, for example, the appropriate response to three different events: police brutality against African Americans; an apparently unjustified war; and sex discrimination by a local city council. *In every one of these contexts, deliberation made group members far more likely to support aggressive protest action.* Group member moved, for example, from support for a peaceful march to support for a nonviolent demonstration, such as a sit-in at a police station or city hall. Interestingly, the size of the shift toward a more extreme response was correlated with the initial mean. When people initially supported a strong response, group discussion produced a greater shift in the direction of a support for a still stronger response. This finding is standard within the literature: the extent of the shift is associated with the strength of the average person's starting point.[18]

People often make individual judgments about fairness and unfairness, including about whether particular people have behaved unfairly; they also make those judgments in groups. What happens to our judgments about unfairness when we speak with one another? The answer should now be clear: when we are individually inclined to believe that unfairness has occurred, our discussion will intensify our beliefs and make us very angry.[19] The most relevant studies had a high degree of realism. People were asked to engage in certain tasks, designed to simulate activities that might actually be undertaken in a business setting—such as classifying budget items, scheduling meetings, and routing a phone message through the proper channels with assignment of the proper level of priority. Good performance could produce financial rewards. After completing the tasks, people were able to ask for their supervisors' judgment and to receive feedback from them. Some of the answers seemed rude and unfair, such as "I've decided not to read your message. The instructions say it's up to me . . . so don't bother sending me any other messages or explanations about your performance on this task," and "If you would have worked harder, then you'd have scored higher. I will not accept your message on this round!"

People were asked to rate their supervisors along various dimensions including fairness, politeness, bias, and good leadership. The ratings occurred in three periods. The first included individual ratings; the second included a group consensus judgment; and the third included individual ratings after group judgment. It turned out that group judgments were far more negative than the average of individual judgments.[20] In many cases, group members decided that the behavior was really very unfair, even though individuals believed that the behavior was only mildly unfair. Interestingly, the groups' conclusions were typically more extreme than were people's individual judgments after deliberation. But such judgments were nonetheless more negative, and thus more extreme, than pre-deliberation individual judgments.

This study does not exactly involve rumor transmission, but it bears directly on that subject. Often, people think that some person or institution has engaged in unfair or outrageous behavior, and when they speak to one another that belief intensifies. False and terrible rumors become entrenched as a result.[21] If people begin with a belief that person X might well have said or done Y, they will become more committed to that (false) belief as they speak with one another. And even if people begin without a clear belief about Y, it may well suffice if they start with some negative judgments about X. Once it is suggested that X said or did Y, the group's antipathy toward X may well be enough to ensure that group polarization entrenches the false rumor.

Why Polarization?

To understand how group polarization solidifies and spreads rumors, we need to ask why like-minded people go to extremes. There are three important reasons:

The exchange of information intensifies preexisting beliefs. The most important reason involves information.[22] People tend to respond to the arguments made by other people—and the pool of arguments, in any group with some predisposition in one direction, will inevitably be skewed in the direction of the original predisposition.

Suppose that you are in a group of people whose members tend to think that Israel is the real aggressor in the Mideast conflict, that eating beef is unhealthy, that some person did in fact engage in sexual misconduct, or that same-sex unions are a good idea. In such a group, you will hear many arguments to that effect, and considerable support for reports, including rumors, that support these tentative thoughts. Because of the initial distribution of views, you will hear relatively fewer opposing views. It is highly likely that you will have heard some, but not all, of the arguments that emerge from the discussion. After you have heard all of what is said, you will probably move further in the direction of being anti-Israel, opposed to eating beef, accepting the claim of sexual misconduct, and favoring civil unions—and you will probably be more inclined to accept supporting rumors. And even if you do not move—even if you are impervious to what others think--most group members will probably be affected.

Corroboration breeds confidence, and confidence breeds extremism.   Those who lack confidence and who are unsure what they should think tend to moderate their views.[23] Suppose that you are asked your view on some question on which you lack information—say, whether some rumor is true. You are likely to avoid an extreme position. It is for this reason that cautious people, not knowing what to do, are likely to choose the midpoint between the extremes.[24] But if other people seem to share their views, people are likely to become more confident that they are correct. As a result, they will probably move in a more extreme direction.

In a wide variety of experimental contexts, people's opinions have been shown to become more extreme simply because their initial view has been corroborated, and because they have been more confident after learning of the shared views of others.[25] Suppose that other people share your view that the United States is not to be trusted, that the attacks of 9/11 were staged, or that Iran poses a serious threat to the rest of the world. If so, your own view will be more deeply felt after you hear what they have to say.

What is especially noteworthy here is that this process—of increased confidence and increased extremism—is often occurring simultaneously for all participants. Suppose that a group of four people is inclined to distrust the intentions of the United States with respect to foreign aid. Seeing her tentative view confirmed by three others, each member is likely to feel vindicated, to hold her view more confidently, and to move in a more extreme direction. At the same time, the very same internal movements are also occurring in *other* people (from corroboration to more confidence, and from more confidence to more extremism). But those movements will not be highly visible to each participant. It will simply appear as if others "really" hold their views without hesitation. As a result, our little group might conclude, after a day's discussion, that the intentions of the United States, with respect to foreign aid, cannot be trusted at all.

We have a clue here about the immense importance of social networks, on the Internet and in ordinary life, in transmitting rumors and in creating movements of various sorts. Social networks can operate as polarization machines, because they help to confirm and thus amplify people's antecedent views.[26] Consider the fact that in one army camp, "the rumor that all men over thirty-five years of age were to be discharged traveled like lightning—but almost exclusively among men over that age."[27] A far more serious example is provided by Islamic terrorism, which is fueled by spontaneous social networks, in which like-minded people spread information and discuss grievances, with potentially violent results.[28] At certain stages, "the interactivity among a 'bunch of guys' acted as an echo chamber, which progressively radicalized them collectively to the point where they were ready to collectively join a terrorist organization. Now the same process is taking place online."[29] The major force here is not websites, which people read passively; it consists of listserves, blogs, and discussion forums, "which are crucial in the process of radicalization."[30] Of course many factors contribute to terrorist behavior, but there is little doubt that social networks, spreading false rumors, play a significant role.

These are examples from the political domain, where rumors run rampant; but there are many other illustrations. Why are some foods enjoyed, or rumored to be especially healthy, in some places, whereas the same foods are disliked, or rumored to be unhealthy, in other places? "Many Germans believe that drinking water after eating cherries is deadly; they also believe that putting ice in soft drinks is unhealthy. The English, however, rather enjoy a cold drink of water after some cherries; and Americans love icy refreshments."[31] A less innocuous example: In some nations, strong majorities believe that Arab terrorists were not responsible for the attacks of September 11, 2001. According the Pew Research Institute, 93 percent of Americans believe that Arab terrorists destroyed the World Trade Center, whereas only 11 percent of Kuwaitis believe that Arab terrorists destroyed the World Trade Center.[32] With respect to daily life, a great deal of what we believe, like, and dislike is influenced by the processes of information exchange that I am exploring here.

People's concern for their reputations can increase extremism. A third explanation involves social comparison. That explanation begins with the claim that people want to be perceived favorably by other group members, and also to perceive themselves favorably. Sometimes our views are, to a greater or lesser extent, a function of how we want to present ourselves. Of course some people are more concerned with others than with their self-presentation. But once we hear what others believe, some of us will adjust our positions at least slightly in the direction of the dominant position, to hold onto our preserved self-presentation. We might contain our opposition;

we might voice somewhat more enthusiasm for the majority view than we really feel.

Some people might want to show, for example, that they are not cowardly or cautious, especially in an entrepreneurial group that disparages these characteristics and that favors boldness and risk taking. In business, people often want to seem to be risk takers. In such a group, people will frame their position so that they do not appear cowardly or cautious by comparison to other group members. And when they hear what other people think, they might find that they occupy a somewhat different position, in relation to the group, from what they hoped. They will shift accordingly.[33] This might be because they want others to see them in a certain way. Or it might be because they want to see themselves a certain way, and a shift is necessary so that they can see themselves in the most attractive light. The phenomenon occurs in many contexts, including acceptance and transmission of rumors.

The Chilling Effect Revisited

In discussions of possible restrictions on free speech, it is standard to speak of, and to deplore, the "chilling effect" that is created by the prospect of civil or criminal sanctions.[34] Libel law, for example, might chill speech about public figures and public issues, in a way that could damage democratic debate. And if there is a "marketplace of ideas," we should be especially concerned about the risk of a chilling effect, because it will undermine processes that will ultimately produce the truth.

Everyone should agree that a chilling effect can be exceedingly harmful to a system of free expression, and that it is important to devise methods to reduce that effect. But the discussion thus far raises doubts about these standard claims, which seem, in their most extreme forms, to be based on empirical blunders and an indefensible optimism about the actual operation of information markets.

There are two points here. First, the chilling effect may be desirable insofar as it reduces damaging and destructive falsehoods, including falsehoods about individuals, famous or not famous, and institutions, public or private. To be sure, some falsehoods are helpful for producing the truth. But many false rumors are not merely damaging but also entirely unhelpful to those who seek to know what is true. Second, the marketplace of ideas will not work well if social influences ensure that false rumors can spread and become entrenched. As we have seen, one consequence of cascade effects and group polarization is to make false rumors widely believed in relevant communities. Under certain conditions, it can be exceedingly difficult to dislodge those false rumors.

Claims about the risks associated with the chilling effect should note that any society needs not an absence of "chill," but an optimal level. To decide on the optimal level, it is necessary to have an understanding of the relationship between the marketplace of ideas and the emergence of truth. Such an understanding would require a great deal of empirical work, which I have not attempted to undertake here. But I hope that I have said enough to suggest that especially in the age of the Internet, the marketplace of ideas will often ensure widespread acceptance of falsehoods.

There are several puzzles here. The first involves the Condorcet Jury Theorem, which shows that under certain conditions, crowds can be extremely wise.[35] To summarize a complex story: If each member of a group is more likely than not to arrive at the right answer, the likelihood that the majority of the group will be right expands to 100 percent as the size of the group expands. We might conclude that in this light, small groups will believe false rumors, but large groups will be able to handle them, in the sense that they will be able to separate error from truth. Undoubtedly this is so under some conditions, and the Condorcet Jury Theorem helps to explain why. But without exploring all of the complexities here, we should notice a single point, which is that the optimistic result of the theorem follows *only if group members are more likely than not to be right.* Suppose, by contrast, that group members suffer from a systematic bias and are hence more likely than not to be wrong. If so, the logic of the theorem suggests a pessimistic result: as the group becomes larger, the likelihood that the majority will be wrong approaches 100 percent. In many contexts, the very mechanisms described here guarantee that group members be more likely than not to be wrong. For this reason, large groups can go astray and crowds will be foolish rather than wise, not in spite of the theorem but by its own logic.

Two of the most important empirical puzzles are these: To what extent do people believe false rumors on the Internet? To what extent are such rumors subject to correction? On a pessimistic view, many or most people follow a simple heuristic, to the effect that people generally do not say things unless they are true. If it is reported that some student or professor engaged in terrible misconduct, or that a candidate for public office is corrupt, many people may be likely to think that the report would not have been unless it had some basis. On this view, there is fire wherever there is smoke. And even if people do not think exactly that, the presence of the bad rumor can leave a residue of suspicion, a kind of negative effect that can ultimately affect beliefs and behavior.

On an optimistic view, there are two safeguards against widespread belief in false rumors, especially in the era of the Internet. The first is the sheer existence of numerous rumors, many of them false. With so much falsity, it might be thought, people will increasingly discount and distrust what they read and hear. Internet "scams" were more effective ten years ago than today; when you read that you have won the lottery, you are unlikely to believe it, even if you might have thought "maybe!" a decade before. Perhaps the culture will generally move toward greater skepticism, especially when the Internet ensures that propagators can easily reach a large audience.

The second safeguard is the greater ability to produce instant corrections. A political figure is able to say, immediately, that the false rumor is false, and to reach numerous people in doing so. Even a private person, lacking any kind of celebrity, may be able to do the same thing. Taken together, the two safeguards might provide a strong correction against belief in false rumors. In my view, this judgment is too optimistic, but it bears empirical testing.

Lives, Pieces of Lives, and the Truman Show (for Everyone)

For democratic discussion about actual and prospective public officials, existing evidence suggests that there is a genuine problem. The Internet is full of reports about what people (supposedly) did and said, and about what they (supposedly) believe. Sometimes those reports are false and are based on nothing at all, other than a desire to obtain attention or to promote or to defeat a cause. Sometimes those reports are false but based on a shred or a kernel of truth, but they produce a palpably incorrect impression, one that harms not only individual people but also institutions that might benefit from their participation.

There is a larger point in the background. People's lives consist of a number of statements and actions, and over a period of years it is nearly inevitable that a particular person will have said something, or done something, that might trigger concern or perhaps even opprobrium if it is broadcast to the world. One of the great risks in the era of bloggers and YouTube is that statements and actions are so closely monitored that any particular one, taken out of context, might seem representative of the whole, or a clue to something dark and bad.

To see the concern, imagine a world, not so very different from what seems to be emerging in our own, in which many lives are monitored and filmed, not by government but by technologies that permit them to be recorded. (This is a generalization of the 1998 movie, *The Truman Show.*) Of course recording would present serious risks to individual privacy.[36] But this is not my concern here; we could suppose that in this imaginable world, recording occurs only for events or statements that are in some sense public. The problem, in any variation in such a world, is that single incidents can obtain real salience. And if this is so, the processes that I have described can greatly magnify that salience. For public figures and members of public institutions, this is a serious problem. It is also a problem for self-government insofar as citizens obtain a false understanding of those people. Of course my topic is false rumors, not true but misleading ones. It is difficult to "chill" reports on particular events that provide a deceptive understanding; the law itself cannot and should not become involved here. But at least we can say that in terms of social norms there is an optimal level of chill on deception as well; and that it is exceedingly important to attempt to convey a social understanding that particular events and statements may badly mislead, even or especially when they become salient.

There is also a problem for ordinary people, who can be greatly injured by false rumors, and all the more easily by virtue of the Internet. Friends, employers, and even family members might well encounter those rumors, based perhaps on a misreading of a single statement or incident. That statement may well come to be taken as representative of some whole, if only because of the operation of human attention; recall the importance of focusing. A chilling effect, at least via social norms, can achieve a great deal of good. The more tractable issue, for purposes of both analysis and policy, involves falsehoods. As we have seen, they can be persistent, not in spite of the marketplace of ideas but because of it.

Of course nothing said here is sufficient to justify any reform of existing practices, even with respect to false rumors. As I have said, any chilling effect on falsehoods is likely to affect truths as well. What counts as a false rumor or true one is often greatly disputed, and we might not trust our institutions to tell the difference with sufficient reliability. Perhaps our norms and our practices will ensure that we discount, to an increasing extent, what we hear. But at the very least, we should be able to see that in the age of the

Internet there is no reason for easy confidence in the power of the market-place of ideas to produce truths, especially when we consider the all-too-comfortable relationship, much of the time, between prior convictions and acceptance of false statements.

Conclusion

False rumors are pervasive on the Internet, and otherwise sensible people believe them. Self-interested and altruistic propagators spread rumors about prominent people and institutions. Such rumors cast doubt on their subject's honesty, decency, fairness, patriotism, and sometimes even sanity; often they portray public figures as fundamentally corrupt. Those who are not in the public sphere are similarly vulnerable. In a matter of seconds, it is easy to portray almost anyone as some kind of wrongdoer, and in that sense to injure their reputation, if only because of the easy availability of information on the Internet. The Internet, then, has two important effects. It allows information to be provided to the world, in an instant, and it allows easy discovery, by anyone, of that information, also in an instant.

Rumor transmission frequently occurs as a result of cascade effects and group polarization. Indeed, rumors spread as a textbook example of an informational cascade: imperfectly or entirely uninformed people accept what they hear from others. Sometimes reputational cascades are involved as well, as people appear to accept rumors, not because they actually believe them but so as to curry favor or not to face opprobrium. Group polarization also plays a large role, as people strengthen their antecedent commitment to a rumor simply because of a process of internal deliberation. When employers come to believe something about an employee, or teachers about a student, or students about a teacher, or voters about a public official, group polarization is typically at work.

I have said little here about how to respond to the existing situation, either through social norms or through legal institutions. The risk of a chilling effect must be taken seriously. But it should be plain that the marketplace of ideas will often fail to produce the truth; the very mechanisms explored here ensure that any marketplace will lead many people to accept damaging and destructive falsehoods. A clear conclusion is that some kind of chilling effect on false statements of fact is important—not only to protect people against negligence, cruelty, and unjustified damage to their reputations—but also to ensure the proper functioning of democracy itself.

CHAPTER 6

Reputation Regulation:
Disclosure and the Challenge of Clandestinely Commensurating Computing

FRANK PASQUALE

There are many reasons to worry about the unsubstantiated rumors, opinions, and evaluations now polluting cyberspace. Viral culture online has made literally true the old bromide, "A lie can be halfway 'round the world before the truth has got its boots on." Although the emancipatory potential of digital connectivity is clear, critical Internet studies have illuminated its role in reinforcing old structures of unfair disadvantage and unearned privilege. Regulation may be necessary to check these trends.

For years, search engines have tried to reassure us that diligent "vanity searching"—that is, entering one's own name as a search query, in order to see what comes up—is the key to good "online hygiene." If an objectionable result comes up about a person, she can litigate against its publisher, or try to "drown it out" with rival information designed to drive the unflattering material to less salient positions in search results. Companies like Reputation Defender offer such services, acting as twenty-first century "reverse private detectives" who specialize in concealing or obscuring damaging information.

The self-help approach always had many shortcomings. Defamation lawsuits are expensive and uncertain projects, especially in the United States. Litigation can backfire, increasing the salience of provocative material if the suit garners media attention. Even the best search engine optimizer cannot guarantee the success of an effort to "bury" unflattering results with other material. But these tactics at least offered some means of trying to "clear one's name" online by detecting, deterring, and occasionally obscuring slurs and innuendo viewable to all.

New search technology has now fatally compromised self-help strategies. As personalization advances, there is no single set of "search results" for a person's name. One searcher may see a collection of positive or neutral results about an individual; another might be presented with compromising material. Screeners within human resources or credit-approval departments may order specialized software that scours the Internet for the most troubling material about any applicant. It is unlikely that the applicants they evaluate will have access to similar software.

In the United States, expansive interpretations of the First Amendment undermine even modest proposals for regulating the results of search engines. However, promoting individuals' access to the Internet results obtained by those making important decisions about them would pass constitutional muster. It would also reduce the reputational "unknown unknowns" that can wreak havoc on careers, credit, and educational opportunities. To the extent that key decision makers know more about us, we need to know exactly what data they have and how they are using it. As David Brin predicted in *The Transparent Society,* further disclosure from corporate entities needs to accompany the scrutiny we all increasingly suffer as individuals.[1]

Reputational systems can never be rendered completely just, but legislators can take two steps toward fairness. The first is relatively straightforward: to ensure that key decision makers reveal the full range of online sources they consult as they approve or deny applications for credit, insurance, employment, and college and graduate school admissions. Such disclosure will at least serve to warn applicants of the dynamic digital dossier they are accumulating in cyberspace. Effective disclosure requirements need to cover more than the users of reputational information—they should also apply to some aggregators as well. Just as banks have moved from consideration of a long-form credit report to use of a single commensurating credit score, employers and educators in an age of reputation regulation may turn to intermediaries that combine extant indicators of reputation into a single scoring of a person. Since such scoring can be characterized as a trade secret, it may be even less accountable than the sorts of rumors and innuendo discussed above. Any proposed legislation will need to address the use of such reputation scores, lest black-box evaluations defeat its broader purposes of accountability and transparency.

Internet-Driven Decision Making

In developed countries, having an online presence is a near inevitability for all but the most marginalized. Classes routinely complete projects online, and profiles on social-networking sites are becoming not only a social but a professional necessity. An individual need not try to create a web presence for herself—detractors or admirers can instantly catapult her into micro-celebrity with or without her permission. Blogging also creates both professional opportunities and dangers, as Heather B. Armstrong, the author of the blog "Dooce," learned when she was fired by her employer for her online commentaries. She ultimately had the last laugh: "getting Dooced" became a slang term for being fired for blogging, and she was able to support herself from advertising as the site became more popular. But many others with online presences may never discover the adverse impact of the "digital person" they appear to be online.[2]

Search engines and social networks offer a tempting trove of data for decision makers. In the college admissions context, "a recent study by the University of Massachusetts-Dartmouth found that 25 percent of college admissions offices admit to using search engines such as Google, Yahoo, and MSN to research potential students and that 20 percent look for the same information on social networking sites such as Facebook and MySpace."[3] Employment lawyers routinely offer guidelines to employers who plan to Google job applicants.[4] There is evidence that "as many as 50% of employers and 77% of job recruiters concerned about alcohol/drug abuse, violence, and similar problems check out potential employees on the Web."[5] Sources for online scrutiny range from Google, Facebook, eBay, and Yahoo to PeopleFinders .com, Local.Live.com, Zillow.com (real estate purchase and sale data), Feed ster.com, Technorati.com (to search for blogs), and Opensecrets.org and Fundrace.org (to search for campaign donations).

Legal efforts to ensure the fairness and accuracy of such reputation-affecting information have not caught up to technological advances in producing it. For example, if a human resources department has "personalized" its results to ensure that the most damaging information available about a person (from its perspective) comes up first, that applicant has no right to learn what information the office considered as it made its negative decision. The applicant would have to avail himself of the same personalizing software to be fully aware of all the negative information such a personalized search was generating. Yet trade secrecy and contracts could easily prevent him from ever accessing an exact replica of the programs used by the educators, employers, landlords, bankers, and others making vital decisions about his future. Even as health reform legislation makes it harder for insurers to discriminate against individuals on the basis of health status, employers or other entities may start to consult personal health data on sites including "Patients Like Me" if users fail to adequately secure their information.[6] Online openness can lead to permanent records of one's weight, health status, and mental health issues.

In popular books like Ian Ayres's *Super Crunchers* and Stephen Baker's *The Numerati*, legal scholars and journalists have celebrated data-driven decision making as a cornerstone of future advances in productivity.[7] However, the individual who is an *object* of such "super-crunching" may fear that a crucial decision about her is being made on the basis of a misunderstanding—an unfair reduction of a complex person to one trait, fact, or record.

In *The Politics of Recognition*, Charles Taylor explores the claims of individuals who felt that they were treated unfairly—or, worse, degraded and subordinated—on account of their ethnic identity.[8] Taylor advanced discussion of multiculturalism by articulating the harm of *misrecognition*—of being understood by others in an untrue or insultingly unflattering light. For example, women are routinely treated unfairly (and even brutally) solely on the basis of gender-based stereotypes.[9] Those dogged by digital scarlet letters may find whole new modes of discrimination blocking their professional or personal advance.

Of course, employers, colleges, and banks have a right to reject or approve applications as they see fit. But while it is one thing to be judged on an identified fault, it is a different experience altogether to to suffer a negative judgment for an unknown reason. While such a problem might seem unlikely now, personalized search technology makes it increasingly possible in the future. As any individual uses a search engine, he gradually trains it to prioritize certain types of results and de-prioritize others.[10] This translation of behavior into a "database of intentions" helps searchers a great deal—but can create uncertainty and anxiety once one is the object searched.[11] While the investigative consumer reports (ICRs) generated by credit-reporting agencies (CRAs) are subject to several strictures, personalized searches are not regulated in the United States.[12] The regulatory framework surrounding extant background checks may unfairly induce the use of informal, digital methods that increase the chance of mis-recognition and reductionism. It is time to develop a consistent regulatory approach for credit bureaus and other sources of reputational information. Antidiscrimination norms may well lead us from legislating against aggregate stereotyping to creating opportunities for individuals to correct misinformation.

Background on the Fair Credit Reporting Act

Much like today's Internet, the files of pre-Fair Credit Reporting Act (FCRA) credit bureaus were often contaminated with irrelevant and inaccurate information, or innuendo. Their dossiers included judgments laced with prejudice; for example, "in 1972, a man in San Francisco discovered that a consumer report about him for life insurance policy included the comment that he used 'his hands in an effeminate manner, also talks in an effeminate manner.'"[13] Senator William Proxmire translated public concern about "erroneous and selective credit reporting" into hearings about credit industry practices and eventual passage of the FCRA.[14]

Congress passed the FCRA in 1970 to protect consumers and regulate the consumer credit-reporting industry. The Congressional findings associated with the act describe the sorry state of the industry as it existed before the passage of FCRA.[15] Congress intended the law "to require that consumer-reporting agencies adopt reasonable procedures . . . for [compiling] consumer credit, personnel, insurance, and other information in a manner which is fair and equitable to the consumer, with regard to the confidentiality, accuracy, relevancy, and proper utilization of such information."[16]

The act regulates the preparation of consumer credit reports by "credit-reporting agencies," as well as the disclosure of those reports, and procedures associated with the maintenance of consumer credit information.[17] When the act applies, it establishes the permissible uses for which an agency may release a report or disclose information, such as by consent of the consumer or for insurance and credit applications. The FCRA also requires that agencies make reasonable efforts to verify information, including the identities of consumers, to increase accuracy.

CRAs must remove information from a report after a certain period of time to reduce the likelihood of reporting obsolete information. If incorrect or inaccurate information is reported, a consumer has the right to dispute the record, at which point the agency must reasonably investigate at no cost to the consumer, and must delete inaccurate data. In addition, consumers are supposed to benefit from mandatory disclosure after an adverse action is taken against them based on a credit report, which gives them the opportunity to dispute inaccuracies under the FCRA. When an agency fails to comply, the FCRA provides a cause of action for civil liability.[18]

Scholars have addressed the policy behind the "second chances" that FCRA mandates are meant to ensure. While "practical obscurity" used to occlude transgressions over time, the CRAs' data storage technology necessitated a legal requirement to restore the old balance between obscurity and publicity. Updating its mandates for the digital age, Jonathan Zittrain has proposed a form of "reputational bankruptcy," giving individuals the ability to block out some features of their online identity.[19] Viktor Mayer-Schonberger's book *Delete: The Virtues of Forgetting in the Digital Age* takes up the difficult task of specifying technical standards for this type of monitoring.[20] Each of these proposals fits into the framework of Danielle Citron's model of "technological due process"—ensuring that the de facto adjudications and rule makings made by software programs live up to some standards of reviewability and revisability.[21]

To complement proposals for "editing by deletion," I have proposed an "annotation remedy" designed to give a more complete picture of persons who object to certain hyperlinks in search results.[22] Such a remedy would permit individuals to add an asterisk to the offending hyperlink, directing web users to their own comment on the objectionable result. Google has recently adopted an "online profiles" program that is one small step toward such annotation rights.[23] My proposal is inspired by Helen Nissenbaum's characterization of privacy as "contextual integrity"—a social condition affording the individual more chances to give a full and complete picture of oneself in a world increasingly driven by scores, snapshots, and sound bites.[24]

Can such ideas be incorporated into a regime like the FCRA? At first glance, the FCRA's focus on the mundane transactional details of credit and debt management has little to offer in the way of solutions to online reputation problems generally. But the very regulatory infrastructure that imposes some minimum standards on credit reports may unfairly elevate the salience of online reputation generators, which can report more provocative (and less vetted) information and rumors. As search engines and other online ratings and rankings entities grow in prominence, some level playing field needs to develop to take into account their roles as data collectors and arrangers. Finland has prevented employers from using Google results (among other unauthorized information sources) in evaluating potential applicants.[25] In this essay, I propose a less draconian solution: requiring important decision makers to reveal the online sources they use in order to evaluate applicants, and revealing the particular information found out about an applicant to that applicant after any decision is made.

A Fair Reputation Reporting Act?

The FCRA is targeted at credit bureaus and the reports they generate. Now that search engines permit anyone to compile a digital dossier on anyone else, can such distributed activity be effectively regulated? Probably not— but at least some elementary steps toward the disclosure of such materials by critical decision makers can curb the most Kafkaesque features of the new reputation systems.

The types of unfairness created by undisclosed reputation dossiers are traditional concerns of three bodies of law: antidiscrimination law, employment law, and fair information practices.[26] None of these laws aspires to cover all human endeavors, and a Fair Reputation Reporting Act would need to be focused, too.[27] Critical decision makers—those with the power to grant or deny applications for employment, credit, insurance, housing, and education—are a logical starting point for such a law. As these decision makers take into account new sources of aggregated information, it would be deeply unfair for applicants not to have a chance to review the digital dossier compiled about them.

Business interests are likely to object to the obligations generated by such a review requirement. However, the same technology that makes so much information available presently can ease the transition to dedicated documentation. As storage costs decline and cloud computing becomes ubiquitous, a decision maker can use software to default to recording the online "leads" pursued as she investigates an applicant. Anyone who has seen a search engine's "web history" knows how revealing and meticulous that documentation can be.

The exact scope of the requirements will need to be worked out by an administrative agency—perhaps the Federal Trade Commission, or perhaps a true privacy regulator to be created pursuant to the proposed act. Regulators will not need to reinvent the wheel. Administrative law has long addressed the record-keeping requirements of government agencies, carefully separating the types of searches for information that constitute forbidden "ex parte contacts" from the run-of-the-mill research no one expects to be recorded.

Though this essay is too brief to flesh out the administrative details of disclosure provisions in a Fair Reputation Reporting Act, it should address three key objections to it. First, while administrative law principles of disclosing the basis of a decision are accepted for government actors, why should the private actors targeted by such legislation also be required to be open about what they are reviewing? Second, should word of mouth or personal recommendations be subject to the same level of review? Third, would the new transparency render reputation reporting as overly positive because individuals will contest negative information, but have no incentive to correct inaccurate positive information?

The first objection merits a layered response. Issuers of credit and insurers are pervasively regulated. As the financial crisis has demonstrated, these entities rely on government as their "ultimate risk manager."[28] After the failure of financial industry deregulation, an ever-closer intertwining of state and the FIRE (finance, insurance, and real estate) industries is a hallmark of the Obama administration.[29] "Coming clean" on the bases of their decisions is a small price to pay for the degree of government subvention they are now receiving.

The case of employers and educators is slightly more complicated. These decision makers are subject to many antidiscrimination laws, and the fair data practices discussed above might better be incorporated into extant regulation on those grounds rather than being a free-standing privacy law. Given the extraordinary targeting of women documented by Danielle Citron and Martha Nussbaum in this volume, there is already a serious civil rights case to be made against indiscriminate reliance on Internet sources.

Citron's documentation of the negative effects of Internet abuse on women is also part of a suite of responses to the second objection. Unlike a recommendation letter written for one or a few readers, or a phone call that is almost never heard by anyone other than the callers, Internet-based rumors and lies are frequently persistent, searchable, replicable, and accessible to any decision maker with access to the right software or database. A negative reference hurts only for as long as a job seeker keeps it on her résumé; a negative comment online is almost always beyond her control. Anyone affected by such expression deserves at least some chance at discovering whether it has been considered by key decision makers.

The third objection above attempts to shift our attention from the rights of the individual to the information environment as a whole. While individuals will likely contest or try to obscure negative data about them, they have no incentive to eliminate incorrect positive information about them. The problem of incorrect positive information has plagued employment references for some time. If decision makers must disclose the reports and research they use to make decisions, the information environment overall could become biased.

To help sort out these problems, it is helpful to examine J. H. Verkerke's work on the law of employment reference practices.[30] Verkerke provides a typology of three problems facing employers and regulators: "falsely negative references, an inadequate supply of reference information, and falsely positive references."[31] At this level of generality, Verkerke's typology also fits the problem of matching customers to insurers and banks, tenants to landlords, and students to schools. Verkerke argues that any effort to improve the quality of references risks reducing the quantity of information available. He concludes that proposed "regulatory measures that would . . . deter [employers] from providing falsely positive references . . . [present an] inescapable trade-off between quantity and quality substantially weakens the case for these reforms." Could the same be said of the fair information practices promoted in this essay? I believe there are many reasons to believe that the information environment and our understanding of reputation have changed sufficiently since Verkerke's piece was published to justify taking special aim at false and negative information.

First, we might want to consider the implications of environmental law for information privacy. Dennis D. Hirsch argues that just as new forms of pollution have caused extraordinary damage to the natural environment, "the digital age is causing unprecedented damage to privacy . . . [as a] 'faceless infrastructure' employs . . . data to deny us jobs, credit, insurance, and other social goods, often without our knowledge."[32] He observes that environmental law has long grappled with the problem of balancing the costs and benefits of regulation. If a given effort to purify the natural environment becomes too costly, state and federal agencies provide many opportunities for feedback designed to subsequently reduce the costs of compliance. Any agency enforcing a Fair Reputation Reporting Act should be open to concerns that its actions have "biased" the information environment, and respond accordingly.

We can already envision some concrete methods of doing so. For example, just as the agency enforcing FCRA could be seen as a guardian of consumers' reputations, a counter-agency dedicated to dispelling false, positive information could arise to assist businesses. Such an agency would investigate suspicious "sock-puppet" behavior designed to create a misleading impression of the authority, talent, or other positive attributes of an individual. Tal Zarsky has noted the problem of manipulative gaming of reputational systems and has recommended deterrence of "gamers" and "sock-puppeteers."[33] The rise of fusion centers and other public-private surveillance initiatives suggests that state actors will assist businesses in such endeavors in exchange for businesses' supplying antiterrorism and other crime-fighting leads.[34]

Even if the state does not become involved on behalf of businesses in this way, information intermediaries can also sniff out false, positive information on their behalf. Verkerke already predicted their rise in his 1998 article, and Lior Strahilevitz has written about their emergence in areas ranging from real estate to insurance.[35] Just as credit bureaus emerged to vet applicants for customers and banks, they and other information intermediaries may start to scrutinize sources of information online. Using algorithms like those employed by Google, they could begin to weight sources of information by reliability in order to give decision makers a clearer sense of exactly how reliable a given positive or negative piece of information is.

Frontiers of Reputation Regulation

Credit bureaus have already gone beyond merely vetting *sources* of information about individuals. They routinely commensurate information into a single score purporting to assess the creditworthiness of applicants for loans. The FCRA may have helped spur the development of this reputation mechanism. After the content of their reports had to be accessible to consumers, credit bureaus became increasingly reliant on opaque credit scoring. Though a credit score is computed via proprietary algorithms protected as trade secrets, it is widely treated as a fair and objective evaluation of an individual's creditworthiness.[36] Disclosure of such secrets can easily amount to a "taking," requiring government compensation for all the business based on it.

After the subprime debacle, the social importance of credit scoring (and its use by predatory lenders) has become more obvious than ever. Nevertheless, the industry remains highly opaque, with scored individuals unable to determine the consequences of late payments, changes in location, or other decisions. Several disturbing reports have alleged racial, geographic, and other inappropriate influences on credit scores. Because of concerns about their unreliability and unfairness, use of credit scores has been regulated by forty-eight states.[37]

Credit scores have also come under attack for having a disparate impact on poor and minority populations.[38] The National Fair Housing Alliance has criticized them as embedding sexist and racist assumptions into an ostensibly neutral process:

> Studies as well as lawsuits continue to demonstrate that African Americans, Hispanics, and elderly women are not treated the same as similarly qualified white males when attempting to purchase products such as cars, or secure mortgage loans or homeowners insurance. The terms and conditions for purchase of these products can be driven by the race, national origin or gender of the consumer rather than by their ability to pay or condition of the home.[39]

The scores themselves may be self-fulfilling prophecies, creating the financial distress they claim merely to indicate.[40] If a scorer determines that one missed $10 payment for a woman with two children earning $30,000 per year lowers her credit score by 200 points, she will be more likely to default because her low score means that she is going to be paying much more in interest for any financing she can find. Since the scores are black boxes, we have no assurance that scorers try to eliminate such endogeneity or whether they profit from such self-fulfilling prophecies.

Could the black-box proprietary models now common in credit scoring spread to reputation scoring? Several Silicon Valley entrepreneurs have already made the connection. For example, Auren Hoffman's company, Rapleaf, offers individuals a bargain—in exchange for plugging in all the details of extant online profiles about them into its system, Rapleaf will give them one-stop access to the information, and will generate a "reputation score" for its members. The Korean site Cyworld has long rated users' "friendliness," "karma," and "sexiness," among other qualities.[41] A company called Gorb "allows, even insists on, anonymous comments and ratings about rated individual's" professional and personal lives.[42] Some of these sites aim not merely to rate the willing, but also to rate everyone within a particular sphere.

So far, the only reported legal case pertaining to such sites has concerned the rating of attorneys by a site called Avvo. As reputation regulation develops, policy makers should examine closely professionals' campaign for accountable rating sites. Though the attorneys ultimately lost their case, physicians have succeeded in forcing insurers that rate them to engage in fair information practices. Both professions' struggles foreshadow future efforts to hold reputation raters more accountable than credit scorers currently are.

In the legal industry, Avvo aims to rate all licensed attorneys within the states it covers.[43] It claims its service gives lawyers the opportunity to increase their exposure and find potential clients. Toward that end, each licensed attorney has a profile on the site. Using public records, Avvo also provides a history of any sanctions or disciplinary measures taken against the attorney. Clients can post reviews of attorneys whose services they have used. Avvo uses this and other information to generate a rating for lawyers, which is a numerical score from 1.0 (the worst—"Extreme Caution") to 10.0 (the best—"Superb"). A rated attorney can add certain information to her profile after "claiming" it by using an identification verification system.

The right to claim the profile is a classic example of Web 2.0 business models. Attorneys listed on the site ignore the profile at their peril, and those critical of Avvo's project are put in a double bind by the profile's very existence. If they ignore the profile, they effectively allow Avvo and others the ability to control this aspect of their online identity. To the extent they tell "their side of the story" on the site, they are feeding data to Avvo and building its reliability. The aggregator acts like Tom Sawyer, inviting others to "paint the fence" by adding to the store of data that increases its authority and comprehensiveness.

Avvo's rating is difficult to assess because the company does not disclose how it is calculated, ostensibly because such disclosure would allow lawyers to manipulate and "game" the rankings in their favor. Avvo does not permit lawyers to pay or purchase ads to help their ratings—however, given the secrecy of its rating algorithm, it is difficult to verify this anti-payola pledge. Partly in order to avoid liability for defamation, Avvo insists that its rankings are merely its opinion, and are not factual.

In 2007, two Washington attorneys filed a complaint against Avvo for violation of the state's Consumer Protection Act (CPA), and sought class certification to include all lawyers rated by Avvo.com. The complaint alleged that "by reporting arbitrary and capricious scores and promoting them to consumers as mathematical calculations and a reliable assessment of a lawyer's competence to handle legal matters, Avvo has engaged in . . . unfair and deceptive acts and practices in violation of" the CPA. The plaintiffs alleged that the rating system treated lawyers unfairly and deceived the consumers who relied on it.

Avvo filed a pretrial motion to dismiss the case, arguing that the complaint was insufficient for several reasons. The court granted the motion, ruling that the "opinions expressed through the rating system . . . are absolutely protected by the First Amendment." The court posited that the site did not deceive consumers because it "contains numerous reminders that the Avvo rating system is subjective," an opinion rather than fact. Since the ratings on the site could not be proven true or false, the court ruled that Avvo was immune from liability for defamation. Avvo did not disclose its algorithm at any time in the suit.

The blanket protection the *Avvo* court would provide for opinions is open to challenge. Internet law expert James Grimmelmann unpacks the leading case on the issue:

> Milkovich v. Lorain Journal Co., while stating the rule that the Constitution shields opinions, leaves in place two significant exceptions. A statement of opinion may imply an underlying fact (the Court's example: "In my opinion John Jones is a liar."), and even a statement of opinion may be false if not honestly held (the Court's example: "I think Jones lied," where the speaker thought nothing of the sort). . . . The relationship of subjective opinion to objective fact . . . is not simple.[44]

Here, the opinion "John Jones is a terrible lawyer" implies certain facts about what Jones did to make him such a rotten attorney. Avvo's disclaimers about its "subjectivity" notwithstanding, no one would take the site seriously if it did not claim to be based on objective and relevant information.

There are examples of challenges to ratings that survived a motion to dismiss,[45] settled out of court,[46] or lost on the merits.[47] These cases demonstrate that there is no absolute First Amendment privilege for opinions or ratings. Therefore, the threat of costly litigation can be used as leverage to persuade raters to accept regulation. This dynamic may have driven resolution of several lawsuits against physician-rating websites.

In the medical field, insurance companies have begun to create "black-box" evaluation, ranking, and rating systems for doctors. Fearing an unfair tiering of its members, the Washington State Medical Association (WSMA) filed suit against Regence BlueShield, an insurance company that evaluated doctors using allegedly inaccurate and outdated information.[48] The doctors claimed that Regence used four-year-old data, small sample sizes, and focused on cost of claims rather than quality of care.[49] The complaint alleged defamation and violation of the CPA, among other causes of action.[50] After ten months of litigation, Regence agreed to settle with the WSMA "in an effort to better understand physician concerns,"[51] voluntarily withdrawing the Select Network program. The settlement agreement, effective for at least two years, promises transparency in evaluations, as well as fair methodology.[52]

In New York, the state attorney general, Andrew Cuomo, launched an investigation of insurers' physician ratings that culminated in settlement agreements in 2007. Cuomo claimed that the evaluation programs were confusing and unfair to both physicians and consumers.[53] After negotiating with his office, insurance companies eventually agreed to follow the ranking guidelines in a national model provided by the Office of the Attorney General (OAG) (in cooperation and consultation with the American Medical Association and other provider trade organizations). The model agreements require "insurers to fully disclose to consumers and physicians all aspects of their ranking system."[54] Since there is mandatory disclosure of all data and methodologies, the problem of the "black-box" evaluation system is reduced under the model agreements. Attorney General Cuomo has advocated the codification of the model based on his written agreements with insurance companies, and several prominent members of the New York legislature have agreed to support the bill.[55] The proposed bill suggests a trend toward transparent, quality-based rankings. CIGNA has agreed to make its rating methodologies public.[56] A "Patient Charter for Physician Performance Measurement" has also emerged as a project of the Consumer-Purchaser Disclosure Project (CPDP). The specific terms of the charter call for evaluations that are "meaningful to consumers" and bar decontextualized ratings based solely on cost.

Comparing Lawyers' Failures and Doctors' Successes in Regulating Reputation Scoring

Professional ranking programs are here to stay, and may play a vital role in pay-for-performance programs designed to rationalize compensation for physicians and lawyers. The CPDP's approach suggests some principles that could govern reputation regulation more generally. However, the failure of the Avvo lawsuit shows that First Amendment defenses can pose a formidable challenge to accountability here. Why have lawyers so far failed where doctors have succeeded?

Some nonlegal differences in the two cases spring to mind. Avvo.com is far smaller than the settling health insurance companies. There is an obvious conflict of interest in the latter situation: insurance companies have a financial incentive to "rank" doctors based on their cost to the insurance company, not the quality of care they offer. An insurance company might profitably purport to evaluate and rank doctors by quality, but then put the physicians who cost the company the least money at the top of its rankings. On the other hand, more subtle and dispersed conflicts of interest permeate Avvo's business model. It has no direct financial interest in the costs of lawyers' work, but it does have an interest in spurring attorneys to "claim" their profiles and supply the site with more information.

Frequently blamed for making heartless coverage decisions, insurance companies are eager to avoid additional bad press. Avvo.com is a new company without the image problems of the private health insurance industry. Moreover, Avvo's prime business model is to rate attorneys, while the insurers' core profit centers lie elsewhere. Though both attorneys and physicians have successfully protected their economic interests, more compressed income distribution among the bulk of physicians may make the "logic of collective action" more compelling to them. Finally, while attorneys ignore their Avvo profile at their peril, and cannot directly deny Avvo business, physicians can pull out of offending insurers' networks.

Yet there are also significant legal rationales for the divergent results of the two lines of litigation. Insurers are part of a heavily regulated industry where government decisions are crucial to their ongoing profitability. Many Supreme Court decisions have permitted agencies to shape the speech of recipients of governmental largesse. In its 9–0 decision in Rumsfeld v. Forum for Academic and Institutional Rights, Inc., the Court allowed the government to condition certain benefits on beneficiaries' compliance with governmental standards. Had the insurers failed to settle, they would likely have seen the doctors merely shift their case from the courts to state insurance commissioners. Avvo, by contrast, is a mere web start-up, with very little contact with or (apparent) reliance on governmental largesse. But as a closer examination of the complex web of laws that govern cyberspace intermediaries reveals, they may well be as vulnerable as insurers to governmental pressure designed to ensure basic protections for the individuals they rank and rate.

Free Speech and the Regulatory State

Internet service providers and search engines have mapped the web, accelerated e-commerce, and empowered new communities. They also pose new challenges for law. Individuals are rapidly losing the ability to affect their own image on the web—or even to know what data others are presented with regarding them. Technology's impact on privacy and democratic culture needs to be at the center of Internet policy making. Regulators should promote individuals' capacity to understand how their reputations— and the online world generally—are shaped by dominant intermediaries.

Heraclitus wrote that "for the waking there is one world, and it is common; but sleepers turn aside each one into a world of his own." In our age of fragmented lifeworlds, narrowcasting, and personalization, Internet searchers are increasingly like Heraclitus's sleepers, each turning to customized reports on the persons and events they take an interest in. While many authors have lamented the effects of the "Daily Me" on politics, and others have noted the Kafkaesque implications of data-driven decision making, few have considered the intersection of these trends. This essay has attempted to do so, and has proposed norms of transparency to ensure that the "watched" have some idea of what type of dossier and scoring the "watchers" are compiling about them.

Because First Amendment defenses have so far quashed many tort actions against raters and rankers, this essay has focused on tailored regulatory responses. Although there is no blanket exception from First Amendment protections for regulations, they appear to be less limited by this constitutional privilege than tort suits. This may be because regulations that promote "the social interest in order and morality" can outweigh the First Amendment concerns that have stymied tort suits.[57] As both Robert Post and Fred Schauer have observed, there are a number of examples of speech-restricting regulations that have not been rendered unconstitutional by First Amendment challenges.[58]

For example, commercial speech is one category of expression frequently regulated by the government. The law "accords a lesser protection to commercial speech than to other constitutionally guaranteed expression."[59] When commercial speech is misleading it can be restricted. . . . For example, regulatory actions banning false advertisements are not prohibited by the First Amendment.

Moreover, when the government has a "substantial interest in regulating" commercial speech, it is not necessarily limited by the First Amendment, even if the speech in question is completely lawful and is not misleading.[60] Copyright and trademark law are two instances where the unfettered right to free speech yields to larger "social interest[s] in order and morality."[61] Provisions of the DMCA strictly regulate what an intermediary like YouTube can keep on its site once it receives a notice that certain material infringes on copyrights. It would be deeply troubling if law could simultaneously be so solicitous of copyright owners (who are able to veto many fair uses, at least temporarily, under the terms of the DMCA), and utterly neglect the interests of those whose reputations are harmed by irresponsible intermediaries.

Just as consumers' interests trump a false advertiser's right to "express himself" with lies about products, so too should certain reputational interests take precedence over the bare right to offer scoring of others' reputations. Norms of due process may throw some sand in the wheels of today's lightning-fast generation of information and scores about individuals. However, fair opportunity in the Information Age depends on accountable rating practices and models. More open and accurate systems of evaluation are a legitimate choice for a culture increasingly disillusioned with clandestinely commensurating computing.

CHAPTER 7

Youthful Indiscretion in an Internet Age

ANUPAM CHANDER

Instantaneous photographs and newspaper enterprise have invaded the sacred precincts of private and domestic life; and numerous mechanical devices threaten to make good the prediction that "what is whispered in the closet shall be proclaimed from the house-tops."

—Samuel D. Warren & Louis D. Brandeis, The Right to Privacy, *Harvard Law Review*, 1890

A child born in the twenty-first century will have her life documented in digital form. When the records involve benign conduct, such as the fact that her soccer team made it into the regional finals, there may be little cause for concern. But when the conduct revealed to the world is more intimate or embarrassing there is reason for alarm. In this new century of ubiquitous camera phones and digital communications, a youthful indiscretion might become an albatross a person can never escape. The torts for the invasion of privacy were themselves born of technological developments. But the "instantaneous photography" that moved Warren and Brandeis to formulate legal rights to privacy is now coupled with the instantaneous global dissemination platform of the Internet, magnifying the problem immeasurably. The digital form extends the accessibility of the private sphere not only in space, but in time. The Internet Age can place a person's history, or, worse, a fleeting episode from that history, at the world's call. The past might haunt the twenty-first-century child till the end of her days.

Fear of future ramifications might cause individuals to recoil from any practice that might lead to public humiliation or embarrassment in the decades to come. Their hopes for careers as politicians, judges, prosecutors, executives, or doctors may hang in the balance. The youth of the Internet Age may be strait jacketed—teens and young adults at the mercy of the world—living their lives as if in a fishbowl. Decisions in such a life require consideration not only of the reputational consequences vis-à-vis families, friends, and acquaintances, but also with respect to future employers, partners, and even unborn children. The cognitive task required is forbidding. In such a world, we may risk youthfulness in youth.

The youth facing a fishbowl life might be tempted to adopt either of two strategies: excessive caution or foolhardy fearlessness. The first strategy might limit decisional autonomy now, constraining the choices available now. The second strategy might limit decisional autonomy later, constraining the choices available then. We should not tolerate this unnecessary choice between reduced choice set now, or reduced choice set later. Here I will argue that both law and society more generally must ameliorate the risks inherent in a fishbowl life, especially for youth, in the service of autonomy.

With respect to the legal regime, I will argue that judges must reinvigorate the paradigmatic privacy tort—the tort for public disclosure of embarrassing private fact. Many scholars have offered requiems for the privacy torts, victim to changing social attitudes and greater solicitude to free speech. By contrast, I will argue that new technologies make the public disclosure tort more necessary than ever before. In particular, I will argue that the disclosure tort is especially appropriate to regulate the display of nude photographs and videos not authorized for public dissemination. The special power of the image, particularly sexual images, requires the special attention of the law.

At the same time, society should take into account the elephantine memory of the digital medium when fashioning architectures of communication. Educators in particular should be careful when they require students to blog, or post their writing or art online. We might all be careful about what we post about others, and respect reasonable requests to remove information about others. While the problem I describe requires greater adjustment to private and educational practices than to the law, my focus in this paper is on the legal regime.

The dangers of inattention are becoming increasingly evident. A champion swimmer at the Beijing Olympics was humiliated by the publication on the Internet of nude photos of her "seemingly taken in an intimate moment by a lover." "I've been to hell," she told a magazine, adding, "I no longer dared wear a [swimsuit]. . . ."[1] Paris Hilton's liaison with a boyfriend became the stuff of a DVD that the man later sought to peddle for profit. Most readers may feel far from either the celebrity or activity of Paris Hilton and other similarly famous personages, insulated by our own obscurity and protected by our own discretion. But the Internet does not restrict its attentions to the private lives of the rich and famous. Nor can we all be counted on to act discreetly in all circumstances. Paris Hilton and other celebrities become the canary in the coal mine, an early warning of the dangers of this new age for us all. Internet sites collect "revenge porn"—depicting ex-girlfriends in sexual situations.[2] One site promises "Nude and REAL Ex-Girlfriends and Ex-Wives Photo Blog Submitted by Surfers as Revenge or Braggin[g] Rights."[3] The media have identified the rise of "sexting," the sending of sexually explicit photos electronically, primarily between cell phones. Kiss and tell now becomes show and tell.[4]

In one grave case, the publication of photos might even have contributed to a young woman's death. After her former boyfriend distributed nude pictures of her within her high school, Jessica Logan was tormented by classmates: "The girls were harassing her, calling her a slut and a whore." Months later, she committed suicide.[5]

Youthful experiment—including challenge and rebellion—is often central to the process of growing up, of becoming autonomous, independent adults. We should not yield youthfulness to the merciless memory of digital recorders. No less values than autonomy and human development are at stake. The risks are especially grave for women. In the age of camera phones, handheld video cameras, and the Internet, a fleeting encounter can find its way to the prying eyes of the world. Liberalism would leave certain decisions to individual choice, outside the realm of state coercion. If one knows that entering the public sphere by seeking a position of authority might risk a disclosure that will compromise one's bodily modesty, one's autonomy will be adversely affected. In this sense, bodily privacy serves here to advance decisional autonomy.[6] Life in a fishbowl constrains choices, not through the coercive mechanisms of the state, but through the disciplinary mechanisms of social pressures, limiting access to jobs, friends, and positions of authority.

But is not truthfulness a virtue? Disclosures of private behavior can reveal hypocrisy or expose lying. They can undermine or promote confidence in counterparties to a transaction, whether professional or personal. Revelations of widespread transgressions can even make it clear that societal norms against such behavior might be outdated. They might also lead to ennui—becoming so commonplace as to lack any capacity to embarrass. "Been there, done that," in the words of one state supreme court.[7]

Because these objections have force, I do not propose a general right to wipe the slate clean.[8] Instead, my intervention is limited to two purposes: (1) highlighting the general problem, and by so doing motivating reconsideration of the increasingly public nature of youth life; and (2) arguing that, at least with respect to nude images, the privacy interest should generally prevail over the interest in public display. My goal here is not to promote a Victorian Compromise—of high public rectitude and low private misdeeds.[9] Rather it is to suggest that even nonmorally-reprobate behavior can be embarrassing when it is exposed to the world and available for the remainder of our lives. At times, law will need to provide a remedy; at other times, individuals and the institutions we craft will have to recognize the risks involved, and ameliorate them.

Since the rise of the Internet, many have noted the threat posed by the digital realm to our privacy. In this writing, I consider the dynamic effects of the technological change currently under way. How will people change their behaviors in response to this technology? Many may respond by modifying either their private behavior—risking youthfulness—or their public behavior—avoiding positions that might lead to embarrassing disclosures. I note the special concerns arising from the fact that such disclosures are likely to be visual and the possibility that they might have a disparate impact on women in public life. I suggest that there is a partial response available in the common law in the tort for public disclosure of private facts, and I defend that suggestion against anticipated critiques.

The United States has long been the land of fresh starts. Because of a vast frontier, individuals who faced hard luck where they lived could begin anew, putting their past behind them. With both geographic mobility and urbanization came the ability to forget, a power absent in the small villages where one's neighbors remained the same from birth to death. Bankruptcy provided a legal fresh start for financial obligations.[10] Youthful offenses in particular long received given special treatment. Expungement statutes throughout the country require states to destroy criminal records of minors, sometimes automatically.[11] There may be little reason to rehabilitate oneself, if one's past transgression will be forever worn like a scarlet letter—or so the theory goes.

With the advent of computers, attention turned to their prodigious data-gathering and collating capacities.[12] Credit histories were one of the first areas of concern following the database revolution of the 1960s. The Fair Credit Reporting Act of 1970 classified negative information that was more than seven years old (ten years, in the case of bankruptcy) "outdated."[13] Credit agencies can release such information only for limited purposes. Burgeoning databases of personal information, Congress recognized, require us to be careful that people are not burdened with past errors for the rest of their lives.

Privacy law too has sought to assist the "rehabilitation of the fallen."[14] In the classic privacy case of Melvin v. Reid, a woman who had once been a prostitute sued the producers of a movie titled *The Red Kimono,* which told her life story using her name without permission. The court held in her favor, explaining that she had, years earlier, "abandoned her life of shame, had rehabilitated herself and had taken her place as a respected and honored member of society."[15] By allowing individuals to contain public release of certain information, privacy law permits us to avoid being forever tarred by any embarrassing youthful actions. Privacy law also prevents an individual from being frozen in society's view at a particular moment; it allows the individual to grow and to change.

Privacy law has recently demonstrated special solicitude for youth facing a digital future. Concerned that technology now permitted children to speak directly to strangers even without leaving home, Congress sought to give parents control over such communications.[16] It passed in 1998 the Children's Online Privacy Protection Act (COPPA), an act that requires online service providers to obtain parental consent before collecting personally identifiable information from children. The statute goes further to give children and their parents rights to the use of the information: "parents are ascribed a powerful right to veto primary collection, primary use, secondary use, and even maintenance of data."[17] But this statute limits itself to websites directed at children under the age of thirteen. The painful truth is that COPPA leaves youth precisely when they enter that time in their lives where they need it most. The period of our lives that we might least want exposed to public attention is our teens and early adulthood, when we begin grappling with the complications of sex and responsibility. COPPA was designed to protect children from prying adults, but not from themselves.

Disclosures involving sex often receive special attention from the law. Privacy law has long had a special concern with sex. Lawrence Friedman even describes privacy as "the idea that certain things (notably the sexual side of life) had to be kept secret, kept private."[18]

Images of private or intimate behavior, in particular, seem especially problematic. The visceral quality of the photograph or the video, coupled with the rapidity with which a human mind can comprehend an image, make the publication of images of special concern. Indeed, as I described earlier, Warren and Brandeis, writing in 1890, were especially concerned about the advent of the Kodak camera, then just two years old. The compact, portable camera offered the ability to make publicly available scenes that normally would have been viewed by few. The photos provided long-lasting visual evidence that might prove difficult to disprove. It was the publication of the photos from Abu Ghraib, and not the earlier textual reports of torture, that caused a worldwide scandal. Similarly, the video of the beating of Rodney King may have galvanized public attention to the problem of police brutality in ways that words could not. (These two examples, of course, suggest that there may be times that we clearly do not want law to suppress images.)

Federal law pays special attention to the image, criminalizing the *"visual depiction"* of sexual activity involving minors.[19] Federal law now requires publishers of sexually explicit photographs to maintain certifications that the subjects are adults.[20] Some jurisdictions have gone so far as to prosecute children for nude photos they take of themselves under state law, a seemingly inappropriate use of criminal statutes designed to counter the exploitation of children by adults.[21]

The problem of intrusions with respect to sexual privacy may be more grave for women than men, for at least two reasons. First, society has long allowed men greater latitude in sexual affairs than it affords women. "Boys will be boys" is a mantra repeated to excuse behaviors. Second, women are more likely to be the subject of nude photographs.[22] A recent survey suggests that males are catching up, though the survey's methodology makes it unreliable. Of those who volunteered to participate in an online survey on sex, one out of every five teenagers (22 percent of teen girls and 18 percent of teen boys) and a third of young adults ages twenty to twenty-six (36 percent of young adult women and 31 percent of young adult men) stated that they had shared nude or seminude photos of themselves electronically.[23] One might speculate that reciprocal nude photo sharing between couples might hold the possibility of giving each person a compromising photo of the other, and thus offer the possibility of deterring wrongful release through an implicit tit-for-tat strategy.

Perhaps the most important legal tool to protect youthful indiscretions in the Internet Age is the tort for public disclosure of embarrassing private facts. This tort, recognized by some thirty-six states, allows a cause of action for the public disclosure of a private matter that is "highly offensive to a reasonable person." Truthfulness is not a defense. The action turns on the inappropriate public revelation of a matter deemed properly private.

Other privacy torts may be relevant as well, such as the tort for intrusion upon seclusion, though I will not focus on them here. A woman successfully deployed the seclusion tort, for example, against a boyfriend who secretly videotaped a sexual encounter with her in his bedroom.[24] Yet another privacy tort, the false light tort, has been deployed successfully against adult magazines that publish photographs of individuals without their consent.[25]

Two principal legal hurdles exist with respect to the use of the public disclosure tort to prevent a youthful indiscretion from becoming a scarlet letter. First, the indiscretion may itself be of legitimate interest to the public—it may be "newsworthy," in the terminology of the common law. Second, Section 230 of the Communications Decency Act (CDA) might well insulate claims against online service providers for hosting material provided by others. I consider these two difficulties below.

The Restatement of Torts limits the public disclosure tort to disclosures "not of legitimate concern to the public."[26] Harry Kalven noted that newsworthiness is "the privilege that has virtually 'swallowed the tort.'" But recent cases demonstrate that courts will not always sustain a claim of newsworthiness, especially when it comes to sexual images. When an adult video company obtained an explicit videotape of actress Pamela Anderson Lee and singer Bret Michaels, the two sued for invasion of privacy. The video company asserted in its defense that the material was "newsworthy," more so because of the subjects' celebrity status. Judge Dean Pregerson's decision upholding the privacy claim seems on the mark: "The fact recorded on the Tape . . . is not that Lee and Michaels were romantically involved, but rather the visual and aural details of their sexual relations, facts which are ordinarily considered private even for celebrities."[27] Judge Pregerson thus entered an injunction—doing so over claims that it would amount to a prior restraint of speech: "Furthermore, the privacy of the acts depicted on the Tape cannot be restored by monetary damages after the Tape becomes public. The nature of the Internet aggravates the irreparable nature of the injury. Once the Tape is posted on [the distributor's] web site, it will be available for instant copying and further dissemination by [the distributor's] subscribers." The injunction did not extend to disclosures that the tape existed, or to public discussion regarding the tape. Such an approach still allows kiss and tell—it's the *show* and tell that is most problematic.

Newsworthiness is especially tricky in an age of a hundred million blogs. Where earlier courts were likely to defer to the editorial decisions of news intermediaries to determine whether information was truly newsworthy, in the age of the Internet, there may be no editorial function before information is released to the public at large. Where the costs of newsprint and the limited space available in a limited set of papers once required the careful exercise of discretion in decisions about what to publish, blogs are available for free to self-appointed editors who do not face such constraints. Blogworthiness is not the same as newsworthiness.

Like celebrity Pamela Lee, ordinary individuals should be able to take preemptive action against improper disclosures. Individuals could seek a declaratory judgment against an individual who might possess compromising photographs, enjoining against future publication.

But would not a lawsuit merely circulate the undesirable information further? Because of this concern, courts often permit the plaintiff to proceed under a Jane Doe pseudonym. Even while holding that imposing damages on a newspaper for publishing the name of a rape victim violated the First Amendment, the Supreme Court in Florida Star v. B.J.F. adopted the lower state court's decision to use the rape victim plaintiff's initials instead of her name.[28] In a case involving "sexting," the practice of sending nude pictures of oneself over electronic networks, the Alabama Supreme Court similarly used initials for the male and female high school students involved in the case, as well as for their parents, reasoning that naming the parents would effectively identify the students as well.[29] (Another aspect of that decision is more troubling: the Court in dicta declared that a person could not be charged with a *public* disclosure of a private fact unless he or she shared the information with a wide group. This seems unwise, given that sexual pictures once released to a few have a high likelihood of being disseminated widely.)

As in all potential civil cases, the cost of litigation will deter many from filing suit. Perhaps the cease and desist letter, written with or without a lawyer's signature, might do the trick—letting the offender know of his or her potential legal exposure. And like all potential civil cases, there is the risk that the threat of an action or an action itself will be misused. However, these cases are unlikely to offer the possibility of a class action that might attract plaintiffs' attorneys to file suit with the hope of extracting settlements.

Another difficulty is perhaps the most serious: intermediaries can escape demands to withdraw information posted by others because of a special statutory immunity. How intermediaries must respond to requests to remove information varies by the subject matter of the underlying infraction. An online intermediary facing an allegation of copyright infringement must immediately take down the material, or risk losing the safe harbor promising immunity from secondary liability. An online intermediary facing an allegation of defamation or invasion of privacy, however, can refuse to remove the material, finding refuge within the immunity grant of the ironically named Good Samaritan provision of the CDA. The end result is that the online gossip site might escape liability for invasions of privacy conducted through its service. In a case involving the posting of a nude picture of a woman on a widely accessible website without her consent, for example, a district court ruled that the Good Samaritan provision immunized the website from the traditional privacy torts of public disclosure, false light, and the intrusion upon seclusion.[30] Such sites could offer takedown procedures on their own, however. Facebook, for example, allows users to withdraw content they have posted—though an individual has no similar right to withdraw content posted by others about her, unless it infringes on her intellectual property rights.

The law should allow the individual to find information to lead her to the person who committed the privacy invasion. In recent litigation involving defamatory statements made about two Yale law students on the gossip site AutoAdmit.com, a federal district court was willing to enforce subpoenas requiring the site to help identify the individuals who posted that material. In that case, initially titled Doe I v. Individuals, Whose True Names Are Unknown, the court compelled the site to disclose information about the people who posted the material.[31] In the AutoAdmit case, Judge Droney also rejected the motion of a defendant to proceed anonymously even though, as the court noted, naming the defendant might result in "social stigma, embarrassment, and economic harm." The fact that such suits might lead to the public identification of individuals who post malicious material behind a cloak of anonymity might itself cause some to desist from posting such material.

While the risks of technology to privacy are great, we need to be careful to not overreact by creating overprotective law. Rights to stop people from disclosing truthful information raise significant difficulties. Reputations would be meaningless if they could be subject to a legal right to manipulate.

Accountability, Anita Allen reminds us, often relies upon reputation.[32] Equally important, the specter of harm to children is often trotted out to reach the legal result that some adults desire. We do not want to infantilize our society, making everything child safe. This would require adults to live according to rules for children. A public disclosure tort that simply allowed people to remove unflattering but truthful material about them from cyber-space would go too far.

I consider below a handful of arguments against the disclosure tort. I conclude that each of these objections, while raising meritorious concerns and requiring cautious application of the tort, should not stop us from seeking, at least, to contain nude images within the private sphere when the subjects of those images never intended their public dissemination and where their content lacks special news value.

First Amendment.   The disclosure tort clearly bars certain speech, and thus raises significant First Amendment concerns. The Supreme Court considered the conflict between privacy and speech in Florida Star v. B.J.F., a case in which a rape victim sued a newspaper for revealing her name in the course of a story about the rape. In that case, the Supreme Court upheld the paper's right to publish her name, where the paper had obtained the information lawfully, the information was truthful, the crime report (if not the identification of the individual by name) involved a matter of public significance, and there were no compelling state interests mandating criminal liability of the newspaper.[33] As *Florida Star* itself indicates, First Amendment free speech protections are not absolute, but tolerate certain restrictions when justified by other compelling societal interests. The Court preferred a case-by-case analysis: "We continue to believe that the sensitivity and significance of the interests presented in clashes between First Amendment and privacy rights counsel relying on limited principles that sweep no more broadly than the appropriate context of the instant case."[34]

The law is replete with constraints on speech. The Video Privacy Protection Act of 1988, for example, bars truthful disclosures of video rental records.[35] Securities law bars even truthful priming of the markets prior to the effectiveness of the registration statement. Perhaps these regulations would fall under First Amendment scrutiny, but perhaps also a court would hold that the interests of privacy and proper functioning of the securities markets might justify the speech intrusions.

Moreover, there is a long history of regulation for nude images in the United States. Such images may often meet the definition of obscenity, and are often trafficked on websites devoted to collecting such material for prurient interest.

Doing away with the privacy tort in favor of certain speech might itself imperil certain other speech and even legal behavior. We often fail to recognize that there are chilling effects on either side in the privacy/speech clash. On one side, individuals who might have exposed private facts to the public in a context we might have valued may find themselves deterred by the possibility of liability. But there is a less often identified chilling effect as well: without privacy rights, individuals may fear for the consequences of their behavior, and hew to a safe path, a path not likely to draw controversy or scrutiny in the decades to come. This implicates an autonomy interest, but also a speech interest: individuals may share less information privately as well. The Supreme Court recognized this possible risk from inadequate protection of privacy in its recent opinion in Bartnicki v. Vopper: "the fear of public disclosure of private conversations might well have a chilling effect on private speech."[36] In that case, the Court ultimately sided with the public disclosure of illegally recorded private conversations within a union's leadership, where the publisher itself had not been engaged in the wrongful recording. The Court explained that "[i]n this case, privacy concerns give way when balanced against the interest in publishing matters of public importance."

The popular maxim counseling one to fight bad speech with good speech will prove unavailing in many privacy intrusion contexts. What is the proper counter to a truthful disclosure of a nude photograph? "You have flab, too" or "Lots of people have sex, as children attest" hardly suffices to lessen the sting.

There will, of course, be occasions in which free speech values will require publication, even of nude images. Anita Allen writes, "If President Thomas Jefferson took the public position that blacks were morally inferior and unfit for the society of whites and if he was having an intimate relationship with his black slave Sally Hemings, his hypocrisy would have merited disclosure."[37] A picture evidencing such a relationship merits even a place on the evening news, at least with some bits edited out.

Efficient markets.   Markets run better with more information. Richard Posner goes further, observing that "the tax collector, fiancé, partner, creditor, and competitor" might seek private information.[38] Revelations about private behavior can improve information on counterparties—perhaps helping us avoid, for example, the pitfalls of statistical discrimination by allowing more individualized evaluation.[39]

The point is important, though with respect to the fact of sexual conduct, there may be limited value to the information; indeed, to borrow a concept from another legal domain, the information may be more prejudicial than probative. Posner himself suggests that "most people do not like to be seen naked" and that the law properly gives individuals a property right in their own nudity.[40] Posner explains that reticence to reveal one's body publicly imposes little "social costs" and given that transaction costs are low, an individual can contract away her privacy right in this regard.

Furthermore, the market consequences will not be limited to the increased information available to those who hire or otherwise deal with the data subject. The release of such private information might lead the individual to shy away from certain marketplace transactions, embarrassed at the revelations that would likely follow. While lifetime income-smoothing decisions and human capital investment show that individuals can make major decisions in consideration of lifetime consequences, one suspects that cognitive limits on such an exercise might well be reached when they involve decisions related to the minutiae of intimate life. Even when one can consider them, the lifetime consequences for youthful error would magnify a particular decision beyond its reasonable limits.

Society will become inured to the problem.   It might be argued that publicizing private behavior will, over time, lead society to accept that behavior as normal, and thus not embarrassing. Society, however, has long been well aware of widespread sexual activity before, within, and outside marriage. Yet, the fascination continues. Embarrassment, or even humiliation, does not turn on whether some activity is out of the ordinary or freakish. Rather human bodily functions can themselves be grounds for embarrassment. Ridicule often takes the form of borrowing ordinary activities and exposing and exploiting them in a public setting.

A related argument, the one most popular among today's youth, is that such behavior will soon be no longer worthy of reprobation, its sting gone. One's own indiscretion will perhaps be lost amidst a sea of similar disclosures. In rejecting a disclosure privacy tort, the Indiana Supreme Court explained, "[W]e do not discern anything special about disclosure injuries. Perhaps Victorian sensibilities once provided a sound basis of distinction, but our more open and tolerant society has largely outgrown such a justification. In our 'been there, done that' age of talk shows, tabloids, and twelve-step programs, public disclosures of private facts are far less likely to cause shock, offense, or emotional distress than at the time Warren and Brandeis wrote their famous article."[41] In the Indiana case, an individual sued a fellow postal worker for revealing that he was HIV positive. Whether such a revelation against the individual's wishes has indeed lost its sting in contemporary society is unclear. However, when it comes to nude photographs, there is no guarantee that revelations will be treated as humdrum—entirely unremarkable and without cause for embarrassment. Indeed, to see the continuing power of such images to embarrass, one need only read the sordid facts of a case involving explicit photographs that four fourteen-year-old girls emailed to two male classmates.[42] One picture even appeared subsequently as "'wallpaper' on a computer in the sixth-grade computer lab."

The disclosure tort itself covers only disclosures that are highly offensive to a reasonable person, and thus allows for changes in social standards.[43] If society does indeed believe a particular disclosure to be unobjectionable under an objective, reasonable person standard, then no tort claim will lie.

While it is possible that society will become blasé to such revelations, it is easy to underestimate the dangers. After all, within the community of youth, these behaviors may well be common, so much so that anyone not engaging in them may even be ridiculed as prudish. A natural presumption is that, as the youth age, their peers will share the same past; their closets will share the same skeletons. It is thus easy for youth to feel comfortable that, given how common these behaviors are among their friends and acquaintances, there is little cause for concern for future disclosure. But when one considers that reputation reaches not only one's immediate peers, but also potential employers, current superiors, and professional acquaintances, the risks may look different. Even while parts of society may come to find such a revelation unremarkable, there is reason to suspect that the subject may continue to worry about its impact. What if the individual has children—might she be concerned about what comes to their attention? What of her parents, grandparents, and relatives? What of the snickers of opposing counsel or law clerks when they email photos while a lawyer takes the stand or of business partners when she speaks in a boardroom? Monica Lewinsky did not take pictures (of which we should be thankful). A former paramour of the first woman president may not be so discreet.

Futility.   Even if a privacy tort is available, is it not futile? Some will argue that legal niceties are hardly likely to staunch the distribution of information in cyberspace. After all, trying to stamp out runaway information in cyberspace is like an endless game of Whack-A-Mole, now gone worldwide and viral. This is clearly true of some information. It may be outside the finances of even Paris Hilton to rid cyberspace entirely of unwanted videos, even if she owns them. But this is not true of more run-of-the-mill events. An individual might contact a person whom she believes might hold intimate photographs, and inform that person that release of that information might subject him to liability. Such an act might deter the individual from disseminating the photograph.

Search engines can do their part by creating methods for permitting individuals to seek to remove images and videos from their indices. Search engines could face secondary liability claims if the individual data subject owned a copyright in the work. Section 230 of the Communications Decency Act might make it difficult to hold intermediaries that do not develop the material liable for privacy invasions, but some have argued for expanding the scope of liability even if intermediaries do not develop the material, but fail to act upon knowledge and appropriate testament from the person alleging the wrong.

Protecting private tyrannies.   By demarcating a private realm not readily accessible to the public, society cannot as easily police that realm. Surveillance facilitates enforcement of both government laws and social norms. This has led many to be concerned about the possible tyrannies of private spaces. Privacy, as Martha Nussbaum concisely puts it, protects a "patriarchal sphere of authority."[44] Catherine MacKinnon criticizes the way that the abortion right is constructed, with the result, she says, that it simply reinforces male hegemony: "[U]nder conditions of gender inequality, sexual liberation in this sense does not so much free women sexually as it frees male sexual aggression."[45] She concludes, "Privacy law keeps some men out of the bedrooms of other men."[46]

The disclosure tort, however, does not necessarily create a private zone free from the policing of either the government or society. The tort is not available if the matter is of "legitimate concern" to the public. Private violence and other private behaviors remain available for police and societal sanction. Of course, the tort begs the question of what is of "legitimate concern." Common law judges have elaborated this tort, making difficult and contestable calls between what is of legitimate concern and what is not.

My suggestion is that a narrowly tailored tort can give individuals, including women, a legal remedy if they themselves choose to exercise it. Lacking such a remedy, the risk is that men and women, and particularly women, will take themselves out of the pool of candidates for positions of authority for fear of embarrassing revelations. Thus, autonomy in the public sphere of marketplace employment and politics can be compromised by unwarranted intrusions in the private sphere of sex. Allowing the free dissemination of photos of sexual relations only compounds any patriarchal authority within the bedroom. As Judith Wagner DeCew writes, "While care must be taken to avoid allowing privacy as a cover for abuse, privacy is nevertheless essential for protecting the freedom and independence needed for individuals to develop their identities and values as self-conscious beings."[47] This certainly has been implicit in the stance of the many women plaintiffs in the cases that have thus far been brought. In a Texas case in which an appeals court rejected a woman's claim against a former lover who had exhibited a sexual videotape of the pair, the Women and the Law section of the State Bar of Texas asserted, "If the tables had been turned, and [the female plaintiff] had peddled the videotape as a vignette of [male defendant's] sexual performance . . . , the all-male majority in this case would have reached a decidedly different result."[48]

Many men (and some women) have publicly disclosed private acts to publicly humiliate former lovers or to announce sexual conquests. Granting women (as well as men) a tort for such actions does not reduce women to mere toys of men, but rather grants them a legal right to counter male exploitation.

"Je ne regrette rien." (I regret nothing.) "Je me fous du passe." (I don't give a damn about the past.) Edith Piaf sang these lines with a devil-may-care world weariness. But even if we regret little, we may yet care about the publication of the details.

The public disclosure tort should remain a viable option with respect to, at the minimum, nude images. Courts can weigh the public interest in the disclosure against the harms of subjecting individuals to the invasion of bodily privacy, and decide whether the intrusion is justified. More broadly, the widespread diffusion of the tools for private recording coupled with the Internet's public disclosure and the digital medium's long memory places youth at risk of being haunted by past actions throughout their lives. In our roles as educators, parents, or government officials, we should strive to give youth a measure of decisional privacy.

CHAPTER 8

Academic Administrators and the Challenge of Social-Networking Websites

KAREN M. BRADSHAW AND SOUVIK SAHA

There exists a divide between users and nonusers of social-networking websites. For users, such websites are generally an integral part of social interaction used daily for information sharing, event planning, and reputation building. In contrast, nonusers typically fail to grasp the extent to which social-networking websites influence in-person interactions. Consequently, university professors and administrators who do not participate in online communities may underestimate the extent to which interactions occurring in the virtual realm affect their academic institutions. This divide can produce serious, negative consequences, particularly when students engage in behavior online that would be unacceptable in a traditional, live setting.

Millions of college students are members of social-networking websites and belong to online groups.[1] The majority of groups on social-networking websites are devoted to shared interests, such as a sport or geographical connection. Other groups, however, are focused on individuals, including faculty members and fellow students. Such groups share candid photos and threads of commentary about their targets. Some are complimentary and are of a fan club nature. Others are not. Bitter comments and untruthful rants about students and faculty at a number of educational institutions are easily found using a quick search of social-networking websites. The existence of these groups raises many questions: When does a thread of commentary transform from acceptably critical to abusive? When do unflattering photos taken and posted without permission become a violation of privacy? Why do students feel free to post lewd comments that they would not say in person?

Abusive behavior taking place online, known as "cyber bullying," is easy to dismiss as harmless pestering that is unlikely to affect a serious graduate student or tenured professor. Yet, online communities often engage in targeted hate speech and defamation that academic communities would not accept in a live setting. These abuses have serious consequences, including professional and reputational damage, sexual harassment, and perhaps even increased suicide rates.

What nonusers fail to recognize is the potency of social-networking websites as compared with other virtual communication tools, such as chat rooms or instant messaging systems. Rather than just a means of communication, Facebook and similar websites–like MySpace and Bebo–are functional communities that happen to exist on the Internet. Technological or generational barriers often render these online communities void of administrators and faculty, allowing students to feel removed from the supervision that exists in classrooms or campuses. We argue that, as a result, online communities lack many of the positive social norms found in traditional academic communities. Without these norms, individuals are emboldened to engage in strikingly abusive harassment of students and faculty. Administrators who are not a part of online social networks tend to underestimate the impact online communities have on classrooms and campuses.

In this essay, we survey administrators' attempts to engage with online communities, and argue that many current approaches fail to appreciate that Facebook is a fundamental component of social dynamics among students. Some schools focus on classroom dynamics by limiting or restricting in-class Internet use. Other academic institutions focus more broadly on monitoring and disciplining inappropriate behavior. These approaches are controversial: privacy concerns, free speech issues, and the appropriate reach of institutional authority are all fodder for heated debates. More importantly, continued, widespread cyber bullying demonstrates that these regulations are ineffective as currently applied. In looking to alternative approaches, we argue that methods designed to inject social norms into the online environment and introduce the metaphorical adult into the room are important, achievable steps toward addressing the most blatant online abuses.

Interactions between Online and Academic Communities

We posit that two communities exist simultaneously in the modern academic setting. First, there is the obvious traditional community in which students, faculty, and administrators interact with one another in the physical space of the institution. A second community has arisen among the millions of students who participate daily in social-networking websites. Administrators have yet to fully grasp the extent to which the traditional academic community is affected by what occurs in these virtual communities. Though a multitude of positive outcomes are generated through student participation in online communities,[2] so too are abuses. This essay focuses on two forms of abuse: obvious in-class use of the Internet, and cyber bullying that may impact the academic community even though it occurs outside the physical classroom.

Social-networking websites provide hundreds of millions of users with a forum for online interaction.[3] According to the website of one popular online community, "Facebook helps you connect and share with the people in your life." These websites are stunningly popular and widely used.[4] University students rely on social-networking websites to keep in touch with friends, organize activities, and pursue information and groups that interest them. Social-networking websites are distinct from previous forms of online communications because they do more than facilitate interaction. Unlike chat rooms or instant messaging, social-networking websites continue to convey and send information about participants even when they are not logged on.

Facebook groups are of particular interest because they are an example of online communities that coexist or even supplant traditional communities. Students can create and join groups focused on varied interests. Group "administrators" provide a title and description of the groups and monitor who can join. Members of the group may post pictures, events, and comments viewable by every group member.

Although social-networking websites provide a new forum for interaction, abusive behavior by college students against a particular target is not new. Facebook groups are somewhat like fraternities that engage in targeted rumor spreading and information sharing. Just as fraternity behavior can become abusive toward individual targets–by spreading lies around campus about a fellow student or creating hateful reviews of professors–online groups may also provide a forum that encourages group members to act increasingly abusively toward targeted persons. Such analogies are helpful in contextualizing the problem for administrators, but can minimize the unique features of cyber bullying that can make it especially difficult but important to discourage.

Some features of social-networking websites, particularly the vast audience and constancy of interaction, make them particularly prone to abuse. Social-networking groups constitute a broadcasting mechanism that permits hundreds of students to see the same information simultaneously. The reach of the broadcasting capability is exponentially magnified when coupled with Facebook's ability to synthesize information from multiple sources, such as other groups or applications on Facebook. Unlike traditional academic communities, Facebook groups can span geographical distances, and members may simultaneously view and share information. The number of potential group members is far greater than in physical communities; on Facebook, elementary school friends and potential employers may have access to the same information that would previously have been available only to students in the academic setting. While strangers may care little about a target, people with minimal external context about a person—especially potential employers—may rely upon the information. This becomes especially damaging when the archiving of Internet pages is taken into account; it can take years for negative messages to disappear from search engine results. Combined, these characteristics create a new and powerful communication tool that is different from previous forms of social information sharing.[5]

Educators mistakenly believe that they understand the depth of concerns presented by social-networking websites because the *symptoms* of in-class Facebook use are obvious. Faculty can easily detect inattention, reduced participation, and distraction. It is perhaps too easy to attribute this inattention to Internet use. For example, Norman Garrett, a professor of Computer Information Systems at Eastern Illinois University, wonders: "Are [students] not even in the same universe as I'm in because they're looking at the Internet?"[6] Studies reporting high in-class use of social-networking websites lead administrators to wrongly conclude that the extent of problems caused by the Internet is limited to inappropriate use within the classroom.

Administrators fail to recognize that the *causes* behind the symptoms outlined above are not obvious. It is certainly possible that a student may not participate in class because she is instead looking at a friend's photos or writing a message. But more troubling and less obvious causes of distraction or unwillingness to participate also exist. These problems seem largely unknown to faculty and administrators, even though they have substantial impact on classroom and social dynamics at academic institutions.[7] For example, a student who is *not* online during class may not be willing to participate in class because she fears her comments will be critiqued online.

Studies of cyber bullying among girls indicate that one form of cyber bullying involves being teased by peers for sharing opinions. Unlike the teasing that occurs in traditional academic communities, targeted communications in online communities have the potential to be more widely broadcast, to take place in groups rather than individual capacities, and to occur without monitoring by educators and administrators. Their spread and impact can be even broader, extending well beyond the confines of the traditional academic community. Fear of this particular form of cyber bullying—rather than actual in-class Internet use—may be the true cause of a student's silence. Other, similar causes abound.

It is easy for administrators, particularly those who are unfamiliar with social-networking websites, to be dismissive of how the effects of online harassment may impact the academic setting. Suicide, significant damage to professional and personal reputation, and the inability of instructors to function in their professional capacities are among the many outcomes of extreme cyber bullying.

Facebook groups most threaten academic environments when they are used to bully, defame, or engage in hate speech against students, administrators, and faculty. Recent reports of campus-related cyber bullying highlight the gravity of this problem. At Syracuse University, sixteen students joined a Facebook group solely devoted to criticizing an English doctoral student teaching a writing class. They engaged in crass and sexualized criticism of the instructor. One entry was described by a different instructor as "level[ing] a crude and personal accusation of possessing an infectious disease, which, though meant hyperbolically, crosses a . . . line.[8] At a Canadian University, a post written to a 200-student Facebook group ridiculed a business student and even acknowledged that "[w]e are pretty much ruining someone's life here."[9] Three hundred sixty students in the United Kingdom joined a Facebook group targeting a library worker at Kent University that included physical threats and speculation about his sexual orientation.[10] Students at a high school posted a false profile of a school principal with lewd language implying he was a pedophile who propositioned students. They also leveled attacks on his wife and child.[11]

Significant anecdotal evidence demonstrates that what occurs in online communities affects traditional academic communities. At an extreme, several student suicides have been attributed to cyber bullying.[12] A study conducted by researchers at the Yale School of Medicine found no direct links but indicated that there is a likely association between bullying and suicide.[13] Less dramatic cases illustrate that cyber bullying negatively impacts traditional academic communities. While no studies were found illustrating this point, anecdotal evidence abounds. For example, one postgraduate student who was a victim of cyber bullying reported that online harassment affected his ability to study.[14] Educators targeted by students online have filed suits pursuing claims for intentional infliction of emotional distress.

Cyber bullying is a small but pervasive negative aspect of a social network that produces many positive effects. It is likely, however, that less obvious but more widespread impacts of cyber bullying may harm classroom and academic dynamics. For example, the potential for online harassment may chill class participation. Some Facebook groups are specifically designed to target students who are active classroom participants.[15] Fear of becoming the target of such groups may cause many students to reduce their in-class participation. Studies exploring the link between online cyber bullying and in-class participation are both lacking and necessary. Classrooms and schools no longer exist as a closed, protected sphere with limited outside influence. The extent, detection, and addressing of concerns stemming from social-networking sites present unique problems. Each of these is exacerbated because those responsible for monitoring and enforcing social norms in traditional communities are functionally excluded from online communities.

Academic Response to Online Communities

Given the potential for social-networking tools to disrupt the academic environment, school administrators face a challenge. The first is recognizing the seriousness of cyber bullying. While some administrators have begun to mobilize in response, there exists a legal debate concerning the extent to which administrators may restrict or punish certain forms of online behavior—whether in class or off campus—that disrupt the integrity of the learning environment. Despite a lack of clear legal precedent, school administrators have adopted strategies to combat the negative effects of online communities on students and academic culture. Surveying administrative approaches designed to lessen inappropriate online behavior illustrates both the strengths and shortcomings of current strategies.

Many current strategies demonstrate the failure of administrators to understand the complex and widespread nature of online communities. Some academic institutions believe they have addressed the problems presented by Facebook by taking technological measures to regulate Internet use within the classroom. For example, some institutions allow only selective use of the Internet in the classroom. Modern technology enables administrators to implement Internet "kill switches" that allow selective access to various websites and course management systems, while temporarily banning all other access.[16] While a testament to increased sophistication in science and technology, students can circumvent these "kill switches" through open wireless (WiFi) networks that are not subject to such regulation.[17] Further, as information technology officials at the University of North Carolina-Chapel Hill found, these technological measures can be extremely time-consuming and costly.[18] And as the director of Computing Services at the University of Michigan Business School states, "There's nothing you can do to keep a student from getting on the Internet."[19] Limiting Internet use through selective website blocking presents cost and efficacy concerns.

Another, more radical approach is to ban Internet use altogether. The University of Chicago Law School has adopted this approach. Disconnecting in-class Internet availability reduces the symptoms of inattention and poor participation. Additionally, for the period of time that students are in the classroom, it limits them to a single community, in which the professor plays the central role. However, while this solves the immediate problem of distracting sub-communities within the classroom, it fails to recognize that Facebook dynamics outside of the classroom can still affect in-class dynamics. Banning Internet use entirely in classrooms may provide a partial answer. However, it would be an error to think that by doing so administrators have protected their students. Taking away in-class Internet use to prevent cyber bullying is like unplugging a television set to prevent violence on television: it fails to address the core concern.

Other institutions refrain from banning Internet use in the classroom on principle. They suggest that the benefits of Internet access in the classroom outweigh the potential for distraction and reputational concerns. The argument underpinning this hands-off approach—that students online will be driven by the same social norms as those in traditional settings—fails to capture the unmonitored nature of the Internet. Administrators have firmly established that they will step in if students begin to abuse one another in the classroom or even at the fraternity house. In contrast, most administrators have yet to establish that their school norms extend to the Internet.

While each in-class Internet policy has certain advantages, none fully addresses the extent to which Facebook use—in and out of the classroom—may affect the academic environment. More important, these approaches undercut the value of the Internet as a powerful learning tool. As one official at the University of Louisiana at Baton Rouge states, these solutions are tantamount to "throwing the baby out with the bathwater."[20] It is therefore necessary to evaluate new and more comprehensive approaches to controlling the impact of Facebook in academic settings.

One reason for abuses in online communities is that they do not have a metaphorical adult in the room. Some school officials address this problem by taking an active role in online communities. "Administrators within higher ed[ucation] are finding ways of embracing the technology, using it as a new medium for interacting with students while tackling these very problems rather than ignore them."[21] Administrators join websites like Facebook to monitor or engage with their students online.

Some administrators join online communities to monitor their students. For example, some school officials pose as students online by creating "dummy Facebook profiles."[22] Administrators use these Facebook profiles to "friend" students, so they can view their profile pages. Once they have access to a student's profile, administrators may view their photos, comments, and group memberships. This information may be used to warn or discipline students.[23] For example, "four Northern Kentucky students received University Code of Conduct violations based on pictures posted on Facebook that showed them drinking."[24] Monitoring students' online activities gives administrators information that would be less available if they relied only upon traditional sources.

Should administrators actively monitor students' online behavior? Opponents of monitoring cite privacy concerns, boundaries between school and other areas of life, and chilling of free speech. They suggest it is deceptive for administrators to pose as students, and costly to pay people to do so. Proponents of monitoring assert that schools have an obligation to protect academic communities from online abuses. At Brandeis University, administrators screen student Facebook profiles for campus-related employment.[25] Both academic and outside employers are increasingly using Facebook searches as part of the hiring process.

Other administrators are actively, publically participating in online communities rather than simply monitoring activity. School administrators urge faculty to become members of the Facebook community in order to temper student behavior online by injecting an authority figure into a previously unregulated community.[26] At Brown University, several high-ranking school administrators have Facebook accounts.[27] Participants include the associate dean for judicial affairs, associate vice president of campus life and dean for student life, a psychotherapist, and three members of the Department of Public Safety.[28] This approach addresses one of the fundamental challenges of Facebook by placing an authority figure into the setting. Embedding an authority figure to enforce rules of conduct and assert social norms makes online communities more analogous to traditional communities. One analogy is to the "mother," whose presence checks the behavior of members of the fraternity. However, there are roadblocks to such interactions. A faculty member or school administrator who fails to identify himself on Facebook might later be held to have violated a student's right to privacy. It is possible that student monitoring could fill this void, inasmuch as students surely expect fellow students to be present in the networking site.

Finally, school administrators have adopted punitive measures to mitigate the growing challenge that off-campus Facebook use presents for the academic environment. Increasing awareness of the potential ugliness of online social-networking communities has produced punitive responses to cyber bullying and other forms of inappropriate online student conduct. Students face suspension and expulsion for their actions, as well as potential criminal charges. At Syracuse University, four students were expelled from their writing class and placed under "disciplinary reprimand" for creating a Facebook group with vulgar comments about an instructor.[29] In reacting to the disciplinary measure, the students' primary concern was that the university failed to provide adequate notice that Facebook posts could lead to punishment. As one of the students implicated in the Syracuse scandal said, "The student body needs to be aware of the [the administration's] expectations and if Facebook is fair grounds for policing, they need to make us aware of it."[30] Without clear guidelines, harsh punishment will be controversial.[31] As an associate dean at the Newhouse School of Public Communications at Syracuse University argues, "If [the judicial office] wants to operate on a case-by-case basis, that doesn't seem like a standard process. . . . What can and cannot be said on the internet should be spelled out clearly."[32]

This need for *ex-ante* rule making is illustrated through one student's battle against the administration at Ryerson University; he was expelled for contributing to a Facebook group dedicated to peer discussion of physics homework. The student, who faces 147 violations of the code of conduct, argues, "If this kind of help is cheating, then so is tutoring and all the mentoring programs the university runs and the discussions we do in tutorials."[33] If a school chooses to punish students for their online communication, it must clearly delineate the boundaries of acceptable and prohibited interaction. In response to such criticisms, some administrators have clarified rules to reflect the claim that online behavior is subject to school regulations. By extension, online abuses fall under the purview of acceptable disciplinary action if the behavior disrupts the learning environment.[34]

Administrators and courts face difficult line-drawing questions. May schools discipline students who cyber bully from home? Is it the student's behavior or the school's reaction that disrupts a student body? As academic responses to cyber bullying become more robust, it will be necessary to address these concerns. The challenge Facebook presents to school administrators to monitor online communities highlights the shortcomings of current policies to combat the potential negative effects of online social-networking tools. Disallowing Internet use in the classroom may reduce the symptoms of Facebook use in the real-time classroom. However, this fails to address the extent to which online community dynamics impact traditional communities. Administrators seem unaware of the extent to which Facebook and other online-networking tools permeate the academic culture, and indeed form unmonitored social communities within the classroom. The primary approach to infusing online communities with the norms present in other areas of an institution is to introduce an authority figure into such communities. Regulating and normalizing online behavior is necessary to maintaining cohesive traditional academic environments. Doing so requires accountability for action and involvement by administration when abuses do occur.

Freedom of expression and privacy rights must be balanced against protecting students. One approach is for school administrators to use social-networking tools while continuing to respect student privacy as they would in traditional settings. For instance, the possibility of educating and encouraging students to self-monitor and report instances of cyber bullying can be an important first step in combating the most serious symptoms of Facebook. This would also address the second shortcoming of administrators' current approaches: the failure to understand how off-campus Facebook use affects in-class dynamics.

At present, many administrators fail to appreciate the pervasive nature and potentially harmful impact of Facebook on campus. A crucial first step in tackling this problem is for school officials to clearly amend academic codes of conduct regarding permissible behavior to include online networking both on and off campus. One legal expert argues, "Policies should inform students [and their parents] that disciplinary action may be taken against them when their off-campus speech causes a substantial disruption to the education environment or interferes with another student's rights."[35] This would be an important first step in notifying students that their actions, statements, use, and involvement with social-networking tools such as Facebook are subject to university policing and punitive standards. Clear policies alone may substantially chill online abuses and allow schools to sidestep the costs of dedicated monitoring of online communities. Extending the academic administrative reach to Facebook can inject the social norms of traditional academic communities into the online realm, which in turn will deter students from cyber bullying.

Administrators underestimate the detrimental impacts of social-networking groups on traditional academic communities. First, the negative impacts of inappropriate use of online-networking websites are real and serious. They include reputational damage, inability to function in academic settings, and links to suicide risks. Although similar to fraternity activity that has long been associated with campus life, the danger of cyber bullying lies in its ability to pervade many aspects of a target's life, while flying under the radar of campus administrators who may be reticent to block it. Second, what happens in online communities tangibly affects traditional communities, even if students are not online during class. The technology presented by these networking sites provides a forum for online communities. At present, many such communities are unmonitored by academic administrators, thus providing a haven for those who engage in hate speech or bullying behavior that would be blatantly unacceptable in traditional academic environments.

The responses by academic administrators to the challenges presented by online-networking sites reflect some progress in addressing the most serious concerns. However, much remains to be decided and enacted. First, courts, legislators, and administrators will need to define the role that academic institutions may play in regulating acts of bullying that do not physically occur on school grounds. Next, administrators must find a balance that simultaneously protects the norms of their institutions and protects the privacy and free speech of its students. Doing so without incurring tremendous monitoring costs is a challenge. Among current approaches, attempts to merely ban Internet use at school seem incomplete in addressing the widespread sense of community provided by online-networking sites. Attempts to actively monitor websites present privacy and cost concerns. Clearly defining standards formally through codes of conduct and informally through administrators' public engagement with the issue is a good foundation. Encouraging student monitoring of peers for truly egregious violations provides a backstop against extreme abuse.

Social-networking websites present new and largely unrecognized challenges to academic administrators who are unaware of the pervasiveness and potential for abuse within online communities. Understanding the severity of the problems that may arise, and surveying the available approaches, provides administrators with the information necessary to begin considering and addressing these concerns effectively.

PART III

Speech

CHAPTER 9

Cleaning Cyber-Cesspools:
Google and Free Speech

BRIAN LEITER

I shall use the term "cyber-cesspool" to refer to those places in cyberspace—chat rooms, websites, blogs, and often the comment sections of blogs[1]—which are devoted in whole or in part to demeaning, harassing, and humiliating individuals: in short, to violating their "dignity." Privacy is one component of dignity—thus its invasions represent an attack on dignity. But they are not the only such affront: implied threats of physical or sexual violence also violate dignity; so too non-defamatory lies and half-truths about someone's behavior and personality, so too especially demeaning and insulting language, so too tortious defamation and infliction of emotional distress. Cyber-cesspools are thus an amalgamation of what I will call "tortious harms" (harms giving rise to causes of action for torts such as defamation and infliction of emotional distress) and "dignitary harms," harms to individuals that are real enough to those affected and recognized by ordinary standards of decency, though not generally actionable.

The Internet is currently full of cyber-cesspools. For private individuals without substantial resources, current law provides almost no effective remedies for tortious harms, and none at all for dignitary harms. Dignitary harms are off-limits for legal remedy because U.S. constitutional law effectively subordinates the dignity of persons to a particular conception of liberty. Speech, however, causes real harms (dignitary and otherwise), so much so that the only reason to think government ought not protect against such harms is that government actors have too many obvious incentives to overreach in placing restrictions on speech.[2]

Since cyber-cesspools are in large part beyond the reach of regulation by the state in America because of constitutional protections, a number of commentators[3] have suggested enhancing private remedies by, for example, making intermediaries—those who host blogs or perhaps even service providers—liable for tortious harms on their sites. This would require repeal of Section 230 of the Communications Decency Act (47 U.S.C. §230), which provides that "No provider or user of an interactive computer service shall be treated as the publisher or speaker of any information provided by another information content provider." The effect of that simple provision has been to treat cyber-cesspools wholly differently from, for example, newspapers that decide to publish similar material. Whereas publishers of the latter are liable for the tortious letters or advertisements they publish, owners of cyber-cesspools are held legally unaccountable for even the most noxious material on their sites, even when put on notice as to its potentially tortious nature. But why should blogs, whose circulation sometimes dwarfs that of many newspapers, be insulated from liability for actionable material they permit on their site?[4] Although it is common for cyber libertarians to talk as if *all* speech is immune from legal regulation, even U.S. constitutional law permits the law to impose penalties for various kinds of "low-value" speech, such as defamation. So why should the law, via Section 230, treat cyberspace differently than the traditional media?

Defenders of Section 230 worry about what I shall refer to as "spillover effects": because website owners are more likely to err on the side of caution when facing legal liability, so the argument goes, if they do not have Section 230 immunity, they will be more likely to "censor" speech, including "valuable" speech. This is probably true, but it has a flip side: namely that insulation from liability via Section 230 will increase the prevalence of low-value speech, as well as speech that causes dignitary harms, as anyone familiar with cyberspace can attest. Why think the balance should be struck in one direction rather than the other? In all kinds of contexts— newspapers, classrooms, workplaces, and courtrooms—we restrict speech not only for the sake of legally protected interests but also for the sake of avoiding dignitary harms, no doubt at the cost of spillover effects. If no academic institution or newspaper would permit its classrooms or pages to turn into the analogue of cyber-cesspools, why should the law encourage that outcome in the virtual world?

The harm of speech in cyberspace is sufficiently serious that we should rethink the legal protections afforded cyber speech that causes dignitary harms. Thanks to Google (and similar search engines), cyber speech tends to be (1) permanent, (2) divorced from context, and (3) available to anyone. If the law should not remedy this problem, it must be because the value of speech that inflicts dignitary harms or the value of the speech swept up in the spillover effects is such that legal regulation is not justified. As I argue below, it is not clear whether either case can be made.

Let us first begin, however, with some case studies. I will quote *verbatim*, because too often academic discussion of this topic whitewashes what is really going on in the cyber-cesspools. Those easily offended—even those not so easily offended—are duly warned.

A Tale of Two Cyber-Cesspools

In late 2004, I noticed that my blog[5] was getting hits from what purported to be a pre-law chat room called "AutoAdmit." I followed back some of the links, and so discovered a website that I have since described—generously, I might add—as a "cesspool of infantile morons, racists, and misogynistic freaks." Especially alarming was the fact that, while about half the "threads" in the chat room actually had something to do with law school or the practice of law—suggesting that there were actual law students utilizing this board—another half had as their primary purpose racist, misogynistic, and anti-Semitic abuse or simply vicious harassment, defamation, and implied threats against named individuals, usually other law students.

Oddly, there was no indication who was responsible for the AutoAdmit site, since it was devoid of contact information. In March 2005, after watching AutoAdmit for several months, I wrote a short note about AutoAdmit to Eugene Volokh, proprietor of a well-known right-wing law blog (prompted by a related post on his blog), knowing that many law students read his blog and thinking he might help "shame" the still-anonymous proprietors of the site into cleaning it up. To my surprise, Professor Volokh's posting about the site[6] led the "administrators" to "out" themselves the following day! Professor Volokh posted a response[7] signed by Anthony Ciolli, then a law student at the University of Pennsylvania, and Jarret Cohen, an insurance salesman in Allentown, Pennsylvania, defending the huge amount of racism, sexism, and anti-Semitism on the site on the grounds that,

> We are very strong believers in the freedom of expression and the market-place of ideas. This is why we allow off-topic discussion and almost never censor content, no matter how abhorrent it may be.

We shall return to the contention that "the freedom of expression and the marketplace of ideas" are in any way relevant to the existence of cyber-cesspools. In any case, now that Mr. Ciolli had outed himself, I made my own attempt to shame the proprietors of this cyber-cesspool into cleaning it up, since I had been collecting some interesting, shall we say, statistics on the site over the prior weeks. The day after the AutoAdmit proprietors outed themselves on the Volokh blog,[8] I posted some examples of "the freedom of expression and the marketplace of ideas" to which Mr. Ciolli and Mr. Cohen were so committed. I noted that there were hundreds of threads with the word "nigger" in the subject line, as well as hundreds about Jews, some benign, but the majority of the variety "Are Jews Smarter, or Just Craftier?" and "Did jew bitches give blowjobs in Auschwitz for the protein?" the latter of which introduces another feature of the site perhaps even more prevalent than the racism and anti-Semitism, its vulgar and abusive sexism. Of course, the racism, anti-Semitism, and sexism would not have been complete without abusive remarks about homosexual men, as in the hundreds of threads about "fags."

Similar searches today on what remains of the AutoAdmit site dwarf these numbers. Consider the site exactly three years later (March 11, 2008) and only *in the section of the site that calls itself "school related"*: there were not quite 200 threads here, of which *maybe* 10 percent were actually related to law school and the practice of law. Many were about current events, dozens of threads once again concerned "niggers," while the rest are well represented by such subject lines as "fantasizes about making you cry with the girth of my cock" and "i cum hard each time my cunt shits out a dead baby." All this disturbed, misogynistic adolescent "trash talk" was in the section of the AutoAdmit site that was supposed to be "school related"; if one were to add in the "off-topic" threads, the law school-related chat on this particular cyber-cesspool drops to perhaps 2 to 3 percent of the content.

In retrospect, the idea of shaming Mr. Ciolli and Mr. Cohen was naïve. I had assumed, falsely, that they had humane sensibilities and some minimal amount of prudence. The response of Mr. Ciolli, Mr. Cohen, and the anonymous posters on AutoAdmit to the exposure I gave their site was a torrent of defamation, criminal threats, and harassment directed at me. I contemplated legal redress, but in the end, it did not seem worthwhile given that the website was rather clearly a cyber-cesspool without any credibility in the real world against a quasi-public figure.[9]

Because I was the first adult to write about this cyber-cesspool, I started to receive emails from those who had suffered far worse assaults on their dignity at the hands of the site administered by Mr. Ciolli and Mr. Cohen. There was, for example, the woman at a top law school who was repeatedly subjected to threads demeaning her by name. Initially she was charged with being unqualified to study at her law school, but soon it turned into threads "reporting" her "gang bangs" and other sexual exploits. This woman, understandably, transferred to another law school. Who wants to study at a small school where classmates are cyber stalking you?

Soon, some of the anonymous misogynists posting on AutoAdmit descended on two women studying at Yale Law School. Among the contributions of these anonymous posters to the "marketplace of ideas" were statements like the following, all of which targeted the innocent women by name (I have substituted Doe I and Doe II for the actual names):

*"just don't FUCK her, she has herpes"
　　*"I think I will sodomize her, repeatedly"
　　*"clearly she deserves to be raped so that her little fantasy world can be shattered by real life"
　　*"I wish to rape [Doe I] and [Doe II] in the ass"
　　*"I'm doing cartwheels knowing this stupid Jew bitch is getting her self esteem raped" (this was posted in the context of multiple threads harassing Doe II)

This is but a small selection of the hundreds of postings devoted to defaming, harassing, and threatening or recommending criminal and sexual violence against the Does.

Mr. Ciolli and Mr. Cohen generally reacted with anger and derision to requests from the victims to remove the abusive and threatening threads; in some cases, they threatened to post the email of the complainant—which would, of course, subject them to further abuse and humiliation. In March 2007, the *Washington Post* ran a story about the harassment of the women on AutoAdmit.[10] Not long thereafter, the law firm where Mr. Ciolli had clerked the summer before rescinded its offer of permanent employment to him,[11] stating that "the content of the messages on the [AutoAdmit] board are 'antithetical' to the values of the firm and the 'principles of collegiality and respect that members of the legal profession should observe in their dealings with other lawyers.'" Referring to Mr. Ciolli and Mr. Cohen's defense of the AutoAdmit board on the Volokh blog, the managing partner of the firm wrote:

We expect any lawyer affiliated with our firm, when presented with the kind of language exhibited on the message board, to reject it and to disavow any affiliation with it. You, instead, facilitated the expression and publication of such language. . . .

The increased attention to the plight of the two Yale women, alas, brought a proliferation of new abusive threads directed at them on AutoAdmit. The female victims eventually sued. They were represented pro bono by one of the nation's leading firms and a leading cyber-law expert. After two years, a handful of the harassers had been identified, some settled, and much of the abusive content had been removed from Google. In short, it took legal representation costing, one surmises, hundreds of thousands of dollars already, to achieve some modest success against only a handful of anonymous misogynists on one cyber-cesspool.

Our second cyber-cesspool is less colorful, and the harm it inflicted trivial by comparison. Yet, by way of contrast, it will prove useful for our analysis.

I run a blog that is widely read by philosophers. An obscure, and quite right-wing, philosophy professor at a university in the American South wrote to me asking that I link to his own blog. I had not been in the habit of simply linking to other blogs on request, but I did look at his blog, and it seemed a bit peculiar and not very interesting. I did not link to it. The obscure philosophy professor—I will call him K.[12]—had been writing nice things about my blog, but when I failed to link to him after a couple of months, he became angry. He started attacking me on his blog: he wrote a hundred different items attacking me as a "disgrace," a "buffoon," a "nut," and the like. The attacks became rather vicious and personal. He began making up incidents and hurling wild accusations. He linked to a story about a left-leaning professor in a small Texas town whose home was vandalized and who received other kinds of threats of violence. He suggested that this should be a warning to me (I lived in Texas at the time). My dean reported this incitement to violence to the university system in which K. worked. He calmed down for a while, but then resumed his irrational attacks.

I finally responded on my blog, documenting K.'s history of vicious and irrational attacks on me and others. I did not realize at the time that K. was probably mentally ill, and that my response would cause him to crack. Not quite two months later, K. spent his Christmas day creating a separate blog devoted to insulting, defaming, harassing, and threatening me—*and* my wife, my children, my parents, and anyone who reminded him of me! He wrote several hundred posts to this effect over the next two years, declaring, more than once, that "By the time we're done with this sorry excuse for a human being, he'll be crying," and noting that my having responded at all to his attacks constituted "a terrible mistake, one that will haunt [Leiter] for the rest of his life. At 48 years of age and in great health, I expect to be around for another 25 to 30 years." This adult man, a tenured professor of philosophy, would often link to photographs of me in order to mock my appearance as "effeminate," also pointing out how "lucky" my children were that "President Bush protected them, for their father certainly wouldn't have." He also compared me to Stalin and Hitler, and denounced me as, variously, an "imbecile," a "monster," and a "cretin." He declared that he would humiliate me in front of not only my children, but my grandchildren![13] Soon I began to hear from other academics he had harassed. The whole display was sufficiently strange that my dean asked a psychiatrist to review the blog to try to shed some light on K.'s mental disturbance and whether he was dangerous.

Economists say, correctly, that the "barriers to entry" are low in cyberspace. They are thinking mainly of financial cost, but the barriers are "low" in a more significant way as well. Prior to cyberspace, if you wanted to reach more than your immediate circle of acquaintances, you usually had to have some kind of competence, education, status, intelligence, and ability: otherwise no one would listen to or publish you. Indeed, in the old days, you generally had to be moderately sane to get an audience! That is no more. The K.s of yesteryear were confined to writing letters, or ranting to their friends (if they had any), or handing out leaflets, or doing other things that involve personal contact, the kind of contact that would, in most instances, reveal the profound level of emotional disturbance afflicting the speaker. Now the K.s and the AutoAdmit sociopaths need only a computer in order to abuse their targets, and to do so in a way that permits their defamation and harassment to be visited and revisited again and again by countless people anywhere on the planet, visitors who are often deprived of almost all relevant information about the speaker or his targets.

Google Is Part of the Problem

This brings us to the final villain in our story of cyber-cesspools: Google, the dominant search engine in the market today. (I shall refer in what follows just to "Google," but the same points apply mutatis mutandis to other search engines.) For without Google, every K. and every chat-room sociopath stews in obscurity. It is Google that retrieves the rantings of a friendless madman typing away on his hate blog, or the anonymous smears directed at a female law student by a vicious misogynist in a chat room, and associates those rantings and smears with the victim's name for any Google user to find. How exactly Google decides what search results to return is shrouded in a bit of mystery, though they do reveal[14] using a "PageRank algorithm" that "considers the importance of each page that casts a vote [by linking], as votes from some pages are considered to have greater value, thus giving the linked page greater value" and a "hypertext-matching analysis," which looks at how a particular search term (e.g., "Brian Leiter") figures in a web page's content.

The idea that the "most relevant and reliable results" about a female student at Yale Law School consist of the anonymous rantings of misogynistic sociopaths would be amusing if real people were not involved. Why Google searches give such prominence to blogs and Internet chat rooms—which, as a class, may be among the least reliable sources of information in human history—is puzzling. As the historian and blogger Juan Cole delicately puts the point: Google does not necessarily "put[the most relevant and reliable results first," though it most certainly facilitates what Professor Cole aptly dubs "the Google smear": the discrediting of an opponent by abuse that has a high web profile and is indexed through Google.[15] When the AutoAdmit posters attacked the Does, they were attacking private individuals with hardly any Internet presence at all. But when posted on a highly trafficked site, AutoAdmit, with the names of the victims in the thread titles, the attacks very quickly became the top search results for anyone—a friend, a family member, a prospective employer, a new acquaintance—Googling their names. Google "smearing" someone like me, with a substantial Internet presence (in the form of blogs and university home pages) is a bit more challenging. K., however, had a cyber friend, another far-right racist blogger, also of dubious sanity. This blogger emailed his entire circle of far-right blogging friends to advertise K.'s hate blog, telling them in the process a series of bizarre falsehoods about me and concluding: "[P]lease blogroll the new blog so that it rises in Google's rankings, so that when people type 'Brian Leiter' into Google, the new blog comes up." His network of extremists obliged, and a new Google smear was briefly born.

What, if anything, should Google do about its clear complicity in the viability of cyber-cesspools? What, if anything, should the law do about it? Is the moral value of "free speech" an obstacle? To these issues we now turn.

The Value of "Free Speech"

All young children are advised at some point to remember that "Sticks and stones can break your bones, but names can never hurt you." Like many things told to young children, this isn't true. Indeed, on its face, the advice is a non sequitur: there are harms other than broken bones, and there is no reason at all to think that "names," that is, words, are not capable of causing them. To be sure, "names" do not break bones, but humans are creatures whose lives are suffused in meaning, and these meanings constitute their sense of self and large parts of their well-being. Words may not be the un-mediated cause of a fracture, but they can certainly cause humiliation, de-pression, debilitating anxiety, incapacitating self-doubt, and devastating fear about loss of safety, respect, and privacy. There are three standard rationales offered for permitting speech, even when it causes some harm: individual autonomy, democratic self-governance, and the discovery of the truth ("the marketplace of ideas"). I will assume that something like John Stuart Mill's "Harm Principle" should be a limitation on individual liberty, and that cer-tain degrees of harm can override the value of speech. I will also assume (contra, perhaps, Mill) that "harms" can include psychological ones—such as dignitary harms to reputation and privacy interests, as well as tortious harms that our law does recognize.[16] Since no one contests the propriety of regulat-ing tortious harms, I concentrate on speech that causes dignitary harms, as well as speech that is included in the spillover effects of more effective regu-lation of tortious harms through the abolition of Section 230 immunity for website owners. The question, in short, is what value the speech on cyber-cesspools can be said to have. If there is any legally significant difference between the virtual and actual worlds, it is that speech in the virtual world may be more likely to cause harms because of its ability to reach a wide audience stripped of relevant context thanks, in large part, to Google.

Notice, to start, that cyber-cesspools, at least insofar as they target pri-vate individuals, will get no help from considerations of democratic self-governance:[17] the viability of informed democratic decision making is not at stake when an anonymous poster on AutoAdmit reports that Jane Doe has herpes or that he would like to sodomize her forcibly. That means that if there is a reason not to regulate the kind of abusive speech that is the hall-mark of cyber-cesspools it must come from the other two considerations: individual autonomy and/or the discovery of the truth ("the marketplace of ideas"). Let us consider the "marketplace of ideas" rationale first.

Mill believed that discovering the truth (or believing what is true *in the right kind of way*) contributes to overall utility, and that an unregulated "marketplace of ideas" was most likely to secure the discovery of truth (or believing what is true in the right kind of way). Mill's commitment to the so-called "marketplace" is based on three claims about truth and our knowledge of it. First, Mill thinks we are not justified in assuming that we are infallible: we may be wrong, and that is a reason to permit dissident opinions, which may well be true. Second, even to the extent our beliefs are partially true, we are more likely to appreciate the whole truth to the extent we are exposed to different beliefs that, themselves, may capture other parts of the truth. Third, and finally, even to the extent our present beliefs are *wholly* true, we are more likely to hold them *for the right kinds of reasons,* and thus more reliably, to the extent we must confront other opinions, even those that are false.

For this line of argument to justify a type of speech, the speech in question must be related to the truth or our knowledge of it, and discovering this kind of truth must actually help us maximize utility. Now one might wonder whether some of the purported "truths" that cyber-cesspools proffer—for example, the purported truth that Jane Doe has herpes—are actually truths that contribute to maximizing utility. But, from the utililtarian perspective, that is not even the right way of framing the question: for the real question is whether claims about Jane Doe's alleged herpes on Internet sites by anonymous individuals with unknown motives (it is even unknown whether they have any interest in the truth!) are likely to maximize utility. It would seem not unreasonable, I venture, to be, at most, agnostic about an affirmative answer to this question, especially once we factor in the likely harms in the event that the claim is false.

But Mill, it is important to recall, did not actually accept the thesis about our fallibility in its strongest form. For Mill held that there is no reason to have a "free market" of ideas and arguments in the case of mathematics (geometry in particular) since "there is nothing at all to be said on the wrong side of the question [in the case of geometry]. The peculiarity of the evidence of mathematical truths is that all of the argument is on one side."[18] This is all the more striking a posture in light of the fact that Mill is a radical empiricist, and so denies that there is any a priori knowledge: even logical and mathematical truths are a posteriori, vindicated by inductive generalizations based on past experience. On Mill's view, then, there simply would not be any epistemic case for making room for the expression of opinions on which there is no contrary point of view that could make any contribution to the truth. This point is particularly important to bear in mind when it comes to material on cyber-cesspools aimed at private individuals.

Permit me to take what I hope is not a very controversial position, namely, that there actually are *not* two sides to the question of whether Jane Doe ought to be forcibly sodomized. If there are any moral truths, surely all the epistemic bona fides are on just one side of this issue. In other words, the explicit and implied threats of sexual violence central to cyber-cesspools like AutoAdmit simply have no moral standing based on the "market-place of ideas": they are in the same boat, for any Millian, as a website devoted to establishing that the square of the hypotenuse of a right triangle is equal to the product, rather than the sum, of the squares on the other two sides.

But what of dignitary harms more generally, and what of the spillover effects attendant upon a legal regime in which website owners face inter-mediary liability? Surely some speech that causes dignitary harms actu-ally *does* facilitate the discovery of the truth, and surely much of the speech that falls within the scope of spillover effects from more effective regula-tion of tortious harms in cyberspace would do so as well (and some of it might even affect democratic self-governance). If we are to be genuine utilitarians, we must weigh the competing utilities and disutilities of dif-ferent schemes of regulation of speech. I shall advance two claims: first, dignitary harms are much more harmful in the age of Google; and, sec-ond, spillover effects of more effective regulation of tortious harms in cyberspace will have little effect on the discovery of truth or democratic self-government.

The AutoAdmit sociopath no doubt had his analogue in an earlier era: call him the Luddite Sociopath. The Luddite Sociopath could indeed tell his friends and acquaintances that Jane Doe is a "slut" with herpes, but there is little reason to think the law ought to provide redress, except in extreme circumstances. The reasons are worth emphasizing. The Luddite Socio-path, in the first instance, reaches hardly anyone with his hateful message. We cannot control, and would not in any case want the law to control, the *thoughts* of others. People may think whatever they want, however false, foolish, disgusting, or demeaning. Even when the Luddite Sociopath ar-ticulates his thoughts, the impact is minimal: a small circle of acquain-tances, perhaps, hear it, and some of them, thanks to their familiarity with the Luddite Sociopath, may appropriately discount them. The harm to Jane Doe is still almost nonexistent: she is insulated both by the size of the audience *and* the availability to the audience of their *experience* with the Luddite Sociopath. Jane Doe may prefer, understandably, that no one think these thoughts or express them, but that is not a preference the law can satisfy.

Suppose, now, that the Luddite Sociopath is dissatisfied with his limited audience, and with the fact that his audience generally knows a fair bit about him—for example, his propensity to rant and rave, or his misogyny, or his inability to interact normally with other people, or his membership in fringe political groups, and the like. The Luddite Sociopath wants the *world at large* to "know" about Jane Doe, he wants to *harm* Jane Doe with his words. Our Luddite Sociopath needs an intermediary who can broadcast his words far beyond any audience he can reach, and who can detach his words, and their meaning, *from him* so that they are free-standing meanings that supply no context for interpretation that might defuse their force.[19] The Luddite Sociopath thus sends letters to the editors of newspapers, tries to place ads in magazines, and tries to weasel his way on to radio and cable television programs that will give him a potent forum for his message about Jane Doe.

But now, of course, the law steps in and places some obstacles in his path. For the law declares that any one of these intermediaries who picks up the Luddite Sociopath's "message" about Jane Doe can be liable for defamation and infliction of emotional distress. None of these intermediaries can say, "We did not say those nasty things, the Luddite Sociopath did!" Thus, the law gives every intermediary a significant incentive to be cautious, to investigate what the Luddite Sociopath says before broadcasting it, and to look into the Luddite Sociopath's background and motivations. Notice, too, that even in the absence of intermediary liability, most of the traditional media also give weight to dignitary harms in deciding what ought to be published about private persons.

In the age of blogs, Internet chat rooms, and Google, our formerly Luddite Sociopath has new intermediaries who have no current incentive to place *any* obstacles in his way. With the help of a chat room or blog, he can disseminate his message about Jane Doe to those who know nothing about him, and with the help of Google, the Sociopath's message can now be widely disseminated well beyond the blog or chat room to anyone with any interest in Jane Doe. Because the law, through Section 230, insulates the intermediaries from any liability, the law no longer puts any obstacles in the way of the Sociopath: no blog owner, or chat room administrator, or search engine operator, has any legal reason to make it harder for the Sociopath to express his thoughts about Jane Doe, to express them with no contextual information about the Sociopath or his target, and to do so in ways that are no longer ephemeral, but etched into the Internet's permanent memory, thanks to Google, for anyone, anywhere to discover. Both Tortious harms and dignitary harms are, in consequence, *more harmful* than ever before.

As Internet sources gradually displace or replicate the functions of other media, the reasons for thinking that they, unlike their old media counterparts, should be exempt from familiar forms of legal regulation will seem increasingly bizarre. Let us assume, then, that Section 230 will be repealed or significantly modified. Hopefully we shall then see the application of ordinary tort law not to Internet service providers, but to the intermediaries more proximate to the harmful words: for example, blog proprietors and chat room administrators/owners. The result would unquestionably be a significant reduction in the freedom with which individuals, especially anonymous individuals, are able to speak on the Internet. That effect would be enhanced if the law were also to provide remedies for some dignitary harms in cyberspace.

There would, however, be no reduction at all in the ability of individuals to speak freely, just in their ability to exercise that purported right to speak freely in cyberspace. It is important to emphasize *purported,* since, as with Ciolli and Cohen's defense of AutoAdmit, appeals to "free speech" are invoked on behalf of speech that in fact enjoys no special legal or moral standing (e.g., defamation of private individuals). Repeal of Section 230 together with causes of action for some dignitary harms will undoubtedly reduce, dramatically, the number of comments sections on blogs, since most blog proprietors fail to monitor the content on their sites. Why that would be a greater loss in cyberspace than it is in the traditional media, which do not permit nearly as much unregulated anonymous self-expression, is a question I have not seen addressed. Certainly anyone who has spent much time reading anonymous comments on blogs would not conclude that they are an especially notable repository of human wisdom, rational insight, or moral acuity. Indeed, if the entire Internet vanished tomorrow, we would still have all the traditional media and the traditional fora of communication: not just the so-called "mainstream media," but the alternative newspapers and presses, the foreign newspapers, the libraries, the scholarly periodicals, the satellite radio and the cable television, and on and on.

The issue, though, is not the Internet, but only certain sites on the Internet, like blogs and chat rooms, which are the primary loci of cyber-cesspools. The world is not obviously better because of these parts of the Internet, and in many ways it is obviously worse. Prior to blogs and chat rooms and Google, female law students were not subjected to campaigns of anonymous vicious harassment accessible to thousands of other students and lawyers around the country. Prior to blogs and chat rooms and Google, it was rather harder to irresponsibly invade privacy, circulate defamatory statements, or threaten sexual and criminal violence with seeming impunity. What *precisely* are the contributions to human knowledge and well-being that are attributable *solely* to these aspects of the Internet, that would have been impossible without its existence in its current unregulated form?[20] It is far from obvious that there are any, at least in otherwise democratic societies.

The preceding considerations leave us, it seems, with only one free speech argument for not regulating cyber-cesspools: namely, the value of permitting individuals to express themselves freely. But what exactly is *valuable* about such expressive freedom or autonomy? Consider the idea that the value of autonomy resides not in free choice per se but in choosing wisely or valuably.[21] If *autonomy* or *freedom* per se has value, then we should think it better that Hitler chooses *freely* to kill the Jews of Europe than that he does so because of a chemical imbalance in his brain. But most of us think the opposite: freedom of choice, exercised poorly, has even less value than the same action performed unfreely![22]

The line of thought I am criticizing here trades on an ambiguity about the "value" of an action: between, that is, its blameworthiness (which is increased when one *autonomously* chooses badly) and its utility for the agent. What is really at stake is the idea that an individual is better off when he can "express" himself than if he has to "bottle up" who he is, what he feels, and so on.

There may well be a type of *value* for the agent in his being able to express himself: Hitler feels better, one suspects, if given the opportunity to rant and rave about the Jews. But that fact leaves unanswered key questions. Is Hitler's "feeling better" a relevant criterion of utility? Can his "feeling better" be outweighed by the disutility to others? We should not conceive of utility in terms of preference-satisfaction alone, so that if Hitler's preference is to spew his venom about the Jews, then it creates utility to let him do so. Satisfying many kinds of preferences makes people worse off: the heroin addict's ability to satisfy his preference for more heroin does not add to his well-being

Even if self-expression has utility for the self that gets to express itself—however depraved or ignorant or foolish—we still need to weigh the utility of others. Let us assume the AutoAdmit sociopath gets utility, in the sense of preference-satisfaction, from his ability to express his desire to sodomize Jane Doe. It surely is not plausible that this utility outweighs the harm to Jane Doe of having that message broadcast, repeatedly and widely. But in that case, we no longer have a justification for permitting such speech.

I conclude that there is no clear reason to think that speech about private individuals on cyber-cesspools has any moral standing as free speech that should be protected, and there is no reason to think spillover effects of better regulation of cyber-cesspools will not be offset, many times over, by all the other avenues by which knowledge is shared and opinions expressed, both on the Internet and in the other media of communication. Legal defenses already exist against abuse of legal process, in the form of SLAPP (strategic lawsuit against public participation) suits against meritless defamation actions whose intent is to suppress protected speech. Yet the main prophylactic against such abuse is to restrict remedies against cyber-cesspools to "private" individuals, as understood in American libel law.[23] "Private" individuals, unlike public figures, are less likely to have the resources to mount frivolous assaults on cyber-cesspools and, by the same token, speech about them is less likely to implicate democratic values or truths that really maximize utility. This is, after all, the solution we have preferred in the rest of American law. The real question is why cyberspace should be treated *more protectively* when it comes to tortious harms and why it should not, in fact, be treated more restrictively when it comes to dignitary harms, given how much more harmful they are in cyberspace.

Regulating Google to Reduce Tortious and Dignitary Harms

What *ought* Google to do about its role in facilitating cyber-cesspools? Here are some simple steps an ethical search engine company might take in response to the harms caused by cyber-cesspools:

First, Google could set up a panel of neutral arbitrators who would evaluate claims by *private* individuals that Google is returning search results that might constitute tortious or dignitary harms. I would limit the right of appeal to *private* individuals precisely because speech about public figures is far more likely to implicate actual free speech values such as democratic self-governance. Google might impose a modest fee for this right of appeal, in order to reduce the number of frivolous complaints filed with the panel. But even a modest fee (say, $500) would be miniscule by comparison to the cost to victims of filing a legal action. The Google panel would receive and evaluate whatever materials the complainant deems relevant.

Second, the Google panel would have authority to provide several possible remedies in the event it concurs with the complainant that the material in question is more likely than not to constitute actionable material or a dignitary harm (the panel would apply something akin to a "preponderance of the evidence" standard). Possible remedies might include (1) delisting the material in question from the search engine results or demoting the results so that they turn up after the first page of results (the first page, or the "top five," being the only ones that most search engine users peruse); (2) awarding to the complainant, per a proposal of Frank Pasquale,[24] a "right of reply" in the form of an asterisk attached to the search result that links the searcher to the complainant's response; or (3) requiring the proprietor of the site on which the material in question appears to provide evidence to the Google panel that the material in question is neither actionable nor a dignitary harm; in the event the proprietor fails to do that, either one of the first two remedies would be available.

Imagine how this system would have worked in the case of the Auto-Admit Does. They are private individuals. They could have provided URLs to the offending postings at AutoAdmit, the majority of which, on their face, were actionable. For those not constituting per se libel or obvious inflictions of emotional distress, the Does might have needed to submit some additional information: for example, evidence of actual LSAT scores (which were alleged on AutoAdmit to be extremely low). The Google panel would have, presumably, awarded the delisting remedy, and the whole matter would likely have ended. The anonymous AutoAdmit sociopaths could rant and rave about the Does, but their ranting and raving would be far less likely to reach employers, friends, and relatives, and so would be far less harmful.

On this proposed voluntary scheme, it is less clear whether a quasi-public figure like me would be helped. The likelihood that highly critical speech about a public or quasi-public figure actually has some *value* is prima facie higher; one cannot craft legal rules around freak cases, like mentally ill individuals with delusional obsessions. By the same token, the ability of what is really actionable speech to do damage to a public or quasi-public figure is significantly less, precisely because there is so much other information available.

Google is unlikely to adopt this voluntary scheme, so the law will probably have to create incentives for Google to address its role in the proliferation of cyber-cesspools. The most promising analogue from existing law would make Google liable for its negligence in disseminating tortious material. (A more radical proposal would make Google liable for disseminating material constituting dignitary harms as well; I remain agnostic on whether that would be advisable.) To be sure, under existing law, neutral disseminators of even actionable material are rarely deemed liable, except in cases where they are aware of the tortious nature of the material, the harms are serious and highly probable, and the burdens on the disseminator to deflect the harm are not too great. The Dobbs torts treatise takes the view,[25] for example, that libraries are not likely to be held liable for maintaining on their shelves material that they know to be defamatory. Yet one of the state statutes Dobbs cites, Cal. Civ. Code §48.5, actually does impose liability on a radio broadcaster who fails to exercise "due care" in disseminating tortious material.[26] This is, I think, the right paradigm for the treatment of Google.

Here is the proposal: if Google is put on notice by a private party complainant that material returned in its searches is tortious, it has an obligation to evaluate the claim in accordance with something like the procedure sketched above; if it fails to evaluate the soundness of the claim, then it is liable for negligent dissemination of tortious material, and can be sued by the complainant. If it undertakes a fair review of the complainant's claim about the material, and deems it nonactionable, then it is not liable, unless the complainant can establish negligence in the review process. Google is, after all, a formidable defendant to sue, and one can imagine that will deter many private individuals. On the other hand, if Google, even after being put on notice, continues to disseminate actionable material, why should it not face liability? We already impose similar obligations on Internet intermediaries with respect to copyright infringement,[27] why not accord as much protection for private individuals from tortious harms (and maybe even dignitary ones)?

Conclusion

The rhetoric about "free speech" in cyberspace usually obscures more than it illuminates, even in scholarly discussions. Daniel Solove observes that, with respect to the regulation of speech on the Internet, "We are witnessing a clash between privacy and free speech, a conflict between two important values that are essential to our autonomy, self-development, freedom and democracy."[28] Yet when it comes to cyber-cesspools, most of these values are not implicated at all, except on the side of the victims. Only the incredible view that all expression, regardless of its subject or character, has value could sustain the idea that there is a significant clash here. James Grimmelman writes that "[R]emoving content from a search engine's index at the demand of a third party . . . is offensive to free-speech values."[29] His example is China's demand that search engines block users from finding information about the Falun Gong, a quasi-religious movement banned by the Chinese government. That might, indeed, implicate some free speech values—such as democratic self-governance and the discovery of the truth—but removing AutoAdmit content threatening sexual violence from a search engine implicates no free speech values I can discern. Mark Lemley—who represented pro bono the women suing AutoAdmit—claims that "The amazing diversity of the Internet, with its abundance of user-generated content, would be impossible" without some safe harbors for intermediaries from liability.[30] But is there really an amazing diversity of *valuable speech* in and around cyber-cesspools such that we should give them safe harbors? We do not protect safe harbors in the traditional media for "cesspool speech"; why is cyberspace different?

It would, of course, be a cost not worth bearing if measures like those described here chilled rough-and-tumble political debate and scathing social criticism. There is already too much faux civility in our public discourse, which permits charlatans and villains to claim the patina of legitimacy because no one dares, for fear of being rude, to call them out for what they are. We do not want to regulate speech, on the Internet or elsewhere, in a way that would make it impossible for a modern-day H. L. Mencken to excoriate his targets. But surely it is not hard to draw the line between a Menckensque scathing critique of public figures and calls to sexually assault female law students or to make someone "cry" and humiliate her in front of her children. Recognizing how little moral standing cyber-cesspools have as bastions of "valuable" speech about private individuals ought to encourage us to rethink Section 230 of the Communications Decency Act and rethink tort liability for search engines like Google. The Internet, and the real world, would both be better places if we did so.[31]

CHAPTER 10

Privacy, the First Amendment, and the Internet

GEOFFREY R. STONE

There is a lot of talk these days about the nasty nature of the discourse on the Internet. As the film critic David Denby notes in his recent book, *Snark,* there is a new "strain of nasty, knowing abuse spreading like pinkeye through the national conversation." Discussion threads on websites are often free-fire zones "of bilious, snarling, resentful, other-annihilating rage." The Internet, Denby observes, has allowed "a degeneration of invective" to "metastasize" through our culture, and once such material is there, "it's there forever, since it's easily Googled out of obscurity." The Internet "provides universal distribution of what had earlier reached a limited number of eyes and ears," and "the knowing group has been enlarged to an enormous audience that enjoys cruelty as a blood sport." The result, he predicts, will undermine the quality of public discourse and leave everyone "in a foul mood."[1]

To what extent may the government regulate such expression, consistent with the First Amendment? As the Supreme Court made clear in New York Times v. Sullivan, the First Amendment embodies "a profound national commitment" to the principle that public discourse "should be uninhibited, robust, and wide-open, and that it may well include vehement, caustic, and sometimes unpleasantly sharp" speech.[2] Indeed, the Court has declared that the freedom of speech may "best serve its high purpose when it induces a condition of unrest . . . or even stirs people to anger."[3] The Court has therefore long and consistently held that the First Amendment generally forbids restrictions of speech in public discourse on the ground that it is offensive, unsettling, insulting, demeaning, annoying, snarling, bilious, rude, abusive, or nasty. As the Court held some sixty years ago, free speech is generally protected unless, at the very least, it is "likely to produce a clear and present danger of a serious substantive evil."[4]

This does not mean that speech can *never* be regulated on the Internet. The Court has recognized that there are "certain well-defined and narrowly limited classes of speech"[5] that can be restricted even in the absence of a "clear and present danger of a serious substantive evil." These include, for example, false statements of fact that defame individuals, fighting words, threats, obscenity, commercial advertising, express incitement of unlawful conduct, and child pornography, all of which can be restricted in certain circumstances.[6] Moreover, such speech can be regulated on the Internet in the same way and to the same extent it can be regulated in any other setting. Thus, bloggers who make false and defamatory statements of fact or threaten others with violence can be punished for their speech just as they could if they conveyed such messages in a newspaper, a leaflet, or a public speech.

Indeed, as a general matter speech on the Internet should be no more or less protected than in any other venue. There are, of course, differences between the Internet and leafleting, in the same way that there are differences between newspapers, pamphlets, movies, radio, television, loudspeakers, and soapboxes. But, for the most part, the core First Amendment principles apply in the same manner, regardless of the means of communication.

It is sometimes said that the harm from speech on the Internet is potentially greater than the harm from speech in other media, because the potential audience is much larger, the speech remains indefinitely discoverable, and information can be easily located through search engines like Google. All of this is true. A false and defamatory statement can cause more harm to its victim if it is conveyed on the Internet than if it is communicated over a backyard fence or in a local newspaper, and this is certainly relevant in determining damages or punishment, if the speech is unprotected by the First Amendment. But none of this is relevant to whether the speech should be protected in the first place.

If speech is sufficiently valuable to merit First Amendment protection when it is spoken over a backyard fence or published in a local newspaper, then (at least presumptively) it is also sufficiently valuable to be protected when it is disseminated on the Internet. This is so because just as the harm caused by the speech may be magnified by the power of the Internet, so too is the value of the speech. As a general proposition, as speech reaches a larger audience, its cumulative value will increase in the same proportion as its cumulative harm. Thus, as a matter of first approximation, the fact that speech on the Internet can cause more harm than speech in a local newspaper is not a reason to accord it any less protection under the First Amendment. The balance between value and harm remains more or less constant.

In this essay, I focus on a category of expression whose status under the First Amendment is unclear—non-newsworthy invasions of privacy. As already noted, the general principles that govern such expression are not unique to the Internet. They apply without regard to whether the speech takes place on the Internet, in a newspaper, in a leaflet, or in any other form of public discourse.

General Principles

In what circumstances, if any, may the government penalize an individual for communicating "private" information about another person? The First Amendment forbids the government to abridge "the freedom of speech, or of the press." On its face, the First Amendment would seem to prohibit any effort of government to punish or censor an individual for communicating private information about another person. Any such penalty or censorship would seem literally to abridge "the freedom of speech, or of the press." This was essentially Justice Hugo Black's view of the First Amendment. The First Amendment says what it means and means what it says. The First Amendment is an absolute. The government "shall make no law abridging the freedom of speech, or of the press." End of discussion.[7]

This view of the First Amendment has not carried the day. The First Amendment cannot plausibly give individuals an unlimited right to say anything, at any time, in any place, in any manner. Justice Oliver Wendell Holmes made this point succinctly with his famous hypothetical of the false cry of fire in a crowded theatre.[8] To make sense of the First Amendment, we must define the "the freedom of speech, or of the press" that may not be "abridged."

Three inquiries have framed the Supreme Court's analysis of this inquiry. First, is the challenged law directed at the content of speech? If the law is neutral with respect to content, that is, if it restricts expression without regard to what is being said, then the Court generally balances the state interest against the speech interest to decide whether the restriction is constitutional. Under this approach, a law prohibiting all public speeches in public places is unconstitutional, whereas a law prohibiting the use of loudspeakers after midnight in residential neighborhoods is constitutional.[9] Insofar as the government penalizes an individual for communicating private information about other persons, the restriction is clearly directed at the content of the communication, so content-neutral analysis is irrelevant.

Second, if the restriction is directed at content, does it regulate only "low-value" speech? The Court has held that there are several categories of expression, such as false statements of fact, obscenity, commercial advertising, fighting words, express incitement of unlawful conduct, and threats, that do not appreciably further the central purposes of the First Amendment. If a challenged restriction is directed at low-value speech, the Court employs a form of balancing to determine whether the state interest is sufficiently weighty to justify the restriction. We will return to this doctrine shortly.

Third, if the law is directed at content, and the speech restricted is not of low First Amendment value, then the restriction ordinarily will be upheld only if it is necessary to prevent a clear and present danger of a very grave harm, such as a threat to the national security.[10] No one seriously argues that laws prohibiting the publication of non-newsworthy private information address a sufficiently grave harm to meet this standard. Thus, the central issue with respect to invasion of privacy is whether such expression is low-value speech.

Protecting Privacy at the Source

Before turning to the issue of defining a category of expression as low-value speech, however, it is important to note there are many ways in which the government can constitutionally protect individual privacy without directly forbidding the publication of "private" information. For example, in order to protect the interest in privacy, the government often restricts particularly intrusive means of gathering information about others, such as wiretapping, unauthorized mail opening, and burglary. Such laws protect privacy not by directly restricting expression, but by enabling people to shield actions, communications, and information they deem private from prying eyes and ears. Laws forbidding such invasions of privacy generally do not violate the First Amendment, because they are not only content-neutral, but are not even directed at speech. Rather, they have only an incidental effect on free expression. As a general proposition, the First Amendment does not give individuals a constitutional right to violate laws of general application merely because doing so would enable them to speak or to gather information more effectively. A reporter, for example, has no First Amendment right to break into a public official's home or to wiretap her phone calls in order to learn whether she has taken a bribe.[11]

An important twist on this method of protecting privacy is whether the government can constitutionally prohibit not only the wiretapping, burglary, or unauthorized mail opening, but also the publication of the unlawfully obtained information. A reporter who burgles a public official's home in order to obtain evidence that she has taken a bribe can clearly can be punished for the unlawful break-in, but can the reporter's newspaper also be punished for publishing the fact that the politician took a bribe? The argument for restricting the newspaper's speech in this situation is not that the publication itself violates the politician's right to privacy but that punishing the publication helps to deter the unlawful burglary.

The Supreme Court has wavered on this question. In some instances, the Court has held that the publication can be prohibited in order to reduce the incentive for the underlying illegality. For example, in the context of child pornography, which involves the depiction of actual sexual acts by real children, the Court has held not only that the government can punish the producer of child pornography for the underlying child sexual abuse, but that it can also punish those who knowingly exhibit or disseminate the images, both to eliminate the incentive for the underlying illegality and to protect the child from the continuing harm that would be caused by the ongoing distribution of the speech.[12]

In other situations, however, the Court has separated the punishment of the person who commits the underlying crime from the right of the press to disseminate the information. In Bartnicki v. Vopper, for example, the Court held that the government could not constitutionally punish a radio commentator for broadcasting an unlawfully wiretapped telephone conversation, where the information related to a matter of public concern. The Court left open the question whether the government could constitutionally have punished the commentator if the broadcast had involved only a matter of "domestic gossip of purely private concern."[13]

The law also protects individual privacy by recognizing and enforcing a broad range of confidential relationships. Some of these relationships are created by private contract, others by statute, regulation, or common law. For example, the law generally protects the confidentiality of client-lawyer, patient-doctor, penitent-priest, source-journalist, and inter-spousal communications, as well as the confidentiality of tax, financial, medical, educational, and psychiatric records.[14]

To the extent these relationships are created by private contract, the general understanding is that such contracts are binding even though one of the parties has agreed to contract away what otherwise would be a First Amendment right to disclose information. As the Supreme Court has observed, in the contractual context the "parties themselves determine the scope of their legal obligations, and any restrictions that may be placed on the publication of truthful information are self-imposed."[15] Thus, if X, a public official, tells Y, a friend, that he took a bribe, Y ordinarily is under no legal obligation not to disclose this information to others and cannot be held legally accountable for doing so. But if X reveals this information to Y, an author, as part of a contractual agreement in which Y promises not to disclose the information, then Y can be held liable for violating the contract. This is so because the law of contract, like laws against burglary and wiretapping, is not directed at speech and has only an incidental effect on free expression.[16]

When these relationships are created by statute, regulation, or common law, the analysis is more complex. For example, the law may prohibit employees of the Internal Revenue Service from disclosing the contents of individual tax returns or it may prohibit doctors and other medical personnel from revealing the contents of confidential medical records. Such laws are directed at speech, but because they govern the conduct of individuals in a special relationship with government—public employees or licensees— who have knowingly agreed to limit their First Amendment rights in order to gain access to confidential information, they are generally upheld as long as they serve a substantial government interest.[17]

In these situations, as in the wiretap and burglary situations, an issue can arise about whether the restriction on speech can be enforced not only against the party to the contract or the public employee or licensee, but also against third parties who obtain the information as a result of a breach of a confidential relationship. For example, suppose a doctor impermissibly discloses confidential medical information about his patient, a political candidate, to a reporter. As in the burglary and wiretap situation, the doctor could be held legally accountable for breaching the confidentiality requirement. But can the political candidate sue the reporter's newspaper for publishing the information?

In decisions like the Pentagon Papers case, the Court has held that even if a reporter gains access to confidential information through an unlawful leak, and even if the public employee who leaked the information can be punished for unlawfully disclosing it to the reporter, the government cannot constitutionally prohibit the publication of the information in order to deter the initial leak.[18] Thus, as in *Bartnicki*, if a newspaper published the information leaked by the doctor about the political candidate, it would be constitutionally protected if the information involved a matter of public concern (for example, if the medical condition was relevant to the candidate's fitness for office). As in the burglary and wiretap situations, however, it is unclear whether the publication would be protected if the information concerned only a matter of "domestic gossip of purely private concern" and the purpose of the restriction was to deter the underlying breach of confidence.[19]

Thus, the law protects privacy in a variety of ways. It enables individuals to be reasonably confident that certain places, activities, communications, and relationships, such as one's home, one's phone calls, one's bank records, and one's private communications with doctors and lawyers, will generally be protected against public exposure. The underlying assumption is that individuals who are truly concerned about the privacy of certain information or activities will have a reasonable, though imperfect, way to safeguard their privacy by controlling how, when, where, and to whom they reveal such information. In this way, they can control their privacy at its source.

Warren and Brandeis

This brings me back to the central question, which is whether the government can constitutionally penalize the publication of private information about an individual *in the absence of any underlying wrongdoing*. To get at this question, suppose a law student writes on a law-related blog that one of her professors is gay. In fact, the professor is gay. He has generally been discreet about this fact, however, preferring to keep it to himself. But he has had several lovers, and he has discussed his sexual orientation with close friends. One of the professor's former lovers told his cousin about his affair with the professor, and the cousin then told the student, who published the information on the blog.

The professor sues the student for invasion of privacy. In this case, the student learned the information without any underlying illegality. Neither the student nor anyone else in the story line engaged in an unlawful wiretap, rummaged through the professor's home or office, breached any contractual agreement with the professor, or did anything else unlawful or improper. Is the student liable to the professor for invasion of privacy?

Historically, Anglo-American law did not recognize a common law right of privacy that would cover this situation. It was traditionally assumed that people would guard—or not guard—their own privacy as they saw fit, and that they would assume certain risks, inherent in a free and open society. If they did certain things in public that were observed or if they chose to share certain information about themselves with others, they assumed the risk that the information might be disseminated to others. In this legal regime, those who wanted to preserve their privacy had to act carefully and with discretion. In what was predominantly a rural or small-town society, this was surely an imperfect protection of privacy. But, as with many risks in everyday life, the law generally assumed that individuals were responsible for their own choices and actions, including their decisions about how best and how much to safeguard their privacy.

The idea of a tort of invasion of privacy for the publication of non-newsworthy information was first advanced by Samuel Warren and Louis Brandeis in an 1890 law review article.[20] Warren and Brandeis's critique of the state of the media at the end of the nineteenth century is especially interesting, because it is strikingly similar to the contemporary critique of discourse on the Internet:[21]

> The press is overstepping in every direction the obvious bounds of propriety and of decency. Gossip is no longer the resource of the idle and of the vicious, but has become a trade, which is pursued with industry as well as effrontery. To satisfy a prurient taste the details of sexual relations are spread broadcast in the columns of the daily papers. To occupy the indolent, column upon column is filled with idle gossip. . . . In this, as in other branches of commerce, the supply creates the demand. Each crop of unseemly gossip, thus harvested, becomes the seed of more, and, in direct proportion to its circulation, results in the lowering of social standards and of morality. Even gossip apparently harmless, when widely and persistently circulated, is potent for evil. It both belittles and perverts. . . . Triviality destroys at once robustness of thought and delicacy of feeling.

To remedy this state of affairs, Warren and Brandeis proposed the recognition of a new tort, based on the "right to privacy," that would protect individuals from the "ruthless publicity" caused by the "discussion by the press" of their "private affairs."[22] The idea gradually took hold, and most states now recognize the tort, holding that an individual can be held liable for the public disclosure of even truthful facts about another if the information is "non-newsworthy" and the disclosure would be "highly offensive" to a reasonable person.[23]

The question is whether this tort can be squared with the First Amendment. Harry Kalven once suggested that the freedom of speech protected by the First Amendment is so broad and "overpowering as virtually to swallow the tort."[24] The Supreme Court has never directly addressed the question.[25] As already noted, the critical issue is whether such expression can appropriately be deemed "low-value" speech within the meaning of the First Amendment.

Low-Value Speech

The Supreme Court has never offered a clearly defined theory of low-value speech. The case law, however, suggests that several factors are relevant to the analysis. First, categories of low-value speech (for example, false statements of fact, threats, commercial advertising, fighting words, express incitement of unlawful conduct, and obscenity) do not primarily advance political discourse. Second, categories of low-value speech are not defined in terms of disfavored ideas or political viewpoints.[26] Third, categories of low-value speech usually have a strong noncognitive effect on the audience.[27] Fourth, categories of low-value speech have long been regulated without undue harm to the overall system of free expression.[28]

A defining characteristic of speech that is actionable as an invasion of privacy is that it is "non-newsworthy." In principle, this takes care of the first two criteria. That is, "non-newsworthy" information, by definition, presumably does not primarily advance political discourse and is not defined in terms of a disfavored idea or point of view.

The third and fourth criteria, however, are more problematic. Unlike, say, threats, fighting words, and obscenity, all of which arguably have a powerful noncognitive impact on the audience, non-newsworthy information does not have that characteristic.[29] Some other low-value categories, however, such as false statements of acts and commercial advertising, also do not share this characteristic, so its absence should not be taken to be dispositive.

The fourth criterion is critical. A long tradition of regulating a particular category of low-value expression creates a shared understanding of the contours and definition of the category and demonstrates from experience whether the category can be regulated without doing undue damage to First Amendment interests. Every recognized category of low-value speech has long been subject to legal regulation, and most classes of low-value speech were regulated at common law even before the adoption of the First Amendment.

The importance of this criterion makes considerable sense, for the recognition of novel categories of low-value speech poses serious constitutional dangers. The very concept of low-value speech is inherently problematic. As Thomas Emerson once observed, the doctrine inevitably involves courts in "value judgments concerned with the content of expression," a role that is awkward, at best, in light of "the basic theory of the First Amendment."[30] Placing great weight on experience and tradition in this context is therefore a reasonable way to capture the benefits of the low-value doctrine without inviting freewheeling judicial judgments about constitutional "value."[31] The Court has rightly been very reluctant to recognize new categories of low-value speech, and this reluctance has stood us in good stead.

There is no long-standing tradition of regulating the publication of non-newsworthy private information. Although the tort was first proposed in 1890 and has been adopted by most states, even now, 120 years later, there is no extensive case law defining the boundaries of the tort and no well-developed understanding of how to reconcile the tort with the First Amendment. For the most part, the tort has been enforced rarely and idiosyncratically. As Daniel Solove, a strong advocate of the privacy tort, has conceded, courts have "struggled when applying the newsworthiness test."[32] There is simply no track record to suggest that this category of expression can meaningfully be regulated without unduly impairing the freedom of speech more generally.

The central argument for treating this category of speech as low value is that it is said to be "non-newsworthy" and therefore does not meaningfully contribute to the sort of public discourse that the First Amendment was intended to promote. But the very concept of "non-newsworthy" is exceedingly slippery. Of course, it is easy to hypothesize specific examples of speech that most people would readily agree constitute non-newsworthy disclosures of private information, the publication of which would be highly offensive to reasonable people. Consider, for example, a nude photograph of an otherwise private individual that someone posts on the Internet for no reason other than to embarrass him. It is difficult to see how such an image, standing alone, could be deemed "newsworthy," or how it could be denied that the posting would be deemed highly offensive by reasonable people.

But identifying a few easy cases does not answer the vagueness concern, for it is just as easy to hypothesize a great many difficult cases. Consider a nude photograph of Sarah Palin. Suppose it reveals her sunbathing on a nude beach. Is that non-newsworthy? Suppose the nude photograph shows a professor naked in his backyard with a student.Or, to change the theme a bit, suppose the post reveals that a professor is gay. Is that non-newsworthy? What if the disclosure is part of an accusation that the professor favors gay students or discriminates against students who are Christian fundamentalists? Suppose a post on the Internet discloses that a student is gay. Is that non-newsworthy? What if the post is intended to inform other students about the student's sexual orientation? Is this "none of their business"? What if some students prefer not to socialize with homosexuals? Don't they have a right to make that choice?

Suppose the post reveals that a particular woman has had an abortion. Is that non-newsworthy? What if the woman is running for student body president? What if the woman is a babysitter and the information is posted on a website about prospective babysitters? Don't parents have a right not to hire as a baby-sitter for their children a woman who, in their view, has murdered her own child? Is such information newsworthy or non-newsworthy?

Or consider the identity of an alleged rape victim. Is there anything newsworthy about the publication of her name? Wouldn't the person accused of the alleged rape want the victim's name broadly disseminated so people with relevant knowledge about her might come forward with information that would help prove his innocence? Perhaps she has made false accusations against other people in the past or told other people a different story about what happened. Is her identity non-newsworthy?

My point is not to deny that there are some hard-core situations that would surely qualify as non-newsworthy publications, or that their dissemination would be highly offensive to reasonable people. It is, rather, that "non-newsworthiness" is an extraordinarily vague and open-ended concept. Other categories of low-value speech, like express incitement of unlawful conduct, threats, fighting words, commercial advertising, and false statements of fact, although inevitably vague at the margins, are much more easily defined and identified than "non-newsworthy" speech, which is highly context and value dependent. Even the doctrine of obscenity, which has vexed the judiciary for decades, is at least limited to a relatively narrow category of expression encompassing only the explicit and patently offensive depiction of certain clearly defined sexual acts. The concept of nonnewsworthiness embodies no objective limitations. As Randall Bezanson has aptly observed, the "standards of taste or propriety" that are necessarily embedded in the idea of non-newsworthiness are "simply unascertainable on a societal level" because contemporary society is "too pluralistic and culturally diverse."[33]

Even Warren and Brandeis acknowledged that there would be serious "difficulties" in the articulation of their proposed tort. They conceded, for example, that "the propriety of publishing the very same facts may depend wholly upon the person" about whom they are published," and that "no fixed formula" can be designed to separate the newsworthy from the nonnewsworthy. Indeed, they acknowledged that any effort to enforce the invasion of privacy tort would necessarily require a "rule of liability" that "must have in it an elasticity which shall take account of the varying circumstances of each case,—a necessity which unfortunately renders such a doctrine not only more difficult of application, but also . . . uncertain in its operation."[34]

Warren and Brandeis recognized these obstacles long before the Supreme Court had explored the challenges of creating a truly robust system of free expression, a system in which concerns about vagueness, over-breadth, discretion, and chilling effect have come to play a central role. Ambiguity in the law governing the freedom of speech was commonplace in 1890. Today, in light of our constitutional experience, the Court has rightly insisted on a degree of precision in First Amendment doctrine that renders implausible the idea of holding people legally accountable for *truthful* publications because some court or jury later finds them to be "non-newsworthy."

At this point, it might be useful for me to offer a brief aside on threats, both because they were much discussed, often rather casually, at the conference on which this volume is based, and also because the concept of a threat illustrates the necessity for a clear definition of low-value speech categories. A threat, for First Amendment purposes, is not a statement that is intended to frighten or intimidate another. For example, a statement by a doctor to a patient that if she does not quit smoking she will take years off her life is not a threat, even though it is intended to frighten and intimidate her into action she does not want to take. To constitute a threat, a statement must, among other things, clearly suggest that the harm will be brought about by the speaker or his confederates. Thus, the statement "I will kill you if you don't pay me what you owe me" is a threat. The statement "X deserves to die because he didn't pay me what he owes me" is not a threat under the First Amendment, because the speaker is not suggesting that he or his accomplices will kill X. The specificity of the definition of a threat is necessary to avoid ambiguity that would otherwise chill constitutionally protected expression.[35]

Similarly, incitement to commit unlawful conduct does not mean statements that might cause others to commit crimes or even statements that are intended to encourage others to commit crimes. The former would reach all sorts of criticism of the government (for example, speech criticizing the conduct of the war in Iraq might be thought to encourage terrorists); the latter would afford speakers who criticize the government inadequate protection against jurors who abhor their views and are therefore likely to find bad intent even when that intent was lacking. Thus, as Judge Learned Hand recognized more than eighty years ago, for speech to be punishable as incitement, it must *expressly* incite unlawful conduct. These examples underscore the fatal ambiguity of the "newsworthiness" concept.[36]

Private and Public Speech

Having said all this, I must acknowledge that there are elements of First Amendment doctrine in which the law distinguishes between public and private speech, and that this distinction is, in some instances, somewhat similar to the distinction between newsworthy and non-newsworthy expression. Does this save the invasion of privacy tort from extinction?

At the outset, it is necessary to separate two different public/private distinctions. Some speech is "private" in the sense that it is not part of public discourse. An example might be a conversation between two friends about a mutual acquaintance over a cup of coffee. Although the Court has not embraced any overarching First Amendment principle for dealing with such nonpublic speech, the general assumption seems to be that a libelous statement, or a threat, or a bribe, or an effort to persuade someone to commit a crime in such circumstances would not necessarily be tested by the same First Amendment standards that govern public discourse.[37] But this element of the public/private distinction is not relevant to speech on the Internet (except, perhaps, to private emails between two individuals), because blogs and most other forms of expression on the Internet are disseminated to a large audience and are therefore clearly on the "public" side of the line in terms of this aspect of the public/private distinction.[38]

The other variant of the public/private distinction is more relevant to the non-newsworthiness inquiry. In several areas of First Amendment law, the Court has held that speech will be protected from restriction if it concerns matters of public concern, even though similar speech might be regulated if it involves matters of only private concern. We have already noted one example of this phenomenon in the discussion of *Bartnicki*, in which the Court held that a radio commentator could not be held liable for broadcasting a tape recording of an unlawfully wiretapped telephone conversation, because the tape concerned a matter of public concern, while at the same time noting that the result might be different if the recording dealt only with "domestic gossip of purely private concern." Similarly, in libel law, the Court has indicated that false statements of fact about "matters of purely private concern" are entitled to less First Amendment protection than false statements on "matters of public concern."[39] And in the regulation of speech by public employees, the Court has held that the government has greater leeway to restrict public employee expression that disrupts government activities when the speech concerns only matters of personal interest, rather than matters of "political, social, or other concern to the community."[40]

Thus, although the Court has generally expressed grave "doubt" about "the wisdom of committing" to judges and jurors the task of distinguishing "on an ad hoc basis" between matters of public and private concern in the interpretation and application of the First Amendment,[41] it has, in at least some circumstances, recognized that such an inquiry may be necessary to strike the right balance between the freedom of speech and competing government interests. Put differently, inquiries into whether speech is relevant to matters of public concern have not been deemed so fundamentally incompatible with the basic premises of the First Amendment that they must be ruled out entirely. But it is important to note that the Court has authorized such inquiries only in very narrowly defined circumstances in which the expression at issue is already presumptively subject to regulation—even apart from the public/private distinction. In the *Bartnicki* situation, for example, the information was initially obtained unlawfully and would not have been available at all but for the underlying illegality. In the libel situation, the expression at issue consists of false statements of fact, which are already deemed low-value speech. In the public employee situation, the Court has long recognized that because the government has special interests "in promoting the efficiency of the public services it performs through its employees," it has much greater latitude in regulating speech that may interfere with those interests than in regulating public discourse generally.[42] Thus, in each of these situations, the protection of speech that is relevant to public debate can be seen as an exception to what would otherwise be a presumption of constitutionally permissible regulation.

In the invasion of privacy context, however, the *only* characteristic of the expression that purportedly justifies characterizing it as low-value speech subject to government regulation is its asserted non-newsworthiness. To put so much weight on so subjective, vague, and open-ended a concept goes beyond anything the Court has ever upheld in its First Amendment jurisprudence, and it is therefore no surprise that the Court has never put its imprimatur on this doctrine.

There is one other possible twist worth noting. There was much talk during the conference on which this volume is based about the tort of intentional infliction of emotional distress. Perhaps actions for invasion of privacy can be squared with the First Amendment when they also constitute intentional inflictions of emotional distress.[43] In the traditional invasion of privacy action, a defendant can be held liable if he published the information with reckless disregard for the offensiveness of the disclosure. Suppose, instead, the law limited such actions only to circumstances in which the defendant intended the publication to cause "severe emotional distress." This would cover the most egregious invasions of privacy. But is the tort of intentional infliction of emotional distress consistent with the First Amendment?

In Hustler Magazine v. Falwell,[44] the Supreme Court held that public figures may not recover for the tort of intentional infliction of emotional distress as a result of even "outrageous" publications that insult, degrade, or humiliate them, in the absence of proof of falsity. The Court explained that although a "bad motive may be deemed controlling for purposes of tort liability in other areas of the law," the "First Amendment prohibits such a result in the area of public debate." The Court added that, like the concept of non-newsworthiness, the concept of "outrageousness" in the realm "of political and social discourse has an inherent subjectiveness about it which would allow a jury to impose liability on the basis of the jurors' tastes." The Court therefore concluded that the "outrageousness" standard "runs afoul of our long-standing refusal to allow damages to be awarded because the speech in question may have an adverse emotional impact on the audience."[45]

Falwell dealt only with statements concerning public figures. It did not address the constitutionality of the intentional infliction of emotional distress tort in the context of private individuals. As with the invasion of privacy tort, however, the argument for enforcing the intentional infliction of emotional distress tort in the realm of public—as distinct from private— discourse seems thin. Historically, the common law did not recognize such a tort, in the absence of physical harm. There was great skepticism about such a tort because of the difficulties of proving mental injury, the risk of fictitious claims, and the fear of a flood of litigation over trivial matters. Although the Second Restatement of Torts recognized the tort in 1965, in the years since most courts have continued to take a decidedly negative approach to intentional infliction of emotional distress claims that involve statements in public discourse. As the New York Court of Appeals observed in 1993, it had rejected every such claim over the preceding quarter-century because in no case was the alleged conduct sufficiently "outrageous" to justify liability.[46] Viewed in this light, it seems unlikely that the tort of intentional infliction of emotional distress can be reconciled with the demands of the First Amendment, even as applied to private figures, as long as the speech is in the domain of public discourse.

The Interest in Privacy

Another difficulty with the invasion of privacy tort concerns the strength of the state interest. Even when speech is deemed of low First Amendment value, the Court generally insists that the state must have at least a substantial interest to justify regulating the expression. This is so both because even low-value speech usually has some First Amendment value and because any effort to regulate low-value speech usually has chilling effects on high-value speech.[47] Those problems are especially acute in the invasion of privacy context, because the very concept of non-newsworthiness is so elastic, subjective, fact dependent, and, in the words of Warren and Brandeis, "difficult of application."

Of course, it is easy to romanticize the interest in forbidding the publication of non-newsworthy information about individuals that causes them embarrassment and emotional distress. Warren and Brandeis waxed eloquent about the right "to be let alone," the right to "an inviolate personality," and the right to have one's "social and domestic relations be guarded from ruthless publicity."[48] Similarly, Paul Gewirtz has noted that privacy, in the sense of "the ability to control and to avoid the disclosure of certain matters about oneself," is "an important precondition for human flourishing."[49] Indeed, there are quite clearly legitimate reasons for being concerned with privacy in this sense. The ability of individuals to engage in private conduct without having it broadcast to the world, the capacity of individuals to make mistakes without being haunted by them forever, and the freedom to live one's life without having to answer publicly for every choice, are unquestionably legitimate personal and societal interests.[50]

But there is another side to the issue. As Richard Posner has observed, if as is often the case "what is revealed is something the individual has concealed for purposes of misrepresenting himself to others, the fact that disclosure is offensive to him and of limited interest to the public at large is no better reason for protecting his privacy than if a seller advanced such arguments for being allowed to continue to engage in false advertising of his goods."[51] In many situations, in other words, those who assert an interest in privacy can reasonably be seen as trying to deceive others about themselves. They would rather that other people believe that they are "better" than they are, that they not know that they once had an affair or an abortion, or cheated on a test, or have an embarrassing illness, or drink to excess, or strike their children, or sunbathe in the nude. There may be good reasons for wanting to keep such information private, but Posner is surely right that in many cases people invoke the right of privacy because they want to mislead others into thinking better of them than they would if they knew the truth. In such circumstances, they are engaged in a form of fraud, and we should be careful not to see that claim for more than it really is.[52]

There is at least a partial answer to Posner's insight, for in many cases people who learn negative things about others may exaggerate the significance of the fault and overreact in their judgment about the person. As Jeffrey Rosen has noted, "when intimate knowledge" is taken out of context, and "revealed to strangers, we are vulnerable to being misjudged on the basis of our most embarrassing, and therefore most memorable, tastes and preferences."[53] Moreover, as Daniel Solove argues, in at least some instances the "law protects against disclosures of private information because society believes that such information is not appropriate for making public judgments about people."[54]

Thus, the real trade-off may not be between truth and falsity, but between fair and unfair evaluations of individuals. We recognize this danger in other areas of the law. In the law of evidence, for example, we routinely make evidence of a party's bad character inadmissible, because we know that jurors tend to overvalue the importance of the evidence.[55] The invasion of privacy tort can be understood as an application of the same basic insight about human nature. But, at least in the realm of public discourse, for the government to deny people access to information because they may overvalue it reflects a form of paternalism that is directly incompatible with the basic assumptions of First Amendment theory.[56]

Defenders of the right of privacy in this context will argue further, however, that whether or not the invasion of privacy tort sometimes enables people to deceive others about themselves, the publication of non-newsworthy information serves no legitimate First Amendment purpose, and that the Constitution is therefore simply irrelevant to the social policy question of whether people should be able to know or not to know such information about others. In Edward Bloustein's words, there is no First Amendment right "to satisfy public curiosity and publish . . . gossip about private lives."[57] But this assumes a distinction between legitimate matters of public concern and "gossip about private lives" that is not so easily sustained. Not only, as we have seen, is the concept of "non-newsworthy" speech exceedingly vague and difficult of application, but it is not at all clear that, even if we "know it when we see it,"[58] such speech is in fact of low First Amendment value.

Eugene Volokh argues, for example, that speech about "daily life" is "worthy" of full First Amendment protection,[59] and Diane Zimmerman insists that contemporary society uses "knowledge about the private lives of individual members" to "preserve and enforce social norms." Indeed, by providing people with a rich way "to learn about social groups to which they do not belong, gossip increases intimacy and a sense of community among disparate groups and individuals." Speech that is seen by some as unfairly invading privacy constitutes "a basic form of information exchange that teaches about other lifestyles and attitudes, and through which community values are changed or reinforced." Indeed, "perceived in this way," such expression "contributes directly" to the First Amendment's "marketplace of ideas."[60]

Beyond all this, though, the practical reality is that changes in technology may have largely made moot the very idea of the tort of invasion of privacy.

In 1890, when Warren and Brandeis first promulgated the tort, the notion that the law could meaningfully distinguish between newsworthy and non-newsworthy publications and could effectively regulate those that were non-newsworthy seemed plausible, although difficult even then. Today, however, with the advent of the Internet, the very idea of attempting to regulate such invasions of privacy is beyond the reasonable capacity of the law. Perhaps the professional press that was the principal target of Warren and Brandeis's legal innovation could reasonably have been expected to conform their publications to professional and legal standards of newsworthiness. With a medium like the Internet, however, in which every individual can disseminate information to the world, the concept of the professional press is largely irrelevant. The private conversations that Warren and Brandeis would themselves have exempted from their tort now occur in a forum that instantly reaches everyone in the world with access to a computer.

This makes the legal enforcement of the concept of non-newsworthiness staggeringly problematic. Consider, for example, a student who posts accurately on a blog dealing with her school that a teacher recently had an abortion or had cheated in college or was seen in a gay bar. Within the confines of the school community, it would be difficult to argue that this is non-newsworthy information or that the student could be punished for revealing it to others. But with modern technology, this information will be available not only to those in the particular school community, at that time and place, but to all Internet users and forever. With the availability of search engines like Google, a person thinking of hiring the teacher twenty years later will be able with just a few keystrokes to find this information. This expands profoundly both the potential value and the potential harm of the initial posting. The main point of the hypothetical, however, is that one person's newsworthy information is another's invasion of privacy, and in the world of the Internet it is no longer possible to segregate audiences based on the immediate relevance of information to the community. We are all now part of a universal audience for everything and forever. This may be liberating or it may be unnerving and unwelcome, but in no event is it a state of affairs that can meaningfully be addressed by the invasion of privacy tort. That approach to the issue, which was problematic even in 1890, is no better than quaint today. It is an odd curiosity of an earlier and vastly simpler era.

A useful analogy is the law of obscenity. Through the 1950s and 1960s, the obscenity doctrine had a substantial impact (for better or worse) on the ability of individuals to gain access to sexually explicit expression. In 1973, the Supreme Court, concerned that such expression was becoming too read-ily available, and that it was increasingly exerting "a corrupting and debasing impact" on society, broadened the constitutional definition of obscenity.[61]

Despite this effort to use the law to control sexually explicit expression, technological change simply swamped the capacity of the law. With the coming of video rentals, cable television, and the Internet, sexually explicit material became more easily available on an unprecedented scale. This, in turn, affected (some would say corrupted) community standards of "de-cency" in the depiction of sex, and over time almost no sexually explicit material could be found to violate "contemporary community stan-dards." The effort of government officials to prosecute the exhibition, distribution, or dissemination of obscene matter has effectively ended at the local, state, and federal levels. Put simply, the capacity of the law was overwhelmed by the forces of social and technological change. As a conse-quence, legal efforts have more recently been refocused on more specific problems posed by sexually explicit materials, problems that are both more serious and more plausibly subject to legal regulation, such as zoning and child pornography.[62]

Just as the law can no longer effectively deal with obscenity because of social and technological change, so too can it no longer effectively deal with non-newsworthy invasions of privacy. This is not to deny that there are situations in which invasions of privacy can be harmful to individuals or that, in an ideal world, we might have some way to prevent that harm. It is to say, though, that even if the First Amendment itself is not sufficient in principle to "swallow the tort," the combination of the First Amendment and social and technological change has, for all practical purposes, gobbled it up completely. To argue otherwise is simply to tilt at windmills.

Moreover, it is not clear that the importance Warren and Brandeis at-tached to this sort of privacy is relevant for the future. In the contemporary culture of Facebook, Friendster, and other social-networking websites, people increasingly seem to value transparency over informational privacy. In many ways, this may be a self-adjusting system. If one of the dangers of invasions of privacy by publication was the risk that people would seriously overvalue the importance of relatively minor instances of private miscon-duct that rarely came to light, the much greater visibility of human foibles in the modern era will likely lead people to learn how to put the mistakes of others in their larger context. In this sense, one might hope that the loss of privacy will result in greater tolerance and understanding, which itself might be a major triumph of the First Amendment.

The most realistic way to protect privacy today is at its source. By prohibiting highly intrusive methods of gaining information that people want to keep confidential it is still possible to enable individuals who truly care about their privacy to preserve it, if they act carefully and with discretion. But once information is out of the bottle, once we share it with others, once others know it, we can no longer hope to put it back. If that era ever existed, it is now the past.

CHAPTER 11

Foul Language:
Some Ruminations on
Cohen v. California

JOHN DEIGH

Great advances in technology sometimes directly increase the power of ordinary people. The invention of the telephone and that of the automobile are two obvious examples. The advance in information technology of the past twenty years is a third. Before the development of the Internet, only a small number of people commanded means of communication that could reach an audience larger than a few hundred. Now, however, anyone with access to a personal computer has the power to reach millions not only in his or her own country but around the world. The voices of ordinary people have thus gained a power to be heard that elites cannot ignore, and the benefits of this gain for democracy have been substantial.

At the same time, this gain carries significant costs. A great increase in the power of people's speech brings a corresponding increase in the harm that can be done to people when that power is abused. As a result, cases at law that forty or more years ago expanded freedom of speech in ways that did not then appear to create opportunities for serious harm, that did not, in particular, portend of abuse that could cause severe injury to a person's reputation or emotional stability, now have a different import. In view of this change, they invite renewed examination. One such case is Cohen v. California (USSC, 1971). This essay presents a set of reflections on the holding in this case.

Cohen extended the First Amendment's right of free speech to words that evince the speaker's emotions. The speaker in the case was one Paul Cohen. On April 26, 1968, he wore a jacket in a public place on the back of which were boldly inscribed the words "Fuck the Draft." The public place was a corridor in the Los Angeles County Courthouse, and the law of whose violation he was convicted was part of the California Penal Code. It prohibited offensive conduct that maliciously and willfully disturbs the peace or quiet of any neighborhood or person. On conviction, Cohen was sentenced to thirty days in prison. The California Appellate Court upheld the conviction, noting that women and children were present in the corridor when Cohen wore his jacket. The U.S. Supreme Court overturned the conviction.

The Court, in overturning the conviction, held that the First Amendment protects speech that expresses emotion per se, that is, regardless of whether the expression of the emotion is necessary to the speech's communicating the ideas and opinions it also expresses. The issue in the original case was whether Cohen in wearing his jacket had wrongfully caused a public harm, and the Supreme Court effectively removed this issue by giving First Amendment protection to Cohen's speech. But the Court's holding has broader implications. It gives similar protection to emotive speech that causes personal and private harms. Expletives, slurs, vulgarities, and other forms of speech that express contempt, disgust, animus, and the like toward someone or the members of some group can produce in their target considerable suffering and anxiety and at the same time make him or her the object of uninvited, demeaning attention and publicity. The latter, in particular, especially when it consists in ambushing the victim and forcing him or her into the glare of such humiliation and denigration, represents a gross violation of privacy. The government, then, if the holding in *Cohen* were applied to such speech, could not suppress it. Its victims could not look to the government for protection from these violations. And if they cannot, because of this holding, the case has an odd and unhappy result.

What makes the holding in *Cohen* odd is its mismatch with the leading philosophical defenses of the right to freedom of speech. None of these offers grounds for taking this right as guaranteeing freedom of emotional expression per se. None implies in its justification of a right to the freedom to express one's thoughts and ideas a justification of a corollary right to the freedom to express one's feelings and emotions. For this reason, one can question whether there is a sound basis for the Court's extending the First Amendment's protection of freedom of speech to include the emotive force of the speaker's words regardless of its importance to the thought those words convey. And while we might think there is a sound basis for protecting Cohen's speech in virtue of its being distinctively political speech—a possibility I will consider in the sequel—one can still question whether there is a sound basis for protecting the emotional force of a speaker's words generally, that is, regardless of whether they fall into a category of speech like political speech that ought to receive heightened protection from government interference. For this reason the opinion the Court delivered in support of its decision in *Cohen*, if taken as applying beyond distinctively political speech, seems problematic. And it may be problematic even if it is taken narrowly as applying only to distinctively political speech.

In questioning whether there is a sound basis for the holding, I do not mean to be questioning whether one can find support for it in past Supreme Court opinions regarding the First Amendment's protection of speech. Perhaps one can. What I question is whether one can find support for it in any of the leading philosophical defenses of the right to free speech. By a philosophical defense I understand a defense of a universal right of free speech, one that all men and women, either as individuals or as members of a people, have regardless of the particular state under whose rule they live. My interest, then, in the holding in *Cohen* does not extend to other Supreme Court decisions.[1] No other, as far as I know, speaks directly to the question of whether the First Amendment protects purely emotive speech. And if any others provide indirect support for the holding, then my misgivings about the latter may apply to them. I will not, however, be considering these broader issues.

Let me also state clearly at the outset that I am not questioning whether the right to free speech should include emotional speech. Obviously it has to. Some thoughts and ideas cannot be expressed except in words that convey emotion.[2] One cannot communicate deep personal loss except in language that expresses grief. One cannot protest cruel injustices except in language that expresses indignation. One cannot warn of coming dangers except in language that expresses alarm. Essential to Winston Churchill's famous warning of the dangers confronting Europe and America in the years immediately following World War II, for example, are words heavy with foreboding and threat. "An *iron curtain*," Churchill declared, "has descended across the [European] Continent. Behind that line lie all the capitals of the ancient states of Central and Eastern Europe. . . . And all are subject in one form or another, not only to Soviet influence, but to a very high and in some cases increasing measure of control from Moscow. . . . In front of the *iron curtain* which lies across Europe are other causes of anxiety. . . . [I]n a great number of countries far from the Russian frontiers and throughout the world Communist fifth columns are established and work in complete unity and absolute obedience to the directions they receive from the Communist center. Except in the British Commonwealth and the United States where Communism is in its infancy, the Communist parties or fifth columns constitute a growing challenge and peril to Christian civilization. These are somber facts for anyone to have to recite on the morrow of a victory gained by so much splendid comradeship in arms and in the cause of freedom and democracy, but we should be most unwise not to face them squarely while time remains."[3] Plainly, it is impossible to separate Churchill's thought in this speech from the apprehension and unease that interpenetrates it. Plainly, it would have been impossible for Churchill to have delivered his warning to the West without using dark and chilling language, language designed to arouse fear.

What I am questioning is whether the right to free speech should include use of emotive language in speech when such language has no other point than to vent and arouse feeling. The word "fuck" in Cohen's speech is a clear example. It served to communicate Cohen's animus toward the draft and perhaps also to shock those who were unaccustomed to seeing the word so displayed. It did not convey any idea about the draft that would explain the appropriateness of animus toward it or contribute to the debates about its role in the conduct of a war that many people had come to regard as grossly immoral. Indeed, the idea the word most commonly expresses has no application in the linguistic context in which Cohen used it. You cannot, after all, engage in sexual congress with a legal institution. Its chief purpose, in Cohen's use of it, was to express virulently his contempt for the draft.

To be sure, "fuck" is now such a common epithet that it has lost the power to shock any but the most genteel soul. Indeed, the current range of its usage or that of its cognates is so great that in some cases one couldn't, without knowing the context of the utterance, tell what sort of emotion it expresses. It has taken over from "damn," it would seem, the function of expressing emotion generally or of infusing an exclamation with additional emotion. Accordingly, it may be placed in the class of pure exclamatory terms along with "ooh," "whoopee," and "yech."

It nonetheless continues to have, in many of its uses, the emotive force with which Cohen used it, and this places it in a different class of emotive terms. These are terms that function at once as common names and as mere expressions of emotion. They are mere expressions in that successfully applying the name does not make the emotion one expresses appropriate. Take

for example ethnic slurs like "wop" and "chink." Each is a name for someone who belongs to a specific ethnic group, and each expresses contempt
for people who belong to that group. Yet the contempt a person expresses
for his Italian neighbors by calling them "wops" is not appropriate by virtue of their being Italian. Consequently, because denying the truth of the
person's statement that his neighbors are wops is equivalent to denying
that they are Italian, refusal to share the person's contempt for them or to
think it appropriate does not imply that one denies the truth of what he
says. By contrast, if a person expresses contempt for his neighbors by calling
them "slobs" or "nitwits," then one's refusal to share his contempt or to think
it appropriate does imply that one denies the truth of what he says. For being
slovenly or foolish is a deficiency to which contempt is an appropriate response. "Slob" and "nitwit," though commonly used to express contempt, are
not mere expressions of the emotion. Similarly, Churchill achieves his aim of
eliciting fear through the use of such words as "peril," "somber," and "fifth
column." They express fear by virtue of the conditions they name; they are
not mere expressions of the emotion.[4]

It is clear, moreover, that the Supreme Court also saw the emotive force
of Cohen's language as, unlike that of Churchill's, separable from its cognitive content. Justice Harlan, writing for the Court's majority, set out, early
in his opinion, the distinction between the inscription on Cohen's jacket
and its meaning. There is no question, Harlan observed, that "the State . . .
lacks power to punish Cohen for the underlying content of the message
the inscription conveyed. At least so long as there is no showing of an intent to incite disobedience to or disruption of the draft, Cohen could not,
consistently with the First and Fourteenth Amendments, be punished for
asserting the evident position on the inutility or immorality of the draft his
jacket reflected."[5] The question, as Harlan saw it, is whether the state has
the power to punish Cohen for the linguistic manner in which he expressed
that position, for the words he chose to express it. And since the words
Cohen chose were not, in the context in which he used them, incendiary
or directed at particular individuals with the intention of provoking
them to violence, one precedent allowing the state to punish speech
because of the words its speaker used does not apply. Rather, as Harlan,
toward the end of his opinion, noted, Cohen chose his words for their
emotive force and not merely for their cognitive content, and such force
"may often be the more important element of the overall message sought
to be communicated."

While no one could quarrel with Harlan's point about words often being chosen more for their emotive force than their cognitive content, it does not follow from this point that such choices should always have the same immunity from government interference as choices of words for their cognitive content. When the two cannot be separated, of course, then the same immunity that a right to free speech secures for the ideas and thoughts that are expressed protects the emotive language with which they are expressed. But when the choice of words for their emotive force is superfluous to whatever ideas and thoughts they express, then the question of what justifies the same protection of that choice is genuine and pressing.

The reason is that people can, as I noted earlier, be seriously harmed by such words. The harm consists not only of the immediate pain they suffer and of its lingering in memory, but also of loss of ease and self-possession, which too can be lasting and debilitating. Part of the experience of being the object of another's contempt and animus is to feel naked and vulnerable, and this is especially true when the contempt and animus are arbitrary and leave one defenseless. People have a basic interest in social acceptance and the freedom from disparagement it entails. It is among the several interests that privacy and the respect it requires protect.[6] To be the target of slurs and expletives is, then, to suffer a violation of this interest and so the privacy that protects it when people, despite their differences and deviations from what is seen as normal, are respected.

In view of this harm, it is not obvious why protection of such verbal abuse should be upheld when it is not necessary for guaranteeing freedom to express one's ideas and opinions. And the difficulty in justifying such protection becomes even more apparent when we consider the major philosophical defenses of a right to free speech.

The classical defense in Anglo-American philosophy is John Stuart Mill's argument, in *On Liberty*, for protecting freedom of speech from societal interference. Mill makes his argument in chapter 2 of *On Liberty*. One cannot, however, fully comprehend the argument without taking into account what Mill says at the end of chapter 1 about the way it fits into the larger argument of his essay. The larger argument is his argument for "one very simple principle"—the harm principle.[7] This is the principle that the only purpose for which society can rightfully interfere with the liberty of any of its members, against that person's will, is to prevent him or her from harming others. It is the object of his essay, Mill writes, "to assert [this] principle."[8] Mill then describes the argument he will make in chapter 2 for protecting freedom of speech as offering, with respect to one division of his subject, grounds that he will in later chapters apply generally.[9] In other words, on Mill's own account, the reasons he advances in chapter 2 in support of the absolute liberty of speech are, when suitably generalized, the same reasons he adduces in support of the harm principle. Mill thus instructs us to read the argument of chapter 2 as a prelude to his general argument for the harm principle, and unless we read it as such, we will fail to understand how he conceives of speech as protected actions under that principle. Too often, however, chapter 2 is read as an independent argument. Too often it is taken as a simple utilitarian argument for protection of speech from societal interference and as such one that proceeds along a different line from the line on which Mill makes his general argument.[10]

Mill, to be sure, rests his case for the harm principle ultimately on considerations of utility. But as he says, these must be considerations of "utility in the largest sense, grounded on the permanent interests of man as a progressive being."[11] The promotion of utility is, consequently, for Mill a matter of advancing these interests, and as we learn in chapter 3 of *On Liberty,* their advancement requires securing for men and women liberty necessary for their self-development, the realization of their distinctively human capacities. Such liberty consists at a minimum in leaving each free, within the sphere of wholly self-regarding actions, to do as he or she chooses. Society, therefore, may interfere with only the actions of individuals that directly affect the interests of others, and only if such interference brings about more utility for humankind than leaving the actions unregulated. Thinking is plainly a wholly self-regarding activity, and accordingly the liberty of thought is a liberty whose immunity from societal interference Mill regards as necessary to advancing the permanent interests of humankind as a progressive species. And because the liberty of speech, Mill observes, is a cognate of the liberty of thought and impossible to separate from it, an argument for securing for people the freedom to think and form opinions for themselves requires an argument for securing for them freedom of speech. It too is necessary for individual self-development. Hence, Mill comes to treat speech as if it were a wholly self-regarding action and so to argue for its immunity from societal interference as he argues for the liberty of all actions that the harm principle protects.

To say this is to say that Mill treats speech as a wholly self-regarding action only insofar as it is an instrument for transmitting thought and opinion.

The qualification is essential. For Mill acknowledges that speech loses its immunity to being interfered with when it is delivered in circumstances in which it becomes "a positive instigation to some mischievous act."[12] So Mill is not arguing in chapter 2 for making speech as such immune from societal interference. Rather he is arguing for disabling society, government in particular, from interfering with speech when it interferes for the purpose of preventing the communication of ideas and opinions. Government, in other words, on the principle Mill defends, may not interfere with the transmission of ideas or opinions in order to stop them from being heard or read, though it may interfere with their transmission because of its manner or circumstances. Once one understands this as Mill's thesis, one can see why the argument of chapter 2 proceeds as it does.

The evil of government interference with speech, the harm it does to man's permanent interests as a progressive being, Mill argues, is that by suppressing particular ideas and opinions, it keeps people, both individually and collectively, from gaining knowledge or a sound understanding of the subject at hand. His argument proceeds by separating cases. First, the suppressed ideas and opinions may be true. However confident the government may be that they are false, it may nonetheless, because of human fallibility, be mistaken. And if the ideas and opinions it suppresses are true, their suppression deprives people of opportunities to overcome their ignorance and gain knowledge. It blocks them from exchanging error for truth. Second, even if the government is not mistaken and the ideas and opinions it suppresses are false, people, though they would not be kept from believing what is true, would still suffer a harm that is nearly as bad. For in this case they would be deprived of the opportunity of having their true ideas and opinions confronted with ones that oppose them, and in the absence of such opposition, their understanding of those ideas and opinions will eventually weaken to the point where they are held unreflectively and dogmatically. If not confronted with ideas and opinions opposed to their own, people will have little occasion to review the grounds that support their ideas. They will, in consequence, come to hold them with little understanding of those grounds. Their thought will become stagnant and shallow. In either case, then, Mill maintains, the government's suppression of ideas and opinions deprives people of knowledge and weakens their understanding. Consequently, it stunts the development of human intellect and moral sensibility.

It should be clear, even from this brief sketch of Mill's argument, that for Mill the point of protecting speech from government interference is to promote the interests of those who are its recipients. The evil of government censorship with which Mill is concerned is the harm it does to those who are deprived by the censorship of hearing or reading certain ideas.[13] Whatever harm the censorship does to the speaker qua speaker is not germane to the argument. Accordingly, we should understand Mill's defense of freedom of speech as an appeal to the interests of the audience and not to those of the speaker. And consequently Mill's defense could support our understanding the right to freedom of speech as protecting purely emotive speech only if government interference with such speech would harm the interests of the audience to which it appeals. Since it plainly does not, since interfering with purely emotive speech does not impede the mental development of men and women that Mill believed freedom of speech advanced, the defense offers no basis on which to justify the extension of the First Amendment right to free speech that the decision in *Cohen* brought about.

Mill's defense is a benchmark in being an appeal to interests of the recipients of speech that purely emotive speech does not advance. One finds the same feature in other major philosophical defenses of free speech. Hence, none of them supports the holding in *Cohen*. I will briefly describe two. They have been particularly influential in contemporary political theory. One is T. M. Scanlon's from his paper "A Theory of Freedom of Expression."[14] The other is Alexander Meiklejohn's, which appears in his book *Free Speech and Its Relation to Self-Government*.[15] I will describe Scanlon's defense in this section and Meiklejohn's in the next.

Scanlon, like Mill, argues for the right to free speech on the grounds of its value to individuals. Unlike Mill, however, he does not make considerations of utility the ultimate appeal. Instead, he makes a principle of respect for persons as rational, autonomous beings his ultimate appeal. Accordingly, Scanlon's defense is closer to Kantian ethics than the ethics of utilitarianism. In Kantian ethics, the fundamental principle forbids one from acting toward rational beings in ways that interfere with their freely exercising their rational powers, and Scanlon's principle, the principle he formulates and argues from, is in the spirit of this Kantian principle. On Scanlon's theory, what grounds the right is its facilitation of people's interest in having a government that respects their standing as rational, autonomous beings. Specifically, what grounds it is its making possible people's acceptance of limited government authority in the regulation of their speech consistently with their being treated respectfully as beings whose beliefs and choices are the products of the free exercise of reason. To be treated in this way, to be respected as a rational, autonomous being, while it does not mean that the government never, in the exercise of its authority, places limits on one's freedom to speak, does mean that the government may not impose such limits for the purpose of keeping one from doing harm to oneself that consists either in one's forming certain beliefs or in the consequences of one's determining that certain actions are worth doing. The right thus protects people from having their speech interfered with for this purpose.

As a preliminary to formulating his principle, Scanlon surveys some examples of speech whose legal prohibition is uncontroversial. One is speech whose pitch and volume are so great as to shatter glass. Since property damage is a harm that consists neither in the formation of some belief nor in being the result of concluding that some course of action is worth taking, the government's prohibiting such speech would be consistent with its respecting people as rational, autonomous beings. Having the potential to cause property damage could therefore be the basis for a justified legal limit on speech that could shatter glass. Other examples like speech that defames, speech essential to criminal conspiracies, and assaultive speech amounting to harassment have the same character. So too does speech that mischievously causes a panic, to recall Holmes's famous example of raising a false alarm in a crowded theater, though to see this, Scanlon notes, one must take acting in a panic as an automatism. Because the harm the speech, in each of these examples, causes does not consist in the formation of a belief or the result of one's having concluded that a certain action is worth doing, attempts by the government to prevent such harm are consistent with its respecting people as rational, autonomous beings. Accordingly, Scanlon uses these examples and a few others as guides to formulating the principle he takes to be the chief ground of the right to free speech.

The principle, on Scanlon's formulation of it, is one that excludes certain kinds of harm from the class of harms whose prevention can sometimes justify a legal prohibition on speech. Thus, on this principle, government is justified in enacting a prohibition on speech only if the prohibition is necessary to prevent harm and only if the harm it prevents does not consist in either the formation of a false belief or some harmful consequence of an action done as a result of one's having determined that it was worth doing. While, as Scanlon observes, the principle falls short of yielding a complete theory of freedom of speech, since it gives only necessary conditions for justifying legal prohibitions on speech, we can nonetheless see from this principle that the theory, at its core, takes as the grounds of the right to free speech the need to protect the interests of the recipients of speech in maintaining their standing as rational, autonomous beings when subject to external authority. Like Mill's defense, then, the interests to which the core of Scanlon's theory appeals to ground the right are those of the audience and not those of the speaker and, being interests in having the free exercise of their rational faculties respected, are not advanced by purely emotive speech. Though purely emotive speech can doubtlessly influence belief formation and practical judgment, because it does so by means other than direct engagement of its audience's rational faculties, interference with it is consistent with respecting people as rational, autonomous beings. Consequently, the core of Scanlon's theory too does not yield an understanding of the right on which it protects purely emotive speech.

Meiklejohn's defense of the right, in being an appeal to the value of free speech for people collectively as citizens of a democracy, differs from Mill's and Scanlon's. Meiklejohn makes his argument as part of an interpretation of the U.S. Constitution. The Constitution, he believes, organizes the government of the United States in accordance with the ideal of government by consent of the people. It is an ideal of self-government. To realize this ideal, Meiklejohn argues, the Constitution guarantees certain political rights including, in particular, the First Amendment's right to free speech. The right is necessary in a democracy, for it guarantees open debate among the people on the matters they decide through elections. Without such debate, people's votes would not reflect an informed and deliberative judgment and would therefore fail to be an expression of their collective will as determined by majority rule. Without such debate, elections in a democracy would not, in short, be exercises of self-government.

Meiklejohn presses his interpretive point by comparing the rights guaranteed by the First Amendment with those guaranteed by the due process clause of the Fifth Amendment. He characterizes the latter as personal rights, rights that protect the pursuit of private interests. As such they are subject to lawful abridgment, something that the language of the Fifth Amendment affirms. By contrast, the language of the First Amendment does not imply that the rights it guarantees may be lawfully abridged. To the contrary, regarding the right to free speech, the Amendment declares that Congress shall pass no law abridging this right. Meiklejohn infers from this difference that one must understand the First Amendment's right of free speech as a political rather than a personal right. The reason, he argues, for the Amendment's unqualified protection of free speech from abridgement by Congress is that unfettered speech is essential to the political system the Constitution defines. Self-government would not be possible if Congress could enact laws limiting people's freedom of speech. The basis for the right, then, on Meiklejohn's reading of the Constitution, is not the private interest in self-expression as an element of personal happiness but rather the public interest in full and open debate on the issues that the people decide.

While Meiklejohn develops his argument for the right to free speech through an interpretation of the Constitution, one can extract the argument from the interpretation and consider it separately. Hence, we do not need to be concerned with the merits of his interpretation. One can see the force of the argument, even if his interpretation is unsound. Crudely, the argument is that the right to free speech is necessary in a democracy, for democracy, as a form of self-government, depends on its citizens' making intelligent and informed decisions when they cast their votes. And to be well-informed and to use their knowledge intelligently in making these decisions citizens must be exposed to full and open debate on the issues their votes decide. The right guarantees that such debates can take place. Plainly, then, the right, on Meiklejohn's defense of it, is grounded on its serving the interests of the recipients of speech and not those of speakers. Meiklejohn himself makes this point when, taking the procedures of a town meeting as his model of self-government, he writes, "Now, in that method of political self-government, the point of ultimate interest is not the words of the speakers, but the minds of the hearers. . . . The welfare of the community requires that those who decide issues shall understand them. They must know what they are voting about. . . . As the self-governing community seeks, by the method of voting, to gain wisdom in action, it can find it only in the minds of its individual citizens. If they fail, it fails. That is why freedom of discussion for those minds may not be abridged."[16]

Meiklejohn's defense is, therefore, like Mill's and Scanlon's (at its core) in being a defense that appeals to the interests of the recipients of speech. At the same time, unlike the recipient interests to which Mill and Scanlon appeal, those to which Meiklejohn appeals are the interests the recipients of speech have as citizens of a democracy. Consequently, one cannot immediately infer that purely emotive speech does not serve those interests. The reason is that citizens of a democracy have not only an interest in hearing the full range of views on the issues that their votes decide but also an interest in knowing how strongly those views are held by their supporters. The depth of people's convictions about matters of public policy and how much people care about the outcomes of certain electoral decisions are often important considerations in deciding how one will vote. Thus, one can easily suppose that purely emotive speech serves this second interest, for one can easily suppose that such speech indicates the depth of the speaker's convictions and how much he cares about the matter on which he is speaking. Accordingly, it is easy to conclude that Meiklejohn's defense of the right to free speech supports taking the right as protecting purely emotive speech from government interference, though the protection applies only to purely emotive political speech.[17]

Yet this conclusion, though easy to draw, is mistaken. The expression of strong emotion in speech is not a reliable indicator of how deeply a speaker holds the view he is expressing or how greatly he cares about the outcomes of decisions on the issues on which he is speaking. He may care greatly, of course, but then again he may not. Consider, for instance, words spoken in anger when you have been provoked. Often, such words are instantly regretted. Someone provokes you, and you get angry. You retaliate with words that are meant to hurt, words you do not mean and wish to take back. Your words, in this case, are used as weapons. They are not expressions of views you deeply hold.[18] Or consider, as a second instance, angry words expressed by someone filled with unfocused hostility, someone with a chip on his shoulder, as we say. Hostility colors the attitudes and dispositions this person manifests in the way he conducts his life. Though largely unfocused, the hostility sometimes finds convenient outlets. On these occasions, it becomes focused. Plainly, though, the anger the person displays need not imply any deeply held views about matters he perceives the objects of his anger to have affronted. Nor does it imply that he cares greatly about such matters. His anger may of course indicate that there is something he cares greatly about, but one would have to uncover the source of the hostility that defines his personality to determine what that is. Cohen, after all, might have been such a person. Hence, one cannot infer from the message on his jacket that he greatly cared about ending the draft or that his view on the matter was deeply held. In particular, one cannot infer either proposition from the emotive charge that the word "fuck" gives to his message. His wearing a jacket with this message gives one no reason to believe his opposition to the draft was more strongly held than the opposition to war that others might have expressed by wearing jackets bearing messages that lacked such words, messages like "Peace Now" or "Make Love Not War," to take two popular slogans from that era.

Having seen, then, that the defenses of the right to free speech that appeal to the audience's interests do not support taking the right as protecting purely emotive speech, let us turn to defenses that appeal to the interests of speakers. Do any of them support taking the right as protecting purely emotive speech? Scanlon's wider theory of free speech makes such an appeal, though the appeal is limited to the right to freedom of political speech. Scanlon adds this appeal to his theory because the principle at the theory's core is insufficient for protecting speech from government interference in cases that the right has traditionally covered. One such case is government prohibition of marches on public streets because of the disruption to traffic, commercial trade, and daily life generally that such events would cause. In this case, the government would not be violating the core principle of Scanlon's theory, yet it could still be preventing speech that traditionally the right has protected. For example, a municipal government would be violating the right to free speech that the members of unpopular groups had if it prohibited marches by such groups on the grounds that their marches were more expensive to police than those, which it routinely permits, held by groups that enjoy broad public support. Hence, Scanlon sees the need to widen his theory so as to account for the traditional protection the right to free speech provides in this and similar examples. Accordingly, he appeals to the interests of speakers in participating in their country's political process as grounding this protection. "Access to means of expression is in many cases a necessary condition for participation in the political process of the country, and therefore something to which citizens have an independent right."[19]

Scanlon bases his appeal to the interests of speakers in participating in their country's political process on the high value of political speech in a democracy. Its value is such, Scanlon argues, as to give its protection priority over other values like public convenience. But since he could use Mill's or Meiklejohn's defense to explain why political speech has such value, its having such value does not necessarily derive from the interests of speakers in participating in the political process of their country. Scanlon's appeal to these interests is therefore unsupported in his theory. At bottom, he merely appeals to what he sees as an *intuitively* attractive basis for the right.

Undoubtedly, the right to participate in the political process of one's country is based at least partly on the interests people have in being able to protect their interests generally through participating in that process. The question, though, is whether the right comprises more than the right to vote and the political rights collateral to it, such as the rights to stand for elective office and to serve on juries. These rights guarantee that no citizen is denied the opportunity of having his interests taken into account in the political decisions that affect his life. But whether the right to participate in the political process of one's country includes more is still an open question. Scanlon thinks it does. Meiklejohn, by contrast, does not, or at least he does not think that it includes the right to make one's own case for promoting one's interests. Meiklehjohn thinks it is necessary that someone make that case, but that someone need not be the very person for whose interests the case is made. In a traditional town meeting, Meiklejohn observes, taking such meetings as the model of self-government, every view on the matter under discussion must be heard, but not every citizen present must be given the opportunity to speak. Citizens who would only repeat what the town council has already heard are routinely excluded from speaking. Such limits on debate are necessary for timely decision making and endurable meetings and are thus understood as consistent with each citizen's right to participate in the town's democratic processes.

Fortunately, we do not need to resolve this disagreement between Scanlon and Meiklejohn to move forward. We do not, that is, need to determine whether democratic decision making requires that each citizen be allowed to make his or her own case for his interests or only that the case be heard. There is a different, much older argument for taking the right to freedom of political speech to be based on the interests citizens have in participating in the political processes of their country. We can consider this argument instead. It appears in Plato's *Crito*. In the speech that the Laws of Athens deliver near the end of the dialogue, the Laws reprove Socrates for considering whether to escape his punishment and so disobey the Athenian assembly that lawfully convicted and sentenced him. The Laws insist on obedience from Socrates, though they do not declare that obedience to law is an unconditional requirement of citizenship. Rather they say that each citizen is required to obey the laws of the city if he has not persuaded the city of their injustice.[20]

Clearly, one implication of this statement is that because citizens are liable to sanctions for disobedience to law, because the city enforces its laws coercively, fairness requires that each citizen have the opportunity to argue against any law he opposes. No one, so the argument goes, whom the city, by virtue of the laws it enacts, places in jeopardy of loss of life, liberty, or property for noncompliance should be so placed without first having the opportunity to persuade his fellow citizens not to enact laws with which he disagrees. Fairness, in other words, requires that the city not impose burdens of obedience on its citizens without their having a voice in that imposition, and that voice must include speaking as well as voting. Hence, by invoking this principle of fairness, one can defend the right to free speech in a democracy on the grounds that each citizen has an interest in being able to persuade his fellow citizens to take his view on the issues they ultimately decide.[21] The defense, therefore, is one that appeals to the interests of speakers.

Let us now consider whether the right, on this defense, protects purely emotive speech. Whether it does depends on what counts as giving each citizen a fair opportunity to persuade his fellow citizens to take his view on the issues they ultimately decide. On one view, the opportunity that fairness requires is the opportunity to reason with one's fellow citizens about the issues being debated. Such persuasion excludes demagoguery. On this view, then, fairness is given narrow scope, so the right does not protect purely emotive speech. Alternatively, fairness may be given wide scope. Accordingly, the right is not limited in any way that unfairly puts some people at a disadvantage in their efforts to persuade their fellow citizens to take their view. In particular, the right does not disfavor inarticulate or poorly educated citizens, and arguably, to exclude purely emotive speech from its protection is liable to do just that.[22]

We can thus draw from the speech that the Laws of Athens make in the *Crito* a defense of the right to free speech on which the right protects purely emotive speech. The success of this defense, however, is still uncertain. For it depends on the scope of the requirement of fairness it invokes, and how one determines its scope is open to dispute. More important, though, is that the defense offers grounds for a right to free speech that covers only political speech. It is in this respect like Meiklejohn's defense. Consequently, the purely emotive speech that the right, on this defense, protects is purely emotive political speech. Cohen's speech would therefore be protected. But purely emotive speech that lies outside of the political sphere would not. The racist and homophobic chanting at soccer games, for instance, that were recently prosecuted in Britain under the Football Offences Act of 1991 would not be protected.[23] Nor would slurs and vulgarities on public message boards and in Internet chat rooms that are directed at private individuals. Vituperative language meant to express loathing and disdain for certain people and to expose them to denigration and scorn, though it no doubt serves the interests of speakers in expressing themselves as they wish, does not serve the interests of speakers as citizens of a democracy to which this defense appeals.

We need, finally, to consider whether there is a defense of the right to free speech that appeals to the interests of speakers outside of their interests as citizens of a democracy. Is there such a defense on which the right would be understood as protecting purely emotive speech? Ronald Dworkin has given one in his essay "Why Must Speech Be Free?"[24] It will be useful, in concluding our study, to see why Dworkin's defense and others like it are bound to fail.

Dworkin's argument turns on a distinction he makes between instrumental and constitutive justifications of the right to free speech. Instrumental justifications appeal to the "good effects" the right has for democracy, society, or all of humankind. Constitutive justifications appeal to an essential feature of a just political society: in such a society "government treat[s] all [the] adult members, except those who are incompetent, as responsible moral agents."[25] Dworkin thinks only constitutive justifications provide adequate support for taking the First Amendment right to free speech as protecting all speech. Instrumental justifications, he argues, are too "fragile" and "limited."[26] The essential feature to which constitutive justifications appeal entails, says Dworkin, two conditions on a political society's being just. First, the members must be free to make up their own minds about what to believe and what to take as a good reason for action. In this respect, constitutive justifications correspond to the principle at the core of Scanlon's theory. Second, the members must be free to express their opinions, convictions, social attitudes, and tastes. To be treated as responsible moral agents, they must have as much right "to contribute to the formation of the [society's] moral or aesthetic climate as they do to participate in politics."[27] Clearly, the first condition, being equivalent to the principle at the core of Scanlon's theory, does not support understanding the right to free speech as protecting purely emotive speech. It is the second condition that provides that support. Moreover, on the understanding it supports, the protection the right gives is not restricted to political speech.

This second condition, however, is bizarre. One might even say "Orwellian." To be a responsible moral agent is to be an agent who is morally responsible for his actions. And to be morally responsible for one's actions primarily means that one is rightly held accountable for them when one injures others or invades their rights. Accordingly, a politically just society treats competent adult human beings as responsible moral agents by holding them accountable for actions that injure others or invade others' rights.[28] It does not hold small children or incompetent adults accountable for such offenses, for neither are morally responsible agents. Society holds people accountable for their actions by making them liable to sanctions for the injuries and invasions that their actions cause. And this is true whether it is speech that causes the injury or invasion or some other kind of action. One is no less responsible for injury one causes by verbally abusing someone than for injury one causes by battering him. Dworkin's view, then, that a just society treats its members as morally responsible agents by granting them protection from government interference with their expressions of opinion, conviction, attitudes, and tastes is confused. It amounts to saying that a just society treats people as morally responsible agents by not holding them accountable for their actions even when those actions injure others or invade their rights.

Dworkin, to support his thesis that the right to free speech protects speech that expresses attitudes and tastes in matters beyond politics, appeals to the right to contribute to the formation of one's society's moral and aesthetic climate. But this right, if it exists, is surely too weak to provide any greater protection from government interference with speech than a general right to liberty like that recognized in the Fifth and Fourteenth Amendments.[29] The reason is clear. An action that seriously injures others or invades their rights does not gain protection from government interference merely by being an attempt to influence one's society's moral or aesthetic climate. Surely the government may prohibit setting off fireworks in residential neighborhoods, say, despite the contribution to the aesthetic climate that fireworks displays make. On any sensible view of a government's police powers, the injuries to innocent bystanders risked by letting amateurs set off fireworks in crowded neighborhoods make such prohibitions justifiable. Thus, while people are entitled to protection from their government's *arbitrarily* interfering with their efforts to change the aesthetic or moral climate by means other than speech, those efforts are surely open to government regulation when they risk harm to others.

And the same point applies when their efforts consist in purely emotive speech.

Dworkin's appeal to a right to contribute to the formation of one's society's moral and aesthetic values therefore fails to bring purely emotive speech within the scope of the right to free speech. Indeed, the appeal's implausibility suggests that Dworkin has discounted the injuries and invasions people can suffer when they become the objects of expressions of hatred and contempt. His view, then, may represent an all-too-common blindness to the issue such speech raises. To see it graphically, one need only consider the example described in several of the chapters in this volume of the two women law students who suffered severe emotional distress and egregious invasions of privacy as the result of being made, seemingly without cause, the targets of many vicious, misogynistic postings on a website whose owners allowed these anonymous postings to go on for weeks.[30]

In *Cohen,* Justice Blackmun, answering Harlan's majority opinion, wrote a dissent, which three other justices joined. Blackmun did not think Cohen's speech qualified as speech deserving First Amendment protection. At the same time, he did not think the California courts had given proper consideration to whether Cohen's behavior was sufficiently disruptive to warrant conviction for violating the part of the state's penal code prohibiting malicious disturbance of the peace. He argued for remanding the case back to the state court that had jurisdiction for reconsideration, especially in light of the California Supreme Court's subsequent clarification of this part of the penal code. Blackmun's dissent, I believe, is truer to the understanding of the right to free speech reflected in the leading philosophical defenses of that right.

PART IV

Privacy

CHAPTER 12

Collective Privacy

LIOR JACOB STRAHILEVITZ

Collective action problems arise in privacy law where a single source of confidential information reveals something about multiple individuals, and these people disagree over whether the information should be disseminated. Such collective action problems are all around us. Perhaps the most familiar contemporary example is Facebook "tagging." Multitudes of Facebook users post photographs of themselves with relatives, friends, and acquaintances, and then provide a caption in which the other pictured individuals are tagged (i.e., named in metadata and on-screen). Depending on the privacy settings chosen by Facebook users, the photographs may then show up on the tagged individuals' Facebook pages as well as those individuals' friends' Facebook pages, and they often become a source of embarrassment.[1] For example, the newly nominated chief of MI6, the British central intelligence agency, was tagged in photos on his wife's Facebook page playing Frisbee and wearing short swimming trunks at the beach.[2] Also pictured were the spy chief's children, parents, and friends, in a series of snapshots that could be seen by any member of the general public. Members of Parliament fumed that the country had spent significant taxpayer money to protect the identity of Sir John Sawyers and his family, but these efforts had been compromised thanks to his spouse's Facebook activity (and subsequent tabloid coverage). Privacy has always been interdependent, but the dangers posed by its interdependence are magnified in the information age.

A recent case from the U.S. Court of Appeals for the Second Circuit starkly illustrates some of the thorny legal issues that can stem from privacy collective action problems. In Associated Press v. United States Department of Defense, the court tried to figure out what to do when a news organization requested the identities of detainees who alleged that they had been abused at Guantanamo Bay, Cuba. The government preferred to keep this list a secret. We know that some of the detainees wanted their identities publicized, and we can presume that other detainees (and their relatives) did not. The controversial question before the court was "what should result from this dissensus?"

This essay examines the issues raised by *Associated Press,* as well as another controversial case called Doe v. Quiring. In *Quiring,* South Dakota wanted to publicize on the Internet private information about a man who had been convicted of incest, but the victim of the crime asked the state not to publish such information, based on a reasonable belief that if her father were identified as an incest perpetrator it would be easy for the public to identify her as an incest victim.

In each case, the government got what it wanted. The Department of Defense (DOD) thwarted the Associated Press's (AP's) efforts to obtain the identities of even those Guantanamo detainees who wished to be identified. And South Dakota convinced the courts to let it identify Doe's father as an incest perpetrator, rather than a generic sex offender, as she had requested. I submit that the respective governments should have lost each case. Both pitted important privacy concerns against significant disclosure concerns, but the collective action problems were soluble via reliance on the express consent of the affected individuals.

The *Associated Press* court did not cite *Quiring,* and neither side in *Associated Press* even brought the prior case to the court's attention. That oversight is not surprising. The decisions of the South Dakota Supreme Court obviously do not bind the Second Circuit. Moreover, the former case raised a legal question concerning the Freedom of Information Act's interpretation and the latter case required the court to determine the meaning of South Dakota's Megan's Law statute. But the disconnect between the two opinions should disturb us still. The fragmentation of privacy law routinely results in conceptual incoherence. Given that the same sorts of privacy collective action problems arise in the context of the Freedom of Information Act and Megan's Law, to say nothing of the Fourth Amendment to the U.S. Constitution, privacy tort law, and other important privacy regimes, there is quite a lot to be gained from using a comparative lens to figure out how these sorts of problems ought to be solved. Considering privacy law holistically can improve the content of each of privacy law's parts. To that end, this essay both develops a framework for thinking about, and sometimes solving, recurring collective action problems in privacy law, and begins a larger scholarly project advocating the reunification of information privacy law.

Consent in Privacy Law

Although information privacy law is deeply and unnecessarily fragmented, there are a few blanket statements that can be made about the body of law. One of these is that if an individual validly consents to the widespread dissemination of her previously private information, the information at issue is no longer private. For example, if someone blogs about his medical condition or sexual hang-ups, he cannot complain when others freely discuss what he has voluntarily disclosed, even if he subsequently regrets his earlier statements. This rule is as applicable in the privacy tort setting as it is in the Fourth Amendment search and seizure context.[3]

Why should the unambiguous consent of the individual to the publication of previously private information prove decisive? The most attractive answer to this question stems from an intuition that the question of what sorts of information ought to be made public is a difficult one, and that the individual herself typically will be in a better position than the government to identify the circumstances under which disclosure is appropriate.[4] Although there are individuals who will disclose facts about themselves that make their friends and relatives wince or blush, the law expresses discomfort with paternalistic restrictions on what individuals might say. To be sure, some scholars have argued forcefully that privacy ought to protect individuals against their own wrongheaded or shortsighted decisions, but these arguments should not carry the day in most settings.[5] The law does create categories where people are deemed incapable of consent. The consent of children, intoxicated adults, and people with severe mental disabilities, for example, is not a decisive waiver of their privacy rights because we have reason to believe that in these contexts the state's agents will make better decisions about what information should remain private than the individuals whose information is at issue.

Setting aside special cases like the legal disabilities discussed above, the law's deference to individual consent is appropriate. Just as there are costs to protecting privacy too little, there will be costs from protecting privacy too much. Excessive privacy protection may chill speech in ways that conflict with important First Amendment values. Inordinately severe limitations on individuals' disclosure of information about themselves will hinder intimacy and the formation of friendships. Unduly strict limitations on the voluntary disclosure of information about one's self may exacerbate the problems of discrimination on the basis of immutable characteristics.[6] While there are certainly harms that can arise in the context of voluntary disclosures of information, and some contexts in which individual decisions about privacy may be optimal for them but not for society as a whole, "give people all the privacy they want, and no more" is likely the least problematic rule available to imperfect people and institutions.

Our consideration of consent so far has assumed a solitary actor with a choice about whether to reveal information about himself. Now suppose that multiple people possess a privacy interest in the same information. Whose consent should be required?

That was essentially the issue confronting the Supreme Court in Georgia v. Randolph.[7] In that case, Scott Randolph shared a home with his wife, Janet. The estranged couple was involved in a dispute over their child, and Janet called the police to their home. Shortly after their arrival, Janet told the police that her husband was a cocaine user and that there was drug paraphernalia in the house. The police requested permission to search the Randolph home. Janet immediately consented and Scott contemporaneously and unequivocally refused consent. The police searched the dwelling, found a drinking straw with cocaine on it in Scott's bedroom, and indicted Scott for possession of cocaine. He moved to suppress the evidence. The Supreme Court held that "a warrantless search of a shared dwelling for evidence over the express refusal of consent by a physically present resident cannot be justified as reasonable as to him on the basis of consent given to the police by another resident."[8]

In the process of invalidating the search, the Court admitted that it was creating a fine line between permissible and impermissible police conduct. An earlier Supreme Court decision, Rodriguez v. Illinois,[9] had held that the consent of an apparent cotenant was sufficient to authorize the search, even when the consent of another tenant, who was asleep inside the apartment, was neither solicited nor obtained. In explaining the divergent results, the Court was attuned to the practicalities of police searching and the burdens that the Fourth Amendment might place on law enforcement:

> For the very reason that *Rodriguez* held it would be unjustifiably impractical to require the police to take affirmative steps to confirm the actual authority of a consenting individual whose authority was apparent, we

think it would needlessly limit the capacity of the police to respond to ostensibly legitimate opportunities in the field if we were to hold that reasonableness required the police to take affirmative steps to find a potentially objecting co-tenant before acting on the permission they had already received.[10]

Pragmatic considerations, not first principles, would resolve this problem of consent, at least in the majority's view. The justices in the majority wanted to require unanimous consent where the lack of such unanimity was easy to discern by the police. The *Randolph* dissenters, however, favored a bright-line rule for these cases: the decision to cohabit meant assuming the risk that one cotenant would waive the other's Fourth Amendment privacy rights.[11] The dissenters arrived at this conclusion because they feared the majority's path would yield indeterminate rules across a range of outcomes: for example, what if a supermajority of cotenants consented to a search? As Chief Justice Roberts wrote, "the possible scenarios are limitless, and slight variations in the fact pattern yield vastly different expectations. . . . Such shifting expectations are not a promising foundation on which to ground a constitutional rule."[12]

Strikingly, none of the justices advocated a straightforward and obvious alternative approach: in the event of a conflict, Janet could authorize a search of her quasi-private spaces in the home (e.g., her bedroom, her closet) but she could not authorize a search of Scott's bedroom, where the incriminating evidence was found. Such an approach, which we will call *constructive partition,* resolves a collective privacy problem by fragmenting the collective resource into interests controlled by discrete individuals. The partition might provide imperfect protection when privacy interests are inextricably comingled: Scott could have revealing photographs of Janet in his bedroom, but he might have them in his office at work too, and she would have no legal standing to prevent the police from finding them there.

Perhaps this intuitive constructive partition solution did not appeal to the justices because as a formal matter, Janet and Scott were cotenants who shared ownership of every square inch of the home itself. But informal arrangements and expectations often inform reasonable expectations of privacy. Just as Scott might have been surprised and dismayed had Janet searched through the drawers of his bedroom desk over his objections, he might have had a legitimate expectation that the police would not do so without his consent.

The Freedom of Information Act's Privacy Exceptionalism

In 1966, Congress enacted the Freedom of Information Act (FOIA) to help make available to the citizenry information about the performance of its government. The act, with certain exceptions, enables citizens to request information that federal agencies possess so that they can learn "what their government is up to."[13] Given that federal agencies have a great deal of sensitive information about individuals, Congress exempted from disclosure information whose dissemination "would constitute a clearly unwarranted invasion of personal privacy."[14] Another FOIA provision specifically exempted from disclosure "records or information compiled for law enforcement purposes, but only to the extent that the production of such law enforcement records or information . . . could reasonably be expected to constitute an unwarranted invasion of personal privacy."[15]

FOIA's reference to an "unwarranted invasion of personal privacy" in the statutory language might have indicated congressional intent to have the statute's privacy provisions piggyback on the substantive protections offered by privacy tort law. Several state courts seeking to understand the scope of "personal privacy" under their state freedom of information acts have so held.[16] Nevertheless, the Supreme Court was quick to take FOIA privacy law in a different direction. In its landmark United States Department of Justice v. Reporters Committee for Freedom of the Press case, the Court noted that the disclosure of a compilation of rap sheet information culled from public records could reasonably be expected to constitute an "unwarranted invasion of personal privacy" under FOIA even though a private actor who compiled such information would be immune from liability under tort law and the First Amendment. In a footnote, the Court stated: "The question of the statutory meaning of privacy under the FOIA is, of course, not the same as the question whether a tort action might lie for invasion of privacy or the question whether an individual's interest in privacy is protected by the Constitution."[17]

This "convenient" bit of dicta prompted a sensible reaction of "Why not?" from one commentator, who observed that in the same year the Supreme Court was holding that FOIA's privacy provisions prevented the government from disclosing the rap sheet of an ex-con defense contractor who had close dealings with a corrupt congressman, a Florida statute prohibiting the publication of a rape victim's identity was deemed unconstitutional on First Amendment grounds.[18] The criminal background of the contractor in *Reporters Committee* was certainly of greater interest to the public than the identity of a private figure rape victim in Florida Star v. B. J. F., as evidenced by the Florida newspaper's admission that it had only published the rape victim's identity via an accidental breach of its own policies.

Although an act-omission distinction perhaps explains why privacy prevailed in *Reporters Committee* but not in *Florida Star,* the distinction should not prove decisive. The Supreme Court has held that state laws imposing defamation liability on newspapers implicate the First Amendment by raising the costs of news reporting in ways that will reduce the flow of information to the public.[19] By the same token, the government's refusal to share information it had already aggregated with CBS news reporters pursuing an important story rendered it less likely that newsworthy information would be shared with the public.

A second significant way in which FOIA privacy law has deviated from privacy tort law is its protection of familial privacy rights. The common law rule is quite clear with respect to privacy tort causes of action: dead men have no privacy rights.[20] In contrast to almost all other tort claims, any cause of action for tortious invasion of privacy dies along with the would-be plaintiff. Under FOIA, however, the Supreme Court has expanded the scope of privacy protections. In its recent National Archives and Records Administration v. Favish case, the Court held that the death of Vince Foster did not mean that there was no longer a "personal privacy" interest in images of his dead body, taken after Foster shot himself in a public park. The Court noted that for the purposes of privacy law, his relatives possessed a strong privacy interest in those images, both on dignitary grounds, and because the disclosure of the photographs in response to a FOIA request might subject Foster's next of kin to harassment or the risk of unwilling exposure to the images.[21]

The *Favish* opinion is ambiguous on the question of whether familial privacy interests arise only upon the death of the person whose private facts are at issue. One can read the opinion as a narrow holding that next of kin have privacy interests in images of their deceased relative. Alternatively, one can read the opinion to suggest that relatives would have a personal privacy interest in information that concerns a loved one during their relative's life. Some lower court opinions since *Favish* have hinted that familial privacy interests may arise for the purposes of FOIA even while the individuals whose information is at issue remain alive.[22]

There are other areas in which FOIA privacy deviates from tort privacy, but these two differences—the tendency of FOIA cases to protect privacy interests forcefully and speech interests weakly, and FOIA's recognition of posthumous familial privacy interests—are the nub of the legal problem in a case like *Associated Press.*

In late 2004 and early 2005, the AP was investigating the treatment of detainees at the military detention facility at Guantanamo Bay. Pursuant to that investigation, the AP made a series of FOIA requests for information concerning the identities of Guantanamo inmates who had alleged mistreatment. The DOD provided the AP with responses to the FOIA request that redacted the names of all Guantanamo detainees.[23]

The DOD probably had little inherent concern for the personal privacy of the Guantanamo detainees. Its real motivation for withholding the information likely stemmed from political considerations. Of course, a public relations calculus provides no statutory basis for resisting FOIA requests. As the litigation progressed, the personal privacy of the detainees and their relatives would provide the only colorable legal basis for the government's refusal to provide the AP with the information it was seeking. But even if the government's invocation of FOIA's privacy exception was entirely pretextual, it does not follow that the AP should have won the case. In enacting the statute and its enumerated justifications for resisting a FOIA request, Congress likely anticipated that personal privacy interests would be most fully vindicated if the executive branch could invoke those interests in cases where they really explained the government's reluctance to disclose documents (e.g., private information concerning federal employees), as well as instances in which the invoked privacy interest was a fig leaf (e.g., the privacy rights of suspected terrorists). The statute enables only the government, and not the individuals whose privacy is at issue, to resist a FOIA request. Congress therefore might have wanted the personal privacy interests of even those groups disfavored by the executive to be protected by FOIA, and the law's structure gave the DOD strong incentives to think hard about the privacy implications of the AP's request.

With one important exception, discussed below, the district court ruled against the department on all the contested issues. The court observed that many of the detainees whose identities were redacted had "participated in hunger strikes to protest alleged abuse," three had collaborated to produce a 115-page report alleging mistreatment, and others had sought to publicize their mistreatment via their attorneys.[24] To the district court, these episodes suggested that the detainees "have not hesitated to reveal their identities." The court went further, reasoning that "most people in such a situation—especially individuals detained incommunicado without many procedural safeguards—would want their plights, and identities, publicized."[25]

The government won in the lower court with respect to only one disclosure request, which involved a letter written by the wife of a detainee to her husband. The husband had reluctantly disclosed the letter to the Administrative Review Board in an effort to secure his release. Evidently, the letter was used to buttress the detainee's assertions that he held strongly negative attitudes toward the Taliban. The district court concluded that notwithstanding the husband's disclosure of this letter, she retained a reasonable expectation of privacy in its contents, enabling the government to redact her identity in light of the dangers she might face from pro-Taliban extremists.

The court of appeals reversed. The court characterized the detainees' interest in disclosure as "somewhat speculative" in light of the "limited number of detainees who have opted to come forward."[26] It offered a conflicting intuition that the disclosure of the detainees' names "could certainly subject them to embarrassment and humiliation." Of course, in an instance where some of the detainees wanted their identities disclosed and others did not, an obvious constructive partition solution is available: permit the government to disclose the identities of those detainees who are willing to opt in to disclosure. Sadiq Reza has advocated precisely such an approach.[27]

Reza's approach to the case has genuine appeal, though it is not without drawbacks: a rule tailored to individual inmates will be more cumbersome and costly for agencies to administer. In *Randolph* terms, some of the detainees may be asleep in another room, not objecting loudly at the vestibule. While this concern is mitigated in the case of detainees who are in federal custody, the costs of determining whether the inmates' relatives and other correspondents consent to the release of information would be quite high. The same is true for former inmates. Moreover, individuals in custody might feel pressured to withhold consent to disclosure based on a desire to win favors from their captors. These difficult issues were briefed and argued by the government and the AP. The government's argument was particularly forceful in light of the Supreme Court's previous support for applying categorical rules that forestall individuated inquiries in FOIA privacy contexts. For example, in the aforementioned *Reporters Committee* case, the

Court held that rap sheets were per se immune from disclosure in response to FOIA requests, rejecting a standard tailored to the nature of the request and the particularities of the person whose information was being sought.

The Second Circuit responded to these serious arguments with make-believe. The court began auspiciously enough, observing that the "first question to ask in determining whether [FOIA] Exemption 7(C) applies is whether there is any privacy interest in the information sought." This sentence was immediately followed by a footnote, which is where things went south quickly. It reads as follows:

> In *Reporters Committee*, the Supreme Court held, "as a categorical matter that a third party's request for law enforcement records or information about a private citizen can reasonably be expected to invade that citizen's privacy." The Court reasoned that "categorical decisions may be appropriate and individual circumstances disregarded when a case fits into a genus in which the balance characteristically tips in one direction." DOD argues that the privacy interests at stake here are readily assessed on a categorical basis. The AP counters that individualized consideration of those interests is appropriate. We are cognizant of the Supreme Court's holding in *Reporters Committee*. However, because our disposition of this appeal would be the same regardless of how we considered the privacy interest accommodated in Exemptions 7 and 6 for those persons whose information may be disclosed here, we do not need to decide whether we must analyze them categorically or individually.[28]

This paragraph is deeply wrong. Recall that the Second Circuit held that the government could withhold the identities of all the detainees under FOIA's privacy exemptions, while conceding that some of the detainees wished to make their identities public. In light of those two facts, there was no intellectually coherent way for the court to dodge the question of whether FOIA's privacy protections should be analyzed categorically or individually with respect to detainees. A categorical approach necessarily would result in complete disclosure or nondisclosure, whereas an individuated approach—constructive partition of the list of detainees—necessarily would result in partial disclosure. By ruling in favor of complete nondisclosure, the court had to embrace a categorical basis for deciding the issue, its protests to the contrary notwithstanding.

As the court saw it, the fact that some detainees wanted their identities disclosed was irrelevant. Moreover, under the court's holding, and its categorical-though-ostensibly-not-categorical approach, the objections of one privacy-seeking detainee would trump the desires of scores of other publicity-seeking detainees.

Such a unanimity rule creates problems akin to the "tragedy of the anti-commons" that Michael Heller has identified in property and intellectual property. Heller famously noted the contrast between post-Soviet Russia's thriving commercial kiosks and its empty storefronts. The storefronts were empty because opening a shop there required permit approvals from count-less bureaucrats and other stakeholders, but an entrepreneur needed only to buy off a couple of local government officials and the neighborhood mafia to start up a new sidewalk kiosk.[29] As this tragedy plays out, a resource does not get used efficiently because every individual is legally entitled to block an efficient use, and none of the other interested parties have the authority to "green light" the socially desirable use of a communal good. The same dynamic played out in *Associated Press*, with the names of the de-tainees as the valuable resource that nobody got to use.

In a better-reasoned section of the *Associated Press* opinion, the court noted that it was not oblivious to the danger that an anticommons problem might arise as a result of its FOIA privacy ruling. The court noted that it did "not mean to suggest that detainees should be prevented in any way from coming forward publicly with allegations of mistreatment or abuse at the hands of DOD in Guantanamo; this opinion does not empower the govern-ment to prevent such public disclosure by the detainees themselves based on this recognized privacy interest."[30] Of course, as Reza noted, the detainees were long deprived of access to counsel, contact with relatives, and oppor-tunities to bring their plight to the attention of the outside world.[31] But since the Supreme Court's decisions in Boumediene v. Bush, Hamdan v. Rumsfeld, and Rasul v. Bush, the legal rights available to Guantanamo detainees have increased substantially, and there are stronger reasons to believe that FOIA might not be the only mechanism for the public to learn the identities of those who would wish to have that information made public.[32]

If one supposes that detainees with an interest in publicizing their iden-tities now have alternative channels to communicate with the public, then the question arises as to whether there is any additional public interest served by FOIA disclosure. Three arguments spring to mind. First, the dif-ference in mechanisms for disseminating identities implicates an opt-in versus opt-out issue. As a large literature on privacy already demonstrates, defaults are quite sticky.[33] Protecting the privacy of only consumers who opt in to heightened privacy protections will result in a much lower level of privacy rights than a regime that requires consumers to opt out of heightened protection. Presumably, the FOIA privacy regime that Reza has in mind would require detainees to opt in to privacy or eliminate any default option and force detainees to choose privacy or publicity, with the result being that the press (and public) will have access to a more complete picture of the identities and characteristics of the Guantanamo detainees.

Second, in any coercive setting, let alone Gitmo, there is a significant danger that detainees will feel pressured to conform their privacy preferences to the views perceived to be more welcome among their captors. A system of aggregating information about detainees where the press, rather than the inmates themselves, must take the first step toward publicizing identities could give inmates greater freedom to make choices that reflect their autonomous preferences. Of course, a system of compelled disclosure would fare better on this score, in that inmates would have no choice but to publicize their identities, and thus they could not be subjected to retaliation or pressure from their captors stemming from that publication. This argument, combined with an empirical hunch that most inmates would want their identities revealed, provides the most plausible case for affirming the district court's judgment. But if the Second Circuit's conflicting empirical intuitions were closer to the mark, then a forced choice regime in response to FOIA requests might best balance the competing expressive, monitoring, and privacy interests.

Third, permitting information concerning the identities of detainees to be disclosed in response to a FOIA request, rather than via the affirmative actions of the detainees themselves, may provide aggregation benefits to the media, facilitating the efficient transmission of information to the public. A FOIA response typically has the advantage of containing an aggregated list that is disclosed at one time. By contrast, voluntary disclosures by detainees themselves may trickle out over time, and information dissemination may occur via a multitude of mediums. There are reasons to favor simultaneous and aggregated disclosures. Sometimes a pattern regarding the detainees, which may reveal aspects of government policy, is not evident unless a large data set can be analyzed. The sum of the whole may reveal more than the sum of the parts. Moreover, although journalists can and do aggregate information that has been disclosed in a disaggregated form, doing so is a costly enterprise. As the costs of aggregating information increase, the probability that the media will incur these costs (and report on a particular story) decline. If the media can free-ride on the aggregation work that the government is peculiarly well suited to conduct, the press can pass the savings on to the public.

The Second Circuit dismissed the benefits of facilitating news reporting by the AP, observing that the only benefit they could see from disclosing some of the requested information was providing "AP with leads for investigating the detainees' claims."[34] To the court, this sort of interest did not square with the purpose of FOIA: "inform[ing] the citizens about 'what the government is up to.'" Absent direct evidence of government misconduct, the court saw no justification for denying the government's request for redaction. Bizarrely, the court did not consider allegations that the government may have tortured detainees at Guantanamo to be potential government misconduct.[35] The court instead focused on the absence of evidence to show, say, that the DOD had responded to allegations of abuse in a discriminatory manner, treating people differently based on their religion or national origin.

The court's analysis misconceives the nature of FOIA. FOIA requests are not exclusively a tool of "gotcha journalism." They can be used by the press to document good or bad government performance. If a citizen hopes to use FOIA to show that a government program is well designed and well managed, this motivation does not excuse the government's burden of disclosing information in response to the request. The *Favish* court was properly skeptical of Mr. Favish's request for photographs of Vince Foster's dead body in light of the fact that five separate and independent investigations into his death had all concluded that Foster's death was a suicide, not the result of a nefarious government conspiracy and cover-up. The treatment of detainees at Guantanamo was, at the time of the AP's request, subject to much greater uncertainty and debate.

In short, there are good reasons to believe that the public interest is well served by requiring the government to produce aggregated information about individuals even in a context where those same individuals can reveal duplicative information about themselves through voluntary actions. These concerns become particularly pronounced in settings where these individuals are incarcerated.

Recall that the district court in *Associated Press* also wrestled with the issue of whether detainees' family members had a FOIA privacy interest in administrative board review documents that identified these relatives. The district court concluded that redaction of the relatives' names was warranted where a detainee professed disdain for the Taliban but redaction was not warranted where a detainee's attitudes toward the Taliban were harder to discern, and the potential threat to his relatives from retaliation was therefore more speculative. The appellate court viewed disclosure as inappropriate in both instances—family members' identities and addresses might be the sort of information "that a person would ordinarily not wish to make known about himself or herself" and disclosure would not help "reveal what the government is up to."[36]

Note that under a broad reading of *Favish*, the consent of the detainees to have their names disclosed would not be decisive. The disclosure of detainees' identities quite plausibly could expose their relatives to violent retaliation even if the names and addresses of the relatives were unknown to the government. Disclosing the identities of the detainees themselves would enable extremists with local knowledge to identify and target detainees' relatives living abroad. It is therefore plausible to read Supreme Court case law as conferring upon the government a broad right to block the disclosure of private information based upon the privacy interests of someone other than the individuals whose information is at issue. Under such an approach, the fragmentation of privacy interests provides the government with a broad excuse to withhold data. If even one third party might object to the disclosure of the information, redaction would be permissible. Constructive partition stops being practical when so many people might assert an interest in the private information.

The anticommons tragedy of empty stores and vibrant kiosks has arisen in various settings in which the nonconsent of one of a number of stakeholders can prevent a socially desirable outcome. For example, even where an individual has issued unambiguous advance directives that his organs be used for transplantation upon his demise, hospital administrators commonly refuse to harvest organs if even one of the decedent's next of kin objects to such a procedure.[37] The social harm from a privacy anticommons would be too much privacy. This result seems relatively harmless compared with analogues like too many transplantable organs going to waste or too little innovation in biomedicine. But recall that the reasons why we defer to an individual's choices about what to make public largely underscore the dangers of excessive privacy protections. Privacy competes with other important values, like expressive interests, the need for robust public debate, and nondiscrimination imperatives. In the FOIA context, letting the government withhold information from credible journalistic entities like the AP necessarily deprived the public of information concerning a controversy that would become the subject of significant political debate. Privacy may be an important enough reason to keep this information out of the public's hands, but if privacy interests become too fragmented, public discourse will suffer.

This basic issue—what to do if an individual would like to disclose information about himself that necessarily implicates the privacy of a third party—is not a new one in privacy law. The leading precedent is Haynes v. Alfred A. Knopf.[38] Judge Posner, writing for the Seventh Circuit, astutely noted that if Ruby Daniels, a Chicagoan who was part of the Great Migration and endured an unhappy marriage as well as other tribulations, could not disclose private facts about her ex-husband, then she could not tell her own story: if the defendant "cannot tell the story of Ruby Daniels without waivers from every person who she thinks did her wrong, he cannot write this book."[39]

Judge Posner's analysis does not deny the significant privacy harm that can come from the publication of a kiss-and-tell memoir. Rather, it recognizes that if two participants in an interaction have conflicting views about its private or public nature, the views of each party deserve significant weight. In cases where there was an explicit or implicit meeting of the minds regarding the permissibility of subsequent disclosure, the law ought to enforce that bargain. But in the absence of such an understanding, the public's right to be informed about matters of legitimate public concern should tip the balance against liability for publication. Extreme cases, such as those involving the dissemination of a surreptitiously recorded videotape depicting consensual sex by one of the participants, are easy: the privacy harm to the nonconsenter is grave and the public's interest in the material is likely not weighty. Setting aside these sorts of cases, the public's interest in reading plus the consenter's interest in speaking typically will trump the objector's interest in not being written about.

Having said that, Posner's analysis in the *Haynes* case is not completely satisfying. He wonders whether a biographer needs to get the permission of anyone who is portrayed negatively in a book, but that is not the issue. Biographies rarely disclose intimate and highly offensive details about a very large number of people. The collective action problems presented in cases like *Haynes* are therefore not tragedies of the anticommons, in that no individual can block an entire story from being told. Assuming away broad familial privacy rights, at most one person could block a portion of a story being told in a particularly detailed way. Nevertheless, privacy tort law typically sidesteps the collective action dilemma by giving each potential speaker a rather strong right to disclose sensitive information about her own intimate associations.

Whose Privacy Counts?—Doe v. Quiring

The most wrenching cases implicating collective privacy interests arise in settings where constructive partition is impossible. *Quiring,*[40] a fascinating South Dakota Supreme Court opinion, surprisingly has been ignored by privacy scholars and barely cited in the case law.[41] *Quiring* concerned a challenge to the state's sex offender registry, brought by the daughter of an offender convicted of violating the state's law criminalizing incest. Under South Dakota's Megan's Law, the sex offender's photograph and address were published on the Internet, along with information specifying that he had been convicted of the crime of "incest." The plaintiff in the case continued to live at the same address as her father after his release from prison. South Dakota therefore cannot publicize his precise crime on Megan's Law without calling attention to her victimization. It can do what Doe asked, which is to identify her father as a generic sex offender, rather than an incest perpetrator.

The facts of *Quiring* potentially present two sorts of privacy conflicts of interest. First, the state likely deemed the perpetrator's privacy rights as substantially reduced by virtue of his having committed a serious crime. Courts sometimes refer to criminals as having "waived" their privacy rights in the process of violating the law, with the effects of such a waiver closely resembling those of consent.[42] Indeed, courts conceptualize a waiver as a form of implicit consent. Second, although we do not know whether Doe's father wished to have his crime classified as a generic sex offense, it is plausible that unlike his daughter he would have preferred the more specific designation. The available empirical research suggests that incest perpetrators are less likely to recidivate than sex offenders whose crimes have victimized strangers.[43] Similarly, among "child molesters, those most likely to sexually recidivate are those who offended against unrelated boy victims, followed by those who offended against unrelated girl victims and, finally, incest offenders."[44] We do not know whether the public generally understands that incest perpetrators present a lower recidivism risk than rapists or other sex offenders who target strangers. If the public does understand this, it might explain why notwithstanding the incest taboo, a sex offender would prefer an incest perpetrator designation to a less precise description. Being designated as an incest perpetrator might have subjected Doe's father to less harassment, suspicion, and surveillance than being described as a more threatening generic sex offender.

The plaintiff challenged the law on statutory grounds—basing her argument on a provision in the Megan's Law statute providing that "any identifying information regarding of the victim of the crime" was to remain confidential. The plaintiff also raised constitutional arguments at trial, but chose not to pursue them on appeal. Nevertheless, South Dakota's Supreme Court improperly held that the constitutional arguments would have been unmeritorious had they been pursued.[45] Turning to the statutory arguments before it, the court upheld the law by a three-to-two vote. The justices in the majority concluded that the designation of the victim's father as an incest perpetrator did not constitute "identifying information regarding the victim" because the plaintiff was one of a number of possible victims who were related to the perpetrator:

> [A] victim could be any one of a number of less than 21-year-old relatives of the offender. Under these circumstances, we believe that the mere listing of the offender and type of offense is not the disclosure of the "identifying information" that the Legislature intended to prohibit. It could not have been the Legislature's intent because, if carried to its logical conclusion, Applicant's position would prohibit the public disclosure of *any* detail of any offense. We do not think the Legislature intended such an absurd construction.[46]

The majority in *Quiring*, like the dissent in *Randolph*, uses the specter of a privacy anticommons to diminish the privacy interest of a party with an overwhelming interest in nondisclosure. The daughter is a cotenant adamantly withholding her consent at the front door, but the court does not want to differentiate her from the babysitter who works in the apartment one night every few weeks. In the process, the majority creates a kind of tragedy of the *commons*—the daughter's private information is disclosed excessively, because neither she nor anyone else is given the right to exercise control over the fact of her victimization.

The *Quiring* dissenters, by contrast, noted that the "size of the class of incest victims is limited to family members. The number of family members under the age of twenty-one is even smaller and, in some cases, may include only a couple of children. Publicly identifying the crime as 'incest' significantly increases the risk of providing 'identifying information of the victim' and may bring opprobrium on family members who were not victims."[47] The dissenters are perhaps understandably blind to the possibility that some family members may *want* to have their kinsman accurately identified as an incest perpetrator, perhaps for the same reason that the district court judge in *Associated Press* couldn't imagine why any abused Guantanamo detainee wouldn't want to be identified. The dispute between the majority and the dissenters boils down to a disagreement over whose privacy interests count. To the majority, nothing less than a categorical identification of "Jane Doe, incest victim" implicates the statute's confidentiality provision. The dissenters viewed the language more probabilistically, and also more realistically, given the ease with which data mining could be used to determine Jane Doe's real identity.[48]

The *Quiring* dissent also gets the better of the policy argument that informs the interpretation of the statutory text. Given that recidivism rates for incest perpetrators seem to be relatively low, and assuming that incest perpetrators are likely to recidivate against relatives, and that rapists of strangers are likely to recidivate against strangers, the blurring of incest perpetrators and generic sex offenders might make it harder for the public to take appropriate precautions. But the number of incest perpetrators seems sufficiently small to justify categorical blurring here. In Minnehaha County, where the plaintiff lived, there were a total of six sex offenders who had been convicted of incest. Although the number of sex offenders living in the county at the time of the lawsuit is unknown, there were 474 total registered sex offenders living in the county in June 2009.[49] If incest perpetrators comprise less than 2 percent of sex offenders, then the harm resulting from lumping them in with other sex offenders is unlikely to be great.

Conclusion

The results in both *Associated Press* and *Quiring* seem intuitively troubling, and an examination of the cases and their contexts reveals a neutral basis for questioning both opinions. A more satisfying resolution would ameliorate *Associated Press's* tragedy of the privacy anticommons and *Quiring's* tragedy of the commons by restoring "consent" to the central position it occupies in the rest of privacy law. Namely, the state should be proscribed from identifying someone as an "incest perpetrator" without the consent of the victim, and the government should be unable to withhold the identities of any detainee absent a showing that *either* that particular detainee or a majority of all detainees prefer anonymity.

How should we choose between those decision rules? Privileging individual consent is most appropriate where individuals did not choose to join the group in question. In the case of voluntary associations, there is a much stronger case for subjecting the individual to the preferences of the majority, as we do with corporations, homeowner's associations, student organizations, and university faculties. Such a rule facilitates coordinated action while encouraging people to choose their associates wisely. Doe did not elect to become an incest victim, so her individual consent should be required regardless of how other members of her nuclear family feel. Even if eleven siblings wanted their father designated as an incest perpetrator, and Doe was the lone hold-out, the court might appropriately embrace the *Associated Press* remedy of no disclosure without unanimous consent because Doe didn't choose her siblings. Applying voluntariness to the facts of *Associated Press*, some of the Guantanamo detainees chose to join the Taliban or Al Qaeda, but none of them chose to be abused, so deciding whether individual consent or majority assent is necessary becomes more difficult there. The costs of constructively partitioning the list of abused detainees will likely be determinative.

It is comforting to remember that collective action problems arise in many areas of law. Property law governs jointly owned resources, and typically requires unanimity where one owner's views conflict with those of her co-owners. In corporate law, by contrast, majority shareholders typically prevail over the minority. Privacy rules modeled on property law—where the consent of all affected parties is required—are most appropriate where courts are rather stingy in determining what "counts" as a privacy interest. As courts increasingly recognize familial privacy interests or encounter data sets that implicate the privacy interests of many individuals, either majoritarian decision making or constructive partition will become necessary to prevent tragedies of the privacy anticommons.

The dissemination of sensitive information concerning an individual often affects particular third parties by inferentially revealing information about them. In cases where these third parties are relatively few in number, and absent reason to doubt whether they can consent or withhold their consent effectively, it is tempting to say that the law should strive to treat these third parties as well as it treats the individuals whose privacy is more obviously at stake. This aspiration, however, has the potential to swallow up much of the Freedom of Information Act's disclosure requirements, with attendant losses to speech and transparency interests. As such, where a large number of people each have a low-stake interest in the dissemination of information concerning a particular individual and constructive partition is impractical, it is appropriate for the law to require only the consent of the obviously and primarily interested individual. Such an approach heads off a potential tragedy of the privacy anticommons, while recognizing the legitimate interdependency of information privacy interests. In short, recognizing the multiplicity of interdependent privacy interests should not make us unwilling to prioritize among those interests. There is, after all, sound logic behind our intuitions that the detainee's desire to publicize his captivity and mistreatment should prevail over the wishes of his publicity-shy relatives, and the incest victim's privacy preferences must matter more than the perpetrator's.

CHAPTER 13

Privacy on Social Networks:
Norms, Markets, and Natural Monopoly

RUBEN RODRIGUES

Introduction

Social-networking sites are the newest phenomenon to take the Internet by storm. Sites like MySpace, Facebook, and Twitter have created robust platforms for perpetual communication of all sorts of information: favorite foods and movies, contact information, where you're going, who you're with, and so on. Never before has so much information, traditionally private by nature, been so widely shared. The concerns for privacy in this new era are obvious: Who controls all this data? Who has access to it? What limits are imposed on its aggregation? Currently, competition between various websites provides strong incentives to protect user privacy. The market for social-networking sites, however, might not support such competition for much longer. We could very well be seeing the rise of a single dominant player who is capable of exercising monopoly power. Such a monopolist would not respond to pressure from competitors to protect the privacy of entrenched users. To effectively protect privacy interests in this market, the law must intervene.

Many commentators have discussed the implications this new communication medium poses for user privacy. In his book, *The Future of Reputation,* Daniel Solove portrays a world where once-fleeting harms to reputation, such as saying something incoherent, dumb, or offensive when under pressure, can be forever memorialized on the servers of YouTube. Not only is it permanently archived; but embarrassing, shameful, and intrusive information is also just a Google search away. In a bygone era, one could overcome reputational harms by finding a new social circle, moving to a new location in severe cases, or by simply waiting for time to pass and for people to forget. Those would all seem futile efforts in an online world. The ability to simply move to a new town to avoid shame, or to hope that as time passes people forget, the hope of a "second chance," is gone.

The situations Solove and others in this book worry about are truly disconcerting. However, it is important to note that they often involve a degree of involuntariness on the part of the individual whose privacy is invaded. In fact, these situations might not really pose *privacy* issues in and of themselves. Rather, they often involve statements that are complete fabrications that are more properly the focus of a defamation or libel action.

The focus of this essay is social-network websites, where users often maintain *control* over their own information, even when it is pervasively shared. Users of these sites generally have the ability to control both who they are "friends" with and the manner in which information is shared. They also retain control over what others can say about them on their "profile" page by deleting undesirable comments. This degree of control prevents many of the harms associated with online slander. Furthermore, anonymous postings and accounts are rare in the context of social networks, and companies like Facebook actively purge accounts they suspect of being fake or anonymous.

The lack of anonymity on social networks allows privacy-enhancing social norms to develop. Society relies on these norms, in addition to legal regimes and liability rules, to influence individual conduct in other realms of life. Thus it only makes sense that such norms will have some effect on the Internet as well. Legal rules are usually left to dissuade particularly egregious conduct when social norms fail. Social norms can often be more effective than legal rules at inducing conforming behavior. For example, fines exist for littering; however, the glare you receive from someone who catches you throwing trash on the ground is more likely to create a disincentive to litter than is a $50 fine that is rarely enforced.

Similarly, the power of individual reputation and online social norms can go a long way toward preventing the abuse of personal information among users of social-networking sites. Any given user is generally just as vulnerable to abuse as any other. Any incentive I might have to abuse your information, or to post derogatory statements about you, is countered by the disincentive that you could conceivably do the same to me. In fact, the disincentives might often outweigh the incentives. Posting derogatory information could very well lead to a massive backlash by friends of the original target.

Still, there *are* privacy concerns with social networks. To the extent that a user's control over his or her network, profile, and personal information is an effective means for protecting user privacy, we must ask what the driving force behind user-friendly privacy-enhancing control mechanisms is. In the context of social-networking sites, market competition plays a large role in promoting user control and shaping privacy policies. Market competition also protects users from the possibility that a social-network provider may itself abuse private user information. Social-networking sites have responded rather quickly to consumer demands for greater privacy protection. These controls, however, can be effective only within the context of robust competition in the market for social networks.

The Market for Social Networking

We can break down the market for social networking into two main classes. First there are the *general,* all-purpose, social networks that act as substitutes for each other. Then there are the *niche* sites that do not act as substitutes, but rather can be used in concert with one another or as add-ons to general sites.

The general sites are the ones this essay is most concerned with. These sites provide a variety of user services such as the ability to have a general profile page accessible to others that can contain contact information, a narrative, pictures, lists of friends or connections, and various "status" updates revealing current information about one's activities. Most general sites provide further features such as the ability to add third-party "applications" to a profile, and the ability to use a profile in concert with niche sites (which are described further below). All general sites provide much of the same functionality, the core element of which is an online network of friends with no particular thematic connection. As such, the general sites act as substitutes for each other, and users will rarely actively use more than one. The distinction between actively using and simply "having an account" on a social-networking site is an important one. Over time many people create multiple accounts on multiple networks, even though they only consistently use a single network and account. The reasons for this are varied: some may simply want to guarantee that their desired user names are not taken, while others may be motivated to occasionally see what other networks are like.

Currently, large players among general social-networking sites are Facebook, MySpace, Orkut (Google's social-networking site), and Windows

Live Spaces (Microsoft's new social-networking site). Other general social-networking sites include early entrants like Friendster, whose popularity has diminished substantially. MySpace poses an interesting example of a general "all-purpose" social-networking site. It invested heavily in providing "niche" social-networking services to musicians and bands, and has developed a robust music-interested social network. This aspect of MySpace may more appropriately be regarded as a niche site. However, for the purposes of this essay, it is difficult to separate out this aspect of the network from the larger, general MySpace network.

Sites that should be described as "niche" are those that provide social-networking functions, but do not serve as substitutes to a general all-purpose site. They include LinkedIn, Twitter, and Flickr. LinkedIn provides users with a professional-minded social network focused on résumé building, recommendations, references, and business networking. Facebook allows users to link directly to their LinkedIn profile from within a Facebook page; the niche service is thus easy to use in concert with the general site.

Meanwhile, Twitter provides users with a "micro-blogging" service that allows users to share short 140-character statements with each other. The most common use of Twitter is through cell phones and PDA devices. Facebook also allows interoperability with Twitter, allowing users to make their Twitter feed and Facebook "status" one and the same. Flickr is a social network built around the concept of photo sharing and commenting on shared photos. The general social-networking sites provide some of the same functionality, but Flickr provides additional features, such as enhanced photo-search capabilities and a community specifically interested in photography.

The initial reaction to so much sharing of information on the Internet is often to assume that everything posted on these sites is no longer private. In one sense, things posted on social networks really do cease to be "private," but at the same time it's not completely "public." While it is true that users disclose a vast amount of information, they conduct this disclosure in a very limited fashion. The information becomes "public" in the sense that it is no longer under the exclusive control of the individual, but at the same time it is not public vis-à-vis the entire world. Users retain a good deal of discretion in determining who has access to what information. For example, on Facebook, users have the ability to limit profile visibility to certain networks of friends, and users can control the display of individual messages, "wall posts," and "photo tags" that refer to them. The social network itself generally retains access and certain rights to use this information, but even this is a form of limited, trusted, disclosure.

The use of social networks, and thus the sharing of all this information, is completely voluntary. No one requires that anyone sign up for a MySpace page. Even if you do, you need not use much of the privacy-deteriorating functionality it offers. However, online social networking has become a powerful trend. As social-networking sites become more popular, it may become harder or even impractical for individuals to avoid them.

A legal regime that addresses privacy concerns on social networks should not limit the ability of individuals to willingly give up traditionally private information. After all, the popularity of sites like MySpace and Facebook means that social-networking sites provide a service that users actually value. In fact, these sites can be extremely efficient modes of communications. But in a world where so much private information lies in the hands of others, how does the law protect individuals from abuse? As we will see, the law has an important role in protecting competition, the current force driving privacy protections across the market for general social-networking sites.

Competition in the Social-Networking Market

Social-networking sites compete with each other for users. While this might not always be apparent since no one pays money directly to Facebook or MySpace to use their services, social-networking sites engage in non-price competition over features, add-ons, and most importantly: privacy. The privacy aspect of social-network competition is multifaceted, and can come in the form of *privacy policies, privacy practices, privacy controls,* or *data security.*

Privacy policies reflect the contractual relationship between users and the social-networking site, often included within a site's "Terms of Service." The privacy policy will often also define the extent to which a social-networking site can use private information for the purpose of generating revenue through targeted advertising. Facebook has recently added documents entitled the "Facebook Principles" and "Statement of Rights and Responsibilities" to its website, which should also be considered in defining the site's overall privacy policy.

Privacy practices refer to a social network's actual practices in implementing its privacy policies. The way a site actually implements its privacy policies may differ substantially from what a policy says on its face. For example, are enough resources committed to redressing users' complaints under the terms of service? There may be situations where privacy policies are very friendly to the privacy interests of users, but are poorly applied in practice. Disallowing anonymous user accounts would be another example of a privacy-enhancing practice.

Privacy controls refer to the features social-networking sites make available that enable users to control how much, and what sorts of, information they post on the network. Examples of privacy controls include the manner in which users can limit profile page visibility, the degree to which access is limited to various "networks," the ability to delete, edit, or otherwise control comments and pictures linked to the user's profile, and a plethora of other features tailored to giving a user more control over his private information and online persona.

Data security refers to how diligent a social-networking site is at protecting users' data from external attacks by hackers or internal breaches, such as a leak. Data security breaches are widely discussed in the media when retailers suffer a breach of consumer credit card data, and social-networking sites are susceptible to similar compromises.

In the past few years, privacy, including all these facets thereof, has been increasingly recognized as an attribute of non-price competition, both within the market for social networking and beyond it. Social-networking sites, such as Facebook, have acknowledged that they compete on privacy. Many users have cited privacy as a major reason for switching from MySpace to Facebook. In addition, Facebook has quickly acted to address consumer privacy demands when faced with user backlashes over various privacy-hostile policies. Examples include the backlash against the release of Facebook Beacon, and the rush of users to change their privacy settings after Facebook announced it was going to make profiles searchable on Google. Consumers of social-networking sites care about privacy, and so far Facebook has reacted to meet consumer demands in the privacy space.

The Federal Trade Commission (FTC) also recognized privacy as a valuable form of non-price competition when faced with the merger of two large providers of online targeted advertising services, Google and Doubleclick. The FTC recognized "the possibility that [the] transaction could adversely affect non-price attributes of competition, such as consumer privacy."[1] The FTC ultimately held that the merger could proceed, since both entities operated in sufficiently different markets, and concluded that "the parties do not significantly affect each other's prices, nor non-price product attributes, such as consumer privacy protections or service quality."

While a typical user rarely considers his or her relationship to a social-networking site as commercial in nature, the transaction between user and site is essentially economic. Users contribute private information, in the form of profile content, communications with others, and consent to behavioral tracking, and in return receive useful services such as access to the network, communication tools, photo sharing, data storage, and a variety of other applications.

The market is two-sided. That is, the social-networking site has two separate, but interrelated, groups of consumers (see Figure 13.1). The first consists of the users who contribute private information, contacts, and behavior for analysis. The second contains the advertisers to whom Facebook sells advertising services. The users engage in non-price bargaining over privacy policies and user services, while the exchange between advertisers and the social-networking site is an area of traditional price competition.

Assuming competition in the market for social networking is an effective means for protecting user privacy, instances where the market ceases to operate effectively should be ripe for legal intervention in order to protect the bargaining relationship between the user and a social-network provider. A dominant social-network provider, who may very well be a natural

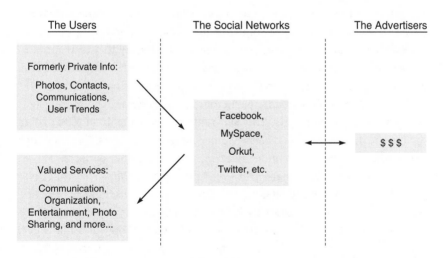

Figure 13.1 The Two-Sided Market for Social Networking.

monopolist, may leverage its monopoly power to provide less-than-desired levels of user privacy protection than would exist under competition.

A social-networking site could also exercise its monopoly power by charging users a price for services. However, it is more likely that it will simply forego investing in privacy protection since its core revenue model is focused on advertising revenue. A successful site enjoys advertising revenue and has little need to spend on privacy protections and other features that users might pay for in a competitive market. Monopoly power aside, it may also be difficult to charge for services consumers expect to receive without (direct) charge.

Social Networks and Natural Monopoly

The social-networking market exhibits *network effects* that make it susceptible to a natural monopoly. A network effect, also called a "network externality," occurs when one user of a good or service directly affects the value that some other user places on the same good or service. A canonical example is the telephone network. The value a particular user receives from a telephone network is directly dependent on how many other users he or she can access through the network. This effectively creates a positive feedback loop. In the end, and holding price aside, it is socially optimal to have a single, all-inclusive, telephone network as opposed to separate, competing, non-interoperable networks.

A natural monopoly in the market for social-networking sites would absolutely negate the ability of robust competition to effectively provide incentives that balance the privacy interests of users with the pecuniary goals of the social-networking site. The value of joining a particular social network derives directly from the ability to connect to all of one's "friends." As such, the more people on a particular social network, the more inherent value that network has. This self-reinforcing principle means that in the long run, a single social-networking site may prevail as all users flock to the site with the most "value" in terms of total number of users.

Social-networking sites are also subject to high *switching costs* that deter entry by new competing sites by making it hard for users of preexisting sites to switch. There may, however, be ways to overcome these costs, as this essay suggests. Users place a great deal of information on the initial social network of their choice. They post profiles, they form "connections," they develop communication routines, they keep track of contacts, and they host photos. After a period of participation, users become *entrenched*. The more information posted on a particular social-networking site, the greater a disincentive for that user to switch to a different site.

Some might perceive the costs of entry into the market for social networking as low. Anyone can cheaply start a website and purchase a domain name. In many ways, that is what Facebook did when it began as a small student-run site at Harvard and then grew to compete with MySpace. However, the costs of entry in the market are more complex than this simplistic model suggests. The costs lie not in creating the website, but in attracting and developing a critical mass of users and growing the overall network. The costs are thus very high when one considers established competitors with preexisting networks, especially if those competitors themselves develop tools and strategies to lock in users and keep switching costs high.

A natural monopolist in the market for social networking can extract monopoly rents on user privacy. A monopolist would have little incentive to respond to the demands of entrenched users concerned about privacy. A monopolist could also erode past privacy practices in exchange for greater income by directly reselling personal information and contact information, despite the interests of its entrenched users. While egregious violations may lead users to switch sites, or abandon social networking altogether, they will do so only once the costs to their privacy outweigh the benefits received from the site. Thus, the natural monopolist will simply engage in monopoly pricing (in regard to the bargaining that goes on between user and social-networking site) and charge "monopoly rents" on user privacy. Ultimately the social-networking site can engage in suboptimal pricing: users pay a lot more in terms of sacrifices to privacy in exchange for social-networking services than they would in a competitive market.

Given the two-sided nature of the social-networking market, this scenario could result even in light of robust price competition between the social-networking monopolist and other sources of targeted advertising. There are many providers of online targeted advertising, including email services (GMail and Hotmail), content distributors (YouTube), online retailers (Amazon), and direct advertisers (Google/Doubleclick). Social-networking sites are but one source of such targeted advertising. A monopolist in the market for social networking could compete strongly with these other players in the market for targeted advertising, while continuing to extract monopoly rents on the privacy of its users.

To put all of this in the context of a real-world scenario, let us look at the development of MySpace and Facebook. MySpace was once the globally dominant social-networking site, but Facebook has since dramatically encroached on MySpace's market share. In June 2008, Facebook had eighty million[2] users in comparison to MySpace's 100 million.[3] MySpace's lead has continued to erode throughout 2008 and 2009. As of September 2008, MySpace grew by six million users to 106 million;[4] while Facebook grew by forty million to achieve 120 million total users by October 2008, and then 200 million in March 2009.[5] Facebook surpassed MySpace to become the number one trafficked social-networking site in the world in 2008, and the fourth most trafficked website overall.[6] However, not all estimates of user traffic have Facebook ahead of MySpace.[7] But Facebook is plainly growing, and might well become the dominant social-networking site.

If social networking is a natural monopoly, why has there been competition between Facebook and MySpace? There are a number of possible explanations. MySpace was dominant only in the early phase of the development of social-networking sites. It is common to see competition in the early stages of a networked industry. There were once competing standards in the construction of railroad gauges and in the distribution of electricity on a national grid. More recently, there was competition between the HD-DVD and Blu-ray standards, with Blu-ray eventually dominating the market. It is possible that market segmentation within MySpace allowed Facebook to gain traction as it developed tools that users found more attractive. The early stage of development in the market also meant that users would be less entrenched than one might see now that the market has matured.

Possible Roles for the Law

There are numerous roles for the law in attempting to counteract the negative effects of a natural monopolist, many of which have been tried in other networked industries. The entirely digital nature of the social-network industry provides an interesting change from older forms of networked industries, and makes options that were impractical with older networks, such as telephones, optimal in the present case.

Standard options for countering the effects of natural monopoly include a command-and-control style regulatory regime or a mandated standard. Both are undesirable in the context of social-networking sites. A better route to keeping a social-networking monopolist in check would be to sim-

ply focus on keeping switching costs low and barring anticompetitive conduct through either an existing or a new antitrust law.

First, let's look at the possibility of mandating a regulatory regime with
specific privacy protections. The Interstate Commerce Commission was one
such command-and-control regime in the era of railroad monopolies. Of
all the options for protecting privacy in light of a social-networking monopolist, this is the most undesirable. A natural monopolist would be able
to charge monopoly "rates" in a number of areas besides privacy that would
also require regulation, such as providing a suboptimal level of new user
features. Dictating legal rules for each extremely technical area of concern
would be highly inefficient, if not impossible.

Furthermore, a government-mandated privacy policy would likely provide either too great or too little protection. It would be difficult for regulators to gauge what sorts of information users are willing to give up, and
what they would like to retain control over. The inability of government
to accurately predict consumer demands is consistent with the history of
command-and-control regulation in the face of a natural monopolist. For
example, the 1996 Telecom Act was an attempt to make the telephone network more competitive, but the period following its passage was replete
with litigation over the appropriate rates to charge competitors. A regulator
is not in a good position to weigh the costs and benefits of various options
and develop an efficient solution. Worst of all, in the context of user privacy, the value of private information is highly subjective. Different users
like to protect or share their information to varying degrees, preferences
that would be impossible for a regulator to fully accommodate.

A regulator might also have difficulty staying aware of the constant innovation in the market for social networking. New features are constantly
added to social-networking sites, and a regulatory body would need to
constantly adjust regulations to these changes.

Industry standards are often suggested as effective means for promoting interoperability among social-networking sites and thus, ideally, a
mechanism for reducing switching costs and maintaining a competitive
environment. Some have proposed the formation of a standard for social-
networking profiles, and Facebook and Google have both signed on to the
DataPortability project at Dataportability.org. Google (Orkut) and MySpace
have also embraced the OpenSocial API as a standard for promoting
interoperability, while Facebook retains its own proprietary systems. A
standard could allow users to easily port information, contacts, and move

from one social-networking site to another. However, for a standard to effectively lower switching costs, it must be accepted by all market participants, including the probable monopolist, and cover *all* aspects of the social network that help entrench users. Given the natural incentive to lock in users, the only way to achieve across-the-board adoption of a comprehensive standard is to impose a government mandate. This option, much like a regulatory regime, is also undesirable.

A mandated standard would likely hamper innovation, as social-networking sites would be discouraged from creating features that do not comply with the standard. To the extent sites would be allowed to develop features *beyond* the standard, it would lose its value in reducing switching costs. Users would be entrenched by the additional add-on features that they cannot port elsewhere via the standard. A mandated standard would also provide too much protection (discouraging innovation) or too little (allowing innovation, but not effectively reducing switching costs). Meanwhile, a voluntary standard would be ineffective since a social-networking monopolist could opt out, design around it, or create new entrenching features beyond the standard's scope.

A better option than a regulatory regime or mandated standard is one that focuses on keeping switching costs low and prohibiting anticompetitive conduct. This sort of regime would ensure that users are allowed to easily port content and contacts from one social-networking site to another, and prohibit sites from imposing artificial barriers to competition.

Competitors have a natural incentive to create scripts and programs that help entrenched users port information from one social-networking site to a competing one. A regime focused on banning anticompetitive behavior need only ensure that the use of such programs is explicitly allowed, and that social-networking sites are not allowed to block programs like these in order to deter competition. Niche sites in particular are well positioned to expand into the general social-network market if they see an opportunity to do so, and could act as an effective threat of entry, deterring a social-networking monopolist from extracting monopoly rents on user privacy.

Some social-networking sites are already embracing low-switching cost regimes, though generally in areas where websites do not act as direct competitors. For example, LinkedIn gives users the ability to search their Google-provided Gmail account for contacts to import onto LinkedIn. Users simply provide LinkedIn their Gmail login information and LinkedIn logs on to Google and acquires a list of possible contacts that LinkedIn users can then choose to add. Google does not block such services, and the model used here (turning over one's password to a trusted social-networking site) has been replicated on many websites.

A general social-networking site, even a monopolistic one, has many valid reasons to block third-party programs, either to protect its own network or in the interests of its users. Social-networking sites can be prone to spam attacks, involving attempts to either directly spam individuals through the network, or gather email addresses for later spamming efforts. Other malicious programs could come in the form of viruses or denial of service attacks designed to overrun the network and bring the system to a crawl.

Some cases may require a difficult determination as to whether a third-party program is a valid attempt to lower switching costs by a legitimate competitor or a malicious attack by a spammer. Blocking the latter should be considered legitimate, while blocking by the former is likely an anticompetitive refusal to deal. The situation between Plaxo and Facebook (described below) may be one such case. Litigation might be necessary to determine the appropriate line between legitimate and anticompetitive blocking in these cases. Some might oppose such litigation as wasteful, but it is a common approach in our legal system when difficult questions of line-drawing arise. Meanwhile, the majority of situations will pose a clear determination that blocking third-party applications by legitimate competitors is an anticompetitive practice. A site such as Facebook could hardly argue that reputable sites like MySpace, Orkut, or LinkedIn are malicious spammers. One could argue that by allowing interconnections of this sort, competitors would be emboldened to begin spamming, or attempt to bring down the monopolistic social-networking site through malicious code. However, such behavior is already prohibited by federal law, and an illicit attempt to bring down a competitor could itself be considered anticompetitive.

Blocking programs developed by competitors is just one way a potential monopolist might try to leverage the network effects of this market and thus artificially raise switching costs in an anticompetitive manner. Other avenues include asserting competitively questionable claims under contract law, while even daring to claim an extreme concern for the privacy interests of users. This could occur through anticompetitive application of a particular social-networking site's terms of service. For example, some sites block users who attempted to use unauthorized programs, while some terms of service prohibit users from sharing their login information with third parties.

In blocking users, and in prohibiting the sharing of login information, Facebook has repeatedly cited the privacy interests of its users as a justification. This could be considered a "false" privacy rationale to the extent a social network uses it to justify the blocking of programs or the banishment of users in ways that raise switching costs to the detriment of competition. Some have pointed out that lowering transaction costs might actually *degrade* privacy.[8] The argument is as follows: users who join a website consent to being connected to each other on a site such as Facebook, but they do not necessarily consent to the prospect of their friends' turning around and redistributing all their information to someone else. Therefore, when someone turns over a friend's user information to a third party, that person violates the friend's privacy interests. This has generally been Facebook's privacy argument. This view fits well with what Professor Lior Strahilevitz calls a "A Social Networks Theory of Privacy," the notion that just because someone has consented to disclosing information to a select group of people, does not mean the individual has consented to broader, public disclosure.[9] Although initially compelling, the argument as applied in this context is flawed, especially when weighed against the competing pro-privacy goal of lowering switching costs and fostering competition and effective threat of entry.

For one thing, it is common practice on many websites to allow users to share their login information in order to port contacts. Google's GMail service arguably contains much more private information about someone than does a Facebook account, yet people share their logins all the time in order to share and import GMail contacts to other services. There has also been no backlash against the use of third-party "Applications" on Facebook, even though use of such applications transmits a great deal of information to third parties without a user's explicit consent. Thus, we should be skeptical of the notion that users feel betrayed by friends who distribute information to third parties in a reasonable manner. Perhaps users have not consented to having their information publicly broadcast to the world (as Strahilevitz's "A Social Networks Theory of Privacy" would suggest), but they likely *have* consented to their friend's use of information to export contacts to Outlook, for example.

Second, Facebook's concerns here fly directly in the face of typical privacy norms. When deciding with whom to share information in everyday fashion, people generally rely on trust with others as a safeguard from abuse of that information. We do not typically feel an affront to privacy if someone passes on the fact that he or she is our friend. Similarly, we generally do not feel harmed if a trusted friend invites us to join a social network, such as LinkedIn, after the friend has imported contacts to the social-networking website via GMail.

Third, Facebook's justifications are directly contrary to its own practices. Facebook allows a growing number of "applications," developed by third parties, to exist on its site. Many of these applications have access to various user and friend information, and the use of such information is consented to only by the friend who adds the application. Facebook has also allowed users to port their contacts and information directly to Microsoft's Windows Live Spaces service, which would presumably pose the same privacy concerns.

In addition to blocking programs or using contracts, a potential monopolist may use questionable claims of intellectual property law to raise the costs of switching or directly attack a competitor. The Supreme Court in Lotus Dev. Corp. v. Borland Int'l, Inc. held that user interfaces in software programs may not be copyrighted, specifically citing the competitive concerns regarding the enforcement of intellectual property rights in user interfaces.[10] Similarly, user interfaces and layouts on social-networking sites should not be subject to copyright (though unique graphical elements may continue to be protected). Facebook recently filed a copyright suit against a German rival, studiVZ. While this site may very well have copied protected elements of Facebook's site (the two sites do, in fact, have a striking resemblance), competitive concerns should be weighed in the analysis as they were in *Lotus*.

With this description of the various ways a natural monopolist might anticompetitively raise switching costs or deter competition, let us look at some more things Facebook has done that could be considered anticompetitive and thus detrimental to privacy. Facebook recently made a questionable move in banning the use of Google's "Friend Connect" application. Friend Connect would go through a user's Facebook profile and port the profile and any contacts the user desired to Google.[11] This is precisely the sort of application designed with an eye toward lowering the switching costs involved in moving from one network to another.

Facebook cited user privacy concerns as a reason for denying access to Google's service. However, Facebook allows many other add-on programs that similarly degrade user privacy by allowing third-party access to user information (via Facebook's "Applications" interface). Facebook may have legitimate claims that a certain application might free-ride on its service, but anticompetitive concerns should be considered in evaluating the legitimacy of Facebook's actions, especially given that Google has its own competing social-networking service, Orkut.

Facebook took similar action against another competitor, Plaxo. Plaxo developed a script that users could use to port profile information and contacts over to its own site and into Microsoft Outlook.[12] Plaxo admittedly has a reputation as a source of unsolicited email, however, the program in question seems to have been narrowly tailored to a legitimate purpose. While Facebook may have justifiably blocked Plaxo, and some have applauded Facebook's blocking of Plaxo's scripts as pro-privacy,[13] anticompetitive concerns should at least be factored into evaluating the appropriateness of Facebook's behavior.

Curiously, Facebook has been much more willing to hand over user-contact information to its business partner, Microsoft, for use in expanding its Windows Live Messenger service.[14] It is unclear how the privacy interests of users are substantially different in this circumstance from those in situations with Google or Plaxo.

To support its claim of being more open and "interoperable," Facebook has created "Facebook Connect." This tool enables any *approved* website to interact with Facebook, by allowing Facebook users to log on to a variety of websites using their Facebook account. Rather than lowering switching costs, however, Facebook Connect actually exacerbates the network effects of Facebook's underlying social network. It makes Facebook an Internet-wide *platform* from which to conduct a large variety of transactions over the Internet, whether logging on to shop at Amazon.com or to chat via instant messaging services like Meebo.

Unlike data-porting tools such as the ones offered by LinkedIn to port contacts from Gmail to LinkedIn, Facebook Connect does not allow a third party wholesale access to a user's information and connections. Rather, Facebook Connect acts as an authentication tool for a variety of services. The difference is important; rather than allow users to share their username and password with third parties, Facebook requires the user to log in to *its* service *first*. The chat-consolidation program Meebo provides a telling example.

Meebo is an instant messaging service that allows a variety of instant messaging clients to communicate through a single interface. The interface accomodates Google's GTalk, Yahoo Messenger, MSN Messaging, AOL's

AIM, and most recently, Facebook. Rather than a user simply entering his or her username and password as with all the other services, and thus giving Meebo wholesale access to the user's account, the Facebook implementation requires the user to log in to Facebook first. Facebook is banning the practice of sharing login information in its terms of service with users as well. The effect is that while Facebook allows interoperability, in that users can use other sites, it ultimately has control over which sites can be used and what information those other sites obtain about a user.

Meebo originally implemented the addition of Facebook in the same way it implemented the incorporation of MySpace, Google, MSN, AOL, and Yahoo; it simply required that users give their passwords and usernames. However, Facebook quickly blocked Meebo and cited the privacy concerns of users as a justification, a rationale that we have already debunked. So what *could* be a justification for Facebook's blocking of Meebo? It is most likely that rather than protecting privacy, Facebook's goal is to increase the costs associated with porting information to a new network, since such portability is not possible through an authentication interface such as Facebook Connect. Requiring that users log in to Facebook first acts to raise the transaction costs of using other social-networking sites. Thus, Facebook Connect actually increases switching costs by deepening the entrenchment of users in the Facebook network and by making Facebook a platform for all sorts of tasks on the Internet.

The fact that Facebook can require another site to use its own authentication tool, rather than allow the site to simply use passwords and usernames (as Google and AIM allow on Meebo), might mean that Facebook is already starting to leverage its monopoly power. Otherwise, one would observe other sites' imposing such authentication measures rather than allowing simple sign-ons.

Facebook recently announced addendums to its terms of service that it calls the "Facebook Principles"[15] and "Statement of Rights and Responsibilities,"[16] which users were allowed to vote on in an "election." The new statement of rights and responsibilities explicitly prohibits users from sharing their login information with third parties. Statement 4.6 states that the user, "will not share your password, let anyone else access your account," while statement 3.2 states that users, "will not collect users' information, or otherwise access Facebook, using automated means (such as harvesting bots, robots, spiders, or scrapers) without our permission."[17] These provisions further inflame the competitive concerns at issue in the Meebo example.

Not only does Facebook block Meebo, but it additionally places a threat on its own users not to share their logins with others, a proven method of effectively porting content from one site to another.

Given the underlying competitive concerns, statements 4.6 and 3.2 can be viewed as diametrically opposed to the more loosely worded pleasant-sounding Facebook "principle" regarding the free flow of information, which states that "People should have the freedom to access all of the information made available to them by others. People should also have practical tools that make it easy, quick, and efficient to share and access this information."[18] It's clear that Facebook does not desire to allow full sharing of information under this principle, or else it would not place such tight restrictions on the sharing of login information with third parties. Perhaps those drafting the principles forgot to condition the words "share" and "access" with the phrase "only within the Facebook network."

All of these anticompetitive concerns have recently come to bear on a lawsuit Facebook filed in early 2009 against Power.com. Power.com is an aggregator of social-networking sites, and it engages in the practice of providing tools to users of social-networking sites, like Facebook and MySpace, that allow them to port content among social networks. These tools are, much like those advocated in this essay, means of keeping switching costs low and minimizing barriers to entry. While the case is still in its infancy, Facebook's complaint alleges questionable claims of copyright and trademark infringement, as well as competitively suspect claims arising out of violations of Facebook's terms of service. In particular, the complaint focuses extensively on Power.com's violation of Facebook's policy against sharing user names and passwords, and Power.com's refusal to cooperate with Facebook Connect as an alternative. Facebook's complaint against Power.com also alleges claims with fewer implications for competition, such as those arising out of the CAN-SPAM Act and misrepresentation. Going forward we should be skeptical of claims by Facebook that threaten competition; courts should weigh heavily the anticompetitive consequences of granting such relief.

Facebook is not a democracy. One common refrain by Facebook users in response to suggestions that Facebook might not have their best privacy interests in mind is that Facebook itself is an empowering tool that allows for user organization and the ability to "petition" Facebook for the redress of grievances through tools like Facebook "groups." This is, in fact, what happened in response to the Facebook Beacon controversy and the push back on changes to Facebook's terms of service. In those situations, Facebook users formed groups and signed online petitions in order to press Facebook for changes. Facebook users, of course, play no role in electing Facebook management, and have no effective check on what Facebook does other than their ability, as consumers, to stop using the service. All these successful online petition campaigns occurred with competition from firms like MySpace and Orkut lurking in the background, even as Facebook continued to increase its share of the market. Petitions may have some effect on a social-networking monopolist, to the extent that a site wants to avoid negative publicity, but in the end the profitable alternative will be the path Facebook takes.

The illusion of Facebook as a form of participatory democracy was further exacerbated with Facebook's recent "election" involving changes to its terms of service. Users were asked to vote on whether to approve a new set of "governing" documents for the site, the Facebook Principles and Statement of Rights and Responsibilities. Very few participated in the voting process. Brilliant marketing aside, it is clear that Facebook is a company, not a democracy. That is how Chris Cox, Facebook's co-founder, put it in an interview with the *New York Times* in March 2009: "It's not a democracy," he said. "We are here to build an Internet medium for communicating and we think we have enough perspective to do that and be caretakers of that vision."[19]

Facebook may already be leveraging its market power to the detriment of user privacy. In December 2009, Facebook announced drastic changes to default user-privacy settings. Facebook took away user control over pictures, contact information, and friend lists and made such information publicly available. It also increased the amount of information available to developers, without the consent of users. Not only do these changes fly in the face of the pro-privacy arguments Facebook has used to justify the blocking of competitors, but it reflects a revolutionary departure from it's original privacy-enhancing business model focused on attracting new users through enhanced user privacy and control. Mark Zuckerberg, Facebook's founder and CEO, has justified these changes by arguing that "social norms" have developed whereby users no longer value online privacy.[20] While more information sharing might be a general trend, it is doubtful that Facebook users, who vastly outnumber users of services like Twitter, would prefer giving up control over their information. Zuckerberg could have structured this change in such a way that people could opt in to more sharing if they wished, rather than make these changes defaults that cannot be opted out from. It may very well be that Facebook has decided to start exploiting the fruits of anticompetitive practices and network effects to the detriment of user privacy, and if that is the case, it may be time for the law to intervene.

Conclusion

Competition among social-networking site operators creates powerful market incentives for protecting user privacy. To the extent that one social-networking site develops monopoly power, and succeeds in raising switching costs and mooting the threat of entry, we can expect such a monopolistic site to engage in suboptimal levels of privacy protection. Because of the two-sided market for social networking, this may be the case even in the face of robust competition for targeted advertising. In order to avoid the loss to society and user privacy that would result, the law should act to ensure switching costs are low and should prohibit the sort of anticompetitive behavior that has been discussed.

While new pro-competitive regulations might be justified, we should not refrain from applying our existing antitrust laws in ways that reflect the important role non-price competition plays in the realm of privacy protection in our modern, networked world. Our laws should adapt to our shifting technological landscape, and protecting privacy via robust competition should become an even greater concern as more and more of our daily life occurs online.

NOTES

CONTRIBUTORS

INDEX

Notes

1. Speech, Privacy, and Reputation on the Internet

1. Danielle Citron, *Cyber Civil Rights*, 89 B.U. L. Rev. 61, 71–72 (2009).
2. John Dewey, *Experience and Nature* 167 (1925) (Jo Ann Boydston ed. 1987).
3. John Hechinger, *College Applicants, Beware: Your Facebook Page Is Showing*, Wall St. J., Sept. 18, 2008, available at http://online.wsj.com/article/ SB122170459104151023.html.
4. Id.
5. Id.
6. Quoted in Daniel J. Solove & Paul M. Schwartz, *Information Privacy Law* 761 (3rd ed. 2009).
7. For example, see Simson Garfinkel, *Database Nation: The Death of Privacy in the 21st Century* (2001); Charles Sykes, *The End of Privacy* (1999); Reg Whitaker, *The End of Privacy* (2000).
8. Neil M. Richards & Daniel J. Solove, *Privacy's Other Path: Recovering the Law of Confidentiality*, 96 Geo. L. J. 123 (2007).
9. David Brin, *The Transparent Society* 8–9 (1998).
10. Pavesich v. New England Life Ins. Co., 50 S. E. 68, 70 (Ga. 1905).
11. 47 U.S.C. §230(c)(1).
12. Daniel J. Solove, *The Future of Reputation: Gossip, Rumor, and Privacy on the Internet* 153–160 (2007). Available as an e-book online at http://futureofrepu tation.com.
13. Id.
14. http://www.juicycampus.com.
15. Jessica Bennett, *What You Don't Know Can Hurt You*, Newsweek, Dec. 17, 2007, http://www.newsweek.com/id/74322.
16. http://www.juicycampus.com/posts/faq.
17. Id.
18. Id.
19. Drake Bennett, *Time for a Muzzle*, Boston Globe, Feb. 15, 2009.
20. Id.

21. 17 U.S.C. §512.

22. *Id.*

23. Amber Taylor, *Partial Book Review: The Future of Reputation,* Prettier than Napoleon, Nov. 18, 2007, http://bamber.blogspot.com/2007/11/partial-book -review-future-of.html.

24. Rebecca Tushnet, *Solove's Future of Reputation,* 43(B)log, Dec. 13, 2007, http:// tushnet.blogspot.com/2007/12/soloves-future-of-reputation.html.

25. Solove, *Future of Reputation.*

26. Lior Strahilevitz makes a compelling argument that social network theory should be used to determine when information exposed to a number of people should still be considered to be private. *See* Lior Jacob Strahilevitz, *A Social Networks Theory of Privacy,* 72 U. Chi. L. Rev. 919 (2005). I agree that social network theory has many useful insights for addressing this issue.

27. *See* Taylor, *Partial Book Review.*

2. Civil Rights in Our Information Age

1. This essay is drawn from my article "Cyber Civil Rights," *Boston University Law Review* 89 (2009): 61–125.

2. "Blog Death Threats Spark Debate," *BBC News,* March 27, 2007, news.bbc.co.uk (accessed May 18, 2009).

3. Secretary of Dep't of Housing and Urban Dev. v. Wilson, 2000 WL 988268 (HUD ALJ July 19, 2000).

4. Azy Barak, "Sexual Harassment on the Internet," *Social Science Computer Review* 23 (2005): 77–92, 81.

5. Plaintiffs' Memorandum of Law in Support of Opposition to John Doe 21's Motion to Quash Plaintiff's Subpoena, DOE I and DOE II v. 39 Individuals Whose True Names Are Unknown, Case No. 3:07-CV-00909, pp. 1, 6 (D. Conn. filed on Mar. 17, 2008).

6. Posting of Jill to Feministe, "What Do We Do About Online Harassment?" www.feministe.us/blog (Aug. 9, 2007, 22:26) (accessed May 18, 2009).

7. Posting of Aletha to Free Soil Party Blog, "Silenced!" freesoil.org/wordpress (Sept. 18, 2007, 1:41 EST) (accessed May 18, 2009).

8. Posting of Alyssaroyse to Blogher, "Rape and Death and Batman, OH MY!" www.blogher.com (Aug. 3, 2008, 11:42) (accessed May 19, 2009).

9. Posting of La Chola to La Alma de Fuego, "Here's What I'm Wondering," brownfemipower.com (Apr. 13, 2007, 11:15 EST) (accessed May 19, 2009).

10. Askthisblackwoman, http://askthisblackwoman.com/2007/10/01/death-threat .aspx (Oct. 1, 2007, 15:20 EST).

11. Roger Brown, *Social Psychology: The Second Edition* (New York: Free Press, 1986).

12. Tom Postmes and Russell Spears, "Deindividuation and Antinormative Behavior: A Meta-Analysis," *Psychological Bulletin* 123 (1998): 238–259.

13. Philip G. Zimbardo, *The Lucifer Effect: Understanding How Good People Turn Evil* (New York: Random House, 2007).

14. David R. Mandel, "Evil and the Instigation of Collective Violence," *Analyses of Social Issues and Public Policy* 2 (2002): 101–108.

15. Robert J. Kaczorowski, *The Politics of Judicial Interpretation: The Federal Courts, Department of Justice, and Civil Rights, 1866–1876* (New York: Fordham University Press, 2005), 66.

16. 47 U.S.C.A. §223(a)(1)(C) (West 2008).

17. Ohio Rev. Code Ann. §2903.211(A)(2) (LexisNexis Supp. 2009).

18. Restatement (Second) of Torts §652D (1977).

19. Martha C. Nussbaum, "Objectification and Internet Misogyny" (see Chapter 4 below).

20. 18 U.S.C. §245(b)(2)(C) (2006).

21. United States v. Syring, 522 F. Supp. 2d 125 (D.D.C. 2007).

22. Partners Against Hate, *Investigating Hate Crimes on the Internet: Technical Assistance Brief* (2003), 5.

23. Ibid.; 28 U.S.C. §994 (2006).

24. 42 U.S.C. §1981 (2000).

25. Vietnamese Fishermen's Ass'n v. Knights of the Ku Klux Klan, 518 F. Supp. 993 (S.D. Tex. 1981).

26. 42 U.S.C. §2000e–6 (2000) (covering gender, race, national origin, color, and religion discrimination); United States v. Original Knights of the Ku Klux Klan, 250 F. Supp. 330, 349 (E.D. La. 1965); see Katzenbach v. McClung, 379 U.S. 294 (1964); Heart of Atlanta Motel, Inc. v. United States, 379 U.S. 241 (1964).

27. Original Knights of the Klan, 349.

28. 42 U.S.C. §1985(3) (2000).

29. 18 U.S.C. §241 (2006).

30. United States v. Cruikshank, 92 U.S. 542 (1876).

31. Griffin v. Breckenridge, 403 U.S. 88 (1971).

32. Bray v. Alexandria Women's Health Clinic, 506 U.S. 263 (1993).

33. Chaplinsky v. New Hampshire, 315 U.S. 568 (1942).

34. Ibid.

35. Varian Med. Sys., Inc. v. Delfino, 6 Cal. Rptr. 3d 325 (Ct. App. 2003), rev'd on other grounds, 106 P.3d 958 (Cal. 2005).

36. 508 U.S. 476 (1993).

37. 505 U.S. 377, 380 (1992).

38. Owen M. Fiss, *The Irony of Free Speech* (Cambridge, Mass.: Harvard University Press, 2006).

39. Cass R. Sunstein, *Democracy and the Problem of Free Speech* (New York: Free Press, 1993).

40. Jack M. Balkin, "Digital Speech and Democratic Culture: A Theory of Freedom of Expression for the Information Society," *New York University Law Review* 79 (2004): 1–58.

41. Diane L. Zimmerman, "Requiem for a Heavyweight: A Farewell to Warren and Brandeis's Privacy Tort," *Cornell Law Review* 68 (1983): 291–367.

42. Abrams v. United States, 250 U.S. 616, 624 (1919) (Holmes, J., dissenting).
43. Robert Post, "Reconciling Theory and Doctrine in First Amendment Jurisprudence," *California Law Review* 88 (2000): 2353–2374.
44. Daniel J. Solove, *The Future of Reputation: Gossip, Rumor, and Privacy on the Internet* (New Haven, Conn.: Yale University Press, 2007).
45. 47 U.S.C. §230 (2000).
46. Solove, *Future of Reputation*, 159.

3. The Internet's Anonymity Problem

1. I use this word because it appears to be the most common on Internet sites I have investigated.
2. Inasmuch as the provider is often an intermediary between author and audience, and because my own earlier work on anonymity emphasized the role of an intermediary in raising the benefit-cost ratio of anonymity, I will use that term here. See Saul Levmore, "The Anonymity Tool," 144 *University of Pennsylvania Law Review* 144 (1996): 2191–2236.
3. In Heller v. Bianco 111 Cal.App. 2d 424 (1952), there was indeed liability for tavern owners who maintained a bathroom, the wall of which contained defamatory material, because knowledge of the existence of the material could be inferred and opportunity to remove the material had passed. A modern judge is more likely to care about the workplace than the washroom, where generations of users have probably come to discount what is written. Thus, Judge Easterbrook, in Tacket v. General Motors Corp., 836 F.2d 1042 (7th Cir. 1987), suggests that readers discount what they read on bathroom stalls, and also that tavern owners would find it costly to paint and repaint bathroom walls.
4. Some speakers would find it difficult to maintain anonymity in a visual medium. Note, however, that handbills appeal to advertisers but not juvenilists.
5. The principle of least cost avoider is embodied in the legal distinction made between "secondary publishers," such as bookstores, and "primary publishers," including broadcasters, on whom legal responsibility is more readily fixed.
6. The soapbox orator is subject to constitutionally permissible time, place, and manner requirements. Similarly, a student's suspension for calling his school's assistant principal a "dick" was upheld because the utterance was insubordinate and not about a political issue or a matter of public concern. Posthumus v. Board of Educ. of Moan Shores School, 380 F.Supp. 2d 891 (2005).
7. 47 U.S.C. §230(c)(1).
8. Such popular games as *World of Warcraft* and *SecondLife* appear to support a substantial infrastructure in order to ward off offensive speakers. In the case of *SecondLife*, anonymity is an important element of the game, which offers the opportunity to experience "life," or at least interactions with other players, as a very different person. An uncontrolled game would disintegrate, much as AOL "chat rooms" lost value; a costly central bureaucracy is required.

9. In my own experience with class discussion boards, I have found that identifi-ability is associated with higher-quality discussion and civility, but also fewer questions. Anonymity can encourage free-riding rather than studious behavior. Discussion board anonymity seems no better than encouraging students to arrive at one's office hours incognito.

10. http://en.wikipedia.org/wiki/Wikipedia:Sock_puppetry.

11. Amazon.com is another site that is able to incorporate the work of many reviewers without falling to juvenile contributors. As compared to Wikipedia, Amazon might be expected to attract less-devoted volunteers, because of its for-profit character; on the other hand, these volunteers provide book reviews and indications of approval, rather than serious research and editing. Both sites use software, or "bots," which delete material containing specified offensive words, but they must also invest in the labor necessary to monitor and delete offensive material and other noise. Other Internet forums have chosen to eliminate interactive comments or anonymity.

12. The comments on these student evaluations can on occasion be quite mean, but in my extensive encounters with them they are rarely crude. Why then was JuicyCampus so much less constructive? One possibility is that evaluative comments are written "for" the instructor, and this brings out munificence rather than offense. Another is that students respond generously to the authoritative status of course evaluations. Perhaps the inability to pile on, or simply to write in reaction to the comments of others, checks juvenile communication.

13. See, for example, Lawrence Lessig, "The Law of the Horse: What Cyber Law Might Teach," *Harvard Law Review* 113 (1999–2000): 501–546; Lawrence Lessig, "Law Regulating Code Regulating Law," *Loyola University of Chicago Law Journal* 35 (2003–2004): 1–14.

14. These arguments play parts in Jack L. Goldsmith, "Against Cyberanarchy," 65 *University of Chicago Law Review* 65 (1998): 1199–1250; Jack L. Goldsmith and Alan O. Sykes, "The Internet and the Dormant Commerce Clause," *Yale Law Journal* 110 (2000–2001): 785–828; Cass R. Sunstein, *Republic.com 2.0* (Princeton University Press, 2007).

15. The notice-and-takedown approach is familiar to students of copyright law. Under the Digital Millennium Copyright Act, there is a safe harbor for online service providers against copyright liability if they adhere to and qualify for certain prescribed safe harbor guidelines and promptly block access to allegedly infringing material (or remove such material from their systems) if they receive notification claiming infringement from a copyright holder or the copyright holder's agent. The act also provides for subpoenas to providers to compel disclosure of their users' identities.

16. Cohen v. California, 403 U.S. 15 (1971) (First Amendment prohibits the state from making the public display of a four-letter word a criminal offense without a more compelling justification than the general disturbance of the peace). Texas v. Johnson, 491 U.S. 397 (1989) (striking down forty-eight state

statutes criminalizing the desecration of an American flag); United States v. Eichman, 496 U.S. 310 (1990) (striking down the federal Flag Protection Act on First Amendment grounds). The Flag Protection Act was passed with the knowledge that most Americans opposed flag burning and favored legal intervention. See S. Rep. 101–152. Polls taken shortly after the *Johnson* decision showed that 65 to 78 percent of respondents disagreed with the holding of the case.

4. Objectification and Internet Misogyny

1. Nietzsche, *Genealogy of Morals,* I.15.
2. Nussbaum, "Objectification," *Philosophy and Public Affairs* 24 (1995), 249–291, reprinted in Nussbaum, *Sex and Social Justice* (New York: Oxford University Press, 1999), 213–239.
3. I draw on my *Hiding from Humanity* (Princeton, N.J.: Princeton University Press, 2004).
4. What follows is a brief summary of the argument in Nussbaum, "Objectification."
5. I continue to refer to the argument I presented in "Objectification."
6. Rae Langton, *Sexual Solipsism* (Oxford: Oxford University Press, 2008).
7. I present these three conditions as Langton gave them ("one treats . . . ," etc.); consequently they don't match the formulations in my own list.
8. Langton, *Sexual Solipsism,* 228–229.
9. See Langton, *Sexual Solipsism,* 231–232.
10. See Erving Goffman, *Stigma* (New York: Simon and Schuster, 1963).
11. http://www.feministe.us/blog/archives/2006/01/04/a-follow-up/. I am grateful to Brian Leiter for this reference.
12. R. Jay Wallace, "Ressentiment, Value, and Self-Vindication: Making Sense of Nietzsche's Slave Revolt," in *Nietzsche and Morality,* eds. Brian Leiter and Neil Sinhababu (Oxford: Clarendon Press, 2007), 110–137.
13. AutoAdmit also features racial objectification. As in the gender-based form: by shaming members of a subordinate group, the objectifier gains power for himself.
14. See Goffman. Empirical work supporting the analysis given here is documented in *Hiding*.
15. See Nancy Chodorow, *The Reproduction of Mothering* (Berkeley and Los Angeles: University of California Press, 1978); Marilyn Friedman, "Autonomy and Social Relationships: Rethinking the Feminist Critique," in Diana Meyers, ed. *Feminists Rethink the Self* (Boulder, Colo.: Westview 1997), 40–61.
16. Kindlon and Thompson, *Raising Cain: Protecting the Emotional Life of Boys* (New York: Ballantine, 1999), chap. 4.
17. Ibid., 75.
18. Ibid., 17.
19. Ibid., 3–10.

20. Ibid., 208–209.

21. Ibid., 210.

22. Ibid., 205. Of course girls masturbate too, but the fantasy of total control over the partner is far less likely to be involved. Indeed, surrender of control is a staple of erotic fiction aimed at women.

23. Ibid., 216.

24. Andrea Dworkin, *Woman Hating* (New York: Dutton, 1974).

5. Believing False Rumors

1. I draw here on David Hirshleifer, The Blind Leading the Blind: Social Influence, Fads, and Informational Cascades, in Mariano Tommasi and Kathryn Ierulli, eds., *The New Economics of Human Behavior* 188, 193–195 (Cambridge: Cambridge University Press, 1995), and on the discussion in Cass R. Sunstein, *Why Societies Need Dissent* 55–73 (Cambridge, Mass.: Harvard University Press, 2003).

2. See Matthew J. Salganik et al., Experimental Study of Inequality and Unpredictability in an Artificial Cultural Market, *Science* 311 (2006)

3. Id.

4. See Fabio Lorenzi-Cioldi and Alain Clémence, Group Processes and the Construction of Social Representations, in Michael A. Hogg and R. Scott Tindale, eds., *Blackwell Handbook of Group Psychology: Group Processes* 311, 315–317 (Oxford: Blackwell Publishing, 2001).

5. See Allport and Postman, *The Psychology of Rumor*, 35 (New York: Holt, 1947) .

6. See Roger Brown, *Social Psychology: The Second Edition* (New York: Free Press, 1986).

7. See J. A. F. Stoner, A Comparison of Individual and Group Decision Involving Risk (unpublished master's thesis, Massachusetts Institute of Technology, 1961).

8. See Lawrence Hong, Risky Shift and Cautious Shift: Some Direct Evidence on the Culture Value Theory, 41 *Social Psych* 342 (1978).

9. See id.

10. Serge Moscovici and Marisa Zavalloni, The Group as a Polarizer of Attitudes, *J. Personality & Soc. Psychol.* 12, 125–135 (1969).

11. Id.; Brown, *Social Psychology*, 210–212.

12. See Hong, Risky Shift.

13. John C. Turner, Michael A. Hogg, Penelope J. Oakes, Stephen D. Reicher, and Margaret S. Wetherell, *Rediscovering the Social Group: A Self-Categorization Theory* (New York: Basil Blackwell, 1987): 142–170.

14. Id., at 153.

15. Id.

16. Paul Cromwell, Alan Marks, James N. Olson, and D'Aunn Wester Avary, Group Effects on Decision-Making by Burglars, 69 *Psychol. Rep.* 579, 586 (1991).

17. See Norris Johnson, James G. Stemler, and Deborah Hunter, Crowd Behavior as "Risky Shift": A Laboratory Experiment, 40 *Sociometry* 183 (1977).

18. Id., at 186.

19. See E. Allan Lind, Laura Kray, and Leigh Thompson, The Social Construction of Injustice: Fairness Judgments in Response to Own and Others' Unfair Treatment by Authorities, 75 *Organizational Behavior and Human Decision Processes* 1 (1998).

20. Id., at 16.

21. Terry Ann Knopf, *Rumors, Race and Riots*, (New Brunswick: Transaction Publishers, 2006) offers examples in the domain of racial conflict

22. See Brown, *Social Psychology*, 200–245.

23. See Robert Baron, Sieg Hoppe, Chuan Feng Kao, Bethany Brunsman, Barbara Linneweh, and Diane Rogers, Social Corroboration and Opinion Extremity, 32 *J. Experimental Soc. Psych.* 537 (1996).

24. See Mark Kelman, Yuval Rottenstrich, and Amos Tversky, Context-Dependence in Legal Decision Making, 25 *J. Legal Stud.* 287–288 (1996).

25. Baron, Social Corroboration.

26. See Tolga Koker and Carlos Yordan, Microfoundations of Terrorism: Exit, Sincere Voice, and Self-Subversion in Terrorist Networks (unpublished manuscript, 2009).

27. Allport and Postman, *The Psychology of Rumor* at 182.

28. See Marc Sageman, *Leaderless Jihad* (Philadelphia: University of Pennsylvania Press, 2008).

29. Id., at 116.

30. Id.

31. See Joseph Henrich, Wulf Albers, Robert Boyd, Gerg Gigerenzer, Kevin A. McCabe, Axel Ockenfels and H. Peyton Young, Group Report: What Is the Role of Culture in Bounded Rationality? in Gerd Gigerenzer and Reinhard Selten, eds., *Bounded Rationality: The Adaptive Toolbox* 353–354, (Cambridge, Mass.: MIT Press, 2001), for an entertaining outline in connection with food choice decisions.

32. Edward Glaeser, Psychology and Paternalism, 73 U Chi L Rev 133 (2006).

33. Id. It has similarly been suggested that majorities are especially potent because people do not want to incur the wrath, or lose the favor, of large numbers of people, and that when minorities have influence it is because they produce genuine attitudinal change. See Baron, Social Corroboration, 82. The demonstrated fact that minorities influence privately held views on such contested issues as gay rights and abortion (see id., at 80) attests to the value of creating institutions that allow room for diverse voices.

34. For a catalogue, see http://www.chillingeffects.org/.

35. For discussion, see Cass R. Sunstein, *Infotopia* (New York: Oxford University Press, 2006).

36. See Daniel Solove, *The Future Of Reputation: Gossip, Rumor, and Privacy on the Internet* (New Haven: Yale University Press, 2007).

6. Reputation Regulation

1. David Brin, *The Transparent Society: Will Technology Force Us to Choose between Privacy and Freedom?* (Basic Books, 1999).

2. Daniel Solove, *The Digital Person* (N.Y.U. Press, 2004).

3. Darby Dickerson, Background Checks in the University Admissions Process: An Overview of Legal and Policy Considerations, 34 *J. College & Uni. Law* 419, 492, n. 514 (2008).

4. Robert Sprague, Googling Job Applicants: Incorporating Personal Information into Hiring Decisions, 23 *Labor Lawyer* 19 (2007); Thomas F. Holt Jr. & Mark D. Pomfret, Finding the Right Fit: The Latest Tool for Employers, 14 *Metro. Corp. Counsel* 29 (2006); Robert Sprague, Rethinking Information Privacy in an Age of Online Transparency, 25 *Hofstra Lab. & Emp. L. J.* 395 (2008).

5. Richard A. Paul & Lisa H. Chung, Brave New Cyberworld: The Employer's Legal Guide to the Interactive Internet, 24 *Lab. Law.* 109 (2008).

6. Jeana H. Frost & Michael P. Massagli, Social Uses of Personal Health Information within PatientsLikeMe, an Online Patient Community: What Can Happen When Patients Have Access to One Another's Data, 10 *J. of Med. Internet Research No.* 3 (2008), available at http://www.jmir.org/2008/3/e15#ref26.

7. Ian Ayres, *Super Crunchers* (Random House, 2008) (discussing data-driven decision making by "number crunchers" enabled by ever-faster computers); Stephen Baker, *The Numerati* (Houghton-Mifflin Harcourt, 2008) ("[S]ome 40 PhDs, from data miners and statisticians to anthropologists . . . comb through [IBM] workers' data").

8. Taylor, *The Politics of Recognition* (Princeton University Press, 2001) 25 ("The thesis is that our identity is partly shaped by recognition or its absence, often by the *mis*recognition of others . . .").

9. Martha Nussbaum, "Legal Weapon," *The Nation* (2006) (reviewing Catharine MacKinnon, "Are Women Human?") ("Inequality on the basis of sex is a pervasive reality of women's lives all over the world").

10. With personalized search, a search engine can use artificial intelligence and other methods to gradually "learn" what a user is most likely to want given his or her pattern of responses to past results. See James E. Pitkow, Hinrich Schütze, Todd Cass, Rob Cooley, Don Turnbull, Andy Edmonds, Eytan Adar & Thomas Breuel, Personalized Search, 45 *Communications of the ACM* 50 (2002) (discussing methods of personalizing search systems).

11. For a prescient examination of objectification resulting from reductionism here, see Julie Cohen, Examined Lives: Informational Privacy and the Subject as Object, *Stan. L. Rev.* 52 (2000) 1373.

12. ICRs are "dossiers on consumers that include information on character, reputation, personal characteristics, and mode of living. ICRs are compiled from personal interviews with persons who know the consumer." See Electronic Privacy Information Center, Fact Sheet on the Fair Credit Reporting Act, available at http://epic.org/privacy/fcra/.

13. Robert Ellis Smith, Ben Franklin's Website 317 (2000) (discussing routine invasions of privacy by CRA's; "countless reports included the fact that a prospective insured was living 'without benefit of wedlock' "; "unverified rumors of homosexuality" were common; the southern-based Retail Credit Co.'s "young, barely trained 'investigators' prepared reports for insurance companies that reported the drinking habits of consumers . . .").

14. *Id.,* at 316.

15. 15 U.S.C. §1681(a)(1)–(4).

16. 15 U.S.C. §1681(b).

17. 15 USCS 1681a(f).

18. 15 U.S.C. §1681o. This paragraph and the last summarize provisions from 15 U.S.C. §1681.

19. Jonathan Zittrain, *The Future of the Internet and How to Stop It* (Yale University Press, 2008), 227.

20. Viktor Mayer-Schonberger, *Delete: The Virtues of Forgetting in the Digital Age* (Princeton University Press, 2009).

21. Danielle Citron, Technological Due Process, *Washington L. Rev.* (2007).

22. Frank Pasquale, Rankings, Reductionism, and Responsibility, *Clev. St. L. Rev.* 54 (2006) 115; Frank Pasquale, Asterisk Revisited: Debating a Right of Reply on Search Results, 3 *Journal of Business & Technology Law* (2008) 61.

23. Kaimipono D. Wenger, Google Profiles and Online Self-Ownership, available at http://www.concurringopinions.com/archives/2009/04/google_profiles.html.

24. Nissenbaum assists us in understanding the use of the term "privacy" in the general sense as the "power to share information discriminately." Helen Nissenbaum, Privacy as Contextual Integrity, *Wash. L. Rev.* 79 (2004) 119, 121 (citing James Rachels, "Why Privacy is Important," in Ferdinand David Schoeman ed., *Philosophical Dimensions of Privacy: An Anthology* (1984) 290, 294).

25. *Act on the Protection of Privacy in Working Life* (759/2004).

26. For a discussion of the last area of law, see Paul M. Schwartz, Beyond Lessig's Code for Internet Privacy: Cyberspace Filters, Privacy Control, and Fair Information Practices, 2000 *Wis. L. Rev.* 743 (2000).

27. For an example of the limits of discrimination law, see Elizabeth Emens, Intimate Discrimination, 122 *Harv. L. Rev.* 1307 (2009) ("legal regulation targeting individual differentiation on these bases [in the intimate domain of sex and love] would be woefully misguided").

28. Ronald Moss, *When All Else Fails: Government as Ultimate Risk Manager* (Harvard University Press, 1999).

29. Richard Posner, *A Failure of Capitalism* (Harvard Univ. Press, 2009); Andrew Ross Sorkin, *Too Big to Fail* (Viking Adult, 2009).

30. J. Hoult Verkerke, Legal Regulation of Employment Reference Practices, 65 *U. Chi. L. Rev.* 115 (1998) ("Prospective employers and regulators confront three analytically distinct problems: falsely negative references, an inadequate supply of reference information, and falsely positive references").

31. *Id.*

32. Dennis D. Hirsch, Protecting the Inner Environment: What Privacy Regulation Can Learn from Environmental Law, 41 *Ga. L. Rev.* 1 (2006).

33. Tal Zarsky, Law and Online Social Networks, 18 Fordham Intell. Prop. Media & Ent. L.J. 741, 780 ("The state should take a proactive role in battling gaming practices transpiring in social networks and move to bring legal action against those engaging in these practices. In doing so, the state could rely on existing legal doctrines and laws, such as fraud, misrepresentation and various laws addressing unfair business practices").

34. Jon D. Michaels, All the President's Spies: Private-Public Intelligence Partnerships in the War on Terror, 96 *Cal. L. Rev.* 901 (2008) (describing in detail favors granted to FedEx and other companies for participation in fusion centers, which combine public and private data about individuals into unified dossiers upon request of homeland security officials); Jack Balkin, The National Surveillance State, 93 *Minn. L. Rev.* 1 (2008).

35. Lior Strahilevitz, Reputation Nation: Law in an Era of Ubiquitous Personal Information, 102 *NW. U. L. Rev.* 1667 (2008).

36. Liz Pulliam Weston, Eight Secret Scores That Lenders Keep, *MSN Money,* available at http://articles.moneycentral.msn.com/Banking/YourCreditRating/8SecretCreditScoresThatLendersKeep.aspx?page=all (describing "complex and largely secret scoring systems"); Liz Pulliam Weston, Your Credit Score, Your Money & What's at Stake (Updated Edition): How to Improve the 3-Digit Number that Shapes Your Financial Future (FT Press, 2009).

37. NAMIC Online, NAMIC's State Laws and Legislative Trends: State Laws Governing Insurance Scoring Practices 1 (2004), available at http:// www .namic.org/reports/credithistory/credithistory.asp.

38. Frank M. Fitzgerald, Comm'r, Office of Fin. and Ins. Serv., "The Use of Ins. Credit Scoring in Auto. and Home Owners Ins.: A Report to the Governor," the Legislature and the People of Mich. (2002), available at www.michigan .gov/documents/cis_ofis_credit_scoring_report_52885_7.pdf; Haw. Rev. Stat. §431:10C–207 (2005).

39. For example, see Birny Birnbaum, Insurer's Use of Credit Scoring for Homeowner's Insurance in Ohio: A Report to the Ohio Civil Rights Commission, 2 (Jan. 2003), available at http://www.cej-online.org/report_to_ohio_civil_rights_commission.pdf.

40. Robert Berners, "Hospitals X-Ray Patient Credit Scores: More and More Are Buying Credit Data to See If the Sick Can Afford Treatment," Businessweek, (December 1, 2008) available at http://www.businessweek.com/magazine/content/08_48/b4110080413532.htm?chan=magazine+channel_what%27s+next.

41. Jonathan Zittrain, The Future of the Internet and How to Stop It (Yale Univ. Press, 2008) 218.

42. Kevin Arrington, Rapleaf Tags, posting to the TechCrunch blog, available at http://www.techcrunch.com/tag/rapleaf/.

43. The next few paragraphs are based on the decision Browne v. Avvo, 525 F. Supp. 2d 1249 (W. D. Wa. 2007).

44. James Grimmelmann, The Structure of Search Engine Law, 90 Iowa L. Rev. 545 (2007).

45. See e.g. Suzuki Motor Corp. v. Consumers Union of United States, Inc., 330 F.3d 1110 (9th Cir. Cal. 2003).

46. See e.g. Complaint & Settlement Announcement, Washington State Medical Association v. Regence BlueShield (2006).

47. See e.g. Bose Corp. v. Consumers Union, 466 U.S. 485 (1984); David J. Grais and Kostas D. Katsiris, Not "The World's Shortest Editorials: Why the First Amendment Does Not Shield the Rating Agencies from Liability for Over-rating CDO's, available at http://www.graisellsworth.com/Rating_Agencies .pdf.

48. See Surgistrategies, Lawsuit: Insurance Commission Physician Tiering Program Flawed, available at http://www.surgicenteronline.com/hotnews/ insurance-commission-physician-tiering.html.

49. Id.

50. Id.

51. Physicians and Regence BlueShield Settle Lawsuit, Press Release, August 8, 2007.

52. Id.

53. Id.

54. Attorney General Cuomo Announces Doctor Ranking Agreement with GHI and HIP: Five Insurers in Three Weeks Adopt Model Created Together with National Medical and Consumer Groups, Press Release, November 20, 2007.

55. Molly McDonough, "Cuomo's Doctor-Ranking Model Gains Political Trac-tion," ABA Journal (November 26, 2007) available at http://www.abajournal .com/news/article/cuomos_doctor_ranking_model_gains_political_traction/.

56. Email from Linda Lacewell, chair of the New York Attorney General's Health Care Task Force, to Frank Pasquale, October 27, 2008 ("CIGNA and other plans have agreed to disclose their methodologies to the public").

57. Chaplinsky v. New Hampshire, 315 U.S. 568, 572 (1942).

58. Robert Post, Recuperating First Amendment Doctrine, Stan. L. Rev. 47 (1995) 1249, 1250; Fredrick Schauer, The Boundaries of the First Amendment: A Preliminary Exploration of Constitutional Salience, Harv. L. Rev. 117 (2004) 1765, 1769.

59. Central Hudson Gas & Electric Co. v. Public Service Comm., 447 U.S. 557 at 561–563 (1980).

60. Id.; see also Metromedia v. City of San Diego, 453 U.S. 490 (1981). The regulation must be reasonably tailored to protect the asserted state interest.

61. Chaplinsky v. New Hampshire, 315 U.S. 568, 572 (1942); Nimmer for locus classicus; Eldred v. Ashcroft, 537 U.S. 186 (2003).

7. Youthful Indiscretion in an Internet Age

1. The rise and fall of a champion in Beijing, Associated Press, Aug. 11, 2008, at http://sports.espn.go.com/espn/wire?section=oly&id=3529287.
2. Richard Morgan, Revenge Porn, Details, Sept. 30, 2008, at http://men.style .com/details/blogs/details/2008/09/revenge-porn.html.
3. http://www.exgfpics.com/blog/ (accessed Nov. 13, 2008).
4. As these examples suggest, this essay focuses on truthful disclosures. For a discussion of false rumors, see Cass R. Sunstein, On Rumors: How Falsehoods Spread, Why We Believe Them, What Can Be Done (2009).
5. Mike Celizic, Her Teen Committed Suicide Over "Sexting," MSNBC.com, Mar. 6, 2009, at http://www.msnbc.msn.com/id/29546030/.
6. For a dissection of different interests often collected under the label "privacy," see Martha C. Nussbaum, Sex Equality, Liberty, and Privacy: A Comparative Approach to the Feminist Critique, in India's Living Constitution: Ideas, Practices, Controversies, eds. Z. Hasan, E. Sridharan, and R. Sudarshan (Delhi: Permanent Black, 2002) 242–283.
7. Doe v. Methodist Hosp., 690 N.E.2d 681, 692 (Ind. 1997).
8. See Jonathan Zittrain, The Future of the Internet 228 (2007) (proposing a right to declare "reputation bankruptcy").
9. Lawrence M. Friedman, Guarding Life's Dark Secrets (2007).
10. Fresh start, generally, in Bankruptcy Service §27:13 (2008).
11. Fred C. Zacharias, The Uses and Abuses of Convictions Set Aside Under the Federal Youth Corrections Act, 1981 Duke L. J. 477.
12. Department of Health Education, and Welfare, Secretary's Advisory Committee on Automated Personal Data Systems, Records, Computers and the Rights of Citizens (1973).
13. FCRA §605. The label "outdated" is used in FCRA §609 to characterize the information excluded by FCRA §605.
14. Melvin v. Reid, 112 Cal. App. 285, 292 (Cal. App. 1931).
15. Id.
16. Federal Trade Commission, Privacy Online: A Report to Congress, 42–43 (June 1998), at www.ftc.gov/reports/privacy3/index.htm.
17. Anita L. Allen, Minor Distractions: Children, Privacy and E-Commerce, 38 Hous. L. Rev. 751 (2001).
18. Friedman, Life's Dark Secrets, at 213.
19. 18 U.S.C. §§2252A, 2256 (criminalizing the visual depiction of explicit sexual conduct by persons under the age of eighteen years); United States v. Williams (2008).
20. 18 U.S.C. §2257.
21. A. H. v. State, 949 So.2d 234 (Fla.App. 1 Dist., 2007) ("16-year-old appellant, A. H., and her 17-year-old boyfriend, J. G. W., were charged as juveniles under the child pornography laws. The charges were based on digital photos A. H. and J. G. W. took on March 25, 2004, of themselves naked and engaged in sexual behavior").

22. See Beth A. Eck, Men Are Much Harder: Gendered Viewing of Nude Images, 17 Gender & Society 691, 692–693 (2003) ("The historical prevalence of female nude images cannot be denied").

23. The National Campaign to Prevent Teen and Unplanned Pregnancy, Sex and Text: Results from a Survey of Teens and Young Adults, at http://www .thenationalcampaign.org/sextech/PDF/SexTech_Summary.pdf (2008).

24. Lewis v. LeGrow, 258 Mich. App. 175 (Ct. App. 2003).

25. Wood v. Hustler Magazine, Inc., 736 F.2d 1084 (5th Cir. 1984); Douglass v. Hustler Magazine, Inc., 769 F.2d 1128 (7th Cir. 1986); Solano v. Playgirl, Inc., 292 F.3d 1078 (2002).

26. Restatement (2nd) of Torts §652D (1977).

27. Michaels v. Internet Entertainment Group, Inc., 5 F.Supp. 2d 823, 840 (1998).

28. Florida Star v. B.J.F., 491 U.S. 524, 527 n.2 (1989).

29. S. B. v. Saint James School, 959 So.2d 72, 79 (Ala. 2006).

30. Doe v. Friendfinder Network, Inc., 540 F.Supp. 2d 288, 302–303 (D.N.H. 2008).

31. Doe I v. Individuals, Whose True Names Are Unknown, 561 F.Supp. 2d 249 (D.Conn. 2008); see also Nathaniel Gleicher, Note, John Doe Subpoenas: Toward a Consistent Legal Standard, 118 Yale L. J. 320 (2008).

32. Anita L. Allen, Why Privacy Isn't Everything: Feminist Reflections on Personal Accountability (2003).

33. 491 U.S. 524 (1989).

34. Id., at 533.

35. 18 U.S.C. §2710.

36. Bartnicki v. Vopper, 532 U.S. 514, 533 (2001).

37. Allen, Privacy Isn't Everything, at 153.

38. Richard Posner, The Right to Privacy, 12 Ga. L. Rev. 393, 394 (1978).

39. Lior Jacob Strahilevitz, Reputation Nation: Law in an Era of Ubiquitous Personal Information, 102 Nw. U. L. Rev. 1667 (2008).

40. Posner, Right to Privacy, at 400.

41. Doe v. Methodist Hosp., 690 N.E.2d 681, 692 (Ind. 1997).

42. Saint James School, 81–83.

43. Lodge v. Shell Oil Co., 747 F.2d 16, 20 (1st Cir. 1984).

44. Nussbaum, Feminist Critique.

45. Catharine A. MacKinnon, Toward a Feminist Theory of the State 190 (1991).

46. Id., at 194.

47. Judith Wagner DeCew, In Pursuit of Privacy: Law, Ethics, and the Rise of Technology 164 (1997).

48. Boyles v. Kerr, 855 S.W.2d 593, 602–603 (Tex., 1993). The plaintiff in the case brought a negligence claim rather than a privacy tort claim, apparently because a negligence claim might have been covered by an insurance policy while an intentional tort would not have been so covered.

8. Academic Administrators and the Challenge of Social-Networking Websites

1. Social-networking websites—such as Facebook and MySpace—are the type of websites featured in this paper because of their widespread popularity among students, not because research indicates that they are more prone to cyber bullying than other websites. Indeed, the primary function of social-networking websites is to help people form positive connections. Facebook, which is repeatedly mentioned in this paper, has taken significant steps toward reducing its capacity to be used for cyber bullying. However, because of their popularity and unique ability to support online communities, social-networking websites continue to be used by students for cyber bullying.

2. Online social-networking sites also present benefits in the form of social capital. See, generally Nicole B. Ellison, Charles Steinfield, and Cliff Lampe, The Benefit of Facebook "Friends": Social Capital and College Students' Use of Online Social Network Sites, 12 *Journal of Computer-Mediated Communication,* Issue 4, 1143 (2007).

3. Facebook, which was started by a Harvard University student in 2004, currently reports having 110 million active users.

4. Facebook tied with drinking beer as the second most popular "in" things on college campuses in 2006. Spring 2006 Lifestyle & Media Study, *Student Monitor.*

5. For example, passing notes, online chatting, and most forms of verbal communication are limited to one-time transactions with limited scope and duration of timing. With Facebook, however, it is feasible for every member of a classroom to have simultaneous access to the same, real-time information.

6. Jeffrey R. Young, The Fight for Classroom Attention: Professor vs. Laptop, *The Chronicle of Higher Education* (June 2, 2006), available at http://chronicle.com/free/v52/i39/39a02701.htm.

7. No studies examining the extent of administrators' awareness of the community aspects of social-networking websites were found. However, "solutions" such as merely disabling Internet use without additional steps indicate that administrators may fail to recognize the unique nature of social-networking websites.

8. Rob Capriccioso, Facebook Face Off, *Inside Higher Ed* (February 14, 2006), available at http://www.insidehighered.com/news/2006/02/14/facebook (relaying specific, vulgar comments, which can be retrieved from this website, and the related .jpg image is available as a link on that web page).

9. Nick Martin, *U of M Probes Cyberbullying on Student Site,* Winnipeg Free Press (March 1, 2008), available at http://winnipegfreepress.com/local/story/3896724p-4506596c.html.

10. Rebecca Camber, "Little Fat Library Man" Ridiculed in Students' Facebook Bullying Campaign, *Mail Online* (July 24, 2007), available at http://www.dailymail.co.uk/news/article-470610/Little-fat-library-man-ridiculed-students-Facebook-bullying-campaign.html.

11. J. S. ex rel. Snyder v. Blue Mountain School Dist., 2008 WL 4279517, *1 (M.D. Pa., 2008).

12. Parents: Cyber Bullying Led to Teen's Suicide, *ABC News* (November 19, 2007), available at http://abcnews.go.com/GMA/Story?id=3882520&page=1; Duncan Gardham, Facebook and Bebo Used to Bully Teachers, Telegraph (June 25, 2008), available at http://www.telegraph.co.uk/digitallife/main.jhtml?xml=/connected/2008/06/25/dlfacebook125.xml. ("Earlier this month Sam Leeson, 13, hanged himself at his parents Gloucestershire home after allegedly being mocked online for being a follower of 'emo' music. And in February it was revealed that a 16-year-old boy from Sussex, who for legal reasons cannot be named, took an overdose of 60 painkillers in a failed suicide bid after being targeted by Bebo bullies.")

13. Tara Parker-Pope, With Bullying, Suicide Risks for Victims and Tormentors, New York Times (July 18, 2008), ("While there is no definitive evidence that bullying makes kids more likely to kill themselves, now that we see there's a likely association, we can act on it and try to prevent it," said lead author Dr. Young-Shin Kim, assistant professor at Yale School of Medicine's Child Study Center).

14. Camber, Library Man ("Mr. Mallaghan has said the bullying had affected his studies and destroyed his confidence").

15. Facebook groups devoted to law school "gunners" (loosely defined as students who talk frequently in class) include: "Law Students against Gunners," "1Ls against Gunners," "2Ls against Gunners," and "Attention All Gunners: Put Your Hand Down and Shut the Fuck Up."

16. Young, Classroom Attention.

17. Katherine Mangan, Cutting the Power, Chronicle for Higher Education (September 2001), available at http://chronicle.com/free/v48/i02/02a04301.htm.

18. Id.

19. Id.

20. Id.

21. Andy Carvin, Facing Up to Facebook, PBS Teachers: Learning Now (December 2006), available at http://www.pbs.org/teachers/learning.now/2006/12/facing_up_to_facebook.html.

22. Id.

23. Id.

24. Stu Woo, The Facebook, Not Just for Students, Brown Daily Herald (November 2005), available at http://media.www.browndailyherald.com/media/storage/paper472/news/2005/11/03/CampusWatch/The-Facebook.Not.Just.For.Students-1044229.shtml.

25. Id.

26. Carvin, Facing Up to Facebook.

27. Id.

28. Woo, The Facebook.

29. Rob Cappriccioso, Facebook Face Off, Inside Higher Ed (February 2006), available at http://www.insidehighered.com/news/2006/02/14/facebook.

30. Id.

31. Id.

32. Id.

33. Louise Brown, Student Faces Facebook Consequences, Thestar.com (March 2008), available at http://www.thestar.com/News/GTA/article/309855.

34. Sameer Hinduja and Justin W. Patchin, Cyberbullying Factsheet: A Brief Review of Relevant Legal and Policy Issues (2009) (available at http://www.cyberbullying.us/01_cyberbullyingfactsheet.pdf.

35. Staff Report, Social Networking Sites Confound Schools, E-School News (November 2006), available at http://www.eschoolnews.com/resources/minimizing-classroom-disruptions/articlesmcs/index.cfm?i=42038&page=3.

9. Cleaning Cyber-Cesspools

1. Other examples include some of the sites discussed in Danielle Citron's contribution to this volume. Among blogs known to lawyers, the comments section of "Above the Law," http://abovethelaw.com/, is an obvious example of a cyber-cesspool. (The comments are so bad that the proprietors of the site, too lazy to actually moderate them, simply require readers to click on a button, after a warning, in order to read them.)

2. See general, Frederick Schauer, *Free Speech: A Philosophical Enquiry* (Cambridge: Cambridge University Press, 1983).

3. For a useful overview of such proposals, see Bradley A. Areheart, "Regulating Cyberbullies through Notice-Based Liability," http://yalelawjournal.org/content/view/581/14/

4. See generally Saul Levmore's contribution to this volume.

5. www.leiterreports.typepad.com. At that time, the blog covered professional news and issues in both academic philosophy and academic law.

6. http://volokh.com/archives/archive_2005_03_06–2005_03_12.shtml #1110478573

7. http://volokh.com/posts/1110500300.shtml

8. http://leiterreports.typepad.com/blog/2005/03/penn_law_studen.html

9. Whether I am really a "public figure" for purposes of American libel law is not entirely clear: hence the hedging locution.

10. "Harsh Words Die Hard on the Web," March 7, 2007, http://www.washingtonpost.com/wp-dyn/content/article/2007/03/06/AR2007030602705_pf.html

11. http://blogs.wsj.com/law/2007/05/03/law-firm-rescinds-offer-to-ex-autoadmit-director/

12. Subsequent evidence suggests the individual in question suffers from mental illness, and so there is no point in embarrassing him further in public.

13. After several years, K. eventually deleted his hate blog altogether. I have no idea why.

14. http://www.google.com/corporate/tech.html
15. http://www.juancole.com/2005/03/googlesmear-as-political-tactic-google.html
16. An alternative route to the same conclusion would be to invoke something like Joel Feinberg's "Offense Principle," though for simplicity of presentation I will focus just on the idea of "harm." See generally, Joel Feinberg, *The Moral Limits of the Criminal Law: Offense to Other* (Oxford: Oxford University Press, 1985).
17. See Alexander Meilkeljohn, *Free Speech and Its Relevance to Self-Government* (1948).
18. John Stuart Mill, ON LIBERTY 104 (New Haven, CT: Yale University Press, 2003).
19. The Luddite Sociopath, in other words, wants to eliminate what Daniel Solove aptly calls "the corrective of familiarity." *The Future of Reputation* 37 (2007).
20. Defenders of Section 230, in a discussion of this paper at New York Law School, could point only to various bits of humor (like "rickrolling": see http://en.wikipedia.org/wiki/Rickroll) as "unique" products of cyberspace. Given the harms, tortious and dignitary, that thrive in cyberspace, it seems like a few jokes aren't really enough to justify the lack of legal regulation.
21. Joseph Raz, *The Morality of Freedom* 381 (Oxford University Press, 1986)
22. As Raz, of course, recognizes.
23. Dan Dobbs, *The Law of Torts* 1169–1172 (2000). See also New York Times Co. v. Sullivan, 376 U.S. 254 (1964).
24. Frank Pasquale, Rankings, Reductionism, and Responsibility, 54 *Clev. St. L. Rev.* 115 (206)
25. Dobbs, *Law of Torts,* 1121–1123.
26. Cal. Civ. Code §48.5(1).
27. Copyright infringement is a strict liability tort whereby all parties in the chain of infringement are jointly and severally liable because "all united in infringing, all are responsible for the damages resulting from infringement." Gross v. Van Dyk Gravure Co., 230 F. 412, 414 (2d Cir. 1916). The infringing parties include both the publisher, Abeshouse v. Ultragraphics, Inc., 754 F.2d 467 (2d Cir. 1985), and the distributor, Parfums Givenchy v. C&C Beauty Sales, 832 F. Supp. 1378 (C.D. Cal. 1993). Some commentators think an extension of liability to search engines is not warranted because the lack of an intent requirement "does not preclude the requirement of volitional conduct." William Patry, *Patry on Copyright* §§21.38, 21.39 (Thomson West Publishing, 2009). Some courts have held that there is a volitional requirement for copyright infringement, see Religious Technology Center v. Netcom On-Line Communication Services Inc., 907 F. Supp. 1361 (N.D. Cal. 1995), and that search engines lack the requisite volitional conduct. Parker v. Google, Inc., 422 F. Supp. 2d 492, 497 (E.D. Pa. 2006). However, the issue of whether the strict liability regime of copyright infringement contains a volitional requirement is not decided. See Perfect 10 Inc. v. Cybernet Ventures Inc., 167 F. Supp. 2d 1114, 1121–1122 (C.D. Cal. 2001). See also Steven J. Horowitz,

"Defusing a Google Bomb," 17 *Yale Law Journal Pocket Part* 36 (2007), http://thepocketpart.org/2007/09/08horowitz.html for related discussion.

28. Solove, *Future of Reputation*, 190

29. James Grimmelman, "The Structure of Search Engine Law," 93 *Iowa L. Rev.* 1, 21 (2007)

30. Mark A. Lemley, "Rationalizing ISP Safe Harbors" in *Internet Service Providers: Law and Regulation* (L. Padmavathi ed., 2008)

31. My thanks to Ben Whiting for helpful research assistance and to the participants in the conference at the University of Chicago Law School, November 21–22, 2008. I am also grateful to questions and comments from a workshop audience at New York Law School, and especially to James Grimmelman, my commentator on that occasion. Finally, this essay was much improved by detailed comments from Martha Nussbaum on the penultimate draft.

10. Privacy, the First Amendment, and the Internet

1. David Denby, *Snark: A Polemic in Seven Fits* (New York: Simon & Schuster, 2009), 1, 3, 5, 10–11. Denby, by the way, does not support the enactment of new laws to deal with these issues, because "censorship in any form . . . will choke legitimate critical speech as well as vicious rant" (ibid., 3).

2. New York Times v. Sullivan, 376 U.S. 254, 270 (1964). Note that this principle applies to public discourse. Whether it applies as well to private speech is unclear. But, except for private email exchanges between individuals, most speech on the Internet clearly falls within the broad category of public discourse because it is intended for a general audience. On private speech, see Frederick Schauer, "Private Speech and the Private Forum: Givhan v. Western Line School District," 1979 *Supreme Court Review* 217.

3. Terminiello v. Chicago, 337 U.S. 1, 3 (1949).

4. Ibid., 4.

5. Chaplinsky v. New Hampshire, 315 U.S. 568, 572 (1942).

6. See Ohralik v. Ohio State Bar Ass'n., 436 U.S. 447, 456 (1978) (commercial advertising); *Chaplinsky,* 572 (fighting words); Roth v. United States, 354 U.S. 476 (1957) (obscenity); *Sullivan,* 254 (false statements of fact); Watts v. United States, 394 U.S. 705 (threats); Dennis v. United States, 341 U.S. 494 (1951) (express advocacy of law violation); New York v. Ferber, 458 U.S. 747 (1982) (child pornography).

7. See Hugo Black, "The Bill of Rights," 35 *New York University Law Review* 865, 874–879 (1960).

8. Schenck v. United States, 249 U.S. 47 (1919).

9. Of course, content-neutral balancing is far more complex than suggested by these two examples. See Geoffrey R. Stone, "Content-Neutral Restrictions," 54 *University of Chicago Law Review* 46 (1987).

10. See Geoffrey R. Stone, "Free Speech in the Twenty-First Century: Ten Lessons from the Twentieth Century," 36 *Pepperdine Law Review* 273, 280–283 (2009).

There are a number of "special circumstances" in which this strong presumption against content-based restrictions does not apply. These range from regulations of speech by government employees to regulations of speech on public property; to regulations of speech by students, soldiers, and prisoners; to regulations of the government's own speech; to regulations that compel individuals to disclose information to the government (see ibid., 285–289).

11. On incidental restrictions on free speech, see Michael Dorf, "Incidental Burdens on Fundamental Rights," 109 *Harvard Law Review* 1175 (1996); Jeb Jubenfeld, "The First Amendment's Purpose," 53 *Stanford Law Review* 767, 769 (2001); Elena Kagan, "Private Speech, Public Purpose: The Role of Government Motive in First Amendment Doctrine," 63 *University of Chicago Law Review* 415, 494–508 (1996); Stone, "Content-Neutral Restrictions," 114; Stone, "Free Speech," 297–298.

12. See New York v. Ferber, 458 U.S. 747 (1982); Ashcroft v. Free Speech Coalition, 535 U.S. 234 (2002).

13. Bartnicki v. Vopper, 532 U.S. 514, 534 (2001).

14. See Daniel J. Solove, *Understanding Privacy* (Cambridge, Mass.: Harvard University Press, 2008), 136–140; Neil M. Richards & Daniel J. Solove, "Privacy's Other Path: Recovering the Law of Confidentiality," 96 *Georgetown Law Journal* 123, 157 (2007); Daniel J. Solove, "The Virtues of Knowing Less: Justifying Privacy Protections against Disclosure,"53 *Duke Law Journal* 967, 971–972 (2003); Susan M. Gilles, "Promises Betrayed: Breach of Confidence as a Remedy for Invasions of Privacy," 43 *Buffalo Law Review* 1, 20–25 (1995); Alan B. Vickery, "Breach of Confidence: An Emerging Tort," 82 *Columbia Law Review* 1426 (1982).

15. Cohen v. Cowles Media Co., 501 U.S. 663, 670 (1991). See Erie Telecommunications, Inc. v. City of Erie, 853 F. 2d 1084, 1096 (3d Cir. 1988) ("[c]onstitutional rights, like rights and privileges of lesser importance, may be contractually waived").

16. See *Cohen*, 663 (reporter has no First Amendment right to violate contract not to disclose confidential information); Eugene Volokh, "Freedom of Speech and Information Privacy: The Troubling Implications of a Right to Stop People from Speaking About You," 52 *Stanford Law Review* 1049, 1057–1061 (2000).

17. See, e.g., Snepp v. United States, 444 U.S. 507 (1980) (CIA employees); Anderson v. Strong Memorial Hospital, 151 Misc. 2d 353 (N.Y. Sup. Ct. 1991) (upholding medical confidentiality); Peter A. Winn, "Confidentiality in Cyberspace: The HIPAA Privacy Rules and the Common Law," 33 *Rutgers Law Journal* 617, 679 (2002). For the argument that statutory and common law restrictions requiring confidentiality may violate the First Amendment, see Gilles, "Promises Betrayed," 72–73.

18. See New York Times v. United States, 403 U.S. 713 (1971).

19. For the argument that the law should prohibit the publication of private information derived from breaches of confidential relationships, see Paul

Gewertz, "Privacy and Speech," 2001 *Supreme Court Review* 139 154–155; Solove, "Virtues of Knowing Less," 1017.

20. Samuel Warren and Louis D. Brandeis, "The Right to Privacy," 4 *Harvard Law Review* 193 (1890).

21. Ibid., 196.

22. Ibid., 213.

23. See *Restatement of Torts* 2d §652D; Solove, "Virtues of Knowing Less," 971.

24. Harry Kalven, "Privacy in Tort Law—Were Warren and Brandeis Wrong?" 31 *Law and Contemporary Problems* 326, 336 (1966).

25. The Court has held, however, that an action for invasion of privacy cannot be sustained, consistent with the First Amendment, where the government itself was the source of the private information. See, e.g., Cox Broadcasting Corp. v. Cohn, 420 U.S. 469 (1975) (holding that the First Amendment prohibits an action for damages for invasion of privacy caused by the publication of the name of a deceased rape victim that was publicly revealed in connection with the prosecution of the case); The Florida Star v. B.J.F., 491 U.S. 524 (1989) (same result where the publisher obtained the name of the rape victim from a publicly released police report); Smith v. Daily Mail Publishing Co., 443 U.S. 97 (1979) (same result where the publisher revealed the name of a juvenile offender obtained from police and prosecutors).

26. For example, blasphemy, hate speech, and pornography have all been rejected as candidates for low-value status in part because they are directed at particular points of view. See Burstyn v. Wilson, 343 U.S. 495 (1952) (blasphemy); R.A.V. v. City of St. Paul, 505 U.S. 377 (1992) (hate speech); American Booksellers Association v. Hudnut, 771 F.2d 323 (7th Cir. 1985), aff'd 475 U.S. 1001 (1986) (pornography).

27. I say "usually" because this characteristic is not present for all categories of low-value speech. False statements of fact, for example, do not share this characteristic. Nonetheless, this seems an important if not a necessary factor in low-value analysis, and it is certainly present with respect to some categories, such as fighting words, obscenity, and threats. See Cass R. Sunstein, "Pornography and the First Amendment," 1986 *Duke Law Journal* 589, 603 (stating that speech "that has purely non-cognitive appeal will be entitled to less constitutional protection").

28. See Geoffrey R. Stone, "Sex, Violence and the First Amendment," 74 *University of Chicago Law Review* 1857, 1863–1864 (2007) (identifying these four factors).

29. The noncognitive impact issue is relevant because the First Amendment is designed to promote expression that engages the thought process and attempts to reinforce or alter opinions by rational persuasion. Threats may literally be "speech," but they affect people's behavior by coercion rather than by persuasion. Its primary effect is akin to twisting someone's arm. Similarly, fighting words are analogous to a physical assault. Hurling a personal insult at another person in a face-to-face encounter is more like spitting in his eye than engaging

him in debate. Obscenity is deemed low-value speech in part because it appeals predominantly to the prurient interest in sex. That is, viewing it creates an immediate physiological response of sexual arousal. See Stone, "Sex, Violence," 1864–1865.

30. Thomas I. Emerson, *The System of Freedom of Expression* (New York: Random House, 1970), 326.

31. Cass Sunstein has astutely observed that the low-value theory is essential to "any well-functioning system of free expression" because without it one of two "unacceptable" results would follow: either (1) "the burden of justification imposed on government" when it regulates high-value speech, such as pure political expression, "would have to be lowered"; or (2) "the properly stringent standards applied to efforts to regulate" high-value speech would have to be applied to low-value speech, with the result that government would not be able to regulate speech "that in all probability should be regulated." Cass R. Sunstein, *The Partial Constitution* (Cambridge, Mass.: Harvard University Press, 1993), 233–234.

32. Solove, "Virtues of Knowing Less," 1001. See Note, "The Newsworthiness Defense to the Public Disclosure Tort," 85 *Kentucky Law Journal* 147, 157–164 (1997) (describing judicial interpretations of newsworthiness). Solove makes an admirable effort to define the concept, but the very complexity of his approach ultimately underscores the problem. See Solove, "Virtues of Knowing Less," 1000–1030.

33. Randall P. Bezanson, "The Right to Privacy Revisited: Privacy, News, and Social Change, 1890–1990," 80 *California Law Review* 1133, 1172 (1992). See Diane L. Zimmerman, "Musings on a Famous Law Review Article: The Shadow of Substance," 41 *Case Western Reserve Law Review* 823, 826 (1991) (noting that it "is difficult to achieve stable and serious agreement on the sort of personal information that can readily be foregone"); Emerson, *Free Expression*, 553 (noting that there is no consensus on "what is or what ought to be a matter of public interest").

34. Warren and Brandeis, "Right to Privacy," 215–216.

35. See Jennifer E. Rothman, "Freedom of Speech and True Threats," 25 *Harvard Journal of Law and Public Policy* 283 (2001). For an excellent debate on the definition of threats, see Planned Parenthood v. American Coalition of Life Activists, 290 F. 3d 1085 (9th Cir. 2002). I should note that I agree with the dissenters in this case.

36. See Masses Publishing Co. v. Patten, 244 F. 535 S.D.N.Y. (1917) (Learned Hand); Bernard Schwartz, "Holmes versus Hand: Clear and Present Danger or Advocacy of Unlawful Action?" 1994 *Supreme Court Review* 209, 240–241; Geoffrey R. Stone, *Perilous Times: Free Speech in Wartime from the Sedition Act of 1798 to the War on Terrorism* (New York: W. W. Norton, 2004).

37. For example, if X tried to persuade Y to murder Z in a private conversation, it seems unlikely that the *Brandenburg* test would apply. See Brandenburg v. Ohio, 395 U.S. 444 (1969) (holding that even express advocacy of law violation

in public discourse cannot be punished unless it is likely to cause imminent harm). See Schauer, "Private Speech," (analyzing private speech).

38. Perhaps ironically, Warren and Brandeis understood that private invasions of privacy, illustrated by a conversation between two friends in which one friend reveals private highly offensive and private information about a third person, would not be governed by their proposed tort. This is ironic in the sense that ordinarily we think that private speech is, if anything, entitled to less protection than public speech under the First Amendment. But in this context, Warren and Brandeis reasoned that it was only public dissemination to a large audience that warranted legal restriction. As they observed, the "law would probably not grant any redress for the invasion of privacy by oral publication," because the "injury resulting from such oral communications would ordinarily be so trifling that the law might well, in the interest of free speech, disregard it altogether." Warren and Brandeis, "Right to Privacy," 217.

39. Dun & Bradstreet v. Greenmoss Builders, 472 U.S. 749, 758–759 (1985) (plurality opinion).

40. Connick v. Myers, 461 U.S. 138, 146 (1983). See Rankin v. McPherson, 483 U.S. 378 (1987) (speech involving a matter of public concern).

41. Gertz v. Robert Welch, Inc., 418 U.S. 323, 346 (1974). See also Rosenbloom v. Metromedia, Inc., 403 U.S. 29, 79 (1971) (Marshall, J., concurring).

42. Pickering v. Board of Education, 391 U.S. 563, 568 (1968).

43. See *Restatement (2d) of Torts*, §46.

44. Hustler Magazine v. Falwell, 485 U.S. 46 (1988).

45. Ibid., 53, 55.

46. Howell v. New York Post, 81 N.Y.2d 115, 612 N.E.2d 699 (1993).

47. See *Sullivan*, 254 (chilling effect); Virginia State Board of Pharmacy v. Virginia Citizens Consumer Council, 425 U.S. 748 (1976) (some value); Stone, "Free Speech," 283–285.

48. Warren and Brandeis, "Right to Privacy," 214.

49. Gewertz, "Privacy and Speech," 139.

50. See Solove, "Virtues of Knowing Less," 1053–1063 (arguing that one of the reasons to protect privacy is to facilitate "growth and reformation").

51. Richard A. Posner, "The Right of Privacy," 12 *Georgia Law Review* 393, 419 (1978).

52. See Richard A. Posner, *Economic Analysis of Law* (Boston: Aspen Publishers, 1998), 46; Richard A. Posner, *Overcoming Law* (Cambridge, Mass.: Harvard University Press, 1995), 532; Richard Epstein, "The Legal Regulation of Genetic Discrimination: Old Responses to New Technology," 74 *Boston University Law Review* 1, 12 (1994).

53. Jeffrey Rosen, *The Unwanted Gaze: The Destruction of Privacy in America* (Friday Harbor, Wash.: Turtleback Books, 2006), 8.

54. Solove, "Virtues of Knowing Less," 1039.

55. See *Federal Rules of Evidence*, 404.

56. See Volokh, "Freedom of Speech," 1093 (noting that "in a free speech regime, others' definitions of me should primarily be molded by their own judgments, rather than by my using legal coercion to keep them in the dark").

57. Edward Bloustein, "The First Amendment and Privacy: The Supreme Court Justice and the Philosopher," 28 *Rutgers Law Review* 41, 56–57 (1974).

58. Jacobellis v. Ohio, 378 U.S. 184, 197 (1964) (Stewart, J., concurring) (with reference to obscenity, "I shall not today attempt further to define the kinds of material I understand to be embraced" within that doctrine, but "I know it when I see it").

59. Volokh, "Freedom of Speech," 1092–1093.

60. Diane L. Zimmerman, "Requiem for a Heavyweight: A Farewell to Warren and Brandeis's Privacy Tort," 68 *Cornell Law Review* 291, 332–334 (1983).

61. See Paris Adult Theatre I v. Slayton, 413 U.S. 49 (1973); Miller v. California, 413 U.S. 15 (1973).

62. See, e.g., Young v. American Mini-Theatres, 427 U.S. 50 (1976) (zoning); City of Renton v. Playtime Theatres, 475 U.S. 41 (1986) (zoning); New York v. Ferber, 458 U.S. 747 (1982) (child pornography); Ashcroft v. Free Speech Coalition, 535 U.S. 234 (2002) (child pornography).

11. Foul Language

1. The decisions, e.g., in Texas v. Johnson and R.A.V. v. St. Paul concerning flag burning and cross burning raise separate issues. Flag and cross burning are acts that demonstrate ideas, the violability of the flag and the supremacy of White Christianity, from which the emotions they conventionally express are inseparable. The holding in Cohen v. California, by contrast, applies to words whose conventional emotional expression is separable from the ideas they express.

2. See my review of Douglas Walton, "The Place of Emotion in Argument" in *Informal Logic* 17 (1995): 113–121.

3. Winston Churchill, "Sinews of Peace," speech at Westminster College, March 5, 1946.

4. On this distinction, see J. O. Urmson, *The Emotive Theory of Ethics* (New York: Oxford University Press, 1968), 117–129.

5. Cohen v. California, 403 U.S. 15 (1971).

6. See my "Privacy" in *Contemporary Debates in Social Philosophy,* Laurence Thomas ed. (Oxford: Blackwell Publishing, 2008), 131–145.

7. John Stuart Mill, *On Liberty,* chap. 1., par. 9.

8. Ibid.

9. Ibid., par. 16.

10. See e.g., Frederick Schauer, *Free Speech: A Philosophical Enquiry* (Cambridge: Cambridge University Press, 1982), 11.

11. Mill, *On Liberty,* chap. 1, par. 11.

12. Ibid., chap. 3, par. 1.

13. "But the peculiar evil of silencing the expression of an opinion is, that it is robbing the human race; posterity as well as the existing generation; those who dissent from the opinion still more than those who hold it" (ibid., chap. 2, par. 1).

14. T. M. Scanlon, "A Theory of Freedom of Expression," *Philosophy & Public Affairs* 1 (1972): 204–226. See also Scanlon, "Freedom of Expression and Categories of Expression," *University of Pittsburgh Law Review* 40 (1978–1979): 519–550.

15. Alexander Meiklejohn, *Free Speech and Its Relation to Self-Government* (New York: Harper and Brothers Publishers, 1948).

16. Ibid., 25.

17. I owe this point to Geoffrey Stone.

18. An example of such anger that received extensive coverage in the news and on TV talk shows was the tirade the comedian Michael Richards launched at a Los Angeles comedy club in reaction to being heckled. See "Richards Tries to Explain His Rant at Comedy Club" by Bill Carter, *New York Times* (November 22, 2006).

19. Scanlon, "Freedom of Expression," 224.

20. Plato, *Crito*, 51b3–51b4, 51b9-51c1, 51e4–52a3.

21. See Peter Singer, *Democracy and Disobedience* (Oxford: Oxford University Press, 1973), 65–68.

22. I am grateful to David Rabban for this point.

23. See "Pair Guilty of Homophobic Chants at Footballer Sol Cambell," *Guardian* (May 15, 2009).

24. Ronald Dworkin, "Why Must Speech Be Free?" in *Freedom's Law* (Cambridge, Mass.: Harvard University Press, 1996), 195–213.

25. Ibid., 200.

26. Ibid., 201.

27. Ibid.

28. See Herbert Morris, "Persons and Punishment," *Monist* 52 (1968): 475–501.

29. Indeed, the right would be redundant in any theory that recognized such a general right to liberty. Elsewhere Dworkin denies that there is such a right. See "What Rights Do We Have?" in *Taking Rights Seriously* (Cambridge, Mass.: Harvard University Press, 1977), 266–278.

30. See the chapters in this volume by Brian Leiter, Martha Nussbaum, Daniel Solove, and Danielle Citron.

12. Collective Privacy

1. Daniel Findlay, Tag! Now You're Really It: What Photographs on Social Networking Sites Mean for the Fourth Amendment, 10 *N.C. J. L. & Tech.* 171, at §III.B. (2008).

2. Sarah Lyall, *On Facebook, A Spy Revealed (Pale Legs, Too)*, N.Y. Times, July 6, 2009, at A1.

3. See, e.g., Gill v. Hearst Publishing, 253 P.2d 441, 444–445 (Cal. 1953) (torts); Schneckloth v. Bustamonte, 412 U.S. 218, 228 (1973) (Fourth Amendment).

4. This point is discussed briefly in Lior Jacob Strahilevitz, A Social Networks Theory of Privacy, 72 *U. Chi. L. Rev.* 919, 920 (2005).

5. See, e.g., Anita Allen, Coercing Privacy, 40 *Wm. & Mary L. Rev.* 723, 729 (1999).

6. Lior Jacob Strahilevitz, Reputation Nation: Law in an Era of Ubiquitous Personal Information, 102 *NW. U. L. Rev.* 1667 (2008).

7. Georgia v. Randolph, 547 U.S. 103 (2006).

8. *Id.*, at 120.

9. Rodriguez v. Illinois, 497 U.S. 177 (1990).

10. *Randolph*, at 122.

11. *Randolph*, at 127, 136 (Roberts, C. J., dissenting).

12. *Id.*, at 130.

13. United States Department of Justice v. Reporters Committee for Freedom of the Press, 489 U.S. 749 (1989).

14. 5 U.S.C. §552(b)(6).

15. 5 U.S.C. §552(b)(7)(c).

16. See, e.g., Perkins v. Freedom of Information Commission, 635 A.2d 783, 788–791 (Conn. 1993); Hearst Corporation v. Hoppe, 580 P.2d 246, 252–254 (Wash. 1978).

17. *Reporters Committee*, at 763 n. 13.

18. Terri Villa-McDowell, Privacy and the Rape Victim: The Inconsistent Treatment of Privacy Interests in Two Recent Supreme Court Cases, 2 *S. Cal. Rev. L. & Women's Stud.* 293, 300–301 (1992).

19. New York Times v. Sullivan, 376 U.S. 254, 287 (1964).

20. Santiesteban v. Goodyear Tire & Rubber Co., 306 F.2d 9, 12 (5th Cir. 1962); Ravellette v. Smith, 300 F.2d 854, 857 (7th Cir. 1962); Restatement (Second) of Torts §6521 (1977).

21. *Favish*, 541 U.S. at 170–171.

22. ACLU v. Dept of Defense, 543 F.3d 59, 86 (2d Cir. 2008) (discussing the Supreme Court's *Ray* case in these terms); Jarvis v. Bureau of ATF, available at 2008 WL 2620741, at *12 (N.D. Fla. June 30, 2008).

23. See Associated Press v. U.S. Dep't of Defense, available at 2006 WL 2707395, at *1–3 (S.D.N.Y. Sep. 20, 2006).

24. *Id.*, at *4.

25. *Id.*

26. Associated Press v. U.S. Dep't of Defense, 554 F.3d 274, 287 n. 12 (2d Cir. 2009).

27. See Sadiq Reza, Privacy and the Post-September 11 Immigration Detainees: The Wrong Way to a Right (and Other Wrongs), 34 *Conn. L. Rev.* 1169, 1177–1179, 1183–1184 (2002).

28. *Associated Press*, at 284 n. 8 (citations omitted).

29. Michael A. Heller, The Tragedy of the Anticommons: Property in Transition from Marx to Markets, 111 *Harv. L. Rev.* 621, 633–650 (1998).

30. *Associated Press*, at 287 n. 13.

31. Reza, *Post-September 11 Immigration Detainees*, at 1179–1180.

32. See Boumediene v. Bush, 128 S. Ct. 2229 (2008); Hamdan v. Rumsfeld, 548 U.S. 557 (2006); Rasul v. Bush, 542 U.S. 466 (2005).

33. See, e.g., Michael E. Staten & Fred H. Cate, The Impact of Opt-In Privacy Rules in Credit Markets: A Case Study of MBNA, 52 *Duke L. J.* 745, 748–750 (2003).

34. *Associated Press,* at 293.

35. *Id.,* at 285 n. 10, 289–291.

36. *Id.*

37. William DeJong et al., Requesting Organ Donation: An Interview Study of Donor and Nondonor Families, 7 *Am. J. Critical Care* 13, 20 (1998).

38. Haynes v. Alfred A. Knopf, 8 F.3d 1222 (7th Cir. 1993).

39. *Id.,* at 1233.

40. Doe v. Quiring, 686 N.W.2d 918 (S.D. 2004).

41. The case was discussed briefly in Daniel Solove & Paul Schwartz, *Information Privacy Law* 574–575 (3d ed. 2009). See also Lindsey Weiss, *All in the Family: A Fourth Amendment Analysis of Familial Searching* (Working Paper 2009).

42. See, e.g., State v. Inciarrano, 473 So.2d 1272, 1275–1276 (Fla. 1985).

43. David Greenberg et al., Recidivism of Child Molesters: A Study of Victim Relationship with the Perpetrator, 24 *Child Abuse & Neglect* 1485, 1487–1491 (2000); Karl Hanson & Monique T. Bussiere, Predicting Relapse: A Meta-Analysis of Sexual Offender Recidivism Studies, 66 *J. Consulting & Clinical Psych.* 348, 351 (1998).

44. R. Karl Hanson et al., Sexual Offender Recidivism Risk: What We Know and What We Need to Know, 989 *Ann. N.Y. Acad. Sci.* 154, 155–156 (2003).

45. *Quiring,* at 925 n. 9. The court declared that the plaintiff would have lost because the information at issue was already part of a public record. The law says otherwise. See Kallstrom v. City of Columbus, 136 F.3d 1055, 1063–1065 & n. 3–n. 4 (6th Cir. 1998).

46. *Quiring,* at 918.

47. *Id.,* at 928 (Meierhenry, J., dissenting).

48. Paul Ohm, Broken Promises of Privacy: Responding to the Surprising Failure of Anonymization, 57 *UCLA L. Rev.* (forthcoming 2010).

49. See https://sor.sd.gov/search.aspx (visited June 17, 2009).

13. Privacy on Social Networks

1. *Google/Doubleclick,* FTC File No. 071–0170, at 2–3 (Dec. 20, 2007).

2. Facebook: Statistics, http://www.facebook.com/press/info.php?statistics (accessed June 2008).

3. Catherine Holahan, "MySpace: My Portal?" *Businessweek.com* (June 12, 2008), http://www.businessweek.com/technology/content/jun2008/tc20080612 _801233.htm

4. Faultline, "MySpace Music Deal Poses Multiple Threats." *The Register* (September 8, 2006), http://www.theregister.co.uk/2006/09/08/myspace_threatens_ record_labels/

5. Facebook: Statistics, http://www.facebook.com/press/info.php?statistics (accessed October, 2008). See, also, Brad Stone, "Is Facebook Growing Up Too Fast?" *New York Times* (Mar. 28, 2009), http://www.nytimes.com/2009/03/29/technology/internet/29face.html?emc=eta1.

6. Facebook: Statistics, http://www.facebook.com/press/info.php?statistics (accessed Nov. 2008 and March 2009).

7. Brian Stelter & Tim Arango, "Losing Popularity Contest, MySpace Tries a Makeover," New York Times (May 3, 2009), http://www.nytimes.com/2009/05/04/technology/companies/04myspace.html?ref=technology.

8. See James Grimmelman, "Facebook and the Social Dynamics of Privacy," New York Law School Legal Studies Research Paper Series 08/09 #7, at 42 (August 2008) (available at http://ssrn.com/abstract=1262822).

9. See Lior Strahilevitz, "A Social Networks Theory of Privacy," University of Chicago Law Review 72 (2005), 919–988.

10. Lotus Dev. Corp. v. Borland Int'l, Inc., 516 U.S. 233 (1996).

11. See Kristen Nicole, "Facebook Blocks Google's Friend Connect. There Goes the Open Web," Mashable, (May 15, 2008), http://mashable.com/2008/05/15/facebook-blocks-friend-connec/.

12. See Erica Naone, "Who Owns Your Friends?" Technology Review (July/August 2008), http://www.technologyreview.com/Infotech/20920/?a=f.

13. See Grimmelman, Facebook and Privacy, at 42.

14. See Michael Arrington, "The Very Curious Microsoft-Facebook Data Relationship," TechCrunch (Nov. 14 2008), http://www.techcrunch.com/2008/11/14/the-very-curious-microsoft-facebook-user-data-relationship/.

15. The Facebook principles can be found at http://www.facebook.com/topic.php?uid=54964476066&topic=7960.

16. The Facebook statement of rights and responsibilities can be found at http://www.facebook.com/topic.php?uid=67758697570&topic=7569.

17. Id.

18. Facebook Principle #3, available at http://www.facebook.com/topic.php?uid=54964476066&topic=7960.

19. Stone, "Facebook Growing Up?"

20. Bobbie Johnson, "Privacy No Longer a Social Norm, Says Facebook Founder" Jan. 11, 2010), http://www.guardian.co.uk/technology/2010/jan/11/facebook-privacy.

Contributors

Karen M. Bradshaw received her J. D. in 2010 from the University of Chicago Law School. She was a comment editor of the *University of Chicago Law Review* and staff member of *The Legal Forum*.

Anupam Chander is a scholar of globalization and digitization. A graduate of Harvard College and Yale Law School, he is professor of law at the University of California, Davis. He clerked for Chief Judge Jon Newman of the Second Circuit Court of Appeals and for Judge William Norris of the Ninth Circuit. He represented sovereigns and corporations at Cleary, Gottlieb, Steen & Hamilton in New York and Hong Kong. In spring 2008, he was visiting professor at Yale Law School, and in 2008–2009, he was visiting professor at the University of Chicago Law School. His recent scholarship has appeared in the *Yale Law Journal*, the *University of Chicago Law Review*, the *NYU Law Review*, the *California Law Review*, and the *American Journal of International Law*. He coedited *Securing Privacy in the Internet Age* (2008). His book, *The Electronic Silk Road*, is forthcoming from Yale University Press.

Danielle Keats Citron is a professor of law at the University of Maryland School of Law, whose work focuses on information privacy law, cyberspace law, and administrative law. Her scholarship has appeared in *California Law Review, Michigan Law Review, Southern California Law Review, Washington University Law Review, Boston University Law Review, George Washington Law Review, U.C. Davis Law Review,* and *University of Chicago Legal Forum*. Danielle is an affiliate fellow at the Yale Information Society Project and blogs at Concurring Opinions. She has presented her work widely, including at Yale Law School, Harvard Law School, University of Chicago Law School, Princeton University, University of Michigan Law School, and New York University School of Law. She received a JD, cum laude, and Order of the

Coif, from Fordham University School of Law and a BA in Comparative Area Studies, cum laude, from Duke University.

John Deigh teaches moral and political philosophy at the University of Texas at Austin. He has a joint appointment in the law school and in the philosophy department. He is the author of *The Sources of Moral Agency* (1996) and *Emotions, Values, and the Law* (2008). He was the editor of *Ethics* from 1997–2008.

Brian Leiter is the John P. Wilson Professor of Law and director of the Center for Law, Philosophy & Human Values at the University of Chicago. He writes primarily on issues in moral, political, and legal philosophy and is the author of more than eighty articles and reviews, as well as two books: *Nietzsche on Morality* (2002) and *Naturalizing Jurisprudence* (2007).

Saul Levmore is the William B. Graham Professor of Law at the University of Chicago. From 2001 to 2009 he was Dean of the Law School. His writing has cut across many fields, and most recently has concentrated on topics in public choice, financial and risk regulation, disaster relief and avoidance, tort law, and corporate law.

Martha C. Nussbaum is Ernst Freund Distinguished Service Professor of Law and Ethics at the University of Chicago, appointed in Law, Philosophy, and Divinity. Her books include *Women and Human Development: The Capabilities Approach* (2000), *Upheavals of Thought: The Intelligence of Emotions* (2001), *Hiding From Humanity: Disgust, Shame, and the Law* (2004), *Frontiers of Justice: Disability, Nationality, Species Membership* (2006), *Liberty of Conscience: In Defense of America's Tradition of Religious Equality* (2008), *From Disgust to Humanity: Sexual Orientation and Constitutional Law* (2010), and *Not for Profit: Why Democracy Needs the Humanities* (2010).

Frank Pasquale is the Loftus Professor of Law at Seton Hall Law School, where he has served as the associate director of the Gibbons Institute for Law, Science & Technology. He is presently associate director of Seton Hall's Center for Health and Pharmaceutical Law and Policy, and editor-in-chief of the blog Health Reform Watch. He has been a visiting professor at Yale and Cardozo Law Schools, and he is presently an affiliate fellow of the Yale Information Society Project. He received his BA degree (summa cum laude) from Harvard, and was a Marshall Scholar at Oxford University. Professor Pasquale clerked on the U.S. Court of Appeals for the First Circuit.

He joined the Seton Hall faculty after practicing at Arnold & Porter LLP. In 2008, he testified before the House Judiciary Committee, along with the general counsels of Microsoft, Google, and Yahoo, presenting "Internet Nondiscrimination Principles for Competition Policy Online."

Ruben Rodrigues graduated with honors from the University of Chicago Law School in 2009. He will be an associate at Foley & Lardner LLP specializing in patent litigation, and is licensed to practice law in Illinois and Massachusetts. He has interned at the Electronic Frontier Foundation and the Massachusetts Governor's Office of Legal Counsel. His areas of research interest include the intersection of intellectual property and antitrust law, privacy law, and patent law. In addition to holding a JD, Ruben has an MPA from Northeastern University focusing on Science & Technology Policy and an SB from Massachusetts Institute of Technology (MIT) in Electrical Engineering and Computer Science, with a minor in Mechanical Engineering.

Souvik Saha is a masters candidate at Columbia University in the School of International and Public Affairs. Prior to attending graduate school, he completed a Fulbright research fellowship to India where he studied foreign direct investment and intellectual property rights, as well as U.S. strategic foreign policy toward India.

Daniel J. Solove is a professor of law at the George Washington University Law School. An internationally known expert in privacy law, Solove is the author of more than thirty articles and essays as well as several books, including *Understanding Privacy* (2008), *The Future of Reputation: Gossip and Rumor in the Information Age* (2007) (winner of the 2007 McGannon Award), and *The Digital Person: Technology and Privacy in the Information Age* (2004). He is also the author of a textbook, *Information Privacy Law* (2005), now in its third edition, with coauthor Paul Schwartz. Professor Solove teaches information privacy law, criminal procedure, criminal law, and law and literature. For more information about Professor Solove, go to http://daniel solove.com.

Geoffrey R. Stone is the Edward H. Levi Distinguished Service Professor of Law at the University of Chicago. After serving as a law clerk to Justice William J. Brennan, Jr., he joined the faculty of the university in 1973. From 1987 to 1994, he served as dean of the University of Chicago Law School and from 1994 to 2002 he served as provost of the University of

Chicago. He has written several books, including most recently, *Perilous Times: Free Speech in Wartime* (2004), *War and Liberty: An American Dilemma* (2007), and *Top Secret: When Our Government Keeps Us in the Dark* (2007). He has served as an editor of the *Supreme Court Review* for the past twenty years, as general editor of a fifteen-volume series, *Inalienable Rights,* that is being published by Oxford University Press between 2006 and 2012, and he is writing a new book, *Sexing the Constitution,* which deals with the intersection of sex, religion, history, and law.

Lior Jacob Strahilevitz is professor of law and the Walter Mander Teaching Scholar at the University of Chicago, and Deputy Dean of the Law School. He teaches and writes about privacy law, property law, and intellectual property law. His recent privacy-related scholarship includes "A Social Networks Theory of Privacy" (2005), " 'How's My Driving?' for Everyone (and Everything?)" (2006), "Reputation Nation: Law in an Era of Ubiquitous Personal Information" (2008), "Privacy versus Antidiscrimination" (2008), "Pseudonymous Litigation" (2010), and *Information and Exclusion* (forthcoming in 2010). He thanks Aziz Huq and Martha Nussbaum for helpful comments on earlier drafts, Katie Heinrichs for outstanding research assistance, and the Morton C. Seeley Fund, Milton and Miriam Handler Foundation, and John M. Olin Foundation for research support.

Cass R. Sunstein is the Felix Frankfurter Professor of Law at Harvard Law School (on leave). Since January 2009, he has been working in the federal government. His essay for this volume was finished before he began federal employment, and nothing said here represents an official position in any way. His many books include *Republic.com* (2002), *Risk and Reason* (2002), *The Laws of Fear* (2005), *Worst-Case Scenarios (2007), Going to Extremes* (2009), and (with Richard H. Thaler) *Nudge* (2008).

Index

A TALE MAGNOLIOUS

A TALE
MAGNOLIOUS

Suzanne Nelson

ALFRED A. KNOPF
NEW YORK

THIS IS A BORZOI BOOK PUBLISHED BY ALFRED A. KNOPF

Visit us on the Web! rhcbooks.com

Educators and librarians, for a variety of teaching tools, visit us at RHTeachersLibrarians.com

Library of Congress Cataloging-in-Publication Data is available upon request.

ISBN 978-1-9848-3174-3 (trade) — ISBN 978-1-9848-3175-0 (lib. bdg.) — ISBN 978-1-9848-3176-7 (ebook)

The text of this book is set in 12-point Adobe Garamond Pro.
Interior design by Jaclyn Whalen

Printed in the United States of America
June 2019
10 9 8 7 6 5 4 3 2 1

First Edition

In loving memory of my grandfather George W. Tallman,
a magnolious farmer who believed in luck and dreaming big
and who always embraced the great unknowable with joy.
And for the many farmers in my family, loved one and all.

—S.N.

A girl,
an elephant,
and a dust storm.
That's how it all began. . . .

CHAPTER ONE

In Which a Thief and a Pachyderm Vanish

Nitty Luce wasn't born a thief. She wasn't born to rescue elephants. Or to make miracles. Nobody ever told her that, though, so she never had reason to doubt. If she'd doubted, none of the bamboozling goings-on in Fortune's Bluff that spring might ever have happened.

But they *did* happen.

The morning started much like any other, with Nitty's empty stomach. It was near on two weeks since she'd run away from Grimsgate Orphanage, two weeks fighting pigs for the slop in their troughs and waiting for breadlines to empty out to scrounge a few dropped crumbs. She wouldn't stoop to begging, not after Headmistress Ricketts's stories of police tossing street urchins into lockup. Just yesterday she'd caught sight of her reflection in a store window, and oh, was she a shambles! Her tumbleweed hair poked out in all directions, crispy with days-old dust. There was a film over her sun-toasted skin and her flour-sack dress, so in the glass she appeared more as a dirt smear than a ten-year-old girl.

"You'll bunk in prison with the likes of Cutthroat Cob," Miz Ricketts had told them at the orphanage. She always gave this sinister warning before lights-out, in case any of her wards got ideas about running away at night. "Or worse, Fang-Toothed Lou."

Nitty didn't believe a word of it. At least, not during daylight hours. Still, she didn't like the idea of fangs of any sort, so whenever she caught sight of police officers, she kept her distance.

But this particular morning, she was doing battle with her hunger again, and it was being a downright bully. When she wandered into the heart of a city, a solid piece west of Grimsgate and north of nowhere, she was too light-headed to worry over police. In fact, on reading the poster nailed to a lone withering tree on Main Street, Nitty had to steady herself against a nearby lamppost.

COME ONE, COME ALL!

WITNESS THE DEATH OF A MURDEROUS FOUR-TON BEAST!

PUBLIC HANGING IN THE SQUARE AT HIGH NOON.

A GUSTO AND GALLANT SPECTACLE NEVER TO BE FORGOTTEN.

Below the words was a gruesome cartoon drawing of a circus elephant trampling a man, with a small caption: GREAT MAGNOLIOUS KILLS TRAINER IN COLD BLOOD.

Nitty leaned closer, studying the fangs and claws drawn on the elephant, the steam pouring from its mouth and trunk, the smoldering rage in its eyes. The picture was nightmarish, the sort of sensational rubbish Miz Ricketts loved to read about in the *Daily Tattler*. Nitty didn't think too harshly of the *Tattler*, though. In fact, she often rescued old editions from the fireplace before they became kindling. They offered the most entertaining reading at Grimsgate.

Now the crowd gathered about the poster was nodding and whispering, heads bobbing like the wind-up tin clowns Nitty had once seen in a toy shop.

"Savage business," one man declared, while two young women fretted about needing to procure smelling salts before the hanging. "The Gusto and Gallant Circus is well rid of the monster. I feel its devilry in my very bones. It would kill again, mark my words."

"Yes," one woman twittered. "I heard its eyes are red as Beelzebub himself."

Nitty frowned. What did these people know about this elephant? Not a speck more than she did, probably. She'd never seen an elephant before, and she doubted any of them had either. She'd once read an account of an elephant in the *Tattler*, a "Just So" story by a man named Rudyard Kipling, that said the animals had an "insatiable curiosity." "Insatiable" made her think of eating chocolate, which would be delicious and wonderful, if there were any chocolate to be had. Which there was not. But if "insatiable" made her think of the delicious and wonderful, then an elephant's curiosity must be those things as well.

Elephants must surely be like orphan girls, she decided: creatures sorely misunderstood and blamed for a host of troubles they had nothing to do with.

She nudged her way through the crowd, glimpsing food carts and tinkers' wagons lining the edges of the square. A barbershop quartet sang at one corner while a clown at another sold balloons. The square had the jaunty atmosphere of a carnival, which seemed even worse than backward to Nitty, given the occasion—especially once she spotted a towering crane rising up from its center. The crane, she guessed, was how they meant to hoist Magnolious from her feet. It was every kind of awful. A chain fashioned into a noose hung from its arm, swaying as a forceful gust of wind hit it.

Nitty shielded her eyes from the grit blasting her face, and others around her held kerchiefs to their mouths and scanned the sky. They were worrying over a dust storm, waiting for the telltale mud-colored clouds to barrel down on them with the force of a bison stampede.

Nitty held her breath, scoping for alleyways where she might take shelter, but the gust soon wheezed out.

She turned away from the crane. She wouldn't watch the hanging, a gawker like the rest. It would be too cruel. But—her stomach whined at wafting scents of roasted peanuts and cotton candy—she would stay close by, in case somebody spilled popcorn or dropped one or two precious peanuts. Most any food had a sandy aftertaste these days anyway, so it wouldn't much matter if she got it from the ground.

She was heading toward the peanut cart when a sudden spark of green caught her eye. She swiveled her head and spotted a wooden wagon. A slatted board in its side was propped open to display an array of colorful oddities. Puppets dangling from strings, jewel-toned bottles full of mysterious potions or exotic perfumes, glass globes holding miniature kingdoms so real-looking that Nitty half expected to see ant-sized people popping out of their cottages and castles. The sign painted along the wagon's side read THE MERRYTHOUGHT WINDOWSHOP.

Nitty stepped closer, and again a twinkle of green flashed. She traced it to a small open pouch full of the strangest objects she'd ever seen. Shaped like question marks no bigger than a fingernail, they were the greenest sight in town. Maybe in the whole county—or state, for that matter. Their bright hue was so cheerful, so incandescent, that Nitty had the urge to climb into the pouch with them.

Her heart reached out to them, rising snugly and pleasantly into her throat. Being inside that pouch would be like being in a proper jungle—a jungle so full up with trees and plants that she could wrap herself in hammocks of leaves and weave herself a home of vines. Nothing would be brown in that jungle. Even dirt and rocks would grow lovely, fuzzy moss.

"I know that look, girl." The tinker—mostly hidden by a threadbare cloak—leaned out over the window. Nitty couldn't see the eyes appraising her, but she felt them spinning her stomach like a whirligig. The voice inside the hood echoed like water over stones. "That's a hungry look," it continued. A knotted hand passed over the pouch. "If it's food you're after, I have none to offer."

"I don't want food," Nitty blurted. She had wanted it, badly, only a minute before, but now . . . she couldn't take her eyes from the green glow of the pouch. "That there in the pouch—"

"These?" The tinker's eyes glittered from the cloak's shadows. "These are seeds. They came from the very first garden on earth. The one that grew before anything else. Before people or animals." The tinker leaned closer. "Before hate and cruelty, before kindness was forgotten. Back when there was only love. And hope. Before time itself."

"There wasn't any such garden," Nitty scoffed.

The tinker smiled, a smile that despite its toothlessness was strangely buoyant. "Oh, but there was, and it was greener than spring grass after a rain, so green that being in the garden was like sitting inside an emerald. It held every dream and every promise of what could be, of what the world wanted to become." The tinker's voice was lullaby soft now, and Nitty felt it again, the urge to be sitting in the midst of that green.

"How much? For the seeds?"

The tinker huffed. "You can't afford them. Few people can."

"But . . . what do they grow?" She couldn't stop staring at the shimmering pods. The longer she stared, the more they looked like they were quivering in the pouch, wanting to be free.

With a crooked finger, the tinker beckoned her closer. "That, girl, depends on the farmer. What do you *need* them to grow?"

Nitty stalled, her thoughts a tangle. She hadn't been thinking about planting them, only keeping them. She felt her Gleam Jar pressed against her side, tied around her waist with twine, and thought how lovely the seeds would look inside. It was only a plain mason jar she'd filched from the Grimsgate kitchen on canning day, but what was inside it . . . well . . . those objects gleamed in all the ways, and with all the colors, that the world—in these days of dust and doldrums—didn't. If Nitty had a second heart, her Gleam Jar was it.

Nitty felt the tinker's hooded gaze, and wanted to be out from under it. She lifted her chin and fixed the tinker with a glare. "I don't need anything."

The tinker straightened with a crowlike cackle. "Ah, but you do. More than you know." Just then, a wisp-thin woman with a passel of knee-high children approached the wagon, asking about cough tonics, and the tinker's focus shifted to her.

Nitty's fingers tingled, itching for that pouch. The wind picked up again, and there was a static hum to the air, the sure sign of a dust storm brewing. Murmurs of excitement suddenly rippled through the crowd, and Nitty turned to see a path being parted by police officers in the square as an enormous creature ambled down the street.

"Great Magnolious!" one of the knee-high boys near her cried out. He yanked on his mother's hand, trying to pry her away from the Merrythought wagon. "Hurry up, Mama, or we'll miss the hanging!"

Nitty stretched onto tiptoe for a better view. The elephant was shackled in chains that gave her a shortened, awkward gait. Her folds of skin bore crisscrossing scars, some puffed and gray like the rest of her, others pink, raw, and fresh. Her head hung low, her long-lashed eyelids half closed in tiredness, or sadness. For no logical reason at all, Nitty longed to go to her, to take that enormous head in her hands and press her face against that trunk. She imagined it feeling tickly with bristles, wrinkled as a raisin but altogether lovelier to touch.

Nitty's fists clenched as jeers and taunts burbled in the crowd. *Poor Old Mag,* she thought, *there's nothing beastly about you.*

"Mama!" the boy beside Nitty shouted. "Come on!"

Nitty's attention turned back to the Merrythought wagon and to the seed pouch. She'd had enough of this town and would be on her way. Any town about to kill such a strange- and wonderful-looking animal was too ugly to stay in, even if there were food pickings to be had. But . . . she hesitated. The seeds. She couldn't leave them. She reached out her hand, fingers buzzing with yearning.

A small dirt devil swirled through the square, making everyone lower their heads just long enough for Nitty to snatch the pouch and scurry into the crowd.

She glanced back once, and she could've sworn the tinker's hood swiveled toward her in a knowing way. Seconds passed, without anyone coming after her. She slowed, wrestling a jab of guilt. The truth of it was, she wasn't cut out for stealing. No more than that elephant was cut out for cruelty. Nitty had goodness in her, she was sure of it. Even if nobody else was.

"Nothing but a scrappy, selfish babe you were, from the moment I set eyes on you," Miz Ricketts liked to remind her. "No wonder you were dropped at Grimsgate's doorstep. Who else would have you? What, with that rat's-nest hair and those peculiar eyes?"

Nitty didn't think her eyes were peculiar. They were simply *very* green. Greener than the seeds she'd just stolen. Greener than the tree frog that Nitty had once hidden atop Miz Ricketts's best Sunday hat. (This might've been the best trick Nitty had ever played on the headmistress, except she wasn't positive the poor frog had recovered from the broom beating Miz Ricketts gave it afterward. Nitty herself had been sore for a week from that broom, and she was much sturdier than a frog.)

"Highly suspicious," Miz Ricketts said whenever the subject of Nitty's eyes came up (and she made sure the subject came up daily). "Suspicious and very probably dangerous."

Miz Ricketts expected nothing but the worst from Nitty,

and that disapproval stuck faster than a bur to a bear. It had spread through the Grimsgate staff and the other orphans until Nitty was blamed for every turn of rotten luck that happened at the orphanage. When the children took sick, it was Nitty's "contagion" that had caused it. If a mouse was discovered in the pantry, it was because "that impish child" had put it there. (Of this offense, Nitty was often actually guilty.) Even if Miz Ricketts's bunion took to swelling, it was because Nitty had given it the "evil eye."

For ten years, Nitty had taken the blame when she was (mostly) blameless. Ten years nearly to the day, and now she hurried through the square with the stolen pouch of seeds. Maybe she'd give up on goodness altogether, since it wasn't being generous with offering her chances to claim it. But then she'd be proving Miz Ricketts right.

Nitty stopped mid-step in the swirling dust, deciding to return the seeds to the Merrythought Windowshop, when an eerie whine rose up from the north. She lifted her eyes to the sky. A telltale wall of toast-colored clouds was charging toward them. Within minutes the square would be choked in dust as thick as pudding. No matter how you tried to catch a gasp of clean air during one of these dusters, none would come. Every breath felt like sucking up a mound of chimney soot.

A shudder passed through the crowd, and some hurried for motorcars, carriages, or storefronts, searching for shelter. Nitty's eyes were scouting for someplace to wait the storm out when a police whistle shrilled the air.

"Stop that girl!" An officer across the square jabbed his stick in her direction. "She's a thief!"

Nitty sprang, darting jackrabbit quick between elbows and legs, slipping through grabbing hands. There was only one spot in the entire square where no crowds dared gather. She headed straight for it, heart clattering. Magnolious stood under the crane with two dozen officers surrounding her. Encircling her neck was a chain as thick around as Nitty's leg. The elephant's feet alone were twice the size of Nitty's head. She remembered the poster, and the man crushed under those feet.

Then another thought struck her. This animal was friendless, as was she. This animal was unloved, as was she.

Surely Magnolious wouldn't hurt a body so like herself?

"Mag!" Nitty cried out, when what she really meant was *Help me.*

The words flew to the elephant's ears. Her drooping eyelids opened; her head lifted. She'd been called many names in her life and remembered all of them. There'd been Great Magnolious, which she'd never liked, because it was usually followed by unnerving cheers and applause. There'd been "beast," "cow," and some others that didn't bear repeating, and, most recently, "murderer." That last was the most loathsome because it was said with tones of such anger, such hatred. She'd never, until this moment, been called Mag. It was the way the name was spoken, in desperation and in kindness, that made her raise her head to see the scrawny girl pushing her way through the crowd.

"Mag," Nitty said again as she broke through the circle of officers surrounding the elephant. A collective gasp swept over the onlookers, and whispers broke out.

"The girl's mad."

"She'll get herself killed."

"Girl! Get back from that beast!"

Nitty ignored them, lifting her eyes to Mag's.

The girl and the elephant regarded each other for a long moment. Then Mag gave the smallest toss of her head and lifted her trunk, and Nitty scooted between her front legs and into the safety of Mag's underbelly.

Stillness fell as everyone watched, waited, and feared the worst.

Mag shifted and straightened her legs over Nitty's crouching form, feeling a new purpose and an odd but not unwelcome responsibility for the charge beneath her.

From under Mag, Nitty peered out at the officers. Would any of them get up the gumption to come after her now?

None did.

Not ten seconds later, the duster hurtled into the square, bellowing heat and spitting grainy sand that pricked the skin and blinded the eyes.

The world turned russet, and Nitty could only see the crowd as ghostly shadows passing through streams of flying earth. Mag's body loomed large above her. Shielding her eyes, Nitty crawled out from under the elephant and to her side, then reached for her ear.

Mag bent her head low in response.

"You're good, Old Mag, aren't you?" Nitty said quietly, holding an open hand out to the elephant. "Nothing like they say you are."

Mag blinked, and the tip of her trunk swung to Nitty's hand, flexing as it explored her fingers and palm.

The trunk brushed ticklishly against her hand, and Nitty felt strangely comforted by it.

"I'm leaving here," Nitty said. "Come with me."

Dirt churned around them, growing thicker. At last Mag gave Nitty the gentlest nudge with her giant head, as if to say, *Step back.* Once Nitty was well clear, Mag rose onto her hind legs and, without much effort at all, pulled the chains that bound her from the ground. Then, with her chains loose and dragging, she lowered herself until she rested on her back haunches with her belly nearly brushing the ground. She bent her front left leg at the knee, as if it were a stepping stool, then stilled. Nitty thought she understood, and she stepped onto Mag's awaiting knee and used it for a boost to clamber behind Mag's head. Mag's spine beneath her was hard, her skin rough and prickly, and Nitty's legs stretched so far across the immensity of Mag's neck that her feet stuck out comically. Nitty took hold of the chain about Mag's neck so she'd have something to keep her steady.

As the sky darkened and dust rained down, Mag began walking. Nitty pulled the collar of her shift up over her mouth and scooted farther down on Mag's back, leaning slightly to one side so that her head was behind one of Mag's flapping ears. The ear shielded her from the worst of the dust.

She felt the pouch of seeds hanging on her twine belt, safe alongside the Gleam Jar; she felt the long, lumbering strides of Old Mag beneath her. She felt the dirt pelting her back, legs, and shoulders. She felt a welcome easing in her feet. They were tuckered out from weeks of running. So was she. In fact, she was sapped from living as a stray.

She'd never go back to Grimsgate, but . . . where *would* she go?

What she needed right now, and maybe what Old Mag needed, too, was for this day to turn out differently from the others that had gone before it. To turn out better, for once.

She pressed her cheek against the bumpy ridges of Old Mag's back and closed her eyes, wanting to believe that something wondrous could happen. Maybe even something miraculous.

CHAPTER TWO

IN WHICH AN ELEPHANT SHOWS GREAT PROMISE AS A COMPASS

It is said that elephants have an extraordinary sense of direction, that they can follow the scent of water from miles away, that they can remember places they've never been, places their ancestors visited before they were ever born.

Nitty didn't know this. Neither did Mag.

As it turns out, thousands of years of elephant instinct come in handy during dust storms. Mag plodded through the squall in much the same way feet might sink into sand at the beach, with dirt heaping and spilling around her, pouring over her head, shoulders, and back. Under other circumstances, the dirt might have felt pleasant, cool and soothing against her skin. *This* dirt felt like a battery of stinging wasps about her eyes and trunk. Not pleasant at all.

She suspected it was much worse for the girl on her back, which was why she kept going, pushing her forehead against the wind, flapping her ears to and fro in hopes of fanning the heaviest blasts of dirt away from the girl's face. The girl was so small, without a trunk to plug from the worst of the grit. Really, such a slight creature wasn't meant for weather like this.

Mag had taken a liking to her the minute she'd seen her running through the square, the minute her trunk had taken in the girl's scent—untamed and sweet. These days, all Mag sniffed on people's skin was the rotten-egg smell of suspicion. Worse than that was the smell of fear and blame—bitter and distasteful as the moldy hay that made up her meals. Meanness, too. Her trainer's skin had stunk with sour-smelling meanness whenever he'd swung the bull hook across her flank. He seemed to think her skin didn't feel hurt the way his did.

He was wrong.

This girl, though, was different. Her eyes were open like a stretch of unbroken grass, with a pinch of wild about them. Mag's sight had grown tired and blurred, but she had been able to see those bright eyes clearly. She liked those eyes. She especially liked that they seemed to understand that Mag didn't want to die, that she shouldn't die.

So Old Mag carried the girl through the storm, all the while listening to the whispers inside her that led her on, this way first and then that way; right, then left; north, then east; and hoping the girl had the sense to keep holding on.

ᢙᢊᡒ

Nitty's throat felt like someone had taken a cheese grater to it, and when she coughed, a gritty mud coated her mouth. Old Mag's sides ballooned outward each time she inhaled, and Nitty's legs hugged tight to them as the elephant's muscles rolled beneath her fingertips.

It seemed like Mag had been walking for hours. In the disorienting vacuum of the storm, though, it might only have been minutes. Nitty couldn't be sure. What she could be sure of was that her own chest was hurting, filling up with dirt.

She opened her eyes a crack and saw nothing but a cyclone of blowing silt. They could be in the middle of towering buildings or on a vast, empty prairie. There was no way to tell. If they stopped, the dirt would be up to Mag's knees in a matter of minutes, and then up to her chest, and then . . .

Nitty swallowed and bent her head closer to Mag's ear.

"We're lost," she whispered.

Then her hand brushed against something solid and run through with ridges. She squinted until she saw planks of wood and hinges.

"Down, please, Mag." She waited, wondering if the elephant would understand.

Mag stretched her body out and down then, like she had before, and offered her bent knee to Nitty.

Nitty climbed from her back, then placed her palms firmly against the object before her.

A door, she thought, and opened it.

⌒ϯ⌒

The barn was dark but welcoming, smelling mustily of hay, damp wool, and warm animals. Nitty heard a cow's lowing, the bleating of sheep, and the comforting clucking of chickens. A mare whinnied nervously at the sight of Old Mag's giant head coming through the door, but Mag must have been used to the animals of the circus, because she didn't give the horse a second glance. Instead she headed for the watering trough on the far side of the barn.

Rust-colored light filtered in through slats in the wood, and after Nitty's eyes adjusted, she glanced at Mag and laughed. "Look at you." The elephant was caked in so much dirt that it rained down to form anthill-like heaps on the floor.

Nitty's laugh was gravelly, and the sound of it made Mag raise her head from the trough and look at Nitty as if to say, *You think* I'm *a mess? You should see yourself.*

"I know." Nitty didn't find it at all strange to be addressing an elephant. So far, Old Mag had proven to be the most well-mannered conversationalist Nitty had ever met. She was certainly an improvement over Miz Ricketts: much less opin-ionated, for one, and far less critical.

Nitty shook out her dress, but the fierce dirt seemed to have burrowed itself under her very skin. She leaned over the trough, only to find nearly all the water gone. After scooping some handfuls into her mouth, she straightened, placing her hands on her hips and eyeing Mag.

"You didn't leave me much to work with, did you?"

Old Mag swung her head toward Nitty, until her right eye was in line with Nitty's face. She brought her trunk within inches of Nitty's skin, moving it purposefully through the air, seeming to trace the outline of Nitty's body, hovering but not touching. Up and down, front to back, Mag's trunk explored, with such thoroughness that Nitty felt compelled to blurt, "Do you mind? If you haven't found something likeable about me by now, it's a hopeless case."

The tip of Mag's trunk dared to push against Nitty's belly button then, and slid its way up until it had reached the top of Nitty's head.

Nitty stood stock-still, feeling the muscular power in that strange strawlike feature and wondering if she'd been foolish to trust an animal of such immense strength. The trunk ruffled her hair, and then blew a powerful shower of water right over Nitty's head.

Nitty sputtered and gasped, laughing as thick red mud ran off her in rivers. There was only enough water in the trough for one more trunkful, and even after that Nitty stayed sticky with mud.

Mag sniffed the empty trough, seeming disgruntled, and Nitty nodded in agreement. "We're going to need more water." She didn't know where they'd get it from, or how. "We'll worry about that later."

She had no idea where they were, whose barn this was, or where they'd go from here. She only knew that she was too tired to run anymore today, and from the looks of things, Old Mag wasn't going anywhere either.

With a huff that sent flurries of dust into the air, the elephant settled onto a nearby mound of hay.

Nitty sat down a safe distance away, then took out her Gleam Jar and held it up to the dim light slanting through the barn's siding. She did this every day with the jar, taking stock of its contents and comfort in its presence. The light bounced off the objects in the jar, sending flecks of blue, yellow, and red spinning about the room. Blue, yellow, red; ribbon, button, marble. These three objects—so small—to a stranger might've seemed unremarkable. To Nitty they were her only link to family, and to a world brimming with color that she'd never seen. *The jar needs green,* Nitty thought sleepily now. *The tinker's seeds.* The barn creaked in the wind, more dust spilling through the wooden slats.

The whole world needs that sort of green, she thought at the sight of the dust.

She'd heard there'd been a time when green had grown up

on its own, straight from the ground. When food and jobs had been as plentiful—even commonplace—as the dust was now. That was before she'd been born. Before jobs and crops had dried up. Before folks had taken to breadlines and bleak stares. Still, she hungered for that green of better times. How much more would others hunger for it, those who'd once seen it coating the bluffs and prairies? There couldn't be much worse than having something so wonderful only to have it taken from you. She knew about that.

Green was wonderful. So were mamas and daddies. Families. Maybe like the one she'd been supposed to have but didn't. It was terrible missing something you didn't remember but knew you'd once loved.

She hugged her Gleam Jar tighter, yawned, and slumped to the floor, several feet from Old Mag. In the hours that passed, in the shifting and turning of slumber, the distance between Nitty and Mag closed. They'd found each other through happenstance, but already being apart seemed unnatural. Soon Nitty's head was cradled in Mag's trunk, girl and elephant curled together.

CHAPTER THREE

In Which an Event of Life-Changing Enormity Befuddles Windle Homes

Windle Homes was stuffing an oil-soaked rag under his front door when the heart-shaped freckle behind his right ear took to itching. He straightened, the way a birch tree might after bowing to the wind, slowly and with a measure of grace. His arms and legs branched from his lean trunk at sharp angles, and it was easy to imagine a timbery creaking accompanying their movements.

The dust kept seeping in around the rag as Windle scratched his freckle.

Strange, that freckle. It had only itched four other times in his life. The moment he'd fallen in love with his sweetheart, Clara; again the moment he'd lost her; a third time when his darling daughter, Lillah, had entered the world; and the fourth time. Well, he didn't like to think about the fourth time at all, so he didn't. Nevertheless, each itch of the freckle had heralded an event of life-changing enormity.

But what could possibly be life-changing about another duster?

The storms had become so commonplace that folks no longer took two lumps of sugar in their tea, but two lumps of prairie sod instead. Some even took to attributing flavors to the different sorts of dirt that blew into their homes and seasoned their every meal. Chokeberry Silt blew down from the Dakotas and left a fruity aftertaste on the tongue, while Oily Loam blazed up from Texas with a sticky stubbornness and tarlike tang. Bison Sward barreled in from Wyoming and left a burly sourness in eyes, mouths, and noses. The worst was the Toeter Grime from Iowa, blowing in with the storm today. Sadly, this particular soil tasted very much of sweaty, unwashed feet, which was why Windle had been trying particularly hard to block it from coming through the door. His itchy freckle distracted him. It made him dread and hope, fear and anticipate.

It made him glance out the window, searching for a sign.

He saw an elephant. Or an elephant-shaped and -sized form. With the storm howling as it was, and whole fields' worth of dirt blowing sideways across the windowpane, it was difficult to tell what, exactly, was lumbering across Windle's yard. But as it drew closer to the barn, he became certain. It was an elephant, and . . . a person. A small person.

It was an elephant and a little girl.

From what he could make out, the girl was a ragamuffin, so toothpick thin that, if the elephant hadn't been there for her to brace against, she would have been blown halfway to Canada by now.

Windle watched the two of them disappear into his barn. Such a pair appearing in his yard during a dust storm could only mean one thing. They were running away.

But from what? Or whom?

He frowned. Windle wasn't keen on runaways. They meant trouble, and he already had enough of that.

He sat down in Clara's empty chair. In his experience, there was no better place for pondering than a rocking chair, and Clara's chair was a fine rocker. He knew. He'd built it. And he needed to ponder for a bit.

What did he know about elephants? Very little. About young girls? Nearly as little. That had been Clara's specialty. His had always been farming. Not that he could do any farming right now.

Windle rocked and pondered, pondered and rocked. His freckle quit itching, and he knew. An event of life-changing enormity *had* happened, and it was—no, *they* were—waiting for him in his barn.

He didn't like it. Not one bit.

⌒ɭ⌒

Nitty woke beneath the shade of a tall but scrawny tree. She blinked and looked again. It wasn't a tree but an old man. He was peering down at her, his thin lips teetering on the edge of a frown.

"Who gave you permission to house a pachyderm in my barn?" The question was demanding, but the rumbly voice didn't sound nearly as stern as she'd expected. In fact, it sounded like a voice trying hard to be something it wasn't. It gave her courage, and as she tucked herself tighter against Old Mag's side, she jutted out her chin and narrowed her eyes, hoping this made her look fierce.

"Who gave *you* permission to be so rude to guests?" she countered.

He lowered his head, his narrow, beaky nose making her think of a crane dipping its head into a creek to nab a fish. "Guests are usually invited by their host *before* they arrive. If I had invited an elephant onto my property, I would've remembered."

"Maybe not." She stared at him, unflinching. "Old folks forget heaps of things." She didn't want to sound hateful, but fear was making her cagey. Not to mention, being woken by a cranky old man right in the middle of a wonderful dream about riding Mag through a lush green meadow struck her as plain unjust.

"*I* am Windle Homes, and rumors of my demise have been highly exaggerated." The man straightened, and when he did,

Nitty realized he might not be quite as age-old as she'd originally thought. His wrinkles sat lightly about his tawny face, as if they were only perched there and could flit away whenever they fancied. Those wrinkles, Nitty guessed, had come on quick. Maybe from some unexpected sadness.

She glanced around and noticed that the light streaming in through the barn's slats was brighter now, more golden than brown.

"Yes, the storm passed hours ago," Windle said, as if reading her thoughts. "Which means you two can be on your way."

"We will be, too." Nitty gave Mag a pat on her side, and they both got to their feet. Mag dipped her trunk into the watering trough and gave a sulky snuffle when it came up empty.

"Come on, Mag. We've got places to be." Nitty held her head high and hugged her Gleam Jar close against her chest, trying her best to ignore the moaning of her stomach and the parched ache in her throat. Mag was surely as thirsty and hungry as she was. But this old man wasn't offering up any cordiality, and Nitty wasn't the begging sort. She nudged the back of Mag's left foreleg, and Mag reluctantly galumphed toward the barn door.

Outside, the sky was a cloudless blue sliding into a fuzzy ocher along the horizon. That fuzziness was leftover dust that hadn't yet settled. It probably wouldn't have the chance to settle before another storm blew through. For now, the day was clear and bright, but drier than a horned toad's tongue. Beyond the barn was a small plank house, its whitewash streaked with dirt and peeling, its window boxes empty and crooked, one half-unhinged and swinging in the breeze. Planters lining the porch still held the remains of bent, shriveled flowers. As far as Nitty could see was nothing but fields of dirt and sand dunes, with a few brittle, mostly dead shrubs poking up here and there.

Nitty had never set eyes on anyplace so withered, so downright lonesome. *Lovelorn* was the word that popped into her head. She'd read that word in the *Daily Tattler,* too. She remembered the sentence perfectly: *Her lovelorn heart searched for solace in starlight.* She thought it must mean a kind of pining for love—maybe love lost, or forgotten. This land had a lovelorn feeling to it, and she didn't think starlight could provide the comfort it needed. That thought made her tighten her grip on her Gleam Jar, wanting to check up on it, as she had a tendency to do, and be reassured by its presence. She imagined it wasn't near as soothing as the kiss of a mother, or the hug of a father. But it was all she had, so she made do with it.

"This is your farm?" she asked Windle, who was standing behind her in grudging silence, as if he'd been taking in the view from Nitty's vantage point and wasn't at all happy with what he saw.

What came from Windle's throat started as a cough and ended as a growl. "It *was* a farm. Once. The finest soil around these parts, some said. Before dusters blew it to bits. Just good-for-nothing dirt now, like every plot of land around the town of Fortune's Bluff."

"Fortune's Bluff!" Nitty blurted. "What a woeful tribulation of a name to have these days!"

Windle's eyes widened. "I suppose that's true." For a second, the corners of his mouth drew upward, though the smile never broke open. "But the place is so dog-eared by dusters it hardly matters what it's called."

"Course it matters. It's your town."

A shadow darkened Windle's face. "It belongs more to Mayor Snollygost than to anybody else now. And it's a sorry sight." He pointed into the far distance at the town—a small, humble brown smudge in the bleak landscape.

"I'm not about to call it that." Nitty stuck her hands on her hips. "It hardly seems fair to harbor such low expectations of a place I've never been. A raindrop's not much to look at either, till it's a river."

"Bah." Windle scowled but then chuckled, a soft, low sound like distant thunder wrapped in velvet. He cleared his throat with a no-nonsense rumble. "Right, then. You *do* . . . have somewhere to be?"

"Oh yes, sir." Nitty made her voice rock-steady. "I mean, as soon as we find it, we'll have it."

His lips flattened, and he drew a hand through the graying shock of hair across his forehead, pacing and mumbling, "Jabbering Jehoshaphat."

"Jumping," Nitty corrected.

He quit pacing and glared ferociously at Nitty. "Listen here, girl. I don't know how you came by this elephant—"

"Her name is Magnolious," Nitty blurted defensively, "and I'm Nitty Luce. But I prefer just Nitty, and *she* prefers Mag."

" 'She prefers . . . ,' " Windle muttered, and took up pacing again. "The girl knows what the pachyderm *prefers*. Confound it all." He shoved his hands into his pockets, giving Nitty side glances every turn he took. "What I'm saying is that you can't stay here." He trudged toward the house while waving one hand behind his back in farewell.

Nitty stared after him. With its cockeyed porch and squeaking window boxes, the house didn't look like it could stand up to anything stronger than the gentlest breeze, but there was something snug about it that made Nitty want to step inside. She turned her eyes to the fields of dirt stretching toward the horizon. If she started walking with Mag through that dirt, she might never reach the end of it.

Nitty looked deep into Mag's eyes, so deep she thought she could see all the way inside Mag's chest. She placed her hand against Mag's side. The elephant's great heart pounded, slow and steady, a comforting strumming beneath Nitty's palm. Mag's heart was surely the size of a watermelon, maybe even a very large pumpkin. How much love could a heart that size hold?

"Wait!" She ran after Windle, with Mag following, and lifted the seed pouch to his face. "We can help you plant crops. Mag and I." Her words tumbled and tripped. "I bet an elephant works twice as fast as any horse and plow. She'll be a good worker. Won't you?"

Mag nuzzled Windle's neck with her trunk, right at the freckled spot behind his ear. Windle pushed her trunk away. "No seeds'll sprout in this dirt. The wind blows them all away. The wind steals everything."

"I have different seeds," Nitty argued. "They'll grow anywhere, in anything."

Windle eyed the seed pouch, the corners of his mouth deep furrows curving down to his stubbled chin. "Argle-bargle."

"It's true!" Nitty persisted, even though she wasn't sure any of what she was saying was true. Still, if wanting made any difference in whether something was true, then this had to be true.

She'd make it true.

"The only plant that grows anywhere and in anything is a weed." Windle dismissed Nitty with another wave. "Keep your seeds."

"They'll grow." She remembered what the tinker had said. "Whatever you *need* them to grow." Nitty jabbed a finger at the green seeds, which juddered in the sunlight like they wanted a chance to prove themselves. "That's the promise of them. That's my promise to you. Just say what you need."

"I need . . . I need . . ." Windle glanced toward the barren fields and back toward the empty house. "I need you . . . I need you and that beast . . ." After a pause, he threw up his hands. "*You* should be the one telling *me* what I need, girl. You're so certain of yourself."

Nitty stiffened. Well! If he wanted to put her to the test,

she'd pass it and then some. She narrowed her eyes and studied him—the drawn lines of his face, the emptiness hanging about his spindly limbs. And she thought she knew. "You," she said matter-of-factly, "need a remedy for a broken heart."

"Bah!" he cried, but there was no anger in it.

What Nitty didn't admit (and never would) was that she hadn't the faintest idea what the remedy for a broken heart was. If she'd known, she'd have swallowed down a dose when she'd been left on the doorstep of Grimsgate as a bawling baby.

"At least let me try to help!" Nitty ran in front of Windle, blocking the path between him and the house. "Let us stay for a handful of days. We'll plant the seeds, and then do whatever work you have for us."

"I don't have any work."

"You do! That windmill needs mending, and . . ." Nitty scanned the farm, ideas fizzing and flashing about her brain like lightning bugs. "And your fields need plowing, and . . . and . . ." She huffed in a breath as Mag nudged her with her trunk. The nudge had a bossy feel, like Mag was trying to tell her something. Nitty swiveled to face her. Mag swung her head from side to side, giving a few short trumpet calls, the first true sounds she'd made so far.

"What is it, Mag?" Nitty asked.

"What's this, now?" Windle groused. "Don't tell me you can understand that beast."

It was true that Nitty had had no experience conversing with elephants. Well, except for the last few hours, and that had been all her own talking and Mag listening. But Nitty wasn't the type to remind herself of what she couldn't do. She'd heard about her can'ts her whole life. Can'ts could chip away at a person's core until she was worn down to a stub of nothingness. She'd never put a lick of credence in them, and she wasn't about to now. So she stared long and hard into Mag's face, watching the elephant's eyelashes brush against the wrinkles bordering deep, black eyes, and she listened. Not with her head, but with her heart, its door wide open and waiting.

She understood then what Mag was telling her.

Windle shuffled his feet impatiently until Nitty turned back to him.

"Mag knows what needs to be done around here," she announced, her voice sure and even. "She'll set everything to right."

"An elephant?" Windle's eyebrows jumped skyward.

"Why *not* an elephant?" Nitty folded her arms.

He shook his head. "I'll give you three nights. But if anyone comes asking after an elephant and a runaway, I'll turn you in quicker than a blink. And I don't have an extra bed in the house either."

"I'll sleep with Mag in the barn," Nitty blurted, not wanting to give him a single reason for changing his mind.

He nodded. "Well, then. Better ask your elephant where she'd like to start first."

CHAPTER FOUR

IN WHICH A COUGH
HERALDS A FRIENDSHIP

It was all well and good for Nitty to declare her faith in the face of Windle's doubts. But once the door to the plank house was shut and she and Mag were left standing in the yard alone, that faith seemed a lot less dependable. It seemed downright flimsy.

But that was the truth of faith, Nitty supposed. The only way to get it to stick fast was to grab it firm by the fist and set it to work proving itself. She planted her hands on her hips and eyed Mag.

"Well?"

Mag lifted her trunk until it formed a perky S shape. Then she set out, with Nitty alongside her, plodding in a westerly direction past the house with what was left of her chains dragging behind her. Her head swung in a wide arc, side to side, as her trunk explored the air. When they reached the windmill, Mag stopped, tracing the walls of the nearly empty water tank at its bottom with her trunk.

"Nothing but a dribble." Nitty shook her head at the water spout. The windmill, missing all but two of its blades, wobbled weakly in the breeze. Nitty scooped a few handfuls of silty water into her mouth before Mag drained the rest. Nitty frowned at her. "What'd you go and do that for? It'll be hours before there's even a puddle in that tank again!"

Mag snuffled Nitty's hair in response, and Nitty heard a deep rumbling that she thought might be elephant laughter. Only it wasn't coming from Mag. It was coming from behind an empty, rotting corn pen. She turned just in time to see a flash of bright blue disappearing behind the corner of the pen.

The sound came again, louder and longer this time.

"Who's there?" Nitty called. When no one answered, she added, "You might be near invisible, but you sure as stars aren't quiet."

Now, Nitty had read about spacemen in the *Daily Tattler,* and the creature that rounded the corner of the pen bore a striking resemblance to one (well, according to *her* imagination, anyway). Ill-fitting, enormous goggles perched on a small, noseless, mouthless head covered in a cheesecloth mask. The creature carried a narrow, rectangular, bright blue box in its arms, with the Morton Salt girl and umbrella printed across the front. So, thought Nitty, *not* a spaceman. Because surely a spaceman wouldn't be carrying something as ordinary as salt.

"Rats and darnation! My stealth is always thwarted by this cough!" a boyish-sounding person mumbled from the depths of the mask, then seemed to remember that he was talking to a stranger and straightened his twig-thin frame. He pulled a notepad and stubby pencil from the back pocket of his dungarees, dropping the blue box along the way.

Nitty scooped up the strange contraption, but the boy snatched it back just as quick. "Hey! Don't you bust my periscope! It took me months to collect enough Morton Salt labels to mail away for it, and it's the finest surveillance equipment I have."

"I didn't want to see it anyway," Nitty huffed, even though she did. Desperately.

The boy tucked the periscope under his arm, then cleared his throat in a no-nonsense way. "Detective Higgler's the name. I have a few questions about the elephant." He bounced fast and light on the tips of his toes, like he was itching to run, or maybe even spring clear into the air the way a cat would, pouncing on a mouse.

"Detective?" Nitty snorted. "You're no more a detective than I'm a princess." She gave Mag a stroke on her trunk and, after a moment's reflection, added, "Not that I'd *want* to be a princess, mind you, always in distress and waiting to be rescued. But that's beside the point. The *point* is . . . I'm not answering questions about Mag. Especially to a stranger I can't look dead-on in the eyes. So. Go snoop someplace else."

He shook his head. "Can't. It's my job, see. Sniffing out danger and foulsome, rotten villainy." He jerked his head toward Old Mag. Now his fingertips were tapping in addition to his toe-bouncing, until soon his entire body was wibbling in jumping-bean fashion. "Old Mag, you say?" He peered around Nitty at Mag, and Mag took the opportunity to inspect his mask and goggles with her trunk. The boy quit wibbling, stood stock-still, and gulped. "Is . . . is she? Dangerous, that is?"

Nitty laughed. She was beginning to enjoy this. "Not with *me*. But then, I don't know what she'll do to boys in frog goggles."

"Criminy!" The boy relaxed then and resumed his wibbling. "I've told Ma a thousand times that nobody could ever take a detective seriously in this getup. But she never lets me leave our house without it. And I barely get out as it is, on account of the mud in my lungs. Doctor says they're so full up with it I could grow a crop on the inside. He says one day corn might bust right out from my ears and belly button. And I told him I wouldn't even mind, as long as it was sweet corn." His laugh was a burbling brook. "But the dusters make it worse, so I wear the mask to keep from breathing more dirt in. It's hot as a skillet inside it, and it itches like the dickens." He yanked off the goggles and mask, revealing walnut eyes set in a face of the very same brown shade. He grinned and shrugged. "Better. There won't be any duster this morning anyway." He stuck out his hand for a shake. "Full name's Angus Higgler, but folks call me Twitch."

Nitty didn't need to ask where the nickname came from. A hummingbird stayed stiller than he did. She introduced herself then, saying simply that she was visiting from out of town. When Twitch asked how she knew Windle, she stiffened. "I don't see how that's any business of yours."

Twitch was undaunted. "I'll uncover it in good time. Always do." He nodded to Mag. "Are you positive she's not dangerous? Even a little?" His voice stretched toward hopeful. "If she were, she could prove invaluable to my operations. My agency's in sore need of a strong-armed interrogator. Er, strong-trunked, in this case."

Nitty stiffened. How dare he leap to offer Mag a job without a second's thought to Nitty's own interrogation experience? Why, she'd set Miz Ricketts to trembling with questions plenty of times—mostly about how Miz Ricketts could eat roast chicken and bread pudding for dinner while Nitty and the other children ate cold porridge. "Mag's not yours to use for whatever you like, you know, and you might've thought to ask about *my* qualifications. I have buckets full! But that's no matter, because *we*—the both of us—are extremely busy and can't be bothered with detectiving nonsense." She spun on her heel to walk away with Mag, but the boy hurried after them.

"Wait! Oh, don't be sore with me." His face was eager and regretful. "You could help, too! I didn't mean for you to think you couldn't. I was overcome by excitement is all. It's not every day a person stumbles on an elephant."

Nitty had to admit this was true.

He turned his periscope in his hands. "I don't leave my house much, you see. Hardly ever, really, unless I manage to sneak by Ma. And even when I do get out, Fortune's Bluff is as exciting as a plank of wood." He paused. "Excepting the dastardly deeds of Mayor Snollygost, of course."

Nitty stopped mid-step, Mag beside her. "What sort of deeds?" She'd learned from the *Daily Tattler* that anything labeled "dastardly" was tremendously interesting.

Twitch's face turned instantly animated at the question. "That's exactly what I'm trying to find out. I heard Ma and Pa say once that Snollygost was never elected mayor square and fair. He owns the loans on most folks' land in Fortune's Bluff. Heck, these days he owns most every corner of Fortune's Bluff. No one ever says it out loud, but they whisper that he forced folks to vote for him. He'd take their land otherwise."

"Whispers about a person don't make truth," Nitty said, thinking about all the whispering Headmistress Ricketts had done over her, and how that whispering had always been just loud enough to be heard.

"Suppose not," Twitch agreed. "But I'm guessing you haven't met Mayor Snollygost yet. Once you do, you'll see it."

"What?"

Twitch leaned closer. "His air of malevolence," he whispered. "Every villain has one. Says so right here in the *Detective*

Comics." He pulled a rolled-up comic book from the back pocket of his dungarees and opened it. The pages were so worn a few loose ones tried to slip out, but Twitch pushed them back into place. He pointed to the top of a page. " 'Ten Ways to Be a Villain, number five: Exude an air of malevolence.' " He nodded once, authoritatively. "Snollygost does that for sure. It sneaks into his smile every once in a while. Nobody else notices. But *I* do. And you will, too."

"If nobody else notices it, why do you think I will?"

He shrugged. "You noticed me, didn't you?"

Nitty didn't think it would be kind to point out that it would be hard not to, what with the cough and the spaceman goggles.

"You're not worn out like the rest," Twitch said decisively, inspecting her from head to toe. "I was watching you. Good detectives get hunches. My hunch tells me you're different." He scrutinized her, then nodded firmly. "I figure it's the elephant. An elephant is exceptional, so maybe you are, too."

Nitty grinned. She was beginning to like Twitch. She appreciated a decent snoop. (She'd been one herself at Grimsgate. That was how she'd discovered that Miz Ricketts wore a wig, and how she'd successfully hung it from the dining hall chandelier.) She liked the words Twitch used, too. Twitch sounded like a living, breathing *Daily Tattler.* It was very entertaining . . . and handy. She'd love to add some more words to her vocabulary. Besides, Twitch had a periscope. A periscope *and* an inspiring vocabulary—those were powerful enticements.

"All right, then, Detective Higgler," she said to Twitch. "Old Mag and I are fixing up this farm. We've got seeds to plant and plants to grow. If you want to get to know my exceptional elephant, how about you give us a hand?"

Twitch opened his mouth, but Nitty held up a finger and added a quick "And *don't* say it can't be done."

Twitch stuck out his chin. "I wasn't about to. But one thing you can't do is use the tractor. The Homes tractor has been clogged with dust for months, same as ours. I helped Pa on our farm plenty before my lungs turned muddy. I was going to point out that for farming these days, you're going to need a horse-drawn plow. That's all."

Nitty smiled. "What about an elephant-drawn plow?"

With that, Nitty and Twitch turned toward the field's edge, where a plow lay on its side, half buried under dirt. Nitty looked at her elephant, then pointed to the plow. She was pleased to see Mag turn in the direction she pointed. "What do you think, Mag? Would you be willing to try it?"

Mag snuffled the abandoned plow and the yoke that lay a few feet from it. She'd seen the likes of that yoke before. She'd worn one to drag stacks of poles through fields and dirt, then to pull the poles to standing to raise the big top, as she'd learned the humans called it. It was pleasant to be out from under that big top, which blocked the sky and snuffed the breeze. It was lovely to be far from her trainer's angry bark and bull hook. Here, alongside this girl, she could see bright blue overhead and feel soft dirt underfoot. Here, alongside this girl, she could

40

move without being commanded; she could do as she pleased without obeying. This made her skin tickle, her trunk swing, her old bones feel young again. It made her want to stay near the girl. And not only that. It made her want to thank the girl, too. She sensed a need in this girl, a canyon of need deep enough to cut a river. She wanted to help fill it. There wasn't anyone barking at her to do it. Just herself, deciding to. That made it feel right.

So Mag bent, slowly, and lifted the yoke with her trunk. Nitty looked at Twitch, and they both grinned.

⌒ᶠ⌒

"Couldn't tell a plow from a pickle, those two," Windle grumbled as he watched Mag and Nitty through the window. And how in darnation she'd finagled Angus Higgler into the mix, Windle didn't want to know. That boy's lungs couldn't handle a sneeze, and he was puffing alongside Nitty trying to fit the yoke onto Mag. Because Mag was roughly five times the size of a horse, it wasn't going at all well.

Windle frowned. He'd banked on the certainty of their failure, sure enough. He just hadn't banked on caring.

This girl couldn't have ever farmed a day in her life. She was walking around the plow, eyeing it from every angle, a riddle she needed to solve.

"She'll give up," Windle said decisively. He knew a thing or two about giving up. Oh, he'd battled that infernal dust, all right. He'd plowed and sown his crops each spring, first with a sturdy hope, then with a seesawing one, and finally with one that had dwindled down to diddly. Each April he'd watched shoots spring from the ground, only to watch them shrivel without rain or be blown to kingdom come by the dust storms.

Despair didn't come naturally to Windle. As a younger man, he'd been brimful of dreams about what he'd do with his farm, how it would grow grain and corn so healthy and tall the tips would sweep the very clouds above. He was certain of his knowledge in farming. He was certain of his future success. He was certain of the path before him.

"Certainty never sticks, not with the world changeable as it is," Clara had told him, resting her head under his chin and patting his hand. "But there's joy to be found in the unknowable, too."

Windle had laughed, for he *knew* soil and crops and farming. He planned; he planted; he grew himself the finest crops for hundreds of miles around. The crops brought the best prices at market, year after year. A "master farmer," the folks of Fortune's Bluff took to calling him. None of them (with one exception) had minded that the Homes fields outshone all others. Instead they'd been proud to claim Windle as their neighbor and as a citizen of Fortune's Bluff.

And Windle had found joy in the certainty of knowing how each and every day would pass, of the path his life was sure to take. He'd found joy in their snug white house, in Clara's peach cheek pressed to his shoulder, in their little girl, Lillah, who had run giggling through the cornfields. But then came the fourth event of life-changing enormity. And on its heels? The dusters.

There was no joy in the dusters. There was no knowing when, or if, they'd ever stop. There was no knowing how much longer the savings he'd stuffed under his mattress with such great care would last. There was no knowing when, or if, he might set eyes on his Lillah again either. There was no certainty at all. Which was why despair stopped in to visit Windle and decided to stay for a spell.

Despair was what made him say again now, "Yes. She'll give up. We all do in time. And the better off she'll be for it, when I haven't a smidgen to offer her."

That's when his eyes fell on the photograph of Clara and Lillah—the one in the smack-dab center of his rickety kitchen table. Clara was smiling, holding a little laughing Lillah in her arms. Their sweet eyes struck Windle as suddenly beseeching.

Windle frowned. He knew confiding in a photograph might strike most as a daffy pastime, but what else did he have to turn to besides a house full of emptiness? "I know what you'd have me do. You two and your sympathetic notions. But somebody's bound to be looking for them. An elephant's not your everyday sort of stray."

The photo said nothing, as photos are prone to do, which was no help at all to Windle.

He glanced back out the window, his wiry paintbrush eyebrows tipping skyward. Nitty Luce did not look like a girl about to give up. With her lips puckered in concentration and her eyes fixed on the plow, she looked like a girl with an uncommon store of pluck. Why, at this very moment, she was trying the yoke on herself, nearly buckling under its weight but still digging her heels into the dirt to try to pull.

He yanked his work hat onto his head, casting a glance back at the photo on the table. "I'll go. Just because I don't want to see my plow broken to pieces by that elephant."

His pronouncement was met by silence. The very same silence he'd heard for near on ten years. He wondered, as he had many times before, if he'd ever get used to it. With sinking spirits, he feared, just as he had so many times before, that he would not.

He stepped onto the front porch and, without a glance in Nitty's direction, headed for the barn. He'd start with fashioning a proper harness for that beast. But that wouldn't mean he was helping. Not a speck.

CHAPTER FIVE

IN WHICH DIRT DISCOVERS
ITS POTENTIAL

It only took the span of a few short minutes for Nitty to discover that Windle Homes didn't want her thanks, or her questions. In fact, he didn't want to be paid any attention at all.
When she tried following him into the barn, he waved her
away. When she asked if he needed anything, he snapped, "Yes.
I need you to leave me be."

"He sure is cantankerous," she said, returning to Twitch,
who sat wheezing beside the immovable plow. "Is there anything in your detective manual about villains being remarkably
bad-tempered?"

Twitch gave her a sideways look. "You're suspicious of
Mr. Homes?"

Nitty shrugged. "Just trying to unpuzzle his moodiness is all."

"It's no puzzle." Twitch jerked his chin toward the white house. "It's on account of his being a hermit. Least, that's the reason Ma gives for it. First, Mrs. Homes passed, and then their daughter, Lillah, traipsed clear across the globe. She sings, and travels for her performances. Windle hasn't seen her in near on ten years. And Ma says when a body's been alone for that long, it's bound to turn ornery. Like a stray cat."

Nitty shook her head, dropping her voice to a whisper. "Hoo-wee. If I had the likes of that sort of sorrow, I suppose I'd be moody, too."

Just then Windle loped out of the barn, carrying a tangle of leather and rope in his hands and a bolt cutter under his arm.

"Shhh," Twitch commanded, nudging Nitty. "Best not talk about it in front of Mr. Homes. It would only worsen his mood."

Windle stopped in front of them, his eyes stern under the shelf of his brow. "Angus?" He bent over Twitch. "Does your ma know you're out of the house? I won't have you suffering any attacks on my account. I know how she frets over your breathing. . . ."

Twitch sent Nitty a quick plea with his eyes. *Don't tell,* his eyes said.

Nitty wouldn't, she decided. She was enjoying his company far too much for that.

"As long as I keep my mask on, Ma says it's fine." Twitch looked Windle dead in the eye.

Nitty felt a stirring of admiration. Twitch was a solid fibber. Not as good as she was, mind, but he could hold his own.

"I'll take your word, then. Man to man," Windle said. "I never did like the idea of you cooped up in that house all day. But the moment you start feeling poorly, you tell me and I'll take you home."

"Yes, sir," Twitch said.

Windle busied himself with the bolt cutter, snapping the chains from about Mag's ankles and neck. When the ankle cuffs thudded heavily to the ground, Mag raised her head higher, as if in relief. Windle gave a nod of satisfaction at his handiwork, then faced Nitty. "This harness won't work." He held it out to Nitty. "That beast'll break through the straps in no time. Don't know why I bothered."

Nitty grinned. "Being bothered is better than being bored."

Windle grunted. "Never said I was bored."

"Well, if *I* was a farmer without fields, I'd be bored as a pirate without a ship." Before Windle could say another word, Nitty scooped the harness from his hands and, as Mag bowed down of her own accord, slipped it over Mag's head and around her chest. She could feel Windle watching her, which only made her more determined to fit it into place to show that she knew a thing or two about harnesses. (She didn't, of course, but who needs expertise when you have confidence?) The harness was fashioned with a broad leather band at Mag's chest and straps running from it along Mag's sides to the front of the plow. Mag seemed comfortable in it, and within seconds she was plodding through the field, pulling the plow behind her.

"Come on, Twitch!" Nitty said triumphantly, hurrying to

catch up to the plow to hold it steady as it churned up dirt. "Let's get to work." She glanced back to see Twitch scrambling toward her and Mag with a wide grin. Windle looked after all of them, frowning and shaking his head.

Nitty paid him no mind, and within minutes she and Mag had plowed two long rows across the field. They weren't straight, but they were better than nothing. She and Twitch followed Mag as she tilled each new row, but every half hour or so Twitch would make for home.

"Got to pester Ma for something or she'll suspect that I'm on the lam," he told Nitty. "The trick is in my cunning. A skilled detective gets your guard down without ever lowering his. See?"

Nitty saw, all right. Twitch darted to and from his house and Windle's with the quick craftiness of a fox. He'd be beside her one minute and gone the next, doing his best to run on those gangly stalks of his. She didn't have the heart to tell him how often his muddy cough gave away his whereabouts.

He helped as much as he could, until his breaths came out in thundery rumbles and Nitty made him quit to rest on the porch. By that time, she'd forgotten all about Windle and his frown until Twitch managed a puffing "Doesn't seem bored anymore, does he?"

Nitty followed Twitch's gaze to the windmill, where Windle, balanced atop a rickety ladder, was hammering on the last of the new blades. The windmill slowly turned in the breeze, then spun faster, and within minutes, water was pouring from the spout at its base into the water tank, filling it up.

"How about that?" Nitty patted Mag's side. "You've got yourself some fresh water." She looked into Mag's right eye, where she could've sworn she saw a glimmer of satisfaction. "All right, all right. I'll never doubt you again." Mag tossed her head, and Nitty laughed. Then Windle whirled on his ladder to face her.

"Are you three going to lollygag or make yourselves useful?" Windle asked.

Nitty turned back to the field, and Twitch stood up from his seat on the porch and returned to the plow.

"He sure is demanding," Twitch said.

But there was something new in Windle's tone that made Nitty feel encouraged. He had expectations for her, accomplishments he was banking on her making.

So she did. She and Mag and Twitch (when he could breathe). They plowed until sundown that first day. Windle studied the half-finished field for a long time before muttering, "Hardly worth the work when a duster's sure to blow it all away. But still . . ." His voice lifted a pinch. "Still . . ." And the cloudless sky stayed dust-free.

After Twitch walked home (for the last time) and Windle busied himself feeding the other animals, Nitty and Mag staggered into the barn, where they found hay and a sparse serving of chipped beef on toast waiting for them.

Nitty was licking the last bits of beef from her fingers when Mag's stomach gave a mighty rumble. She turned to see Mag snuffling the dirt floor, every last morsel of her hay gone.

"I'm still hungry, too." Nitty patted Mag's belly in sympathy. "But I've a suspicion he gave us all he could for tonight. I snuck a peek through the kitchen window a bit ago, and his dinner plate was just as meager as mine."

She sat down and set her Gleam Jar in her lap, and not a moment later, Mag settled down beside her. Nitty rolled the jar in her hands, and the contents chimed quietly against the glass. Blue, yellow, red. Ribbon, button, marble. Nitty closed her eyes and focused until she could see them all—her family—before her. The ribbon twining through her mother's hair, the button tucked into her father's pocket, the marble rolling between her brother's fingertips.

Her chest tightened with the all-too-familiar pains of missing them, but then she felt the strange, bristled softness of Mag's trunk pressing against her chest, in the very spot where it ached.

Nitty opened her eyes to find Mag's enormous head so near her own that winding gullies of gray wrinkles filled Nitty's vision. Mag's right eye was watching her intently, her trunk still pressing against Nitty's chest, right over her heart, as if Mag was wanting to take measure of its beating.

"You had a family once, too," Nitty whispered to her. "Do you remember them?"

Mag blinked and blinked again, never shifting her gaze from Nitty's face. She didn't know what the girl was saying, but her tone was quiet, and more than a little lost-sounding. And her heart . . . her little heart was pounding in a lonely way, like Mag had once heard an injured horse's do after a big-top show. But the longer Mag stayed near, the longer she held her trunk to the girl's chest, the stronger and steadier the little heart sounded. It made Mag feel needed, more than she'd ever been needed before, and that was a feeling that made *her* feel less alone.

Just as Mag thought this, Nitty raised her hand to rub under Mag's chin. When Mag sighed and tilted her chin toward her, Nitty laughed.

"You like that?" Nitty asked, then laughed harder when Mag opened her mouth to expose her pink tongue. "I'll rub your chin as much as you want. *Not* your tongue."

Mag seemed to accept this and let her head sink back against the ground, then flopped entirely onto her side, every ounce of her mountainous self limp. This gave Nitty her first up-close glimpse of the welts Mag bore along her belly and legs. Nitty touched the scars gingerly, tracing her fingertips along their ridges. Then she placed her palms against Mag's rough, thick skin and rubbed her underbelly and sides.

"They'd no right to do it," Nitty whispered fiercely. "And as long as I'm with you, no one will hurt you like that ever again."

Whether from this pledge or from the feel of the hands caressing her, Nitty didn't know, but Mag heaved a contented sigh. Her great eyelids fluttered and half closed, and as they did, Nitty yawned, too.

She tucked her Gleam Jar tight against her belly, then lay down in the curl of Mag's trunk.

Mag, close to drifting off to sleep herself, felt the small, still warmth of the girl pressed against her, and made her own pledge. That she'd protect the girl's lost and lonely heart with her own for as long as she was able.

Then, almost at the same moment, the two fell into a heavy, woolly sleep.

The next morning, Nitty woke with a crisp apple under her nose, cans of white paint beside her head, and Mag tickling her toes with her trunk. Nitty could see the scant remains of the fresh bale of hay that had been left for Mag, which the elephant had already made neat work of finishing.

Rise and shine, Mag's trunk insisted.

"All right already." Nitty sat up, stretching. "I'm getting there."

Still, a spray of cold water from Mag's trunk made certain.

Nitty sputtered, jolting awake. "You could've asked more politely."

Mag patted Nitty's head, once, twice, and then, tucking her trunk under Nitty's armpit, pulled her gently to her feet. Nitty smiled and rubbed under Mag's chin. "I take it you like it here, then?" she asked, leaning her head against Mag's chest. "I do, too," she whispered. "But don't let on just yet."

Nitty and Mag emerged from the barn to the sight of Windle scraping the last curl of old peeling paint from the house. Twitch was there, too, his nose (out of the dust mask, for the time being) stuck in a *Detective Comics.*

"Morning, Twitch," Nitty said.

"It says here that villains can go easily undetected. 'Ten Ways to Be a Villain, number eight: Disguise yourself as a patron of philanthropy and good citizenship.'" He tapped his comic with a finger. "Neezer Snollygost is the *mayor*."

Nitty yawned.

"Don't you see?" Twitch's knees bobbed up and down so violently that the comic threatened to slide off his lap. "Posing as mayor is the perfect disguise."

Windle quit scraping, his limbs stiffening. "No time for comics and villains today. Mask on, Twitch. We've work to do." He slapped paintbrushes into both their hands as soon as Twitch reluctantly donned his mask, then led Mag toward the field. "You paint while the pachyderm and I finish plowing."

Nitty and Twitch painted until Nitty's face and Twitch's mask were covered in white freckles. Nitty's arms burned like she'd gotten into a patch of fire ants. By sundown the house shone clean and bright against the endless toasted landscape, and the field was plowed into expectant rows.

"Waste of paint, this, when a duster's going to turn it brown in a blink," Windle said. "But still . . ." And the sky beamed down blue over the glowing house, which, from the sky's vantage point, must've looked like a perfect white egg, waiting to hatch.

On the third day, with no dusters in sight, Nitty woke well before sunrise. A biscuit sat under her nose, wrapped in a kerchief, but Nitty ignored it.

Her pouch of green seeds was juddering. She pressed the pouch against her heart, feeling the seeds' vim and verve warming her from the outside in.

"I know," she told them. "It's time you were planted."

She opened the barn door onto a still-purple sky. Last night's stars were waltzing with the sun's first rays, seeing who could outshine the others. It was the enchanted in-between time, when minutes hover without passing, when the universe holds its breath, waiting to see what will happen beyond the crest of the brand-new day.

The seeds juddered faster.

"Mag." That was all Nitty needed to say, because Mag felt it, too.

Mag felt the humming expectancy in the air, under her feet, in her heart. She nuzzled the girl's cheek and felt the girl's excitement rising from her skin. It had the scent of a fresh, clear watering hole. She stuck her trunk into the girl's bag of seeds and felt the tiny life inside them, whirring with wanting to get out. She understood what needed to be done.

The two of them walked to the edge of the field. Nitty picked up a pile of dirt in her palm and held it, wondering, worrying. The dirt was loose and dry as a desert, hardly fertile for planting. The smallest breeze might blow the seeds away, and a duster . . . a duster would . . .

"No it won't either," Nitty said aloud, wanting to make sure the dirt, the air, and the sky heard her loud and clear. Windle's glum thinking would never be hers. Not if she could help it. She knelt down and dug a hole in the soil with her finger.

Mag snuffled that hole and, using her trunk like a spoon, scooped out another small hole a ways down from it. She took a few steps into the row, then dug another, and another. While Mag dug, Nitty took the first seed from the pouch. Its new-born green shimmered beneath the sun and stars, eager and exultant.

She laid the seed into a hole and covered it with a blanket of dirt. She bent toward the earth. She was about to say *Grow,* but stopped. Growing seemed so . . . unimpressive. She wanted the seed to do more than grow. Much, much more. She thought for a long minute, then whispered, "Triumph," giving the dirt one more encouraging pat.

So they planted during the in-between time, Nitty and Mag, until the entire field was sown and all but a handful of seeds were snug under the soil. After considering for several minutes, Nitty tucked that last handful into the planters along the porch and under the windowsills. Maybe something bright and lovely would sprout in them—something to lure a hermit from his lonely lair. Soon enough, all the seeds were planted save one. That one seed Nitty tucked into her Gleam Jar, not able to part with its green. Blue, yellow, red, green. Ribbon, button, marble, seed. She smiled. The seed fit in perfectly.

Then she and Mag sat down at the field's edge.

Just about the time that the marigold sun finally bested

the stars, Windle appeared on the porch, coffee in hand. He nodded at the planted field.

"It'll need water, and we'll spread some hay over the top, to keep the soil from blowing." He took a sip of coffee, peering at Nitty and Mag over the cup's rim. "How is your elephant at irrigating?"

Nitty had no idea, but she answered confidently, "She's magnolious. How else would she be?"

Windle harrumphed, but the harrumph came out garbled. Nitty suspected there might've been a laugh corked up under it somewhere. "We'll see about that."

Nitty rubbed Mag behind an ear. "You're not going to let him offend you like that, are you?"

Mag straightened her legs and lifted her head. She most certainly was not.

"Good," Nitty said. "Let's draw some water."

At first Mag hung back, studying Nitty and her bucket intently. Then she went to the trough and mimicked Nitty's process, using her trunk. Nitty did her best to keep up, but there was no rivaling Mag. That trunk could draw twice as much water from the trough as the bucket and could irrigate six seeds to Nitty's three. The windmill kept spinning, water kept flowing into the trough, and Mag kept drawing it into her trunk and fountaining it onto the seeds. At some point, Twitch showed up to watch, but his cough was much muddier than in the days before, so watching was about all he could do. As Mag walked the rows, darkening the soil with damp, Windle spread the hay after her, until the sun was high overhead.

"It's on the verge," Nitty announced when the water trough had been emptied and refilled a dozen times and the last inch of soil was strewn with hay.

"On the verge of what?" Twitch asked.

Nitty stared at him, then sighed. "Of happening."

"What's going to happen?"

"Everything that needs to. Am I the only one who feels it coming? It has a certain smell, like . . ." She raised her head toward the sky. "Like the sweetness of morning dew."

Twitch paused over his *Detective Comics,* then grinned, nodding. "That is a fine smell."

"Hogwash and hornswoggle," Windle said. "I smell nothing but"—he sniffed the air—"unwashed feet." He grimaced. "Mark my words, there'll be a Toeter Grime duster here within the hour." They raised their eyes to the sky. Creeping over the horizon were the brown clouds—nothing but toadstools now, but soon they'd be billowing titans. The animals, too, seemed to sense what was coming, because the horses left the corral for their stalls and the chickens left their coop, fluttering to the safety of the barn's rafters instead. "Twitch, I'll take you home before it hits. Nitty, you and Mag head back to the barn and stay put."

"But the seeds," Nitty and Twitch said together.

Windle peered into their waiting, wide-eyed faces. His

common sense tolled a doomsday bell. But what came out of Windle's mouth wasn't doom. What came out of his mouth was "If the seeds are worth their salt, they will reveal their merits in a timely manner. For now, they would do well to dig in snug and hold on tight."

Nitty and Twitch stared at him.

"Are you *sure* you're a curmudgeon?" Nitty cocked her head at Windle.

Windle's frown was back before Nitty could blink, and then he stomped away to fetch the truck. Mag rested her trunk on Nitty's shoulder as they watched him go.

"He likes you," Twitch told Nitty. "And Mag, too."

"He's hardly said boo to either one of us." But Nitty's heartstrings pinged like wind chimes stirring in a breeze. "How do you know he likes us?"

Twitch nodded toward the repaired windmill and the freshly painted house. "He's fixing things. He's trying. Trying isn't a small thing. Especially when everybody around you is giving up." Twitch peered toward the barn. "I've got to hightail it before he comes with the truck."

Nitty's eyes settled on the horizon. The brown toadstools in the sky were taller, looming closer. "Twitch, let him take you home."

"And have Ma catch me?" He shook his head. "Nah."

"Doesn't she notice you disappearing?"

"Remember what I told you? About folks not noticing?" Twitch said. "It's funny about parents. They're the worst about noticing. Oh, they see the dirt behind your ears, or when your toenails could stand clipping. But they don't always see *you.*" He stared down at his toes. "Ma's been different since Pa went west to look for work. She spends most of the time anymore fretting over money." His voice sank a notch, and his mouth sagged. "When she quits hearing my muddy cough for a spell, she's so relieved she never thinks to wonder why." He grinned. "I disappear, my cough disappears, too. Ma hardly comes to my room at all anyway. Besides, I'm mostly supposed to stay in bed, sipping the turnip soup she fixes." He wrinkled his nose. "Can't stand the stuff. I don't trust turnips any more than I trust Miz Turngiddy."

"Miz Who?" Nitty asked.

"Mayor Snollygost's secretary. She comes around our house most weeks wanting to know when we'll pay Mayor Snollygost what we owe him."

"What do you owe him for?"

"Our land, for one. And all the goods we buy from Snollygost General Store." He studied his feet. "Ma's pride doesn't like buying on credit, but she says it's either that or empty bellies."

Nitty nodded. There'd never been enough to eat at Grimsgate either, at least not for anyone besides Miz Ricketts. Plenty of times, late into the night, she'd heard whining stomachs echoing in the dorm. "Lately it feels like the whole world's emptied out. It needs to be filled again, don't you think?"

"With what?"

Nitty shrugged. "I'm not sure. But Mag and me. We're going to try to fill it up."

"Me too," Twitch added, and Nitty nodded. He tucked his comic under his arm and waved to Nitty. "See you tomorrow," he hollered, then took off, trotting and wheezing.

A moment later, the slight breeze turned into a proper blow. Squinting against the wafting grit, Nitty and Mag reached the barn door just as Windle drove up. He frowned when she told him that Twitch had already gone.

"I have a mind to speak to Mrs. Higgler about the boy's ramblings," he groused. "His lungs can't take it."

"You don't know that," Nitty said. "Maybe they can."

Windle stared at her, his dark eyes sorrowful. "Limitations are as plentiful in this world as the air we breathe. You think you can beat them. We all do, at one time or another. But we can't." He sighed. "Might as well get used to it now."

Nitty stared right back at him. "If I wanted to get used to that kind of thinking, I would've stayed back at—" *Grimsgate,* she finished in her head. She wasn't about to let that slip. But she knew all about limitations.

"You would've stayed where?" Windle peered down at her.

"Nowhere." She stuck out her chin. "All I meant was, if you're going to live expecting nothing but letdowns, might as well not live at all." He harrumphed, and she added, "I bet you never said such a thing to your daughter. I bet you used to tell her that she could do anything—"

"And she left, confound it! That's what she did!" Windle paled, his body ramrodding. "Enough. I've heard enough." He got out of the truck, adding gruffly, "You had your three days. Time's up in the morning." With that, he turned toward the house, ushering Nitty and Mag into the barn's shelter as he went.

Nitty sighed as the barn door banged shut and the wind took to whining through its cracks. She glanced at Mag, who bobbed her head up and down, like she was already agreeing with what Nitty hadn't yet said out loud. Then it came.

"Three days isn't near enough time to change his mind."

⟨⁌†⁍⟩

As the dust barreled through Fortune's Bluff that evening, the residents of the Homes farm dreamed.

A curmudgeonly farmer dreamed of corn sweeping the clouds above, of his sweet Clara resting her chin on his shoulder, of their young girl who used to giggle as she ran through the fields. He dreamed that, at long last, the infernal freckle behind his right ear quit itching.

An elephant dreamed of mountains of fresh, sweet hay and of the snug warmth of the girl whose head rested against her belly. She dreamed of a world without bull hooks or sour-smelling trainers. She curled her trunk around the girl as a blanket.

And the girl. The girl dreamed of walking with Mag through

a flourishing garden, a stalwart farmer and a twitchy detective beside them. Her hands tightened around her Gleam Jar, where, even though nobody noticed, a single green seed glowed.

Dreams are forces in themselves, strong enough to leave footprints behind in the imagination. But there was another, greater force at work. A force stirring beneath the dirt where the green seeds lay, damp, contented, and juddering. Some might call it magic. Whatever it was, it woke a long-forgotten feeling in the earth that moved her to her very core.

The world felt the green seeds tickling her surface. She felt them juddering. She felt the wind and dust pulling and tearing at her soil, wanting to rip the seeds away from her. She held them closer. They reminded her of something. A garden. An ancient garden that had once belonged to her. A garden greener than spring grass after rain, so green that being in it was like sitting inside an emerald. A garden full of *her* dreams.

Then, all at once, the world remembered. She remembered every dream and every promise of what could be, of what she— the world—wanted to become.

She whispered her memories to the juddering seeds, and they dug in and broke open. Their roots, tiny tendrils fine as angel hair, curled into the damp earth. The seeds began to grow.

CHAPTER SIX

In Which a Spectral Smile
Prevents an Untimely Departure

There was no breakfast under Nitty's nose in the morning. No hay for Mag either. Nitty sighed.

She tucked her Gleam Jar into the pocket of her flour-sack dress and then slid a hand onto the end of Mag's trunk. Mag's trunk curled gently over it. If Nitty had to face defeat, she reasoned, it was best to do it while holding tight to another living being. If that living being happened to be an exceptional elephant, so much the better.

They stepped out of the barn together, blinking into the sooty sunlight. Everything—the newly painted house, the windmill, the silo—was smudged in brown all over again. Everything, that is, except for one field. Every inch of that field was covered in sproutlings of such an astonishing green that Nitty had to squint at the sheer radiance of it.

"It's happening!" Nitty whooped and hugged Mag's trunk. She ran to the edge of the field with Mag galumphing close behind.

She brushed her fingertips over the curling tops of the little plants, feeling tiny hairlike fibers covering each one. Mag did the same, running the tip of her trunk over the sproutlings and sneezing with great gusto.

Nitty grinned. "They tickle like a caterpillar's fuzz." She tilted her head. "I haven't seen them around in ages, but I just love the way caterpillars scoot across a hand. They have a determined air. It must be on account of all they want to accomplish before turning into butterflies." Nitty leaned over to get a closer look at the sproutlings. Like their seeds, they had a question-mark shape and, every few seconds, juddered from root to tip. They were bigger than the seeds, of course, and—strange—seemed to be growing taller even as Nitty looked on. "These sproutlings have that determined air, too. They're aiming to go places."

The moment she thought of going places, a knot clogged her throat. She reached for her Gleam Jar, turning it over and over in her hands until the colors swirled inside. Ribbon, button, marble, seed. Blue, yellow, red, green. She hugged the jar, wishing a family could sprout whole and loving from it the way the seeds were sprouting from the ground. Even if that never happened, her Gleam Jar would never leave her side.

It would never tell her she wasn't welcome, or that she wasn't loved.

At least she had that. And Mag.

"We'd best be on our way," Nitty whispered to her now, standing on tiptoe to rub Mag's leathery ear. "He doesn't want us here."

She cast a final glance at the sproutlings, her chest wrenching with the pain of walking away from all the glorious green. Then she cupped her hand under the tip of Mag's trunk and turned her back on the little farmhouse to face the wide expanse of barren brown land ahead.

"Come, Mag." She stepped off, head high, expecting Mag to follow.

Mag did not. She lifted her trunk into the air, snuffling. The air around her smelled sweet, alive with chickens and horses, water and sproutlings. The air ahead, in the direction the girl was walking, smelled bitter, parched and lifeless. Ahead there would be nothing but hunger and thirst. Ahead there would be no place to hide herself from those who spoke in hard, hateful tones, who called her "murderer." There would be no place to hide the girl from the dust.

She could not take the girl to such a place. She would not. Her enormous feet rooted firmly in the spot.

"Mag, come!" Nitty said again, louder this time. Mag did not move, but instead lowered her head to the ground, trailing her trunk through the dirt. Nitty wrapped her arms about Mag's right foreleg and gave it an experimental tug. But while a determined ten-year-old is one thing, a determined elephant is quite another. "Suffering sardines! You're immovable as a mountain."

Nitty planted her hands on her hips, staring Mag down. Her pulse sprinted, and for the first time since she'd arrived on the farm, Nitty felt scared. What if Mag didn't want to follow? What if she didn't want to stay with Nitty after all? Nitty swallowed, the knot in her throat tightening. She stepped nearer Mag and took her trunk in her hands, stroking it. "I'm not happy about it either," she said to her, "but he didn't give us much choice. We're leaving—"

"What's this about leaving?" Windle's gruff voice interrupted. Nitty spun to see Windle standing in the farmhouse doorway. His paintbrush eyebrows pulled into a V above his nose, but his eyes . . . Nitty tilted her head to get a better view. Yes, she'd thought as much. His eyes *were* a smidge less curmudgeonly than they'd been yesterday, and something in them calmed her sprinting pulse a bit.

Windle stepped onto the porch, surveying the field, his twiggy fingers wrapped around his tin coffee cup.

"I told you they'd grow," Nitty said.

Windle grunted. "The question is for how long? Our well water's turning muddy, which means it's running low. If the well goes dry—"

"No ifs," Nitty pronounced as she moved to stand beside him, with Mag following. "Not today. Not with *that*." She pointed to the field. "That's some kind of viridescent splendor, right there." Windle's left eyebrow arched in her direction, so Nitty clarified. "'The emerald necklace nested in her bosom, a viridescent bird I longed to cage.' That's from the *Tattler*'s serial *The Countess and the Convict*. I read every installment but the last one. You'd be astounded by the number of times the word 'bosom' appears in the *Daily Tattler*. Once I counted over fifty in a single Saturday-morning edition!"

Windle sighed, keeping his eyes on the field. "First, I much prefer your use of 'viridescent' to the *Daily Tattler*'s. No doubt I'd find plenty to astound me in its pages, but I'm partial to the works of Robert Louis Stevenson. I expect you'll have your own opinion about *Treasure Island* once you're finished reading it."

Windle pulled a frayed edition of the book from his back pocket and handed it to Nitty.

"Second," Windle continued as Nitty clutched the book to her chest, "if you're coming to town with me, you best take a bath directly. And . . . here." He cleared his throat, reached around the kitchen door, and retrieved a girl's dress, which he pushed awkwardly toward Nitty. His cheeks reddened. "It belonged to my daughter, Lillah, back when she was about your age. It's a mite musty, but more tolerable than burlap, I reckon."

Nitty's heart jumped. Hoo-wee, what a dress! It was a proper one of red-and-white gingham, with a wide ribbon at the waist and a pleated skirt. It was fancier than anything anyone at Grimsgate wore, and certainly looked much less itchy than Nitty's own flour-sack shift.

"Thanks for the dress," Nitty offered, then searched her

mind (and her *Daily Tattler* reserve) for a word that would show her manners and smarts all at once. When she decided on one, she used it alongside her most gracious smile. "It's utterly resplendent."

Windle sputtered into his coffee, and Nitty thought she caught the specter of a smile peeking from behind his cup.

A remedy for a broken heart, she'd guessed Windle needed, that first day. No doubt about that, Nitty thought now, hanging newfound hope on that specter of a smile. If there was a specter of a smile, a real one might follow. And then perhaps a broken heart mended. Not unscarred, mind you. Never that. But maybe stitched up enough to carry the beat of the living. The question now was: Would one sprouting field be enough?

Windle straightened, and the spectral smile faded as quickly as it had come. "Third, there's a cot in the kitchen. *You* may sleep in it. *Not* the pachyderm. She sleeps in the barn."

A twizzle of emotions, light and ticklish as confetti, whirled inside Nitty. Windle was offering her a cot, a book, decent clothes (how delicious!), and a bath (not quite as delicious, but, even she had to admit, a necessity). That meant she was staying put, at least for the time being. Three words hummed happily in her head. *From now on . . . from now on . . . from now on.* Didn't they have a forever sort of ring to them? No, Nitty scolded herself. She'd make do with day-by-day gladness. Better to do that than hang hopes on a future nobody could pin down.

"Thank you." She took a step toward Windle. She wasn't

sure what she planned to do, but something along the lines of hugging crossed her mind.

He held up his hands before she reached him, backing against the door. In recent years, hugging for Windle had become a risky business. You never knew when a hug might soften a part of the heart that couldn't stand any more weakening. "No thanks needed," he said hurriedly. "This is strictly a business arrangement. You'll be working for your room and board, you understand."

Nitty grinned. "I do understand."

"Fine, fine." Windle finished his coffee. "We're wasting daylight. Setting foot in Neezer Snollygost's store always tilts my axis, but we'll need hay for your elephant." Windle eyed Old Mag, then sighed. "A lot more hay."

Well, Nitty thought, at least he hadn't called Mag a beast this time. This was progress. In the meantime, however, a new worry had presented itself. The last time she'd set foot in any town, she'd stolen an elephant and some rather unusual seeds. It seemed like she and Mag had traveled a fair piece from that city to find Windle's farm, but what if someone here in Fortune's Bluff had heard of what she'd done? Even more worrying was the possibility that the police were searching for her and Mag. She instinctively hugged Mag's trunk, thinking of how Windle had called Mag *her* elephant. As if the two of them were a pair and went together as well as salt and pepper.

"Maybe it would be more prudent for me to stay here?" Nitty suggested to Windle now.

The sound that tunneled up through Windle's throat might have been a laugh, or a growl. Nitty couldn't be sure. "Prudence doesn't seem to suit elephants, or crops that sprout overnight in dusters. I'm inclined to overlook it today."

He paused, watching Nitty for long enough that Nitty wondered if he was waiting for her to confess. She wouldn't, though her tongue (which had as much potential for goodness as the rest of her) was itching to tell the truth.

"We'll leave your elephant here." Windle stepped off the porch and toward the barn without another word.

Whether his decision was based on suspicions he had about Mag's origins or on convenience, Nitty didn't know. Whatever his reason, she was grateful. Besides, from the keen way Mag's trunk was exploring the nearby chicken coop, it didn't look like she had plans to go anywhere soon. In fact, it looked for all the world like she might be hoping to make some friends of the feathered variety.

Don't worry about us, Mag's long-lashed eyes seemed to say as she snuffled the clucking chickens. *We'll be busy getting acquainted.*

So with that settled, Nitty jumped off the porch, running after Windle.

"Mr. Homes!" she called first, but when he didn't turn, she blurted, "Windle!"

He stopped at that, and Nitty waited for him to scold. He didn't. Instead, he arched an eyebrow. "And what leads you to believe you may call me by my first name?"

"Well, seeing as we're going to be sleeping under the same roof, I thought it would be cozier. And besides, it's a friendly sort of name and should be used whenever opportunity arises. Don't you agree?"

His eyebrow rose higher. "I've never given it a thought."

"You should." She grinned. "In the meantime, I'll try it out on a trial basis, to see if it strikes your fancy." When he didn't argue, Nitty straightened with the sense she'd made commendable progress. "Now . . . about *Treasure Island.* I could stand to improve on my elocution." It was another line she'd taken from the *Daily Tattler,* this time from *The Education of Miss Valancy.* She'd fancied it because of the smart-sounding manner in which "elocution" rolled through her lips. "I'd like to read it aloud. To you and Mag. If you don't mind."

Windle gazed down at the girl before him, at her earnest eyes the very color of the field sprouting behind her. "I don't mind." His heart galumphed.

CHAPTER SEVEN

IN WHICH A NOSE EXHIBITS A PECULIARLY WORRISOME TALENT

To call Fortune's Bluff a proper town would've been an embellishment bordering on an out-and-out falsehood. Nitty supposed it had been a proper town once. There were signs here and there of the care it had been given in years past—a swath of peeling blue paint curlicuing down the front of the Palace Nickelodeon, storefronts with hand-painted signs that were now faded and dangling, crooked and broken. There was a boarded-up schoolhouse, too, bearing a sign that read: CLOSED. TEACHER LEFT TOWN.

The townsfolk looked just as poorly, dragging themselves through the streets, heads hanging low.

Most windows were layered so thick with dust that they

were impossible to see through. The window of Crispin Sigh's bakery, however, was busy getting scrubbed into spotlessness by a half dozen children. It offered a view of dangling ropes, strung like curtains across the glass, and empty shelves, save two, which were lined with the sorriest, saggiest loaves of bread Nitty had ever seen. The children weren't any better off either, their clothes so threadbare and flimsy that Nitty was suddenly embarrassed by her red gingham dress. She'd washed the stubborn dirt from her limbs and combed the weeks-old knots from her hair, and she'd been secretly pleased with the result, even if the washing and combing had been a nuisance. On seeing the children, though, she wished she hadn't. It was nothing more than sheer luck that she wasn't still wearing her own flour-sack dress.

A slight, olive-skinned man with a mass of tousled black curls walked out of the bakery to hold up a trembling hand to Windle, and Windle stopped the truck at the curb.

"That'd be Crispin. Waiting on me." Windle plunked a nickel into Nitty's palm. "Fetch us two loaves of bread."

Nickel in hand, Nitty crossed the street. As she got closer to the bakery, she realized that what she'd thought were ropes in the window were, instead, the skins of snakes. Her palms turned butter slick, but when she glanced over her shoulder at Windle, he only nodded her onward.

Nitty didn't hesitate again. When she reached the bakery door, Crispin was already holding out the loaves, wrapped in newspaper. His hands shook so badly the loaves slipped from the paper. Nitty caught them seconds before they hit the ground. Then, when she saw that they were covered in a pale green fuzz of mold, she nearly dropped them for a second time.

"You're new." Crispin's voice shook as badly as his hands.

The way he said it, Nitty could've sworn he was accusing her of a crime. In her defense, she said simply, "I'm just Nitty." She glanced sideways at the children, who were beginning to whine about being hungry.

The tallest of the girls glowered at Nitty. Crispin took no notice. His eyes were fixed on the ocher sky overhead.

"Rain? Rain? Where is the rain?" he muttered, then tapped the side of his temple. "Rain wears the marble, you see. Worry and rain, rain and worry." He pulled a rolling pin from his back pocket and shook it, then held it up to his ear. He seemed both discouraged and relieved to discover that the rolling pin remained mute.

He leaned toward Nitty, his eyes red-rimmed and watery. "The yeast won't rise; the air's too dry. I need a recipe. A rain recipe!" He disappeared into the back of the shop, tapping his temple and mumbling, "Flour, stratus, sugar, salt, cumulonimbus . . ." He broke into waves of laughter.

"Thank you for the bread!" Nitty called after him.

He didn't seem to hear.

"You!" The frowning girl stepped in front of Nitty, blocking her way back to Windle. "Just to be clear, Papa didn't do any wrong. No matter what anyone says." The hardness of the girl's expression made Nitty think of a clenched fist, ready to throw a punch.

Nitty recognized the look. She'd given it plenty of times herself at Grimsgate. "It's no business of mine what your papa did or didn't do," she said quietly. Then she left before the girl had a chance to change her frown into a fistful of action.

Back at the truck, she handed Windle the bread. "Only . . . it's molded through and through."

He nodded, not the least bit surprised. "It'll do just fine as chicken feed."

How many times, Nitty wondered then, had Windle bought Crispin's bread knowing it would only do for the chickens?

"Windle," she whispered, "why is Crispin's bakery strung with snakeskins? And why does he shake so awful?"

Windle cast sharp eyes on her. "Desperation." Then he set the bread in the truck's cab and turned abruptly down the sidewalk. Nitty followed, knowing well enough that he wouldn't say another word on the matter.

"What a mumpish shadow this town's under!" she blurted.

"It's under a shadow, to be sure." Windle motioned beyond the north end of Main Street, and Nitty gaped into the distance, at what she hadn't noticed before. An enormous building towered over all else, blocking out the morning sun with its bulk. The word SNOLLYGOST blazed across the front in swirling copper letters. It was the only building in sight that wasn't decrepit with shabbiness. In fact, it looked so well cared for, it had a sheen to it, as if someone took pains to polish it daily. From the building came a periodic and reverberating *WHUMP*, exactly like the sound Nitty imagined a giant's foot might make as it struck the ground. *WHUMP! WHUMP! WHUMP!*

It was an ugsome, ominous sound. It was a sound, Nitty thought, foretelling misfortune.

She stared. "What in the indecipherable cosmos *is* that?"

"*That*"—Windle's eyes darkened under his brow—"is the headquarters and warehouse of the Snollygost Institute. The mayor built it some ten years ago."

"What for?"

Before Windle could answer, a small child being toted down the street by her mother paused to answer with dutiful somberness, "For community progress, fulfillment, and the betterment of all." The little girl, pressing her hands over her ears to dampen the whumping, continued on her way while her mother praised her for remembering "the Snollygost motto."

"There you have it," Windle mumbled. "It didn't always make that cursed rumpus. The noise started up a few months ago."

Nitty's eyes flitted from the Snollygost Institute to the rest of the main street. "There's nothing but melancholy as far as the eye can see. Where is the betterment and fulfillment?"

"According to Neezer Snollygost, we're awaiting its imminent arrival."

"And according to you?"

Windle worked his jaw, contemplating, before finally responding with "That is a matter I keep to myself. And you'd prove wise to do as I do and pay that institute no mind."

But Nitty's eyes lingered on the Snollygost Institute. As she watched, a line of dust-covered trucks drove up to the imposing structure and then disappeared through two enormous doors, open and waiting, at its side. The doors swung shut just as Nitty and Windle reached the front of the Snollygost General Store.

Nitty vowed to ask Twitch about the institute when she saw him next. Especially its whumping. It was simply too peculiar to ignore, and she was sure that, unlike Windle, Twitch would be raring to share an opinion on it.

She stared at the general store's window displays. They were gleaming with pyramids of canned goods, sacks of grain, and bottles of fresh milk. It was more food than Nitty had ever seen in one place—in fact, more food than she'd ever seen at all.

"Hooooo-wee and codswallop!" Nitty exclaimed. "You could live off that for years."

"Not at Snollygost's prices," Windle muttered. "Let's be quick about it. Remember our objective."

"We have an objective?"

Windle nodded. The freckle behind his right ear was itching something fierce, as was its habit whenever the fourth event of life-changing enormity crossed his mind. (It was the very decade-old event Windle preferred never to think about, but often *did* think about at Snollygost General Store.) "Mind our business. Buy our goods. Leave before we're called on to converse."

"What's wrong with conversing?" Nitty asked, at the same

time wondering why he kept scratching at that spot behind his ear.

"Conversing leads to questions. Questions lead to chin-wagging, and I've had enough of that to last my lifetime. Besides, people could mistake a simple, unassuming hello as friendliness."

"Better than mistaking you for friendless." Nitty cast a side-long glance at him.

"Humph," Windle said in response, and then he was loping through the doors of the store with Nitty scrambling to catch up to him.

It took less than a minute for Windle's objectives to be compromised. During that minute, an anguished howl rang out, and something that bore a striking resemblance to a small rodent flew over Nitty's head and hit Windle with a squelch, sticking to the front of his shirt.

"Is it a bat?" Nitty asked excitedly. Bats were the one creature that had eluded her capture at Grimsgate, although she'd often thought that letting one loose in Miz Ricketts's bedroom would've been great fun.

"Could be a rabid mole," a shopper remarked, giving Windle a wide berth as she passed with her children.

Windle raised his eyes to the ceiling as he pulled the strange object from his shirt. "It's a mustache."

"Without a face?" Nitty only had a moment to inspect the drooping, furry thing dangling from Windle's fingers before it was snatched away by a bearish fist.

The fist belonged to a squat, barrel-shaped man with apple-red cheeks. He had a mustache, too, one lying limp and droopy across his upper lip, full of bald patches and shedding more strands of hair even as Nitty watched.

"Without a face indeed!" the man bellowed. "And therein lies the calamity. What face would want to be seen wearing such a travesty as this? I ask you." He shook the mustache clenched in his fist at Nitty, then pressed it against his eyes, his head sagging. His own face took on the shade of an overripe plum.

"Having trouble with the mustaches again, Ferdinand?" Windle asked, then introduced Nitty to the man, explaining, much to Nitty's relief, that she was a visitor passing through town. Windle added as an aside, "Mr. Klempt owns the Schnurr-bart Emporium down the street. He's a mustache maker."

"A pogonologist, in fact," Ferdinand said somberly, his shoulders straightening. "A student of beards, and, more importantly, an avid admirer and creator of that most superb and refined of all hairs." He paused, bowing to the word he was about to say, which was uttered reverentially. "The mustache. The walrus, the pencil, the handlebar, the imperial. But it was my father who was the true mustachio virtuoso. Papa's mustaches were like no others. Beauteous creatures, crafted of the finest corn silk in these parts."

"But . . . why make mustaches when people can grow their own?" Nitty asked.

"Pah! And what of the poor soul who can't? Must he lead a mustacheless existence?" He shook his head with such violence that the right side of his mustache slid down over his lip. He quickly pressed it back into place. "Of course not! The Schnurrbart Emporium sells mustaches for all. You see?"

Nitty could only nod as Ferdinand rushed on: "There is so much in this confounded existence that is beyond our reach. Lonely hearts want company but remain alone; loving couples want children but remain childless; kindly people want great suffering to cease, but cease"—he sighed—"it does not." He peered into Nitty's eyes. "Why, then, should anyone want for a perfectly groomed mustache, if we have the means to provide it? Don't you agree that it's our duty to use our talents to bring what's beyond reach into being?"

Nitty thought of the seeds sprouting back at Windle's. "I do. Only I had no idea people suffered over mustaches."

Ferdinand closed his eyes. "There are tremendous sufferings and trifling ones. It's all suffering just the same. As my dear papa, inventor of the Super-Duper Triple-Crimp Mustache, used to say, 'Who is to judge one person's dearest wishes against another's?' For some, a mustache is as defining as a fingerprint. There is quite a demand among funambulists and ringmasters. Why, only last month I sold Papa's best horseshoe mustache to Gusto and Gallant's ringmaster. Mr. Percival Gallant himself."

Nitty froze at the mention of Gusto and Gallant. That was the circus troupe Mag had been a part of. She remembered seeing the names on the poster announcing Mag's hanging. Her muscles clenched. Nitty trained her eyes on the floor, avoiding Windle's hawkish gaze, as Ferdinand kept talking.

"Even Windle here wore one of Papa's walrus masterpieces when he was courting Clara." He smiled at the memory. "Do you remember, my friend?"

Nitty dared a glance at Windle, but his gaze now seemed suddenly lost in some far-off place. "She fancied it dashing," he muttered, "until it fell into her glass of iced tea." He arched an eyebrow at Ferdinand, but Ferdinand dismissed the look with a wave of his hand.

"A mere malfunction with the glue." Ferdinand scrutinized Nitty. "Tell me, young lady, what is your opinion of the mustache?"

Nitty thought on that. "It depends entirely on the person wearing it."

Ferdinand Klempt clasped his hands together and nodded until his thick brown curls bounced about his head. "Ah . . . just so! An unworthy scallywag can ruin the effect of a respectable British upper lip, while a respectable gentleman might never live up to the pointed shiftiness of a scallywag's pencil. But—oh! None of that matters now." His eyes dulled; his face crumpled. "All is lost! Lost! Papa's mustaches are in ruins. The dusters have withered them all, and my own creations are only sorry imitations. Dear Papa, forgive me! I've failed you again." He lifted his eyes to the ceiling, and then issued a series of mutterings that very well might've been German, but to Nitty sounded like "Embittered ants should eat me!"

"Oh no, Mr. Klempt." Nitty laid a hand on his arm. "Surely you don't deserve such an awful fate as that."

Ferdinand sniffed and blinked through streaming tears. "Do you know what it's like to *be* someone's disappointment? There is no fate more awful." With that, he gave Nitty's hand a squeeze and rushed from the store with the droopy mustache pressed over his eyes as a kerchief.

Nitty looked at Windle, who was shaking his head as he watched Ferdinand leave.

"Darn these dusters and what they're doing to all of us."

"What did Mr. Klempt mean just then?" Nitty asked him. "Was it his papa he disappointed?"

Windle rubbed at the stubble caught in the cleft in his chin. "Mr. Klempt's father was a hard man. Upstanding, surely, but hard. Sooner notice a stain on your collar than a smile on your face. And Ferdinand . . ."

"Was a stain." Nitty saw it clear as day. If Miz Ricketts had ever thought to add "stain" to the long list of inflammatory remarks she'd made at Nitty's expense, Nitty surely could've counted herself as one, too. "It sets my innards scalding to think on it."

Windle fixed her with a warning glance. "It's not for us to think on at all."

Nitty shut her mouth while deciding firmly that she could think on it as little or as much as she fancied. How was Windle to know as long as she kept those thoughts to herself? Except, she feared, that might prove a trial.

"Time's wasting and we have supplies to get," he said briskly, straightening. Then he strode to the back of the store, heading for the sign marked FEED.

Nitty followed at a much slower pace.

There was far too much of interest to see along the way. If she was going to stay in Fortune's Bluff for the time being, she wanted to understand it. Understanding a place and its people, she reasoned, was the best way to stay out of mischief when you didn't want it and to find it when you did.

"Only one can of tomatoes today," a mother was saying to her nearly grown daughter, who was struggling with two sobbing babies in her arms. "And some bologna to fry up for dinner."

Mother, daughter, and babies all wore earmuffs, much to Nitty's bafflement. With cold weather having left some time ago, Nitty couldn't figure why, except that the earmuffs quieted the incessant whumping from the Snollygost Institute. Nitty could hear it even from inside the store. She'd only had to endure it a little while, but it was already becoming annoying.

A little farther down the aisle, a man and his earmuffed son debated between canned beans and Spam, but when they checked the prices, they put them both back and left empty-handed, with the man saying, "We'll make do with milk toast for another few days."

While every shelf in the store was piled with food, most people (some earmuffed, some not) chose only one or two items. One little girl let her fingers trail across the food as she walked the aisle, as if touching it might satisfy her hunger. Nitty guessed she was probably imagining tasting it, too. But with empty pockets, imagining was all folks could do.

The wrongness of it pestered like a giant skeeter bite on Nitty's spirit. Weren't times hard enough without having mountains of canned peaches rubbed in your face? It made her want to march right out of the store, but the sound of a muddy cough stopped her.

Twitch, she thought. She followed the sound down an aisle until a hand grabbed her, pulling her behind a pyramid of canned condensed milk.

"Hiya—" Nitty started, near to bursting with all the questions she wanted to ask him about mysterious trucks and whumping and moldy bread. Twitch pressed a finger to his lips. He motioned to her to join him as he hunkered down behind the cans.

"Don't blow my cover," he whispered. "I'm doing reconnaissance." Twitch was on his hands and knees, crawling toward the back of the store, his lungs wheezing accordions. He paused for only a second in his crawling to eye Nitty's dress suspiciously. "What happened to you?"

"It was Lillah's, but Windle let me borrow it." She shrugged as she fell into a crawling stride beside him. "It's tolerable." Nitty tried to keep her pleated skirt from dragging along the floor, not ready to admit how much she relished the dress's crisp fabric and the softness of it against her knobby knees.

"So he's warming to you, then." Twitch nodded knowingly. "I figured as much, alone as he is all the livelong day."

Nitty nodded. "It's not me so much as the seedlings."

Twitch would've made a fine fish, right then, the way he was gawking. "You mean—"

"They're sprouting dandy." Nitty smiled. "You have to come see . . ."

Her words died as Twitch yanked her unceremoniously through a partially opened doorway into darkness. "Twitch," Nitty hissed, making out the gray silhouette of a mop and bucket in the corner of the tiny room. "Why are we in a broom closet?"

"It could be a secret passage disguised as a broom closet," he said, pulling a cord dangling from the ceiling to illuminate a dim bulb overhead. He pressed against the walls with his palms, and when that revealed nothing, settled to inspecting the supply shelves. His head disappeared deep into the recesses of one shelf, then reappeared with a triumphant smile. "Eureka!" He wrestled to keep hold of the shiny brass contraption (nearly half his size) in his arms. "Does *this* look like a broom to you?"

"Hoo-wee! It looks like a euphonium," Nitty said admiringly, already searching for a mouthpiece so she might give it a try. She'd seen a picture of one in the *Daily Tattler*'s "Music from Around the World" edition and thought it a marvelous-looking instrument.

Only on closer inspection did Nitty see that the contraption before her had no mouthpiece, but instead was shaped into an enormous funnel at the top, narrowing to a spoutlike opening at the bottom. "What *is* it, exactly?"

"I've never seen the likes of it," he said, "but I'd wager it's a gadget made by the mayor himself. Pa used to talk about how Snollygost built all manner of oddities, back in his boyhood. He recalled that most resulted in mishaps of one sort or another." Twitch studied the instrument, and his eyes lit up. "Look here! There's a red button on its side."

"Push it," Nitty urged without a moment's hesitation, because buttons, of any sort or color, always begged to be pushed, if only to see what unexpected event might unfold as a result of the pushing.

Twitch did, and they both jumped as a vacuous *sssslurp!* filled the closet. Nitty didn't jump far enough away from the contraption, which wasted no time in sucking a substantial amount of her hair right down its funneled gullet.

"Get! Off! Me! You! Diabolical! Entity!" she said through clenched teeth as she gripped its neck (or what she surmised was its neck) and attempted to choke it into submission.

Twitch clamped a hand over Nitty's mouth and jabbed a finger at the door in warning, even as he grappled with the wriggling contraption. Strangely, the air in the room seemed to be getting sucked into the funnel's great mouth, and Nitty and Twitch soon found themselves gasping for breath. At last Twitch found the red button again and, once more, pushed it. As quick as it had started, the vacuum inside the closet died, and Nitty and Twitch were left breathless, staring at the brass instrument with a mixture of awe and trepidation.

They had no chance to examine it further, because suddenly voices sounded outside, approaching the closet door. Twitch opened the door a crack and peeked through, then opened it wider and motioned for Nitty to follow him as he headed for the safe haven of a stack of canned tomatoes.

"Here comes Miz Turngiddy with Mayor Snollygost. Listen," he hissed, once they were hidden to his satisfaction. "Observe." His eyes darkened somberly. "Probe."

Nitty pressed her head against Twitch's, and together they peered through a narrow gap between the cans.

A woman scurried into Nitty's line of vision, walking in the shadow of the burly man beside her. Miz Turngiddy was short and stooped, wearing a dreary dress the same mud shade as the Fortune's Bluff landscape. The notepad she scribbled on was held so close to her squinting eyes it nearly brushed the tip of her narrow, pointed nose, giving her the impression of a studious weasel.

On the other hand, Neezer Snollygost, broad-shouldered, with a neck and forearms as wide around as telephone poles, put Nitty in mind of a buffalo.

"Henshaw, Higgler, Hilder," Miz Turngiddy muttered as she scribbled. "Late, late, late. Jackford, Jenson, Johnson." She jabbed her pen against the notepad. "Late."

"All of them late with their payments, you say?" Neezer's voice had a stuffy-nosed, bagpipe quality. He shook his head slowly. "A shame, a shame. *Such* a shame." He patted his brawny hands against his purple waistcoat as if he'd just finished a most satisfying meal.

"There's more, sir. Many, many more." Her lips quivered as she murmured a string of numbers under her breath. "Eighty-five percent of Fortune's Bluff, to be exact."

People paused in their shopping upon hearing that troubling news.

Neezer looked at the shoppers watching, and his teeth spread a crescent moon across his face. "Well, we must determine how best to help our struggling townsfolk." He bowed his head to the shoppers deferentially. "We must do our civic duty."

Miz Turngiddy nodded. "About that, sir . . ." Her voice lifted enthusiastically. "I'm anxious to do my part, and I've been studying the newest advancements in farming techniques." She flipped through the pages of her notebook. "I've done some calculations, and—"

"No time to waste on that at the moment, Miz Turngiddy. Now is the time for a stoic commander to listen to the needs of his citizens."

"Of course it is." Miz Turngiddy's voice sank, but she waited, pen poised, for the citizens in the Snollygost General Store to speak their needs.

Nitty waited, too. Would they protest the exorbitant prices in the store? Or that whumping that surely kept them up nights?

Not a single citizen spoke.

"Thank you. Your silent contentment speaks volumes." Neezer nodded appreciatively, breathing slowly in and out. As he breathed, his nose whistled. Softly, at first, and then not so softly.

The whistling began to take on a familiar tune. Nitty tilted her head to get a better listen. "Is that 'My Country, 'Tis of Thee'?"

Twitch nodded. "We hear that one when he gives speeches in the town square, too." His eyes narrowed at Neezer. "I don't trust a nose that makes music. See here." He whipped a *Detective Comics* from his back pocket. " 'Ten Ways to Be a Villain, number three: Develop a signature peculiarity or mannerism that easily distinguishes you from other villainy.' "

Nitty listened to the whistling. "He can't help what his nose does."

Twitch didn't look convinced. "If you ever hear Beethoven's Fifth whistling from that snout, clear out quick. The last time I heard it whistle that tune was the day Crispin Sigh was packed away to—"

Twitch's words were cut off as he was abruptly yanked from the floor by his suspenders.

"Angus Higgler! What did I say about busybodying?" The voice was low, silk smooth, and commanding. The woman it belonged to was only as tall as Nitty, and nearly as thin. She clutched a blue bottle of Mr. Moop's Cough Tonic in her hand. Her heart-shaped face and tired—oh, so tired—eyes seemed far too delicate for such a voice. But from the speed with which Twitch was shuffling his feet, Nitty understood that that voice was made to be minded.

"A great detective's always on duty, Ma," Twitch said, as Miz Turngiddy and Neezer turned their eyes toward them.

"Angus Higgler!" There was a dash of menace in the way the mayor boomed Twitch's name. "Show yourself." He swept his lapels aside to put his hands on his hips as Mrs. Higgler brought Twitch to stand before him. All eyes were on Twitch now, especially Neezer Snollygost's.

He loomed over Twitch with a too-bright, too-white smile. "What's this I hear about you playing detective?" His smile stretched wider. "I do so admire an individual with aim. Ambition is the fortress on which to build success." He clapped Twitch on the back, and the nose's "My Country, 'Tis of Thee" shifted into "Puttin' on the Ritz." "And what sort of sleuthing might you be up to, my young friend?"

Twitch stood tall, staring into Neezer's face. "I am suspicious of evildoings in Fortune's Bluff."

The nose emitted a whinny of laughter. "As mayor, it's my duty to make sure our town is safe and snug as a turtle shell."

"That noise," Twitch persisted, "coming from the institute. What are you hiding that makes such a noise?"

Neezer laughed again. "That noise, my boy, is the sound of progress. The sound of an innovation the likes of which no one has ever seen." He bent nearer Twitch, until they were eye to eye. "That is the sound of this town's salvation."

Mutterings arose from the shoppers.

"That's right, citizens," Neezer continued. "As we speak, I am hard at work on a solution to our woes. A machine to end the dusters." Hopeful gasps winged about the room, and folks clasped hands in gratitude. "You've heard the music of its inner workings for some time now. A few of you besides Angus here even broached the subject with me before, only I thought it best not to divulge details until I was sure of the machine's success. Now, you can let the sound of it soothe your worries." Neezer nodded encouragingly. "And know that all will be revealed in good time." He clamped a hand on Twitch's shoulder. "And thank you, young Angus, for your inquiry. Rest assured that if there *were* evildoings in our beloved town, I would be the first to uncover them."

"Unless . . ." Twitch sucked in a gurgled breath. "Unless you—"

A cough stopped him before he could finish, and within seconds he was bent over, gasping. Mrs. Higgler held up the bottle of cough elixir. "All right, Twitch, honey. Doc Grant says this tonic will do you wonders. Just let me go put it on our account—"

"Mrs. Higgler, one moment, if I may." Miz Turngiddy placed her hand over the blue bottle. "Your account, as I was just informing Mayor Snollygost, is overdrawn."

Twitch's mama twisted the bottle in her hands. "Yes, yes, I know," she said quietly. "Only I thought . . . I was hoping . . . if we could have an extension on our credit . . ."

Folks paused around them, busy trying *not* to look like they were eavesdropping as they hung on every word. Mrs. Higgler continued, "A few more weeks and a little rain . . . When my husband returns, we can get another crop to seed—"

"No need for that, no need at all," Neezer interjected. "Times like these we must keep the wells of kindness overflowing." He swept Miz Turngiddy's notepad into his fist and turned a circle, including each person in his gaze. "The Snollygost General Store will waive payments on credit accounts through the end of the month."

Murmurs of relief and applause swept the room. Miz Turngiddy's applause was the last to come, but come it did. Rather stiffly, Nitty thought.

"Your magnanimity knows no bounds, sir." Miz Turngiddy's face puckered as if a sour grape were stuck to the roof of her mouth. She motioned to Twitch and his ma to follow her to the front of the store.

As they left, Twitch waved to Nitty over his shoulder, wheezing out a barely audible, "Remember. Beware Beethoven's Fifth!"

Nitty might've giggled, but now that Twitch and his ma were gone, Nitty found Neezer's eyes focused entirely on her. Peering into those wily eyes drained the cheer right out of her.

"Who do we have here?" Neezer's nose-whistling rose an octave. "Am I to surmise you are new to Fortune's Bluff?" A single clap of his enormous hands and the floor beneath Nitty's feet shuddered. "Welcome! Welcome!"

"Thank you." Nitty suddenly wished Mag were beside her,

and then, seconds later, wished Mag were even farther from Neezer than she already was. "I'm Nitty Luce. I'm . . . I'm . . ."

"She's with me," Windle said, rounding the corner of the aisle to join her.

"Windle." Neezer gave him a single nod, and Windle did the same.

"Neezer."

For a long moment, the two men's eyes locked in a staring duel. Watching them, Nitty wondered how many unspoken words were piling up behind those stares. Months of them, maybe. Even years. What the words were, Nitty couldn't tell, but one thing was certain from the eyes keeping them at bay. Those words had heaps of things to say, and not all good either.

"Nitty's a guest at my place," Windle said. "For the time being."

"A guest, you say?" Neezer's eyebrows rose. "I don't recall the Homes farm ever entertaining guests before."

"Haven't had any reason to before," Windle replied.

"And what reason have you now?"

"None that I care to divulge," Windle said simply.

Neezer's cheek twitched for a hairsbreadth, and then he clapped a hand on Windle's shoulder. "Well, knowing how you've suffered from my niece's absence, I'm certain having a visitor will do you good."

Nitty stared at him. Was it possible? "Your niece? You mean you and Windle are—"

"Brothers," Neezer finished for her. "Indeed we are."

"Brothers-in-law," Windle corrected quietly. He was scratching his freckle again, rather furiously this time.

"No point quibbling over semantics," Neezer barreled on. "Alas, we two don't spend nearly as much time together as I'd like. Do we, Windle? And where has dear Lillah's singing taken her now?" Then he added as an aside to Nitty, "Did you know my niece is an accomplished opera singer?"

"Last I had word, she was in Spain," Windle said.

"Serenading the bullfighters with her arias, no doubt." Neezer smiled as Windle scratched at his freckle. "Well, it's understandable that a person of her great talent would grow weary of your little farmhouse. Don't you agree?"

Windle said nothing.

"But you've become downright reclusive since Lillah's departure!" Neezer mopped his brow as his nose swung into a jaunty "When the Saints Go Marching In." "I've been sick with worry. Simply sick!"

"You don't look sick at all," Nitty blurted.

"Sick at heart, child." He ruffled Nitty's hair, spoiling its careful combing.

Nitty ducked out from his hand. *After all that effort, too!* she thought grumpily.

"Well. A visitor to ease your solitude. This *is* splendid news!" Neezer's teeth blazed at Nitty. "And how are your crops coming? I heard from Miz Turngiddy that a duster swept away the corn seed you planted last month. A travesty, that. But perhaps now you'll consider my offer to buy the farm?"

Windle was on the cusp of frowning, but then he looked at Nitty. Nitty thought of the green sproutlings. *Their* sproutlings. And—she couldn't help herself—she grinned. She waited for Windle to tell Neezer that nothing could grow in Fortune's Bluff but weeds. She waited for Windle to tell Neezer of the host of reasons why the crop they had growing might fail. Instead Windle grinned back at Nitty.

"My crop," he finally said, "will be something to behold. And I am not a man who considers. I am a man who does."

Neezer bellowed out a chuckle, and his face purpled to the very shade of his satin vest. "As am I, Windle! As am I."

Windle turned to Nitty. "We'd best get the hay home before a duster blows it off the truck." He started down the aisle with Nitty beside him, then paused. "Oh, and Neezer." He grinned again. "You'll be needing more hay directly."

Neezer blinked. "More? We stocked forty bales yesterday!"

"Yes." Windle winked at Nitty. "I bought them all."

CHAPTER EIGHT

In Which a Hand Is Taken and a Great Gulf Crossed

As Windle's truck slogged along under the weight of the hay, Nitty asked the question that had been pestering her since back at the store.

"If Neezer's your brother—"

"In-law," Windle added.

"Why don't you get along?"

Windle glanced at her, his brows exclamation points. "You didn't see us arguing, did you?"

"Your mouths might not have been feuding, but your eyes sure were."

He stared out the window. "It was a long time ago. Hardly worth the words it would take to explain it."

"Seems like no fight should take that long to fix."

Windle gave a single, hard "Ha!" then added, "I see I'll have to teach you about the Hundred Years' War in addition to Robert Louis Stevenson." He stared through the windshield. "There was a time when Neezer and I were friends." His voice softened. "Good friends. Then . . . we weren't."

"I imagine Lillah didn't like that. The two of you fighting." A grimace flickered across Windle's face. "Is that part of why she left?"

"She left to sing." He glowered over the steering wheel. "Now let that put an end to your inquisition."

"But—"

"That is all."

A million questions buzzed in Nitty's brain. Like why Windle's face had suddenly sunk in on itself with sadness. Like what had caused Windle and Neezer to fight in the first place. Like how two people could fall into and out of friendship, when friendship was such a rarity to begin with. At least, it had been a rarity in *her* life. She had a million questions, but Windle's stony face said he wouldn't be answering a single one of them today. So she resigned herself to living with the mystery for now, and thought instead about how happy Old Mag would be with the hay they were bringing home for her. Nitty couldn't help giggling.

"What's given you a case of the twitters?" Windle asked with relief at the change of subject.

"Did you see Neezer's face when you told him about the hay?" She giggled again. "Wasn't he just stupefied?"

She grinned at Windle, but he only shook his head, muttering, "I was a fool to say such a thing. Next he'll be wanting to know what the hay is for, instead of leaving us to our own affairs. Next he'll be asking how we came by an elephant in the first place."

"Oh," Nitty mumbled as this sank in. Then she sat up straighter as a simple solution presented itself. "We don't have to tell him about Mag at all." She swallowed and studied Windle, hoping for a sign of solidarity. "Do we?"

Windle frowned. "Anybody who knows more than Neezer is somebody who knows too much. And your elephant . . . well . . . she can't be kept secret for long."

"I *know* that. Only . . . she can't go back to . . . to where she came from either." She hoped that was all she'd have to say on the matter, but Windle looked at her long and hard.

"Why not?" he asked.

"She wasn't happy with her old way of life." The crane, with its dangling noose, came to her mind, and then an image of Grimsgate, with its barred windows and storm-gray stones. She shivered and reached for her Gleam Jar, which today she'd tied about her neck with the old twine from her flour-sack dress. How many nights at Grimsgate had she only had her Gleam Jar to ward off her loneliness or Miz Ricketts's harsh words? Mag had never had a Gleam Jar—or anything, probably—to offer her comfort. "No one thought much of her. Back where she came from."

Windle harrumphed. "I suspect Neezer may take issue with an elephant in Fortune's Bluff."

"Why?" Nitty asked.

"Because she wasn't his idea." He sighed.

They drove on a piece in silence, and then Windle slowed the truck and turned toward her, his eyes grave knots in the grain of his face. "Your elephant. How do you know she wasn't happy?"

"Because . . ." Nitty's voice was wind-through-a-cornfield soft. "She wasn't loved."

"Elephants don't need love."

Nitty glared at him then. "What sort of catawampus idea is that? I believe everything needs love."

Windle cleared his throat gruffly. "Best not believe too deeply. Better to protect your heart."

"What's the point of that?" A heart wasn't like a canned good, meant to sit on the shelf of some darkened cupboard for years, shut up tight. No. Hearts were meant for opening.

Windle blinked, then studied the steering wheel for a long minute. "After love comes loss. And loss brings more unhappiness."

"Until?" Nitty asked. "There *has* to be an 'until.'"

She waited, but Windle returned his eyes to the road and drove on without another word. Maybe he didn't know what was on the other side of loss, Nitty decided then. Maybe he didn't know because he hadn't reached the other side yet.

That thought made her lean across the seat to take his hand.

He turned stock-still, the tips of his ears reddening. "Thanks for the hay." Her hand sat pint-sized in his great, furrowed one.

A muffled growl rose from his throat, which Nitty understood to mean, *You're welcome.* A second later, he released her hand to grip the steering wheel.

But not without first giving it the smallest, fleetingest of squeezes.

⌒⋏⌒

Nitty had to admit that a cot was much preferable to a barn floor when it came to comfort, but still, as she lay among the slanting shadows of the farmhouse kitchen that night, she decided that a cot was not at all preferable to the curl of an elephant's trunk.

She rolled over on the cot for the dozenth time, but it was no use. All she could think about was Mag in the barn, without her. She slid the cot across the floor, opened the kitchen window, and, propping herself up on her elbow, peered out at the darkened barn. Was Mag lonely without her? she wondered. Or worse, was she frightened?

Nitty flopped onto her back with a sigh, pangs of missing Mag needling her heart. She'd just about made up her mind to go to her when, suddenly, slinking through the open window came an inquisitive trunk. Its tip swished at the air for a moment and then, as if it had managed to determine its exact location, lowered itself onto Nitty's forehead to deposit a damp, snouty kiss.

Nitty giggled, and Mag's head appeared at the other side of the kitchen window, peering in.

"There isn't much point to Windle latching the barn door, is there?" she asked then, guessing that Mag had unlatched it with her trunk (which, in truth, was exactly what she *had* done). She smiled into the dark as she rubbed Mag's trunk. "Were you missing me, too?"

Mag blew a puff of air across Nitty's forehead, and a rolling rumble—almost like a purr, only much louder—sounded from deep in Mag's throat. It was a pleasant sound, lulling and rhythmic, like water lapping on a shore, and Nitty noticed that it grew the longer she rubbed Mag's trunk.

"I'm glad you're here," she whispered. "I was having a time of it trying to get to sleep without you." She turned on her elbow to face Mag's blinking eyes. "Would you . . . stay here with me? Until I fall asleep?"

Mag's trunk eased the open window higher so that she could squeeze the bottom of her head and chin through. Nitty, laughing, obliged the effort with a chin rub.

"I've never had anyone to tuck me in properly," Nitty went on, feeling herself settling more comfortably into the crook of her cot. "I always imagined it would be lovely." She studied Mag's patient face, her dark eyes. "I suppose you never had either."

She thought on this a spell, trying to discern what might be the best way to tuck in an elephant. "I could tell you a story. One of my own, if you like. Maybe about my time at

Grimsgate? It'd have to stay our secret, mind, because no one here can know where I came from. But I don't suppose you'll tell anyone, will you?"

Mag trilled a soft *Brrt* with her trunk, and that was enough to satisfy Nitty.

"All right, then." Nitty nodded, cupping her palm around the tip of Mag's trunk. "One of my favorites is about the time I dumped an entire inkwell into Miz Ricketts's tea, on account of her locking me in the attic for a week. . . ."

Mag's ears lifted as the girl began talking. The rise and fall of the girl's voice was pleasant. She'd missed that voice tonight in the darkness of the barn. She liked it here well enough, but mostly she simply liked being near the girl. No one—animal or human—had ever treated her so gently, or ever spoken to her in such soft tones. It almost made her forget about her trainer. Almost.

Now the girl's voice sounded heavy with sleep, and Mag herself felt a drowsiness stealing over her. Still, she stayed, not wanting to leave the girl's side.

At last the girl fell silent, calm, and peaceful.

Ever so slowly, using her trunk, Mag pushed the blanket up to the girl's chin. Then, with deep satisfaction, she plodded slowly back to the barn and latched the door behind her.

CHAPTER NINE

In Which the Nature of Bottomless Hunger and Whumping Is Explored

Neezer Snollygost was musing over Nitty. And hay. And the Homes farm. And the whumping, which sounded at regular intervals from behind the locked door beside his office. In fact, as he sat behind his desk at the Snollygost Institute with his nose whistling "I'm a Jolly Banker," Neezer was musing over a great many things.

He leaned back in his chair, his hands drumming his chest. Musing had a habit of making him hungry.

"Miz Turngiddy!" he bellowed over the whumping.

Seconds later, Miz Turngiddy scampered through his office door. "Yes, sir?" she shouted. "What can I do for you, sir?"

Nearly every conversation between Neezer Snollygost and

Miz Turngiddy involved shouting, because of the incessant whumping.

"I am in need of sustenance," Neezer said.

Someone other than Miz Turngiddy might've been surprised by this declaration. Especially someone glancing at the top of Neezer's desk, as Miz Turngiddy was doing now.

On this desktop, spread before Neezer, was a lavish meal of more than a dozen courses. A feast the likes of which no other soul in all of Fortune's Bluff had ever seen. Steak and potatoes, watermelon, a platter of corn piled two feet high, fritters, sweet cakes, pies. It was enough to feed an entire Fortune's Bluff family. Four or five families, in fact. But Neezer Snollygost was dining alone.

Miz Turngiddy was *not* surprised by Neezer's declaration. Her skills of observation were much keener than Neezer understood them to be, due to the fact that the mayor didn't fancy thinking of anyone's skills except his own. This was fine by Miz Turngiddy. She was not in the habit of revealing the whole of her impressive intellect to her supervisor, as she always suspected he would dislike it. And Miz Turngiddy needed to keep her job so that she might use this intellect to help alleviate the dire circumstances she found her beloved town of Fortune's Bluff facing. She needed her job, too, for its pay, which she mailed out west to her son and grandbabies. But if Fortune's Bluff could be revived, then her grandbabies, with their sweet-cream scent and apricot-fuzz curls, might someday move back to town. It was this hope that kept Miz Turngiddy's skills keen and her wit sharp. And it was with these keen skills of observation that she had come to understand one inexorable certainty about Neezer Snollygost: his hunger was as bottomless as his hubris was great.

From the moment he'd arrived in the world with a demanding holler, Neezer had hungered. One bottle of milk was never as good as two, two never as good as three. It might've been because he was born early and small and he needed to gain strength and girth. It might've been because just as Neezer was brought into this world, his mama passed from it.

Even though Neezer had a loving older sister in Clara, his mama's passing carved a hollow in his heart. And when his papa passed, too, and Neezer and Clara were taken in by their grandfather, the hollow deepened.

"No need to be as big as a mountain to move one," his grandfather told him when Neezer's small size made it impossible for him to fetch water buckets or push the plow.

Whatever chores Neezer couldn't manage, Clara did for him, and he loved her all the more for it. Clara had a way of making him forget his hunger with her kindness. But Neezer had his share of tormentors, too—schoolmates who chided him for his smallness and his unusual ideas. Where Clara's love filled a portion of the hollow in Neezer's heart, others' misjudgments made it impossible for the hollow to heal entirely. It remained, and so did Neezer's cravings, growing as he did.

It wasn't simply food that Neezer craved. Neezer Snollygost craved admiration. What he couldn't achieve with physical strength, he tried to achieve with innovation.

He was eight when he locked himself in his grandfather's barn and emerged, two days later, with the Speedy Seed-Spitter, his first brainchild. "Guaranteed to plant seeds faster than any man or plow."

When the Speedy Seed-Spitter delivered the battery of seeds into the chicken coop instead of the field (where the hens promptly ate the would-be crop), Neezer's grandfather smiled and squeezed his shoulder, saying as gently as he could, "Perhaps farming isn't your calling."

But Neezer wanted it to be. Oh, did he want it to be! So at nine, Neezer built the Self-Propellant Plow. The plow propelled itself right through the side of the barn, which delighted the horses, who promptly escaped to spend a week gallivanting with the mares across town. At ten, he created the Refracting Rain-Catcher, which flooded the fields.

And so it went as the years passed. One calamitous invention after another.

"Someday you'll succeed," his grandfather told him. "At something besides farming."

Neezer refused to give up, and when he met Clara's beau, Windle Homes—Windle, with all his confidence and certainty and great farming talent—his heart buoyed. For Windle was a man who understood what it was to aspire to greatness, a man who would put his faith in Neezer's farming inventions as Neezer's grandfather never had.

Neezer didn't mind that it was to Clara and Windle that his grandfather left the farm, because they still offered him a partnership in it. He believed that, in time, his inventions would convince them of his worth, and then he might buy a portion of the farm for himself. He loved them and Lillah, too, when she came along. His hunger, in the face of friendship, family, and newfound possibility, began to fade.

But then came the Fantastic Farm-O-Matic catastrophe—a failure of such enormity there could be no recovering from it. It was after this that Neezer finally saw he would never succeed at farming. It was after this that he saw he had been wrong to put his faith in friendship and family. It was after this that his heart's hollow—which had been ever so slowly healing—ruptured into an unconquerable chasm. His hunger—which had been fading—grew exponentially in size and ferocity.

It was after this that Neezer, at last, found success.

First he succeeded in banking. He succeeded at lending farmers money to buy land and seed, and then at collecting the money they made. Next he succeeded in gaining their trust. As he grew in stature and strength, his smile grew, too, widening until it drew in just about every person in town. Which was how, finally, he succeeded in becoming mayor.

Neezer's successes, though, didn't satisfy him. Perhaps they had come too late, and at too great a price. Perhaps it was watching Clara and Windle continue to grow their farm and family without him. Or perhaps the irreparable rupture to Neezer's heart had made it that he was never satisfied with anything, that he was always seeking an idea of happiness that could never exist. No matter whether it was all or none of those reasons, or some other reason entirely, Neezer hungered and hungered.

And since his hunger was not an ordinary one, it could never be satisfied by ordinary means. Miz Turngiddy suspected this, which was why she considered the tending of Neezer's bottomless hunger one of her most pivotal tasks. The cogs and wheels of Miz Turngiddy's mind were in constant motion, striving to learn as much about civic service and mayoral duties as she could.

Truth be told, Neezer's hunger frightened her. It had frightened her son, too, enough to send him, with the grandbabies, out west. But Miz Turngiddy, like so many other folks, remembered Fortune's Bluff in its glory days, long before Neezer, and she loved it as much now as then, even in its decrepitude. It was the home of her own childhood—a place she couldn't leave. She vowed to stay behind to help it, so that someday her grandbabies could come home to it as it used to be: green and welcoming. Helping Fortune's Bluff, she believed, meant curtailing Neezer's hunger.

She thought she might curtail it if she could only succeed in finding that most elusive of foods that could satisfy it.

Which she set about doing now, flipping the pages of her

notepad, her pursed lips quivering. "Oranges!" she cried hopefully above the whumping. "You said yourself that a delivery arrived earlier today, sir, and one truck was full to the brim with oranges. Straight from California! Perhaps a freshly peeled orange, then, sir?"

"Oranges, you say? Hmmm." Neezer mulled this over as he finished a second helping of rhubarb pie. "It *has* been several weeks since I've had an orange." He nodded. "I will have oranges, then, Miz Turngiddy. Bring me half a dozen."

"Very good, sir!" Miz Turngiddy hollered over the whumping.

For Neezer Snollygost, the whumping was symphonic in its sweetness. It was a sound like no other. A sound that brought him one step closer to community progress, fulfillment, and the betterment of all. A sound that meant he would be remembered forever. A sound that, at long last, one day very soon, might sate his bottomless hunger.

On the other hand, the whumping was a source of annoyance for Miz Turngiddy. How could it not be, when, for months now, it had whumped its eternal *WHUMP* every minute of every hour, day and night? At times the whumping seemed no better than a mallet striking at Miz Turngiddy's temples. In fact, she secretly hoped that one day it would stop altogether, once Neezer's machine was, at last, complete. This was why she asked now, "Mr. Snollygost, how is progress on the Whirlybog coming?"

"Exemplary! Couldn't be better," Neezer said between bites

of mashed potatoes. "It is only the briefest matter of time now. A mere twinkling away from stopping the dusters, I should say."

Miz Turngiddy had come to understand that to Neezer, the "briefest matter of time" could mean days, or months, or—worst of all—years. Neezer had already been toiling over his invention for ten years (although it was only in the last months the *WHUMP* had started), and he was forever making promises of its nearing completion. She stared at the locked door as the whumping rattled her teeth. Behind it lay the Whirlybog, something she had yet to set eyes on but guessed was as enormous in its size as its sound. The machine was not seen by anyone other than Neezer himself. Ever. Those were his strict orders, and, to keep her job, Miz Turngiddy obeyed. Still, she longed to set eyes on it, to study it, to put the cogs and wheels of her mind to work improving it. For she was sure she could improve it, as she was sure she could improve so many things in Fortune's Bluff, if only given a proper chance. She took a deep breath. "It's heartening to think that your invention could save Fortune's Bluff. I wonder if we might, too, think of securing the soil itself? To prevent it from blowing away? Perhaps by plowing terraces in the land?"

"Terraces! The very idea is absurd!"

Miz Turngiddy pinched her lips together at that. She tried again. "Mr. Snollygost, if you'd permit me entrance to your workshop, I might examine the machine and help—"

Her words were cut short by Neezer's chuckle, a disquieting

sound somewhere between sneezing and blowing one's nose. "No need to tax yourself. My efforts are nothing more than the humble fruits of an inspired mind. I'm only doing my duty."

Miz Turngiddy had her response ready, as she always did, although it tended to taste like rotten cabbage on her tongue. "You do much more than that, sir. So much more!"

Neezer shook his head. "To business, Miz Turngiddy, before you embarrass me further. Have you made an inventory of today's deliveries?"

"Of course, sir. Potatoes, canned peas, corn, peaches, Spam . . . oh, and some chocolate." Miz Turngiddy checked off each food on her list as she read it. Of course she had not been present for the deliveries. She never was. They arrived both day and night, but Neezer always insisted on taking care of them himself, always while Miz Turngiddy was out. Miz Turngiddy was only able to inventory the items *after* the delivery trucks had come and gone.

There were questions Miz Turngiddy could not ask Neezer, though she often wanted to. Questions about why the machine he promised was taking so long to complete, when it managed to whump very completely and successfully already. Questions about why dusters seemed to be getting worse in Fortune's Bluff but not, according to her recent research, anywhere else. Questions about where their food deliveries came from, and why she never saw bills of sale for them.

"Not matters to trouble your mind," Neezer had said once, when she'd posed these questions to him.

She was suspicious of his answer, and of the offhand way in

which his nose struck up "It Don't Mean a Thing" afterward. She was suspicious, in general, of Neezer Snollygost himself. Often she wondered about the sincerity of his smile *and* his whistling nose.

But since the biggest trouble of Miz Turngiddy's mind was keeping her job to help Fortune's Bluff and to bring back her grandbabies, she vowed to stifle her suspicions and her questions.

"Well." Neezer sat back in his chair now, smiling. "Folks are bound to be tickled by the chocolate. I can't remember when anyone in Fortune's Bluff last saw chocolate! Can you?"

She shook her head. "You must have paid a fortune for it." Neezer kept his accounting ledgers locked in his workshop alongside the Whirlybog. Miz Turngiddy would've loved to study those as well.

Neezer waved a hand. "Think nothing of it, Miz Turngiddy. I live to be of service to our community. I'm just thankful there's still food to be had." Neezer tapped the tips of his fingers together.

"Only . . ." Miz Turngiddy consulted her notes. "We do seem to have a shortage of hay at the moment. As a result of Windle's visit to the store today."

"Hay! Yes. I was aware of that, of course."

When she was sure Neezer wasn't paying attention, Miz Turngiddy raised her eyes to the ceiling.

Neezer's nose changed its tune to "Worried Man Blues." "A peculiar purchase, that enormous amount of hay. And a peculiar girl, that Nitty Luce, with those odd green eyes. Do you agree?"

Miz Turngiddy had noticed Nitty's eyes, to be certain, as she noticed everything else in Fortune's Bluff. For her part, she'd found Nitty's eyes refreshing in their greenness—cheery, even. She didn't dare say so to Neezer. What she did say was, "Decidedly odd. Most certainly."

"I do wonder how Windle came by his guest. This Nitty Luce." He chewed thoughtfully on a roasted leg of chicken. "We must keep a watchful eye, Miz Turngiddy. To ensure that Windle shares our goals of community progress and fulfillment, as all our citizens should." He focused his eyes on Miz Turngiddy with the gravity of a colonel giving his soldier a mission. "Can I entrust you with this task?"

"You can," Miz Turngiddy assured him.

"But first. The oranges?"

"Oranges, oranges, yes, yes." With that, Miz Turngiddy scurried away. It might've been her feet's way of trying to keep pace with her whirring mind, but Miz Turngiddy, as it happened, was a very adept scurrier.

As she scurried, Neezer returned to his musings. He abandoned his feast, much of which was still untouched, and focused his attention on the locked door beside his office. *WHUMP! WHUMP! WHUMP!* The Whirlybog was calling him.

With a few adjustments to the Dustometer, some tightening of screws here and there, it could be more powerful. The Whirlybog, indeed, would be the solution to all the problems of Fortune's Bluff. Neezer smiled. Then he unlocked the door and disappeared behind it.

CHAPTER TEN

In Which Sleuthing and Snakeskins Collide

By the time sleep overcame Nitty and Mag that night, the sproutlings had already grown a foot tall. By the next day, they brushed Nitty's shoulder, and by the day after that, they were taller and fuller than any cornstalk ever seen in those parts. Soon stalks as big as Nitty's arm branched into leaves as wide and round as umbrellas.

Windle didn't know what to make of it. He stood on the porch every morning, bewildered, while his coffee turned cold in its cup.

"It can't last," he'd finally mutter. Especially with the well turning muddier every day, and not a drop of rain in sight.

But it *did* last. Dusters came each afternoon, howling and nipping, sometimes bending the stalks to the ground with their winds. But once the storms were over, the stalks sprang up, determined and sprightly, juddering until the dust was shaken from each and every leaf.

Nitty liked to watch the stalks in the evening hours after the storms, when it was safe for her and Mag to take up their stations on the porch again. It was at this time of day, with chores done and supper over, that Nitty would read aloud from *Treasure Island* while Mag rested her trunk on her shoulder.

More often than not, Nitty discovered items waiting for her and Mag on the windowsill beside the front door, left there as if by some mysterious hand. One evening, Nitty discovered a peppermint. The next, she found a hairbrush and two barrettes that she suspected Lillah had once worn as a young girl. An old croquet ball appeared one evening for Mag, and she spent the better part of an hour rolling it across the porch with her trunk.

Only once, Nitty tried offering thanks to Windle for a spinning top he'd left for her, but she was met with such a formidable stare she vowed never to say boo about it again.

Instead she made sure to pronounce her admiration for the offerings aloud to Mag, knowing Windle would hear it, even if he wouldn't acknowledge it. "You're one lucky elephant today," Nitty would say when Mag found peanuts or apple slices on the sill. "And nobody ever asks you to share," she added teasingly. "Even luckier."

Of course Mag always shared, dropping a peanut or apple slice in Nitty's lap before returning her trunk to Nitty's shoulder. There her trunk would stay, until a page in *Treasure Island* needed turning. Mag, Nitty was delighted to discover, was both an eager listener and adept page turner. The moment Nitty paused at a page's end, Mag's trunk would slowly push the page upward until it flipped. This never failed to make Windle's specter smile appear as he sat in his rocking chair just inside the screen door.

When Nitty stumbled over a word, Windle called out the correct pronunciation instantly. His corrections were gruff, but they pleased Nitty all the same, for that was how she was sure he was listening.

When Nitty paused in her reading to gaze out on the juddering emerald field, when she whispered to Mag, "You know what I think? I think those stalks are dancing, that's what. They're dancing because they're strong, they're tended, and they're here," she knew Windle heard, too.

It was far better, she thought, to have him listening to a book than staring forlornly at the photo on the kitchen table. She'd noticed him doing this often, and she'd even, at times, overheard him murmuring to it when he thought her out of earshot. Seeing him like that—so sad, and scratching at his freckle— made her more determined than ever to help him.

Even as she waited on Windle's change of heart and the field's triumph, she discovered that there was no lack of tasks for her to accomplish. This was partly due to Windle's belief in productivity, but mostly due to Twitch's belief in mischief. Each morning, Twitch appeared on the front porch, pacing, a

Detective Comics issue under one arm, his Morton Salt periscope under the other, and his notepad and pencil in his pocket.

As he posited theory upon theory about Neezer (so far, he'd considered that Neezer was building a torture chamber, a speakeasy, and an oubliette), Nitty hurried through chores, knowing that, all too soon, Twitch would get antsy for town. She only paused long enough to laugh at Mag, who'd assigned herself the morning chore of rousing the chickens from their roosts. Mag accomplished this by slyly sneaking up on the chickens with her trunk and blasting them with a stream of hot air. The chickens would explode from their coop, squawking, as Mag puckishly swung her trunk at them. Then Twitch would turn too fidgety, and he and Nitty would go in search of Windle.

"Can we run any errands for you in town today?" Twitch would ask Windle impatiently. Nitty knew that what he really meant was *Can we go sleuthing today?*

"Mind you don't fribble the time away," Windle always warned sternly after he'd finished listing the errands. "Be back before noon so you steer clear of dusters."

Nitty promised they would. Windle's errands, Nitty came to realize, were less errands and more acts of kindness. Some days she and Twitch delivered the one or two eggs Windle's chickens had laid to the Johnsons or the O'Reillys. Other days they took a fresh pail of Bessie's milk to the Steins. Each and every day they left another handful of wilting corn silk (scrounged from Windle's rotting corn crib) for Ferdinand Klempt, who could always be found sagging over his worktable at the Schnurrbart Emporium, crying over another failed mustache.

Whatever meager offerings the Homes farm still produced, Windle gave away.

"Leave it on the doorstep" was Windle's instruction for each delivery. "No need to call attention to yourselves."

This was fine by Nitty and Twitch, because the less attention they were paid, the greater their chances of sleuthing success. Together they'd spotted a half dozen more mystery trucks coming and going from the Snollygost Institute, though these trucks were so coated in dust it was impossible to decipher any signage on them that might offer a hint as to their purpose. Twitch had also observed Neezer carrying a book under his arm titled *Sublime Skyscrapers: The Beauty of a Metropolis.*

"I've never seen him reading anything before, let alone a book," Twitch had said. "Why would he want a book on skyscrapers?"

Neither of them knew, but afterward Twitch vowed to double their visits to town *and* their sleuthing efforts.

Nitty didn't like leaving Mag behind for these errands, but Mag didn't seem to mind, and knowing it was for Mag's own good helped ease the pain of it. As Nitty walked down the road away from the farm, she'd look back to see that Mag, with a chicken or two in tow, had taken up post beside Windle.

Windle never discussed what he and Mag did while Nitty and Twitch made their daily rounds about town. From the repairs and improvements that were made, slowly but surely, to the Homes farm, Nitty decided they made a productive team.

Window boxes were rehung and straightened, broken railings mended, and splintered porch stairs replaced. She suspected that it suited Windle just dandy to work with an elephant, since hours could pass without so much as a single word spoken between them.

On the other hand, there was never any shortage of words passing between Nitty and Twitch, especially on the particular day their errands included a stop at Crispin's Bakery.

"I've been waiting for this for ages." Twitch's breaths were coming in excited, whining puffs like a steam whistle. "Ma won't get within ten feet of those snakeskins. Nobody in Fortune's Bluff will." He grinned. "I bet they're rattlers, too, with fangs near a foot long!"

"Sure as bats in a belfry they are," Nitty affirmed as they reached Main Street, where she fought the urge to plug her ears against the incessant noise coming from the Snollygost Institute. The *WHUMP* was whumping, louder and longer than it had yesterday or the day before. "I saw them up close myself. After the first shock of it, they didn't bother me any. I was far more worried about getting pummeled by Crispin's daughter. The oldest one."

"You mean Bernice." Twitch said her name quietly and with guarded respect, as if the simple act of saying it might incur Bernice's wrath. "If only she'd commit a crime, she would make a stellar villain."

"Bernice didn't strike me as a villain. But she sure struck me as angry."

"Well, she only meets one of the villainous criteria so far. 'Ten Ways to Be a Villain, number one: Suffer an alleged wrong or injustice that leaves you embittered of the world and its every occupant.'"

"What sort of wrong did she suffer?"

"It was Crispin who suffered it, not Bernice, but she's angry enough for the whole Sigh family. It was a while back, maybe two or so years ago. Right after the last Sigh baby was born and Mrs. Sigh passed. Fortune's Bluff was in a sorry state. Crops blown away, no food to be found. And then the Snollygost General Store opened and offered everyone free store credit. Only, Crispin didn't think anybody should be beholden to Neezer. He didn't trust him. Same as me." Twitch patted the *Detective Comics* rolled up in his back pocket. "Intuition, see." He tapped his temple knowingly, then broke into a coughing fit.

As Nitty waited for it to pass, she shook her head. "What does any of this have to do with injustice?"

"I'm getting to that!" Twitch blurted, breathless, glowering at her. "So Crispin starts giving his bread away for free, and for a while people quit shopping at Snollygost's, just eating bread and whatever else Crispin mustered up to offer them. Neezer never said a word about it, but everybody knew he was fit to be tied. Then, one day, a duster blew through and brought a twister with it. And wouldn't you know, that twister touched down right on Crispin's storehouse, taking almost all his flour, eggs, everything he needed for his bread. Then it left, without touching another building in town." Twitch leaned toward Nitty, whispering conspiratorially, "*Almost* like that twister was planned."

Nitty stared at Twitch. She might've been tempted to laugh, but the gravity in Twitch's eyes made her think twice. "A twister can't pick where it's going to land."

"No, but what if a person could tell it where to land?"

"That's imposs—" She caught herself. To say that one mysterious happening was impossible meant that others were, too. Wasn't the crop growing on the Homes farm mysterious? Nitty didn't want to be a skeptic. A skeptic could take something mysterious and squelch the magic right out of it. Instead she said, "That would be bewildering, to be sure."

"Well, that's what Crispin believes. After the twister, Crispin took to wandering outside the Snollygost Institute at all hours. He was convinced that Neezer was behind the twister. That the proof was hidden somewhere at the institute."

"Did he find anything?"

"No one knows for sure. Miz Turngiddy never would let him inside, so finally one night Crispin broke in. Neezer caught him, of course, and sent him to the Kickapoo Asylum, saying Crispin was imagining things, making up stories."

"An asylum." Nitty swallowed. Asylums featured in some of the *Daily Tattler*'s most sensationalistic stories. Nitty imagined them as dismal places haunted by the moans and cries of the wronged and misjudged. Asylums were the sort of places that only belonged in made-up stories, never in real life. They were far too terrible for that. "How long was Crispin there for?"

"Two months." Twitch nodded slowly. "And when Neezer saw Crispin loaded into the asylum's wagon, his nose whistled Beethoven's Fifth. I witnessed it myself. Swear on my muddy lungs."

Nitty gasped. "And that whole time Bernice and the other Sigh children were alone?" She shook her head, brushing her hand over her Gleam Jar for reassurance. "How awful." She felt a sudden surge of anger toward Neezer Snollygost. What right did he have to turn children into orphans?

Twitch nodded. "It was awful. Whatever Crispin saw inside the Snollygost Institute changed him. Now he rambles on about whirlybogs and wind. Mostly, though, he talks about rain. Why, last month he launched a balloon full of lit dynamite over Fortune's Bluff to see if it could make rain. It didn't." Twitch grinned. "But it sure made for some dandy fireworks."

"Twitch!" Nitty scolded, but she could hardly blame him for his enthusiasm. It would've been a sight!

"It's not just dynamite either," Twitch said. "That's why Crispin hangs those snakeskins. He chants to the sky, too. All for rain."

"And I bet nobody believes a word he says about the Snollygost Institute," Nitty guessed.

"Oh, some wondered when Crispin got taken away, and

then again when the *WHUMP* started up months back. But they only whispered over it. They didn't dare speak up to Neezer for fear of him demanding payments on their loans and store credits. And now Neezer's got everyone hoodwinked with promises of that invention to stop the dusters."

"What makes folks think Neezer's ideas are so much better than Crispin's, anyway?" Nitty asked.

"Power." Twitch nodded knowingly. "That's what Pa used to say. Mostly, I think folks are too worn for questioning anymore. 'Cept me." He shrugged. "If I could make heads or tails of Crispin's words, I would, but others think he's gone balmy. Neezer's told everyone to steer clear of the bakery. He says it's dangerous, that Crispin's a threat. And the snakeskins and dynamite spook people."

Nitty stopped mid-step. "So nobody eats Crispin's bread anymore?"

"Crispin can't bake much these days. He won't buy supplies from the Snollygost General Store, so I don't know where he gets his ingredients. Windle buys what little Crispin bakes, but he . . . he's the only one." Twitch turned suddenly sheepish. "I told you Ma doesn't let me go near the bakery!"

Anger fizzed in Nitty. "Isn't that just the way! A person devises an uncommon solution to a problem, such as snakeskins or dynamite, and folks turn a cold shoulder." Here she was, all this time thinking that Miz Ricketts might be the only one suffering from a stagnant imagination! When really it was a voluminous horde! She stalked toward the bakery now, tripling her pace.

"Nitty?" Twitch was running to keep up, huffing beside her. "What are you going to do?"

"I'm going to rid Bernice Sigh of her pricklies, that's what."

Nitty found Crispin standing in the bakery's doorway, scanning the sky, holding his rolling pin up to his ear.

"Rain. Rain. Where's the rain?" Crispin's hands trembled fiercely. "Cans of sauce, from the cross; hide them all, says the boss."

He blinked his red-rimmed, watery eyes at Nitty. "Do you have a recipe for rain? I need a recipe for rain. The dough's too starched; the sky's too parched."

"No recipe today, Mr. Sigh." Nitty smiled. At the sight of his trembling and sad eyes, her anger started fresh. She didn't know for certain if Neezer Snollygost was truly to blame. It hardly mattered in the face of Crispin's torment. "I've come to buy some bread."

Crispin blinked, then blinked again. At last he nodded and turned toward the bakery's shelves. "Only one loaf today. My barrel's near empty, and I've nothing to grind."

Nitty couldn't make any sense of that until Bernice stepped from the back of the bakery, trailing three sniffling, smudge-covered little Sighs from her tattered apron.

"He means the flour," Bernice said. "We've only one barrel left."

Nitty thought Bernice looked like a sentry when she stepped protectively in front of Crispin. She folded her arms and glared from Nitty to Twitch and back again, as if daring them to make a wrong move.

Nitty eased to the left of Bernice and gently took the loaf from Crispin's outstretched arms, depositing the nickel Windle had given her in its place. Crispin clutched the coin to his chest, then disappeared with it into the back of the store, the littlest Sighs trailing behind him. Bernice stayed where she was.

"The bread looks delectable. Doesn't it, Twitch?" Nitty nudged Twitch in the ribs, which prompted his enthusiastic "Yes!"

Bernice glared harder. Her hands curled into fists. "Are you poking fun? If you are—"

Nitty didn't give her time to finish. She chose not to think about the spots of fuzzy mold she'd seen on the loaf. It wouldn't be the first time she'd eaten food that had turned. Instead she closed her eyes and sank her teeth into a sizable chunk of the loaf. It was hard as stone, but after chewing for some time, she swallowed it down.

"Perfectly palatable," she said. She opened her eyes and saw Bernice. She wasn't glaring anymore, just staring.

"You don't really like it." Bernice's tone was more surprised than angry. "Any fool knows it tastes like dirt."

As Nitty saw it, she was faced with two options. The first was to construct a lie, hold her breath, and await Bernice's fist in her nose. The second was to confess to the truth, hold her breath, and await Bernice's fist in her nose. Since the outcome of either option seemed inevitable, she decided to try her hand at the truth.

"Well." She took a deep breath, then glanced at Twitch for some sign of encouragement. He nodded her on in stalwart detectiving fashion, but edged toward the door, probably in case there was pummeling and they needed to run for it. "If you want to know," Nitty pressed on, "the bread could do with a little more seasoning and a little less Toeter Grime."

A long silence followed this pronouncement, and then Bernice snorted. It was a hiccup of a snort. Bernice quickly stopped it, covering her mouth with her hand. Only it was too late.

"You laughed," Nitty proclaimed.

"Did not." Bernice's face turned flinty again.

Twitch narrowed his eyes at her. "We're onto you. You are *not* what you seem."

Bernice spun on her foot and made to stomp away, but Nitty called after her. "We're detectives! We don't put any credence in gossip."

"But we believe in papas," Twitch added. "And in the possibility of evildoings in Fortune's Bluff."

Bernice stopped, whirling to face them. "What do you know about any of it?"

"Not much," Nitty said.

"Yet," Twitch added. "But we're on the case. And the case involves Neezer Snollygost."

"He's got everyone in this town fooled except for Papa." At the mention of her papa, Bernice's voice turned soft around its jagged edges. "He's the only one who knows the truth. Or knew the truth." She dropped her eyes. "These days he only talks in gibberish riddles."

Nitty thought of the poems and riddles she'd read in the *Daily Tattler*. No matter how hard they were to decipher, in the end they always said *something* that mattered. "Maybe he's trying to tell you something with the riddles. Maybe he wants you to solve them. He said one just as we walked in. Twitch, do you remember?"

"It had to do with cans and crisscrosses, I think."

He pulled his notepad and pencil from the front pocket of his dungarees and wrote as much of it down as they could remember. As he was scribbling, a movement outside the bakery window caught Nitty's eye.

"It's Neezer!" she hissed, then ducked under the window, pulling Twitch down alongside her. Bernice stood with her arms crossed before her, glaring down at them, unmoving.

Nitty didn't dare yank on her the way she had Twitch, but she did glare back. "You may not like us any yet, but at least don't hamper our gumshoeing!"

At that Bernice grudgingly dropped to her knees beside them.

Twitch put his notepad away and lifted his Morton Salt periscope up to his goggles, directing it at the Snollygost General

Store. He lowered it a second later with a frustrated sigh. "Can't ever see a thing through these goggles."

As he took off his goggles, Nitty raised the periscope to her own eyes, delighted, as she always was, by the sheer sneakiness of such an instrument. Her breath hitched as Neezer came into focus. He was standing outside the store, loading a crate of mason jars into the back of his automobile.

"What do you see? What do you see?" Twitch was tugging on her arm, apt to pull it off entirely if she stayed mum a second longer.

"He's got jars full of something . . . I can't tell what. But . . ." She shifted the periscope slightly to get a better look. "Whatever's inside the jars is murky-colored . . . and *moving!*" Bernice scoffed doubtfully, until Nitty handed her the periscope for a turn.

Bernice was silent for a long moment as she stared through the eyepiece, and then she mumbled, "There's writing on the jars, but I can't make out what it says." Her voice was less guarded, but only for the second before a dark shadow descended over them.

As Bernice shoved the periscope behind her back, Nitty glanced up to see Miz Turngiddy, her arms full of newspapers, peering at them from the other side of the bakery window.

"It's Neezer's cloak-and-dagger," Twitch whispered. "Beware."

Miz Turngiddy strode into the bakery just as Neezer drove away in the direction of the institute, taking the mysterious crate of jars with him.

"Good morning." Miz Turngiddy nodded to the three of

them, setting down her newspapers on the counter and pulling her notebook from her pocket. She scanned the bakery's shelves. "And how is your father today, Bernice? Is he making any progress on his weather studies?"

Bernice stared at Miz Turngiddy. "I wouldn't tell you if he were." Her words were as impenetrable as a wall. *Impressive bravado,* noted Nitty silently.

Miz Turngiddy, though, was not impressed. She frowned, and her pen shook over her notebook—whether in fury or disappointment, it was hard to say. "No matter," she said briskly. "Mayor Snollygost considers it his duty to keep abreast of the health and well-being of each citizen. He'll look in on your father personally. Another day."

With that, she was through the door and scurrying up Main Street toward the institute.

"She's going to give a report to Mayor Snollygost," Bernice said drily.

"About your father?"

"About you. Being here." Bernice shrugged. "Neezer won't like it, just you wait and see. He doesn't like anyone paying visits to the bakery."

"Well, well, well." Twitch had turned his attention to the bakery's tall counter. "Look what she left behind." He held up the pile of newspapers.

Bernice rolled her eyes. "They're just a bunch of papers, Twitch."

He gaped in horror at the remark. "There is no 'just' in

detectiving. Papers might seem insignificant, but they *could* turn out to be irrefutable evidence. I don't ever take what looks ordinary for granted." He folded them under his arm with great formality. "I'll read through them for clues later. In the meantime, our next step is to get inside the Snollygost Institute. Whatever's in those jars, whatever Neezer's hiding . . . we'll uncover it." He held out his hand to Bernice for a shake. "If your papa says anything else of import, you'll inform us at once?"

Bernice's eyes slivered. "How can I trust you won't snitch to the mayor and Miz Turngiddy?"

Nitty and Twitch looked at each other, then back at Bernice. "We'll be as silent as a sarcophagus," Nitty vowed solemnly. "The sort without an accursed, moaning mummy inside." *That* tale in the *Daily Tattler* had kept her up plenty of nights.

At that moment, a child's cry rang out from the room over their heads, and Bernice glanced up wearily. "I don't have time to concern myself with mummies." She frowned. "That'd be Verna wanting her rattle. Papa never remembers where he sets it down." She started to walk away, then turned back to Nitty. "I can't believe you ate the bread."

Nitty grinned, then shrugged. "I can't believe you didn't pummel me."

Bernice grinned. "I can't either."

CHAPTER ELEVEN

In Which the Pogonologist Tells a Tale of a Mustache and Its Nits

Nitty had barely put a single foot outside Crispin's door, but Twitch was hurrying down the street, already a dozen steps ahead of her.

"Where are you going?" Nitty ran to catch up with him.

"Where do you think?" His march was full of purpose. "The Snollygost Institute. We're going to figure out a way in and—"

A cough overtook Twitch before he could finish. He reached into his pocket for the bottle of Mr. Moop's Cough Tonic he'd taken to keeping there, for just such occasions. He swallowed down a gulp as Nitty looked on, worry niggling her insides.

She wanted to investigate the institute as much as he did, but what if his lungs couldn't take it? The building sat atop the bluff in the distance, and getting there would mean they'd have to walk through the rest of town and then uphill until they reached the institute's formidable iron gates. Just the walk into town had left Twitch wheezing worse than usual. But pointing that out to him would only make Twitch sore at her.

Nitty grabbed his arm, stopping him mid-step. "We can't go up there. Not in the middle of the day like this. We'll be too easily spotted."

Twitch opened his mouth to protest, but the sound Nitty heard was the distant rumble of wind galloping over prairie.

"A duster's coming." She glanced up at a towering wave of dust, its first gritty blasts already stinging her face. She'd seen plenty like it before, barreling past the windows of Grimsgate. "A bad one, by the looks of it. We need to get back to the farm."

Twitch was coughing again, this time doubled over with the effort. As fast as this duster was moving, it would consume Main Street in minutes. The sky darkened to near night as clouds blocked the sun, and dirt hurtled against their skin in frenzied, stinging bites. She tugged on Twitch's arm, aiming to take him back to Crispin's, but then she heard Ferdinand Klempt calling to her.

"Come, come!" He beckoned to them from the doorway of the Schnurrbart Emporium. "Before you're blinded by the storm."

It was with some effort that the two of them reached Ferdinand's door, and by the time they did, the rest of the buildings and houses on the street were hidden. They shook the dust from their clothes as Ferdinand fetched them water.

While Twitch recovered his breath, Nitty used the opportunity to study the inside of the emporium. On previous visits she'd found Ferdinand sobbing and not in any mood for company, so she hadn't yet been able to take in the shop properly.

Now, upon inspection, she found it fascinating. Corn-silk mustaches by the dozens—dyed brightest silver to darkest obsidian and every shade in between—adorned the walls and workbench, giving Nitty the impression that there were countless faces hidden in the woodwork, their upper lips the only parts of themselves they were brave enough to show.

When she said as much to Ferdinand, he sighed. "It is only one face I see watching me . . . Papa's. And his lips are forever frowning."

"But these mustaches are beautiful," Nitty said encouragingly.

Ferdinand howled, his head dropping to his worktable. "They are! Because I didn't make them. Papa did! But look." He lifted one of his father's mustaches from its place on the wall and set it in Nitty's open palm. "See what the dusters have done."

As Nitty cautiously took the corner of the mustache between her fingertips, the corn silk crumbled to dust. "Oh," she said quietly.

Ferdinand nodded. "And this . . ." He cupped a droopy, moplike bunch of corn silk in his hands. "This is *my* craftsmanship. Another failure."

"Have you never sold a single mustache of your own?"

Nitty asked gently, suddenly wishing she had money to buy one herself.

Much to her relief, he nodded, holding up a single finger. "One. Just one. Months ago, to an elephant trainer passing through town with the Gusto and Gallant Circus."

Nitty's heart twittered at the mention of the circus, and she lifted her water cup to her mouth to mask whatever emotions might be showing on her face. She discovered she'd been too late to escape Twitch's notice, however. She hadn't breathed a word about Mag's origins to Twitch, but it became clear from his wide, knowing eyes that he'd just figured it out. He coughed over his own cup—a little too loudly, Nitty thought—and she gave him a hefty pat on the back as a warning not to say a word about Mag. When he gave a nearly imperceptible nod, Nitty felt awash with relief and gratitude.

"It could hardly even be considered a mustache," Ferdinand went on, oblivious to Nitty and Twitch's exchange of glances. "It was the most pathetic toothbrush mustache—uneven and riddled with nits."

Nitty paused over her cup, wondering if she'd heard right. "Did you say . . . nits?"

Ferdinand nodded. "I couldn't help myself, you see. Not after he told me what he'd done to his elephant. He was a braggart, and went on and on about how he had to keep his beast in her place. 'A bone-breaking wallop every few days does the trick,' he said. 'To remind her who's the master.'"

Nitty's hands were shaking, and she set her cup down on the

worktable before she sloshed it over herself. She felt Twitch's eyes on her face, and when he came to stand beside her, Nitty saw that his eyes looked as sorrowful as her heart felt. *Oh Mag,* she silently cried, *how they hurt you.*

"So . . . you sold the trainer a lemon?" Twitch said to Ferdinand, because Nitty couldn't find her voice to speak.

"I did. I gave him the moldiest, most nit-infested mustache I could find in my trash bin. One I never would've sold to a decent soul. I should've had the gallantry to give him a wallop instead, but . . ." Ferdinand shook his head. "I never could stand up for myself. Let alone anyone else."

Nitty wondered if Ferdinand was thinking of his own father, instead of the trainer. She laid a hand on Ferdinand's arm. "Well. I for one hope those nits itched him to kingdom come and back." No sooner had the words left her mouth than Nitty felt a nudge of guilt, wondering if it was wrong to say such a thing about a person no longer living. Maybe it was, but it was also wrong to treat any living being the way he'd treated Mag. She sighed.

Ferdinand stared at his pile of failing corn-silk mustaches. "How do you make peace with certain sorts of cruelty?"

"Maybe you never do," Twitch said.

"Maybe you bury them with your own better doings," she said, thinking of Mag's sweetness. She handed Ferdinand one of his works in progress.

His eyes filled, and Nitty feared he'd start crying again and possibly *never* stop, so she grabbed a handful of corn silk and motioned for Twitch to do the same. "Twitch and I can't go anywhere until the storm's passed, so why don't we help you with your work?"

Twitch's eyes lit up. "Could you fashion me one for detectiving? One that says I'm hard-boiled and meant to be taken seriously?"

Ferdinand hesitated, then scanned the mustaches covering the walls. "You don't want one of my disasters. And now the dust is making Papa's masterpieces fall apart at the slightest touch. The corn silk can't withstand it."

"Of course he wants one of your mustaches." Nitty exchanged a look with Twitch that was meant to stifle any protests. "He needs an original worthy of his investigating genius."

Twitch grinned at that, as Nitty had guessed he would.

Ferdinand looked hesitant, then nodded slowly. "All right, but I'd be obliged if you'd keep your expectations low." He inspected the shape of Twitch's face, jotting down some measurements. "A chevron for you, I think. Sober, intelligent, and, when need be, intimidating as well."

"Yes," Nitty said enthusiastically. "That sounds exactly right."

As dirt screeched past the store's window panes and the wind howled, the three of them set to work, with Ferdinand trimming and shaping corn silk, Nitty gluing it into place on a felt band, and Twitch applying a finishing sheen with warm wax.

At last Twitch's chevron mustache was finished, and so was the storm. Once Ferdinand glued it into place beneath Twitch's nose, he and Nitty scrutinized it.

"I loathe it," Ferdinand moaned. "It's yours at no charge. Papa would say the curl of the tips is askew and that it's poorly trimmed."

"He's not here, though," Nitty replied, "and *I* say it looks dashing and inspective."

Twitch admired his reflection in the emporium's mirror, turning this way and that. "It says 'sleuth' from every angle!" He grinned at Ferdinand. "Thank you."

The red of Ferdinand's plum cheeks deepened, and Nitty thought he looked almost happy. She was about to say as much, but only a moment later the emporium's door flew open, and Windle stormed in, pale and windblown.

"*Here* you are!" he cried breathlessly. "The duster blew in, and I thought you'd been caught out in it, but then the truck wouldn't start . . ." He ran a hand through his mussed hair. "I've been searching creation for you two."

"Ferdinand took us in," Nitty said. "We were safe."

"This may have been the worst one yet," Ferdinand said to Windle. "And to come so early in the day. There's no rhyme or reason to any of it at all."

"There is, too," Twitch blurted. He turned to Nitty. "Did you notice that the duster sprang up right on the heels of Miz Turngiddy spotting us at Crispin's?" Nitty nodded. "I'd call that more than coincidence. There was conniving involved. . . ."

Windle's brow furrowed. "Twitch, you don't mean to say that Miz Turngiddy summoned the storm, do you? That's as far-fetched a theory as I've ever heard."

"Not Miz Turngiddy, but maybe Neezer himself." Twitch's eyes narrowed. "I'd say this storm's reeking with shiftiness."

He said it with such conviction that Nitty had to smile into her sleeve. Windle, however, didn't seem the least bit convinced.

"That's enough flapdoodle for one day, Angus," he said. "Your ma is beside herself. She came looking for you before the storm hit, and she was none too happy to hear you were in town." He raised an eyebrow at Twitch. "I suppose you forgot to tell her about the errands I've been sending you and Nitty on?"

"Forgot." Twitch fidgeted with his periscope. "Y-yes."

"Well." Windle clapped a hand on Twitch's shoulder. "I didn't see any harm in the errands either. But I fear we're all in a heap of trouble now."

"She's not right blaming you for my disappearing," Twitch said. "She can't coop me up forever, and I'll tell her so."

"A word of warning." Windle held up a finger. "It's never wise to start an argument with a mother when she's spent hours fearing for her child's life." Twitch groaned at that, but the groan turned into a cough, which only made the worry lines on Windle's forehead deepen. "I'm under strict orders to get you home and to bed," Windle went on, "and I won't hear any buts about it."

So, with the sinking feeling that their adventures were at an end, Nitty walked to the door with Twitch beside her. Still, she'd have plenty to relay tonight when Mag paid her nightly visit to the kitchen window to tuck Nitty in for the night. They'd made a habit of it, the two of them, and Nitty looked forward to their nighttime conversations all day long.

"Adults can find more ways to ruin a decent caper . . . ," Twitch mumbled now, but he didn't look too downtrodden as he stroked his chevron mustache. "It's a fine mustache, isn't it?" Even as the words were spoken, a few strands of corn silk loosened and fell from his upper lip.

"It is," Nitty whispered as they walked to Windle's truck, "only, it may not last the day." She put a finger to her lips. "Don't tell Ferdinand or he'll likely give up altogether."

"Not a word," Twitch whispered back.

CHAPTER TWELVE

IN WHICH A MOTORCAR IS DRIVEN BY TWO LOAVES OF BREAD

Mag might've been kept a secret for at least a bit longer if it hadn't been for the sheer immensity of green that overtook the Homes farm during the next few days. Out in the field, fuchsia-colored buds, still shut tight, clustered under leaves like bright lanterns waiting to be lit for a party. Under the house's windowsills, great fuchsia flowers bloomed in petaled clouds of such profusion that the window boxes bulged and strained under their weight.

One morning upon waking, Nitty opened her eyes to find Windle sitting at the kitchen table, staring at the photo of Clara and Lillah, gripping a postcard in his hands. She guessed, without needing to ask, that it was from Lillah.

"Hoo-weee! Paris!" Nitty exclaimed when she caught sight

of the picture on the front of the postcard. "The *Daily Tattler* says Parisians are 'the very zenith of sophistication and creativity.'" Windle's harrumph was so melancholic that Nitty quickly added, "I have my doubts about that, mostly on account of folks there eating snails and liking them."

She wrinkled her nose, and one corner of Windle's mouth curled, but that was as far as his smile ventured.

Nitty couldn't help herself then. She snuck a peek at what Lillah had written. "But, Windle! Lillah writes that she hasn't heard from you in months!" She held tight to her Gleam Jar, thinking of all the calamities Lillah might be imagining had befallen her father. "Why haven't you written to her?"

"Haven't had anything to say," he muttered, and when Nitty glared at him, opening her mouth to argue, he stopped her by adding, "At any rate, I had no news to share besides dusters and drought."

"But you have *good* news now," she said in a rush. She *almost* added, *Tell her about me and Mag,* but caught herself. Because . . . what if he didn't think her worthy of mentioning? That thought made her breath hitch. Instead she ventured, "Tell her about the new crop growing."

Windle thought on this. There was a world of wanting in his eyes. The difference between wanting and doing, though, is the difference between a paintbrush and a masterpiece.

Windle's silence stretched, a rope pulled taut with sadness. "Can't."

Nitty saw then, plain as day. The problem was that Windle

was scared—scared to pen his hopes for the crop onto paper. Even now, with the crop growing prettier and sturdier each day, he was scared of losing it.

His voice was gruff as he stood abruptly. "I'd best go feed the animals."

Nitty knew better than to try to dissuade him. She figured a person could be on the brink of change for some time. Maybe even a long time. His heart could only tiptoe around its fears for now, but sooner or later it'd have to stomp all over them. He'd write to Lillah when he was good and ready.

Still, Windle's gloom was a nut that wouldn't crack. It usually brightened by the daily appearance of Twitch. But since their visit to Crispin's Bakery and the Schnurrbart Emporium, Twitch hadn't been back to the farm. Nitty suspected it was more the persistence of his ma than his cough that was keeping him away, especially when Windle had word from Mrs. Higgler on the matter.

"Another fever," Windle muttered with a shake of his head. "Best hope it's not dust pneumonia."

Nitty thought it wasn't, mostly due to a note she'd found wedged in the slat of the barn door addressed to "Detective Nitty and Her Exceptional Sidekick." The note made no mention of fever or pneumonia.

I come under cover of darkness. I've eluded my captor for now, but time is of the essence. I've unearthed some information of import. But it's too risky to divulge on paper. As my official assistant, you must be my eyes and ears. Upon my return, I expect a full report on any developments in the Snollygost Case. Remember: A villain is a keen observer who seeks out and preys on the weakness of others. (Ten Ways to Be a Villain, number four.) PS. Keep a sharp lookout for spies.

Mag, Nitty soon noticed, suffered from Twitch's absence on the farm as much as Windle did. She'd gotten into all manner of mischief of late, tickling the horses' haunches with her trunk until they whinnied in annoyance and spending inordinate amounts of time around the chicken coop, hoping for the hens to perch on her ears (which they'd taken a fancy to doing). Nitty missed Twitch, too, and especially missed their sleuthing trips into Fortune's Bluff. It might've been only three days since their last visit to town, but that felt as spun out as an eternity to Nitty.

It wasn't often—or ever, really—that people passed by the Homes farm. It sat on the farthest outskirts of Fortune's Bluff, and there was nothing between the farm and California except fifteen hundred miles of desert-dry dirt. If you happened past the farm, you were either going to Fortune's Bluff or getting as far away from it as possible. Nitty couldn't bank on passersby, and this was both a curse and a blessing. A curse because it only compounded her loneliness for Twitch; a blessing because it meant no one had yet caught on to the fact of Mag's existence.

So when, early one morning, a dilapidated Tin Lizzie

sputtered down the lane leading to the Homes house, Nitty was torn between burning curiosity and an inclination to hide and be quick about it. She eyed the driver's silhouette suspiciously, thinking that if Miz Ricketts had found her out, she still stood a chance at escape, if only she could wrangle Mag away from the chicken coop.

She was mid-jump off the front porch when a shaft of sunlight exposed the face behind the steering wheel. Nitty skittered to a stop, staring. The driver was none other than Bernice Sigh!

"Flabbergast and render me thunderstruck!" Nitty cried as Bernice brought the automobile to a jerky stop. "You can drive an automobile?"

"Course I can." Bernice faced Nitty's stare with an indomitable one of her own. "Have ever since Papa . . ." She stiffened in her seat as the younger Sighs tumbled helter-skelter from every corner of the motorcar. "How else were we supposed to get to Kickapoo and back for visits?"

Nitty guessed then what she meant. Bernice must've driven to Kickapoo to visit her papa in the asylum, maybe even with the passel of young Sigh children in tow. This, compounded by the novelty of her driving a motorcar at all, made Bernice instantly rise a thousand times higher in Nitty's estimation.

"It's rumbustious," she uttered appreciatively. "It could be a getaway car, like in *The Swashbuckler's Plunder*."

"The what?" Bernice snorted. "Never mind. I just did what needed doing is all." She stepped from the car, revealing a pile of Sears, Roebuck catalogs on the driver's seat and two thick loaves of bread strapped to her feet for reaching the pedals. Her eyes fell on the sprouting field, where the younger Sighs were marveling at the fuchsia buds. Bernice barely gave the crop a second glance. Her mind seemed to be somewhere else entirely. "I need to see Mr. Homes."

A thousand questions tickled Nitty's tongue: Was Bernice here with news of Neezer? Had Crispin said something of import? But Bernice's stony expression warned against any questions.

"He's in the barn." That was all Nitty had the chance to say before Bernice was marching to the barn, loaved feet and all. Not a minute later, Windle was hurrying out the barn door for his truck, calling out to Nitty that he'd be back in due course and that under no circumstances was any other youngster to drive Crispin's motorcar until further notice.

Nitty's disappointment at this dictum (for she'd been wondering how she might convince Bernice to let her do just that) was squelched as soon as she saw Bernice sag onto the front-porch steps, chin in her hands. It was difficult to tell by her swallowed-a-bug disgruntlement if she was angry or sad. It hardly mattered, Nitty decided, because Bernice looked, most of all, in need of a lending ear.

She wasn't the only one who sensed this, because just as Nitty took a step toward Bernice, Mag rounded the corner of the barn, heading straight for her. Nitty had already witnessed firsthand Mag's ability to make an impressive entrance, but today Mag outdid herself. All twelve of the Homes chickens roosted on her back and atop her head, ornamenting her with a feathered headdress. Nitty thought it beautiful, but Bernice?

She shot from the steps with the speed of a rattler striking, and within seconds had baby Verna hoisted onto her hip and the younger Sighs herded up behind her.

"An elephant!" they squealed in astonishment and delight, peeking around Bernice even as she tried to barricade them.

"I can see that," Bernice groused, then stared, with unbridled suspicion, as Nitty greeted Mag with a rub under the chin.

"I know you're eager to make the Sighs' acquaintance," Nitty whispered in Mag's ear. "Only give them a chance to get used to the idea first."

Mag swung her trunk to and fro, then raised its tip into the air, as if she was taking in the Sighs in the best way she knew how, with a proper and thorough sniffing.

To Bernice, Nitty added, "This is Magnolious. She's enormous, to be sure, but gentle as a baby."

Bernice didn't seem convinced, until Mag plucked a fuchsia bud from the field's edge and, ever so slowly, tucked the bud into Bernice's hair.

Just as slowly, Bernice raised a hand to touch the bud, blushing as she did. "She's all right, I guess," she finally mumbled. At that the other Sighs whooped and sprang from behind Bernice's back, each eager to greet Mag themselves. Within minutes, Mag had curled her trunk into a swing for the younger Sighs while Nitty, Bernice, and Verna watched from the porch steps.

"You could ride her," Nitty offered. "If you wanted."

Bernice shook her head as she bounced Verna on her knee. "And leave these five running wild?" She nodded toward the younger Sighs. "A duster'd likely blow them to the moon without me keeping watch." She stared down at the loaves on her feet and shook her head, as if she'd only just remembered she was wearing them in the first place. She slid Verna to Nitty's knee as she undid the twine holding them in place. "Papa . . . he had a bad spell this morning."

Nitty held her breath. Bernice might be skittish as a deer, but if Nitty stayed still and patient, she guessed Bernice would say more. Sure enough, after near-torturous minutes of silence, Bernice kept on.

"Neezer paid us a visit, first thing, saying he needed to inspect the bakery. To check on its cleanliness, for the sake of customers, he said." She scowled. "He really came to threaten Papa with closing the shop. And after he left . . . Papa flew into a frenzy. That's why I came to fetch Mr. Homes. He looks in on him from time to time. He might calm him, like he's done before."

"I'm sure he will." Nitty expected nothing less of him, even with all his grousing. Windle's kindness was the sly sort that shied from acclamation. She felt the stirrings of a pride in it, and wondered if this was how a daughter might feel about her papa, if he was a good, upstanding papa. She tucked the thought into a cozy corner of her heart, for safekeeping.

"I haven't seen Papa like that in . . ." Bernice swallowed and pressed her lips into a fixed line. She held up the loaves for

Nitty to see. "He baked these, and I can't make heads or tails of what it means."

Nitty passed Verna back to Bernice and took the loaves. For the first time, she noticed their unusual design. On top of each loaf was a starlike shape etched into the bread, with a round knob set in the dead center of the star.

"This reminds me of something." Nitty traced the lines of the star with her finger, noting how the two lines running through the center, horizontally and vertically, were longer than the others. Her mind whirred with *Daily Tattler* stories of pirates, conquistadores, pioneers. . . . "A compass!" she cried exultantly. "This looks exactly like the lines on the face of a compass that show direction." She clutched the bread. "Did your papa say anything about it? One of his riddles, maybe?"

Bernice nodded as she set the fussing Verna on the ground. "He said . . . 'North is silt; south is oil. Turn the dial; pick the soil.'"

"The dial?" Nitty repeated.

"I want to believe he's talking sense, but . . ." Her words were drowned by the earsplitting hollers of two of the Sigh boys, who were now tussling on the front porch, each with a firm grip on the other's hair and ears. Bernice was on her feet in an instant, looming over them with a scowl. "What in the crab apple are you two fighting over now?"

Between shouts of "It's mine!" and "I saw it first," Bernice dauntlessly dove into the fray of punching fists and kicking feet, and soon had a hand firmly atop each of the boys' moppy heads, holding them apart.

She nodded to a small brown object lying at her feet, saying to Nitty, "They told me they found it under the porch." She glared at both boys. "But that does *not* mean it's yours. And it's only a rusty key, besides."

Disappointed at the loss of their prize, the boys scooted from the porch while Nitty picked up the object. She knew from the *Daily Tattler* that rusty, old keys were always emblematic of some great secret. Her pulse pranced at the pure romance of it. "Horsefeathers, Bernice, keys like this unlock secret chambers and mummies' tombs, not to mention treasure chests! This key is a clue!"

Bernice, who'd turned to tending a fresh scrape on Verna's knee as the baby clung to her ankle, paused just long enough to frown. "Don't have time to waste deciphering clues when there are noses to wipe and squabbles to quash." But she cocked her head, looking more closely at the key.

That was when Nitty caught the tiniest spark of curiosity light Bernice's eyes. She snatched at it.

"What if this key proves a help to your papa? Would you snub it then?"

Bernice stared at Nitty. She stared at the key. She snorted.

Nitty took this as a sign of her open-mindedness in the matter. She grinned, an idea hatching as she did. Twitch could prove a fine remedy for Bernice's melancholy over her papa, if only she could spring him from his convalescence. And besides, she and Twitch and Mag were overdue for some muck-raking for certain.

Nitty leaped off the porch, beelining for the Higgler farm. "Stay put!" she told Bernice. "I'll be back with Twitch in a wink."

Bernice hollered after her, "Just what is it you plan to do?"

Nitty wondered at such a question. If Bernice had read even a single issue of the *Daily Tattler,* the answer would've been obvious. Didn't the poor girl have a speck of mischievery left at all? Or had the wiping of all those little noses worn it out of her? Whatever the case, Nitty decided then and there that Bernice could benefit from some adventuring.

Nitty called over her shoulder as she ran, "We're going to find the lock to fit that key."

CHAPTER THIRTEEN

In Which There Is Much Cogitation on Secrets and Speedy Seed-Spitters

"This is *exactly* the sort of key to hide a fiendish secret," Twitch confirmed the moment Bernice laid the key in his hand.

"I knew it." Nitty grinned as she sat down on the porch, motioning for Twitch to do the same. The walk from his house back to the Homes farm had winded him, and she wanted to give him a chance to catch his breath.

As he sat, Twitch lifted the key to his nose and sniffed. "Smells like criminality."

Bernice guffawed at that. She set Verna down on the ground, letting the baby crawl to her brothers, who were rolling the croquet ball back and forth to Mag, whooping raucously each time Mag returned it with a shove of her trunk. "Don't go spouting that criminality has a smell."

"It does, too," Twitch said indignantly. He fingered the chevron detecting mustache he had insisted on wearing over his cheesecloth mask. As soon as he touched it, a substantial chunk of its silk fell into his lap. Twitch shrugged at the mishap, and Nitty guessed he was determined to wear the mustache until it deteriorated entirely. "*Detective Comics* calls it 'the repellent stench of treachery.' *I* think it bears the distinct odor of rotten eggs and turnips."

Bernice shook her head. "I don't give a weevil's snout what odor it bears. What do you plan to do, dig up every scrap of dirt from here to Fortune's Bluff in search of some hidden bunkum?"

Twitch hopped up, puffing, and within seconds was nose to nose with Bernice, bouncing on his tiptoes like a boxer. "I am a seasoned detective, and seasoned detectives do not go on wild-goose chases."

Bernice stuck a hand to her hip. "What *do* they do, then?"

"Look here." He pulled a pile of papers from where they'd been tucked into the waist of his pants.

"Aren't those the newspapers Miz Turngiddy left at the bakery?" Nitty asked, peering over Twitch's shoulder.

He nodded. "I told you I had information of import, didn't I?" With no small measure of satisfaction, he spread the papers onto the porch, jabbing his finger at several headlines. "These articles all say the same thing: that dusters are dying down in plenty of places."

Nitty read the headlines. DUST STORMS DIMINISHING read

one, while another exclaimed DUSTERS IN NORTH DAKOTA ARE GONE WITH THE WIND. She frowned. "How can that be? When they're getting worse here by the day?"

"I don't know. There's got to be an explanation, and I bet it has to do with Neezer Snollygost. I bet there's an explanation for why Miz Turngiddy had all those papers in the first place, too." He held up the key. "Neezer used to live on this farm, and now we have this key. It's bound to reveal something, and I—"

Twitch tried to finish what he was saying, but no sound came except a bubbling cough. Nitty cringed. It had taken all her powers of persuasion, and Twitch promising not to remove his cheesecloth mask, to convince Mrs. Higgler to let Twitch venture outside. She'd been none too happy about him having to forgo her fresh batch of turnip soup, but she'd finally relented.

"Mind you stay quiet," she'd said. "Read your comics. *Calmly.* No running or horseplay."

Twitch had promised, but instead of keeping him quiet, the matter of this mystery key had increased his twitchiness tenfold. Nitty could hardly blame him. She was feeling twitchy herself, itching to look for the key's lock.

She went to Twitch now, and stood by his side while she waited for the coughing fit to pass. She had a mind to holler at Bernice for provoking him in the first place, until she saw that Bernice looked as worried over Twitch's coughing as she was herself. Mag, too, had forgotten her ball (and abandoned her chickens, flapping her ears to set them aflight) and was lumbering toward Twitch.

She issued a scolding *Brrrt!* as if to say, *He has no business being up and about.*

"Don't look at me like that," Nitty mumbled to Mag, dropping her eyes. "It's the key he's worked up about. We can't force him into invalidism if his mind's set on capers."

Once Mag reached Twitch, she stroked his back with her trunk until his cough subsided, then calmly snuffled the key for a moment and perfunctorily plucked it from his hand. She turned and headed confidently, and without hesitation, toward the barn. Nitty looked on in satisfaction as Bernice's mouth fell open.

"You and Mag are still getting acquainted, but you should know, she has a habit of proving that elephants, as a whole, are a rather spectacular species." She started after Mag, saying over her shoulder, "Come on. She wants us to follow her."

Twitch caught up to Nitty as quick as he could, but Bernice hung back, hesitating, arms crossed. Twitch shook his head at Nitty. "She wants to be ornery about it, so leave her be," he wheezed. He added, loud enough for Bernice to hear, "If she wants to let her papa be defeated by a charlatan like Neezer, that's her decision."

Nitty snuck a glance at Bernice, aghast at Twitch's rebuke and sure that Bernice's swift retribution would follow.

Bernice clasped and unclasped her fists, her face revealing

her quandary. Then, using the twine she'd discarded from her loaf pedals earlier, she quickly tethered baby Verna by her bitty waist, then tied the other end of the twine to the front-porch railing. She leveled a stern gaze at the other Sighs. "Keep watch over Verna, or I'll make you change her next diaper." After issuing that command, she fell into step alongside Nitty and Twitch. "I'll not stand by one more second watching Papa suffer his fits and my brothers and sisters go wanting. Daft as these hijinks strike me, if this ends up having anything to do with Neezer, I'm coming."

Nitty didn't let on how pleased she was by this development, especially when she noticed a new liveliness to Bernice's step that had been missing when she'd first arrived. Instead she turned her attention to Mag and her unwavering stride.

"That's the way, Mag." She smiled up at her as they moved into the shadows of the barn. "You know where you're going."

Mag didn't hesitate a moment, but plodded to a far corner of the barn Nitty hadn't yet explored—a corner where cobwebs veiled a menagerie of discarded hoes and scythes, a dust-riddled tractor, and even an old rocking horse. Tattered sheets covered other objects, and Mag made for one sheet in particular. After setting the key down beside it, she drew the sheet back with her trunk to reveal a large, weather-beaten chest underneath.

She swiveled her head toward Bernice, her mouth curling upward into what might've been an elephantine smile.

"You're better than a bloodhound," Twitch said. "The most indispensable sidekick I've come across." He patted Mag's side appreciatively.

"The *only* sidekick you've come across," quipped Bernice, to which Twitch offered her an impressive glower.

Before another argument could break out (and she expected one any second), Nitty snatched the key from the floor and slid it into the tarnished keyhole in the chest's front. The lock protested with a tinny groan but then gave way, the chest spewing dust as it rasped open.

"'And so the cavernous gateway to enigmas opens,'" Nitty whispered. It was a quote from *The Cursed Treasure of Captain Blackbeard,* one she thought most fitting for the occasion.

There was nearly a collision of heads as Nitty, Bernice, and Twitch bent over for a look inside. The chest brimmed with musty items: books, a moth-eaten quilt, a yellowed pair of delicate crocheted gloves. There was a smattering of tatty photos, most of people Nitty didn't recognize. She was the first to dare reach a hand into the chest, but soon Twitch and Bernice were sifting through its contents, too.

Nitty spotted a photo that struck her as familiar somehow, and she held it up to a shaft of sunlight. Three figures stared out from it: two young men with a petite fair-haired lady seated between them. The lady Nitty recognized as Clara, but a younger Clara than the one from the photo in Windle's kitchen. Nitty peered closer at the taller of the two men, then sucked in her breath. There was Windle—a younger Windle, as spindly as ever but with a shock of dark hair and merry eyes—his hand resting on Clara's shoulder. And on the other side of Clara . . . Could it be?

"Neezer!" she blurted. He was younger and scrawnier, no sign of his brawn about him yet. Twitch and Bernice crowded around the photo, staring.

"Neezer looks different. Not like the puffed-up peacock he usually does." Bernice tilted the photo in the light, studying it from different angles.

"He's smiling." Twitch shook his head in confusion. "Almost an honest smile, too."

"All three of them look happy." Nitty slid the photo back into the chest. "What happened that ruined it all?"

"Keep digging" was Twitch's response. "We're hot on the trail. I feel it."

"What about this?" Bernice pulled a ragged leather-bound notebook from the chest's depths. "It's full of notes and drawings. . . ." She flipped through the dog-eared pages.

"A . . . Refracting Rain-Catcher?" Nitty read the handwriting from over Bernice's shoulder. "And . . . the Speedy Seed-Spitter? Here's another one . . . a Fantastic Farm-O-Matic. The oddest contraptions, by the looks of them. It's a journal, I think."

"May I?" Twitch held out his hand for the notebook, his tone suddenly the epitome of an investigative professional. He opened the cover to the first page. "The dates are from long before any of us were born." His eyes widened. "'An account of the inspired ideas and inventions of Neezer Snollygost,'" he read from the first page, "'as written by the creator himself.'"

Bernice snorted as Twitch skimmed the pages. "So he never was one for humbleness, then. Even before he was mayor."

Twitch froze, staring, then turned an open page toward Nitty. "He calls it the Wind Whiffler, but what does that look like to you?"

Nitty scrutinized Neezer's sketch, and as she did, her blood surged. "That's the brass contraption that nearly balded me in the Snollygost broom closet!"

"Indubitably." Twitch nodded an affirmation. "But what is its purpose?"

"I'll tell you what it is!" Nitty exclaimed, the unpleasantness of the incident in the closet returning to her full force. "It's to cause all manner of scalp suffering to unsuspecting girls!"

Twitch was too consumed with the journal to respond, and a moment later he shouted, "Rats and darnation!" He jabbed his finger at the page. "There's a drawing in here titled 'Whirlybog.'"

The sketch was of the strangest machine Nitty had ever seen. Dozens of blades resembling windmills jutted from the top of the machine, and at its center was an enormous, clear canister labeled HOLDING TANK. None of those peculiar features, though, caught Nitty's attention. What did was a large dial in the middle of the machine's control panel, labeled DUSTOMETER, with lines spreading from its star-shaped center.

"Bernice." Nitty pointed to the dial. "What does that Dustometer remind you of?"

Bernice stared, eyes widening. "It's the compass lines Pa baked in the bread."

Nitty nodded. "Your pa was baking a copy of that dial, which means—"

"He's seen it before," Bernice finished. "When he broke into the Snollygost Institute." She sat back on her heels, relieved and exultant. "The Whirlybog that Papa talked about actually exists."

"But Neezer's admitted as much," Nitty said. "He's already told everyone himself that he's building something that will save the town from dusters."

Bernice scrutinized the sketch in the notebook. "He hasn't written anything here about what the Whirlybog does. But with a Dustometer, it's got to involve dust in some way or other."

Twitch coughed, then sputtered, "There's a shadiness to it. Make no mistake. We have to see this Whirlybog. The real one. For ourselves."

While each of them thought on this, Mag snuffled her trunk past the chest and into the deepest reaches of the shadowy corner of the barn. She rummaged with such enthusiasm that the old rocking horse and scythes toppled, and Nitty and Bernice were unceremoniously pushed to the side.

"Mag," Nitty scolded, "if you want to share in the snooping, use better manners."

But Twitch, seeing an opportunity for further investigating, crawled between Mag's forelegs and into the corner to inspect some newly unearthed objects, while Bernice kept paging through Neezer's journal.

Nitty, thinking that maybe Twitch was onto another flummoxing discovery, followed him. She scooted under Mag's chin and through the narrow space to find Twitch, his back to her, kneeling before a small wooden trough.

"What did you fi—"

Twitch turned to her, and his look stopped her cold. It made her think of Grimsgate, of the looks on the orphans' faces whenever they weren't chosen for adoption. It was a look she'd seen so often before. On Windle's face, on Crispin's, on Ferdinand Klempt's.

It was a look of loss. But what had Twitch lost, and why had he never told her?

It made an ache start inside Nitty's chest, and she pressed her Gleam Jar closer. Blue, yellow, red, green. Ribbon, button, marble, seed. It should've made her feel better, but this time it didn't.

Mag's trunk swung worriedly back and forth from Nitty to Twitch, touching her shoulder, then his. It was as if she sensed a darkening mood, but wasn't sure whom to comfort first.

Nitty started to ask Twitch what was wrong, but he leaped up before she could get the words out. "I'm going outside."

Nitty sank onto her heels, entirely stumped. Then she saw,

and her heart wilted in dismay. What Twitch had found wasn't a trough after all. It was a little wooden cradle.

"Twitch, wait!" Nitty jumped up to follow him, her chest wrenching, but Windle caught her by the arms. He stood before her, a fence post of rigidity.

"What have you done?" His voice was thunderous as he looked from her to the open chest before him, its contents strewn on the floor. Bernice stood behind him, her face the very portrait of entrapment and misery. "You had no business opening this. No business at all."

Nitty could scarce meet his eyes, so icy with anger were their depths. Still, she needed him to know it hadn't been entirely her fault. Or Twitch's and Bernice's either. "We found the key by accident," she explained quietly. "Under the porch."

"Confound it." Windle scratched the freckle behind his right ear. "I lost it years ago and was none too sorry for the loss."

"But there are photographs in there of Clara. Of you. Why would you lock those away?" It seemed incomprehensible to her to have something of a real family and want to be rid of it. Clara's fingers must've touched that quilt. Lillah must've worn those gloves. The chest was better than any Gleam Jar. Much, much better. Why didn't Windle understand that?

He glowered. "It should've been left alone. All of it. Some things are better off locked away. Do you understand?"

Bernice started at his words, and Nitty watched as the flintiness returned to her eyes. Bernice spun and ran from the barn, and as she did, Mag swung her trunk toward Windle, trumpeted one short but definitively cross *Brrrt!* and lumbered after Bernice and Twitch. Windle's anger wilted into regret.

Nitty glanced down at the photographs and the notebook. There were stories that needed telling here, secrets that needed sharing. She locked eyes with Windle. "I don't like saying so, because I've taken a liking to you, crabbiness and all. But . . . you're wrong."

With that, she straightened her shoulders, set her jaw, and marched from the barn.

CHAPTER FOURTEEN

In Which an Accomplice Prophesies Calamity

The ride back to the Homes farm from the Sighs' shop was a quiet one.

Ever since Windle had stomped from the barn declaring that it was time for the Sighs to be on their way home, the collective mood of the entire group was nothing short of wretched. Windle insisted on driving Bernice and the other Sighs back to town, saying he'd return Crispin's Tin Lizzie to the bakery later, but Nitty wasn't about to let Bernice endure Windle's brooding without her. After all, Bernice could hardly be blamed for anything except the gumption to drive a motorcar. Twitch must've shared Nitty's sentiment, because, though he said not a word, he piled into Windle's truck for the ride, too.

But even after Bernice had offered him a bracing shoulder nudge and a whispered "Don't quit the case, whatever you do" as her encouraging goodbye, Twitch remained mute.

Now he sat beside Nitty in the truck's bed, staring straight ahead, producing a tired, leaky balloon of wheezing from underneath his cheesecloth mask. Even the pages of his *Detective Comics* couldn't entice him. Nitty hugged her Gleam Jar tightly as the truck rumbled, thinking about Windle's ire and worrying over Twitch, although her Gleam Jar wasn't a balm this time.

She tried to be patient with Twitch. She spent approximately four minutes trying. For the first minute, she counted the number of times Windle harrumphed (five). For the second minute, she counted the number of times Twitch's muddy lungs squeaked (twelve). For the third and fourth minutes, she decided counting was an entirely futile distraction that did nothing except create *impatience*. After this revelation, she gave up trying altogether.

"Well?" she blurted to Twitch. "If you're sore at me, I wish you'd come out and say it!"

Twitch's shoulders scrunched in surprise. "I'm not sore at you." His voice sounded far away with sadness.

Nitty swallowed, knowing she'd have to bring up the topic sooner or later, but dreading what might come of it. "Was it . . . was it something to do with the cradle in the barn?"

For the first time since she'd met him, Twitch went entirely still. Not a single muscle moved. "That cradle . . . it belonged to our baby." His voice turned so quiet now that Nitty had to stop her own breath to hear proper. "Windle carved it for my sister. Anna."

"You had a sister?" Nitty's insides were suddenly slick and nervous. She wasn't sure she wanted to hear any more. But if Twitch had the courage to tell it, then she'd have to have the courage to listen.

Twitch slid his mask and goggles from his face. His mouth crumpled at its edges. "She was born in the middle of a duster." He cupped his hands together. "She was no bigger than a teacup. Seemed like her lungs were muddier than mine before she even took her first breath. She only lived a day."

There it was again. The look of loss.

"That's why Ma frets over me. And why Pa didn't stay. He loves Fortune's Bluff, or the way it used to be, anyway. Before the dusters. He was set on keeping us here. Sure things would get better. But then last year, Anna . . ." He sighed. "That was when Pa left to look for work out west. I believe he just couldn't bear the melancholy. I suppose he could come back once he forgets." Twitch looked at Nitty. "Only . . . I don't think he'll forget."

"It's the worst kind of funny, isn't it? If I had any memories of my family, I'd give anything to keep them. But your pa . . . he has his memories and wants to lose them."

"Anna was beautiful," Twitch said. "I would never want to forget that."

Nitty couldn't think of a single thing to say to this. She took Twitch's hand.

"The worst villains are the ones you can't see," Twitch whispered then. "'Ten Ways to Be a Villain, number ten: Strike silently, swiftly, and ruthlessly.'"

Together they watched ocher clouds mushrooming along the horizon. Windle frowned as he looked through the windshield. A duster was coming.

When the truck at last reached the lush green stalks of Nitty's crop, Nitty nearly cried with gratefulness at the sight of Mag lumbering from the barn to greet them. If ever there was a time when she needed the comforting warmth of Mag's trunk resting on her shoulder, it was now.

Then a movement at the edge of the field caught Nitty's eye. At first Nitty mistook it for a walking tumbleweed. But, suddenly, the tumbleweed jumped. "An elephant!" it yelped.

"Miz Turngiddy," declared Nitty.

"Miz Turngiddy," lamented Windle.

"Spy," said Twitch. The sadness in his voice was replaced with sudden keenness, and he nodded toward the spot where Miz Turngiddy had parked her automobile, nearly out of sight among the field's forest of stalks. "An intriguing development in our case."

Nitty jumped from the bed of the now-stopped truck, moving to stand between Mag and Mayor Snollygost's rapidly approaching secretary.

Mag's ears lifted into stiff flags. Her heart became a cannon, booming in her chest. This human's scent was sickly sweet with nervousness, but Mag didn't understand why. The woman wasn't afraid of *her*. But she *was* afraid of someone. And that made Mag cautious and put her on alert for danger. She was ready to protect her girl. Her girl, though, seemed to want to protect *her*.

"It's all right." Nitty patted the underside of Mag's trunk. "She can't do a thing to you." Nitty hoped she was right about that.

"Afternoon, Miz Turngiddy," Windle said slowly, looking even broodier than he had minutes before (if that was possible). "What brings you from town?"

Miz Turngiddy stopped some distance away from Nitty and Mag, gripping her notepad in both hands. Her eyes darted from the field to Mag and back again. "I was making rounds on Mayor Snollygost's behalf. Paying friendly calls to neighbors and their lands."

"Demanding people's money." Twitch coughed. Loudly. It wasn't his muddy cough, but a scornful one.

Miz Turngiddy looked momentarily injured by Twitch's words, but her expression quickly transformed into a frown. "Young man, I am merely doing what my job requires of me. And Mayor Snollygost does not demand that debts be repaid today, or even tomorrow. Only that we work toward community progress, fulfillment, and the betterment of all." She leaned over Twitch, her eyes looking more beseeching than threatening, as if she were about to give him a test she hoped he'd pass. "You *do* know the Fortune's Bluff motto, don't you?"

"Nefarious deeds are afoot." Twitch was stiff as a soldier,

staring at Miz Turngiddy. "And *you* know that dusters are disappearing everywhere but here, don't you? Tell me. Do you know *why*?"

Nitty felt a rush of pride. Horsefeathers, her friend was brave! Possibly foolish, too, if the disappointment on Miz Turngiddy's scarlet face was any indication, but definitely brave.

Miz Turngiddy's mouth fell open, but no sound came from it. Finally she blustered, "I don't know what you're implying, but—"

"Miz Turngiddy." Windle placed himself between Miz Turngiddy and Twitch, diverting all her attention to him. "I'm afraid we've only just returned from an outing to town. I wasn't expecting you to pay a call—"

"Of course not!" Miz Turngiddy seemed to recover herself, and redirected her focus to the field. She touched one of the field's green stalks, as if to test its sturdiness. "I was only passing by your farm, and your field stopped me short. Why, nothing's grown in Fortune's Bluff in a decade! It's simply fascinating. And now this." Her weasel eyes squinted up at Mag's approaching form. "Mr. Homes! You are in possession of an elephant!"

"So it would seem."

Miz Turngiddy's nose twitched. She scribbled furiously in her notebook. "What is the purpose of this elephant?"

"I would think the answer to that would be obvious." Windle glanced at Nitty, and to her astonishment and relief, she saw his broodiness weakening. There was the hint of a twinkle in his eyes. A genuine twinkle! Nitty's heart lifted. "Farming."

"I thought as much."

There was something feverish in the way Miz Turngiddy eyed the field and Mag, her pinprick eyes glinting zealously. It made Nitty's palms gummy with sweat.

"How very unconventional," Miz Turngiddy continued. "Ingenious, really. And your crop. Its root system must be unusually sturdy to withstand the dusters. It will be of great interest to the mayor." Miz Turngiddy cupped one of the bulbous pink buds in her hand. "I'm not familiar with this particular . . ." Her voice faltered. "What is it, exactly?"

Windle glanced at Nitty again. "I couldn't rightly say."

"Well." Miz Turngiddy scribbled. "Well." She scribbled some more. "I'd love to obtain a sample, if I might—"

"You might not." Windle glanced toward the dust clouds building to their east. "Miz Turngiddy, there's a duster coming, and our elephant is in need of watering."

"Of course, of course." Her hand still cupped the fuchsia bud, but now tightened, as if it could barely stand letting the bud drop. "I will stay abreast of this. Such an anomaly for a crop to survive duster after duster," she mumbled to herself. "Such a streak of luck. I'd calculate the odds of it continuing to be one in a thousand. Time will tell."

As Miz Turngiddy's automobile rattled back toward Fortune's Bluff, spitting dust in its wake, Mag trumpeted. Rather indignantly, Nitty thought.

"I agree," Nitty responded. "I don't trust her either."

"We haven't heard the end from her," Windle said morosely.

Twitch looked at Nitty. " 'Ten Ways to Be a Villain, number two: Rely on a shrewd accomplice to be your eyes and ears.' " When Nitty looked at him blankly, Twitch added, with some chagrin, "She'll be telling Mayor Snollygost about Mag before the day's out."

"What should we do?" she asked him.

"Crack the case. As soon as possible."

Yes, thought Nitty. *Very soon.* Because one thing was sure: Miz Turngiddy was not entirely at ease with an elephant in Fortune's Bluff. And Neezer Snollygost, Nitty suspected, wouldn't be either.

CHAPTER FIFTEEN

In Which an Eggplant Is Mistaken for an Elephant

"An elephant!"

Those were the words spoken by Neezer Snollygost that evening as he sat in his office at the Snollygost Institute, only moments after Miz Turngiddy informed him of the unusual happenings at the Homes farm. Because of the ever-present *WHUMP! WHUMP! WHUMP!* resonating at regular intervals from the Whirlybog in the locked room beyond Neezer's office, because Neezer's mouth was full of steak and potatoes as he spoke, and because his nose was whistling "How Many Biscuits Can You Eat?" what Miz Turngiddy heard him say was, "An eggplant!"

Miz Turngiddy's frazzled hopes lifted. Could it be that eggplant was the answer, at last, to Neezer's bottomless hunger? If it was, perhaps Neezer would see reason at last and allow her to help restore Fortune's Bluff to its former glory. Then she might be able to write her son that all was again right and well in Fortune's Bluff. Her grandbabies, with their sweet-cream scent and apricot-fuzz curls, might come back.

If eggplant was the answer, perhaps Neezer, having been satiated, would see the logic in Miz Turngiddy's studying weather patterns and soil erosion. Perhaps he could be persuaded to visit other towns to find out why dusters were dying down everywhere but Fortune's Bluff. (She knew, as Angus Higgler had correctly and embarrassingly guessed, that this was undeniably the case.) Perhaps, most pressingly, he would let her into his Whirlybog workshop, where she was confident that, if given the opportunity, she could fix the machine so that, at last, it stopped the dusters. And what she wouldn't give to stop its infernal whumping!

If eggplant was to prove the solution to all, then—by gum!—Miz Turngiddy had her mission.

"Of course, sir," she said. "Right away, sir. If you're craving eggplant, I'm sure one can be found in the warehouse." She began to scurry from the office.

"Miz Turngiddy!" Neezer bellowed over the incessant *WHUMP!*

Miz Turngiddy stopped mid-scurry.

"It is a perilous thing, confusing an eggplant with an elephant when one is much more likely to cause turmoil than the other." He took another hefty bite of steak and potatoes, dipping it in the gravy boat beforehand to ensure that every morsel dripped with thick, rich sauce.

"No eggplant, then, sir?"

"Not as of yet, Miz Turngiddy." Neezer's nose swung into "I Heard the Voice of a Pork Chop" as he moved on to the next course of biscuits and grits. He motioned to the chair across from his desk. "Have a seat. Notes should be taken."

Miz Turngiddy sat, her notepad perched in readiness on her knees.

"We must ask ourselves some questions about Windle's elephant." He dabbed at his mouth with the napkin tucked under his chin. "For instance, how does the elephant work toward the betterment of all? Is this elephant contributing to our community's progress?"

"The answer is simple, sir. The elephant is helping Windle with his farming. Windle is part of our community."

Neezer propped his elbows onto the table and pressed his fingertips together in what he thought of as a pose of stately wisdom. Miz Turngiddy noted (silently, of course) that it was a pose that put his elbows into gravy. "Windle is one of many. Is it fair for him to prosper while others suffer?"

Miz Turngiddy paled at the idea of what she was about to say, but decided it would not put her job in too much jeopardy to venture this one truth. "Excuse me for saying so, sir, but I did not see him prospering. Only trying, which he can't be faulted for."

"Can't he?" Neezer tapped his fingertips together. "You say

his crop is flourishing. How is it, do you think, that his crop flourishes when everyone else's fails?"

"It is most unusual," Miz Turngiddy admitted. "But then, we *do* want crops to grow."

"We want Fortune's Bluff to reach its potential. To reach the pinnacle of fulfillment." Neezer's nose struck a fittingly high note of triumph, as if it agreed. "The people of Fortune's Bluff have every manner of food available to them already. What Fortune's Bluff craves, the Snollygost General Store provides, does it not?"

"Of course, sir," Miz Turngiddy said. "Except . . ."

"Yes?"

"Except many can't afford the food."

"Because folks are stuck on farmland that will *not* be farmed. Fortune's Bluff doesn't need more failing crops. What we need is progress of a concrete sort. Invention. Expansion." Neezer's stomach growled. "Fortune's Bluff could be a place of renown. Is it too much to ask that others share my vision for its evolution?"

"Of course not, sir. Here." Miz Turngiddy, whose own stomach stirred uneasily at this "evolution" he spoke of, offered him a chocolate éclair from the remnants of his feast. "Eat this."

Neezer bit into it, then heaved a weighty sigh. "I strive. I toil. I give. My mission is to serve Fortune's Bluff." His nose struck up the piteous first notes of "Swing Low, Sweet Chariot." "I've been patient, have I not? Extending loans and credit? Waiting for folks to realize that their debts can't be paid with farming? Waiting for them to turn to me for solutions? And I have solutions, Miz

Turngiddy! Indeed I do." He tapped his temple knowingly. "But now this. An elephant! A crop that serves one but not all." His head sank to his desk. "It is exhausting, Miz Turngiddy, bearing the shoulders on which an entire town rests."

Miz Turngiddy, for her part, was beginning to feel exhausted from bearing Neezer Snollygost. "I am sorry, sir." Her teeth clenched. "But if you'd permit me to at least help with your accounts, sir, and perhaps write to some other towns to learn *their* methods for preventing dusters—"

"You think other towns have solutions we lack?" Neezer's eyes blazed. "Solutions better than my Whirlybog, which I labor over day and night?"

Miz Turngiddy straightened, her doubts a battalion behind her clenched teeth. All she had to do was open her mouth and the words would pour forth. What a relief that would be! But she did not open her mouth. Neezer, instead, opened his.

"Take care that you don't forget yourself, Miz Turngiddy." His voice was slither smooth. "It's not like you. Not like you at all."

"Of course. Sir," she managed at last. "What I meant to say was that I hate to see you so burdened by the news of this elephant. With not a soul to ease your suffering."

Neezer offered her a renewed, albeit beleaguered, smile. "I'm relieved you understand my plight, Miz Turngiddy. Just as you understand the hazard of this elephant. Thus far, how- ever, we have not asked ourselves the most significant ques- tion about the elephant." He folded his hands across his chest. Often he took comfort in the sheer strength and broadness of it, but tonight, he discovered, he could not. "*How* did Windle come by this elephant?"

"Ingenuity and skill, sir?" Miz Turngiddy suggested.

Neezer's face purpled. "Windle Homes? A possessor of ingenuity? I should think not." Neezer slapped a hand down onto the table. "No. This elephant came to Windle by dubious, conceivably unlawful means."

"How—how dismaying." Miz Turngiddy forced the words out, but in fact, she wasn't dismayed at all. She was electrified. Electrified by the idea of doing something as unconventional— as downright revolutionary!—as procuring an elephant by unlawful means. Not to mention, there was no end to the improvements an elephant might make to a farm, or even a town, for that matter. But her task, she reminded herself, was not to revolutionize. Her task was to keep Neezer Snollygost happy so that his hunger would stay confined to food and not turn to the whole of Fortune's Bluff. Although, with each day that passed, she doubted more and more that this was possible. With each day that passed, her misgivings and distrust of Neezer Snollygost grew.

Now the cogs and gears of her mind whirred until they produced a vision of an elephant—the very same elephant, in fact—standing behind the bars of a circus wagon. Even as it pained her to do it, she admitted, "I have it, sir. I remember. The Gusto and Gallant Circus. It passed through Fortune's Bluff a couple months ago, on its way to Kickapoo. Just before the horrible death of that elephant trainer."

A gradual smile slicked across Neezer's teeth. "Great Magnolious?" he mumbled to himself. "Could it be she?"

Miz Turngiddy approached Neezer's desk and pulled last week's edition of the *Kickapoo Gazette* from its top drawer. Neezer was not in the habit of reading the *Gazette,* or any other papers, for that matter, but he fancied that having a newspaper in his desk made him appear well-informed. Miz Turngiddy, on the other hand, regularly read over a dozen papers weekly, which was how she stayed abreast of stories surrounding dusters and their imminent extinction from everywhere but Fortune's Bluff. Her avid reading was a fact, of course, that she'd decided would be wise to keep to herself.

Now, with some reluctance, she opened the paper and read aloud the ad she'd remembered seeing some days before:

On the lookout for savage elephant!! Escaped from Gusto and Gallant Circus caravan. Whereabouts currently unknown. Extremely dangerous. Last seen with runaway orphan. Girl approx. age ten or eleven, average height, brown hair, abnormally green eyes. If seen, telegraph Percival Gallant in Kickapoo, Kansas, immediately. Substantial reward if found.

Neezer's stomach gave a raucous growl. "Miz Turngiddy, what was the name of that girl Windle brought into the store a couple weeks past?"

Miz Turngiddy flipped through the pages of her notepad. "Nitty Luce, sir."

"Her eyes *were* curious, weren't they?"

Miz Turngiddy swallowed. "Greener than grass."

Neezer's smile widened. "Miz Turngiddy, a telegram must be sent. To Percival Gallant."

"Yes, sir." Despite Miz Turngiddy's hand shaking, she took up her notepad. "What should it say?"

Neezer dictated. Miz Turngiddy's pen trembled, but still did Neezer's bidding. When they were finished, Neezer's stomach gave a fretful rumble. Miz Turngiddy turned for the door.

"Before you go," Neezer said. "From what you saw of Windle's crop, do you think a duster could destroy it?"

She paused over this, recalling the sturdiness of those green stalks. "I suppose if the duster were bad enough, the crop could be destroyed. But it would have to be a very strong duster."

"Mmmm." Neezer nodded. "I see. The worst yet." His nose struck up "Oh! It's a Lovely War!" "Well done, Miz Turngiddy. Well done." He patted his stomach. "I'm ravenous. In fact, eggplant sounds delightful."

"Right away, sir." Miz Turngiddy scurried from the office, the wheels and cogs of her brain whirring. Given the fact that elephants in this part of the world were extremely rare, if not altogether unheard of, she calculated the probability of the Gusto and Gallant elephant and the Homes elephant being one and the same as 98.256 percent. Still, this statistic was not the reason for her mind's pinwheeling.

Miz Turngiddy's thoughts, instead, were consumed with how she might feel roaming free as a runaway elephant. Doing as she liked, saying what she liked. The elephant she'd seen at the Homes farm hadn't struck her as savage. On the contrary, that elephant had struck her as peacefully contented.

As Miz Turngiddy contemplated the nature of contentment, and how she might obtain it, Neezer was also contemplating. While the whumping serenaded his ears, Neezer rose from his chair, slid a large brass key from the top drawer of his desk, and walked to his locked workshop door. He slid the key into the lock, then slipped through the door, shutting it firmly behind him.

On a drafting table just inside the door sat a miniature model of Fortune's Bluff. Now Neezer leaned over it. With a feverish gleam in his eyes, he inspected the matchbox-sized buildings of Main Street, the smaller homes on the surrounding farms. His nose began whistling the *William Tell* Overture. Then he reached his fingers down and lifted the little white house from Windle's farm. He held it to his face, pinching it between his thumb and forefinger as he might a pesky fly.

He pinched until the house splintered into toothpicks. In the empty spot where the house had been, Neezer set an imposing building, a dozen stories high. Then several more beside it, until it looked as if a tiny city were rising on the exact spot where Windle's crop was flourishing.

"The pinnacle of fulfillment," he whispered. He smiled and turned from his model to the great machine whumping a few feet from where he stood. He had much work to do, and his Whirlybog was waiting.

When Miz Turngiddy returned to the office a little while later, holding a plate of delicious-looking eggplant Florentine in her hands, Neezer wasn't at his desk. From behind the workshop's door came sounds of hammering, clanging, and Neezer's occasional mutterings of "if I adjust this" or "if I raise the internal pressure."

Miz Turngiddy, who was still thinking, rather wistfully, about the benefits of doing and saying all she pleased, glared at the locked door. Her mind craved to examine what lay beyond it, but she was losing hope of Mayor Snollygost's ever allowing her access, just as she was losing hope in the mayor's promises about the Whirlybog itself. Now, to make matters worse, the eggplant Florentine she'd painstakingly made was growing cold. She set the plate down on Neezer's desk with a clatter, and as she did, she noticed one acutely annoying new development.

In the time she'd been gone fixing Neezer's supper, the whumping of the Whirlybog had grown considerably louder.

CHAPTER SIXTEEN

In Which a Confession Is Made and a Leap Taken

That night, not a soul at the Homes farm could sleep. It might've been on account of the duster, howling for hours, bringing with it a dark that felt sinister in its soupiness. Or it might've been the memories of each of the farm's occupants, roused from hibernation by the day's troubling events. Memories—particularly ones we'd prefer to forget—can be pesky this way.

Some memories tumbled, moth-eaten and fusty, from a closet in Windle's mind, and he took to scratching that freckle behind his right ear. One thorny memory pricked at Mag's pumpkin heart as she paced inside the barn, making her keen a low, resonant refrain.

Nitty's memories were of a different sort. Oh, there were the all-too-real memories of Grimsgate and Miz Ricketts. But the rest? Well, they weren't so much proper memories as long-ings for ones. These jangled, unfinished and impatient, in the Gleam Jar as Nitty wriggled wakefully on her cot. Before she'd found Mag, before Windle and Twitch and Bernice, the Gleam Jar was all she'd had in the whole wide world. Once, it had seemed like enough. Tonight, it seemed different. Tonight, it couldn't make anything right.

Windle had been remote and distracted since the afternoon, and even though he'd stood by Nitty and Mag in the face of Miz Turngiddy's scrutiny, Nitty worried she'd done irreparable damage to his opinion of her. Maybe she had tried too hard when she shouldn't have.

Mag's sad keening reached her ears on the blowing wind then, and Nitty's heart cramped at the sound. Mag was trou-bled tonight, too, and Nitty wondered why. She longed to go to her, to have Mag's trunk ruffle her hair from her forehead, to laugh when Mag startled a dozing chicken from her back by blowing a blast of air at it with her trunk. But there was no going to Mag now. Not with the dust nearly reaching the top of the windowsills.

Nitty flipped in her cot, and her Gleam Jar pressed into her rib, irritating her for the dozenth time in so many minutes.

"Oh, won't you leave me be!" Nitty cried out at last.

She never expected her outburst would startle Windle so badly that he would rush headlong from his bedroom, in his red woolen union suit, to come to her aid. Nitty stared in disbelief.

Her first thought was *Windle wants to protect me.*

This made her smile.

Her second thought was *Windle looks ridiculous in woolens.*

This made her laugh.

Then Windle, looking down at his union suit, laughed, too. A boisterous, donkey bray of a laugh that was as unlikely a sound as any to hear from a man who resembled a tree.

"Oh, Nitty girl." Windle slapped his knees, bent over as he was with laughing. "Here I thought you needed me."

Nitty looked at him for a long moment. Her heart chimed. "But I do." Nitty waited to let this sink in, waited to see if her saying that would turn Windle back into wood.

It didn't. Instead Windle wiped his laughing tears from his eyes and settled into Clara's rocker. He glanced at the photo of Clara and Lillah atop the kitchen table. What would they say, if they'd heard his laughter? He knew. Clara would declare that it was near on ten years since he'd laughed like that. Then Lillah would pronounce that *that* was ten years too long. And maybe, just maybe, they'd be right.

"Are you done, then?" Nitty asked him.

"With what?"

"Your brooding. I suppose you're entitled to a bit of it, since it was your property we rifled through. Still, the brooding's getting a mite tiresome."

Windle stiffened at this. He opened his mouth. He shut it again. He wished for the hundredth time that he could call on his Clara for consultation on how best to handle precociousness in little girls. A thought struck him. Maybe it didn't need handling at all. This thought was so alarming in its lawlessness that Windle nearly slapped the side of his head to shake it out. *Maybe,* said one of these lawless thoughts, *Nitty isn't the one who needs correcting.*

"I wouldn't say I'm done entirely," he finally uttered as he took up rocking. "But it's fair to say the worst of it has passed." He cleared his throat. "That chest in the barn's stayed locked for years. I wasn't prepared for its opening."

"Well." Nitty stared at him, unflinching. "You can't be prepared for everything all the time. And who wants that, besides?"

Windle harrumphed.

"And, like it or not, ever since we opened it, I've been pondering."

"A dangerous pastime." Windle rocked.

"Don't I know it." She sat up in the cot. "But I can't put a stop to it. Mostly I've been pondering the dangers of villains and accomplices. The difference between truth and wishing." She tapped her chin, wanting to make sure she'd remembered everything. "Oh. And muddy lungs, too."

"That is a sizable amount of pondering for one night." The floorboards whined under Clara's rocker.

Nitty nodded. "And what I want to know is: Why? Why do Mr. Klempt and Mr. Sigh have to suffer so? And why do you, with your lonely, broken heart?"

"Bah!" Windle blurted. "Who said anything about—"

"I'm not finished," Nitty interjected, then added for good measure, "And you do *too* have one."

Windle puffed his chest but stayed silent, after which Nitty, satisfied, continued. "Why did Twitch get a baby sister only to have her taken away?" Her Gleam Jar rattled in her lap, and she sucked in a breath. Then she asked the question that had been stuck like a nettle to her heart for as long as she could remember. "Why did I have parents who didn't want me?" She hated that her voice shilly-shallied over that last one, but there it was. Out of her mouth and into the world, where it hung in the silty air between her and Windle.

Windle quit rocking altogether. It was his turn to ponder. *So,* he thought, *it was as I suspected all along. The girl has no one but her elephant.* Then a loud, insistent voice inside him added, *And you. The girl has you.*

Windle clasped his hands, tucking them under his chin as he frowned at the floor. What had his craggy, brassbound self to offer up to her open, asking eyes? The truth. Windle Homes was a commendable truth teller.

"Sometimes," he said quietly, "there are no answers. People make choices. But that's never the whole of it. Life is as much happenstance and folly as decision. Chance, providence, fate—whatever infernal name you wish to call it—packs a mighty wallop."

Nitty thought on this as the wind screeched and fingers of dust stretched from under the front door. "I don't like it. Not one iota."

Windle nodded. "Didn't expect you to. I don't like it myself."

"So which was it, then? Choice or folly that made you and Neezer sworn enemies?"

Windle's freckle was afire now. For ten years he'd vowed not to dwell on Neezer and the fourth event of life-changing enormity. Only, tonight, with the wind and the memories and all this talk of folly and hearts, he *was* dwelling on it. Tonight it was not going to leave him be until he was out with it, once and for all.

"Neezer was never my enemy." Windle's voice was tired. "There was a time we ran this farm together. Neezer never had a knack for it, but he helped me with the business end of it, and I worked the land. We were partners. It gave my Clara joy to have us all together, with Lillah passed about from knee to knee each night. The crops grew; Lillah grew. We were happy. But Neezer wanted more."

"More of what?" asked Nitty. She understood wanting more. She'd wished for more so many times in the gray rooms of Grimsgate.

Windle sighed. "More success in his own right. We loved him as he was—Clara and I. But what he thought of most days wasn't the love. It was his failures. He wanted to prove himself, to show he could farm as well with his methods as I could with mine. He meant to help and thought he could make farming easier, better. He invented a machine. He called it the Fantastic Farm-O-Matic."

"I saw a drawing of it in Neezer's old journal."

Windle nodded. "He told me the machine would do everything a farmer could. Plant crops, irrigate them, even harvest. It would do it all. With the machine, anyone could be a farmer." His brow furrowed. "I had doubts, to be sure. But I saw the hopes Neezer pinned on that machine. Saw how badly he wanted to succeed, just once, at farming. So when he asked me to let him try the machine on my fields for an entire year . . ." Windle's shoulders sagged. "Of course I said yes. I hoped it would work, for his sake."

Windle's voice was so drenched in gloom that Nitty could already guess what had happened. "The machine didn't work?"

Windle harrumphed. "The machine tore up my fields one end to the other. What few crops grew failed in days, and worse, the soil turned rancid. It was two years before I could get anything to grow again." He shook his head. "Neezer was sick over it. Not just the machine's failure, but what it had done to the farm. He apologized over and over again, but I . . ." Windle's voice choked, and his face reddened. "I let my temper and pride overtake my common sense. I was embarrassed over what had happened, humiliated that I wasn't a master farmer anymore. I blamed Neezer, and minced no words telling him so. I spoke spiteful words that anyone would be ashamed to repeat. . . . I've never behaved so dishonorably. I called him a failure and broke off our partnership. He left the farm after that to go his own way."

"Oh," Nitty whispered. It wasn't easy to swallow, the knowing that Windle had brought on that sort of hurt. But Nitty could see from his drawn face how much he'd been hurt by *doing* the hurting, too. "And you never . . . you never set it right with him?"

"I tried, after I'd calmed down." His voice was hoarse. "I went to him with apologies, after the farm recovered and I grew a fresh crop. But by then he'd changed. He'd . . . turned ugly. His whole life, he'd wanted more. It started out with aspirations, but after our fight, it turned to greed. He took to hating farmland. Farming was too humble, he decided, and the town of Fortune's Bluff too small. Irrelevant, he called it. He said he wanted enterprise. A proper city instead of farmland. He offered to buy the land from me and Clara."

"For community progress, fulfillment, and the betterment of all," Nitty recited. "The Snollygost motto."

Windle's face was grim. "The betterment of all, fiddlesticks. It's the betterment of the Snollygost Institute that Neezer's concerned with now. Which is why we told him no when he offered to buy the farm. It should've stopped there. But then he turned on Clara, who'd never stopped loving him or hoping the two of us would make our peace. He called her greedy for wanting to keep the farm for herself. He accused her—both of us—of never having loved him in the first place. After that . . ." He sighed. "I had no use for him at all."

Nitty thought about the mystery crop just beyond the front door, the only speck of green for miles, maybe even for states. "I'm glad you kept the farm. Even if it *was* the cause of the kerfuffle between you and Neezer."

"I was glad, too, in the beginning. While Neezer ran for mayor and built his institute, I brought in the best crop I'd ever had. But I paid a painful price for it." Windle's face darkened. "Clara grew heartsick over what had happened. Lillah wanted us to make amends, for Clara's sake. But I refused to keep trying. I couldn't trust the man Neezer had become, even if I missed the man he'd been. Then the first duster blew through, right at harvest-time. It destroyed my entire crop." His voice quieted into a whisper. "Clara's health was already failing, and the dusters ruined what was left of it. Lillah left town soon after Clara's passing. She said she wanted to see the world, that she needed to travel for her singing. She just wanted to be out from under the sadness of it all."

"Well . . . Neezer was wrong to turn on Clara. You were only trying to protect her, and the farm." Nitty's heart panged at the sorrow in Windle's eyes, so bottomless there seemed to be no end to it at all.

"I said plenty that was wrong, too, and I've no excuse for it."

"But you could've tried making amends again and it would've done no good at all."

"Could've. Would've. Should've." Windle's freckle stung fiercer than a wasp on his skin. "Three words full of wasted wishing. There was much I might've done besides insisting on my own rightness. Was my stubbornness worth the grief of what was lost? Seems to me that humility might've served me better than pride."

Nitty and Windle sat together for a long time after Windle

finished talking. When Nitty spoke at last, it was with the certainty that she could never bring even an ounce more suffering to Windle Homes, that she had to do what she could to protect him, and that this began with absolute and total honesty.

She swallowed. "Windle?"

"Hmmmm?"

"I have some dire confessions to make."

Windle's paintbrush eyebrows drew together. "I'm waiting."

Nitty sucked in a breath and, in a headlong rush of words, listed every last one of her wrongdoings. Running away from Grimsgate seemed the least offensive, so she began with that, then moved on to her thievery and Mag's escape from the noose.

"I did steal the seeds, but I didn't steal Mag so much as rescue her," Nitty cried as she finished. "Just like she rescued me! And you can hardly blame me, can you? When she was about to be murdered? When she was so magnificent and in such great need?"

She sank back on her cot after that and waited. What if Windle sent her out the door and into the throes of the wailing duster? What if she never saw her crop, or Mag, or Windle again? But no. She would not cry. She set her mouth and shoulders. Whatever judgment awaited her, she'd meet it with as much mettle as she could muster.

Windle stood. Nitty's heart galloped.

"It occurs to me," he said matter-of-factly, "that at this late hour, there is only one sensible solution before us."

"I'm prepared," Nitty responded bravely, although, perhaps

truly, being only ten and on the verge of possible exile, she was not.

"A decent dose of sleep," he pronounced. "Won't be worth a hill of beans come morning without it."

Nitty blinked. "But . . . you're not frightened, then? Of me being a criminal, that is?"

Windle harrumphed. "To bed with you."

He turned for his room then, not wanting to let on that he was *plenty* frightened. For something uncanny was happening to Windle Homes. When he'd first set eyes on Nitty and Mag, he'd feared keeping them. Now, for the first time, he feared losing them.

He gave a backward glance to the photo of Clara and Lillah before shutting his door. He hadn't been able to keep Lillah from leaving, or his Clara from dying. How, then, could he protect anyone?

He lay down and closed his eyes. His heart clattered. *Try,* it told him. *Just try.*

And back in the kitchen, on her cot, Nitty smiled. She understood what Windle couldn't say.

Windle wanted her and Mag to stay.

CHAPTER SEVENTEEN

IN WHICH MOONLIGHT BRINGS BLOSSOMING

It had been many years since the little farmhouse had felt like a proper home—many years since it had been filled with anything other than Windle's despair. On this night, though, as Windle made his unspoken promise to Nitty, a change swept over the farmhouse. No longer was it forlorn, or "lorn" of any sort. While Nitty and Windle slipped into sleep, a newfound warmth—some might even have called it the beginnings of love—swept through the little farmhouse, then wound its way from house to porch and beyond.

The milky goliath moon felt it, and drew nearer, sending the few remaining tawny-brown clouds scudding away. The stars felt it, and shone so mightily over the farm that it was bathed in a silvery glow. The earth felt it, and gave the bending green stalks above her an encouraging prod that straightened them up and shook the dust from their leaves.

The warmth twined and twirled itself around the green stalks of Nitty's mystery crop. It paused over the lantern-like, fuchsia buds, giving each the gentlest of coaxing caresses. Then, like newborn babies opening their eyes for the very first time to gaze upon the world, the buds began to bloom.

Nitty sat up in her cot as the first bud unfurled. It woke her with its unexpected whisper—a tiny but jubilant *Whee!* as if there were nothing better than to be born among starlight and moonshine in a field of emerald green.

Nitty heard the second bud unfurl and went to the door. The third and she was off the porch and running to the field. Never, in all of her life, had Nitty seen moonshine like this. Bright as daylight but the palest, prettiest of blues, it made everything look freshly washed and new.

She found Mag at the field's edge, strutting happily with her trunk tickling the stalks.

"I can see your mood's improved." Nitty laughed, standing on tiptoe to rub under Mag's chin. "And I'm glad to see it. So has mine."

All around them now, the soft cries of the flowers' delight filled the air.

Nitty crouched before one bud, watching it tremble in antici-pation.

"Come on, then," she whispered to it. "Come see the world." As she did, the lantern of petals burst open into a cloud of pinks. At the center of the flower hung a cluster of round, fuchsia . . . What were they exactly? Fruits? Berries? Vegetables? Nitty had never seen the likes of them before. Each was the size of a cherry, with a pink frond like corn silk hanging from its top. Whatever they were, they shone sumptuously in the moonlight. And what a scent they had! A fresh-baked-cookie, fresh-picked-strawberry sort of smell that warmed Nitty's heart.

She was sorely tempted to pick one and taste it. Mag, too, was exploring one of the clusters with her trunk.

"Do they smell as heavenly to you as they do to me?" Nitty asked her.

Mag bowed her head to Nitty's height, and Nitty stroked her trunk, looking deeply into Mag's left eye. She thought she saw a glimmer of delight there, as if Mag were just as excited by this turn of events as she was.

Then, curious and hopeful, they walked straight into the stalks together. The stalks, for their part, didn't seem to mind the intrusion in the least, and sprang back up the moment Mag's enormous feet passed.

Nitty spread her arms like wings as she walked, rustling the stalks with her fingertips. Green was everywhere and everywhere was green, glowing in the moonlight.

Before long, the two of them reached the middle of the field. Then, because at that moment Nitty couldn't think of a single thing she wanted to do more, she lay down. Her bare toes and fingers tickled pleasantly from the cool stalks cushioned beneath her.

Seconds later, there was a momentous rustling and sighing as Mag lay down beside her.

Above their heads, the stalks formed a canopy with the cascading stars. Their green blazed, and Nitty sucked in a breath. *What would it feel like,* she'd wondered when she'd stolen the seeds, *to be in the middle of all that green?* Now she knew beyond any doubt. It was like being inside an emerald.

Nitty plucked one of the strange-looking clusters from a nearby stalk and pulled off three of the mystery fruits. Just in the last minutes, the fruits had grown bigger, and they were now the size of small plums. As she pulled each one from its cluster, its silky tassel came off in her hand, leaving a star-shaped opening at the top.

She held one of them out to Mag. "What do you think?"

Without a second's hesitation, Mag took the fruit with her trunk and scooped it into her mouth. There was a pulpy crunching, followed by Mag's single, short trumpet of satisfaction.

The taste of the fruit stirred an instinctive memory in Mag's heart—one that didn't belong to her but to her ancestors before her. A memory of sweeping gold grass that tickled the belly. Of a sprawling savanna dappled with other animals—animals that seemed foreign but familiar all at once. Animals that shared the open space with one another, roaming, hunting, living, dying. Everything in balance. Every creature free. The fruit tasted like all these things.

Mag picked a second bundle of fruit from the field and gently set it in Nitty's lap.

"You want me to eat it?" Nitty asked.

Mag nudged the bundle encouragingly with the tip of her trunk.

Nitty raised the fruit to her lips. Now that the fruit was right under her nose, its scent was even more enticing.

Nitty took a bite, and a tangy sweetness burst over her tongue. The outer skin of the fruit was thin but crisp. The inside was juicy, tart, and pudding smooth all at once. Its flavor was like nothing she'd ever known—as if every flower and fruit in the world had melded into every cookie, cake, and chocolate. It tasted like a found family. Like green growing in desert dryness. Like a smile. It tasted like everything the world should have been but often wasn't. There was something else, too. Something she couldn't quite pin down.

Nitty laughed. She took another bite, and another. As she ate, a strange feeling came over her, until she felt like one of those fuchsia buds before they'd opened—pent-up and near to bursting with everything she'd kept bottled inside her for these many years. She untied her Gleam Jar from around her neck and set it carefully between her and Mag.

"I know you can't tell me what happened to you in the circus," she said to Mag. "You might not want to even if you could, and I can hardly blame you. There are some things I don't talk about either. Like what's in this jar." She tapped the lid and opened it. "There's not a soul on earth who's heard about it. But tonight I'd like to tell you, because . . ." She rubbed Mag's chin. "Because you're the first friend I ever had. And you're a mighty fine listener."

Beside Nitty, Mag raised her head. Her girl's voice was soft and warbly. A bird's voice. She liked listening to it. She gently traced the lid of the Gleam Jar with her trunk, spending some minutes smelling its contents. The scent of her girl—a wonderful fresh-grass, cool-dirt scent—covered the jar. There was the scent of salt and sadness, too—the scent of tears. Mag moved her trunk from the jar to her girl's cheeks, searching for tears but finding none. The tears on the jar were old, then, but they were also many. What had caused her girl such sadness, and what could she do to take it from her? She moved the tip of her trunk over the girl's hair, sweeping it from her forehead. Slowly she stroked her girl's hair and listened to her story. It wasn't in a language she could understand, but that hardly mattered, for she could hear the yearning in it all the same.

The first object Nitty took from the jar was the satin ribbon of robin's-egg blue. She set it in her palm, where it lay like a curl of captured sky. "This ribbon was tucked into my blanket when I was left at Grimsgate Orphanage." She brushed it against her cheek. "I believe my mama used to tie her hair back with this ribbon. She would've had luminous hair, Mama would've, the cool blue-black of a river at night. Mama is tiger tough, and she fought to protect me from hunger and wanting as long as she could. That's how she lost her ribbon. Fighting to protect me."

The second object was the daffodil-yellow button, smaller than a penny.

"This button I found buried in the yard at Grimsgate. My pa left it there for me to find. To bring me luck. He is a man who believes in luck and dreaming big. Until the day he buried it for me to find, he carried that button in his own pocket, hoping his luck would turn so he could keep me."

Nitty reached into the jar again and brought out the third object—the cardinal-red agate marble. "This marble belonged to my brother. The day I left Grimsgate, I saw it in a roadside ditch. He was so upset about me being left at Grimsgate, he up and dropped his favorite marble. He's an expert at shooting marbles."

Nitty held the marble up to the moonlight, and its center glowed, skittering fractured red light across her face and Mag's.

"They're made-up stories," she said softly. "Course I know that." It was the first time she'd ever said that aloud, and it made a sadness steal over her as she did. "I used to tell them before I came here, when I was lonesome. The more I did, the more they struck me as true, until I could barely tell the difference between what was true and what I wished to be true." She stroked the blue ribbon with her finger. "Only, lately, I haven't had much use for the stories. In fact"—she heaved a sigh—"they've been causing me all manner of grief and consternation. They're nothing but mirages playing tricks on me. But I wanted to tell you about them, before they're gone for good."

Even though Nitty had given it specific orders not to, her

voice disobeyed her by wobbling. Mag paused in her stroking of Nitty's hair, and Nitty pressed her face into Mag's trunk, holding on tight.

"Did your family make you promises? Back before the circus?" Nitty whispered to her. "I bet they did. I bet they would've done anything to keep you from chains, if they could've."

Nitty turned the Gleam Jar in her hands, and as she did, its contents caught the starlight, sending a shower of color across the ground. She thought about her mama and daddy. Had they made promises to each other? To her, back before they left her at Grimsgate? Had they promised to keep her safe and warm and fed? Had they promised to give her the best life they could? Had Twitch's mama made that promise to his little sister?

Though she fought it, a single tear leaked from one of her eyes. Before she could move to brush it away, Mag, with a caress as gentle as any mother's, did it for her.

"Maybe," Nitty said, "there are ways of keeping promises that don't make much sense." She sniffled, then gave a little laugh when Mag did the same. "I'll tell you what else. Elephant or person, I don't think anybody, if she's honest and true, ever means to break a promise."

Mag gave a *whoomph* of a sigh and took up stroking Nitty's hair again for a long stretch of minutes as Nitty stared up into the star-freckled dark. Mag couldn't say it aloud, but Nitty felt she understood. She leaned against Mag's mountain belly. Mag's pumpkin heart drummed a rich, faithful beat against her cheek.

"I've been thinking," Nitty whispered. "That we could be family. Together." She stilled, turning to Mag. "So do you . . ." Her pulse skipped. "Do you like the idea?"

Mag lifted her trunk to Nitty, and in the moonlight it looked to Nitty like a welcoming, open arm. Nitty tucked into it, fitting snugly and seamlessly against its curled warmth. Sleep soon slipped over them, and for the briefest twinkling in time, the two hearts beat in unison.

CHAPTER EIGHTEEN

In Which Fruit Is Given a Most Unusual Name

"Rats and darnation! We have sleuthing to do, and I find you sawing logs in the middle of a field?"

Nitty blinked her eyes open to see Twitch standing over her, hands on hips, one foot hammering the ground loud and fast as a woodpecker's peck.

"Quit your grousing, Twitch." She sat up beside Mag, who was already stretching her trunk toward more fuchsia fruit, perky and alert in the early-morning light. Gone were last night's clear skies, replaced with a sooty, mustard haze. "Can't you see we've got our crop?" She picked a piece of fruit, which had tripled in size overnight. She tossed it to Twitch, who caught it against his stomach with an *oof.*

Twitch coughed, and Nitty winced at the sound, wishing

she hadn't been so careless. It wasn't a pebbles-tumbling-under-water cough anymore so much as a barking rattle-rasp.

Twitch's cough was getting worse.

He raised his goggles, and he stared at the fruit. "It's as big as your head!"

"Well, are you going to try it or not?" Nitty said impatiently.

Twitch didn't hesitate another second. Pink juice dribbled down his chin in syrupy rivers. He took another bite and another. Then he plunked down beside Nitty and Mag. His eyes glistened, and he swiped at them quickly. Nitty guessed he didn't want anyone to notice, so she kept her eyes on Mag's trunk, which was snuffling the rest of the fruit in Twitch's hand.

"It tastes like Anna's tiny fist, curled around my finger. Like Pa coming home." He laughed softly, but the laugh soon turned into a cough.

"Eat more," Nitty encouraged, a notion taking shape in her head. The fruit seemed to have a delightful effect on her, and Mag couldn't seem to get enough of it either. Mightn't it help Twitch's cough?

Twitch was poised to take another bite when a sudden rustling in the field made them all turn.

Windle burst through the stalks with phrases like "What in blazes" and "Pachyderm trampling my crop," but stopped short at the sight of Nitty and Twitch, their mouths and chins bright pink, grinning amid the abundance of fruit. Nitty stood to place a piece of fruit in his hand.

"Morning, Windle," Nitty chirped, as if this were a perfectly ordinary day and there was nothing at all unusual about a pink, melon-sized mystery crop ripening overnight. "Have some fruit."

There were a great many things Windle might've done in this moment. He might've cried with relief at his strange but bountiful crop—the first crop he'd grown in years. He might've laughed at Nitty, Twitch, and even Mag, with their chins and cheeks dribbling with fuchsia juice. He might've whooped and hollered and bounded for joy at his farm returning to life after being buried, for so long, in dust. In his heart, in fact, Windle *was* doing all of these things. But because his boggled mind hadn't quite caught up with his rhapsodizing heart, he was only capable of taking the simplest, easiest action. Windle ate some fruit.

He chewed slowly, solemnly. Nothing about his expression gave the slightest hint at his thoughts.

Nitty held her breath.

At last Windle harrumphed. It was a different sort of harrumph, puny with crankiness but robust with joy. "Tastes like the sight of my sweet Clara sitting in her rocker. Like a little girl giggling, running through cornfields."

A remedy for a broken heart, Nitty thought. "Do you see?" She grinned, because she suddenly understood what it was about the fruit that she hadn't been able to pin down before. "It tastes like triumph, sure as can be."

Nitty waited for Windle to argue. He didn't. No one did. Because they were beginning to see. Every one of them.

"It needs a proper name," Twitch said then.

"Yes. For when we take it to town." Nitty's eyes met Twitch's in a moment of unspoken understanding. She'd thought, too, about the mountains of food in Snollygost General Store that no one could pay for, about Miz Turngiddy's list of names. She'd had the very same idea that she saw forming on Twitch's face now.

Nitty held a piece of fruit under her nose. She breathed in its blissful scent. Then it came to her—a name as unexpected and singular as the fruit itself. "Froozle. It's froozle fruit."

"Froozle's a fine name." Twitch grinned, bouncing on his toes.

"Who said anything about taking it to town?" Windle's eyebrows were flapping wings, dipping and diving.

"Well, of course we have to take it to town!" Nitty stared at Windle. "Everyone in Fortune's Bluff needs it. Right away. Then they don't have to worry over food they can't afford."

Windle said nothing, but a light flickered on in his eyes. His gaze swept the field, and as it did, the hazy sunlight caught the green stalks in just a certain way, until the stalks' tips seemed to be sweeping the very clouds above. A lightning bolt of realization struck Windle. He had grown a crop worthy of his younger, braver self. A crop worthy of the land and the town he'd once loved. What good did any crop do a farmer unless it was put to proper use? Crops were meant for harvesting. Meant for eating.

"I'll get the truck," he said.

CHAPTER NINETEEN

IN WHICH A FARM TAKES A
TRIP INTO TOWN

Windle's truck hadn't made it halfway down the main street of
Fortune's Bluff when its occupants started staring.

Windle stared at the roof of the Palace Nickelodeon. Or,
rather, he stared at the hole atop the nickelodeon where the
roof had once been. He stared at the broken windows of the
homes lining the street. Nitty and Twitch stared at a dozen
streetlamps that were snapped in half or uprooted entirely.

"Last night's duster," muttered Windle, shaking his head as
he stopped the truck across from the Snollygost General Store.

Twitch started to lift his periscope to his goggles to assess
the damage, then stopped, seeming not to have the heart for it.
Instead he turned his head toward the Snollygost Institute, with
its ever-present *WHUMP.* " 'Ten Ways to Be a Villain, number

seven,'" he wheezed. "'If something or someone stands in your way, destroy it.'"

Nitty climbed down from the seat, making a mental list of all the damage within sight. A portion of her spirit sank in on itself, like a cake falling after a violent noise. So much of Fortune's Bluff was broken now. It was hard to imagine anything beyond its splintered roofs and shattered windows. But Nitty tried, and as she did, she remembered the triumph of the froozle crop. After some time, her shoulders straightened. "Well. It has to be fixed, of course. All of it. We can help."

"No point in that." Ferdinand Klempt appeared in the doorway of the Schnurrbart Emporium, hoisting the corner of a slumping walrus mustache. "It will only be blown to pieces again with the next duster." He bowed his head, his sagging mustache trembling woefully. "All is lost. Lost, I tell you."

Murmurs of assent rose from dozens of earmuffed folks around them. There were sighs, too, and mournful tears trailing down countless cheeks. No one made a move to start fixing. Instead the people of Fortune's Bluff were staring, their faces perfect portraits of misery.

Folks walking by who hadn't worked in years but still wanted to appear as if they had someplace important to go; children who'd been hungry for so long their bellies had given up rumbling; children who hadn't slept in months on account of their teeth rattling all night from the whumping at the Snollygost Institute; parents who cried each night for their hungry, teeth-rattled children. All, each and every one, stared at the hurts of Fortune's Bluff. The only movement was a collective flinching—painful to watch—that came with each relentless *WHUMP* reverberating from the bluff overlooking the town.

This is what giving up looks like, Nitty thought.

"Notice anything unusual?" Twitch whispered to Nitty then.

Nitty frowned. "Nothing is usual about this dismal predicament."

Twitch jerked his head toward the institute. "The only two buildings untouched by the duster? The institute and the general store." He bounced on his toes. "Coincidence? I think not."

"You're right." Nitty's thoughts whirled. "But we can't investigate that now. Not with everyone in this state." She turned to Windle. "Why isn't anyone doing anything?"

Windle's brow furrowed. "There are limits to what people can bear. And when there's too much broken for you to see any clear path to fixing—"

"You clear a path yourself," Nitty blurted, unwilling to accept any other answer. The question now was, What did the town of Fortune's Bluff need?

Verve and vim and courage, and a great many other things besides, Nitty thought. But right now, she only had one thing to offer.

She scooped a mound of froozle fruit into her arms. Out of the corner of her eye, she saw Twitch and Windle do the same.

She held out a piece to a dust-smudged little girl who barely came up to her knee. "For you."

The little girl hesitated just long enough to get a nod from her mother, then snatched the fruit and took a hearty bite. She giggled. "Tastes like chocolate."

Murmurs of curiosity and eagerness rose from the crowd, so Nitty didn't waste a second. "It's froozle fruit. Help yourselves. Take as much as you'd like. There's plenty."

She held out more fruit, and within moments her arms were empty. So were Twitch's.

From all around them came the crackling of crisp froozle fruit being bitten into, and then contented sighs and gasps of wonder.

"Tastes like a bubble bath," said an old woman.

"Tastes like the smell of a new baby," said a woman whose belly bulged beneath her skirt.

"Tastes like finding a job," said a man.

"Tastes like respect," said another.

Faces that, a few minutes before, had been ashen and dull suddenly brightened. Children who'd been wailing for food all morning now laughed at their hearty, satisfied belches. As folks ate their fill of fruit, they glanced about Main Street, seeming to take it in with a fresh eye. There was talk of getting hammers and nails and paint buckets to fix what had been torn away by the duster.

There isn't a single soul who should be forgotten, Nitty thought. *Everyone needs the froozle fruit.*

Which is why, when Nitty saw Bernice and Crispin watching from the doorway of the bakery, looking out at all the happenings with yearning but reluctant to endure stares or questions, she didn't hesitate. Tucking a melon-sized froozle fruit under each arm, she hurried toward the bakery before the Sighs could retreat entirely.

Crispin greeted her with his usual "Rain. Rain. Where's the rain? Salt, nimbostratus, flour, altostratus . . ." He worried the knobs of his rolling pin in his hands. "The Whirlybog whumps, makes the sky gust. The nose sings out, 'Blow! And turn all to dust.'"

Nitty tried making sense of what he'd said, but when she discovered she couldn't, and Bernice's cheeks were growing brighter with embarrassment with each passing second, she plunked the froozle fruit into Bernice's arms. "I brought you a new ingredient. For your bread."

Bernice frowned. "We're out of flour. Used the last of it yesterday."

Nitty searched her store of ideas, not ready to let this small problem stand in the way of bigger prospects. "In that case, maybe you can make froozle flourless bread."

"Flourless," Crispin mumbled. "Froozle." He lifted the fruit to his mouth and took a bite.

At Nitty's nod of encouragement, Bernice grudgingly did the same.

"Tastes like not having to scrub dishes or change diapers," Bernice mumbled. "Tastes like having fun again." She snorted her snort-laugh.

Nitty ventured a smile. Then she and Bernice both stared

as Crispin stopped trembling and gazed down at the froozle fruit. "Tastes like rain. And fresh, rising dough." He looked at Bernice. "Baking. Today is a fine day for baking."

He turned on his heel and disappeared into the bakery with the rest of the froozle fruit.

"I don't understand it." Bernice looked after him, mystified. "Just this morning he swore he'd never bake again."

Nitty shrugged. "Maybe he should take more care with his swears." She caught Bernice's eyes, and Bernice snort-laughed again, louder this time.

"Would you like to help hand out the rest of the froozle fruit?" Nitty asked. "It's probably not the best fun you've ever had, but—"

Bernice was two steps out the door before Nitty could finish, calling over her shoulder, "I'll help. Long as nobody says boo about Papa."

Soon Nitty, Bernice, and Twitch fell into a rhythm at the truck, passing the heaviest of the fruits through their arms and out to folks eager and waiting. The only person in the crowd who wasn't bustling for the fruit was Ferdinand Klempt, who was hanging back, wringing his hands.

"Aren't you going to take some?" urged Nitty, offering him a fruit that gleamed with fuchsia splendor.

"How can I possibly? My father would say a man without creative vision cannot eat. A man without a muse is too pitiful for food." He waved away the fruit.

Nitty wasn't ready to give up. "Mr. Klempt, I've had such

verminous language used against me, you'd scarce believe it. My spirit might've been reduced to a measly dust mote." Nitty looked him square in the eyes. "It wasn't. Because my spirit is my own."

"My father—" Ferdinand Klempt started, his voice cracking.

Nitty dangled a fruit before his eyes, holding it by its silken, fuchsia tassel. Ferdinand Klempt stared at the tassel, his eyes widening.

"My father—" He stopped. He touched the fuchsia tassel, testing its texture with his fingers. He held it over his upper lip. His eyes took on the light of sun breaking through clouds. He smiled, grabbing as many froozle fruits as he could carry, and hurried into the Schnurrbart Emporium, slamming the door behind him.

"Is he all right?" Nitty asked Windle.

Windle nodded. "He will be. It's been years since I've seen that look on his face."

"What does it mean?"

"It means the muse is upon him." Windle stared at the Schnurrbart Emporium for a long minute, then grumbled, "He'll want me to try some newfangled mustache of his before the week's out. Just you wait."

Nitty placed her hand on his arm. "And you will, won't you?"

Windle sighed. "I suppose I'll have to." He didn't seem nearly as disgruntled about it as he was trying to sound. In fact, Nitty could've sworn she saw him smile as he turned back toward the truck bed to give out more fruit.

Bernice, too, was smiling, albeit warily and mostly into the sleeve of her shirt. Twitch was the only one, Nitty noticed then, who was not smiling.

Twitch's eyes were fixed on the Snollygost General Store, where two shadowy figures stared out from the window. "It's Miz Turngiddy and Mayor Snollygost," he whispered. "And Neezer's not happy."

Nitty looked again at the figures in the window and saw that Twitch was right. Miz Turngiddy was scribbling frantically on her notepad, her head bobbing like a doll's that had come loose. Neezer's expression—dark, turbulent, unpredictable— bore all the signs of a brewing storm. In a heartbeat, his eyes registered Nitty's and the storm lifted.

"He's coming." Nitty straightened her shoulders and set her jaw as Neezer strode toward their truck with Miz Turngiddy close behind.

"And what sort of merriment do we have here?" he asked.

With the booming of Neezer's voice, each person took a step away from the truck. Except Windle, Nitty, Twitch, and Bernice. They stood, unmoving, before the crop.

"The sort of merriment that our town should have but never does." Twitch narrowed his eyes at Neezer.

"Windle," Neezer began again, ignoring Twitch entirely, "what is all this ruckus?"

"Nothing to turn anyone's tide," Windle said slowly. "Only sharing our harvest."

"What a harvest it is!" Neezer picked up a piece of froozle

fruit, turning it over and over in his hands. "I've never seen the likes of this before."

"No one has." Nitty raised her chin in pride. "It's froozle fruit."

"Unorthodox, to be sure." Neezer's smile made a wide stretch of piano keys. He tossed the fruit up and down in his palm. His nose whistled "Conquering Now and Still to Conquer," the same song Nitty had once heard Miz Ricketts humming as she'd locked Nitty in the Grimsgate attic.

"Try it," she challenged, holding fruit out to Neezer and Miz Turngiddy.

"This froozle fruit . . ." Neezer eyed it. "There is much we don't know or understand about it as of yet. It is a crop never seen before, much less consumed before."

"It does look delicious." Miz Turngiddy lifted her piece to her nose and breathed deeply. "And what an extraordinarily fast growing cycle! Why, just the other day, this fruit was no more than a bud. A study of its internal structure might—"

"Delicious?" boomed Neezer, drowning out Miz Turngiddy. "We shall see." He took a froozle fruit from Nitty, and then, using a pocketknife retrieved from his purple waistcoat, cut himself a hefty slice of fruit and promptly popped it into his mouth.

He chewed some long seconds, then bent over with sudden, violent coughing.

"Mayor Snollygost?" Miz Turngiddy hovered over his bowed form. "What is it, sir?"

Murmurs of "Is he all right?" and "He's choking" rustled through the townsfolk as Neezer gasped and gripped his throat. "My tongue. It's . . . swelling. Need . . . water."

A flurry of activity and alarm erupted on the street as folks scattered to fetch water, but it was Miz Turngiddy who was quickest, hurrying into the Snollygost General Store to return mere seconds later with a cup.

Neezer gulped down several swallows of water, then leaned against Windle's truck for support until his rasping breaths calmed. He mopped his brow with a handkerchief but waved away the worried inquiries of the folks surrounding him. "I'll . . . recover momentarily," he managed with what appeared to be some difficulty. "Fortunately, I took only the smallest bite. Anything bigger and . . ."

He coughed mightily, and every person on Main Street stilled. Every mouth ceased chewing. Every face paled. Except for Nitty's, Twitch's, and Bernice's. They were studying Neezer intensely.

"It's a ruse," Twitch hissed into Nitty's ear. "A sleight of hand. I saw him do it with my own eyes. . . ."

"What do you mean?" Nitty asked.

Twitch didn't have a chance to respond before one young mother stepped forward, blurting, "It made the mayor sick." Several others nodded in agreement. "Did you see?" The woman dropped her fruit to the ground, where it broke open, splattering froozle juice over the sidewalk.

Neezer waved a dismissive hand. "Now, now . . . no need for alarm. I'll be all right in due course . . . I'm certain." He did not, however, *sound* certain. He straightened with effort, trembling slightly, his eyes sweeping the crowd. "It's only the slightest dizziness now, and numbness of the fingers."

"Look what it's done to him. What if the fruit's poison?" someone in the crowd cried out. "No one should eat it."

"No! The fruit's perfectly safe to eat!" Nitty blurted. "Twitch, Windle, and I ate stomachfuls this morning, and we're fiddle fit as can be."

"How can you be sure?" one father asked, shielding his children from the truck full of fruit.

"I'm sure." Bernice took another enormous bite of fruit.

"Me too," said Twitch.

Nitty gave them grateful smiles.

Worried mutterings spread through the rest of the crowd, however, and Neezer weakly nodded in sympathy. "Caution is sensible, friends," he said, seeming to rally as several families, with sadness, returned their fruits to the truck bed. "Better to get your food from trustworthy sources, and right now the Snollygost store has the most delicious oranges."

"Trustworthy as toadstools and turnips," muttered Twitch, and then he marched up to Neezer, heaving accordion breaths as he went. "You didn't taste the fruit. It never even touched your lips. I *saw* you slip it up your shirtsleeve—"

"Come now, Angus." Windle put his hands on Twitch's

shoulders, steering him back toward the truck. Twitch was panting heavily. "Save your breath before you have an attack."

Nitty scrutinized Neezer's sleeves then, and she was sure she saw an unidentifiable lump under Neezer's left cuff. Her pulse clanged in her ears.

Neezer, who'd paid no attention to Twitch's outburst, breezed past them, directing people toward his store. He seemed nearly recovered, save for the tentative way he was walking and massaging his fingers, as if to alleviate their numbness. "This way, friends. Herein lies the familiar. The trusted."

"Wait!" Nitty hurried after people as they walked away from Windle's truck empty-handed. "Froozle fruit won't make you sick. Come back."

Most folks did not come back. Parents began inspecting their children's mouths and throats and asking how their bellies felt. There were a few—a very few—who still went home with fruit, but their jubilation was gone, replaced with worry. Out of the whole of Fortune's Bluff, it was only Crispin and Ferdinand, in the end, who returned to the truck to stand their ground.

Crispin, unusually clear-eyed and calm, declared, "I'll take as much of the fruit as you can spare." Then he locked eyes with Neezer in a gaze that Nitty could only interpret as one of sheer defiance.

"And I'll take the tassels," Ferdinand said. "If you've no use for them."

"Take however much you need" was Windle's encouraging response.

For one small second, Neezer couldn't mask his surprise and annoyance, but he quickly covered both up with a smile.

Nitty stared at his smug smile and felt she might explode in fury. "How could you do that? How could you take this away from them?"

Neezer seemed not to hear, already turning to leave with Miz Turngiddy, who was frowning, eyes downcast. Nitty picked up a piece of froozle fruit the exact size of Neezer's head. She contemplated throwing it at him. She smiled at the thought of how the froozle juice would run down his purple waistcoat, likely staining it beyond repair.

"Nitty." Windle's voice broke through her thoughts, sparing her the loss of her temper and Neezer the possible loss of his head. "It's best that we go."

"But—" She looked at Windle, and her protests fizzled. His eyes were telling her it was no use, that no one would be back for more fruit. Slowly she said goodbye to Bernice, Crispin, and Ferdinand.

"I'll keep a staunch lookout from the bakery," Bernice promised.

Nitty was too angry to take much encouragement from this, although she appreciated Bernice's dedication to their cause. She climbed into the truck bed beside Twitch and a mountain of leftover froozle fruit. "That—that splenetic rapscallion!" she blurted as soon as the truck pulled away from the curb. "I'd just as soon eat slug pie as look at him!"

"Haven't I been saying as much this entire time?" Twitch

coughed, and she handed him a piece of froozle fruit. "I know he was hiding that slice of fruit in his shirtsleeve. I should've wrestled him to the ground to prove it."

"Couldn't any of them see they were being steamrollered?"

Twitch shrugged. "Fear blinds folks from lots of wrongs they should see."

Nitty wanted to argue that it should be easy to step over that fear, or leap over it, if need be. Still, she knew that it wasn't an easy thing, dealing with fear. If it were, Mag might not have been sentenced to hang, Twitch's pa might never have left for California, and the whole of Fortune's Bluff might never have been caught in this predicament in the first place.

"I tell you what," she said then. "And I don't need to consult your *Detective Comics* to know it either. Fear is the very worst villain of them all."

"That's the truth of it," Twitch agreed.

They rode the rest of the way home in silence, the uneaten froozle fruit that surrounded them smelling ripe with deliciousness, but also with missed opportunity.

⚓︎

Mag was sliding another bunch of the delicious pink fruit into her mouth when her girl came back to her. She expected Nitty to run to her, as she usually did, trilling in that chirpy voice Mag liked, offering a chin rubbing, which Mag liked even better. This time, the girl was quiet, and slow to come to her, her head down. It was so unlike her girl that Mag dropped the fruit in alarm.

She nuzzled the girl's hand with her trunk, breathing in her scent. There was still a green-grassiness to it, but there was also the bitterness of anger and—she sniffed more deeply this time—sadness, too. Something was wrong.

Mag sounded a low rumble of concern, and then the girl burst into a flood of words. The words were hard and clipped, like stones clattering over stones. Mag didn't like the tone of them, because there was pain to them. It was the same kind of pain she'd smelled yesterday, when the boy Twitch had come upon the small wooden trough in the barn.

Mag had gone to that trough because its scent had at first confused and then troubled her. It was not a hay or water scent, like the other troughs Mag had known. This trough held the milky-sweet scent of a baby—a human baby. It was a faint scent, an old one, and one that was tinged with sickness. The baby had been ill, and it hadn't been near the trough in a long time.

Now Mag wondered if her girl's sadness had to do with that trough, too.

Her girl began pacing, her voice louder, and Mag grew worried.

She'd seen pacing like that before. The lion had paced like that, in his cage, back at the big top. He'd paced day and night—restless, angry, not having anywhere to go or knowing what else to do.

Maybe her girl didn't know what to do now either.

Mag wanted to help. She thought of that trough, with its milky scent. She thought of filling it with something that might bring her girl comfort. Something that might make her girl's voice chirp happily, like before. She turned to the field and picked several of the biggest clusters of flowers that she could find. She pressed a cluster into her girl's arms.

At first her girl spoke, her tone rising in surprise, but then Mag slowly led her to the back corner of the barn, where the trough sat in shadow. Mag laid her flowers in the trough and waited. Her girl hesitated, then nodded. Slowly, quietly, her girl sat down beside the trough and laid her flowers in its bottom. She set the trough to a gentle rocking. Her girl's voice turned singsongy. It wasn't bird-chirp happy, but instead was whisper-soft and soothing.

Mag felt a rightness in what they'd done, and she stayed there with her girl for some time.

When at last she snuffled her girl's palm again, this time her girl answered the snuffle with an ear rub. Mag smelled some of the anger lifting from the girl's skin.

Mag offered her trunk, and her girl sat down in its curl, swinging. The evening wore on, but Mag didn't tire.

When her girl slid into sleep, Mag laid her down on a pile of hay and stood nearby to keep watch. It was only when the man Windle came in quietly to find the girl that Mag stepped aside. The man lifted her sleeping girl and gently carried her to the house.

He was the only one Mag would've let take her.

He wanted to protect her as much as Mag did. She sensed it in his strong, tree-bark scent, and in the low, rumbling tones of his voice—not threatening, but guarding. As long as he had care of her girl, Mag, at last, would sleep.

CHAPTER TWENTY

IN WHICH A TOWN AND AN ELEPHANT ARE PROPERLY INTRODUCED

Fear is a powerful oppressor, to be sure, but it is safe to say that, in all of history up to this point, fear had never encountered the irresistible allure of froozle fruit. All that night and into the next morning, the thoughts of the folks of Fortune's Bluff were consumed with that beautiful fuchsia bounty. For those who had tasted the fruit, its sweetness lingered on their lips, making them smile when they otherwise might have frowned. Those who had not yet tasted it saw the smiles on the faces of those who had and wished they had tasted it themselves.

As the hours passed and night turned to day, it became obvious that eating the fruit caused no ill effects. It was not poisonous. It was edible, delicious, and, in fact, exactly what the folks of Fortune's Bluff needed after so many long and cheerless years.

Which is why it was not at all surprising that at eight o'clock the next morning, Nitty opened the Homes door to find Crispin, Bernice, and the troop of little Sighs standing on the front porch. What *was* surprising was that Crispin didn't utter a single word or rhyme about rain.

Instead he smiled shyly and, with steady hands free of trembles, offered Nitty a perfectly fresh, crisp loaf of fuchsia bread. It was still warm.

"For you," he said, "in thanks."

"But I thought you had no more flour," Nitty said.

"We don't." Bernice's voice was airy light. She shrugged. "Turns out when we used froozle fruit in the recipe, we didn't need any."

The tantalizing smell of the bread reached Nitty's nose, and her mouth watered. "It looks delicious."

"Try it," Bernice blurted impatiently, an uncharacteristically optimistic grin spreading on her face. Before Nitty could do it herself, Bernice broke off a piece for her.

The bread zinged in Nitty's mouth, the perfect blend of cozy doughiness and tart froozle sweetness. "That . . . is some bread," she said. "A mouthful of mellifluousness."

That made Bernice giggle, which was so surprising that it brought Windle to the door.

"The Sighs brought us fresh bread." Nitty gave him a piece, and soon everyone was sitting on the porch, eating bread in companionable contentment. Everyone, that is, except Mag, who up until that point had been dozing with the chickens, horses, and cows in the barn.

When the scent of the bread reached her trunk, she ambled out from the open barn door, shaking roosting chickens from her head as she went, her trunk lifted playfully, following the trail of the scent.

"Magnolious!" the younger Sighs cried jubilantly, and they shrieked with delight when Nitty offered Mag a piece of bread and the elephant popped it into her mouth, then gave a short trumpet of satisfaction. Seeming to enjoy the attention, Mag soon settled herself into the dirt below the porch and rolled in it, spraying herself with a dirt shower that made the children laugh even more. Several of them sprang off the porch and ran to Mag, who happily lay there as they rubbed her ears and trunk.

Bernice was the only one who hung back, looking torn between longing to join in the fun and wanting to stay near Crispin in case he needed her.

"Ride her today," Nitty said. "Won't you?"

Bernice's eyes lit, but then she glanced at Crispin, doubtful.

Crispin, who'd been deep in conversation with Windle over the many culinary qualities of froozle fruit, smiled at Bernice. "Go on," he said steadily. "Have some fun for a change."

That was that. Nitty didn't wait for Bernice to hesitate, but instead pulled her from the porch toward Mag, as Bernice laughed in spite of herself. The other Sigh children looked on

224

in awe and not a little jealousy as Nitty climbed onto Mag's neck, then helped Bernice up in front of her. There was a moment when Bernice gasped as Mag rose to her feet, but after Mag settled into a steady, plodding walk, Bernice relaxed and even ventured a tentative rub of Mag's ear.

The three of them took several turns around the froozle field. At some point during the ride, Nitty noticed that Twitch had arrived with Mrs. Higgler and was helping himself to a sizable hunk of bread and reading one of his comics aloud to the other Sighs. She called out to him that his turn with Mag was next, but Mrs. Higgler put a stop to that idea instantly, on account of the fragility of Twitch's lungs. Then Mag's chickens took to missing their perch, and they squawked and fussed until Mag came to a stop in front of the coop and knelt for Bernice and Nitty to climb down.

"What did you think of the ride?" Nitty couldn't resist asking.

Bernice stood, silent for a moment, watching as the chickens flew to Mag. She shook her head. "The ride was bumpy. But . . ." Her sulky mouth gave in to a smile. "Your elephant is great."

Nitty gazed up at Mag, whose ears, head, and trunk were covered in a fluttering, fluffing headdress of chickens. Yes, Mag was most certainly great. Not great because she befriended chickens, or because she offered rides to lonely, angry girls, or even because she showed a promising fondness for decent books. She was great because she was Mag—the elephant who'd carried Nitty through a dust storm, who'd planted the seeds of the greenest crop Nitty had ever set eyes on, who'd brought her to Windle Homes.

As for Mag, she was thinking that there was nothing greater than being an elephant covered in birds, standing near the girl she loved. She pressed her trunk into her girl's palm, breathing in her green-grass scent. There was a honeyed happiness about her girl today, so different from the sadness of yesterday, and Mag felt a relief at it. She remembered how rarely she'd smelled happiness on the other animals of the circus. Mostly they'd smelled prickly with pain or sadness. Mag hadn't been able to help those animals with their suffering. But she was here, helping her girl. She blew a blast of air against her girl's hair, just to hear her bird-chirp laughter, and was about to do it again when she felt a low vibration under her feet. Her ears perked, and she listened. Her girl stilled beside her, and Mag knew she heard it, too.

It was the echoing racket of a line of automobiles and wagons on the horizon, heading toward the farm. Nitty placed her hand against Mag's side, and together they watched the procession advance.

"What's this now?" Windle asked as the unusual parade came to a stop beside the froozle field.

Crispin walked over. "Seems half of Fortune's Bluff is paying you a visit." He wrung his hands, which gave the briefest tremble, the only one they'd had all morning.

Windle's brow zigzagged with worry. "What do you pro-pose we do with your elephant?" he asked Nitty.

Nitty thought on this for a long minute. She thought on this as she watched Mag playing hide-and-seek with the Sighs, tapping them with her trunk when she found them hiding be-hind the corn crib and the plow. She thought on Mag, and the good she'd already brought Fortune's Bluff by helping to sow the seeds for the froozle-fruit crop. She thought on the fact that Miz Turngiddy, and surely Neezer, too, knew about Mag now. What would be the purpose of keeping her hidden? Maybe it was time to let Fortune's Bluff meet Mag.

Nitty went to her. "What do you think? It'll be a hullabaloo, no question. But they won't harm a hair on your head. I swear it. And if they can brave meeting you, maybe they'll learn to brave Neezer as well."

Mag swung her trunk up and down and offered a brief *Brrt!* as if to say she was of exactly the same mind and that a hullabaloo—if it was a happy one—was in tall order. Then she moved off toward the froozle field, not an ounce of uncertainty in her purposeful step.

"I propose we give Mag a proper introduction," Nitty said to Windle. "You'll be called on to converse. Quite a lot, by the looks of it."

"Jumbling Jehoshaphat," Windle mumbled reluctantly.

"Jumping." Nitty grinned as Windle harrumphed.

"There's not enough well water to brew coffee," he said. "And we don't have any food to offer."

While Nitty thought on this, her eyes fell on Mag, who at that moment was curling her trunk around one especially large froozle fruit. Mag squeezed, crushing the fruit and letting its liquid run into her mouth.

"That's it!" Nitty went to Mag and proudly patted her chin. "Mag has the simplest solution. She'll crush some fruit for us to make juice."

"Yes." Windle nodded, fortified. "Juice. We'll make do with that."

Mrs. Higgler turned toward the house. "I'll slice up some of the fruit for everyone, too," she said, stepping inside.

"And we have my bread," added Crispin.

"We should leave," Bernice said to Crispin then, her expression suddenly full of its old wariness. "I won't have them gossip over Papa," she whispered to Nitty. "And nobody will want us here."

"*I* want you here." Nitty squeezed her hand. "Stay." She nodded toward Mag, who was in the field crushing fruit as Windle collected the juice in a pitcher. "Besides, what are a few snakeskins next to a bona fide elephant?"

Bernice opened her mouth but found she couldn't argue with that. And then she lost the chance to argue altogether, because Ferdinand Klempt was leaping out from one of the automobiles, waving brilliantly fuchsia mustaches. "I've done it! I've done it! Behold the beauty!"

He ran to Twitch first, pulled what little remained of

Twitch's failing corn-silk chevron from his face, and stuck a full, lustrous pink handlebar mustache in its place. Twitch immediately hurried inside to show Mrs. Higgler while Ferdinand ran to the Sigh children next. He stuck them each with a mustache, laughing jovially as he did.

"Froozle mustaches for all!" he hollered.

Windle wagged a warning finger at Ferdinand when it was his turn, but Ferdinand was undeterred. "Windle Homes, you are a true and loyal friend who is in need of a mustache that mirrors the greatness of your spirit." He planted the mustache on Windle's upper lip and an enthusiastic smack of a kiss to each of Windle's cheeks. "Enjoy! Enjoy!"

"It does give you a daring air," Twitch said to Windle with a grin as he stepped onto the porch alongside Mrs. Higgler. He held a plate of froozle-fruit slices, which Nitty set out for the incoming guests next to the pitcher of froozle juice.

"Like a knight errant," Nitty seconded. "Though the effect would be improved by a sword and armor."

"Humph" was Windle's response to that, but it was the most half-hearted *humph* Nitty had ever heard.

It was at this moment that Mag, who'd been watching Ferdinand's mustache distribution with some interest from the shelter of the froozle field, burst from the towering green stalks and, with an excited bugle from her trunk, announced her presence to the crowd of folks just arriving.

Ferdinand turned, took a long, wide-eyed look at Mag,

then clapped his hands in delight. "Froozle fruit and elephants. Windle Homes, just how many marvels have you stowed away on this farm?"

Windle humphed again. "That's the whole of it." He paused, considered, then added, "That I know of. For now."

As Ferdinand beamed up at her, Mag wasted no time in taking the remaining mustaches from his hands and setting them all atop her head in a hairpiece of sorts.

"A magnificent coiffure for a magnificent creature!" Ferdinand cried gleefully. "Just so."

Without further ado, he hurried to his automobile for more mustaches. Meanwhile, a dozen other folks walked tremulously toward the Homes front porch, eyeing Mag and the froozle field with both cautiousness and expectation.

"Would you look at that crop!" a handful whispered. Many more whispered, "Would you look at that elephant!"

Nitty stood protectively at Mag's side, ready to defend her if anyone should so much as blink at her askance.

Mag raised her trunk, taking in the scents on the air. She lifted her ears, listening to these people's voices. Their tones were hesitant but also curious. She heard no blame in the tones, no anger. Her ears relaxed. She nuzzled her girl's neck with her trunk to let her know that all was well.

Nitty, taking the nuzzle as a vote of confidence, led Mag nearer. "If you'll offer it, she'd be pleased to snuffle your hand," she encouraged folks. "Even more pleased with a rub to her trunk. And if you've come for froozle fruit . . ." She smiled. "The field is full as full can be. Take as much as you want."

Relief passed over the faces of everyone present. There were plenty of people who greeted Mag then, and Nitty and Mag both were gratified to see their smiles and hear their laughter. Afterward, people took to the field, picking bundles of froozle fruit and filling aprons, arms, and pockets with as much as could be carried.

As folks harvested the fruit, Mrs. Higgler and Windle moved among them, offering froozle juice, while Crispin shyly followed, offering up his bread. Some initially eyed Crispin and his bread with suspicion, but then, as these few nibbled their fruit, suspicions eased into tentative friendliness. A few others persisted in refusing Crispin's bread entirely. These misguided souls, Nitty noted, were met with such vehement glares from Bernice that even they eventually offered Crispin polite, if not entirely comfortable, nods.

Folks whiled away the minutes eating fruit and talking, mostly about possibilities. Aspirations folks hadn't thought about in years burbled fresh in their minds, and a restful peace settled over the farm, as if each person there had been reassured, in some unspoken way, that all that was amiss could still be set right.

Nitty spent her time keeping close watch over Mag, making sure she was treated with the utmost respect and gentleness.

Mag felt the joy resonating in the air and heard the laughter of the children, and she, too, felt joyful. Her girl, she sensed by her scent, was happy, and the bustling, boisterous mood about the farm, though noisy, was different from the harsh chaos of the circus tent. Eventually she grew tired, and then she lay down in the midst of the froozle field and let the chatter around her fade into the background.

Everyone else, seeming to understand, left her alone there.

By then, morning had stretched lazily into afternoon, and everyone, young and old, had eaten their fill of froozle fruit and had enough to bring home to last them for days. Nitty smiled from her perch on the front porch, taking in the view. Crispin, Windle, and Ferdinand stood at the field's edge, cheerfully debating which of the froozle fruit's qualities—its pulp, its flavor, or its tassels—was the best. Mrs. Higgler sat on the porch steps with Bernice, sipping froozle juice and braiding Bernice's hair, as the other Sigh children rough-and-tumbled about their feet. Mrs. Higgler spoke to Bernice in low, soft tones, and a comfortable calm came over Bernice's face. Bernice, Nitty suspected, was warming to the notion of being mothered again, even if it was only for a little while.

Everywhere Nitty looked she saw contentment. So much so that it was on the tip of her tongue to declare the day a definitive success, until Twitch came bursting from the froozle field, goggles pulled down about his neck, panting and calling her over.

"Neezer's here," Twitch choked out as he pulled her into the field where no one else could hear. "I saw him. Just now."

Anger welled in Nitty as she remembered Neezer's behavior in town the day before. He'd already tried to turn folks against the froozle fruit. Did he have to ruin today's fun as well? "What's he doing?" Nitty asked.

"Leaving now, from the looks of it." Through a break in the froozle stalks, Twitch pointed into the distance toward the field's far edge, and Nitty could just make out the flash of Neezer's purple waistcoat as he climbed into his automobile and drove away, kicking up a cloud of dust as he went. "But he's been nosing about." Twitch frowned. "Likely masterminding sabotage."

"Sabotage!" Nitty repeated, disbelieving.

"Sabotage, to be sure." Twitch nodded soberly. Then he pulled a folded paper from his back pocket, and a mischievous glint shone in his eyes. "While Neezer was snooping around the froozle field, I did my own snooping. In his motorcar. And I found *this*."

"You stole something from his car?" Nitty was both impressed and worried by the idea.

"Borrowed. I'll sneak it back into the general store next time I'm there with Ma. I'll make it look like he dropped it. I'm always thinking one step ahead of him, outwitting him, see?" He grinned, then unfolded the paper and laid it flat on the ground. "It's a map of Fortune's Bluff, but that's not all. . . ."

He pointed to a dozen penned *X*s on the map.

Nitty took a closer look. "The *X*s are marked on buildings. The Palace Nickelodeon, the bakery, Ferdinand's emporium—"

"All buildings that were damaged by dusters," Twitch said victoriously. "More and more, it looks like those dusters were planned. Doesn't it?"

"Twitch." Before, she hadn't been sure what to make of his theory, but after yesterday it seemed possible, and the thought dampened her fine mood. What dampened it more, however, was the darkening of the horizon not more than fifteen minutes later.

"I told you so." Twitch jabbed a finger at the sky. "Sabotage."

Nitty frowned. "It *is* an unusually convenient coincidence. I'll warrant that."

Just then Windle called for them, and Nitty and Twitch met him on the porch, where he was worriedly taking in the rusty cast of the sky. "Let's help everyone get on their way before the duster hits."

Nitty didn't need to be told twice. She and Bernice were off the porch and helping folks load up babies and froozle fruit even as the wind turned from a breeze to a blow. Twitch was hurried away by Mrs. Higgler, who was pouring such copious amounts of Mr. Moop's tonic down his throat as they departed that Twitch could scarcely gurgle out a farewell.

There wasn't time for any proper goodbyes or well-wishes as folks turned their automobiles back toward Fortune's Bluff, but at least, Nitty knew, there had been time to fill bellies beforehand.

Bernice and the Sighs were the last to leave. Bernice approached Nitty with an uncommon shyness.

"That braid looks so picturesque on you, Bernice," Nitty announced.

Bernice blushed and scoffed all at once. "Won't last the day around Verna," she said as the baby yanked one of its tendrils loose. "But it's tolerable." She kissed the top of Verna's head, and Nitty saw how much she loved the baby, even as she groused about her.

Her pulse gave a sudden, expectant quiver. It struck her that, in the fading light, Bernice's hair was the blue-black of a river at night. And Bernice was tiger tough, fighting to protect the smallest Sighs, even though it was a job she might never have wished for. Nitty glanced down at her Gleam Jar, hung about her neck, and at the ribbon of robin's-egg blue curled at its bottom. She hadn't yet given up carrying the jar around, because she'd been waiting for the right moments to empty its contents. The jar's treasures had seen her through much, and they deserved new owners worthy of them. She unscrewed the lid, slipped her hand into the jar, and ever-so-gently lifted the ribbon from it.

Maybe it hadn't belonged to Nitty's *own* mother, but it could still belong to one, all the same. And wasn't that what Nitty had always wished for, besides? That the ribbon, button, and marble belong to a real, flesh-and-blood family? She held the ribbon out to Bernice.

"You could use it to tie your hair back, if you wanted. To keep it free from Verna's pulling," Nitty said softly.

Bernice looked to be on the verge of snorting, but she hesitated. "Pretty things aren't of any use to me."

Nitty laughed. "Well. How about if its use is just being yours? You wouldn't have to share it with anybody else."

Bernice's face turned eager at that. "One thing . . . that's just mine," she murmured.

Nitty nodded. "I think it suits you, too."

Bernice's eyes lingered over the ribbon for a long moment. Slowly she lifted it from Nitty's palm and tied it into her hair. A gradual smile spread over her face, and she turned to watch Crispin tickling the other children as they piled into the Tin Lizzie. "I haven't seen Papa this peaceful in ages." She grabbed Nitty in a quick hug, then jumped into the car, muttering "Thank you" before slamming the door shut.

Nitty grinned as the Sighs drove away, and kept on grinning as she took Mag to the safety of the barn, planting a kiss on her trunk as she did. She was still grinning later as, from her cot, she heard Windle tiptoe to the kitchen table. She pretended to sleep, but opened one eye a crack to see Windle seated before the photo of Clara and Lillah, a pen scratching across the paper under his hand. After all this time, Windle was writing a letter to Lillah. Which meant, Nitty suspected, that he finally had something worth sharing. Maybe something about the froozle fruit, or Mag. Maybe something about *her*. This, above all else, kept the grin on Nitty's face.

Even the duster that howled over the farm in the next hours couldn't dampen her mood. She—the contagion, the evil eye, the selfish, scrappy thing—had helped folks with her froozle fruit. She—Nitty Luce—*had* done good.

CHAPTER TWENTY-ONE

In Which Friends and Foes Come to Blows

The next morning, when Nitty sat up in her cot, she was greeted by a world smothered in dust. The windowpanes were layered in dirt so thick that the inside of the house was steeped in midnight shadows. A single shaft of light broke through one windowpane, and Nitty saw Mag's trunk on the other side of the glass, wiping at the dirt with a rag.

"Your elephant makes fine work of cleaning," Windle said.

Nitty opened the window, sending down a rain of dirt, and tickled Mag's trunk. "Good morning, girl," she whispered. Mag snuffled her palm in answer.

Nitty turned to Windle, who was busy sweeping foot-high mounds of dirt from the kitchen out the front door. Inches of fine rust-colored silt piled in every corner of the house. Beyond the open door, Nitty saw that the froozle field was still there, but the old corn crib and windmill were not.

"The well's bone-dry," Windle said softly, coming to stand beside her. "The storm yesterday blew the windmill to bits, and our water's gone."

"It'll be all right, won't it?" Nitty said. "Mag can crush more fruit for froozle juice. We'll fill pitchers with it first thing this morning. We can drink that."

"For now, but not forever. Fortune's Bluff is likely worse for the wear this morning, too."

Nitty stiffened as she imagined an even more tattered Fortune's Bluff than the one she'd seen two days before.

"At least folks have the froozle fruit now."

"Froozle fruit may stave off hunger, but it can't stop dusters." His voice was low and tired. "And there's no telling how much more Fortune's Bluff can survive."

Nitty wanted to argue but found she couldn't. Not this time. There was too much truth in his words. She'd seen it with her own eyes already. Beyond the froozle field lay a bleak landscape, brown and desolate. The world had grown drearier, and the cheery atmosphere of yesterday's froozle harvest suddenly seemed impossible to recollect.

Nitty spent most of the day working to clear the house of dust, but it seemed a bootless and never-ending task.

It was well on afternoon when she dumped the final mound of dirt into the yard, and that was when she spotted Mrs. Higgler hurrying down the lane, a kerchief pressed to her eyes. She called to Windle, who met the crying Mrs. Higgler just as she reached the porch.

"What's wrong, Rachel?" Windle asked her. "Is Angus ailing?"

"He's—he's home in bed with a fever again," Mrs. Higgler stammered, shaking her head. "But that's not why I'm here." She glanced up, her eyes red with tears. "Mayor Snollygost himself stopped by our house just now." Her voice cracked. "He's demanding total payment immediately on all loans. On store credits, too."

"What?" Windle's face paled to birch white. "But . . . there's not a person in Fortune's Bluff who can pay."

Mrs. Higgler nodded, crying softly again. "He says that anyone who can't pay will forfeit and their land will belong to Snollygost."

Windle scratched violently at the freckle behind his ear. "Why would he have a hornet in his hat over this now?"

Mrs. Higgler could only dab at her eyes with the handkerchief, shaking her head.

Windle sighed. "Come inside," he said at last. "We'll talk it over." Together, the two adults stepped into the house.

Nitty had a mind to run to Twitch's place straight off, but stopped herself, thinking that if he had a fever, it was best to leave him to his rest. Worrying over this wouldn't do his lungs a bit of good. Instead she tried to distract herself by taking up a game of hide-and-seek with Mag in the froozle field.

Mag trudged to the middle of the field as Nitty counted to

one hundred, and then waited, still as a statue, for Nitty to find her. Nitty never let on that Mag's head cresting the tops of the froozle stalks was a dead giveaway. What would've been the fun of that? Instead she made a big to-do over calling Mag's name and searching all around the barn and porch for her.

The first few attempts, the chickens found Mag well before Nitty, flapping topsy-turvy through the field to perch on Mag's back and squawk her whereabouts. But when the chickens tired of playing, Mag peeked the tip of her trunk above the field and, every few minutes, gave a clipped, tooting call, as if to hint at her hiding spot.

When it was Nitty's turn, she hardly offered any sort of contest, for when Mag gave chase, the elephant's pursuit was so loud, with pounding feet and excited trumpeting, that Nitty couldn't quit giggling.

Mag had just found Nitty hiding behind the barn door when, suddenly, she swung her head in the direction of the froozle field. Her ears lifted to attention as she listened intently, and then, after prodding Nitty with her trunk to follow, she took off resolutely for the far end of the field.

"What is it?" Nitty ran to catch up with her. But she soon heard the answer in Twitch's telling wheeze. He was crouched low among the froozle stalks, goggled and wearing an absurdly large suit jacket and fedora, along with Ferdinand's fuchsia mustache over his cheesecloth mask.

"What do you think?" He cocked his hat to one side, and it promptly slid down over his left eye. This caused his goggles and cheesecloth mask to slip, too, until his getup was in complete disarray. "Is my disguise convincing?"

"Twitch!" she hissed as he yanked her into the shelter of the stalks. "You're supposed to be sick in bed!" Without his goggles and mask on, Twitch looked sick, for certain, and Nitty was alarmed to hear his breath coming so short and fast.

Twitch, however, was impervious to her worry. "Nah. Detectives don't catch fevers. They catch outlaws." He muffled a cough in the sleeve of his jacket, then thrust a bundle into Nitty's hands. "Here. Put these on over your clothes. But take care. Ma will have your head if you tear her best Sunday dress."

Nitty held up a long blue lady's dress and a black-veiled pillbox hat. "Why am I putting these on?" she asked as she slid the dress over her clothes.

"Because . . ." Twitch glanced around, checking to make sure they weren't being overheard. "We're going undercover. When Neezer left our house, he drove straight to the old dried riverbed across the way." He nodded across the flat land that stretched from the Homes farm to Fortune's Bluff. In the middle of it, marked by the smallest outcropping of withered scrub brush, was a speck that Nitty could only assume was Neezer's motorcar. "His motorcar's trunk was full of mason jars, like the ones we saw him with at the Snollygost General Store. So full it wouldn't shut and was tied closed with twine. I saw it all from my bedroom window." He was so twitchy now that he was hopping from one foot to the other. "We have to find out what's in those jars, and then we've got to get to the Snollygost Institute."

Tiny droplets of fever sweat were forming on Twitch's forehead, and Nitty didn't like the glassiness of his eyes. Mag didn't seem to either. She was shifting from foot to foot, dabbing at his forehead with her trunk, sending small puffs of air across it. "Maybe we should wait till another day—"

"There is no other day. Ma took me to town this morning to see Doc Grant, and there wasn't a soul shopping at the Snollygost General Store. Mr. Klempt told me it's been empty two days now. Ever since we brought that truckload of fruit into town."

Nitty's heart was lifted by this news about the Snollygost General Store, but only for a fleeting moment. "So," she said, her face heating with anger, "no one is buying Snollygost's goods anymore, and he's going to make everyone pay."

"He's not either, because we're going to stop him. Today." He stood, then wobbled unsteadily for a moment before straightening. "We'll have him on the lam in no time."

Nitty looked at Mag, wishing she could give a sign of approval for the mission. Instead, Mag only warbled, soft and concerned, her trunk hovering protectively around Twitch. "I can't let him go alone," Nitty whispered to her. "You know that. And you know you can't come along. You keep watch here, all right?" Nitty pointed toward the house. "Go on."

Mag hesitated, offering a few snorts that sounded to Nitty like protests. Finally, after touching her trunk to each of their foreheads, Mag turned for the house.

The two detectives set out for the riverbed, eyes fixed on the target in the distance. "Onward," Twitch wheezed as they went, "to face the foe."

⌒ᵢ⌐

Facing the foe, as Nitty soon discovered, involved a good deal of lying facedown in the dirt. They'd walked a decent portion of the distance to the riverbed, but then Twitch had dropped to his belly, arguing they needed to shimmy the rest of the way.

"So as to remain unseen. Maintain our anonymity at all costs." Twitch explained this in halting whispers. Halting because of his wheezing, but also because when a body is facedown on the ground, it is extremely difficult to talk without ingesting mouthfuls of dirt. "Observe the skill with which I make my noiseless approach."

Nitty waited as Twitch wriggled across the ground. She observed two things: His approach was as skilled as a madcap three-legged lizard's. His approach was as noiseless as a harmonica played through a megaphone.

Nitty believed it was only because Neezer's nose was whistling "Buckin' the Wind" with as much vigor as Twitch's lungs were wheezing that they were able to go unnoticed. In fact, she heard Neezer's nose long before she saw his person. His motorcar sat at the crest of a small embankment flanked by pitiable bushes and tumbleweeds.

It wasn't until Nitty caught up to Twitch where he hunkered, behind the largest of the pitiable bushes, that she spotted Neezer down in the riverbed. Mason jars sat at his feet, and he held one in his hand. In the cradle of his other arm he held a brass contraption that Nitty recognized as looking uncannily like a euphonium.

She elbowed Twitch. "That's the Wind Whiffler! From the store's broom closet!"

Twitch nodded with an air of exasperation, as if he'd figured that out some time ago. Nitty, though irritated, decided now was not the time to say anything to him about it, as they seemed on the cusp of some significant discovery. Instead she lay down beside him, focusing her attention on Neezer.

There was an air of merriment to Neezer's demeanor as he scanned the sky, then stuck a finger in his mouth and held it up to the air, turning it this direction and that.

"Feels like a breeze today," Neezer said to himself. "Or, better yet, a blow or even a strong gust." Neezer opened the mason jar and set it on the ground, then positioned the Wind Whiffler directly over it. The Whiffler's bottom spout fit perfectly over the jar's opening.

"What is he doing?" Nitty whispered.

Twitch jabbed a finger to his lips for quiet.

Minutes passed, and Nitty's right shin took to itching something awful, but she dared not scratch it for fear the movement would incur Twitch's wrath. Then, suddenly, she felt it.

The slightest tickle of a breeze across her cheek. At the same moment, Neezer pushed the Whiffler's red button. A familiar *ssslurp!* sounded from the contraption as bits of fine dust from the air were sucked into its funneled top. When the breeze died abruptly, Neezer turned off the Whiffler and, quick as lightning, snapped a lid over the jar. He gave the jar a mighty shake, and Nitty and Twitch watched, bewildered, as the tiniest of tornadoes began spinning inside it.

"He caught it!" Twitch hissed, latching onto Nitty's arm. "He caught the wind."

Nitty could scarce believe it, and nearly said *Impossible,* but stopped herself. Who was she to think that, with the crop she'd grown? Instead she wordlessly followed Twitch, heart hammering, as he shimmied to Neezer's motorcar.

Together they rose to their knees to peek inside the open trunk. More mason jars sat in the trunk, all full of dusty air moving about in a mishmash of speeds and patterns. Each jar had a label scrawled on its lid.

DRAFT was a white haze drifting lazily around its jar. PUFF was a minuscule cloud that waxed and waned. There was a ZEPHYR, which spun (rather prettily, Nitty thought) about its jar. There was a GALE, a MISTRAL, and even a CHINOOK.

Nitty was so entranced by the vacillating brown, ocher, and white winds in the jars that she didn't notice Twitch unscrewing the lid on a jar marked BLAST until it was too late. A violent surge of air shot from the jar with a deafening howl, hitting

Twitch square in the face with such force that his cheeks ballooned outward like a chipmunk's.

Nitty might've doubled over laughing if not for Neezer's bellow from the riverbed.

By the time he shouted "Who goes there?" Nitty had grabbed Twitch's hand and they were running for the Homes farm, a discouragingly small speck in the distance.

"He'll never recognize us," Twitch puffed confidently.

Nitty was worried much less about that than she was about Twitch making it all the way back to the farm at all. He was panting already and they were only yards from the riverbed. The growl of a motorcar behind them made Nitty triple her pace, pulling Twitch along as best she could. But he was flagging, and soon Neezer would overtake them.

She expected Neezer's mighty voice to barrel over her at any second. Or for his hand to grab both of them by the collars and toss them into his motorcar, never to be seen or heard from again. What she did not expect was to see Bernice behind the wheel of Crispin's Tin Lizzie, screeching to a haphazard stop beside them.

"What a rip-roaring getaway car!" Twitch exclaimed dazedly between heaving breaths.

"Get in already," Bernice muttered.

In a fit of detectiving melodrama, Twitch dove headfirst through the open window while Nitty scrambled for the door. With a spin of tires, a spray of dust, and great force applied to the two loaves of bread strapped to her feet, Bernice blazed away.

It was only after a solid piece of driving that Nitty dared a glance back at the riverbed. Neezer, his motorcar, and his jars of wind were speeding furiously toward Fortune's Bluff, where, Nitty had a dreaded hunch, the day of reckoning was at hand.

CHAPTER TWENTY-TWO

IN WHICH A NINCOMPOOP RECKONS AND IS RECKONED

"He nearly had us in his clutches! Did you see?" Twitch bounced on the seat of the Tin Lizzie with such exuberance, Nitty lifted off her seat, too. "But our retreat was swift, and the archnemesis foiled."

Bernice jerked the motorcar to a stop at the edge of the froozle field. "What I saw was you two about to be in a mammoth pickle." She snorted as she took in their clothes. "What sort of getups are you wearing, anyway?"

Twitch sniffed. "They were imperative to our covert operations."

Bernice raised a skeptical eyebrow. "Seemed like their imperative was to give you two left feet. What if I hadn't been there?"

"You saved our hides, no doubt about it." Nitty grinned at

her in thanks. "But what were you doing out there in the first place?"

"What do you think?" Bernice shook her head as if the answer were obvious already. "I was spying on Neezer, same as you. I've been tracking his movements about Fortune's Bluff, and let me tell you, he's in a state. Most folks lost their windmills in the last storms, but I could've sworn I saw him unloading a whole truckful of windmill blades at the institute."

"He's working on his Whirlybog," Nitty said.

"He's up to something. So today, when I saw him leave town, I followed in the motorcar. Only Verna lost her rattle again, so I was late leaving. Plus I had to sneak past Pa. Now that he's feeling better, he's laid down the law about my driving." She sighed.

Nitty sighed, too. Even just now she'd been admiring the authoritative way Bernice's hands rested on the steering wheel, hoping she might get a feel of the wheel herself. Oh, she'd wager she could put some speed into that gas pedal. "That is lamentable hard luck."

"I know it," Bernice responded gloomily. "Anyhow, by the time I got out of Fortune's Bluff, it was only to see you two running pell-mell from Neezer, and I guessed you might need a mode of escape."

"That's a fine use of deductive reasoning," Twitch said with an officiousness that had Nitty and Bernice *both* snorting.

Just then, Windle's voice rose up, calling Nitty inside and startling them all. Nitty scrambled out of her disguise and tossed it to Twitch, then opened the car door. "We'd all better hightail it home before they catch on to our delinquency."

"It's not delinquency. We're in pursuit of wrongdoers." Twitch climbed out, too, already turning in the direction of his house. He faltered, paling, and gripped the door for support. Nitty leaned toward him, worry hammering her chest, but he waved her off. "We have to corner Neezer. Apprehend him. At the stroke of midnight."

"Twitch," Nitty started, "you're not—"

"I'm fine. Keep alert, and await my signal." With that he took off, half staggering, half running toward home.

A second later, Bernice was squealing away in the Tin Lizzie, and Nitty was staring after them both, wondering what sort of scrape they were in for. She soon found out when she climbed the porch steps to find Windle waiting, his eyes dark with foreboding. Mag was quick to leave her antics at the chicken coop to join them, first emitting a joyous tootle at the sight of Nitty, but following it with an anxious whiffle as Windle began to speak.

"Do my eyes deceive me?" His voice was so grave, Nitty shivered to hear it. "Did I, or did I not, just see Bernice Sigh operating a motorcar?"

Nitty dropped her eyes, knowing there was no point lying. "You did."

"And did I, or did I not, also see an infirm Angus Higgler *running* for home?"

"You saw that, too." Nitty sighed, then added in a rush, "We only wanted to see what Mayor Snollygost was up to."

"That is *not* our affair."

Nitty glared at him. "It's everybody's affair."

Windle threw up his hands, stomping across the porch. "What do you propose I do with such bald-faced disobedience? Have you no care for that boy's lungs, or his mother's peace of mind?"

"Course I do!" Nitty blurted it loudly and angrily enough that Mag raised her ears and flapped them in concern. How dare Windle suggest she didn't care? Why, practically all she *did* was care! "That's why we're trying to stop Mayor Snollygost, before he takes everyone's land—"

Windle's hand pressed Nitty's shoulder, cutting her words short. "You'll do no such thing."

Nitty stared at him, wondering at the fact he didn't seem angrier about Neezer when he should've been absolutely inflamed. "We have to stop him! He's robbing folks of their land—"

"It's not robbing." Windle's voice was bone-tired. "Folks agreed to the loans. They signed the papers."

"They never had a choice." Nitty was looking to Mag now, wishing, as impossible as it was, that the elephant could argue her side. Mag only shifted worriedly from one foot to the other, snuffling Nitty's hair. "They had to feed their families and have a roof over their heads. And Neezer . . . he's cheating them. I know he is. Twitch does, too! We just need proof."

Windle looked at her. It was the look an adult gives a child when he thinks the child is fabricating stories. It was a look Nitty had received countless times from Miz Ricketts, but never from Windle. It was a look that made Nitty's very blood turn to fire.

"You don't believe me!" She locked eyes with Windle, wanting him to say something—*do* something—to prove her wrong. He only stood there, motionless.

Nitty directed the full force of a glare at Windle. "How can you let this happen?"

In the distance, a low rumble sounded, and Mag moved protectively to Nitty's side. *Another duster coming,* Nitty thought, scanning the darkening sky. That made two in less than twenty-four hours. The storms were getting closer together and more frequent. She caught the deepening concern on Windle's face and wondered if he was thinking the same thought.

Then his concern shifted into irritation. "There's nothing we can do."

"There is! But you're too afraid!" she yelled. "Too afraid of everything to do anything at all, you . . . you insufferable nincompoop!"

It wasn't exactly the biting insult she'd wanted to use, but she could see from the stricken look on Windle's face that she'd said it with an effective amount of wrath.

He turned toward the door, shoulders sagging.

"I'm tired of do-nothings all around," Nitty shouted after him. She whirled on her heel and, with Mag following, marched straight to the barn. She slammed the barn door shut with a clang that startled the horses and cows from their napping, then pressed herself against it. As an hour, and then another and another passed, she waited for Windle to come.

He didn't.

Even as the wind moaned fearfully, she risked a peek outside to see that night had fallen.

"Let him stew in his do-nothing juices!" Nitty hollered, kicking a pile of hay. "Suits me."

Mag huffed and tossed a pile of hay with her trunk, too.

Together they walked the length of the barn and back, throwing hay, hollering and trumpeting as they went, until Nitty's hair was tangled with yellow stalks. Nitty sank to the floor in a pile of dishevelment and dismay. Mag, in an effort to be helpful, loosened the hay from her hair and ate it.

Nitty threw up her hands. "How can you possibly eat while I'm in an abyss of despair?"

Mag swallowed and, with a flick of her trunk, dumped an entire mound of hay over Nitty's head.

"Hey! What'd you do that for?" Nitty's anger flared fresh, then fizzled as Mag set her trunk atop the crown of her head. Nitty could've sworn she saw a playful glint in Mag's eyes, and knew she meant well. But she couldn't bring herself to laugh. Not tonight.

Mag, who had been waiting, ears perked, for the bubbling sound of her girl's laughter, did not give up when the laughter didn't come. Instead she curled her trunk into an inviting hammock and waited. This, she noticed, made her girl's stomping feet quiet, the heat coming off her skin cool. Soon her girl curled into the hammock's curve, her small hands holding on tight.

Mag swayed her trunk, back and forth, back and forth, crooning a low rumble. She sighed. She had a memory of another of her own kind crooning this same rumbling song to her, long ago. Before she'd known her trainer, or any other human. It had made her feel warm and safe. This she could give to her girl now.

Nitty pressed her ear against Mag's trunk, listening. The elephant's susurrant rumbling had the soothing, drawn-out tones of a lullaby. It spoke to Nitty's heart and to all the disappointment she felt in that moment. Surely Mag was telling her she understood, that she'd always understand.

Soon the wind was screeching through the slats in the barn and dust was spilling through cracks and crevices. Nitty nestled against Mag, listening to that strange, gently thunderous lullaby and seeking the comfort of Mag's warmth. Only tonight, she had too many troubling thoughts for lasting comfort.

CHAPTER TWENTY-THREE

In Which a Sigh Is a Hopeful Sign

In the darkness of the barn, Nitty waited for midnight. When the duster's shrieking quieted, there came a certain suspense to the stillness. Then she heard a series of convoluted raps on the barn door, followed by a most uncanny "ca-caw, ca-caw," and a wheeze.

"Twitch." Nitty stood with relief as he peered around the door. "You sound like a tap-dancing, accordion-playing parrot."

"The sign's meant to confuddle. So only you and Bernice recognize it." His voice sounded small and pinched in the darkness. "I saw your cot in the kitchen was empty and figured you'd be out here with Mag." Before he could say anything else, he coughed.

Nitty stiffened at the sound. It was a horrible, drowning choke. "You're too sick," she whispered. "You shouldn't be here."

Emitting three short blats from her trunk, Mag began stroking Twitch's back. The cough took a full minute to end.

"Haven't sprouted any corn yet, so I imagine I'll get by." Twitch rasped. "The time for action is now."

A shaft of dust-mottled moonlight caught his face, and Nitty nearly gasped. His nut-brown skin was chalky, his forehead shining with a film of sweat. The hand holding his Morton Salt periscope trembled, even though the duster had left the air tepid. All in all, he looked even worse than he sounded. Nitty wished he would sit down to rest, but the sober determination in his eyes warned her not to even suggest such a thing. He'd likely march straight out the door in a rage.

Instead she asked, "What's the plan?"

Even as his teeth chattered, Twitch grinned. "We find a way into the Snollygost Institute. We witness firsthand Neezer's evildoings." He reached under his shirt and pulled a large burlap sack from it. "Then trap Neezer."

"In . . . a potato sack?" Nitty tried hard not to let her tone betray her reservations (and at the moment, her reservations were many).

"I know. It's a sorry substitute for handcuffs, but it'll have to do. And . . ." He pulled something from his back pocket. "I brought this, too. It's Ma's."

"A hairpin?"

"For picking locks, of course!" Twitch cried, incredulous. "It's in practically every issue of *Detective Comics*."

"But how can we stop Neezer from collecting payments on loans?"

"We find proof of his villainy," Twitch answered. "We need to get up close to this Whirlybog, find out how it works and what it really does. We can search the institute for hard evidence of Neezer's deceit. That'll be enough to get folks to stand up to him."

Nitty hesitated. "I don't like Neezer any more than you do. But . . . what if we don't find any proof?"

Twitch stared at her, anger flickering across his features. "What if your seeds never grew?" he countered. "You had a hunch about those seeds, just like I have a hunch about this. I never doubted *you*."

Nitty considered this, and her heart floundered. He was right, of course. He'd been there, beside her, those first few days of planting when Windle groused about the impossibility of her crop. He'd been beside her nearly every day, helping her and believing. No matter how ill he looked, or how worried she was for him, she had to see this through with him. "You're right." She locked her eyes on his. "Let's go."

They stepped toward the door but discovered that Mag had barricaded herself against it.

"Mag, you can't come with us." She tried to nuzzle Mag's trunk with her forehead, but Mag would have none of it. Her dark eyes were reproachful. *Don't go,* they seemed to plead, and this made Nitty's insides lurch.

What if this was Mag's way of warning her that, if they went, calamity would strike? But no . . . Twitch needed Nitty tonight.

"Mag. Please," she whispered. "For Twitch."

At last Mag moved from the door, her ears down, her trunk drooping, issuing a series of agitated blats. Then Nitty slipped around the door with Twitch, unable to glance at Mag for fear of seeing the elephant's distraught eyes staring back. Leaving Mag this way felt disloyal, but she had to see this through, no matter what.

༺ঌ༻

The walk into Fortune's Bluff was painstakingly long. Twitch's staunch resolve was no match for his flagging lungs, and they could only walk in short intervals, stopping for Twitch to rest in between.

The moon shone dimly through the hazy brown clouds, and Fortune's Bluff itself lay in almost total darkness, making it difficult for them to find their way toward Main Street. Not for the first time, Nitty reflected with regret that Mag might've carried them to the institute in a quarter of the time. But it was too late for that now, she told herself, and better that Mag stayed safe.

When they were halfway down Main Street, Twitch doubled

over in a coughing fit so loud that it brought a shadowy figure running toward them.

Nitty's pulse drummed. "We're caught, Twitch." She wrapped an arm protectively around his shoulders. "Doomed."

There was no chance of running for it. The figure was moving too quickly, and Twitch was still hunched over, trying to catch his breath. Nitty braced herself and set her jaw, vowing that she'd stand her ground, an immovable force against tyranny.

"For cripes' sake, Twitch," the figure hissed, "some sign *this* is. You're liable to wake the dead with that coughing."

Nitty nearly whooped with relief as Bernice thrust a bottle of Mr. Moop's Cough Tonic toward Twitch.

"Take a swallow and hush already," Bernice ordered. As Twitch did as instructed, she glared at both of them. "What took you two so long getting here? The whole town's in a dither. Everybody's weeping. Folks are giving up." She wrinkled her nose. "And if Neezer has his way—"

"He won't," Twitch eked out, then swigged more cough tonic.

Nitty noticed a rolling pin protruding from Bernice's back pocket. "What's that for?"

Bernice slid it from her pocket and raised it like a baseball bat. "Defense."

Nitty grinned. "Resourceful. Wieldy, too. I like it."

Bernice stood a little taller at that. "Let's get this mission underway."

Another coughing fit shook Twitch, and Nitty had to help him keep standing. She and Bernice exchanged a glance.

"What will we do if he keeps on this way?" Bernice whispered over Twitch's stooped frame. "We can't carry him home."

"We can," Nitty answered firmly. She'd carry Twitch clear across the state if she had to. "But it won't come to that. Not if we hurry." She turned toward the looming shadow of the Snollygost Institute. Then, remembering one of her favorite lines from the *Daily Tattler*'s *The Countess and the Convict*— a line that, she felt, might instill anyone with greater bravery— she added, "'And onward they strode, not knowing the perils that lay ahead but believing that their unity could conquer all.'"

CHAPTER TWENTY-FOUR

IN WHICH FOULSOME ROTTEN VILLAINY IS AT LONG LAST REVEALED

A few minutes and a lot of coughing later, they stood before the imposing and dauntingly high iron-spiked fence surrounding the Snollygost Institute.

"How do you suppose we'll manage to climb that?" Nitty wondered aloud with floundering confidence.

"Why in blazes would you want to risk a limb climbing that?" Bernice scoffed. "Follow me." Bernice didn't wait to see if they were following but searched the length of the fence until she reached a spot where the iron bars had been warped into an opening big enough to slip through. Her teeth shone in a rare smile as she gestured toward the opening. "Pa mentioned this once in his ramblings. I suppose it's how he snuck into the institute himself."

"Fine work," Twitch said with an air of superiority, as if he were Holmes complimenting Watson, but his wheeze diminished the effect. Which was just as well.

The three of them crept low to the ground as they climbed the small knoll leading to the institute. The building sat in darkness, save for a faint glow from two small windows set high in its outer wall. It was, however, whumping its incessant *WHUMP,* loud as ever, and with what seemed like greater urgency and frequency. As they drew closer, Nitty saw several trucks parked beside the building.

"More of the trucks," Twitch said. "The ones that are always coming and going."

Nitty could barely make them out until the haze over the moon lifted for a moment. Dust clung thickly to the trucks, covering them all in a uniform brown, except for a strange, indecipherable red symbol on their sides, barely visible under the dirt.

"Hey." Nitty nudged Twitch. "There's some sort of symbol on those trucks. I'm going to get closer." Before Twitch could say a word (which, in his current state of breathlessness, was unlikely anyway), Nitty dropped to her stomach and shimmied.

She reached the first in the line of trucks, and, standing on tiptoe, brushed the inches-thick dust from its side. The symbol emerged, and Nitty gasped. It was a familiar bright red cross.

She shimmied her way back to Twitch and Bernice. "They're Red Cross trucks! Only . . . why are they here?"

Twitch shrugged. "Bet we'll find out when we get inside."

He nodded toward Bernice, who was eyeing one of the institute's windows.

"It looks to be open," she said. "Just a crack."

Nitty moved along the wall until she stood under the window. It was much too high for her to reach on her own, but then she spied the ivy—nearly dried out to the point of death—clinging to the wall beneath the window. She gave it an experimental tug and, when it held, pulled on it with the full force of her body. It seemed sturdy enough.

"This way," she whispered to Twitch and Bernice. She began to climb.

Once she reached the window's ledge, she was able to pry the window open just enough to squeeze through. It might've been a much greater drop to the floor inside had her fall not been broken by the sacks of flour piled beneath the window. Her landing sent a cloud of flour puffing into the air, but otherwise her arrival inside the institute was mostly silent. Even if she had made a sound, it wouldn't have been heard over the whumping, which was coming at regular intervals from somewhere nearby. Twitch and Bernice entered just as stealthily, although Twitch seemed to be holding his breath in an effort not to cough.

Twitch slid his goggles up onto his forehead while Nitty scanned the room from atop their flour pile, making sure they'd gone undetected. As she took in her surroundings, her mouth fell open.

"Would you look at all of this food!" she whispered. Canned

goods, sacks of flour, fresh melons, eggplant, corn—food by the ton was stacked from the floor to the ceiling. "There's enough here to feed an army!"

Bernice frowned. "This must be where Neezer keeps food before he takes it to the Snollygost General Store."

There was a sound, then, of voices approaching, and Twitch's wheezing quickened beside Nitty. Nitty scooted backward to take cover behind one of the larger sacks of flour, and Twitch and Bernice did the same. From the hiding place, if Nitty strained, she could just make out the voices above the whumping.

"There will be another truckload of donations delivered sometime next week," one voice was saying. "We want to make sure no one goes hungry."

"Speaking for all of Fortune's Bluff," came Neezer's familiar, nasal voice, "you and the Red Cross have our eternal gratitude."

As Neezer said his goodbyes to the deliverymen, Twitch gripped Nitty's arm.

"Those trucks," he whispered in Nitty's ear. His eyes looked wild, either with fever or excitement—Nitty couldn't tell which. "They're coming with donations!"

Bernice's eyes widened in understanding. "That's what Papa was trying to tell us with his rhyme. Remember? 'Cans of sauce, from the Cross . . .'"

"'Hide them all, says the boss,'" Twitch finished. "Neezer hides the donations here and then sells them at the store!"

"Papa wasn't talking nonsense at all." Bernice's voice was

more hopeful than Nitty had ever heard it before. "He was trying to tell everyone . . ."

"Only no one would listen," Nitty finished quietly. Her chest was a furnace of anger. "Of all the pernicious, deceitful escapades—"

"Shhhh!" Bernice hissed as Neezer—or rather the whistling of Neezer's nose—drew closer. His footsteps, and his whistling, breezed past them, and it was only then that Nitty dared peek around the sack of flour. She saw Neezer unlock a door not far from their hiding place. The door only opened a sliver, but as it did, the sound of whumping intensified. Neezer slipped through the door and shut it firmly behind him.

Nitty waited a moment, and when she was sure they were alone in the storage room, she ventured a whisper. "The Whirlybog. It's got to be in that room."

Instantly Bernice stood and began picking her way carefully down the mountain of flour, her rolling pin in her hand, ready for battle.

Twitch still lay atop the sacks, heaving tired breaths, his face pricked with sweat. "On . . . my . . . way . . . ," he sputtered.

Nitty frowned when she saw that he'd grown even paler since they'd left Windle's barn. She hurried to Bernice. "Twitch . . . he's getting worse. We should take him home."

"Not yet." Bernice looked back at Nitty and Twitch with dogged determination. "Papa knew about the Red Cross. He was right. He knew about the Whirlybog before anyone else, too. And I'm not leaving here until I find out what it does. For Papa's sake."

"Bernice, wait." Nitty started after her, and saw that Twitch was struggling to get to his feet to do the same.

"I'm fine." Twitch gave Nitty a warning look. "Bernice is right. We came here to get hard evidence, and we can't leave without it. Otherwise no one will ever believe us."

Nitty hesitated as she watched Twitch moving unsteadily down the flour mound. *This is wrong,* she thought. But if Twitch kept going, the only thing she could do was stay with him.

Reluctantly, she followed him and Bernice as they snuck through the storage room, staying hidden behind the piles of food as much as they could. Nitty's heart hammered as they drew closer to the whumping.

The three of them got down on their knees and crawled the last few feet to the door.

Twitch handed Nitty the burlap sack, then slid the hairpin from his pocket. "Ready the instrument of capture," he said to Nitty, solemnly.

Nitty raised the burlap sack. Beside her, Bernice raised the rolling pin—prepared, Nitty guessed, to give Neezer a thorough pummeling.

With temporarily renewed energy and a true stealth Nitty found masterly, Twitch slid the hairpin into the door's lock. His eyes, though glazed, gleamed with exhilaration when he touched the doorknob and it turned under his grasp.

Silently, he pushed the door open a crack and lifted his periscope to his face. Together they peeked inside.

The Whirlybog was the oddest-looking machine Nitty had ever set eyes on—a massive structure of wood and metal covered in the blades of windmills. It was a large-scale replica of the sketch they'd discovered in Neezer's invention notebook. But the machine before them struck Nitty as much more ominous in reality than on paper.

"Look there." Bernice pointed toward the Whirlybog's control panel. There, at its center, was the very Dustometer dial Crispin had baked into his bread loaves. Each point on the dial had a name, and Nitty's pulse raced as she read them: Chokeberry Silt, Oily Loam, Bison Sward, Toeter Grime.

"Duster names," Twitch confirmed. "But what do they mean? And what is *that*?" He pointed to a drafting table, where a model full of miniature houses and taller buildings sat. His eyes narrowed. "Wait . . . that reminds me of the map I found in Neezer's car. It's . . . it's a model of Fortune's Bluff! But some buildings are missing—"

He swallowed the rest of his words as Neezer suddenly came into view, walking toward the giant clear holding tank at the center of the Whirlybog. He held three mason jars in his arms. He climbed a small stepladder, set the jars on the ladder's top step, and opened the Whirlybog's holding tank.

"A half a jar of Blast, I think," he mumbled as he opened one of the jars and poured a portion of its churning contents into the holding tank. "A third of a jar of Gale, and a full jar of Cyclone."

Down from the ladder, he turned the Dustometer on the Whirlybog to the Toeter Grime setting. Then he raised a large red lever to the side of the control dial, and as he did, the blades of the Whirlybog spun faster.

"More power." Neezer smiled triumphantly. "More wind. And we'll have the biggest duster yet!"

Nitty's eyes became saucers, and she glanced at Bernice and Twitch, who were both looking on with a mixture of anger and astonishment. "The Whirlybog's not ridding the town of dusters," she whispered. "It's causing them!" She'd seen enough— enough to tell Windle and everyone else in Fortune's Bluff what Neezer was doing. Now they could leave before they were discovered. "Let's go!"

Proof! Bernice mouthed then, pointing to one of the mason jars still sitting on Neezer's stepladder.

"Bernice. No!" But before Nitty could stop her, Bernice inched through the door, heading for the jar.

Nitty held her breath, not daring to move, as she watched Bernice's painstaking progress across the floor. Neezer's back was still safely turned to them, and Bernice's fingers were within inches of the jar when it happened.

Twitch covered his mouth with his hand.

Nitty braced herself against him, hoping she could muffle what she knew was coming. Twitch's cheeks ballooned with the effort of trying not to cough, but still, the smallest gurgle rose from his throat.

All three of them froze, because the gurgle had come in between *WHUMP*s, and, though small, it had been distinct. Nitty held her breath as she watched Neezer stiffen. She waited for him to turn around, but he didn't. Instead he reached for the red lever. The windmill blades spun furiously, and the whumping grew louder and faster. Much faster.

Then Nitty heard it. A sound much worse than the Whirlybog's ominous whumping. It was the sound of whistling—a high-pitched, nasal whistling. But it was the tune being whistled that struck fear in Nitty's heart: a tune Twitch had once warned her must never be heard from the likes of the villainous mayor. Or else.

What Nitty heard was the sound of Neezer's nose whistling Beethoven's Fifth.

༼ᚺ༽

Nitty sprang to her feet as Twitch hollered to Bernice, "Run!"

Bernice, however, did not run. She lifted her rolling pin and brought it down with a conquering *crack!* against the Whirlybog's holding tank. Nitty waited for a splinter, a shatter, anything. Bernice, eyes expectant and vengeful, waited, too. But the holding tank did what it was built to do. The holding tank *held*.

With the surprise and disappointment of her failure scored

on her face, Bernice snatched up Neezer's Cyclone jar and was through the door in seconds.

Nitty wanted to follow but was momentarily mesmerized by the sight of Neezer turning toward them, an impossibly congenial smile spreading across his lips.

She did the only thing she could think to do. She grabbed the burlap sack and launched it, with all the might she could muster, directly at Neezer's head. Then she too ran. She pulled Twitch, who had begun coughing as soon as he'd hollered his command and now couldn't seem to stop, along with her.

The Whirlybog's whumping had grown to a deafening bellow, and through the walls of the institute Nitty could hear the telltale whine of a duster brewing.

"He's making a duster!" Bernice cried. "With the Whirlybog."

Strange, thought Nitty, that Neezer wasn't yelling after them, or pursuing them at all. But that smile of his . . . Nitty shuddered. His smile could only mean one thing: he *would* get them, one way or another. She knew now that the beginning of Beethoven's Fifth had been the portent of an indomitable *end*.

They reached the bottom of the mound of flour, but Twitch was panting and weak. He'd never be able to climb up the sacks to the window.

Nitty's eyes flew about the room, looking for another exit, and they at last spotted a large door along the north wall. She could only hope it led to the outside.

"There!" she called to Bernice over the whumping, and

propping Twitch up between the two of them, they half stumbled, half ran toward it.

Nitty didn't look behind her as she ran. She couldn't hear footsteps. She couldn't hear anything over the Whirlybog. Every second that passed, she expected to feel Neezer's pawlike hand clamping down on her shoulder.

But then she was flinging the door open and barreling into the darkness of night with Twitch and Bernice beside her.

Safe was her first relieved thought. Her second was *Duster.*

A duster, already fierce in its violent winds and blinding dirt, was whirling around them. She tried to run into the wind, but it overpowered her, knocking her to the ground, wrenching her arms from Bernice and Twitch. Neezer hadn't let them go, Nitty realized. He'd sent the storm to catch them.

"Twitch!" She reached out in the darkness. Her words disappeared into the wind the moment she spoke them. "Bernice!"

She glimpsed Bernice for only a second, just long enough to watch Neezer's Cyclone jar get wrenched from her hands in the wind and fall to the ground, shattering. Her heart sank. Their proof was gone. Then a thick cloud engulfed Bernice, and Nitty lost sight of her.

She pulled the collar of her shirt up over her mouth and nose and shielded her eyes against the stinging grit. There—barely visible—was a shadowy form.

The dust swirled faster, flying into her nose and eyes, even through her shirt's fabric. She squinted, barely able to make out Twitch where he stood a few feet away.

271

"Bernice!" Nitty called. "Help!"

Bernice had disappeared completely into the darkness. And Twitch . . . Twitch couldn't stop coughing. He was hunched over, clutching his sides.

"I'm . . . not . . . breathing so good," he wheezed. He coughed again, and his bright blue periscope slipped out of his hand. It rolled the second it hit the ground, the wind making it spin and skitter in the dirt. A ferocious gust tore the periscope from the ground and into the air. Before Nitty could cry out, it was gone. Twitch, too, was gone, his form vanishing behind a black wall of dust.

"Nitty!" Twitch's voice was the tiniest mouse in the lion's roar of the storm.

"I'm here!" Nitty pushed the words from her open mouth, but as soon as she did, clots of dirt and dust choked her throat. She leaned into the wind, pulling her feet forward, step by step, reaching her outstretched hands toward the sound of Twitch's voice.

"Nitty." The mouse was tinier, weaker.

Bernice, Nitty was certain, would be fine. Wherever she was in the storm now, Bernice would find shelter, or some way to stay safe. But Twitch, with his fever and his cough . . .

Please, Nitty thought. *Please let me reach him.*

There was a crushing weight in Nitty's chest, as if a boulder were sitting atop it, and she fell to her knees, struggling to breathe. She began crawling. But which way to go?

She could hear no sound from Twitch. The only sound was the screaming wind. She tried, once more, to call out, but her voice failed her. She closed her eyes and reached out her arms, sweeping the piling dust through her fingers. She couldn't reach Twitch. She wouldn't find him.

She gathered all the thoughts in her head and stretched them toward the Homes farm, toward Windle. And even more toward Mag.

Mag! she thought then. *Mag, come to me. Help me.*

If there was ever a time for Mag to be magnolious, it was now.

⌒ᡭ⌒

Through the miles of dust and wind, through the vastness of the wide, blowing world, Mag heard her girl call out to her.

She raised her head.

She lifted her ears.

Her pumpkin heart tolled a clanging alarm.

Her girl was in danger.

She lowered her head like a battering ram, and she ran.

⌒ᡭ⌒

Nitty's breath was coming in shallow gasps. The dust was building a blanket, a heavy blanket smothering her. . . .

But then the blanket was yanked away by a sweeping trunk. A trunk that gave the briefest stroke to Nitty's cheek. A stroke that said, *I am here. I am here. I am here.*

Mag.

Nitty raised her head and, from the corner of her eye, saw the blur of a wooden plank tearing through the air. Then— *whack!*—it landed a jarring blow to her skull. The world spun with stars, but she fought to right it. Through the murky curtain of dust appeared the outline of the elephant, and a small, curled mound between Mag's legs.

The storm subsided just enough for Nitty to make out Mag's trunk lifting Twitch into the air, raising him up until he was umbrellaed under her enormous left ear.

Nitty sighed. Safe. Twitch was safe with Mag.

Now, at last, Nitty could sleep.

She closed her eyes.

But before she gave in to the warmth of her dust blanket, she heard a distant, nasal voice booming, "Beast! Murderous beast!"

CHAPTER TWENTY-FIVE

In Which Matters Are Complicated by Mayors and Missing Elephants

When Nitty next opened her eyes, she found herself under a willow tree. The willow was weeping, silently but stormily.

"Don't cry, Windle," Nitty whispered hoarsely. For it was Windle whose head was bent low over Nitty in grief. He was seated in Clara's rocker by her side. Nitty put out a shaky hand to touch the top of his uncombed hair. "Don't cry."

This only made Windle cry harder. "You're all right, then! All right." He brushed at his eyes to no avail. "You've been sleeping near on a full day now. Blast it if you didn't give this crotchety ticker a fright."

"But, Windle." Nitty's own eyes blurred. "You're crying for me."

Windle's paintbrush eyebrows knit together. He straightened

from a willow into a birch. "A momentary lapse of willpower, and I'll thank you not to make a fuss about it."

Nitty smiled at him, relieved to see that his crying had done nothing to diminish his terseness. She'd grown to like it (most of the time). Slowly she lifted her head to take in her surroundings. Why, she was back in the Homes kitchen in her cot! And—hoo-wee!—did she have a headache. Her throat was raw with grittiness, too, and she gratefully accepted the cup of froozle juice that Windle offered.

As she sipped it, she cautiously touched her forehead and discovered a sizable goose egg.

She raised her eyebrows, questioning, and Windle nodded. "You hit your head. Before we found you and Twitch. Probably hit it on some flying debris. The storm was a real whopper." He frowned.

Nitty's thoughts, which up until now had been fuddled and musty, turned suddenly sharp.

"The storm." She sat up in alarm. "Twitch and Mag! Bernice!"

Windle laid an arm across her shoulders, gently but firmly lowering her back onto the cot. "They're out of harm's way. Bernice ran all the way here in the storm to get help. She tried to drive—confound her—but Crispin's car was full up with dust. She got a lungful herself, and could hardly speak by the time she blew in the door, but she's safe with Crispin now. All I understood was that you and Twitch were caught in the storm outside the institute. I ran for my truck, but its engine was dust-plugged. By the time the truck finally started, Mag was already gone." He shook his head. "She broke down the barn door to get to you faster."

Nitty's relief lasted only until she noticed that Windle was skirting her gaze. Nitty glanced out the kitchen window, searching. The emerald green and fuchsia of the froozle field—still standing, if bowed—were marred by grimy layers of inches-thick dust. Nitty guessed it was getting on dusk. Still, it was hard to tell with the brown pea-souper hovering as a leftover from last night's duster. The porch, though shadowy, was clearly empty. If Twitch and Mag were all right, then Mag would be there at the window, looking in on her. Twitch would be here, too, likely reading her one of his *Detective Comics.*

Her limbs jellified.

"What happened?" Her voice was small. "Where are they? Twitch and Mag?" Windle stared at his toes, until Nitty grabbed the pillow from underneath her head, bursting out with "I swear I'll wallop you with this if you don't tell me right now!"

At that Windle's eyes widened, a near smile pulling at the corners of his mouth. Then he did something that surprised both of them. He took her hand. Not just for a second. No. He took her hand and held on tight.

"Oh, Nitty girl, you walloped me good and hard already, the very first day you showed up here on this farm. Me, Twitch . . . the whole of Fortune's Bluff." He shook his head. "Now we're all in a bind." He heaved a breath. "Twitch is ailing, but Mrs. Higgler's tending to him. She's fixed him some froozle soup, if you can believe that."

"His muddy lungs?" Nitty asked, and Windle nodded. She swallowed, remembering. "When we got caught out in the duster, Twitch couldn't breathe. He couldn't breathe at all."

Windle stared at the floor. "Nitty, he's got dust pneumonia."

Nitty's heart was a mallet, striking her ribs fast and fierce. "Well, he needs more cough tonic, that's all. And more froozle fruit. Rest, too, and then he'll be fine." She made her voice say the words, as a way of convincing her mind of their truth.

"Doc Grant has seen him already, but there's nothing much to be done for Angus. I'm afraid your froozle fruit won't cure him. His illness is too far gone for that. The fact is, his lungs can't bear any more dusters."

Silence fell between them. Nitty's eyes filled.

Poor Twitch. Poor, brave Twitch. Here he'd finally uncovered proof of Neezer Snollygost's villainy, only to have his muddy lungs betray him.

Nitty swung her legs over the side of the bed. "First I'll see Mag in the barn. And then I need to talk to Twitch. Right away. We discovered something at the institute. Something so shuddersome you'll scarce believe it."

Windle frowned. "I *thought* Bernice kept saying Neezer's name, but I couldn't understand much else through her coughing fits. What's he gone and done now? Built himself a throne?" Nitty shook her head, and she guessed she must've turned several shades paler, because Windle's eyes widened. "What is it?"

With halting breaths, she explained all she, Twitch, and

Bernice had seen at Neezer's institute. Windle's face, as she spoke, went through several stages of transformation—the bleached-bone look of shock, the grim acceptance of a difficult truth, and then, at last, the purpling bluster of anger. "No!" was his frequent exclamation, along with "He didn't dare!" and "He wouldn't," and, finally, a resigned "The scoundrel."

Nitty barely finished the dreaded recounting before a coughing fit overtook her. As she coughed, Windle shook his head, muttering, "How could I not have known?"

Nitty nearly blurted that he might've known earlier had he bothered to listen properly to Twitch's and her hunches. But his pained expression and trembling hands stopped her. She couldn't gloat at the sight of his suffering, not even if he *had* behaved like a thickheaded grown-up.

"All these years, right under our noses!" he said now. "And I saw the trucks coming and going. We all did."

"The dust did its job disguising them," Nitty managed to rasp. "It's not all your fault."

"More mine than most. I knew who Neezer had become. Better than anyone else. And I stuck my head in the sand and let Fortune's Bluff suffer through his skullduggery. I should've stood against it." He pounded a fist into his palm. "By balderdash, I should've stood for *something*!"

"We have to stop him," Nitty said. Then she coughed again, and the taste of sweaty, unwashed feet filled her mouth. Curse those Toeter Grime dusters!

Windle squeezed her hand. "You need to rest. You sucked up a mountain of dust yourself. Doc Grant was none too happy with the way your lungs were sounding either."

"I'm fine." Nitty gasped, straining to make her breath sound steady. "I'll be even better once I see Twitch and Mag. Once we have a plan."

Windle's mouth sagged. "About Mag. She's not here. Neezer—"

Suddenly the front door swung open and a voice boomed into the room. "Nitty Luce, alive and well!" Neezer Snollygost barreled through the doorway, his smile wide and slick as ever. "I thought I'd look in to see how the patient is faring today." The blazing purple of his waistcoat pained Nitty's eyes. "Just an amicable stop on my mayoral circuit of duties."

"You." Nitty frowned, suddenly wishing she had something more effective than a pillow for walloping. "What did you do with my elephant?"

"May I?" Neezer swept a box of chocolate out from behind his back, setting it beside Nitty on the bed. "A gift to brighten your convalescence."

Unbidden, Nitty's mouth began to water, but she turned her head away. "I won't touch one morsel of that contraband."

Neezer clucked his tongue. "Such a shame. Windle, I see you've had as much trouble imparting good sense to this girl as you did to Lillah. The both of them wild as lions."

Windle stood up, straightening. At his full height he was

nearly two heads taller than Neezer, but his newborn air of tenacity made him appear even taller. "On the contrary." His voice struck Nitty as suddenly impressive with authority. "Lillah had the sense to move on when I couldn't, and Nitty . . . well, the girl has more good sense than I've had in years."

Neezer's crescent-moon smile narrowed to a sliver. "Harboring a dangerous animal certainly doesn't strike me as good sense."

"My Mag wouldn't hurt a flea." A fire lit in Nitty's belly, then spread to her cheeks.

"Is that so? Well." Neezer moved to the foot of the bed. "Your Mag cost Angus Higgler dearly. She strangled him to within a hairsbreadth of his life."

"That's a lie!" Nitty's ragged breath came in hot, shallow gasps. "Mag was trying to help Twitch. She picked him up to keep him safe from the dust."

"The elephant's a gentle soul," Windle said. "I've never seen her behave with anything other than tenderness."

"Ah, but I have." Neezer's nose struck up a languid, morose rendering of Chopin's Funeral March. "She crushed the institute's fence in her fury, and then I saw her choking the boy with my own eyes. If I hadn't stepped in, tragedy surely would've struck. Miz Turngiddy witnessed the event firsthand. She can testify as to what happened. Can't you, Miz Turngiddy?"

Neezer nodded toward the doorway, and Nitty saw Miz Turngiddy hanging back on its threshold, her hands clasped tightly at her waist.

"She wasn't there," Nitty protested. "I saw as much for myself!"

"Miz Turngiddy?" Neezer prodded.

Miz Turngiddy looked pained. "I—I arrived just as the duster was waning. Truth be told, my view was obscured by the flying dirt—"

Neezer cleared his throat. Loudly. His nose struck up "Vigilante Man."

Miz Turngiddy paled. "It's true!" she blurted. "The elephant's trunk was wrapped around Angus. There is a ninety-nine-point-five percent probability that, with its strength, it could've done harm—"

"There!" Neezer's nose emitted a victorious *tweet!* "As I said, the elephant is a danger. A threat to us all."

Miz Turngiddy looked away, her expression drooping.

For a moment Nitty pitied the woman, as she'd pity anyone who blindly took up another's cause without, first, understanding the truth and, second, knowing her own opinion of it. Once the moment was over, Nitty maddened.

"Shame on you," she burst out. "Shame on both of you!"

Neezer ignored her. "Needless to say, the elephant is being kept in my custody, under the strictest of scrutiny, to assure the safety of everyone in Fortune's Bluff."

"You've locked her up, haven't you?" Nitty wanted to shout, but her voice was still weak, and all she could manage was a frustrated bark. "You can't chain her again! I won't let you. It's the worst sort of cruelty."

Dear Mag. Her heart wasn't meant to endure more deceit.

Nitty looked Neezer square in the eye and, with thoughts of Twitch in mind, said, " 'Ten Ways to Be a Villain, number nine: Undermine all that is good, fair, and just with treachery.' "

"On the contrary, young lady, what is more just than making a criminal answerable to her crime?" Neezer sighed heavily and with great import. "I'm afraid this is what comes of stealing an animal from a circus. Misery all around."

Nitty glanced at Windle, worried what she might see in his face. He'd never asked for an elephant and a thief to descend upon him. He might easily regret it now. But he didn't look regretful. He looked proud.

"I had to steal her to save her," Nitty said then. "She was about to be hanged!"

Neezer pulled a telegram from his pocket and passed it to Windle. "Yes, I know all about it. The beast killed her trainer."

"She didn't! I'm sure it was an accident. You can ask Mr. Klempt if you like. He met her trainer. He swears the man mistreated Mag awfully. She bears the scars as proof!"

Windle, who'd been reading over the telegram again and again, lifted forlorn eyes from the paper. "Says here that Magnolious is lawfully owned by the Gusto and Gallant Circus. And . . . Percival Gallant will be coming to Fortune's Bluff to collect his property. Tomorrow."

"Tomorrow!" Nitty gasped. "We can't let him take Mag away. He'll kill her." She looked at Windle, imploring. "We can talk to Mr. Gallant. Maybe he'll let her go free as long as we promise she won't be a danger to anyone. We have to make him see."

"We'll do all we can," Windle said solemnly. He turned to Neezer. "We're going to put a stop to this, Neezer. We've had our differences, you and I, but this goes beyond the two of us. This is about doing right."

"Twitch knows what happened," Nitty continued. "He can explain how she rescued him."

Neezer shook his head. "I've just come from visiting Angus. The boy can barely breathe, let alone talk. Why, Mrs. Higgler is busy packing up their belongings as we speak."

At Nitty's blank look, Neezer added, "Oh. Didn't Windle tell you? Doc Grant has recommended a change of climate for Angus, as soon as possible. They leave for California at first light tomorrow. The best thing you can do for your friend now is to let him recuperate in peace."

The fire under Nitty's skin broke loose, burning her eyes until they watered. But no. If there was one thing she refused to do, it was to cry in front of Neezer Snollygost. She would not let him ever believe that he could reduce her to tears.

She lifted her chin. "The only person you know what's best for is yourself, Mr. Snollygost. I'll thank you to leave any other opinions about my friend *and* my elephant to yourself."

Neezer's nose commenced "The Battle Hymn of the Republic," and Nitty was struck with an almost irrepressible desire to stuff a sock up Neezer's nostrils.

"Regretfully," Neezer said, "as mayor I cannot allow a threat such as this elephant to remain in my town."

At that moment, Windle reached for the freckle behind his right ear. Then he stopped, for he'd had enough of the itching. He'd had enough of Neezer altogether. He lowered his hand and locked eyes with Neezer. "Know this." His voice was steady and strong. "You cannot stop us from keeping our elephant. She belongs here, with Nitty. With us."

Neezer might almost have looked startled by Windle's display of fortitude had he not remembered that enterprising swindlers, such as he, made a point of never looking startled. Instead he smiled. "Have you forgotten who owns Fortune's Bluff, Windle? Who owns the deeds on every parcel of farmland?"

"Except mine," Windle countered.

"Yes. Except yours. Such a shame, that. I could do wonders with this property." He clapped Windle on the back. "But I'll not let such a trifle stand in the way of our town's betterment. Indeed not. Other folks have seen reason these last few days. Why, just yesterday four families at last agreed to give me their land in return for the promise of new jobs."

"What jobs?" Windle scoffed. "You can't promise what you don't have."

Neezer waved a dismissive hand. "Once Fortune City is built over the ruins of Fortune's Bluff, I'll have jobs to offer. Bellboys, concierges . . . cooks for gourmet restaurants." His eyes glinted. "Imagine a high-rise hotel where the Higgler farm stands. Can you see it?"

Windle and Nitty said nothing. But Nitty understood now why Twitch had seen Neezer with that *Sublime Skyscrapers* book. Neezer had been plotting this all along.

"Fortune's Bluff, a metropolis," Miz Turngiddy whispered. She clutched her notebook, her knuckles whitening, and a sickly pallor swept her face.

Windle clenched his jaw. "You'll never have this farm."

"Oh?" Neezer tapped his chin, as if deep in thought. "And what would happen if a duster destroyed this farm? Would you still be so dead set on keeping it then?" Neezer's smile widened. He patted his stomach, which Nitty could hear grumbling.

"Now if you'll excuse me. A public servant's work is never done." He nodded toward Nitty in farewell. Then he and Miz Turngiddy left the room, and soon the dust-choked putter of Neezer's motorcar signaled their departure into the inky dark.

Nitty wasted no time in getting out of bed and starting to dress.

"Oh no you don't." Windle nodded toward the window. "It's six o'clock but might as well be midnight. The dust is still thick as tar. There won't be any rescue missions tonight."

"But, Windle—" She stopped short at his warning glance.

"I need to ponder and feed the animals. You need to sleep." He turned for the front door, and Nitty saw him eyeing Clara's rocker, and then the photograph on the kitchen table. He cleared his throat awkwardly. "I . . . posted a letter to Lillah."

His voice was a near whisper. "I told her about a young orphan girl whom she should like to meet, if ever she finds herself back this way. I told her . . ." His voice creaked like age-old floorboards. "How much you remind me of her."

Nitty's heart warmed through her sorrow. "Thank you. For showing me such kindness. I'd like to meet Lillah someday, too." Only now, she thought, this could never happen. But she didn't say so aloud.

Windle nodded and turned away, then hesitated. "I'm sorry about Twitch. And Mag. This is my fault. I . . . I never have known what to do with little girls, especially little girls with elephants." He sighed—a sigh so heavy Nitty thought it might drag him clear down through the floor.

"It's not your fault," Nitty whispered as he quietly shut the door. "It's mine."

She clenched her eyes shut, and a picture came to her of her own dear Mag, alone and frightened in a dark corner of the Snollygost Institute. Maybe Mag thought Nitty had abandoned her. Or worse. Maybe Mag thought Nitty didn't care what happened to her at all.

Nitty's heart wrenched. Then, at last, she began to cry.

CHAPTER TWENTY-SIX

IN WHICH TEARS, LARGE IN SIZE AND AMOUNT, ARE SHED

Elephants, it is believed by some, cannot cry. They may shed tears, but some say this is simply to wash dirt from their eyes. Neezer Snollygost was just such a skeptic, for that is exactly what he said when he and Miz Turngiddy walked into the Snollygost Institute to find their captive crying.

Mag stood in a dark corner, her head bowed, her ears drooping, her marble-sized tears rolling from her eyes to the tip of her trunk. The tears pooled around the chains binding her feet.

"Would you look at that elephant?" Miz Turngiddy shook her head, a redness creeping over her cheeks. "I believe she's crying!"

Neezer, who was preoccupied with brushing the dust from his coattails, chortled. "Pish! As if such a simple-minded beast could cry! It's just clearing the grit from its eyes." He gave her a stern look. "Really, Miz Turngiddy. What an unwarranted display of sentimentality."

"I—I'm sorry," Miz Turngiddy stammered, but she wasn't looking at Neezer when she said it. Instead her eyes were on Mag's. Mag's eyes, she discovered, were sweet and . . . even innocent. She did not like that the elephant was chained. Nor did she like all she'd witnessed of the mayor's behavior in recent days. She'd seen him hide that slice of froozle fruit in his sleeve. And though the elephant was strong, she did not truly think it would have harmed Angus Higgler. Nor did she think Neezer had seen the elephant do anything other than come to Angus's aid. She could not believe, after all she'd seen, that any of what he said was true, or that any of what he did was for good. But . . . her job. What would happen to Fortune's Bluff if she did not continue working to stand between it and Neezer?

For the first time in Miz Turngiddy's life, the cogs and wheels of her mind jammed, giving her an awful headache.

"I'll overlook it for now." Neezer turned his back to Mag and, with purposeful strides, headed for his office. "I have much work to do in preparation for the arrival of our guests."

"Guests, sir?" Miz Turngiddy consulted her notebook. "I thought it was just Percival Gallant coming."

Neezer smiled. "Percival Gallant is not the only individual interested in a return of property. There is also the matter of Nitty Luce. There are a host of individuals, myself and one headmistress in particular, who would be happy to have her returned to the orphanage."

Miz Turngiddy frowned. "Sir, I've researched such institutions in the interest of improving my knowledge of civic service. I doubt very much that one small orphan girl would be missed at an orphanage, when it means one less mouth to feed."

Neezer's smile widened. "She's missed exactly as much as I pay to have her missed . . . and returned."

Miz Turngiddy stared at him, her face paling. Her grandbabies appeared in her aching mind's eye, complete with their sweet-cream scent and apricot-fuzz curls. Her grandbabies, so far from her, their own kin. Nitty Luce . . . so far from her own kin. Miz Turngiddy's head pounded. "You won't send her away, not with Windle Homes having taken her in as his own. Why, he could be planning to adopt—"

"Remember the Snollygost motto, Miz Turngiddy. Know that all I do, I do for community progress, fulfillment, and the betterment of all." He patted his stomach. "Now, I'm famished, Miz Turngiddy, and in need of sustenance. As soon as possible."

"Yes . . . sir." Miz Turngiddy pressed her fingertips to her temple. Her head was splitting, and all it could do at the moment was envision orphans, farmers, and the whole of the population of Fortune's Bluff squashed under an enormous purple skyscraper. "And . . . the elephant?"

"What of it?" Neezer huffed from his doorway.

"Will it be needing water?" Miz Turngiddy clutched her

notepad in one hand, her forehead in the other. Neezer did not notice. "Or food?"

"I'll not waste one bit more of the town's food and water supply on this murderous animal. She belongs to Percival Gallant. Let Percival Gallant foot the cost of her care." He gazed down his nose at Miz Turngiddy in a way that made her feel no bigger than a bug at his shoe tip. "Don't give that monster another thought."

But, as Neezer's office door shut with an authoritative click, Miz Turngiddy *did* give Mag another thought.

Poor creature was her thought.

She glanced at Mag one last time, just as another tear plunked to the floor, then quickly looked away. The elephant would survive the night, at least, she reasoned, and by tomorrow morning, with the arrival of Percival Gallant, the elephant would no longer be her problem at all. Tomorrow morning, she would double her efforts and, perhaps at last, stop Neezer's hunger in order to save Fortune's Bluff. Yes, that was what she would do, if only her head didn't ache so. . . .

Miz Turngiddy scurried off in search of sustenance for Neezer and a cool rag for her forehead, and Mag was left alone.

༺༻

Mag shuffled her feet, and the hollow rattling of her chains made her tears fall faster. Make no mistake: Mag was indeed crying.

She was crying for herself—for her hunger, her thirst, her loneliness. She was crying for the chains that bound her feet again. She was crying for the night of her trainer's accident, months past now.

She'd been bound like this when he'd come at her with the bull hook. Her flanks and heels were still raw and sore from other beatings, and each swing of the hook brought another wave of pain. She'd backed up against her circus wagon, pressing into one of its wheels. She heard the splintering of wood and felt the wheel beneath her haunch give a little. A second later, she forgot about the wheel and the wagon, because the hook was raised and sharp and painful and it was being swung directly at her chest. She raised her trunk.

Then, all at once, the hook was in her trunk and out of her trainer's hands. She held it over him. She knew what the hook would do if she brought it down with a hard *thwack* on her trainer's head. It would be as easy as splitting a tree trunk.

She only wanted to be free of that hook.

She tossed it under the wagon, out of his reach.

She didn't expect him to crawl under the wagon to look for it. She didn't expect the splintering wheel to suddenly snap, or for the wagon to come buckling to the ground with her trainer caught underneath its weight.

She knew he'd stopped breathing. His warm, pungent, alive scent disappeared, replaced by a soured, dried-leaves scent.

She still tried to help. She pulled her chains from their stakes in the ground. Using her head and shoulders, she pushed at the wagon with all her might until, with a thundering crash, it tipped over, freeing her trainer from its weight.

It was too late.

Voices shouted in the darkness, and though the words made no sense to her, their hard, cold tone made her remember and fear them. "The beast!" the cold words came. "The beast has crushed him!"

There was running and shouting and dozens of hands and whips and bull hooks in her face. It was frightening, but not nearly as frightening as the stagnant stillness of her trainer.

Nor was it as frightening as the blame they placed on her for his death.

There was no one who saw what had happened, who understood that it had been the wagon, and not Mag, that had crushed the trainer. There was no one who could speak for her. No one who understood her enough to know, with certainty, that she would never do harm no matter how she herself might be harmed.

No one until the girl—*her* girl—came along. Tonight, Mag cried for her girl, too. She wanted to be by her side to keep her safe. She wanted to be far from her to keep her safe. Her girl was all that mattered.

Mag sank to the floor. The chains dug into her ankles and forelegs, making every move painful. What she would've given to be back in the sweet-smelling barn with her girl curled into her trunk!

Mag closed her eyes. Her tears fell, one by one, in silence to the floor. Alone and frightened, Mag cried. Her great pumpkin heart was breaking.

CHAPTER TWENTY-SEVEN

In Which Escapes Are Made and Farewells Spoken

Nitty stood in the silty shadows of the Homes kitchen, watching Windle sleep. Her head and chest still ached. Her flour-sack dress scratched her skin, but she'd made up her mind to leave her decent clothes behind. They were from Lillah's girlhood, and she didn't feel right taking them. It felt akin to stealing, and her stealing days were over and done with. She'd stolen those green seeds from the Merrythought Windowshop. But what about all she'd hoped would come from them?

When the seeds had sprouted and grown with the froozle fruit, she'd believed in their triumph. But now Twitch was sick, so morbidly sick that he was leaving. The Homes farm was back to being lovelorn. Windle was back to being hopeless. And Mag . . . dear Mag was back in chains.

Even with her froozle fruit, her Twitch, her Windle, *her* Mag . . . nothing had triumphed except Neezer Snollygost. She'd never been one to bemoan her misfortunes, but—oh!— she bemoaned them tonight.

Windle looked so mournful, sleeping in the rocker with his chin to his chest. It was his disappointment in her, no doubt, that stooped his shoulders and sagged his mouth into its doleful horseshoe.

Nitty wished she could tell him where she was going. She wished she could tell him she was sorry she'd happenstanced into his life, that she'd only meant to bring good to him instead of all this vexation. She wished she didn't have to leave him. But she did.

She opened her Gleam Jar and took from it the daffodil-yellow button. She gently set it in Windle's open palm.

"Because you believe in luck and dreaming big," she whispered, "even though you don't always remember that you do."

She went to the door, looking back once to see a scant, sad smile cross Windle's dreaming face. Then, before her willpower could abandon her, she left.

༻✧༺

The walk to Twitch's house didn't wear Nitty out as much as the sight of his pallid face through the window did.

"You look unequivocally cadaverous!" Nitty declared as she

climbed over the window ledge into his bedroom. She wrinkled her nose. "*And* you smell of camphor."

"Ma's putrid chest liniment." Twitch's voice was spoon-strumming-a-washboard hoarse, but he managed a weak smile, which brought no end of relief to Nitty. "At least she's not pouring turnip soup down my throat. Froozle soup is heaps better." He sat back against his pillows, seeming exhausted from the few words he'd spoken. "I didn't think you'd come."

"What did you think? That I'd leave you a captive?" Nitty sat down at the end of Twitch's bed, trying to smile. Smiles are difficult to keep when you're sad and scared and sitting at the sickbed of someone you love. Still, she hoped to appear stalwart, as all dependable partners should. She pulled a froozle fruit from her pocket—a small one, because only the smaller ones were left. The folks of Fortune's Bluff had harvested the rest. She'd brought several with her, having picked them on her way to Twitch's, but she needed to save some for Mag, too.

"Here." She set the froozle fruit beside Twitch. "This will do you some good. It might taste better than Mr. Moop's Cough Tonic, too."

"Might?" Twitch scoffed. "Anything tastes better than that tarlike slop."

He took a weak bite while they both giggled.

"You should've seen me skulking past your mama," she kept on. "She's outside packing the motorcar right now."

Twitch sank deeper into his pillow. His nutmeg skin had

a pearly sheen that frightened Nitty even more. "Doc Grant doesn't like me being moved at all, but he says my lungs can't take even one more duster. Ma's set on going before another comes."

"That may be." Nitty crossed her arms. "But *I'm* set on springing you. We have to close this case, once and for all. First, though, we have to rescue Mag."

Twitch's eyes widened. "What happened to Mag?"

"Neezer's got her locked up. He's giving her back to the circus." She quickly explained what had happened, and watched Twitch turn several shades paler. "I'm on my way to the Snollygost Institute right now. To rescue her. But I can't do it alone."

Twitch coughed, and Nitty thought that, for the rest of her life, nothing would ever sound as horrid as that cough. When it was at last over, Twitch lay panting and damp with fever. "This time," he finally managed, "you have to defeat the villain without me."

"No." Nitty's nerves were a jumble of sweat and vinegar. "It wouldn't be fair, seeing as how this was your case long before I came here. Besides, you can't move away. Don't you want to stay?"

"I want to stay. But I want to go, too." Twitch raised a shaking hand from the sheets. In it was a piece of paper. "It's a letter. From my pa. It came today. He's found work in California. He wants us to come to him."

"Oh." Nitty stared at the floor. Her head was suddenly throbbing again. Or it could've been that her heart's throbbing was spreading to her head. It was hard to tell. At any rate, the throbbing was relentless and terrible.

"Nitty, you'd do the same. You know you would." Twitch's eyes were dark and glassy, sorrowful and hopeful. "It's my pa."

Yes, Nitty's heart whispered to her, *you'd do the same. For your pa. For a family.*

Twitch was leaving for one family. She was running from another. And it was all to try to save them.

She nodded. "I understand. But I don't have to like it."

Twitch managed a squeak of a laugh. "I didn't figure you would."

She sighed and kicked at the dust motes floating about the toe of her shoe. "Just how am I supposed to manage Mag's liberation without you?" Before she could stop herself in time to remember how sick Twitch was, she glared at him.

Twitch squeaked again. "Nitty Luce, you're the most effervescent individual I've ever met. You rescued Mag once already. You'll do it again, to be sure."

Nitty felt a burst of bubbles rise and pop happily inside her. She wasn't used to being complimented. And "effervescent" sounded so much more pleasant than "suspicious" or "scrappy." "Effervescent" had an emerald-green feel to it, like the seeds, like the froozle field, like her own eyes. "Effervescent," she decided, was something she felt proud to be.

"Thank you," she said softly. Then, for the second time in so many hours, she opened her Gleam Jar. "I'd like you to have this." She set the cardinal-red agate marble in Twitch's

trembling hand and closed her fingers over his. *Brother,* her
heart whispered. "You are a true friend. I—I used to wish for a
brother. A brother like you." The marble grew warm between
them. "It's meant to belong to you."

Twitch rolled the marble around in the cup of his palm.
Even in the sooty air, the red of the marble fought to gleam.
"I'll take good care of it."

"Isn't saying goodbye an abysmal affair!" she cried then,
swiping at her eyes in frustration. A trough of lonesomeness
for Twitch was already being plowed through her, and he hadn't
even left yet. She could feel it there—bruise tender—in her
heart. If Twitch went, his dust pneumonia could clear. He
could see his pa. But if Twitch went, he'd be gone from her. It
was a quandary. "Why is it that caring for another soul means
you want to do what's best for them, even when it's hurtful
to you?" She crossed her arms and glared at him again. "By all
rights I should be incensed at you."

Twitch grinned weakly. "You can't stay sore at me, Nitty
Luce. It's my muddy lungs that are maddening, not me."

"Well." She huffed, thinking this over. "I can't blame you."
The hotness leaked out of her anger. "If I had a pa who wanted
me with him, I'd go in a blink."

"You better write to me." Twitch heaved a determined
breath. "I want to hear every detail of Neezer Snollygost's come-
uppance."

"You're assuming he'll have one."

Twitch nodded. "He will. Every villain does."

At that moment, Mrs. Higgler's voice sounded outside Twitch's bedroom door.

"Go! Hurry!" Twitch wheezed. "Before she comes."

Nitty scrambled off the bed and hurried to the window. Twitch rasped out her name.

He was propped up on his elbow, looking as mischievous and determined as ever, even in the midst of his trembling and coughing. "Remember: 'Ten Ways to Be a Villain, number six: Hide your Achilles' heel from those who would destroy you. The moment you expose your weakness is the moment of your downfall.'" He clutched the red marble in his fist. "Neezer has an Achilles' heel. Find it."

He sank back, exhausted, onto his pillow, just as his bedroom door flew open.

"What on earth?" Mrs. Higgler exclaimed as she took in the open window and Nitty dropping over the side of the sill. "Nitty Luce, how did you sneak in here? Angus Higgler, what do you think you're doing getting yourself into such a state in your condition?"

"Stay eagle-eyed and sure-footed, Nitty!" Twitch hollered hoarsely over Mrs. Higgler's cries of distress. "Neezer's defeat is within your grasp!"

Mrs. Higgler called after Nitty, "Where are you going? You shouldn't be out of bed! There's bound to be another duster. Nitty, come back!"

"Goodbye, Twitch," Nitty whispered as her feet pounded the dirt beneath them.

For she was already running toward Fortune's Bluff, the Snollygost Institute, and Mag, solemnly pledging, as she ran, to make Twitch proud.

CHAPTER TWENTY-EIGHT

In Which There Are Reunions, Happy and Unhappy

Nitty ran through the deserted streets of Fortune's Bluff, more disheartened with each passing second. In the hazy early light, the town looked in far worse shape than ever before. Dust drifts nearly as tall as she was covered most windows and even some doors. The brown fog blanketing Main Street made it difficult to see more than a few feet at a stretch, but still, Nitty saw plenty. Roofs were torn to pieces; windows were broken and gaping; motorcars and wagons were buried.

No one dared set foot outside for risk of not being able to find the way back home. Or, worse, for fear of getting caught in a duster so fierce a person might be buried alive. No one dared. Except Nitty Luce.

When she passed the Sigh bakery, she saw its windows

gaping, its shelves buckled. She half hoped Bernice would appear at her side, offering her help, but then decided it was better for Bernice to stay safe where she was. Crispin and the Sigh children couldn't do without her. Today, Nitty would have to face the foe alone.

As she ran, she remembered the leather graininess of Mag's skin, the warmth of her trunk wrapped around her. She remembered that this was how the two of them had begun, she and Mag, like this, under a blinding shadow of dust, each of them searching for a sympathetic soul.

It could've stayed that way, just the two of them. But they'd stumbled into a barn. They'd met Windle and Twitch. Ferdinand Klempt, and Bernice and Crispin Sigh. Where she'd wished for one sympathetic soul, Nitty had been granted Fortune's Bluff. Only now, it seemed, she would have to leave Fortune's Bluff worse off than she'd found it, instead of better. The very thought cleaved her heart in two.

When she set eyes on the Snollygost Institute, untouched by the storms, looming menacing and black against the sod-laden sky, whumping its infernal, ever-lasting *WHUMP,* Nitty's every hair stood on end.

Mag was her one thought. *I have to save Mag.*

Theirs, Nitty believed in her bones, was meant to be a great and timeless friendship. And in all great and timeless friendships, momentous rescues occur. Mag had rescued her once before, and Nitty understood that it was now her chance to return the favor.

It was this thought that pushed her forward, this thought that made her ignore the grittiness filling her lungs, this thought that made a locomotive of bravery steam through her veins. This thought that made her, without hesitation, race over the now-flattened fence of the Snollygost Institute, scale the withered vines clinging to the building, and sneak through its tallest window.

It was at this moment that Nitty found herself grateful for the Whirlybog's teeth-rattling *WHUMP*, because it was the *WHUMP* that muffled the sound of her dropping, not very gracefully, onto the sacks of flour below. She was back in the storage room, surrounded by canned foods, the sacks of rice and flour, and a pyramid of cantaloupes. There was no sign of Mag. But in the brief seconds of silence between each of the Whirlybog's *WHUMP*s, Nitty heard muffled voices.

Nitty tiptoed across the storage room toward Neezer's office, listening all the while.

WHUMP! . . . The low mumble of voices . . . *WHUMP!* . . . A whistled version of "Happy Days Are Here Again," which meant that Neezer's nose was nearby . . . *WHUMP!* . . . The wretched clank of chains dragging along the floor.

Mag. Nitty was getting closer to Mag.

Slowly, slowly, slowly, Nitty inched forward through the maze of canned goods. Then she went down on her knees, listening for the clanking, and crawled, following the sound and keeping to the shadows, hoping she'd find Mag before Neezer found her.

On the hard, cold floor a dozen feet from Neezer's office, Mag lay in a restless slumber. Her throat was parched and her stomach empty, and for these very reasons, her sleep was disturbed with nightmares involving circus wagons, bull hooks, and blame.

She was always blamed, one way or another, for many wrongs. First by her trainer. Then by her ringmaster. Now by that man who sat in his office, feasting on food that made Mag's mouth water and her stomach whine, talking in his too-loud, too-hungry voice. Occasionally he stood in the doorway of his office, simply, it seemed, to scowl at her.

She did not like the man. It was unnatural for a man to trumpet through his nose like an elephant. Yet he did trumpet. She did not trust his trumpeting, or his scowl. Both frightened her.

But it was the blame he directed at her with his accusing tone and his bitter, angry scent that frightened her most of all.

She had no defense against the blame. She could never explain it away. No one could understand her language. No one could understand her. Except her girl.

Nitty. Her girl was called Nitty.

My girl, Mag thought then. *I will dream of my girl.*

The dream was vivid. In it, her girl was by her side, whispering in her ear, calling her name.

"Mag," her girl whispered. "Mag, wake up. It's Nitty. I'm here."

Mag opened her eyes. She blinked.

Nitty was by her side, whispering in her ear, calling her name. "Mag," Nitty whispered again. "I'm here, Mag. I'm here."

Slowly Mag raised her trunk to touch her girl's cheek, soaking up her beloved green-grass scent.

Her girl had come for her.

Her girl pulled a bunch of froozle fruit from her pocket and slipped it into Mag's mouth.

Mag chewed the pulpy fruit, swallowed, then sighed contentedly.

Her great pumpkin heart warmed, as if it were resting in a field of bright, golden sunshine. Her girl had come for her, and her heart was mending.

She lifted her head to look into her girl's eyes. What she saw, though, was not Nitty's eyes. What Mag saw was the man with the trumpeting nose, standing over them both.

⌒﹖⌒

"Nitty Luce the orphan!" Neezer bellowed. "I suspected you'd come."

Miz Turngiddy hovered behind him, wringing her notebook in her hands, her expression caught in an uncomfortable tug-of-war between duty and doubt.

Nitty lifted her chin, meeting Neezer's gaze. Her locomotive of bravery was steaming on strong. "I've come for Mag."

"Of course you have." Neezer lowered his head, his nose-whistling turning shrill and insistent. "You can't possibly take her, however, because you see . . ." He waved a hand toward his office door. "Someone, in fact, has come for *you*."

There was nothing, in that moment, that could've surprised Nitty more than the sight of Miz Ricketts standing in the doorway of Neezer's office. Her head-to-toe black dress was as dour as her expression, and her expression clearly said, *The hour of your demise has come at last.*

"I've been looking for you." Miz Ricketts clasped and unclasped her hands. "All of us at Grimsgate have been most concerned for your welfare since your hasty departure."

"That's a change, then." Mag rose to her feet, and Nitty pressed against her side, taking comfort in the steadfast thud of Mag's heart against her back. "I don't recall you showing interest in my welfare at any time at all."

Miz Ricketts clasped her hands tighter, her knuckles whitening. She stepped toward Nitty, but stopped a safe distance from Mag. "You always were a scrappy, selfish thing. With such peculiar eyes." Her own eyes narrowed hawkishly as she spoke. "Now I hear you've brought this poor town to the brink of tragedy with your reckless behavior, nearly killing a hapless boy."

Nitty shook her head. "It's not true. But it hardly matters what *you* believe about me." She understood that now. She straightened her spine and curled her arm around Mag's trunk. "You never did think I had a spot of goodness, but all it needed was a chance to grow. Away from the likes of you."

For a moment Miz Ricketts was a codfish, gasping for air.

Then, in a swift, catlike movement, she pounced on Nitty, grabbing her by the hair at the nape of her neck. Her mouth snapped down on the words "Why you—"

"Mag!" Nitty cried as Miz Ricketts and Neezer pulled Nitty away from Mag's side.

"Come now!" Neezer's voice boomed. "Struggles are so unseemly."

But Nitty struggled, thrashing against the viselike hands gripping her and steering her toward the front door of the building. Mag struggled, too, pulling at her chains, which were bolted to the cement floor. Mag trumpeted loudly enough to drown out the Whirlybog's whumping. But nothing lessened Neezer's and Miz Ricketts's hold on Nitty.

Once outside in the mustardy daylight, Nitty saw a motorwagon waiting, black and foreboding. This made her pull even more fiercely against her captors' grasp.

"Miz Ricketts," Neezer said (with some difficulty due to the immense and impressive battle Nitty was waging against them both). "Our meeting of minds is drawing to a close." He crooked a finger at Miz Turngiddy, who had been following the threesome with hesitant steps. She was clutching a bulky envelope against her waist, her lips quivering.

Neezer stared at her. "Give the headmistress the envelope, Miz Turngiddy."

Miz Turngiddy did not move. Her hold on the envelope tightened.

"Miz Turngiddy!" barked Neezer. He wrenched the envelope from her and deposited it into Miz Ricketts's one free and outstretched hand.

Miz Turngiddy took a step backward, then another. She turned from the scene, sinking her head into her hands, while Neezer nodded to Miz Ricketts. "I am eternally grateful for your willingness to take back the child."

The headmistress's frown kinked upward unnaturally, and Nitty supposed it was the closest she could come to a smile. "And I, sir, am grateful for your donation." While Neezer clamped down on Nitty's arms, Miz Ricketts, panting with exertion, was able to slip the envelope into her pocketbook. "It will improve our meager orphanage tenfold."

Miz Ricketts brushed a damp hair from her forehead, looking increasingly weathered, and resumed her hold on Nitty. "In you go. Now," Miz Ricketts said in a low, clenched-toothed tone. "My ship's come in at last, and even *your* evil eye can't ruin it for me."

"That money in the envelope," Nitty said. "It belongs to the people of Fortune's Bluff! And *you'll* never use it to help the orphans of Grimsgate."

"Shut. Your. Mouth." Miz Ricketts raised her hand, as she had so many other times while Nitty was in her care (if "care" was what her wretched failure at guardianship could be called), and prepared to bring it down with the full force of her weight across Nitty's cheek.

This time the intended blow was blocked from its target

by a resolute fist, which wrapped itself around Miz Ricketts's hand and would not let go. The fist, Nitty stopped struggling long enough to notice, belonged to none other than Windle Homes.

"Release your hold on my daughter." Windle's voice was solid and immovable as an oak as he planted himself before Miz Ricketts.

Daughter. The word flew from Windle's mouth so easily, without a second's faltering, and as it did, a window in Nitty's heart opened to catch it.

"As *if* that feral creature could be anybody's daughter!" Miz Ricketts snapped, while Neezer clutched his sides at the hilarity of the idea. Still, because Miz Ricketts stood two feet shorter than Windle, and also because she had no wish to stoke the flames she saw in Windle's eyes into a wildfire, she released her hold on Nitty.

"Good riddance to her," the headmistress spat. After colliding with Miz Turngiddy, who blustered apologies as she handed Miz Ricketts back the pocketbook she'd dropped in the crash, Miz Ricketts hurriedly climbed behind the wheel of the motorwagon. The wagon snarled to life.

"Miz Ricketts, wait!" Neezer might've stopped her had it not been for the wagon's spray of exhaust hitting him square in his face. "We had a bargain!" he coughed.

"I have all I care to take!" Miz Ricketts waved her pocketbook out the window in farewell. Neezer watched, puffing from rage as the wagon, and the money, rattled away.

Nitty looked at Windle then and for the first time noticed that he was wearing the daffodil-yellow button, pinned to the collar of his shirt. "Windle. You bested Miz Ricketts."

"So I did," he responded. There was a certain giddy lilt to his voice, as if he'd very much enjoyed it.

Nitty grinned. "Such a display of heroic steeliness puts the *Daily Tattler* to shame!"

Windle opened his arms to Nitty. She flew to him, letting the spindly branches of his arms enfold her. *Daughter,* Nitty thought. *He called me daughter.* Of the many impressive words Nitty had tucked into the dictionary of her mind, none could ever match the splendor or comfort of that simple one. *Daughter.*

But the rapture in Nitty's soul could only last the smallest second before Neezer burst out with "The girl does not belong with you."

"She does, and so does her elephant. If the idea appeals to her." Windle looked down at Nitty with bright eyes.

"Appeal to me?" Nitty laughed. "The idea has me teeming with euphoria!"

Windle harrumphed, but simply because he was at a loss for what else *to* do with such a bombardment of emotion. "No time to waste. We have negotiations to make and an elephant to retrieve." He straightened with resolve. "First . . . I plan to have some words with Neezer."

He and Nitty glanced around and noted several things at once. The first was the ominous moan of wind heralding from the east, the second was the fortress of dust plunging toward them across the barren horizon, and the third was Neezer, or the sudden *absence* of Neezer.

The door to the institute stood open. From its yawning darkness came the ever-present, ever-loudening *WHUMP!* and a foreboding, nasal trill. Neezer's nose was whistling "Dust Can't Kill Me."

CHAPTER TWENTY-NINE

In Which Machine Betrays Master

It took only seconds for Nitty and Windle to reach the door, but in those seconds the air turned sludgy and the wind savage. Never had any duster descended so quickly and with such ferocity. This was a duster of reckoning, of demolition, of extermination. This was a duster to end all dusters.

Inside, a dirt-pudding fog permeated the warehouse, and Nitty and Windle inched their way forward blindly. The lamentable whumping grew louder and faster.

"The Whirlybog," Nitty said between coughs. "Neezer's using it to bring on the storm." Her heart quickened. "I have to get to Mag."

"Stay with me, Nitty." Windle's voice came, choked and

muffled, from somewhere to Nitty's right. His hand had hers, holding tight. "Let Mag find us."

Nitty itched to set off on her own to search for Mag. Mag was chained and alone and in danger. Very real danger. As was the entirety of Fortune's Bluff.

But Windle had spoken the word: *daughter.* He was wearing the daffodil-yellow button. She would not let go of his hand.

So instead, as Windle and Nitty made their way toward Neezer and his Whirlybog, Nitty called to Mag.

Find us was the thought she sent out to Mag through the brown stew and deafening whumping. *Find us.*

She was still thinking this when, suddenly, the curtain of dust before them was swept aside to reveal Neezer standing before the monstrous, galumphing Whirlybog. Neezer set the Whirlybog's Dustometer to Oily Loam and then began pouring the contents of jar after jar into the machine's holding tank.

Nitty cringed. Neezer was emptying every single jar of wind into the holding tank. The tank was beginning to shake violently as a black, dangerous funnel churned inside it.

"Neezer," Windle called over the Whirlybog's frenzied whumping. "Turn off the machine."

Just then, Miz Turngiddy rushed past Windle and Nitty, scurrying to Neezer's side with a tray of food, a look of determined purpose on her face. As she did this, she nodded at Nitty to make her way toward the large red lever on the Whirlybog.

Nitty could scarce believe it. Could Miz Turngiddy be

trying to help? Miz Turngiddy gave her the answer in a pointed wink. She *was*!

Nitty took a step toward the lever while Miz Turngiddy held the platter under Neezer's nose. "Mayor Snollygost, sir, might I offer you some sustenance? Perhaps a bite of eggplant Florentine?"

Neezer looked at Miz Turngiddy. He laughed. "There are times for eggplant, Miz Turngiddy, and there are times for hegemony. You would do wisely not to confuse the two."

"Brother," Windle said to Neezer then, "won't you see reason?"

Neezer laughed again. It was not a kind laugh, but a greedy laugh. It was a laugh filled with hunger. "You choose this moment, of all moments, to call me brother again? Have you forgotten how you called me a failure and a fool?"

"It was long ago. It was wrong of me." Windle bowed his head. Given his past penchant for unbridled aspirations and sky-high cornfields, he'd never gotten into the habit of admitting wrongs. But how else can anyone make amends, except by being humble and honest? "Some words spoken can't be forgotten, I know. But can't they be forgiven? Clara would've wanted that."

At the mention of Clara's name, Neezer paused. His fingers hovered, hesitating, over the Whirlybog's Dustometer, and a wistfulness passed over his features. "Clara," he said softly. "She loved me."

Nitty paused in her advance toward the red lever, remembering

Twitch's words about Neezer's Achilles' heel. Might the memory of Clara weaken Neezer's resolve? She waited, watching, only to see Neezer stiffen, his face harden. "Clara loved me, and even she refused to give me what I asked for."

"What you wanted was too much," Windle said.

"Some biscuits and gravy, perhaps?" Miz Turngiddy interjected loudly. This time her suggestion was met with not even a glance in her direction.

Nitty took another tiptoe step toward the red lever.

Windle pressed on. "We wanted our farm kept the way it was—open and wild and free. Not suffocated by cement and skyscrapers."

"Suffocated . . . pish!" Neezer scowled. "It's progress, but no one here has vision for that. The people of Fortune's Bluff are the *true* fools and failures, and I've suffered them long enough! When there's nothing left in Fortune's Bluff, there will be nothing left to stand in my way."

"No!" Miz Turngiddy gave a banshee battle cry and raised her tray above her head like a catapult ready to launch. At the very moment the tray flew from Miz Turngiddy's hands, Nitty lunged for the red lever, and Neezer lunged for Nitty.

The eggplant Florentine missed Neezer's head but did, Nitty was delighted to see, hit him square in the chest, spelling disaster for his purple waistcoat. Nitty ducked from Neezer's grasp, but his elbow caught her in the shoulder, knocking her away from the red lever and clearing the path for Neezer to reach it.

Reach it he did, and he slid it upward. A thunderous roar echoed through the building.

Timbers snapped and cracked overhead, and when Nitty looked up, she saw a hole in the building's roof and shingles tearing away and fluttering into the burned-brown sky. Wind tunneled its way down through the holes in the roof, papers and bits of food flew from Neezer's desk into the air, Miz Turn-giddy's notebook was whisked from her pocket, and soon a cyclone of shingles, paper, and food spun with worrying rapidity around the Whirlybog.

Neezer raised the lever several inches more. The force of the twister made Nitty's feet slide across the floor and then lifted them from it completely. She rose into the air with the ease of a feather. She might've been blown away entirely had it not been for the sudden grip of Mag's trunk, firm but gentle, about her middle.

"Mag," Nitty breathed. "You heard me."

Mag's chains were gone. Of course she'd heard her girl. Of course she'd broken her chains to get to her.

The elephant gently swung Nitty sideward and onto her neck. Relieved, Nitty discovered Windle there, too, holding on tightly, having just been saved by Mag's trunk as well.

"Do you know," Windle hollered into Nitty's ear, "sitting astride an elephant isn't nearly as uncomfortable as I believed it would be."

"Of course not," Nitty hollered back. "And it gives a person all manner of fresh perspective." Nitty looked at Neezer, whose hands gripped the red lever as the rest of him floated above it, and Miz Turngiddy, who, having paused in her battle against Neezer for fear of being blown away, had tethered herself to Mag's sturdy tail. "From up here, they seem so small and ordinary. Not villains so much as people. Plain, unhappy people who've lost their way."

"Seems all of us do," Windle said. "Lose our way. One time or another."

Nitty considered that. She considered the hours and days she'd spent at Grimsgate, staring into her Gleam Jar, contemplating the entire family she'd lost before she'd ever known them. And then more hours and days contemplating how she might get good and lost herself. There were times and reasons, she decided, for losing yourself. Not all the reasons might be sensible, worthy, or even right, but where was it ever written that humans were sensible creatures in the first place? Why, there would never have been anything at all of interest to read in the *Daily Tattler* if that were the case! It surely hadn't been sensible of Nitty to steal the green seeds or an elephant, but if she hadn't . . . well, if she hadn't lost her way, how might she have ever found her goodness?

Yes, there were times for losing yourself. But the better times—the best times of all—were when you were found. Not found by the likes of Miz Ricketts, but found by those who cared. Who wanted you, no matter how lost you were, how thieving, how greedy, how—Neezer's nose gave a whistle—adenoidal.

Nitty made up her mind then, and before Windle had the chance to grab hold of her, she slid down from around Mag's neck. She'd never known anyone as lost as Neezer Snollygost. Or as greedy. But there was one thing Neezer had never had, one food he'd never tasted. Could that one thing be enough to weaken his resolve? Windle called her name, reaching for her, but Nitty, holding tight with one hand to Mag's foreleg, kept her eyes trained on Neezer and his red lever. With her other hand, she reached into her pocket for the very last piece of froozle fruit.

"Mr. Snollygost." Nitty held the fruit toward him. "You don't need to destroy Fortune's Bluff. Wouldn't you rather try some froozle fruit instead? *Really* try it, I mean?"

Neezer stared at the froozle fruit, then at Mag, and lastly at Nitty.

"You—" Neezer took one hand off the lever long enough to jab a finger at Nitty. "You and that elephant. If you hadn't come along, growing that nuisance of a crop, filling everyone's heads with notions of faith and promise and other such twaddle, this town would've bent to my will. You think you can change the course of its destiny, but you can't. Because you're nothing. You will always be nothing."

Nitty had heard such words before. They'd once stuck fast to her. She'd once—almost—believed them. Now she raised her chin. She locked eyes with Neezer. "I don't have faith in destiny. I have faith in green seeds and elephants and froozle fruit. And I am not nothing. I am effervescent."

She stretched to the limit of her reach, holding the froozle fruit out to Neezer.

Neezer, who was perspiring from the effort of holding the red lever and also from the distasteful sensation of being seen through by Nitty's unsettling green eyes, hesitated. Under his eggplant-splattered waistcoat, his stomach rumbled. *What might froozle fruit taste like?* he wondered. Would it taste like the glory of skyscrapers and cement? Or would it taste like sitting about the table with Windle and Clara so many years past, bouncing a baby Lillah on his knee and laughing?

He considered tasting the froozle fruit. He considered accepting Nitty's offering.

But how could one small piece of fuchsia fruit possibly sate him? Neezer's hunger was bottomless. It hungered for more—much more—than what Nitty and Windle and all of Fortune's Bluff could offer.

Neezer reached for the froozle fruit and, with one swoop of his fist, knocked it from Nitty's hand and into the swirling vortex. The fruit circled overhead once, twice, and then disappeared through the now-sizable hole in the roof.

With both hands on the red lever, Neezer slid it all the way upward, unleashing the full power of the Whirlybog.

Every sound after that was drowned out by the blusterous fury of the storm. The rampant wind tore and yanked and pummeled, and several things happened all at once.

Neezer's perspiring palms slipped from the red lever, and he became airborne.

Nitty's grip on Mag's foreleg loosened and then came undone entirely, and Nitty, too, shot into the air.

Miz Turngiddy screamed, Windle hollered, and Mag trumpeted, but each of their distress calls was sucked away into the gale.

Nitty's fingers scavenged the air until, suddenly, they found the Whirlybog's red lever and grasped it, hanging on for dear life. She saw Mag's form through the wind tunnel, her trunk reaching for her. She saw Neezer spiraling through the air with nothing to anchor him.

In Neezer's ogling eyes, Nitty saw bottomless hunger. She saw his true Achilles' heel. Even as he twisted and twirled, even as he lifted higher and higher toward the cavernous hole in the roof, Neezer hungered for everything he wanted and could not have, everything he longed to take that was not his for the taking. This was his downfall—that he'd give up everything for a chance at more. More upon more upon more. But in his eyes, Nitty also saw fear.

"Help!" Nitty cried.

"Help!" Neezer cried.

Mag's trunk swung up into the gusts and billows, reaching toward Nitty. Mag tried—oh, she tried—battling the wind with every muscle in her beautiful gray bulk of a body. An elephant, though, even an exceptional one, has limitations, and a trunk can only stretch so far.

The Whirlybog whumped one tremendous, final *WHUMP*, the cyclone loosed a colossal burst of wind, and Neezer shot higher into the air. At the very same moment, just as Mag's trunk brushed her heel, Nitty pulled down mightily on the Whirlybog's red lever.

The Whirlybog sputtered, then fell silent.

The whirlwind, though it slowed, was not so easily stopped. It began a bellowing ascension into the sky, taking the contents of its vortex with it.

The last Nitty saw of Neezer was the blur of his ruined waistcoat caught in the tempest, climbing higher and higher. The last she heard of him was his nose, whistling "Farewell Blues."

Neezer Snollygost was gone.

CHAPTER THIRTY

IN WHICH A TOWN IS LOST BUT JUICE IS FOUND

The Fortune's Bluff that Nitty saw upon leaving the now roof-less, wind-battered Snollygost Institute was vastly different from the one she'd passed through hours earlier. The town, if it could still be called that, was as flattened and bare as an unbut-tered, syrupless pancake, and indeed just as sorry to take in.

Nitty and Windle surveyed the damage from the slight knoll where the institute sat, and for a time, neither could muster a single word to say.

Miz Turngiddy, who still, out of a need for support or reas-surance, held tightly to the end of Mag's tail, was the first to make a sound. All she could manage was a mournful "Oh."

Nitty laid a hand on Mag's side, and then leaned in to her entirely, needing to feel the nearness of her heart. She pressed her face into Mag's neck as tears pricked her eyes. Mag's trunk curled around Nitty's shoulders and stroked her back.

Nitty couldn't bring herself to look a second time at the disaster Neezer's Whirlybog had wrought. She'd seen enough in her first glance. Crispin Sigh's bakery gone, Ferdinand Klempt's Schnurrbart Emporium gone, the Palace Nickelodeon and even the Snollygost General Store, all gone. Every store, home, and business in Fortune's Bluff had splintered into rubble. Folks were slowly climbing up from storm cellars and out from under piles of timber to stare at what was left, which, it seemed, was next to nothing.

"Behold." Windle's voice was dry and tired. "The product of Neezer's progress, betterment, and fulfillment."

Miz Turngiddy covered her face with her hands. "Betrayal!" she moaned. "Deceit! Treachery!"

"A hard truth," Windle said, his voice gentler this time. "One I wish I could've prevented. I'm as much to blame as Neezer in this."

Nitty's head sprang up at that, and she stared at Windle. "How can you say that? You tried to stop him, you tried to make amends—"

Windle held up his hand to silence her. "Too late. I tried too late. Windows for doing can open and close in a blink, and if you miss them . . ." He sighed. "I did nothing at all for far too long."

"I'm to blame more than most." Miz Turngiddy purpled with shame. "I fed him when I should've fought. I thought

325

I could curb him if I stayed close and paid attention. That I could protect and help our town. But I failed it instead."

"No." Nitty swiped at her eyes. "This is my fault. If I hadn't come here, none of this would've happened. I needed . . ." Her voice cracked and broke. "I had my mind set on saving Mag and fixing Fortune's Bluff, but I only brought ruination."

Windle shook his head and frowned, looking like he was about to argue otherwise, but then, suddenly, a rasping horn and wildly screeching tires sounded in the distance.

Nitty, Windle, and Miz Turngiddy all looked toward Fortune's Bluff, or what had *been* Fortune's Bluff. They stared, eyes agog, as Crispin Sigh's automobile—the worse for wear from dust and dents—wheezed, sputtered, and then died, swerving to a haphazard stop in the place where Main Street had once stood.

The door swung open and from it burst a landslide of dirt and then Bernice, covered head to toe in dust but grinning with ebullient pride. For one small second, Nitty bolstered herself enough to say, "That Bernice makes an entrance worthy of the best of the *Daily Tattler*'s daredevils."

Bernice started toward them but was instantly hampered in her approach by Crispin and the younger Sighs, who hurried from behind a sky-high pile of rubble and, seconds later, engulfed Bernice so entirely that all that could be seen of her was a puff of dust rising from her hair. The younger Sighs clung to Bernice's arms and legs with shrieks and hollers while Crispin bowed his head, crying in relieved silence.

When Bernice, at last, reached Nitty, it was to quip, "The rip-roaring getaway car conquers all."

"We *cannot* give it up," Nitty whispered so only Bernice could hear.

"What in blazes happened that you're driving about in the wake of a duster?" Windle demanded.

Bernice shrugged, dauntless in the face of Windle's sternness. "I snuck out, headed for your place. Before the duster hit. I . . ." She blushed. "Needed to pay a visit."

"You were worried about me and Twitch!" Nitty declared.

Bernice raised eyes to the sky. "Well. It would've been a waste to save your hides if you'd up and kicked the bucket afterward." She snorted. "Only you weren't home. Twitch either. And his house was emptied out, too."

"He's gone already then." Nitty's eyes welled fresh. "To California."

"Oh," came Bernice's forlorn reply. She frowned over this for a long moment, then nodded. "California's a sight better fate for him than what I imagined. I was sure Neezer had kidnapped you both and was about to head straight for the institute. Then the duster hit, and I had to wait at the farm for it to end."

Windle frowned. "There will be no more operating of motorcars. Under any circumstances. By any youngster. Ever." He arched an eyebrow, first at Bernice, then at Nitty.

Nitty, in turn, arched an eyebrow at Bernice, who gave an almost imperceptible nod. Oh, they'd make plans aplenty for that motorcar, Nitty understood that nod to mean. Only they'd best not inform any grown-ups of these plans for the foreseeable future.

Bernice smiled at her, and more dust rained from her hair. Then she looked back toward Crispin, who was mumbling as he held his rolling pin to his ear. Her smile quit her faster than a blink. Crispin, it seemed, had taken a turn for the worse.

"What of the farm?" Windle asked a moment later, and Bernice dropped her eyes.

"The house and barn are still standing," she said quietly as she took Crispin's hand. "But the froozle crop . . ." She shook her head solemnly.

Nitty's eyes filled. Could it be true? And if it was true, why? Why would she—all of them—have been given such a gift only to have it taken away? It didn't make sense.

Mag gave her a worried snuffle, and Nitty burrowed into Mag's great chest, pressing her face into her raisiny skin. Mag dipped her head and wrapped her trunk about Nitty in an all-encompassing elephant embrace. Nitty heard Mag's pumpkin heart resonating a deep and steady *I'm here. I'm here. I'm here.* Being held didn't make anything right, but it reminded Nitty that she wasn't alone in the wrongness of it all.

"I did salvage something," Bernice said then.

Nitty glanced at Bernice, who motioned for them to follow her to Crispin's motorcar.

Since they were at an utter loss as to what else to do at that very moment besides shed copious amounts of tears for the town and the froozle fruits that were no more, they walked down the knoll after Bernice.

⚮

Once they had picked their way across the expanse of debris to Bernice's side, they watched as she carefully removed two covered pitchers from Crispin's car.

To Nitty's questioning look, Bernice answered, "It's froozle juice!"

"The last two pitchers of it," Nitty whispered in disbelief. She'd set them on Windle's kitchen table herself, right after the froozle harvest.

"I know it," Bernice said with no small amount of pride. "And I wasn't about to let a single drop spill to a duster. My gut told me that, this being the worst duster yet, the juice might come in handy about town."

She cast a worried glance toward Crispin and slid her arm through his. Crispin, who'd given up on conversing with his rolling pin for the time being, now held a dusty fuchsia loaf of bread in his hands, mumbling, "Two parts hope, one part pain, that's the recipe for rain." Bernice's eyes turned watery as the smallest Sighs hugged her ankles and dress, seeming to shiver in unison, as if they were standing coatless in the dead of winter.

Nitty couldn't bear their sorrow, but neither could she bear to take in the despondent looks on the faces of the other folks surrounding them. Tears were flowing fast as rivers, and the air was full of whispered regrets and what-ifs.

"Should've left here long ago," one husband lamented to his wife.

"No reason to stay anymore," muttered a young mother, clutching her baby.

Mag went from person to person, snuffling at their tears with her trunk and letting the smaller children hug her legs. Ferdinand clutched fistfuls of fuchsia mustaches to his eyes, moaning, "All is lost. All is lost."

Nitty hung her head. There was simply too much sadness to swallow. "I'm not sure it's the right time for juice." Her voice quivered against her will.

At that, Bernice marched over to her, fists clenched at her sides. "Listen here. I don't know about the juice, but it's sure as spitfire not the right time for you to turn into a doomster." Her watery eyes turned flinty. "I'm not about to let Papa slip away again when he's only just come back to us. The froozle juice is near about all we have left, anywise, so might as well make use of it."

She dug through the rubble that had once been the Sigh bakery and enlisted the younger Sighs to do the same among the other piles of debris, until they'd unearthed a dozen tin cups. She shoved some at Nitty, motioning for her to fill them. Nitty hesitated, glancing back at her uncertainly. But when Bernice gave her another pummeling look, Nitty set to work alongside her. Windle, too, took up the cause, administering a sharp warning of "No lollygagging" if Nitty began to yield to sadness.

Although her heart was hurting and her faith floundering, Nitty filled the cups and passed them out to the folks of Fortune's Bluff, young and old.

"Take a sip and pass it on," she told them.

The whispered regrets and what-ifs quieted, until the only sound to be heard was the soft slosh of juice being lifted to lips and swallowed.

Then, when only one cup remained, she offered sips to Windle and Ferdinand, Crispin and Bernice and the smallest Sighs, even Miz Turngiddy. She scooped some into Mag's mouth. Finally she took the last sip for herself.

The juice touched Nitty's lips and slid down her throat with a cool, enveloping comfort. She closed her eyes. It tasted exactly like her first bite of froozle fruit. It tasted like triumph.

CHAPTER THIRTY-ONE

In Which Hope Is a Thing with Froozles

For years to come, the people who were present on the dilapidated Main Street that day would try to describe what happened in those moments as the cups were passed around. No one could ever come close to an accurate recounting.

As the froozle juice flowed sweetly down the throats of the folks of Fortune's Bluff, a change came over them. Their spirits, at first floundering, began to flutter and slowly rise. As they did, a baby's breath of a breeze blew the remaining dust from the sky, chasing away the burned-toast haze. The juice soothed the soul of every person in Fortune's Bluff and whispered, *Hope, hope, hope,* to their hearts.

Hope was what made Windle and Nitty clasp hands. Hope

was what made Mag raise her trunk to blow a long, sonorous note into the sky.

Hope was what each person tasted, sipping the froozle juice. Fortune's Bluff, which a moment before had been teetering at the edge of what surely would've been an irreversible despair, slowly began to right itself. Folks sipped and sighed, sighed and sipped. They let their gazes wander over the Fortune's Bluff ruins, they let their tears fall on the rubble, but they let their hearts linger in hope.

This hope proved especially serendipitous when, as the very last sip of juice from the very last froozle fruit was swallowed, a red-and-yellow circus wagon appeared on the horizon, the words GUSTO & GALLANT emblazoned on its side. A figure in a top hat drove the wagon, his red face determined and covered with a decidedly worn and ragged mustache.

"I'd recognize that horseshoe mustachio anywhere, even in its current calamitous state of disarray." Ferdinand Klempt stepped forward, suddenly stalwart where a few minutes before he'd been tear-sodden. "That's none other than Percival Gallant himself."

Here, thought Nitty, was another villain needing vanquishing. "He's come for Mag." She set down her cup and planted herself staunchly in front of Mag. Windle, Ferdinand, and then Crispin, Bernice, and the Sigh children did the same.

Windle took one of Nitty's hands while Bernice took the other. Bernice narrowed her eyes at Percival Gallant, who had just stopped the wagon and was climbing down from it with a purposeful air. "They took Papa to the asylum in a wagon like that. It's not a wagon so much as a jail."

Nitty nodded, frowning. "He means to send Mag to her death."

Mutterings stirred around her and Mag, and soon there was a circle of people surrounding them, much like the one Nitty remembered from the day Mag was meant to be hanged. This time, though, Nitty heard no utterance of "monster" or "murderer." This time, the folks surrounding her and Mag weren't jeering gawkers. This time, they were a shield.

Behind her, Nitty felt Mag shift nervously from side to side as Percival Gallant approached.

"We've been searching for you, beast," he said to Mag, tapping a bull hook against the ankle of his black boot. "Where's Mayor Snollygost?"

"Due to the unfortunate ferocity of the recent duster, Neezer Snollygost is no more." Windle's words were flat as stone.

The effect they had on the folks of Fortune's Bluff was strange. Upon hearing that the harbinger of progress, betterment, and fulfillment had disappeared, people first blinked in bewilderment. Slowly, those who'd worn earmuffs for all the livelong days of Snollygost's reign slid them from their ears. They raised their heads to the blessed quiet. They breathed in the dust-free air, and they felt the first stirrings of a long-overdue relief.

"I owed the mayor my thanks," Percival Gallant went on,

"for locating and returning what by rights belongs to me. Now if you'll excuse me, I'll take what's mine and be on my way."

Percival stepped toward Mag. The folks of Fortune's Bluff stepped toward Percival Gallant.

"She's not yours." Nitty pressed herself against Mag's chest. "She's not anybody's. But we love her, and she can stay with us as long as she likes."

Beside her, Bernice nodded her agreement, her expression resolute.

Percival chuckled. He might've patted Nitty on the head in the manner he had of patting all children on the head to illustrate how much taller and stronger he was than they. Only, Nitty was barricaded by Ferdinand Klempt, Crispin Sigh, and Windle Homes. Percival patted Bernice's head instead, for which he received a swift kick in the shin in response.

"Now see here." Percival grimaced, rubbing his shin. "That elephant is dangerous, a threat to public safety. She was meant to be disposed of some time ago. She's useless as a performer, but I might still gain a profit from her yet."

"You mean to sell tickets to her execution." Nitty glared at him. If she'd been close enough, she would've kicked Percival Gallant's other shin.

"Spectators will pay good money for the macabre." Percival shrugged, as if it were nothing to send another living creature to her death, as if *Mag* were nothing.

Nitty's hands balled into fists. "She's not going."

Percival snorted. "Little girl, you have no say in the matter."

"I do," Nitty said. "Each and every one of us has a say when it comes to what is right. I don't know what happened to her trainer, but Mag was not at fault."

Percival scoffed. "You know nothing of what happened."

"No," Nitty said. "But I know Mag. I know her heart." She looked deep into Mag's left eye then, so deep it felt as if she were gazing into the very well of Mag's soul. There she saw what she'd always felt—the gentleness of Mag's great pumpkin heart, her kindness, her love. "She didn't kill her trainer."

"Mr. Gallant." Ferdinand leveled unflinching eyes at him. "I knew this elephant's trainer. I heard him boast of breaking her, of beating her and worse. No animal deserves such cruelty. No animal can be blamed for defending itself against it either." He stepped closer to Percival, until the two of them were nose to nose. "I wonder, how often did you notice wounds on the elephant? How often did you notice and do nothing?"

Percival Gallant fell silent, but Ferdinand held his ground until, at last, Percival stepped back, clearing his throat and dropping his eyes to the ground.

"I thought as much," Ferdinand said.

Seeing Percival's sudden shame, Nitty felt the hope she'd swallowed burgeoning. There was a chance for Mag. . . . there was . . . there was . . .

"I need Mag," Nitty said then. "Fortune's Bluff needs Mag. And I say she stays."

"I do, too," said Windle.

"So do I," said Bernice.

"And I," said Ferdinand.

"And I," said Crispin.

And so it went, until every person in Fortune's Bluff had had a say in favor of Mag staying.

"This is preposterous!" Percival blustered. "The beast is Gusto and Gallant property. And there is nothing you can do to prevent my taking her."

Nitty glanced at Windle. "There has to be something we can do."

Hope, Nitty was certain, would not have led them this far for nothing. Hope was never an end, but always a beginning.

The whole of Fortune's Bluff fell silent in the next few moments, each person searching their mind for a solution. Only Ferdinand Klempt seemed distracted, suddenly paying particularly close attention to Percival Gallant's horseshoe mustache.

"Mr. Gallant." He took Percival for a stroll, arm in arm. "I can't help but notice that your mustache has—how shall I put this delicately?—passed its prime."

Percival bristled at this, his cheeks reddening. "What what?" He patted his mustache worriedly.

Ferdinand nodded knowingly. "It's looking reprehensibly dowdy. Why, there's no telling what effect a mustache in such deplorable condition would have on circusgoers. Surely a man in your profession understands the necessity of a mustache that offers as much in the way of grandeur as in comfort."

"Of course," Percival said worriedly, "but traveling on the road wreaks such havoc on mustaches, and with all the sawdust and animals—"

"Say no more!" Ferdinand was aglow with enthusiasm and confidence. "For I have, here in my pocket, some of the sturdiest, most dazzling mustaches you'll ever lay eyes on. Built to withstand hours, days, weeks—even months!—of showmanship."

Ferdinand held one of his fuchsia handlebar mustaches out to Percival, who touched it reverently. "What a striking shade. A novel shape, too."

"My own creation." Ferdinand's shoulders heightened with pride. "Inspired by the arc of a flamingo's wing."

Percival's eyes could not leave the mustache. "And such softness . . ."

"Perfectly suited to you." Ferdinand clapped him on the back. "I believe we may have a bargain to strike. What would you say to a lifetime's supply of froozle mustaches in exchange for the life of one elephant?"

⚘

Not more than twenty minutes later, Percival Gallant and his circus wagon were shrinking specks on the horizon, carrying with them bags full of Ferdinand Klempt's Famous Froozle Flying Flamingo mustaches and a promise for more mustaches to come.

The children of Fortune's Bluff had made quick work of

salvaging mustaches from the wreckage of the Schnurrbart Emporium, and Percival Gallant had left in a state both cheery and allayed.

"The elephant would've proved more burdensome than profitable to be sure," Ferdinand had assured Percival as he climbed aboard the wagon, "but these mustaches, they'll assure your success. I guarantee it."

"But, Mr. Klempt," Nitty said once Percival and the circus wagon were beyond earshot, "the froozle crop is gone. What will you do when you run out of the froozle silk?"

Ferdinand shrugged. "Percival Gallant has enough mustaches in that trunk to last at least a decade, maybe even two. After that . . . well . . . I'll have to await an epiphany. Or"—he smiled—"I won't wait. I'll make my own epiphanies."

Nitty motioned him to lean down to her height, after which she gave him a peck on his cheek. "Thank you," she whispered.

The Gusto and Gallant wagon winked out of sight. Then, with a soft, sweet whisper, rain began to fall in Fortune's Bluff for the first time in ten years.

"Just as I said." Crispin looked with approval at the sky above. "Two parts hope, one part pain. That's the recipe for rain." The Sigh children gathered around him, and he planted kisses atop each of their heads, one by one.

"Everything was just like you said, Papa." Bernice smiled at him.

He nodded. "I knew it was. All along." He took the rolling pin from his back pocket. "And now, if Miz Turngiddy approves, I will go search the food stores at the Snollygost Institute for some flour."

"Help yourself," Miz Turngiddy said. "Most of the institute was destroyed, but some of the food stores survived. The food should have been given to Fortune's Bluff some time ago, and I intend to right that wrong straightaway."

Crispin nodded his thanks, then turned to look at the pile of lumber that had once been his bakery. "In the end, I think we'll do better without the snakeskins, don't you?" he asked Bernice.

Bernice hugged him. "Leaps and bounds better."

Then she smiled at Nitty, who was more than happy to return the smile with one of her own. Nitty felt a kinship with Bernice, after all they'd weathered together these last few days, and with Twitch gone, it struck her that she and Bernice would now be a duo in mischief and mayhem.

"Bernice," Nitty said, "I've a mind to tell you some tales from the *Daily Tattler*. How do you feel about pirates and convicts?"

"Is there pummeling involved?"

"And then some. Swashbuckling, too."

Bernice shrugged. "Sounds tolerable enough." But her grin confessed her enthusiasm, and so Nitty began a retelling of *The Countess and the Convict*.

Meanwhile, the rain kept on, wetting noses and eyelashes. It kerplunked harmoniously onto the thirsty, grateful ground. It sank beneath the dirt, far down through the rocks and prehistoric strata below, and whispered to the world, *Triumph*.

As it whispered, Nitty, along with the rest of Fortune's Bluff, turned her attention to the piles of rubble surrounding them.

This time, it was Windle who spoke first. Not Windle the curmudgeon. No. This Windle stood taller for the storms he'd weathered and more joyful for the fact that they'd now, at last, passed him by.

"This town is long overdue for a rejuvenation," he announced, and every head nodded in agreement.

"We'll rebuild," said Ferdinand. "With more mustaches."

"More bread," said Crispin.

"More Magnolious," said Nitty. Beside her, Mag trumpeted an enlivening *Brrt!* Then she scooped up some stray pieces of timber with her trunk and dropped them into a pile. Nitty laughed. "She knows what to do. She'll help."

"There is a small problem," Crispin said softly. "Neezer had every cent, every deed, we owned."

"Not so!" Miz Turngiddy scurried to the front of the crowd. "Every scrap of paper in the Snollygost Institute blew away with the duster. Therefore there are no records of debts, no loans to repay. And . . . I still have this!" From the pocket of her skirt she pulled a bulky envelope—the very same bulky envelope that Nitty had seen Miz Ricketts slip into her pocketbook.

"But Miz Ricketts took that money," Nitty said.

"I took it back when Miz Ricketts dropped her pocketbook," Miz Turngiddy announced, and then her perpetually pursed lips pulled back to reveal a proud smile—the first Nitty had ever seen her give. "The money belongs to Fortune's Bluff, and"—she blushed—"note-taking makes for nimble fingers."

"Miz Turngiddy!" Nitty laughed. "You're a proper pickpocket!"

Miz Turngiddy winked. "I read the *Daily Tattler* on occasion. I find it offers a host of practical information." Then she sobered. "I only ever wanted to help our town." There was a drop of sadness in her voice. "And to have my far-off family come back to me. I overlooked our mayor's foibles for too long. But . . ." She held out the envelope. "I did salvage this. I suppose that's something."

"That is a commendable something." Nitty smiled at her.

"It's not much," Miz Turngiddy said, "but it's a start. And I have ideas. For new farming ways, irrigation, terraces . . ." She paused. "If anyone cares to hear."

"We do," came several voices.

Miz Turngiddy smiled as the cogs and wheels of her mind whirred joyfully at the prospect of sharing, at last, the fruits of their labors.

Then Windle clapped his hands together with a decisive bang, and everyone moved in different directions all at once, piling up rubble, searching for hammers and nails and paint cans among the debris, and talking of new businesses, new crops, and new lives.

It was some minutes, however, before Windle himself went to work. He spent those minutes pondering. He pondered that, at last, the heart-shaped freckle just below his right ear had quit itching for good. He pondered his sweet Clara, and how happy she'd be to see him restored to himself, and happy besides that he had Nitty (and, yes, her elephant, too) to keep him company in the coming years. He pondered the possibility of Lillah's return, if or when her singing brought her westward, and how she'd delight in getting to know Nitty. Mostly, though, he pondered something he'd once told Nitty—something that he now realized he'd said wrongly and unjustly. Something he needed to correct.

Now he put his arm around Nitty, as together they watched a town set to work rebuilding itself.

"Nitty, I once told you that after love comes loss. And that loss brings more unhappiness."

"Until?" Nitty looked up at him through the pitter-pattering rain, waiting. She'd known all along there had to be an "until," and she could see from the promise in Windle's eyes that he finally knew what it was.

Windle smiled. "Until more love comes along."

Yes, thought Nitty, twining her hand around Mag's trunk. Love could always be found lingering, waiting to blossom, sooner or later. And that was exactly as it should be.

CHAPTER THIRTY-TWO

IN WHICH A GIRL AND AN ELEPHANT PONDER TRIUMPHS AND THE GREAT UNKNOWABLE

Time passed, as it is apt to do, and dusters were never again seen in Fortune's Bluff. On the other hand, one particularly congenial elephant *was* seen with great regularity, always in the company of a green-eyed girl and, on occasion, some adventurous chickens.

There was still one shuddering green seed in Nitty's Gleam Jar, but she never planted it. She suspected that if she did, nothing would grow but a plain and common lima bean. Which was why, one fine summer day, when Nitty heard tell of a tinker passing through Fortune's Bluff, she bundled her last green seed into her pocket and rode Mag into town.

The Merrythought Windowshop was just as she remembered

it, charmingly cluttered with potions, perfumes, and tiny globed kingdoms.

The tinker—barely visible under a threadbare cloak—cackled upon seeing Nitty standing in Mag's great shadow. "I remember you, girl. You had such a hungry look about you, you did." The tinker leaned toward Nitty. "Not anymore, though." A single, shaded eye looked Magnolious up and down, and another cackle rose from the cloak. "Did you find what you needed, then?"

Nitty nodded. "Yes." She held out the green seed to the tinker, who accepted it with a wrinkled, craggy hand. "This belongs to you."

"And what am I to believe will come from such a small, unimportant seed as this?" the tinker asked.

"Anything. Everything." Nitty smiled as Mag's trunk tickled her palm. "It depends on the farmer. It depends on what you *need* it to grow."

Nitty climbed onto Mag's neck again then, and as she did, she could've sworn she heard the tinker laughing. Whether or not the seed would ever grow, Nitty couldn't say. But she believed, and maybe someone else, someday, would believe, too. It might be enough, just enough, to believe something wondrous—even miraculous—into being.

Riding Mag down Main Street, Nitty took in the whole expanse of Fortune's Bluff and smiled. The once-rubbled town had rebuilt itself, one timber at a time. It had taken months of hard work and patience. It had taken all the money in Miz Turngiddy's envelope. It had taken all the food and wood that was salvaged from the wreckage of the Snollygost Institute. It had taken sore muscles, tired eyes, and hungry bellies aplenty, but it had happened.

In time, Fortune's Bluff had grown into a cheerful, welcoming place once more. Thanks to Miz Turngiddy's innovative ideas on farming, fields of bounteous corn, beans, and grain sprouted, surrounding the town in a pool of green so vivid folks often had the urge to stop and sit right in the middle of it. And, of course, they did just that.

That green never left Nitty's field of vision as she and Mag lumbered down Main Street. But the green wasn't all she savored either. There was Ferdinand Klempt waving to her and Mag from the fuchsia doorway of the Schnurrbart Emporium. He was sporting an enormous mustache shaped like a bow tie.

"Stop in soon!" he called to her. "You must try my latest model: the Funambulist Funicular."

There was Miz Turngiddy posting VOTE TURNGIDDY FOR MAYOR signs in front of the new schoolhouse, her grandbabies toddling happily about her feet.

There was Crispin, with the smallest Sighs, setting freshly baked bread in the window of his bakery just as customers approached to buy it. And there was Bernice, her feet propped against the steering wheel of the parked Tin Lizzie, her nose stuck in the copy of *Great Expectations* that Nitty had lent her the day before.

Bernice paused just long enough in her reading to offer a trunk tickle to Mag and a whispered "Twitch's new case—I'll be by at sundown" to Nitty.

Nitty nodded, already antsy to hear Bernice's notions about the case. Twitch's latest letter sat in Nitty's pocket, and as Mag trundled past the freshly painted Palace Nickelodeon, Nitty read it once again.

To: Detective Nitty, Detective Bernice, and the exceptional sidekick Magnolious,

I'm investigating a case of a highly secretive nature, involving a one Miz Millicent Crottle, former traveling magician turned farmhand. Two weeks ago, she arrived here in Visalia to help with the harvesting. Since then, all manner of strange events have occurred. Horrid Mr. Vermix told a coarse joke in Miz Crottle's presence, and afterward he took sick with a twelve-hour pox! When I was grousing over taking my daily dose of Mr. Moop's Cough Tonic, Miz Crottle winked at me. The next thing I knew, the tonic had turned my tongue orange and Ma was swearing she'd never give it to me again. (Fine by me, for I haven't suffered a single cough or wheeze in months!) And just yesterday the carrot field was hot as a griddle . . . until Miz Crottle did a jig in the dirt. Not a minute later, a cloudburst cooled everybody off. I also have reason to believe Miz Crottle is harboring a white rabbit underneath her unusually large straw hat. Now I ask you:

Does Miz Crottle possess magical abilities? Does her shifty
rabbit? Or am I falling prey to nothing but smoke and
mirrors? I'm relying on your powers of deductive reasoning.
Waste no time writing back with your hypotheses.

Your partner in sleuthing,
Detective Angus "Twitch" Higgler

Nitty thought on shifty rabbits and on Twitch's commendable nose for detecting. Hoo-wee, she missed him terribly at times! But she knew she'd see him again. She felt it in her heart, just the way she felt Mag's love, unspoken but true all the same. Until then, she had his frequent letters. Twitch, no matter the miles separating them, would always remain one of her greatest friends.

She tucked the letter away for safekeeping just as Mag reached the edge of their farm. Windle, Nitty knew, would be waiting for them in the rocker, husking corn for supper from their sky-high crop.

She climbed down from Mag and slipped off her shoes. Together she and Mag walked barefoot into the field that had once been plowed with juddering green seeds, where once had grown a crop of froozle fruit.

Nitty pressed her face against Mag's side to feel her pumpkin heart beating. She felt the world's great garden of love wriggling under her toes—seeds of friendship and family triumphing. She felt the joy of all that is great and unknowable, and the joy of all that is great and known. She felt that there was nothing better than to pass the days with an elephant she loved, who loved her in return.

Mag twined her trunk through Nitty's hand, and together through the field of emerald green they walked home.

AUTHOR'S NOTE

An elephant, a dream, and a farm. That's how this book began.

Several years ago, I was doing online research for another book and stumbled across an extremely unsettling photograph of an elephant hanging from a crane (rarehistoricalphotos.com/murderous-mary-1916). The Asian elephant, named Mary, belonged to the Sparks World Famous Shows circus, and she was publicly executed in Erwin, Tennessee, in 1916 after killing her trainer. Though there is still much uncertainty over the exact details of the events surrounding her execution, there is no doubt that her death was a painful and tragic one.

I could not tear my eyes from the horrible photograph and, for hours afterward, found myself asking how Mary's fate might have been different if she'd been better understood and loved. That same night, I dreamed of a little girl running through a town square, a mysterious stolen object in her arms. Dust was blowing fiercely all around her. The terrified girl was being chased by police officers and faceless townsfolk. She didn't know where to run, until she saw an elephant in the middle of the square. She ducked between the elephant's front legs, finding safety there.

I woke up in the morning with the dream still vivid in my mind, and I felt a sudden conviction that I needed to rewrite Mary the elephant's story, giving her a much happier fate. That was the moment when Magnolious the elephant and Nitty Luce were born. Their story is fictional, but born of my wish that we all—every one of us—foster a greater open-mindedness toward, and empathy and understanding for, one another, human and animal alike.

Elephants, as Nitty says in the story, are a "rather spectacular species." Although we don't yet know how much they comprehend of us and our language, we know they are highly intelligent and emotional beings. They can remember places, other elephants, and people they have close relationships with. They establish profound family ties within their herds and can develop strong bonds with people as well. It is not beyond the realm of possibility that Magnolious would sense Nitty's emotions through the sound of her voice and her intonation and would respond to Nitty with her own body language. In fact, recent studies have found that herds of elephants in Africa can identify potential threats simply by perceiving certain inflections in people's voices. In short, there is much we have yet to learn about the extent of elephants' intelligence and intuition, and much we can learn from them.

An elephant's trunk is incredible, too, and serves many purposes. It has the strength to uproot trees but also the finesse to turn (by using a pushing motion) the pages of this book. Elephants use their trunks for both smelling and touching, and for exploring and playing with a variety of objects, as Magnolious does.

While Magnolious and Nitty Luce were inspired by a real elephant and a dream, the Homes farm was inspired by my family's ancestral farm in Pennsylvania. The farm has been in my family for over 150 years, through five generations of farmers. It did not grow froozle fruit. It grew potatoes instead. Because I was raised in Southern California, where the hills remained brown and dry for the better part of each year, visiting my grandpa's Pennsylvania potato farm seemed like visiting the inside of an emerald. The farm was greener than anything I'd seen in California, and I loved it so much that it truly felt magical.

Though the dusters Nitty, Magnolious, and Fortune's Bluff experience have magical origins, the dusters that occurred during America's Dust Bowl were, unfortunately, very real and very destructive. They were a result of the overfarming of America's Central Plains. Native grasslands were plowed under to make way for agricultural crops, and much of the plains soil was left open and exposed on flat land. Without enough trees or hills to shield the soil from wind, when drought came, the soil blew away with the wind until it formed ominous dust storms. The Dust Bowl years, which lasted for approximately eight to ten years during the 1930s, brought suffocating storms that barreled across many states of the central United States. The storms made it nearly impossible for farmers to grow crops, and dust filled houses and even buried cars and small buildings. A number of people suffered from "dust pneumonia," as Twitch does in the story. Many people found it difficult to continue living in states affected by dusters, and some migrated westward to California in search of jobs and fertile farmland.

Because there was a shortage of food during this time as well, many songs from this period focused on hunger, dust, or food. In fact, most of the songs Neezer's nose whistles in the story are real, including "Dust Can't Kill Me," "Farewell Blues," and "I Heard the Voice of a Pork Chop." Some of these were specifically inspired by the Dust Bowl, while others were songs written in the 1920s and 1930s. Twitch's *Detective Comics,* too, were real, first debuting in the late 1930s, although the "Ten Ways to Be a Villain" are fictionalized. These comics featured some of the first "hard-boiled" detective stories, and eventually introduced some well-known superheroes, like Batman and Robin.

For a fascinating look at the bond one conservationist had with a particular herd of elephants in South Africa, consider reading *The Elephant Whisperer: My Life with the Herd in the African Wild* (Young Readers Adaptation) by Lawrence Anthony. For an in-depth and interactive exploration of the Dust Bowl years, inspired by Ken Burns's documentary film *The Dust Bowl,* visit pbs.org/kenburns/dustbowl/legacy.

In many parts of the world today, wild elephants are facing grave threats from poaching and habitat destruction. Some elephants, exploited for tourism, are also still subject to harsh treatment and poor living conditions. For more information about how to help save elephants or support elephant sanctuaries, visit these informative websites:

The Elephant Valley Project of Mondulkiri, Cambodia:
elephantvalleyproject.org

Space for Elephants Foundation of KwaZulu-Natal, South Africa:
spaceforelephants.com

The Elephant Sanctuary in Hohenwald, Tennessee:
elephants.com

ACKNOWLEDGMENTS

The seed for a story begins in the mind of an author, but it takes hope and heaps of helpful, encouraging, and talented people for that seed to sprout and, ultimately, to blossom into a book. My sister and best friend, Christina Howe, was the first person I told about the dream I'd had of Nitty and Magnolious running away together. When I asked her if she thought it was ridiculous for me to write a story about the girl and elephant from my dream, her answer was an immediate no. For her faith in my ideas and her faith in me when my own faith fails, and for her willingness to read (and reread *and* reread) my stories, I'm forever grateful.

My agent, Joan Paquette, enthusiastically cheered on *A Tale Magnolious* even when all she had to go on was a mere four-sentence synopsis. She's ever ready and willing to offer fortification and positivity, and without her in my corner I might never have had the stamina to persist as a writer, or the courage to continue trying out new story ideas in the face of potential failure.

357

My thanks go to the entire Erin Murphy Literary Agency "family" of agents, authors, and illustrators, who offer endless support and inspiration. This talented group was the first audience to hear the beginning of *Magnolious* read aloud, and their kind applause and smiles stayed with me—a vote of confidence as I continued writing the story.

I have the tremendous good fortune to have Michelle Frey as my editor and friend. Her insightful feedback made this book stronger and better. Discovering one of her smiley faces or a "Ha!" written on my manuscript felt as sweet as discovering one more Hershey's Kiss at the bottom of a supposedly empty bag. I clung to those little treasures with the sense that they were cheering me ever onward toward the finish line.

I'm thankful to the entire team at Knopf Books for Young Readers for its copyediting, proofreading, and design skills, especially Artie Bennett, Karen Sherman, Marianne Cohen, and Katrina Damkoehler. I'm also in awe of Emilia Dziubak and the truly magnolious cover and interior art she created for this book.

Natalie H. Hall, doctor of veterinary medicine, diplomate ACZM, shared with me her impressive expertise on elephants, and I'm indebted to her for her careful reading of the story, and for allowing me to ask her numerous questions about elephants and their amazing abilities.

I'm blessed to have many incredible friends in my neighborhood, who keep me supplied with ample laughter, hugs, walks, and coffee while I'm writing. To "The Fraus"—thanks for giving me perspective and keeping me sane.

I will never stop thanking the educators of my childhood and young adulthood for emboldening me to hone my writing skills, or my parents for endowing me with the bravery and persistence to pursue my dreams.

My biggest thanks go to my husband and children—Chad, Colin, Aidan, and Madeline. Chad, for your unwavering support, your commitment to our family, your goodness of heart, and your love. Colin, for your keen observations on life, your wicked chess game, your beautiful cello music, and your sense of humor. Aidan, for your adventurous spirit, your drawings, your impish smile, your empathy toward all living creatures, and your winged feet. Madeline, for your sweet hugs and kisses, your kind heart, your imagination, and your intuitive understanding of when I need peace and quiet, or chocolate. I love you all.